THE
PUBLIC GENERAL ACTS
AND GENERAL SYNOD MEASURES
1986

[IN FIVE PARTS]

PART IV
(Chapters 60–68 and Measures 1–4)

with
Lists of the Public General Acts
Local Acts and an Index

LONDON
HER MAJESTY'S STATIONERY OFFICE
1987
£200·00 net

HMSO publications are available from:

C 02 0140187

HMSO Publications Centre
(Mail and telephone orders only)
PO Box 276, London SW8 5DT
Telephone orders 01-622 3316
General enquiries 01-211 5656
(queuing system in operation for both numbers)

HMSO Bookshops
49 High Holborn, London, WC1V 6HB   01-211 5656 (Counter service only)
258 Broad Street, Birmingham, B1 2HE   021-643 3757
Southey House, 33 Wine Street, Bristol, BS1 2BQ   (0272) 24306/24307
9-21 Princess Street, Manchester, M60 8AS   061-834 7201
80 Chichester Street, Belfast, BT1 4JY   (0232) 238451
13a Castle Street, Edinburgh, EH2 3AR   031-225 6333

HMSO's Accredited Agents
(see Yellow Pages)

and through good booksellers

ISBN 0 11 840272 2

c

THIS PUBLICATION
relates to
the Public General Acts
and General Synod Measures
which received the Royal Assent in 1986
in which year ended the THIRTY-FOURTH
and began the THIRTY-FIFTH YEAR
of the Reign of HER MAJESTY
QUEEN ELIZABETH THE SECOND
and
ended the Third session
and began the Fourth session
of the Forty-Ninth Parliament of the
United Kingdom of Great Britain
and Northern Ireland.

PRINTED IN ENGLAND BY J A DOLE
Controller and Chief Executive of Her Majesty's Stationery Office and
Queen's Printer of Acts of Parliament

e

CONTENTS

PART I

PART II

PART III

CONTENTS

PART IV

PART V

TABLE I
Alphabetical List of
the Public General Acts of 1986

Alphabetical List (contd)

Alphabetical List (contd)

TABLE II
Chronological List of
the Public General Acts of 1986

*Consolidation Act

Chronological List (contd)

*Consolidation Act

TABLE III

Alphabetical List of
the Local and Personal Acts of 1986

TABLE IV
Chronological List of
the General Synod Measures of 1986

Measures passed by the General Synod of the Church of England which received the Royal Assent during the year 1986

Financial Services Act
1986

1986 CHAPTER 60

An Act to regulate the carrying on of investment business; to make related provision with respect to insurance business and business carried on by friendly societies; to make new provision with respect to the official listing of securities, offers of unlisted securities, takeover offers and insider dealing; to make provision as to the disclosure of information obtained under enactments relating to fair trading, banking, companies and insurance; to make provision for securing reciprocity with other countries in respect of facilities for the provision of financial services; and for connected purposes.   [7th November 1986]

BE IT ENACTED by the Queen's most Excellent Majesty, by and with the advice and consent of the Lords Spiritual and Temporal, and Commons, in this present Parliament assembled, and by the authority of the same, as follows:—

PART I

REGULATION OF INVESTMENT BUSINESS

CHAPTER I

PRELIMINARY

1.—(1) In this Act, unless the context otherwise requires, "investment" means any asset, right or interest falling within any paragraph in Part I of Schedule 1 to this Act.

Investments and investment business.

(2) In this Act " investment business " means the business of engaging in one or more of the activities which fall within the paragraphs in Part II of that Schedule and are not excluded by Part III of that Schedule.

(3) For the purposes of this Act a person carries on investment business in the United Kingdom if he—

    (*a*) carries on investment business from a permanent place of business maintained by him in the United Kingdom; or

    (*b*) engages in the United Kingdom in one or more of the activities which fall within the paragraphs in Part II of that Schedule and are not excluded by Part III or IV of that Schedule and his doing so constitutes the carrying on by him of a business in the United Kingdom.

(4) Parts I to IV of that Schedule shall be construed in accordance with Part V.

2.—(1) The Secretary of State may by order amend Schedule 1 to this Act so as—

    (*a*) to extend or restrict the meaning of investment for the purposes of all or any provisions of this Act ; or

    (*b*) to extend or restrict for the purposes of all or any of those provisions the activities that are to constitute the carrying on of investment business or the carrying on of such business in the United Kingdom.

(2) The amendments that may be made for the purposes of subsection (1)(*b*) above include amendments conferring powers on the Secretary of State, whether by extending or modifying any provision of that Schedule which confers such powers or by adding further such provisions.

(3) An order under this section which extends the meaning of investment or extends the activities that are to constitute the carrying on of investment business or the carrying on of such business in the United Kingdom shall be laid before Parliament after being made and shall cease to have effect at the end of the period of twenty-eight days beginning with the day on which it is made (but without prejudice to anything done under the order or to the making of a new order) unless before the end of that period the order is approved by a resolution of each House of Parliament.

(4) In reckoning the period mentioned in subsection (3) above no account shall be taken of any time during which Parliament is dissolved or prorogued or during which both Houses are adjourned for more than four days.

(5) Any order under this section to which subsection (3) above does not apply shall be subject to annulment in pursuance of a resolution of either House of Parliament.

(6) An order under this section may contain such transitional provisions as the Secretary of State thinks necessary or expedient.

CHAPTER II

RESTRICTION ON CARRYING ON BUSINESS

3. No person shall carry on, or purport to carry on, investment business in the United Kingdom unless he is an authorised person under Chapter III or an exempted person under Chapter IV of this Part of this Act.

Persons entitled to carry on investment business.

4.—(1) Any person who carries on, or purports to carry on, investment business in contravention of section 3 above shall be guilty of an offence and liable—

Offences.

   (*a*) on conviction on indictment, to imprisonment for a term not exceeding two years or to a fine or to both ;

   (*b*) on summary conviction, to imprisonment for a term not exceeding six months or to a fine not exceeding the statutory maximum or to both.

(2) In proceedings brought against any person for an offence under this section it shall be a defence for him to prove that he took all reasonable precautions and exercised all due diligence to avoid the commission of the offence.

5.—(1) Subject to subsection (3) below, any agreement to which this subsection applies—

Agreements made by or through unauthorised persons.

   (*a*) which is entered into by a person in the course of carrying on investment business in contravention of section 3 above ; or

   (*b*) which is entered into—

      (i) by a person who is an authorised person or an exempted person in respect of the investment business in the course of which he enters into the agreement ; but

      (ii) in consequence of anything said or done by a person in the course of carrying on investment business in contravention of that section,

shall be unenforceable against the other party ; and that party shall be entitled to recover any money or other property paid or transferred by him under the agreement, together with compensation for any loss sustained by him as a result of having parted with it.

2A

(2) The compensation recoverable under subsection (1) above shall be such as the parties may agree or as the court may, on the application of either party, determine.

(3) A court may allow an agreement to which subsection (1) above applies to be enforced or money and property paid or transferred under it to be retained if it is satisfied—

(*a*) in a case within paragraph (*a*) of that subsection, that the person mentioned in that paragraph reasonably believed that his entering into the agreement did not constitute a contravention of section 3 above ;

(*b*) in a case within paragraph (*b*) of that subsection, that the person mentioned in sub-paragraph (i) of that paragraph did not know that the agreement was entered into as mentioned in sub-paragraph (ii) of that paragraph ; and

(*c*) in either case, that it is just and equitable for the agreement to be enforced or, as the case may be, for the money or property paid or transferred under it to be retained.

(4) Where a person elects not to perform an agreement which by virtue of this section is unenforceable against him or by virtue of this section recovers money paid or other property transferred by him under an agreement he shall repay any money and return any other property received by him under the agreement.

(5) Where any property transferred under an agreement to which this section applies has passed to a third party the references to that property in subsections (1), (3) and (4) above shall be construed as references to its value at the time of its transfer under the agreement.

(6) A contravention of section 3 above shall not make an agreement illegal or invalid to any greater extent than is provided in this section.

(7) Subsection (1) above applies to any agreement the making or performance of which by the person seeking to enforce it or from whom money or other property is recoverable under this section constitutes an activity which falls within any paragraph of Part II of Schedule 1 to this Act and is not excluded by Part III or IV of that Schedule.

Injunctions
and
restitution
orders.

6.—(1) If, on the application of the Secretary of State, the court is satisfied—

(*a*) that there is a reasonable likelihood that a person will contravene section 3 above ; or (*b*) **that any person has contravened that section and that** there is a reasonable likelihood that the contravention will continue or be repeated,

the court may grant an injunction restraining the contravention or, in Scotland, an interdict prohibiting the contravention.

(2) If, on the application of the Secretary of State, the court is satisfied that a person has entered into any transaction in contravention of section 3 above the court may order that person and any other person who appears to the court to have been knowingly concerned in the contravention to take such steps as the court may direct for restoring the parties to the position in which they were before the transaction was entered into.

(3) The court may, on the application of the Secretary of State, make an order under subsection (4) below or, in relation to Scotland, under subsection (5) below if satisfied that a person has been carrying on investment business in contravention of section 3 above and—

(*a*) that profits have accrued to that person as a result of carrying on that business ; or

(*b*) that one or more investors have suffered loss or been otherwise adversely affected as a result of his contravention of section 47 or 56 below or failure to act substantially in accordance with any of the rules or regulations made under Chapter V of this Part of this Act.

(4) The court may under this subsection order the person concerned to pay into court, or appoint a receiver to recover from him, such sum as appears to the court to be just having regard—

(*a*) in a case within paragraph (*a*) of subsection (3) above, to the profits appearing to the court to have accrued ;

(*b*) in a case within paragraph (*b*) of that subsection, to the extent of the loss or other adverse effect ; or

(*c*) in a case within both paragraphs (*a*) and (*b*) of that subsection, to the profits and to the extent of the loss or other adverse effect.

(5) The court may under this subsection order the person concerned to pay to the applicant such sum as appears to the court to be just having regard to the considerations mentioned in paragraphs (*a*) to (*c*) of subsection (4) above.

(6) Any amount paid into court by or recovered from a person in pursuance of an order under subsection (4) or (5) above shall be paid out to such person or distributed among such persons as the court may direct, being a person or persons appearing to the court to have entered into transactions with that person as a result of which the profits mentioned in paragraph (*a*) of subsec-

A3

tion (3) above have accrued to him or the loss or other adverse effect mentioned in paragraph (*b*) of that subsection has been suffered.

(7) On an application under subsection (3) above the court may require the person concerned to furnish it with such accounts or other information as it may require for establishing whether any and, if so, what profits have accrued to him as mentioned in paragraph (*a*) of that subsection and for determining how any amounts are to be paid or distributed under subsection (6) above ; and the court may require any such accounts or other information to be verified in such manner as it may direct.

(8) The jurisdiction conferred by this section shall be exercisable by the High Court and the Court of Session.

(9) Nothing in this section affects the right of any person other than the Secretary of State to bring proceedings in respect of any of the matters to which this section applies.

CHAPTER III

AUTHORISED PERSONS

Members of recognised self-regulating organisations

Authorisation by membership of recognised self-regulating organisation.
7.—(1) Subject to subsection (2) below, a member of a recognised self-regulating organisation is an authorised person by virtue of his membership of that organisation.

(2) This section does not apply to a member who is an authorised person by virtue of section 22 or 23 below or an insurance company which is an authorised person by virtue of section 31 below.

Self-regulating organisations.
8.—(1) In this Act a " self-regulating organisation " means a body (whether a body corporate or an unincorporated association) which regulates the carrying on of investment business of any kind by enforcing rules which are binding on persons carrying on business of that kind either because they are members of that body or because they are otherwise subject to its control.

(2) In this Act references to the members of a self-regulating organisation are references to the persons who, whether or not members of the organisation, are subject to its rules in carrying on the business in question.

(3) In this Act references to the rules of a self-regulating organisation are references to the rules (whether or not laid down by the organisation itself) which the organisation has power to enforce in relation to the carrying on of the business in question or which relate to the admission and expulsion of members of the organisation or otherwise to its constitution.

(4) In this Act references to guidance issued by a self-regulat-
ing organisation are references to guidance issued or any recom-
mendation made by it to all or any class of its members or
persons seeking to become members which would, if it were
a rule, fall within subsection (3) above.

9.—(1) A self-regulating organisation may apply to the Secre-   Applications
tary of State for an order declaring it to be a recognised self-   for
regulating organisation for the purposes of this Act.   recognition.

(2) Any such application—

    (*a*) shall be made in such manner as the Secretary of State
          may direct ; and

    (*b*) shall be accompanied by such information as the Sec-
          retary of State may reasonably require for the purpose
          of determining the application.

(3) At any time after receiving an application and before
determining it the Secretary of State may require the applicant
to furnish additional information.

(4) The directions and requirements given or imposed under
subsections (2) and (3) above may differ as between different
applications.

(5) Any information to be furnished to the Secretary of
State under this section shall, if he so requires, be in such form
or verified in such manner as he may specify.

(6) Every application shall be accompanied by a copy of the
applicant's rules and of any guidance issued by the applicant
which is intended to have continuing effect and is issued in
writing or other legible form.

10.—(1) The Secretary of State may, on an application duly   Grant and
made in accordance with section 9 above and after being   refusal of
furnished with all such information as he may require under   recognition.
that section, make or refuse to make an order (" a recognition
order ") declaring the applicant to be a recognised self-regulating
organisation.

(2) Subject to subsection (4) below and to Chapter XIV of this
Part of this Act, the Secretary of State shall make a recognition
order if it appears to him from the information furnished by the
organisation making the application and having regard to any
other information in his possession that the requirements of subsection (3) below and of Schedule 2 to this Act are satisfied as
respects that organisation.

(3) Where there is a kind of investment business with which
the organisation is not concerned, its rules must preclude a
member from carrying on investment business of that kind unless
he is an authorised person otherwise than by virtue of his mem-

A 4

bership of the organisation or an exempted person in respect of that business.

(4) The Secretary of State may refuse to make a recognition order in respect of an organisation if he considers that its recognition is unnecessary having regard to the existence of one or more other organisations which are concerned with investment business of a kind with which the applicant is concerned and which have been or are likely to be recognised under this section.

(5) Where the Secretary of State refuses an application for a recognition order he shall give the applicant a written notice to that effect specifying a requirement which in the opinion of the Secretary of State is not satisfied, stating that the application is refused on the ground mentioned in subsection (4) above or stating that it is refused by virtue of Chapter XIV.

(6) A recognition order shall state the date on which it takes effect.

Revocation of
recognition.

11.—(1) A recognition order may be revoked by a further order made by the Secretary of State if at any time it appears to him—

> (a) that section 10(3) above or any requirement of Schedule 2 to this Act is not satisfied in the case of the organisation to which the recognition order relates (" the recognised organisation ") ;

> (b) that the recognised organisation has failed to comply with any obligation to which it is subject by virtue of this Act ; or

> (c) that the continued recognition of the organisation is undesirable having regard to the existence of one or more other organisations which have been or are to be recognised under section 10 above.

(2) An order revoking a recognition order shall state the date on which it takes effect and that date shall not be earlier than three months after the day on which the revocation order is made.

(3) Before revoking a recognition order the Secretary of State shall give written notice of his intention to do so to the recognised organisation, take such steps as he considers reasonably practicable for bringing the notice to the attention of members of the organisation and publish it in such manner as he thinks appropriate for bringing it to the attention of any other persons who are in his opinion likely to be affected.

(4) A notice under subsection (3) above shall state the reasons for which the Secretary of State proposes to act and give particulars of the rights conferred by subsection (5) below.

(5) An organisation on which a notice is served under subsection (3) above, any member of the organisation and any other person who appears to the Secretary of State to be affected may within three months after the date of service or publication, or within such longer time as the Secretary of State may allow, make written representations to the Secretary of State and, if desired, oral representations to a person appointed for that purpose by the Secretary of State ; and the Secretary of State shall have regard to any representations made in accordance with this subsection in determining whether to revoke the recognition order.

(6) If in any case the Secretary of State considers it essential to do so in the interests of investors he may revoke a recognition order without regard to the restriction imposed by subsection (2) above and notwithstanding that no notice has been given or published under subsection (3) above or that the time for making representations in pursuance of such a notice has not expired.

(7) An order revoking a recognition order may contain such transitional provisions as the Secretary of State thinks necessary or expedient.

(8) A recognition order may be revoked at the request or with the consent of the recognised organisation and any such revocation shall not be subject to the restrictions imposed by subsections (1) and (2) or the requirements of subsections (3) to (5) above.

(9) On making an order revoking a recognition order the Secretary of State shall give the organisation written notice of the making of the order, take such steps as he considers reasonably practicable for bringing the making of the order to the attention of members of the organisation and publish a notice of the making of the order in such manner as he thinks appropriate for bringing it to the attention of any other persons who are in his opinion likely to be affected.

12.—(1) If at any time it appears to the Secretary of State—

(*a*) that subsection (3) of section 10 above or any requirement of Schedule 2 to this Act is not satisfied in the case of a recognised organisation ; or

(*b*) that a recognised organisation has failed to comply with any obligation to which it is subject by virtue of this Act,

he may, instead of revoking the recognition order under section 11 above, make an application to the court under this section.

(2) If on any such application the court decides that subsection (3) of section 10 or the requirement in question is not satisfied or, as the case may be, that the organisation has failed to comply with the obligation in question it may order the

PART I
CHAPTER III

organisation to take such steps as the court directs for securing that that subsection or requirement is satisfied or that that obligation is complied with.

(3) The jurisdiction conferred by this section shall be exercisable by the High Court and the Court of Session.

Alteration of
rules for
protection of
investors.

13.—(1) If at any time it appears to the Secretary of State that the rules of a recognised organisation do not satisfy the requirements of paragraph 3(1) of Schedule 2 to this Act he may, instead of revoking the recognition order or making an application under section 12 above, direct the organisation to alter, or himself alter, its rules in such manner as he considers necessary for securing that the rules satisfy those requirements.

(2) If at any time it appears to the Secretary of State that the rules or practices of a recognised organisation which is concerned with two or more kinds of investment business do not satisfy any requirement of Schedule 2 to this Act in respect of investment business of any of those kinds he may, instead of revoking the recognition order or making an application under section 12 above, direct the organisation to alter, or himself alter, its rules so that they preclude a member from carrying on investment business of that kind unless he is an authorised person otherwise than by virtue of membership of the organisation or an exempted person in respect of that business.

(3) Any direction given under this section shall, on the application of the Secretary of State, be enforceable by mandamus or, in Scotland, by an order for specific performance under section 91 of the Court of Session Act 1868.

1868 c. 100.

(4) Before giving a direction or making any alteration under subsection (1) above the Secretary of State shall consult the organisation concerned.

(5) A recognised organisation whose rules have been altered by or pursuant to a direction given by the Secretary of State under subsection (1) above may apply to the court and if the court is satisfied—

    (a) that the rules without the alteration satisfied the requirements mentioned in that subsection ; or

    (b) that other alterations proposed by the organisation would result in the rules satisfying those requirements,

the court may set aside the alteration made by or pursuant to the direction given by the Secretary of State and, in a case within paragraph (b) above, order the organisation to make the alterations proposed by it ; but the setting aside of an alteration under this subsection shall not affect its previous operation.

(6) The jurisdiction conferred by subsection (5) above shall be exercisable by the High Court and the Court of Session.

(7) Section 11(2) to (7) and (9) above shall, with the necessary modifications, have effect in relation to any direction given or alteration made by the Secretary of State under subsection (2) above as they have effect in relation to an order revoking a recognition order.

(8) The fact that the rules of a recognised organisation have been altered by or pursuant to a direction given by the Secretary of State or pursuant to an order made by the court under this section shall not preclude their subsequent alteration or revocation by that organisation.

14.—(1) The Secretary of State may make regulations requiring a recognised organisation to give him forthwith notice of the occurrence of such events relating to the organisation or its members as are specified in the regulations and such information in respect of those events as is so specified.

Notification requirements.

(2) The Secretary of State may make regulations requiring a recognised organisation to furnish him at such times or in respect of such periods as are specified in the regulations with such information relating to the organisation or its members as is so specified.

(3) The notices and information required to be given or furnished under the foregoing provisions of this section shall be such as the Secretary of State may reasonably require for the exercise of his functions under this Act.

(4) Regulations under the foregoing provisions of this section may require information to be given in a specified form and to be verified in a specified manner.

(5) Any notice or information required to be given or furnished under the foregoing provisions of this section shall be given in writing or in such other manner as the Secretary of State may approve.

(6) Where a recognised organisation amends, revokes or adds to its rules or guidance it shall within seven days give the Secretary of State written notice of the amendment, revocation or addition; but notice need not be given of the revocation of guidance other than such as is mentioned in section 9(6) above or of any amendment of or addition to guidance which does not result in or consist of such guidance as is there mentioned.

(7) Contravention of, or of regulations under, this section shall not be an offence.

Persons authorised by recognised professional bodies

15.—(1) A person holding a certificate issued for the purposes of this Part of this Act by a recognised professional body is an authorised person.

Authorisation by certification by recognised professional body.

(2) Such a certificate may be issued by a recognised professional body to an individual, a body corporate, a partnership or an unincorporated association.

(3) A certificate issued to a partnership—

(a) shall be issued in the partnership name ; and

(b) shall authorise the carrying on of investment business in that name by the partnership to which the certificate is issued, by any partnership which succeeds to that business or by any person who succeeds to that business having previously carried it on in partnership ;

and, in relation to a certificate issued to a partnership constituted under the law of England and Wales or Northern Ireland or the law of any other country or territory under which a partnership is not a legal person, references in this Act to the person who holds the certificate or is certified shall be construed as references to the persons or person for the time being authorised by the certificate to carry on investment business as mentioned in paragraph (b) above.

Professional bodies.

16.—(1) In this Act a " professional body " means a body which regulates the practice of a profession and references to the practice of a profession do not include references to carrying on a business consisting wholly or mainly of investment business.

(2) In this Act references to the members of a professional body are references to individuals who, whether or not members of the body, are entitled to practise the profession in question and, in practising it, are subject to the rules of that body.

(3) In this Act references to the rules of a professional body are references to the rules (whether or not laid down by the body itself) which the body has power to enforce in relation to the practice of the profession in question and the carrying on of investment business by persons practising that profession or which relate to the grant, suspension or withdrawal of certificates under section 15 above, the admission and expulsion of members or otherwise to the constitution of the body.

(4) In this Act references to guidance issued by a professional body are references to guidance issued or any recommendation made by it to all or any class of its members or persons seeking to become members, or to persons or any class of persons who are or are seeking to be certified by the body, and which would, if it were a rule, fall within subsection (3) above.

Applications for recognition.

17.—(1) A professional body may apply to the Secretary of State for an order declaring it to be a recognised professional body for the purposes of this Act.

(2) Subsections (2) to (6) of section 9 above shall have effect in relation to an application under subsection (1) above as they have effect in relation to an application under subsection (1) of that section.

18.—(1) The Secretary of State may, on an application duly made in accordance with section 17 above and after being furnished with all such information as he may require under that section, make or refuse to make an order ("a recognition order") declaring the applicant to be a recognised professional body.

(2) The Secretary of State may make a recognition order if it appears to him from the information furnished by the body making the application and having regard to any other information in his possession that the requirements of subsection (3) below and of Schedule 3 to this Act are satisfied as respects that body.

(3) The body must have rules which impose acceptable limits on the kinds of investment business which may be carried on by persons certified by it and the circumstances in which they may carry on such business and which preclude a person certified by that body from carrying on any investment business outside those limits unless he is an authorised person otherwise than by virtue of the certification or an exempted person in respect of that business.

(4) Where the Secretary of State refuses an application for a recognition order he shall give the applicant a written notice to that effect, stating the reasons for the refusal.

(5) A recognition order shall state the date on which it takes effect.

19.—(1) A recognition order under section 18 above may be revoked by a further order made by the Secretary of State if at any time it appears to him—

   (a) that section 18(3) above or any requirement of Schedule 3 to this Act is not satisfied in the case of the body to which the recognition order relates ; or

   (b) that the body has failed to comply with any obligation to which it is subject by virtue of this Act.

(2) Subsections (2) to (9) of section 11 above shall have effect in relation to the revocation of a recognition order under this section as they have effect in relation to the revocation of a recognition order under subsection (1) of that section.

20.—(1) If at any time it appears to the Secretary of State—

   (a) that subsection (3) of section 18 above or any requirement of Schedule 3 to this Act is not satisfied in the case of a recognised professional body ; or

(*b*) that such a body has failed to comply with any obligation to which it is subject by virtue of this Act,

he may, instead of revoking the recognition order under section
19 above, make an application to the court under this section.

(2) If on any such application the court decides that subsection (3) of section 18 above or the requirement in question is not
satisfied or, as the case may be, that the body has failed to
comply with the obligation in question it may order the body
to take such steps as the court directs for securing that that
subsection or requirement is satisfied or that that obligation is
complied with.

(3) The jurisdiction conferred by this section shall be exercisable by the High Court and the Court of Session.

Notification
requirements.

21.—(1) The Secretary of State may make regulations requiring a recognised professional body to give him forthwith notice
of the occurrence of such events relating to the body, its members or persons certified by it as are specified in the regulations
and such information in respect of those events as is so specified.

(2) The Secretary of State may make regulations requiring a
recognised professional body to furnish him at such times or in
respect of such periods as are specified in the regulations with
such information relating to the body, its members and persons
certified by it as is so specified.

(3) The notices and information required to be given or furnished under the foregoing provisions of this section shall be
such as the Secretary of State may reasonably require for the
exercise of his functions under this Act.

(4) Regulations under the foregoing provisions of this section
may require information to be given in a specified form and to
be verified in a specified manner.

(5) Any notice or information required to be given or furnished under the foregoing provisions of this section shall be
given in writing or in such other manner as the Secretary of State
may approve.

(6) Where a recognised professional body amends, revokes
or adds to its rules or guidance it shall within seven days give
the Secretary of State written notice of the amendment, revocation or addition ; but—

(*a*) notice need not be given of the revocation of guidance
other than such as is mentioned in section 9(6) above or
of any amendment of or addition to guidance which
does not result in or consist of such guidance as is
there mentioned ; and

(b) notice need not be given in respect of any rule or   PART I
    guidance, or rules or guidance of any description, in CHAPTER III
    the case of which the Secretary of State has waived
    compliance with this subsection by notice in writing to
    the body concerned ;

and any such waiver may be varied or revoked by a further
notice in writing.

(7) Contravention of, or of regulations under, this section shall
not be an offence.

Insurance companies

22. A body which is authorised under section 3 or 4 of Authorised
the Insurance Companies Act 1982 to carry on insurance business insurers.
which is investment business and carries on such insurance busi- 1982 c. 50.
ness in the United Kingdom is an authorised person as respects—

   (a) any insurance business which is investment business ;
    and

   (b) any other investment business which that body may
    carry on without contravening section 16 of that Act.

Friendly societies

23.—(1) A society which—   Registered

   (a) is a friendly society within the meaning of section 7(1)(a) friendly
    of the Friendly Societies Act 1974 ;   societies.
                               1974 c. 46.

   (b) is registered within the meaning of that Act as a society
    but not as a branch of a society ;

   (c) under its rules has its registered office at a place situated
    in Great Britain ; and

   (d) carries on investment business in the United Kingdom,

is an authorised person as respects any investment business
which it carries on for or in connection with any of the purposes
mentioned in Schedule 1 to that Act.

(2) A society which—

   (a) is a friendly society within the meaning of section 1(1)(a)
    of the Friendly Societies Act (Northern Ireland) 1970 ; 1970 c. 31

   (b) is registered or deemed to be registered as a society (N.I.).
    but not as a branch of a society under that Act ;

   (c) under its rules has its registered office at a place situated
    in Northern Ireland ; and

   (d) carries on investment business in the United Kingdom,

is an authorised person as respects any investment business
which it carries on for or in connection with any of the purposes
mentioned in Schedule 1 to that Act.

PART I
CHAPTER III
Operators and
trustees of
recognised
schemes.

Collective investment schemes

24. The operator or trustee of a scheme recognised under section 86 below is an authorised person as respects—

(a) investment business which consists in operating or acting as trustee in relation to that scheme ; and

(b) any investment business which is carried on by him in connection with or for the purposes of that scheme.

Persons authorised by the Secretary of State

25. A person holding an authorisation granted by the Secretary of State under the following provisions of this Chapter is an authorised person.

26.—(1) An application for authorisation by the Secretary of State may be made by—

(a) an individual ;

(b) a body corporate ;

(c) a partnership ; or

(d) an unincorporated association.

(2) Any such application—

(a) shall be made in such manner as the Secretary of State may direct ;

(b) shall contain or be accompanied by—

(i) information as to the investment business which the applicant proposes to carry on and the services which he will hold himself out as able to provide in the carrying on of that business ; and

(ii) such other information as the Secretary of State may reasonably require for the purpose of determining the application ; and

(c) shall contain the address of a place in the United Kingdom for the service on the applicant of any notice or other document required or authorised to be served on him under this Act.

(3) At any time after receiving an application and before determining it the Secretary of State may require the applicant to furnish additional information.

(4) The directions and requirements given or imposed under subsections (2) and (3) above may differ as between different applications.

(5) Any information to be furnished to the Secretary of State under this section shall, if he so requires, be in such form or verified in such manner as he may specify.

27.—(1) The Secretary of State may, on an application duly made in accordance with section 26 above and after being furnished with all such information as he may require under that section, grant or refuse the application.

(2) The Secretary of State shall grant the application if it appears to him from the information furnished by the applicant and having regard to any other information in his possession that the applicant is a fit and proper person to carry on the investment business and provide the services described in the application.

(3) In determining whether to grant or refuse an application the Secretary of State may take into account any matter relating to any person who is or will be employed by or associated with the applicant for the purposes of the business in question, to any person who is or will be acting as an appointed representative in relation to that business and—

(a) if the applicant is a body corporate, to any director or controller of the body, to any other body corporate in the same group or to any director or controller of any such other body corporate ;

(b) if the applicant is a partnership, to any of the partners ;

(c) if the applicant is an unincorporated association, to any member of the governing body of the association or any officer or controller of the association.

(4) In determining whether to grant or refuse an application the Secretary of State may also have regard to any business which the applicant proposes to carry on in connection with his investment business.

(5) In the case of an applicant who is authorised to carry on investment business in a member State other than the United Kingdom the Secretary of State shall have regard to that authorisation.

(6) An authorisation granted to a partnership—

(a) shall be granted in the partnership name ; and

(b) shall authorise the carrying on of investment business in that name (or with the Secretary of State's consent in any other name) by the partnership to which the authorisation is granted, by any partnership which succeeds to that business or by any person who succeeds to that business having previously carried it on in partnership ;

and, in relation to an authorisation granted to a partnership constituted under the law of England and Wales or Northern Ireland or the law of any other country or territory under which a partnership is not a legal person, references in this

Act to the holder of the authorisation or the authorised person shall be construed as references to the persons or person for the time being authorised by the authorisation to carry on investment business as mentioned in paragraph (b) above.

(7) An authorisation granted to an unincorporated association shall apply to the carrying on of investment business in the name of the association and in such manner as may be specified in the authorisation.

(8) The Secretary of State shall give an applicant for authorisation written notice of the grant of authorisation specifying the date on which it takes effect.

Withdrawal and suspension of authorisation.

28.—(1) The Secretary of State may at any time withdraw or suspend any authorisation granted by him if it appears to him—

    (a) that the holder of the authorisation is not a fit and proper person to carry on the investment business which he is carrying on or proposing to carry on ; or

    (b) without prejudice to paragraph (a) above, that the holder of the authorisation has contravened any provision of this Act or any rules or regulations made under it or, in purported compliance with any such provision, has furnished the Secretary of State with false, inaccurate or misleading information or has contravened any prohibition or requirement imposed under this Act.

(2) For the purposes of subsection (1)(a) above the Secretary of State may take into account any such matters as are mentioned in section 27 (3) and (4) above.

(3) Where the holder of the authorisation is a member of a recognised self-regulating organisation the rules, prohibitions and requirements referred to in paragraph (b) of subsection (1) above include the rules of that organisation and any prohibition or requirement imposed by virtue of those rules ; and where he is a person certified by a recognised professional body the rules, prohibitions and requirements referred to in that paragraph include the rules of that body which regulate the carrying on by him of investment business and any prohibition or requirement imposed by virtue of those rules.

(4) The suspension of an authorisation shall be for a specified period or until the occurrence of a specified event or until specified conditions are complied with ; and while an authorisation is suspended the holder shall not be an authorised person.

(5) Any period, event or conditions specified under subsection (4) above in the case of an authorisation may be varied by the Secretary of State on the application of the holder.

29.—(1) Where the Secretary of State proposes—

    (*a*) to refuse an application under section 26 or 28(5) above ; or

    (*b*) to withdraw or suspend an authorisation,

he shall give the applicant or the authorised person written notice of his intention to do so, stating the reasons for which he proposes to act.

(2) In the case of a proposed withdrawal or suspension the notice shall state the date on which it is proposed that the withdrawal or suspension should take effect and, in the case of a proposed suspension, its proposed duration.

(3) Where the reasons stated in a notice under this section relate specifically to matters which—

    (*a*) refer to a person identified in the notice other than the applicant or the holder of the authorisation ; and

    (*b*) are in the opinion of the Secretary of State prejudicial to that person in any office or employment,

the Secretary of State shall, unless he considers it impracticable to do so, serve a copy of the notice on that person.

(4) A notice under this section shall give particulars of the right to require the case to be referred to the Tribunal under Chapter IX of this Part of this Act.

(5) Where a case is not required to be referred to the Tribunal by a person on whom a notice is served under this section the Secretary of State shall, at the expiration of the period within which such a requirement can be made—

    (*a*) give that person written notice of the refusal, withdrawal or suspension ; or

    (*b*) give that person written notice of the grant of the application or, as the case may be, written notice that the authorisation is not to be withdrawn or suspended ;

and the Secretary of State may give public notice of any decision notified by him under paragraph (*a*) or (*b*) above and the reasons for the decision except that he shall not do so in the case of a decision notified under paragraph (*b*) unless the person concerned consents to his doing so.

30.—(1) An application under section 26 above may be withdrawn before it is granted or refused ; and, subject to subsections (2) and (3) below, an authorisation granted under section 27 above may be withdrawn by the Secretary of State at the request or with the consent of the authorised person.

(2) The Secretary of State may refuse to withdraw any such authorisation if he considers that the public interest requires

any matter affecting the authorised person to be investigated as a preliminary to a decision on the question whether the Secretary of State should in respect of that person exercise his powers under section 28 above or under any other provision of this Part of this Act.

(3) The Secretary of State may also refuse to withdraw an authorisation where in his opinion it is desirable that a prohibition or restriction should be imposed on the authorised person under Chapter VI of this Part of this Act or that a prohibition or restriction imposed on that person under that Chapter should continue in force.

(4) The Secretary of State may give public notice of any withdrawal of authorisation under subsection (1) above.

Persons authorised in other member States

Authorisation
in other
member State.

31.—(1) A person carrying on investment business in the United Kingdom is an authorised person if—

    (*a*) he is established in a member State other than the United Kingdom ;

    (*b*) the law of that State recognises him as a national of that or another member State ; and

    (*c*) he is for the time being authorised under that law to carry on investment business or investment business of any particular kind.

(2) For the purposes of this Act a person is established in a member State other than the United Kingdom if his head office is situated in that State and he does not transact investment business from a permanent place of business maintained by him in the United Kingdom.

(3) This section applies to a person only if the provisions of the law under which he is authorised to carry on the investment business in question—

    (*a*) afford to investors in the United Kingdom protection, in relation to his carrying on of that business, which is at least equivalent to that provided for them by the provisions of this Chapter relating to members of recognised self-regulating organisations or to persons authorised by the Secretary of State ; or

    (*b*) satisfy the conditions laid down by a Community instrument for the co-ordination or approximation of the laws, regulations or administrative provisions of member States relating to the carrying on of investment business or investment business of the relevant kind.

(4) A certificate issued by the Secretary of State and for the time being in force to the effect that the provisions of the law

of a member State comply with the requirements of subsection (3)(*a*) above, either as respects all investment business or as respects investment business of a particular kind, shall be conclusive evidence of that matter but the absence or revocation of such a certificate shall not be regarded as indicating that those requirements are not complied with.

(5) This section shall not apply to a person by virtue of paragraph (*b*) of subsection (3) above unless the authority by which he is authorised to carry on the investment business in question certifies that he is authorised to do so under a law which complies with the requirements of that paragraph.

32.—(1) A person who is an authorised person by virtue of section 31 above shall be guilty of an offence unless, not less than seven days before beginning to carry on investment business in the United Kingdom, he has given notice of his intention to do so to the Secretary of State either in writing or in such other manner as the Secretary of State may approve.

(2) The notice shall contain—

    (*a*) information as to the investment business which that person proposes to carry on in the United Kingdom and the services which he will hold himself out as able to provide in the carrying on of that business ;

    (*b*) information as to the authorisation of that person in the member State in question ;

    (*c*) the address of a place (whether in the United Kingdom or elsewhere) for the service on that person of any notice or other document required or authorised to be served on him under this Act ;

    (*d*) such other information as may be prescribed ;

and the notice shall comply with such requirements as to the form in which any information is to be given and as to its verification as may be prescribed.

(3) A notice by a person claiming to be authorised by virtue of subsection (3)(*b*) of section 31 above shall be accompanied by a copy of the certificate required by subsection (5) of that section.

(4) A person guilty of an offence under subsection (1) above shall be liable—

    (*a*) on conviction on indictment, to a fine ;

    (*b*) on summary conviction, to a fine not exceeding the statutory maximum.

(5) In proceedings brought against any person for an offence under subsection (1) above it shall be a defence for him to prove

that he took all reasonable precautions and exercised all due diligence to avoid the commission of the offence.

Termination and suspension of authorisation.

33.—(1) If it appears to the Secretary of State that a person who is an authorised person by virtue of section 31 above has contravened any provision of this Act or of any rules or regulations made under it or, in purported compliance with any such provision, has furnished the Secretary of State with false, inaccurate or misleading information or has contravened any prohibition or requirement imposed under this Act the Secretary of State may direct—

(a) that he shall cease to be an authorised person by virtue of that section ; or

(b) that he shall not be an authorised person by virtue of that section for a specified period or until the occurrence of a specified event or until specified conditions are complied with.

(2) In the case of a person who is a member of a recognised self-regulating organisation the rules, prohibitions and requirements referred to in subsection (1) above include the rules of that organisation and any prohibition or requirement imposed by virtue of those rules ; and in the case of a person who is certified by a recognised professional body the rules, prohibitions and requirements referred to in that subsection include the rules of that body which regulate the carrying on by him of investment business and any prohibition or requirement imposed by virtue of those rules.

(3) Any period, event or condition specified in a direction under subsection (1)(b) above may be varied by the Secretary of State on the application of the person to whom the direction relates.

(4) The Secretary of State shall consult the relevant supervisory authority before giving a direction under this section unless he considers it essential in the interests of investors that the direction should be given forthwith but in that case he shall consult the authority immediately after giving the direction and may then revoke or vary it if he considers it appropriate to do so.

(5) The Secretary of State shall revoke a direction under this section if he is satisfied, after consulting the relevant supervisory authority, that it will secure that the person concerned will comply with the provisions mentioned in subsection (1) above.

(6) In this section " the relevant supervisory authority " means the authority of the member State where the person concerned is established which is responsible for supervising the carrying on of investment business of the kind which that person is or was carrying on.

34.—(1) Where the Secretary of State proposes—

   (*a*) to give a direction under section 33 above ; or

   (*b*) to refuse an application under subsection (3) of that
      section,

he shall give the authorised person written notice of his intention to do so, stating the reasons for which he proposes to act.

(2) In the case of a proposed direction under section 33 above
the notice shall state the date on which it is proposed that the
direction should take effect and, in the case of a proposed direction under subsection (1)(*b*) of that section, its proposed duration.

(3) Where the reasons stated in a notice under this section
relate specifically to matters which—

   (*a*) refer to a person identified in the notice other than the
      authorised person ; and

   (*b*) are in the opinion of the Secretary of State prejudicial
      to that person in any office or employment,

the Secretary of State shall, unless he considers it impracticable
to do so, serve a copy of the notice on that other person.

(4) A notice under this section shall give particulars of the
right to require the case to be referred to the Tribunal under
Chapter IX of this Part of this Act.

(5) Where a case is not required to be referred to the Tribunal
by a person on whom a notice is served under this section the
Secretary of State shall, at the expiration of the period within
which such a requirement can be made—

   (*a*) give that person written notice of the direction or refus-
      al ; or

   (*b*) give that person written notice that the direction is not
      to be given or, as the case may be, of the grant of the
      application ;

and the Secretary of State may give public notice of any decision
notified by him under paragraph (*a*) or (*b*) above and the reasons
for the decision except that he shall not do so in the case of a
decision within paragraph (*b*) unless the person concerned consents to his doing so.

Chapter IV
Exempted Persons
The Bank of England

35. The Bank of England is an exempted person. The Bank of
England.

Recognised investment exchanges and clearing houses

36.—(1) A recognised investment exchange is an exempted Investment
person as respects anything done in its capacity as such which exchanges.
constitutes investment business.

(2) In this Act references to the rules of an investment exchange are references to the rules made or conditions imposed by it with respect to the matters dealt with in Schedule 4 to this Act, with respect to the admission of persons to or their exclusion from the use of its facilities or otherwise relating to its constitution.

(3) In this Act references to guidance issued by an investment exchange are references to guidance issued or any recommendation made by it to all or any class of its members or users or persons seeking to become members of the exchange or to use its facilities and which would, if it were a rule, fall within subsection (2) above.

Grant and
revocation of
recognition.

37.—(1) Any body corporate or unincorporated association may apply to the Secretary of State for an order declaring it to be a recognised investment exchange for the purposes of this Act.

(2) Subsections (2) to (5) of section 9 above shall have effect in relation to an application under subsection (1) above as they have effect in relation to an application under subsection (1) of that section ; and every application under subsection (1) above shall be accompanied by—

    (*a*) a copy of the applicant's rules ;

    (*b*) a copy of any guidance issued by the applicant which is intended to have continuing effect and is issued in writing or other legible form ; and

    (*c*) particulars of any arrangements which the applicant has made or proposes to make for the provision of clearing services.

(3) The Secretary of State may, on an application duly made in accordance with subsection (1) above and after being furnished with all such information as he may require in connection with the application, make or refuse to make an order (" a recognition order ") declaring the applicant to be a recognised investment exchange for the purposes of this Act.

(4) Subject to Chapter XIV of this Part of this Act, the Secretary of State may make a recognition order if it appears to him from the information furnished by the exchange making the application and having regard to any other information in his possession that the requirements of Schedule 4 to this Act are satisfied as respects that exchange.

(5) Where the Secretary of State refuses an application for a recognition order he shall give the applicant a written notice to that effect stating the reasons for the refusal.

(6) A recognition order shall state the date on which it takes effect.

(7) A recognition order may be revoked by a further order made by the Secretary of State if at any time it appears to him—

(*a*) that any requirement of Schedule 4 to this Act is not satisfied in the case of the exchange to which the recognition order relates ; or

(*b*) that the exchange has failed to comply with any obligation to which it is subject by virtue of this Act ;

and subsections (2) to (9) of section 11 above shall have effect in relation to the revocation of a recognition order under this subsection as they have effect in relation to the revocation of such an order under subsection (1) of that section.

(8) Section 12 above shall have effect in relation to a recognised investment exchange and the requirements and obligations referred to in subsection (7) above as it has effect in relation to the requirements and obligations there mentioned.

38.—(1) A recognised clearing house is an exempted person as respects anything done by it in its capacity as a person providing clearing services for the transaction of investment business.

Clearing houses.

(2) In this Act references to the rules of a clearing house are references to the rules made or conditions imposed by it with respect to the provision by it or its members of clearing services under clearing arrangements, that is to say, arrangements with a recognised investment exchange for the provision of clearing services in respect of transactions effected on the exchange.

(3) In this Act references to guidance issued by a clearing house are references to guidance issued or any recommendation made by it to all or any class of its members or persons using or seeking to use its services and which would, if it were a rule, fall within subsection (2) above.

39.—(1) Any body corporate or unincorporated association may apply to the Secretary of State for an order declaring it to be a recognised clearing house for the purposes of this Act.

Grant and revocation of recognition.

(2) Subsections (2) to (5) of section 9 above shall have effect in relation to an application under subsection (1) above as they have effect in relation to an application under subsection (1) of that section ; and any application under subsection (1) above shall be accompanied by—

(*a*) a copy of the applicant's rules ;

(*b*) a copy of any guidance issued by the applicant which is intended to have continuing effect and is issued in writing or other legible form ; and

(c) particulars of any recognised investment exchange with which the applicant proposes to make clearing arrangements and of any other person (whether or not such an exchange) for whom the applicant provides clearing services.

(3) The Secretary of State may, on an application duly made in accordance with subsection (1) above and after being furnished with all such information as he may require in connection with the application, make or refuse to make an order (" a recognition order ") declaring the applicant to be a recognised clearing house for the purposes of this Act.

(4) Subject to Chapter XIV of this Part of this Act, the Secretary of State may make a recognition order if it appears to him from the information furnished by the clearing house making the application and having regard to any other information in his possession that the clearing house—

(a) has financial resources sufficient for the proper performance of its functions ;

(b) has adequate arrangements and resources for the effective monitoring and enforcement of compliance with its rules or, as respects monitoring, arrangements providing for that function to be performed on behalf of the clearing house (and without affecting its responsibility) by another body or person who is able and willing to perform it ;

(c) provides or is able to provide clearing services which would enable a recognised investment exchange to make arrangements with it that satisfy the requirements of Schedule 4 to this Act ; and

(d) is able and willing to comply with duties corresponding to those imposed in the case of a recognised investment exchange by paragraph 5 of that Schedule.

(5) Where the Secretary of State refuses an application for a recognition order he shall give the applicant a written notice to that effect stating the reasons for the refusal.

(6) A recognition order shall state the date on which it takes effect.

(7) A recognition order may be revoked by a further order made by the Secretary of State if at any time it appears to him—

(a) that any requirement of subsection (4) above is not satisfied in the case of the clearing house ; or

(b) that the clearing house has failed to comply with any obligation to which it is subject by virtue of this Act ;

and subsections (2) to (9) of section 11 above shall have effect in relation to the revocation of a recognition order under this subsection as they have effect in relation to the revocation of such an order under subsection (1) of that section.

(8) Section 12 above shall have effect in relation to a recognised clearing house and the requirements and obligations referred to in subsection (7) above as it has effect in relation to the requirements and obligations there mentioned.

40.—(1) Any application under section 37(1) or 39(1) above by a body or association whose head office is situated in a country outside the United Kingdom shall contain the address of a place in the United Kingdom for the service on that body or association of notices or other documents required or authorised to be served on it under this Act.

(2) In relation to any such body or association sections 37(4) and 39(4) above shall have effect with the substitution for the requirements there mentioned of the following requirements, that is to say—

(*a*) that the body or association is, in the country in which its head office is situated, subject to supervision which, together with the rules and practices of that body or association, is such that investors in the United Kingdom are afforded protection in relation to that body or association at least equivalent to that provided by the provisions of this Act in relation to investment exchanges and clearing houses in respect of which recognition orders are made otherwise than by virtue of this subsection ; and

(*b*) that the body or association is able and willing to co-operate, by the sharing of information and otherwise, with the authorities, bodies and persons responsible in the United Kingdom for the supervision and regulation of investment business or other financial services ; and

(*c*) that adequate arrangements exist for such co-operation between those responsible for the supervision of the body or association in the country mentioned in paragraph (*a*) above and the authorities, bodies and persons mentioned in paragraph (*b*) above.

(3) In determining whether to make a recognition order by virtue of subsection (2) above the Secretary of State may have regard to the extent to which persons in the United Kingdom and persons in the country mentioned in that subsection have access to the financial markets in each others' countries.

(4) In relation to a body or association declared to be a recognised investment exchange or recognised clearing house by a recognition order made by virtue of subsection (2) above—

> (*a*) the reference in section 36(2) above to the matters dealt with in Schedule 4 to this Act shall be construed as a reference to corresponding matters ;
>
> (*b*) sections 37(7) and (8) and 39(7) and (8) above shall have effect as if the requirements mentioned in section 37(7)(*a*) and in section 39(7)(*a*) were those of subsection (2)(*a*) and (*b*) above ; and
>
> (*c*) the grounds on which the order may be revoked under section 37(7) or 39(7) above shall include the ground that it appears to the Secretary of State that revocation is desirable in the interests of investors and potential investors in the United Kingdom.

(5) In this section " country " includes any territory or any part of a country or territory.

(6) A body or association declared to be a recognised investment exchange or recognised clearing house by a recognition order made by virtue of subsection (2) above is in this Act referred to as an " overseas investment exchange " or an " overseas clearing house ".

Notification
requirements.
41.—(1) The Secretary of State may make regulations requiring a recognised investment exchange or recognised clearing house to give him forthwith notice of the occurrence of such events relating to the exchange or clearing house as are specified in the regulations and such information in respect of those events as is so specified.

(2) The Secretary of State may make regulations requiring a recognised investment exchange or recognised clearing house to furnish him at such times or in respect of such periods as are specified in the regulations with such information relating to the exchange or clearing house as is so specified.

(3) The notices and information required to be given or furnished under the foregoing provisions of this section shall be such as the Secretary of State may reasonably require for the exercise of his functions under this Act.

(4) Regulations under the foregoing provisions of this section may require information to be given in a specified form and to be verified in a specified manner.

(5) Where a recognised investment exchange—

> (*a*) amends, revokes or adds to its rules or guidance ; or
>
> (*b*) makes, terminates or varies any clearing arrangements,

it shall within seven days give written notice to the Secretary of
State of the amendment, revocation or addition or, as the case
may be, of the matters mentioned in paragraph (*b*) above.

(6) Where a recognised clearing house—

    (*a*) amends, revokes or adds to its rules or guidance ; or

    (*b*) makes a change in the persons for whom it provides
       clearing services,

it shall within seven days give written notice to the Secretary of
State of the amendment, revocation or addition or, as the case
may be, of the change.

(7) Notice need not be given under subsection (5) or (6) above
of the revocation of guidance other than such as is mentioned
in section 37(2)(*b*) or 39(2)(*b*) above or of any amendment of
or addition to guidance which does not result in or consist of
such guidance as is there mentioned.

Other exemptions

42. The Society of Lloyd's and persons permitted by the   Lloyd's.
Council of Lloyd's to act as underwriting agents at Lloyd's are
exempted persons as respects investment business carried on in
connection with or for the purpose of insurance business at
Lloyd's.

43.—(1) A person for the time being included in a list main-   Listed money
tained by the Bank of England for the purposes of this section   market
(" a listed institution ") is an exempted person in respect of, and   institutions.
of anything done for the purposes of, any transaction to which
Part I or Part II of Schedule 5 to this Act applies and in respect
of any arrangements made by him with a view to other persons
entering into a transaction to which Part III of that Schedule
applies.

(2) The conditions imposed by the Bank of England for
admission to the list referred to in this section and the arrangements made by it for a person's admission to and removal from
the list shall require the approval of the Treasury ; and this
section shall cease to have effect if that approval is withdrawn
but without prejudice to its again having effect if approval is
given for fresh conditions or arrangements.

(3) The Bank of England shall publish the list as for the time
being in force and provide a certified copy of it at the request of
any person wishing to refer to it in legal proceedings.

(4) Such a certified copy shall be evidence or, in Scotland,
sufficient evidence of the contents of the list ; and a copy purporting to be certified by or on behalf of the Bank shall be
deemed to have been duly certified unless the contrary is shown.

44.—(1) An appointed representative is an exempted person as respects investment business carried on by him as such a representative.

(2) For the purposes of this Act an appointed representative is a person—

> (a) who is employed by an authorised person (his " principal ") under a contract for services which—
>
>> (i) requires or permits him to carry on investment business to which this section applies ; and
>>
>> (ii) complies with subsections (4) and (5) below ; and
>
> (b) for whose activities in carrying on the whole or part of that investment business his principal has accepted responsibility in writing ;

and the investment business carried on by an appointed representative as such is the investment business for which his principal has accepted responsibility.

(3) This section applies to investment business carried on by an appointed representative which consists of—

> (a) procuring or endeavouring to procure the persons with whom he deals to enter into investment agreements with his principal or (if not prohibited by his contract) with other persons ;
>
> (b) giving advice to the persons with whom he deals about entering into investment agreements with his principal or (if not prohibited by his contract) with other persons ; or
>
> (c) giving advice as to the sale of investments issued by his principal or as to the exercise of rights conferred by an investment whether or not issued as aforesaid.

(4) If the contract between an appointed representative and his principal does not prohibit the representative from procuring or endeavouring to procure persons to enter into investment agreements with persons other than his principal it must make provision for enabling the principal either to impose such a prohibition or to restrict the kinds of investment to which those agreements may relate or the other persons with whom they may be entered into.

(5) If the contract between an appointed representative and his principal does not prohibit the representative from giving advice about entering into investment agreements with persons other than his principal it must make provision for enabling the principal either to impose such a prohibition or to restrict the kinds of advice which the representative may give by reference

to the kinds of investment in relation to which or the persons with whom the representative may advise that investment agreements should be made.

(6) The principal of an appointed representative shall be responsible, to the same extent as if he had expressly authorised it, for anything said or done or omitted by the representative in carrying on the investment business for which he has accepted responsibility.

(7) In determining whether an authorised person has complied with—

(a) any provision contained in or made under this Act ; or

(b) any rules of a recognised self-regulating organisation or recognised professional body,

anything which a person who at the material time is or was an appointed representative of the authorised person has said, done or omitted as respects investment business for which the authorised person has accepted responsibility shall be treated as having been said, done or omitted by the authorised person.

(8) Nothing in subsection (7) above shall cause the knowledge or intentions of an appointed representative to be attributed to his principal for the purpose of determining whether the principal has committed a criminal offence unless in all the circumstances it is reasonable for them to be attributed to him.

(9) In this Act "investment agreement" means any agreement the making or performance of which by either party constitutes an activity which falls within any paragraph of Part II of Schedule 1 to this Act or would do so apart from Parts III and IV of that Schedule.

45.—(1) Each of the following persons is an exempted person to the extent specified in relation to that person—

Miscellaneous exemptions.

(a) the President of the Family Division of the High Court when acting in the exercise of his functions under section 9 of the Administration of Estates Act 1925 ;

1925 c. 23.

(b) the Probate Judge of the High Court of Northern Ireland when acting in the exercise of his functions under section 3 of the Administration of Estates Act (Northern Ireland) 1955 ;

1955 c. 24 (N.I.).

(c) the Accountant General of the Supreme Court when acting in the exercise of his functions under Part VI of the Administration of Justice Act 1982 ;

1982 c. 53.

(d) the Accountant of Court when acting in the exercise of his functions in connection with the consignation or deposit of sums of money ;

Part I
Chapter IV
1906 c. 55.

1983 c. 20.

1896 c. 35.

1960 c. 58.
1964 c. 33
(N.I.).
1961 c. 62.
1982 c. 53.

1958 No. 1.

1986 c. 45.

(e) the Public Trustee when acting in the exercise of his functions under the Public Trustee Act 1906 ;

(f) the Master of the Court of Protection when acting in the exercise of his functions under Part VII of the Mental Health Act 1983 ;

(g) the Official Solicitor to the Supreme Court when acting as judicial trustee under the Judicial Trustees Act 1896 ;

(h) a registrar of a county court when managing funds paid into court ;

(i) a sheriff clerk when acting in the exercise of his functions in connection with the consignation or deposit of sums of money ;

(j) a person acting in his capacity as manager of a fund established under section 22 of the Charities Act 1960, section 25 of the Charities Act (Northern Ireland) 1964, section 11 of the Trustee Investments Act 1961 or section 42 of the Administration of Justice Act 1982 ;

(k) the Central Board of Finance of the Church of England or a Diocesan Authority within the meaning of the Church Funds Investment Measure 1958 when acting in the exercise of its functions under that Measure ;

(l) a person acting in his capacity as an official receiver within the meaning of section 399 of the Insolvency Act 1986 or in that capacity within the meaning of any corresponding provision in force in Northern Ireland.

(2) Where a bankruptcy order is made in respect of an authorised person or of a person whose authorisation is suspended under section 28 above or who is the subject of a direction under section 33(1)(b) above or a winding-up order is made in respect of a partnership which is such a person, the trustee in bankruptcy or liquidator acting in his capacity as such is an exempted person but—

(a) sections 48 to 71 below and, so far as relevant to any of those provisions, Chapter IX of this Part of this Act ; and

(b) sections 104, 105 and 106 below,

shall apply to him to the same extent as they applied to the bankrupt or partnership and, if the bankrupt or partnership was subject to the rules of a recognised self-regulating organisation or recognised professional body, he shall himself also be subject to those rules.

(3) In the application of subsection (2) above to Scotland—

(a) for the reference to a bankruptcy order being made in

respect of a person there shall be substituted a reference to the estate of that person being sequestrated ;

(b) the reference to a winding-up order in respect of a partnership is a reference to such an order made under section 72 below ;

(c) for the reference to the trustee in bankruptcy there shall be substituted a reference to the interim trustee or permanent trustee within the meaning of the Bankruptcy (Scotland) Act 1985 ; and

1985 c. 66.

(d) for the references to the bankrupt there shall be substituted references to the debtor.

(4) In the application of subsection (2) above to Northern Ireland for the reference to a bankruptcy order there shall be substituted a reference to an order of adjudication of bankruptcy and the reference to a trustee in bankruptcy shall include a reference to an assignee in bankruptcy.

Supplemental

46.—(1) The Secretary of State may by order provide—

Power to extend or restrict exemptions.

(a) for exemptions additional to those specified in the foregoing provisions of this Chapter ; or

(b) for removing or restricting any exemption conferred by section 42, 43 or 45 above ;

and any such order may contain such transitional provisions as the Secretary of State thinks necessary or expedient.

(2) An order making such provision as is mentioned in paragraph (a) of subsection (1) above shall be subject to annulment in pursuance of a resolution of either House of Parliament ; and no order making such provision as is mentioned in paragraph (b) of that subsection shall be made unless a draft of it has been laid before and approved by a resolution of each House of Parliament.

CHAPTER V

CONDUCT OF INVESTMENT BUSINESS

47.—(1) Any person who—

Misleading statements and practices.

(a) makes a statement, promise or forecast which he knows to be misleading, false or deceptive or dishonestly conceals any material facts ; or

(b) recklessly makes (dishonestly or otherwise) a statement, promise or forecast which is misleading, false or deceptive,

is guilty of an offence if he makes the statement, promise or forecast or conceals the facts for the purpose of inducing, or is reckless as to whether it may induce, another person (whether or not the person to whom the statement, promise or forecast is made or from whom the facts are concealed) to enter or offer to enter into, or to refrain from entering or offering to enter into, an investment agreement or to exercise, or refrain from exercising, any rights conferred by an investment.

(2) Any person who does any act or engages in any course of conduct which creates a false or misleading impression as to the market in or the price or value of any investments is guilty of an offence if he does so for the purpose of creating that impression and of thereby inducing another person to acquire, dispose of, subscribe for or underwrite those investments or to refrain from doing so or to exercise, or refrain from exercising, any rights conferred by those investments.

(3) In proceedings brought against any person for an offence under subsection (2) above it shall be a defence for him to prove that he reasonably believed that his act or conduct would not create an impression that was false or misleading as to the matters mentioned in that subsection.

(4) Subsection (1) above does not apply unless—

> (*a*) the statement, promise or forecast is made in or from, or the facts are concealed in or from, the United Kingdom;
>
> (*b*) the person on whom the inducement is intended to or may have effect is in the United Kingdom; or
>
> (*c*) the agreement is or would be entered into or the rights are or would be exercised in the United Kingdom.

(5) Subsection (2) above does not apply unless—

> (*a*) the act is done or the course of conduct is engaged in in the United Kingdom; or
>
> (*b*) the false or misleading impression is created there.

(6) A person guilty of an offence under this section shall be liable—

> (*a*) on conviction on indictment, to imprisonment for a term not exceeding seven years or to a fine or to both;
>
> (*b*) on summary conviction, to imprisonment for a term not exceeding six months or to a fine not exceeding the statutory maximum or to both.

Conduct of business rules.

48.—(1) The Secretary of State may make rules regulating the conduct of investment business by authorised persons but those rules shall not apply to members of a recognised self-regulating organisation or persons certified by a recognised professional body in respect of investment business in the carrying on of which they are subject to the rules of the organisation or body.

(2) Rules under this section may in particular make provision—

(a) prohibiting a person from carrying on, or holding himself out as carrying on—

(i) investment business of any kind specified in the rules ; or

(ii) investment business of a kind or on a scale other than that notified by him to the Secretary of State in connection with an application for authorisation under Chapter III of this Part of this Act, in a notice under section 32 above or in accordance with any provision of the rules or regulations in that behalf ;

(b) prohibiting a person from carrying on investment business in relation to persons other than those of a specified class or description ;

(c) regulating the manner in which a person may hold himself out as carrying on investment business ;

(d) regulating the manner in which a person makes a market in any investments ;

(e) as to the form and content of advertisements in respect of investment business ;

(f) requiring the principals of appointed representatives to impose restrictions on the investment business carried on by them ;

(g) requiring the disclosure of the amount or value, or of arrangements for the payment or provision, of commissions or other inducements in connection with investment business and restricting the matters by reference to which or the manner in which their amount or value may be determined ;

(h) enabling or requiring information obtained by an authorised person in the course of carrying on one part of his business to be withheld by him from persons with whom he deals in the course of carrying on another part and for that purpose enabling or requiring persons employed in one part of that business to withhold information from those employed in another part ;

(i) as to the circumstances and manner in which and the time when or the period during which action may be taken for the purpose of stabilising the price of investments of any specified description ;

(j) for arrangements for the settlement of disputes ;

(k) requiring the keeping of accounts and other records, as to their form and content and for their inspection ;

(*l*) requiring a person to whom the rules apply to make provision for the protection of investors in the event of the cessation of his investment business in consequence of his death, incapacity or otherwise.

(3) Subsection (2) above is without prejudice to the generality of subsection (1) above and accordingly rules under this section may make provision for matters other than those mentioned in subsection (2) or further provision as to any of the matters there mentioned except that they shall not impose limits on the amount or value of commissions or other inducements paid or provided in connection with investment business.

(4) Rules under this section may also regulate or prohibit the carrying on in connection with investment business of any other business or the carrying on of any other business which is held out as being for the purposes of investment.

(5) In paragraph (*e*) of subsection (2) above " advertisement " does not include any advertisement which is subject to section 154 below or which is required or permitted to be published by listing rules under Part IV of this Act and relates to securities which have been admitted to listing under that Part ; and rules under that paragraph shall have effect subject to the provisions of Part V of this Act.

(6) Nothing done in conformity with rules made under paragraph (*h*) of subsection (2) above shall be regarded as a contravention of section 47 above.

(7) Section 47(2) above shall not be regarded as contravened by anything done for the purpose of stabilising the price of investments if it is done in conformity with rules made under this section and—

    (*a*) in respect of investments which fall within any of paragraphs 1 to 5 of Schedule 1 to this Act and are specified by the rules ; and

    (*b*) during such period before or after the issue of those investments as is specified by the rules.

(8) The Secretary of State may by order amend subsection (7) above—

    (*a*) by restricting or extending the kinds of investment to which it applies ;

    (*b*) by restricting it so as to apply only in relation to the issue of investments in specified circumstances or by extending it, in respect of investments of any kind specified in the order, so as to apply to things done during a specified period before or after events other than the issue of those investments.

(9) No order shall be made under subsection (8) above unless a draft of it has been laid before and approved by a resolution of each House of Parliament.

(10) Rules under this section may contain such incidental and transitional provisions as the Secretary of State thinks necessary or expedient.

49.—(1) The Secretary of State may make rules requiring Financial persons authorised to carry on investment business by virtue of resources rules. section 25 or 31 above to have and maintain in respect of that business such financial resources as are required by the rules.

(2) Without prejudice to the generality of subsection (1) above, rules under this section may—

  (*a*) impose requirements which are absolute or which are to vary from time to time by reference to such factors as are specified in or determined in accordance with the rules ;

  (*b*) impose requirements which take account of any business (whether or not investment business) carried on by the person concerned in conjunction with or in addition to the business mentioned in subsection (1) above ;

  (*c*) make provision as to the assets, liabilities and other matters to be taken into account in determining a person's financial resources for the purposes of the rules and the extent to which and the manner in which they are to be taken into account for that purpose.

50.—(1) The Secretary of State may, on the application of any Modification person to whom any rules made under section 48 or 49 above of conduct of apply, alter the requirements of the rules so as to adapt them business and to the circumstances of that person or to any particular kind financial of business carried on or to be carried on by him. resources rules for particular cases.

(2) The Secretary of State shall not exercise the powers conferred by subsection (1) above in any case unless it appears to him that—

  (*a*) compliance with the requirements in question would be unduly burdensome for the applicant having regard to the benefit which compliance would confer on investors ; and

  (*b*) the exercise of those powers will not result in any undue risk to investors.

(3) The powers conferred by subsection (1) above may be exercised unconditionally or subject to conditions.

51.—(1) The Secretary of State may make rules for enabling a person who has entered or offered to enter into an investment agreement with an authorised person to rescind the agreement or withdraw the offer within such period and in such manner as may be prescribed.

(2) Without prejudice to the generality of subsection (1) above, rules under this section may make provision—

(a) for requiring the service of notices with respect to the rights exercisable under the rules ;

(b) for the restitution of property and the making or recovery of payments where those rights are exercised ; and

(c) for such other incidental matters as the Secretary of State thinks necessary or expedient.

52.—(1) The Secretary of State may make regulations requiring authorised persons to give him forthwith notice of the occurrence of such events as are specified in the regulations and such information in respect of those events as is so specified.

(2) The Secretary of State may make regulations requiring authorised persons to furnish him at such times or in respect of such periods as are specified in the regulations with such information as is so specified.

(3) Regulations under this section shall not apply to a member of a recognised self-regulating organisation or a person certified by a recognised professional body unless he carries on investment business in the carrying on of which he is subject to any of the rules made under section 48 above.

(4) Without prejudice to the generality of subsections (1) and (2) above, regulations under this section may relate to—

(a) the nature of the investment business being carried on ;

(b) the nature of any other business carried on with or for the purposes of the investment business ;

(c) any proposal of an authorised person to alter the nature or extent of any business carried on by him ;

(d) any person becoming or ceasing to be a person of the kind to whom regard could be had by the Secretary of State under subsection (3) of section 27 above in deciding an application for authorisation under that section ;

(e) the financial position of an authorised person as respects his investment business or any other business carried on by him ;

(f) any property managed, and any property or money held, by an authorised person on behalf of other persons.

(5) Regulations under this section may require information to be given in a specified form and to be verified in a specified manner.

(6) Any notice or information required to be given or furnished under this section shall be given in writing or in such other manner as the Secretary of State may approve.

53.—(1) The Secretary of State may make rules concerning Indemnity indemnity against any claim in respect of any description of rules. civil liability incurred by an authorised person in connection with his investment business.

(2) Rules under this section shall not apply to a member of a recognised self-regulating organisation or a person certified by a recognised professional body in respect of investment business in the carrying on of which he is subject to the rules of the organisation or body unless that organisation or body has requested that rules under this section should apply to him ; and any such request shall not be capable of being withdrawn after rules giving effect to it have been made but without prejudice to the power of the Secretary of State to revoke the rules if he thinks fit.

(3) For the purpose of providing indemnity the rules—

(*a*) may authorise the Secretary of State to establish and maintain a fund or funds ;

(*b*) may authorise the Secretary of State to take out and maintain insurance with insurers authorised to carry on insurance business under the law of the United Kingdom or any other member State ;

(*c*) may require any person to whom the rules apply to take out and maintain insurance with any such insurer.

(4) Without prejudice to the generality of the foregoing provisions, the rules may—

(*a*) specify the terms and conditions on which, and the extent to which, indemnity is to be available and any circumstances in which the right to it is to be excluded or modified ;

(*b*) provide for the management, administration and protection of any fund maintained by virtue of subsection (3)(*a*) above and require persons to whom the rules apply to make payments to any such fund ;

(*c*) require persons to whom the rules apply to make payments by way of premium on any insurance policy maintained by the Secretary of State by virtue of subsection (3)(*b*) above ;

(*d*) prescribe the conditions which an insurance policy must satisfy for the purposes of subsection (3)(*c*) above ;

(*e*) authorise the Secretary of State to determine the amount which the rules require to be paid to him or an insurer, subject to such limits or in accordance with such provisions as may be prescribed by the rules ;

(*f*) specify circumstances in which, where sums are paid by the Secretary of State or an insurer in satisfaction of claims against a person subject to the rules, proceedings may be taken against that person by the Secretary of State or the insurer ;

(*g*) specify circumstances in which persons are exempt from the rules ;

(*h*) empower the Secretary of State to take such steps as he considers necessary or expedient to ascertain whether or not the rules are being complied with ; and

(*i*) contain incidental or supplementary provisions.

Compensation fund.

54.—(1) The Secretary of State may by rules establish a scheme for compensating investors in cases where persons who are or have been authorised persons are unable, or likely to be unable, to satisfy claims in respect of any description of civil liability incurred by them in connection with their investment businesses.

(2) Without prejudice to the generality of subsection (1) above, rules under this section may—

(*a*) provide for the administration of the scheme and, subject to the rules, the determination and regulation of any matter relating to its operation by a body appearing to the Secretary of State to be representative of, or of any class of, authorised persons ;

(*b*) establish a fund out of which compensation is to be paid ;

(*c*) provide for the levying of contributions from, or from any class of, authorised persons and otherwise for financing the scheme and for the payment of contributions and other money into the fund ;

(*d*) specify the terms and conditions on which, and the extent to which, compensation is to be payable and any circumstances in which the right to compensation is to be excluded or modified ;

(*e*) provide for treating compensation payable under the scheme in respect of a claim against any person as extinguishing or reducing the liability of that person in respect of the claim and for conferring on the body administering the scheme a right of recovery against that person, being, in the event of his insolvency, a right not exceeding such right, if any, as the claimant would have had in that event ; and

(*f*) contain incidental and supplementary provisions.

(3) A scheme under this section shall not be made so as to apply to persons who are members of a recognised self-regulating organisation except after consultation with that organisation or, except at the request of a recognised professional body, to persons who are certified by it and subject to its rules in carrying on all the investment business carried on by them ; and no scheme applying to such persons shall be made unless the Secretary of State is satisfied that the rules establishing it make sufficient provision—

(*a*) for the administration of the scheme by a body on which the interests of those persons are adequately represented ; and

(*b*) for securing that the amounts which they are liable to contribute reflect, so far as practicable, the amount of the claims made or likely to be made in respect of those persons.

(4) Where a scheme applies to such persons as are mentioned in subsection (3) above the rules under this section may—

(*a*) constitute the recognised self-regulating organisation or recognised professional body in question as the body administering the scheme in relation to those persons ;

(b) provide for the levying of contributions from that organisation or body instead of from those persons ; and

(*c*) establish a separate fund for the contributions and compensation payable in respect of those persons, with or without provision for payments and repayments in specified circumstances between that and any other fund established by the scheme.

(5) A request by a recognised professional body under subsection (3) above shall not be capable of being withdrawn after rules giving effect to it have been made but without prejudice to the power of the Secretary of State to revoke the rules if he thinks fit.

(6) Rules may be made—

(*a*) for England and Wales, under sections 411 and 412 of the Insolvency Act 1986 ;

1986 c. 45.

(*b*) for Scotland—

(i) under the said section 411 ; and

PART I
CHAPTER V

1985 c. 66.

S.I. 1986/1032
(N.I.6)
1978 c. 23.

(ii) in relation to the application of this section where the persons who are or have been authorised persons are persons whose estates may be sequestrated under the Bankruptcy (Scotland) Act 1985, by the Secretary of State under this section; and

(c) for Northern Ireland, under Article 613 of the Companies (Northern Ireland) Order 1986 and section 65 of the Judicature (Northern Ireland) Act 1978,

for the purpose of integrating any procedure for which provision is made by virtue of subsection (2)(e) above into the general procedure on a winding-up, bankruptcy or sequestration.

Clients'
money.

55.—(1) The Secretary of State may make regulations with respect to money (in this section referred to as " clients' money ") which authorised persons, or authorised persons of any description, hold in such circumstances as are specified in the regulations.

(2) Without prejudice to the generality of subsection (1) above, regulations under this section may—

(a) provide that clients' money held by an authorised person is held on trust ;

(b) require clients' money to be paid into an account the title of which contains the word " client " and which is with an institution of a kind specified in the regulations or, in the case of a member of a recognised self-regulating organisation or a person certified by a recognised professional body, by the rules of that organisation or body ;

(c) make provision with respect to the opening and keeping of clients' accounts, including provision as to the circumstances in which money other than clients' money may be paid into such accounts and the circumstances in which and the persons to whom money held in such accounts may be paid out ;

(d) require the keeping of accounts and records in respect of clients' money ;

(e) require any such accounts to be examined by an accountant having such qualifications as are specified in the regulations and require the accountant to report to the Secretary of State, or in the case of a member of a recognised self-regulating organisation or a person certified by a recognised professional body, to that organisation or body, whether in his opinion the provisions of the regulations have been complied with and on such other matters as may be specified in the regulations ;

(f) authorise the retention, to such extent and in such cases as may be specified in regulations, of so much of clients' money as represents interest.

(3) Where an authorised person is required to have an auditor, whether by virtue of any provision contained in or made under any enactment (including this Act) or of the rules of any such organisation or body as is mentioned in paragraph (b) of subsection (2) above, the regulations may require the examination and report referred to in paragraph (e) of that subsection to be carried out and made by that auditor.

(4) An institution with which an account is kept in pursuance of regulations made under this section does not incur any liability as constructive trustee where money is wrongfully paid from the account unless the institution permits the payment with knowledge that it is wrongful or having deliberately failed to make enquiries in circumstances in which a reasonable and honest person would have done so.

(5) In the application of this section to Scotland for the reference to money being held on trust there shall be substituted a reference to its being held as agent for the person who is entitled to call for it to be paid over to him or to be paid on his direction or to have it otherwise credited to him.

56.—(1) Except so far as permitted by regulations made by the Secretary of State, no person shall in the course of or in consequence of an unsolicited call— Unsolicited calls.

    (a) made on a person in the United Kingdom ; or

    (b) made from the United Kingdom on a person elsewhere,

by way of business enter into an investment agreement with the person on whom the call is made or procure or endeavour to procure that person to enter into such an agreement.

(2) A person shall not be guilty of an offence by reason only of contravening subsection (1) above, but subject to subsection (4) below—

    (a) any investment agreement which is entered into in the course of or in consequence of the unsolicited call shall not be enforceable against the person on whom the call was made ; and

    (b) that person shall be entitled to recover any money or other property paid or transferred by him under the agreement, together with compensation for any loss sustained by him as a result of having parted with it.

(3) The compensation recoverable under subsection (2) above shall be such as the parties may agree or as a court may, on the application of either party, determine.

(4) A court may allow an agreement to which subsection (2) above applies to be enforced or money and property paid or transferred under it to be retained if it is satisfied—

(a) that the person on whom the call was made was not influenced, or not influenced to any material extent, by anything said or done in the course of or in consequence of the call ;

(b) without prejudice to paragraph (a) above, that the person on whom the call was made entered into the agreement—

(i) following discussions between the parties of such a nature and over such a period that his entering into the agreement can fairly be regarded as a consequence of those discussions rather than the call ; and

(ii) was aware of the nature of the agreement and any risks involved in entering into it ; or

(c) that the call was not made by—

(i) the person seeking to enforce the agreement or to retain the money or property or a person acting on his behalf or an appointed representative whose principal he was ; or

(ii) a person who has received or is to receive, or in the case of an appointed representative whose principal has received or is to receive, any commission or other inducement in respect of the agreement from a person mentioned in sub-paragraph (i) above.

(5) Where a person elects not to perform an agreement which by virtue of this section is unenforceable against him or by virtue of this section recovers money paid or other property transferred by him under an agreement he shall repay any money and return any other property received by him under the agreement.

(6) Where any property transferred under an agreement to which this section applies has passed to a third party the references to that property in this section shall be construed as references to its value at the time of its transfer under the agreement.

(7) In the application of this section to anything done by a member of a recognised self-regulating organisation or a person certified by a recognised professional body in carrying on invest-

ment business in the carrying on of which he is subject to the rules of the organisation or body the reference in subsection (1) above to regulations made by the Secretary of State shall be construed as references to the rules of the organisation or body.

(8) In this section " unsolicited call " means a personal visit or oral communication made without express invitation.

57.—(1) Subject to section 58 below, no person other than an authorised person shall issue or cause to be issued an investment advertisement in the United Kingdom unless its contents have been approved by an authorised person.

(2) In this Act " an investment advertisement " means any advertisement inviting persons to enter or offer to enter into an investment agreement or to exercise any rights conferred by an investment to acquire, dispose of, underwrite or convert an investment or containing information calculated to lead directly or indirectly to persons doing so.

(3) Subject to subsection (4) below, any person who contravenes this section shall be guilty of an offence and liable—

(a) on conviction on indictment, to imprisonment for a term not exceeding two years or to a fine or to both ;

(b) on summary conviction, to imprisonment for a term not exceeding six months or to a fine not exceeding the statutory maximum or to both.

(4) A person who in the ordinary course of a business other than investment business issues an advertisement to the order of another person shall not be guilty of an offence under this section if he proves that he believed on reasonable grounds that the person to whose order the advertisement was issued was an authorised person, that the contents of the advertisement were approved by an authorised person or that the advertisement was permitted by or under section 58 below.

(5) If in contravention of this section a person issues or causes to be issued an advertisement inviting persons to enter or offer to enter into an investment agreement or containing information calculated to lead directly or indirectly to persons doing so, then, subject to subsection (8) below—

(a) he shall not be entitled to enforce any agreement to which the advertisement related and which was entered into after the issue of the advertisement ; and

(b) the other party shall be entitled to recover any money or other property paid or transferred by him under the agreement, together with compensation for any loss sustained by him as a result of having parted with it.

(6) If in contravention of this section a person issues or causes to be issued an advertisement inviting persons to exercise any rights conferred by an investment or containing information calculated to lead directly or indirectly to persons doing so, then, subject to subsection (8) below—

   (a) he shall not be entitled to enforce any obligation to which a person is subject as a result of any exercise by him after the issue of the advertisement of any rights to which the advertisement related ; and

   (b) that person shall be entitled to recover any money or other property paid or transferred by him under any such obligation, together with compensation for any loss sustained by him as a result of having parted with it.

(7) The compensation recoverable under subsection (5) or (6) above shall be such as the parties may agree or as a court may, on the application of either party, determine.

(8) A court may allow any such agreement or obligation as is mentioned in subsection (5) or (6) above to be enforced or money or property paid or transferred under it to be retained if it is satisfied—

   (a) that the person against whom enforcement is sought or who is seeking to recover the money or property was not influenced, or not influenced to any material extent, by the advertisement in making his decision to enter into the agreement or as to the exercise of the rights in question ; or

   (b) that the advertisement was not misleading as to the nature of the investment, the terms of the agreement or, as the case may be, the consequences of exercising the rights in question and fairly stated any risks involved in those matters.

(9) Where a person elects not to perform an agreement or an obligation which by virtue of subsection (5) or (6) above is unenforceable against him or by virtue of either of those sub-sections recovers money paid or other property transferred by him under an agreement or obligation he shall repay any money and return any other property received by him under the agreement or, as the case may be, as a result of exercising the rights in question.

(10) Where any property transferred under an agreement or obligation to which subsection (5) or (6) above applies has passed to a third party the references to that property in this section shall be construed as references to its value at the time of its transfer under the agreement or obligation.

58.—(1) Section 57 above does not apply to—

    (*a*) any advertisement issued or caused to be issued by, and relating only to investments issued by—

        (i) the government of the United Kingdom, of Northern Ireland or of any country or territory outside the United Kingdom ;

        (ii) a local authority in the United Kingdom or elsewhere ;

        (iii) the Bank of England or the central bank of any country or territory outside the United Kingdom ; or

        (iv) any international organisation the members of which include the United Kingdom or another member State ;

    (*b*) any advertisement issued or caused to be issued by a person who is exempt under section 36, 38, 42, 43, 44 or 45 above, or by virtue of an order under section 46 above, if the advertisement relates to a matter in respect of which he is exempt.

    (*c*) any advertisement which is issued or caused to be issued by a national of a member State other than the United Kingdom in the course of investment business lawfully carried on by him in such a State and which conforms with any rules made under section 48(2)(*e*) above ;

    (*d*) any advertisement which—

        (i) is subject to section 154 below ; or

        (ii) consists of or any part of listing particulars, supplementary listing particulars or any other document required or permitted to be published by listing rules under Part IV of this Act or by an approved exchange under Part V of this Act.

  (2) Section 57 above does not apply to an advertisement inviting persons to subscribe in cash for any investments to which Part V of this Act applies if the advertisement is issued or caused to be issued by the person by whom the investments are to be issued and either the advertisement consists of a prospectus registered in accordance with that Part or the following matters (and no others that would make it an investment advertisement) are contained in the advertisement—

    (*a*) the name of that person and his address or particulars of other means of communicating with him ;

    (*b*) the nature of the investments, the number offered for subscription and their nominal value and price ;

(*c*) a statement that a prospectus for the purposes of that Part of this Act is or will be available and, if it is not yet available, when it will be ; and

(*d*) instructions for obtaining a copy of the prospectus.

(3) Section 57 above does not apply to an advertisement issued in such circumstances as may be specified in an order made by the Secretary of State for the purpose of exempting from that section—

(*a*) advertisements appearing to him to have a private character, whether by reason of a connection between the person issuing them and those to whom they are issued or otherwise ;

(*b*) advertisements appearing to him to deal with investment only incidentally ;

(*c*) advertisements issued to persons appearing to him to be sufficiently expert to understand any risks involved ; or

(*d*) such other classes of advertisement as he thinks fit.

(4) An order under subsection (3) above may require any person who by virtue of the order is authorised to issue an advertisement to comply with such requirements as are specified in the order.

(5) An order made by virtue of paragraph (*a*), (*b*) or (*c*) of subsection (3) above shall be subject to annulment in pursuance of a resolution of either House of Parliament ; and no order shall be made by virtue of paragraph (*d*) of that subsection unless a draft of it has been laid before and approved by a resolution of each House of Parliament.

(6) Subsections (1)(*c*) and (2) above do not apply to any advertisement relating to an investment falling within paragraph 5 of Schedule 1 to this Act.

Employment of prohibited persons.

59.—(1) If it appears to the Secretary of State that any individual is not a fit and proper person to be employed in connection with investment business or investment business of a particular kind he may direct that he shall not, without the written consent of the Secretary of State, be employed in connection with investment business or, as the case may be, investment business of that kind—

(*a*) by authorised persons or exempted persons ; or

(*b*) by any specified person or persons, or by persons of any specified description, falling within paragraph (*a*) above.

(2) A direction under this section (" a disqualification direction ") shall specify the date on which it is to take effect and a
copy of it shall be served on the person to whom it relates.

(3) Any consent by the Secretary of State to the employment
of a person who is the subject of a disqualification direction may
relate to employment generally or to employment of a particular
kind, may be given subject to conditions and restrictions and
may be varied by him from time to time.

(4) Where the Secretary of State proposes—

    (*a*) to give a disqualification direction in respect of any
        person ; or

    (*b*) to refuse an application for his consent under this sec-
        tion or for the variation of such consent,

he shall give that person or the applicant written notice of his
intention to do so, stating the reasons for which he proposes
to act and giving particulars of the right to require the case to
be referred to the Tribunal under Chapter IX of this Part of
this Act.

(5) Any person who accepts or continues in any employment in contravention of a disqualification direction shall be
guilty of an offence and liable on summary conviction to a fine
not exceeding the fifth level on the standard scale.

(6) It shall be the duty of an authorised person and an
appointed representative to take reasonable care not to employ
or continue to employ a person in contravention of a disqualification direction.

(7) The Secretary of State may revoke a disqualification
direction.

(8) In this section references to employment include references to employment otherwise than under a contract of service.

    60.—(1) If it appears to the Secretary of State that a person
who is or was an authorised person by virtue of section 22, 24,
25 or 31 above has contravened—

     Public
statement as
to person's
misconduct.

    (*a*) any provision of rules or regulations made under this
        Chapter or of section 56 or 59 above ; or

    (*b*) any condition imposed under section 50 above,

he may publish a statement to that effect.

(2) Before publishing a statement under subsection (1) above
the Secretary of State shall give the person concerned written
notice of the proposed statement and of the reasons for which
he proposes to act.

(3) Where the reasons stated in the notice relate specifically to matters which—

> (*a*) refer to a person identified in the notice other than the person who is or was the authorised person ; and
>
> (*b*) are in the opinion of the Secretary of State prejudicial to that person in any office or employment,

the Secretary of State shall, unless he considers it impracticable to do so, serve a copy of the notice on that other person.

(4) A notice under this section shall give particulars of the right to have the case referred to the Tribunal under Chapter IX of this Part of this Act.

(5) Where a case is not required to be referred to the Tribunal by a person on whom a notice is served under this section the Secretary of State shall, at the expiration of the period within which such a requirement can be made, give that person written notice that the statement is or is not to be published ; and if it is to be published the Secretary of State shall after publication send a copy of it to that person and to any person on whom a copy of the notice under subsection (2) above was served.

Injunctions
and restitution
orders.

61.—(1) If on the application of the Secretary of State the court is satisfied—

> (*a*) that there is a reasonable likelihood that any person will contravene any provision of—
>
> > (i) rules or regulations made under this Chapter ;
> >
> > (ii) sections 47, 56, 57, or 59 above ;
> >
> > (iii) any requirements imposed by an order under section 58(3) above ; or
> >
> > (iv) the rules of a recognised self-regulating organisation, recognised professional body, recognised investment exchange or recognised clearing house to which that person is subject and which regulate the carrying on by him of investment business,
> >
> > or any condition imposed under section 50 above ;
>
> (*b*) that any person has contravened any such provision or condition and that there is a reasonable likelihood that the contravention will continue or be repeated ; or
>
> (*c*) that any person has contravened any such provision or condition and that there are steps that could be taken for remedying the contravention,

the court may grant an injunction restraining the contravention or, in Scotland, an interdict prohibiting the contravention or, as the case may be, make an order requiring that person and any other person who appears to the court to have been knowingly concerned in the contravention to take such steps as the court may direct to remedy it.

(2) No application shall be made by the Secretary of State under subsection (1) above in respect of any such rules as are mentioned in subsection (1)(*a*)(iv) above unless it appears to him that the organisation, body, exchange or clearing house is unable or unwilling to take appropriate steps to restrain the contravention or to require the person concerned to take such steps as are mentioned in subsection (1) above.

(3) The court may, on the application of the Secretary of State, make an order under subsection (4) below or, in relation to Scotland, under subsection (5) below if satisfied—

(*a*) that profits have accrued to any person as a result of his contravention of any provision or condition mentioned in subsection (1)(*a*) above ; or

(*b*) that one or more investors have suffered loss or been otherwise adversely affected as a result of that contravention.

(4) The court may under this subsection order the person concerned to pay into court, or appoint a receiver to recover from him, such sum as appears to the court to be just having regard—

(*a*) in a case within paragraph (*a*) of subsection (3) above, to the profits appearing to the court to have accrued ;

(*b*) in a case within paragraph (*b*) of that subsection, to the extent of the loss or other adverse effect ; or

(*c*) in a case within both paragraphs (*a*) and (*b*) of that subsection, to the profits and to the extent of the loss or other adverse effect.

(5) The court may under this subsection order the person concerned to pay to the applicant such sum as appears to the court to be just having regard to the considerations mentioned in paragraphs (*a*) to (*c*) of subsection (4) above.

(6) Any amount paid into court by or recovered from a person in pursuance of an order under subsection (4) or (5) above shall be paid out to such person or distributed among such persons as the court may direct, being a person or persons appearing to the court to have entered into transactions with that person as a result of which the profits mentioned in paragraph (*a*) of subsection (3) above have accrued to him or the loss or adverse effect mentioned in paragraph (*b*) of that subsection has been suffered.

(7) On an application under subsection (3) above the court may require the person concerned to furnish it with such accounts or other information as it may require for establishing whether any and, if so, what profits have accrued to him as mentioned in paragraph (*a*) of that subsection and for determining how any

amounts are to be paid or distributed under subsection (6) above ; and the court may require any such accounts or other information to be verified in such manner as it may direct.

(8) The jurisdiction conferred by this section shall be exercisable by the High Court and the Court of Session.

(9) Nothing in this section affects the right of any person other than the Secretary of State to bring proceedings in respect of the matters to which this section applies.

Actions for
damages.

62.—(1) Without prejudice to section 61 above, a contravention of—

> (a) any rules or regulations made under this Chapter ;
>
> (b) any conditions imposed under section 50 above ;
>
> (c) any requirements imposed by an order under section 58(3) above ;
>
> (d) the duty imposed by section 59(6) above,

shall be actionable at the suit of a person who suffers loss as a result of the contravention subject to the defences and other incidents applying to actions for breach of statutory duty.

(2) Subsection (1) applies also to a contravention by a member of a recognised self-regulating organisation or a person certified by a recognised professional body of any rules of the organisation or body relating to a matter in respect of which rules or regulations have been or could be made under this Chapter in relation to an authorised person who is not such a member or so certified.

(3) Subsection (1) above does not apply—

> (a) to a contravention of rules made under section 49 or conditions imposed under section 50 in connection with an alteration of the requirements of those rules ; or
>
> (b) by virtue of subsection (2) above to a contravention of rules relating to a matter in respect of which rules have been or could be made under section 49.

(4) A person shall not be guilty of an offence by reason of any contravention to which subsection (1) above applies or of a contravention of rules made under section 49 above or such conditions as are mentioned in subsection (3)(a) above and no such contravention shall invalidate any transaction.

Gaming
contracts.

63.—(1) No contract to which this section applies shall be void or unenforceable by reason of—

(*a*) section 18 of the Gaming Act 1845, section 1 of the
Gaming Act 1892 or any corresponding provisions in
force in Northern Ireland ; or

(*b*) any rule of the law of Scotland whereby a contract by
way of gaming or wagering is not legally enforceable.

(2) This section applies to any contract entered into by either
or each party by way of business and the making or performance
of which by either party constitutes an activity which falls within
paragraph 12 of Schedule 1 to this Act or would do so apart from
Parts III and IV of that Schedule.

CHAPTER VI

POWERS OF INTERVENTION

64.—(1) The powers conferred on the Secretary of State by
this Chapter shall be exercisable in relation to any authorised
person or, except in the case of the power conferred by section
65 below, any appointed representative of his if it appears to
the Secretary of State—

(*a*) that the exercise of the powers is desirable for the protection of investors ;

(*b*) that the authorised person is not fit to carry on investment business of a particular kind or to the extent to
which he is carrying it on or proposing to carry it
on ; or

(*c*) that the authorised person has contravened any provision of this Act or of any rules or regulations made
under it or, in purported compliance with any such
provision, has furnished the Secretary of State with
false, inaccurate or misleading information or has
contravened any prohibition or requirement imposed
under this Act.

(2) For the purposes of subsection (1)(*b*) above the Secretary
of State may take into account any matters that could be taken
into account in deciding whether to withdraw or suspend an
authorisation under Chapter III of this Part of this Act.

(3) The powers conferred by this Chapter may be exercised
in relation to a person whose authorisation is suspended under
section 28 above or who is the subject of a direction under section 33(1)(*b*) above and references in this Chapter to an authorised person shall be construed accordingly.

(4) The powers conferred by this Chapter shall not be exercisable in relation to—

(a) an authorised person who is a member of a recognised self-regulating organisation or a person certified by a recognised professional body and is subject to the rules of such an organisation or body in carrying on all the investment business carried on by him ; or

(b) an appointed representative whose principal or, in the case of such a representative with more than one principal, each of whose principals is a member of such an organisation or body and is subject to the rules of such an organisation or body in carrying on the investment business in respect of which his principal or each of his principals has accepted responsibility for his activities ;

except that the powers conferred by virtue of section 67(1)(b) below may on any of the grounds specified in subsection (1) above be exercised in relation to such a person at the request of any such organisation of which he or, in the case of an appointed representative, any of his principals is a member or any such body by which he or, as the case may be, any of his principals is certified.

Restriction of business.

65.—(1) The Secretary of State may prohibit an authorised person from—

(a) entering into transactions of any specified kind or entering into them except in specified circumstances or to a specified extent ;

(b) soliciting business from persons of a specified kind or otherwise than from such persons or in a specified country or territory outside the United Kingdom ;

(c) carrying on business in a specified manner or otherwise than in a specified manner.

(2) A prohibition under this section may relate to transactions entered into in connection with or for the purposes of investment business or to other business which is carried on in connection with or for the purposes of investment business.

Restriction on dealing with assets.

66.—(1) The Secretary of State may prohibit an authorised person or appointed representative from disposing of or otherwise dealing with any assets, or any specified assets, of that person or, as the case may be, representative in any specified manner or otherwise than in a specified manner.

(2) A prohibition under this section may relate to assets outside the United Kingdom.

67.—(1) The Secretary of State may impose a requirement that all assets, or all assets of any specified class or description, which at any time while the requirement is in force—

(a) belong to an authorised person or appointed representative ; or

(b) belong to investors and are held by or to the order of an authorised person or appointed representative,

shall be transferred to and held by a trustee approved by the Secretary of State.

(2) Where a requirement is imposed under this section it shall be the duty of the authorised person or, as the case may be, appointed representative to transfer the assets to the trustee and to give him all such other assistance as may be required to enable him to discharge his functions in accordance with the requirement.

(3) Assets held by a trustee in accordance with a requirement under this section shall not be released or dealt with except in accordance with directions given by the Secretary of State or in such circumstances as may be specified by him.

(4) A requirement under this section may relate to assets outside the United Kingdom.

PART I
CHAPTER VI
Vesting of assets in trustee.

68.—(1) The Secretary of State may require an authorised person or appointed representative to maintain in the United Kingdom assets of such value as appears to the Secretary of State to be desirable with a view to ensuring that the authorised person or, as the case may be, appointed representative will be able to meet his liabilities in respect of investment business carried on by him in the United Kingdom.

(2) The Secretary of State may direct that for the purposes of any requirement under this section assets of any specified class or description shall or shall not be taken into account.

Maintenance of assets in United Kingdom.

69. The Secretary of State may, either of his own motion or on the application of a person on whom a prohibition or requirement has been imposed under this Chapter, rescind or vary the prohibition or requirement if it appears to the Secretary of State that it is no longer necessary for the prohibition or requirement to take effect or continue in force or, as the case may be, that it should take effect or continue in force in a different form.

Rescission and variation.

70.—(1) The power to impose, rescind or vary a prohibition or requirement under this Chapter shall be exercisable by written notice served by the Secretary of State on the person concerned ; and any such notice shall take effect on such date as is specified in the notice.

Notices.

(2) If the Secretary of State refuses to rescind or vary a prohibition or requirement on the application of the person to whom it applies he shall serve that person with a written notice of the refusal.

(3) A notice imposing a prohibition or requirement, or varying a prohibition or requirement otherwise than on the application of the person to whom it applies, and a notice under subsection (2) above shall state the reasons for which the prohibition or requirement was imposed or varied or, as the case may be, why the application was refused.

(4) Where the reasons stated in a notice to which subsection (3) above applies relate specifically to matters which—

    (*a*) refer to a person identified in the notice other than the person to whom the prohibition or requirement applies ; and

    (*b*) are in the opinion of the Secretary of State prejudicial to that person in any office or employment,

the Secretary of State shall, unless he considers it impracticable to do so, serve a copy of the notice on that person.

(5) A notice to which subsection (3) above applies shall give particulars of the right to have the case referred to the Tribunal under Chapter IX of this Part of this Act.

(6) The Secretary of State may give public notice of any prohibition or requirement imposed by him under this Chapter and of the rescission and variation of any such prohibition or requirement ; and any such notice may, if the Secretary of State thinks fit, include a statement of the reasons for which the prohibition or requirement was imposed, rescinded or varied.

Breach of prohibition or requirement.

71.—(1) Sections 60, 61, and 62 above shall have effect in relation to a contravention of a prohibition or requirement imposed under this Chapter as they have effect in relation to any such contravention as is mentioned in those sections.

(2) In its application by virtue of this section, section 62(2) shall have effect with the substitution—

    (*a*) for the reference to the rules of a recognised self-regulating organisation of a reference to any prohibition or requirement imposed by it in the exercise of powers for purposes corresponding to those of this Chapter ; and

    (*b*) for the reference to the rules of a recognised professional body of a reference to any prohibition or requirement imposed in the exercise of powers for such purposes by that body or by any other body or person having functions in respect of the enforcement of the recognised professional body's rules relating to the carrying on of investment business.

(3) This section is without prejudice to any equitable remedy available in respect of property which by virtue of a require- ment under section 67 above is subject to a trust.

CHAPTER VII
WINDING UP AND ADMINISTRATION ORDERS

72.—(1) On a petition presented by the Secretary of State by virtue of this section, the court having jurisdiction under the Insolvency Act 1986 may wind up an authorised person or ap- pointed representative to whom this subsection applies if—

(a) the person is unable to pay his debts within the mean- ing of section 123 or, as the case may be, section 221 of that Act; or

(b) the court is of the opinion that it is just and equitable that the person should be wound up.

(2) Subsection (1) above applies to any authorised person, any person whose authorisation is suspended under section 28 above or who is the subject of a direction under section 33(1)(b) above or any appointed representative who is—

(a) a company within the meaning of section 735 of the Companies Act 1985;

(b) an unregistered company within the meaning of section 220 of the Insolvency Act 1986;

(c) an oversea company within the meaning of section 744 of the Companies Act 1985; or

(d) a partnership.

(3) For the purposes of a petition under subsection (1) above a person who defaults in an obligation to pay any sum due and payable under any investment agreement shall be deemed to be unable to pay his debts.

(4) Where a petition is presented under subsection (1) above for the winding up of a partnership on the ground mentioned in paragraph (b) of subsection (1) above or, in Scotland, on a ground mentioned in paragraph (a) or (b) of that subsection, the court shall have jurisdiction and the Insolvency Act 1986 shall have effect as if the partnership were an unregistered com- pany within the meaning of section 220 of that Act.

(5) The Secretary of State shall not present a petition under subsection (1) above for the winding up of any person who is an authorised person by virtue of membership of a recognised self-regulating organisation or certification by a recognised pro- fessional body and is subject to the rules of the organisation or

PART I
CHAPTER VII

body in the carrying on of all investment business carried on by him, unless that organisation or body has consented to his doing so.

Winding up orders: Northern Ireland.

S.I. 1986/1032 (N.I.6).

73.—(1) On a petition presented by the Secretary of State by virtue of this section, the High Court in Northern Ireland may wind up an authorised person or appointed representative to whom this subsection applies if—

    (*a*) the person is unable to pay his debts within the meaning of Article 480 or, as the case may be, Article 616 of the Companies (Northern Ireland) Order 1986 ; or

    (*b*) the court is of the opinion that it is just and equitable that the person should be wound up.

(2) Subsection (1) above applies to any authorised person, any person whose authorisation is suspended under section 28 above or who is the subject of a direction under section 33(1)(*b*) above or any appointed representative who is—

    (*a*) a company within the meaning of Article 3 of the Companies (Northern Ireland) Order 1986 ;

    (*b*) an unregistered company within the meaning of Article 615 of that Order ; or

    (*c*) a Part XXIII company within the meaning of Article 2 of that Order ; or

    (*d*) a partnership.

(3) For the purposes of a petition under subsection (1) above a person who defaults in an obligation to pay any sum due and payable under any investment agreement shall be deemed to be unable to pay his debts.

(4) Where a petition is presented under subsection (1) above for the winding up of a partnership on the ground mentioned in paragraph (*b*) of subsection (1) above, the High Court in Northern Ireland shall have jurisdiction and the Companies (Northern Ireland) Order 1986 shall have effect as if the partnership were an unregistered company within the meaning of Article 615 of that Order.

(5) The Secretary of State shall not present a petition under subsection (1) above for the winding up of any person who is an authorised person by virtue of membership of a recognised self-regulating organisation or certification by a recognised professional body and is subject to the rules of the organisation or body in the carrying on of all investment business carried on by him, unless that organisation or body has consented to his doing so.

74. A petition may be presented under section 9 of the In- PART I
solvency Act 1986 (applications for administration orders) in CHAPTER VII
relation to a company to which section 8 of that Act applies Administration
which is an authorised person, a person whose authorisation is orders.
suspended under section 28 above or who is the subject of a 1986 c. 45.
direction under section 33(1)(*b*) above or an appointed representative—

    (*a*) in the case of an authorised person who is an authorised
        person by virtue of membership of a recognised self-
        regulating organisation or certification by a recognised
        professional body, by that organisation or body ; and

    (*b*) in the case of an appointed representative or an autho-
        rised person who is not authorised as mentioned in
        paragraph (*a*) above or is so authorised but is not sub-
        ject to the rules of the organisation or body in question
        in the carrying on of all investment business carried on
        by him, by the Secretary of State.

CHAPTER VIII
COLLECTIVE INVESTMENT SCHEMES
Preliminary

75.—(1) In this Act " a collective investment scheme " means, Interpretation.
subject to the provisions of this section, any arrangements with
respect to property of any description, including money, the purpose or effect of which is to enable persons taking part in the
arrangements (whether by becoming owners of the property or
any part of it or otherwise) to participate in or receive profits or
income arising from the acquisition, holding, management or
disposal of the property or sums paid out of such profits or
income.

(2) The arrangements must be such that the persons who are
to participate as mentioned in subsection (1) above (in this Act
referred to as " participants ") do not have day to day control over the management of the property in question, whether
or not they have the right to be consulted or to give directions ;
and the arrangements must also have either or both of the
characteristics mentioned in subsection (3) below.

(3) Those characteristics are—
    (*a*) that the contributions of the participants and the profits
        or income out of which payments are to be made to
        them are pooled ;
    (*b*) that the property in question is managed as a whole by
        or on behalf of the operator of the scheme.

(4) Where any arrangements provide for such pooling as is mentioned in paragraph (*a*) of subsection (3) above in relation to separate parts of the property in question, the arrangements shall not be regarded as constituting a single collective investment scheme unless the participants are entitled to exchange rights in one part for rights in another.

(5) Arrangements are not a collective investment scheme if—

    (*a*) the property to which the arrangements relate (other than cash awaiting investment) consists of investments falling within any of paragraphs 1 to 5, 6 (so far as relating to units in authorised unit trust schemes and recognised schemes) and 10 of Schedule 1 to this Act ;

    (*b*) each participant is the owner of a part of that property and entitled to withdraw it at any time ; and

    (*c*) the arrangements do not have the characteristics mentioned in paragraph (*a*) of subsection (3) above and have those mentioned in paragraph (*b*) of that subsection only because the parts of the property belonging to different participants are not bought and sold separately except where a person becomes or ceases to be a participant.

(6) The following are not collective investment schemes—

    (*a*) arrangements operated by a person otherwise than by way of business ;

    (*b*) arrangements where each of the participants carries on a business other than investment business and enters into the arrangements for commercial purposes related to that business ;

    (*c*) arrangements where each of the participants is a body corporate in the same group as the operator ;

    (*d*) arrangements where—

       (i) each of the participants is a bona fide employee or former employee (or the wife, husband, widow, widower, child or step-child under the age of eighteen of such an employee or former employee) of a body corporate in the same group as the operator ; and

       (ii) the property to which the arrangements relate consists of shares or debentures (as defined in paragraph 20(4) of Schedule 1 to this Act) in or of a member of that group ;

    (*e*) arrangements where the receipt of the participants' contributions constitutes the acceptance of deposits in the course of a business which is a deposit-taking business for the purposes of the Banking Act 1979 and does not constitute a transaction prescribed for the purposes of section 2 of that Act by regulations made by the Treasury ;

(f) franchise arrangements, that is to say, arrangements under which a person earns profits or income by exploiting a right conferred by the arrangements to use a trade name or design or other intellectual property or the good-will attached to it ;

(g) arrangements the predominant purpose of which is to enable persons participating in them to share in the use or enjoyment of a particular property or to make its use or enjoyment available gratuitously to other persons ;

(h) arrangements under which the rights or interests of the participants are investments falling within paragraph 5 of Schedule 1 to this Act ;

(i) arrangements the purpose of which is the provision of clearing services and which are operated by an authorised person, a recognised clearing house or a recognised investment exchange ;

(j) contracts of insurance ;

(k) occupational pension schemes.

(7) No body incorporated under the law of, or of any part of, the United Kingdom relating to building societies or industrial and provident societies or registered under any such law relating to friendly societies, and no other body corporate other than an open-ended investment company, shall be regarded as constituting a collective investment scheme.

(8) In this Act—

" a unit trust scheme " means a collective investment scheme under which the property in question is held on trust for the participants ;

" an open-ended investment company " means a collective investment scheme under which—

(a) the property in question belongs beneficially to, and is managed by or on behalf of, a body corporate having as its purpose the investment of its funds with the aim of spreading investment risk and giving its members the benefit of the results of the management of those funds by or on behalf of that body ; and

(b) the rights of the participants are represented by shares in or securities of that body which—

(i) the participants are entitled to have redeemed or repurchased, or which (otherwise than under Chapter VII of Part V of the Companies Act 1985 or the corresponding Northern Ireland provision) are redeemed or repurchased from them by, or out of funds provided by, that body ; or

(ii) the body ensures can be sold by the participants on an investment exchange at a price related to the value of the property to which they relate ;

" trustee ", in relation to a unit trust scheme, means the person holding the property in question on trust for the participants and, in relation to a collective investment scheme constituted under the law of a country or territory outside the United Kingdom, means any person who (whether or not under a trust) is entrusted with the custody of the property in question ;

" units " means the rights or interests (however described) of the participants in a collective investment scheme ;

" the operator ", in relation to unit trust scheme with a separate trustee, means the manager and, in relation to an open-ended investment company, means that company.

(9) If an order under section 2 above amends the references to a collective investment scheme in Schedule 1 to this Act it may also amend the provisions of this section.

Promotion of schemes

Restrictions on promotion.

76.—(1) Subject to subsections (2), (3) and (4) below, an authorised person shall not—

(a) issue or cause to be issued in the United Kingdom any advertisement inviting persons to become or offer to become participants in a collective investment scheme or containing information calculated to lead directly or indirectly to persons becoming or offering to become participants in such a scheme ; or

(b) advise or procure any person in the United Kingdom to become or offer to become a participant in such a scheme,

unless the scheme is an authorised unit trust scheme or a recognised scheme under the following provisions of this Chapter.

(2) Subsection (1) above shall not apply if the advertisement is issued to or the person mentioned in paragraph (b) of that subsection is—

(*a*) an authorised person ; or

(*b*) a person whose ordinary business involves the acquisition and disposal of property of the same kind as the property, or a substantial part of the property, to which the scheme relates.

(3) Subsection (1) above shall not apply to anything done in accordance with regulations made by the Secretary of State for the purpose of exempting from that subsection the promotion otherwise than to the general public of schemes of such descriptions as are specified in the regulations.

(4) The Secretary of State may by regulations make provision for exempting single property schemes from subsection (1) above.

(5) For the purposes of subsection (4) above a single property scheme is a scheme which has the characteristics mentioned in subsection (6) below and satisfies such other requirements as are specified in the regulations conferring the exemption.

(6) The characteristics referred to above are—

(*a*) that the property subject to the scheme (apart from cash or other assets held for management purposes) consists of—

(i) a single building (or a single building with ancillary buildings) managed by or on behalf of the operator of the scheme ; or

(ii) a group of adjacent or contiguous buildings managed by him or on his behalf as a single enterprise,

with or without ancillary land and with or without furniture, fittings or other contents of the building or buildings in question ; and

(*b*) that the units of the participants in the scheme are either dealt in on a recognised investment exchange or offered on terms such that any agreement for their acquisition is conditional on their admission to dealings on such an exchange.

(7) Regulations under subsection (4) above may contain such supplementary and transitional provisions as the Secretary of State thinks necessary and may also contain provisions imposing obligations or liabilities on the operator and trustee (if any) of an exempted scheme, including, to such extent as he thinks appropriate, provisions for purposes corresponding to those for which provision can be made under section 85 below in relation to authorised unit trust schemes.

Authorised unit trust schemes

77.—(1) Any application for an order declaring a unit trust scheme to be an authorised unit trust scheme shall be made by the manager and trustee, or proposed manager and trustee, of the scheme and the manager and trustee shall be different persons.

(2) Any such application—

> (a) shall be made in such manner as the Secretary of State may direct ; and
>
> (b) shall contain or be accompanied by such information as he may reasonably require for the purpose of determining the application.

(3) At any time after receiving an application and before determining it the Secretary of State may require the applicant to furnish additional information.

(4) The directions and requirements given or imposed under subsections (2) and (3) above may differ as between different applications.

(5) Any information to be furnished to the Secretary of State under this section shall, if he so requires, be in such form or verified in such manner as he may specify.

78.—(1) The Secretary of State may, on an application duly made in accordance with section 77 above and after being furnished with all such information as he may require under that section, make an order declaring a unit trust scheme to be an authorised unit trust scheme for the purposes of this Act if—

> (a) it appears to him that the scheme complies with the requirements of the regulations made under section 81 below and that the following provisions of this section are satisfied ; and
>
> (b) he has been furnished with a copy of the trust deed and a certificate signed by a solicitor to the effect that it complies with such of those requirements as relate to its contents.

(2) The manager and the trustee must be persons who are independent of each other.

(3) The manager and the trustee must each be a body corporate incorporated in the United Kingdom or another member State, the affairs of each must be administered in the country in which it is incorporated, each must have a place of business in the United Kingdom and, if the manager is incorporated in another member State, the scheme must not be one which satisfies

the requirements prescribed for the purposes of section 86 below.

(4) The manager and the trustee must each be an authorised person and neither must be prohibited from acting as manager or trustee, as the case may be, by or under rules under section 48 above, by or under the rules of any recognised self-regulating organisation of which the manager or trustee is a member or by a prohibition imposed under section 65 above.

(5) The name of the scheme must not be undesirable or misleading; and the purposes of the scheme must be reasonably capable of being successfully carried into effect.

(6) The participants must be entitled to have their units redeemed in accordance with the scheme at a price related to the net value of the property to which the units relate and determined in accordance with the scheme; but a scheme shall be treated as complying with this subsection if it requires the manager to ensure that a participant is able to sell his units on an investment exchange at a price not significantly different from that mentioned in this subsection.

(7) The Secretary of State shall inform the applicants of his decision on the application not later than six months after the date on which the application was received.

(8) On making an order under this section the Secretary of State may issue a certificate to the effect that the scheme complies with the conditions necessary for it to enjoy the rights conferred by any relevant Community instrument.

79.—(1) The Secretary of State may revoke an order declaring a unit trust scheme to be an authorised unit trust scheme if it appears to him—

Revocation of authorisation.

> (a) that any of the requirements for the making of the order are no longer satisfied;
>
> (b) that it is undesirable in the interests of the participants or potential participants that the scheme should continue to be authorised; or
>
> (c) without prejudice to paragraph (b) above, that the manager or trustee of the scheme has contravened any provision of this Act or any rules or regulations made under it or, in purported compliance with any such provision, has furnished the Secretary of State with false, inaccurate or misleading information or has contravened any prohibition or requirement imposed under this Act.

(2) For the purposes of subsection (1)(b) above the Secretary of State may take into account any matter relating to the scheme,

the manager or trustee, a director or controller of the manager or trustee or any person employed by or associated with the manager or trustee in connection with the scheme.

(3) In the case of a manager or trustee who is a member of a recognised self-regulating organisation the rules, prohibitions and requirements referred to in subsection (1)(c) above include the rules of that organisation and any prohibition or requirement imposed by virtue of those rules.

(4) The Secretary of State may revoke an order declaring a unit trust scheme to be an authorised unit trust scheme at the request of the manager or trustee of the scheme ; but he may refuse to do so if he considers that any matter concerning the scheme should be investigated as a preliminary to a decision on the question whether the order should be revoked or that revocation would not be in the interests of the participants or would be incompatible with a Community obligation.

Representa-
tions against
refusal or
revocation.

80.—(1) Where the Secretary of State proposes—

> (a) to refuse an application for an order under section 78 above ; or
>
> (b) to revoke such an order otherwise than at the request of the manager or trustee of the scheme,

he shall give the applicants or, as the case may be, the manager and trustee of the scheme written notice of his intention to do so, stating the reasons for which he proposes to act and giving particulars of the rights conferred by subsection (2) below.

(2) A person on whom a notice is served under subsection (1) above may, within twenty-one days of the date of service, make written representations to the Secretary of State and, if desired, oral representations to a person appointed for that purpose by the Secretary of State.

(3) The Secretary of State shall have regard to any representations made in accordance with subsection (2) above in determining whether to refuse the application or revoke the order, as the case may be.

Constitution
and
management.

81.—(1) The Secretary of State may make regulations as to the constitution and management of authorised unit trust schemes, the powers and duties of the manager and trustee of any such scheme and the rights and obligations of the participants in any such scheme.

(2) Without prejudice to the generality of subsection (1) above, regulations under this section may make provision—

(a) as to the issue and redemption of the units under the scheme ;

(b) as to the expenses of the scheme and the means of meeting them ;

(c) for the appointment, removal, powers and duties of an auditor for the scheme ;

(d) for restricting or regulating the investment and borrowing powers exercisable in relation to the scheme ;

(e) requiring the keeping of records with respect to the transactions and financial position of the scheme and for the inspection of those records ;

(f) requiring the preparation of periodical reports with respect to the scheme and the furnishing of those reports to the participants and to the Secretary of State ; and

(g) with respect to the amendment of the scheme.

(3) Regulations under this section may make provision as to the contents of the trust deed, including provision requiring any of the matters mentioned in subsection (2) above to be dealt with in the deed ; but regulations under this section shall be binding on the manager, trustee and participants independently of the contents of the deed and, in the case of the participants, shall have effect as if contained in it.

(4) Regulations under this section shall not impose limits on the remuneration payable to the manager of a scheme.

(5) Regulations under this section may contain such incidental and transitional provisions as the Secretary of State thinks necessary or expedient.

82.—(1) The manager of an authorised unit trust scheme shall give written notice to the Secretary of State of— Alteration of schemes and changes of manager or trustee.

(a) any proposed alteration to the scheme ; and

(b) any proposal to replace the trustee of the scheme ;

and any notice given in respect of a proposed alteration involving a change in the trust deed shall be accompanied by a certificate signed by a solicitor to the effect that the change will not affect the compliance of the deed with the regulations made under section 81 above.

(2) The trustee of an authorised unit trust scheme shall give written notice to the Secretary of State of any proposal to replace the manager of the scheme.

(3) Effect shall not be given to any such proposal unless—

(a) the Secretary of State has given his approval to the proposal ; or (*b*) one month has elapsed since the date on which the notice was given under subsection (1) or (2) above without the Secretary of State having notified the manager or trustee that the proposal is not approved.

(4) Neither the manager nor the trustee of an authorised unit trust scheme shall be replaced except by persons who satisfy the requirements of section 78(2) to (4) above.

Restrictions
on activities
of manager.

83.—(1) The manager of an authorised unit trust scheme shall not engage in any activities other than those mentioned in subsection (2) below.

(2) Those activities are—

(*a*) acting as manager of—

(i) a unit trust scheme ;

(ii) an open-ended investment company or any other body corporate whose business consists of investing its funds with the aim of spreading investment risk and giving its members the benefit of the results of the management of its funds by or on behalf of that body ; or

(iii) any other collective investment scheme under which the contributions of the participants and the profits or income out of which payments are to be made to them are pooled ;

(*b*) activities for the purposes of or in connection with those mentioned in paragraph (*a*) above.

(3) A prohibition under section 65 above may prohibit the manager of an authorised unit trust scheme from inviting persons in any specified country or territory outside the United Kingdom to become participants in the scheme.

Avoidance of
exclusion
clauses.

84. Any provision of the trust deed of an authorised unit trust scheme shall be void in so far as it would have the effect of exempting the manager or trustee from liability for any failure to exercise due care and diligence in the discharge of his functions in respect of the scheme.

Publication of
scheme
particulars.

85.—(1) The Secretary of State may make regulations requiring the manager of an authorised unit trust scheme to submit to him and publish or make available to the public on request a document (" scheme particulars ") containing information about the scheme and complying with such requirements as are specified in the regulations.

(2) Regulations under this section may require the manager of an authorised unit trust scheme to submit and publish or make available revised or further scheme particulars if—

    (a) there is a significant change affecting any matter contained in such particulars previously published or made available whose inclusion was required by the regulations ; or

    (b) a significant new matter arises the inclusion of information in respect of which would have been required in previous particulars if it had arisen when those particulars were prepared.

(3) Regulations under this section may provide for the payment, by the person or persons who in accordance with the regulations are treated as responsible for any scheme particulars, of compensation to any person who has become or agreed to become a participant in the scheme and suffered loss as a result of any untrue or misleading statement in the particulars or the omission from them of any matter required by the regulations to be included.

(4) Regulations under this section shall not affect any liability which any person may incur apart from the regulations.

Recognition of overseas schemes

86.—(1) Subject to subsection (2) below, a collective investment scheme constituted in a member State other than the United Kingdom is a recognised scheme if it satisfies such requirements as are prescribed for the purposes of this section.

Schemes constituted in other member States.

(2) Not less than two months before inviting persons in the United Kingdom to become participants in the scheme the operator of the scheme shall give written notice to the Secretary of State of his intention to do so, specifying the manner in which the invitation is to be made ; and the scheme shall not be a recognised scheme by virtue of this section if within two months of receiving the notice the Secretary of State notifies—

    (a) the operator of the scheme ; and

    (b) the authorities of the State in question who are responsible for the authorisation of collective investment schemes,

that the manner in which the invitation is to be made does not comply with the law in force in the United Kingdom.

(3) The notice to be given to the Secretary of State under subsection (2) above—

(a) shall be accompanied by a certificate from the authorities mentioned in subsection (2)(b) above to the effect that the scheme complies with the conditions necessary for it to enjoy the rights conferred by any relevant Community instrument;

(b) shall contain the address of a place in the United Kingdom for the service on the operator of notices or other documents required or authorised to be served on him under this Act; and

(c) shall contain or be accompanied by such other information and documents as may be prescribed.

(4) A notice given by the Secretary of State under subsection (2) above shall give the reasons for which he considers that the law in force in the United Kingdom will not be complied with and give particulars of the rights conferred by subsection (5) below.

(5) A person on whom a notice is served by the Secretary of State under subsection (2) above may, within twenty-one days of the date of service, make written representations to the Secretary of State and, if desired, oral representations to a person appointed for that purpose by the Secretary of State.

(6) The Secretary of State may in the light of any representations made in accordance with subsection (5) above withdraw his notice and in that event the scheme shall be a recognised scheme from the date on which the notice is withdrawn.

(7) Rules under section 48 above shall not apply to investment business in respect of which the operator or trustee of a scheme recognised under this section is an authorised person by virtue of section 24 above except so far as they make provision as respects—

(a) procuring persons to become participants in the scheme and advising persons on the scheme and the exercise of the rights conferred by it;

(b) matters incidental to those mentioned in paragraph (a) above.

(8) For the purposes of this section a collective investment scheme is constituted in a member State if—

(a) it is constituted under the law of that State by a contract or under a trust and is managed by a body corporate incorporated under that law; or

(b) it takes the form of an open-ended investment company incorporated under that law.

(9) If the operator of a scheme recognised under this section
gives written notice to the Secretary of State stating that he
desires the scheme no longer to be recognised under this
section it shall cease to be so recognised when the notice is
given.

87.—(1) Subject to subsection (3) below, a collective invest- Schemes
ment scheme which is not a recognised scheme by virtue of authorised in
section 86 above but is managed in and authorised under the designated
law of a country or territory outside the United Kingdom is a territories.
recognised scheme if—

> (*a*) that country or territory is designated for the purposes
> of this section by an order made by the Secretary of
> State ; and
>
> (*b*) the scheme is of a class specified by the order.

(2) The Secretary of State shall not make an order designating
any country or territory for the purposes of this section unless
he is satisfied that the law under which collective investment
schemes of the class to be specified by the order are authorised
and supervised in that country or territory affords to investors
in the United Kingdom protection at least equivalent to that
provided for them by this Chapter in the case of an authorised
unit trust scheme.

(3) A scheme shall not be recognised by virtue of this section
unless the operator of the scheme gives written notice to the
Secretary of State that he wishes it to be recognised ; and the
scheme shall not be recognised if within such period from receiving the notice as may be prescribed the Secretary of State notifies the operator that the scheme is not to be recognised.

(4) The notice given by the operator under subsection (3)
above—

> (*a*) shall contain the address of a place in the United King-
> dom for the service on the operator of notices or other
> documents required or authorised to be served on him
> under this Act ; and
>
> (*b*) shall contain or be accompanied by such information
> and documents as may be prescribed.

(5) Section 85 above shall have effect in relation to a scheme
recognised under this section as it has effect in relation to an
authorised unit trust scheme, taking references to the manager
as references to the operator and, in the case of an operator who
is not an authorised person, references to publishing particulars
as references to causing them to be published ; and regulations
made by virtue of this subsection may make provision whereby
compliance with any requirements imposed by or under the law

PART I
CHAPTER VIII

of a country or territory designated under this section is treated as compliance with any requirement of the regulations.

(6) An order under subsection (1) above may contain such transitional provisions as the Secretary of State thinks necessary or expedient and shall be subject to annulment in pursuance of a resolution of either House of Parliament.

Other
overseas
schemes.

88.—(1) The Secretary of State may, on the application of the operator of a scheme which—

(a) is managed in a country or territory outside the United Kingdom ; but

(b) does not satisfy the requirements mentioned in section 86(1) above and in relation to which there is no relevant order under section 87(1) above,

make an order declaring the scheme to be a recognised scheme if it appears to him that it affords adequate protection to the participants, makes adequate provision for the matters dealt with by regulations under section 81 above and satisfies the following provisions of this section.

(2) The operator must be a body corporate or the scheme must take the form of an open-ended investment company.

(3) Subject to subsection (4) below, the operator and the trustee, if any, must be fit and proper persons to act as operator or, as the case may be, as trustee ; and for that purpose the Secretary of State may take into account any matter relating to—

(a) any person who is or will be employed by or associated with the operator or trustee for the purposes of the scheme ;

(b) any director or controller of the operator or trustee ;

(c) any other body corporate in the same group as the operator or trustee and any director or controller of any such other body.

(4) Subsection (3) above does not apply to an operator or trustee who is an authorised person and not prohibited from acting as operator or trustee, as the case may be, by or under rules under section 48 above, by or under the rules of any recognised self-regulating organisation of which he is a member or by any prohibition imposed under section 65 above.

(5) If the operator is not an authorised person he must have a representative in the United Kingdom who is an authorised person and has power to act generally for the operator and to accept service of notices and other documents on his behalf.

(6) The name of the scheme must not be undesirable or misleading; and the purposes of the scheme must be reasonably capable of being successfully carried into effect.

(7) The participants must be entitled to have their units redeemed in accordance with the scheme at a price related to the net value of the property to which the units relate and determined in accordance with the scheme; but a scheme shall be treated as complying with this subsection if it requires the operator to ensure that a participant is able to sell his units on an investment exchange at a price not significantly different from that mentioned in this subsection.

(8) Subsections (2) to (5) of section 77 above shall apply also to an application under this section.

(9) So much of section 82 above as applies to an alteration of the scheme shall apply also to a scheme recognised under this section, taking references to the manager as references to the operator and with the omission of the requirement relating to the solicitor's certificate; and if the operator or trustee of any such scheme is to be replaced the operator or, as the case may be, the trustee, or in either case the person who is to replace him, shall give at least one month's notice to the Secretary of State.

(10) Section 85 above shall have effect in relation to a scheme recognised under this section as it has effect in relation to an authorised unit trust scheme, taking references to the manager as references to the operator and, in the case of an operator who is not an authorised person, references to publishing particulars as references to causing them to be published.

89.—(1) The Secretary of State may at any time direct that a scheme shall cease to be recognised by virtue of section 87 above or revoke an order under section 88 above if it appears to him— *Refusal and revocation of recognition.*

(a) that it is undesirable in the interests of the participants or potential participants in the United Kingdom that the scheme should continue to be recognised;

(b) without prejudice to paragraph (a) above, that the operator or trustee of the scheme has contravened any provision of this Act or any rules or regulations made under it or, in purported compliance with any such provision, has furnished the Secretary of State with false, inaccurate or misleading information or has contravened any prohibition or requirement imposed under this Act; or

(c) in the case of an order under section 88 that any of the requirements for the making of the order are no longer satisfied.

(2) For the purposes of subsection (1)(*a*) above the Secretary of State may take into account any matter relating to the scheme the operator or trustee, a director or controller of the operator or trustee or any person employed by or associated with the operator or trustee in connection with the scheme.

(3) In the case of an operator or trustee who is a member of a recognised self-regulating organisation the rules, prohibitions and requirements referred to in subsection (1)(*b*) above include the rules of that organisation and any prohibition or requirement imposed by virtue of those rules.

(4) The Secretary of State may give such a direction or revoke such an order as is mentioned in subsection (1) above at the request of the operator or trustee of the scheme ; but he may refuse to do so if he considers that any matter concerning the scheme should be investigated as a preliminary to a decision on the question whether the direction should be given or the order revoked or that the direction or revocation would not be in the interests of the participants.

(5) Where the Secretary of State proposes—

  (*a*) to notify the operator of a scheme under section 87(3) above ; or

  (*b*) to give such a direction or to refuse to make or to revoke such an order as is mentioned in subsection (1) above,

he shall give the operator written notice of his intention to do so, stating the reasons for which he proposes to act and giving particulars of the rights conferred by subsection (6) below.

(6) A person on whom a notice is served under subsection (5) above may, within twenty-one days of the date of service, make written representations to the Secretary of State and, if desired, oral representations to a person appointed for that purpose by the Secretary of State.

(7) The Secretary of State shall have regard to any representations made in accordance with subsection (6) above in determining whether to notify the operator, give the direction or refuse to make or revoke the order, as the case may be.

Facilities and information in the United Kingdom.

90.—(1) The Secretary of State may make regulations requiring operators of recognised schemes to maintain in the United Kingdom, or in such part or parts of it as may be specified in the regulations, such facilities as he thinks desirable in the interests of participants and as are specified in the regulations.

(2) The Secretary of State may by notice in writing require the operator of any recognised scheme to include such explanatory information as is specified in the notice in any investment adver-

tisement issued or caused to be issued by him in the United
Kingdom in which the scheme is named.

Powers of intervention

91.—(1) If it appears to the Secretary of State—

  (a) that any of the requirements for the making of an order
      declaring a scheme to be an authorised unit trust
      scheme are no longer satisfied ;

  (b) that the exercise of the power conferred by this subsec-
      tion is desirable in the interests of participants or
      potential participants in the scheme ; or

  (c) without prejudice to paragraph (b) above, that the man-
      ager or trustee of such a scheme has contravened any
      provision of this Act or any rules or regulations made
      under it or, in purported compliance with any such
      provision, has furnished the Secretary of State with
      false, inaccurate or misleading information or has con-
      travened any prohibition or requirement imposed under
      this Act,

he may give a direction under subsection (2) below.

(2) A direction under this subsection may—

  (a) require the manager of the scheme to cease the issue or
      redemption, or both the issue and redemption, of units
      under the scheme on a date specified in the direction
      until such further date as is specified in that or another
      direction ;

  (b) require the manager and trustee of the scheme to wind
      it up by such date as is specified in the direction or,
      if no date is specified, as soon as practicable.

(3) The revocation of the order declaring an authorised unit
trust scheme to be such a scheme shall not affect the operation
of any direction under subsection (2) above which is then in
force ; and a direction may be given under that subsection in
relation to a scheme in the case of which the order declaring it
to be an authorised unit trust scheme has been revoked if a
direction under that subsection was already in force at the time
of revocation.

(4) Sections 60, 61 and 62 above shall have effect in relation to
a contravention of a direction under subsection (2) above as
they have effect in relation to any such contravention as is mentioned in those sections.

(5) If it appears to the Secretary of State—

> (a) that the exercise of the power conferred by this subsection is desirable in the interests of participants or potential participants in a scheme recognised under section 87 or 88 above who are in the United Kingdom ;
>
> (b) without prejudice to paragraph (a) above, that the operator of such a scheme has contravened any provision of this Act or any rules or regulations made under it or, in purported compliance with any such provision, has furnished the Secretary of State with false, inaccurate or misleading information or has contravened any prohibition or requirement imposed under this Act ; or
>
> (c) that any of the requirements for the recognition of a scheme under section 88 above are no longer satisfied.

he may direct that the scheme shall not be a recognised scheme for a specified period or until the occurrence of a specified event or until specified conditions are complied with.

(6) For the purposes of subsections (1)(b) and (5)(a) above the Secretary of State may take into account any matter relating to the scheme, the manager, operator or trustee, a director or controller of the manager, operator or trustee or any person employed by or associated with the manager, operator or trustee in connection with the scheme.

(7) In the case of a manager, operator or trustee who is a member of a recognised self-regulating organisation the rules, prohibitions and requirements referred to in subsections (1)(c) and (5)(b) above include the rules of that organisation and any prohibition or requirement imposed by virtue of those rules.

(8) The Secretary of State may, either of his own motion or on the application of the manager, trustee or operator of the scheme concerned, withdraw or vary a direction given under this section if it appears to the Secretary of State that it is no longer necessary for the direction to take effect or continue in force or, as the case may be, that it should take effect or continue in force in a different form.

Notice of
directions.

92.—(1) The power to give a direction under section 91 above in relation to a scheme shall be exercisable by written notice served by the Secretary of State on the manager and trustee or, as the case may be, on the operator of the scheme and any such notice shall take effect on such date as is specified in the notice.

(2) If the Secretary of State refuses to withdraw or vary a direction on the application of the manager, trustee or operator of the scheme concerned he shall serve that person with a written notice of refusal.

(3) A notice giving a direction, or varying it otherwise than on the application of the manager, trustee or operator concerned, or refusing to withdraw or vary a direction on the application of such a person shall state the reasons for which the direction was given or varied or, as the case may be, why the application was refused.

(4) The Secretary of State may give public notice of a direction given by him under section 91 above and of any withdrawal or variation of such a direction ; and any such notice may, if the Secretary of State thinks fit, include a statement of the reasons for which the direction was given, withdrawn or varied.

93.—(1) In any case in which the Secretary of State has power Applications to give a direction under section 91(2) above in relation to an to the court. authorised unit trust scheme or, by virtue of subsection (3) of that section, in relation to a scheme which has been such a scheme, he may apply to the court—

> (*a*) for an order removing the manager or trustee, or both the manager and trustee, of the scheme and replacing either or both of them with a person or persons nominated by him and appearing to him to satisfy the requirements of section 78 above ; or
>
> (*b*) if it appears to the Secretary of State that no, or no suitable, person satisfying those requirements is available, for an order removing the manager or trustee, or both the manager and trustee, and appointing an authorised person to wind the scheme up.

(2) On an application under this section the court may make such order as it thinks fit ; and the court may, on the application of the Secretary of State, rescind any such order as is mentioned in paragraph (*b*) of subsection (1) above and substitute such an order as is mentioned in paragraph (*a*) of that subsection.

(3) The Secretary of State shall give written notice of the making of an application under this section to the manager and trustee of the scheme concerned and take such steps as he considers appropriate for bringing the making of the application to the attention of the participants.

(4) The jurisdiction conferred by this section shall be exercisable by the High Court and the Court of Session.

(5) Section 83 above shall not apply to a manager appointed by an order made on an application under subsection (1)(*b*) above.

Supplemental

94.—(1) The Secretary of State may appoint one or more competent inspectors to investigate and report on—

(a) the affairs of, or of the manager or trustee of, any authorised unit trust scheme ;

(b) the affairs of, or of the operator or trustee of, any recognised scheme so far as relating to activities carried on in the United Kingdom ; or

(c) the affairs of, or of the operator or trustee of, any other collective investment scheme,

if it appears to the Secretary of State that it is in the interests of the participants to do so or that the matter is of public concern.

(2) An inspector appointed under subsection (1) above to investigate the affairs of, or of the manager, trustee or operator of, any scheme may also, if he thinks it necessary for the purposes of that investigation, investigate the affairs of, or of the manager, trustee or operator of, any other such scheme as is mentioned in that subsection whose manager, trustee or operator is the same person as the manager, trustee or operator of the first-mentioned scheme.

1985 c. 6.   (3) Sections 434 to 436 of the Companies Act 1985 (production of documents and evidence to inspectors), except section 435(1)(a) and (b) and (2), shall apply in relation to an inspector appointed under this section as they apply to an inspector appointed under section 431 of that Act but with the modifications specified in subsection (4) below.

(4) In the provisions applied by subsection (3) above for any reference to a company or its affairs there shall be substituted a reference to the scheme under investigation by virtue of this section and the affairs mentioned in subsection (1) or (2) above and any reference to an officer or director of the company shall include a reference to any director of the manager, trustee or operator of the scheme.

(5) A person shall not under this section be required to disclose any information or produce any document which he would be entitled to refuse to disclose or produce on grounds of legal professional privilege in proceedings in the High Court or on grounds of confidentiality as between client and professional legal adviser in proceedings in the Court of Session except that a lawyer may be required to furnish the name and address of his client.

(6) Where a person claims a lien on a document its production under this section shall be without prejudice to the lien.

(7) Nothing in this section shall require a person carrying on the business of banking to disclose any information or produce any document relating to the affairs of a customer unless—

    (*a*) the customer is a person who the inspector has reason to believe may be able to give information relevant to the investigation ; and

    (*b*) the Secretary of State is satisfied that the disclosure or production is necessary for the purposes of the investigation.

(8) An inspector appointed under this section may, and if so directed by the Secretary of State shall, make interim reports to the Secretary of State and on the conclusion of his investigation shall make a final report to him.

(9) Any such report shall be written or printed as the Secretary of State may direct and the Secretary of State may, if he thinks fit—

    (*a*) furnish a copy, on request and on payment of the prescribed fee, to the manager, trustee or operator or any participant in a scheme under investigation or any other person whose conduct is referred to in the report ; and

    (*b*) cause the report to be published.

95.—(1) A person who contravenes any provision of this Chapter, a manager or trustee of an authorised unit trust scheme who contravenes any regulations made under section 81 above and a person who contravenes any other regulations made under this Chapter shall be treated as having contravened rules made under Chapter V of this Part of this Act or, in the case of a person who is an authorised person by virtue of his membership of a recognised self-regulating organisation or certification by a recognised professional body, the rules of that organisation or body. *Contra-*
ventions.

(2) Subsection (1) above applies also to any contravention by the operator of a recognised scheme of a requirement imposed under section 90(2) above.

CHAPTER IX

THE TRIBUNAL

96.—(1) For the purposes of this Act there shall be a Tribunal known as the Financial Services Tribunal (in this Act referred to as " the Tribunal "). *The Financial*
Services
Tribunal.

(2) There shall be a panel of not less than ten persons to serve as members of the Tribunal when nominated to do so in accor-

dance with subsection (3) below; and that panel shall consist of—

> (*a*) persons with legal qualifications appointed by the Lord Chancellor after consultation with the Lord Advocate, including at least one person qualified in Scots law; and

> (*b*) persons appointed by the Secretary of State who appear to him to be qualified by experience or otherwise to deal with the cases that may be referred to the Tribunal.

(3) Where a case is referred to the Tribunal the Secretary of State shall nominate three persons from the panel to serve as members of the Tribunal in respect of that case and nominate one of them to be chairman.

(4) The person nominated to be chairman of the Tribunal in respect of any case shall be a person with legal qualifications and, so far as practicable, at least one of the other members shall be a person with recent practical experience in business relevant to the case.

(5) If while a case is being dealt with by the Tribunal one of the three persons serving as members in respect of that case becomes unable to act the case may, with the consent of the Secretary of State and of the person or persons at whose request the case was referred to the Tribunal, be dealt with by the other two members.

(6) Schedule 6 to this Act shall have effect as respects the Tribunal and its proceedings.

References to
the Tribunal.

97.—(1) Any person—

> (*a*) on whom a notice is served under section 29, 34, 59(4), 60(2) or 70 above; or

> (*b*) on whom a copy of a notice under section 29, 34, 60(2) or 70 above is served or on whom the Secretary of State considers that a copy of such a notice would have been served if it had been practicable to do so,

may within twenty-eight days of the date of service of the notice require the Secretary of State to refer the matter to which the notice relates to the Tribunal and, subject to the provisions of this section, the Secretary of State shall refer that matter accordingly.

(2) The Secretary of State need not refer a matter to the Tribunal at the request of the person on whom a notice was

served under section 29, 34, 59(4) or 60(2) above if within the period mentioned in subsection (1) above he—

   (*a*) decides to grant the application or, as the case may be, decides not to withdraw or suspend the authorisation, give the direction or publish the statement to which the notice relates ; and

   (*b*) gives written notice of his decision to that person.

(3) The Secretary of State need not refer a matter to the Tribunal at the request of the person on whom a notice is served under section 70 above if—

   (*a*) that matter is the refusal of an application for the rescission or variation of a prohibition or requirement and within the period mentioned in subsection (1) above he—

      (i) decides to grant the application ; and

      (ii) gives written notice of his decision to that person ; or

   (*b*) that matter is the imposition or variation of a prohibition or requirement, being a prohibition, requirement or variation which has not yet taken effect, and within the period mentioned in subsection (1) above and before the prohibition, requirement or variation takes effect he—

      (i) decides to rescind the prohibition or requirement or decides not to make the variation ; and

      (ii) gives written notice of his decision to that person.

(4) Where the notice served on a person under section 29 or 34 above—

   (*a*) proposed the withdrawal of an authorisation or the giving of a direction under section 33(1)(*a*) above ; or

   (*b*) proposed the suspension of an authorisation or the giving of a direction under section 33(1)(*b*) above,

and at any time within the period mentioned in subsection (1) above the Secretary of State serves a new notice on that person in substitution for that previously served, then, if the substituted notice complies with subsection (5) below, subsection (1) above shall have effect in relation to the substituted notice instead of the original notice and as if the period there mentioned were twenty-eight days after the date of service of the original notice or fourteen days after the date of service of the substituted notice, whichever ends later.

(5) A notice served in substitution for a notice within subsection (4)(*a*) above complies with this subsection if it proposes—

   (*a*) the suspension of an authorisation or the giving of a direction under section 33(1)(*b*) above ; or

(b) the exercise of the power conferred by section 60 above ;

and a notice served in substitution for a notice within subsection (4)(b) above complies with this subsection if it proposes a less severe suspension or direction under section 33(1)(b) or the exercise of the power conferred by section 60 above.

(6) The reference of the imposition or variation of a prohibition or requirement under Chapter VI of this Part of this Act to the Tribunal shall not affect the date on which it comes into effect.

Decisions on references by applicant or authorised person etc.

98.—(1) Where a case is referred to the Tribunal at the request of a person within section 97(1)(a) above the Tribunal shall—

> (a) investigate the case ; and
>
> (b) make a report to the Secretary of State stating what would in its opinion be the appropriate decision in the matter and the reasons for that opinion ;

and it shall be the duty of the Secretary of State to decide the matter forthwith in accordance with the Tribunal's report.

(2) Where the matter referred to the Tribunal is the refusal of an application the Tribunal may under this section report that the appropriate decision would be to grant or refuse the application or—

> (a) in the case of an application for the variation of a suspension, direction, consent, prohibition or requirement, to vary it in a specified manner ;
>
> (b) in the case of an application for the rescission of a prohibition or requirement, to vary the prohibition or requirement in a specified manner.

(3) Where the matter referred to the Tribunal is any action of the Secretary of State other than the refusal of an application the Tribunal may report that the appropriate decision would be—

> (a) to take or not to take the action taken or proposed to be taken by the Secretary of State or to take any other action that he could take under the provision in question ; or
>
> (b) to take instead or in addition any action that he could take in the case of the person concerned under any one or more of the provisions mentioned in subsection (4) below other than that under which he was acting or proposing to act.

(4) Those provisions are sections 28, 33 and 60 above and Chapter VI of this Part of this Act ; and sections 29, 34, 60(2) and (3) and 70(2) and (4) above shall not apply to any action

taken by the Secretary of State in accordance with the Tribunal's report.

(5) The Tribunal shall send a copy of its report under this section to the person at whose request the case was referred to it ; and the Secretary of State shall serve him with a written notice of the decision made by him in accordance with the report.

99. Where a case is referred to the Tribunal at the request of a person within section 97(1)(*b*) above the Tribunal shall report to the Secretary of State whether the reasons stated in the notice in question which relate to that person are substantiated ; and the Tribunal shall send a copy of the report to that person and to the person on whom the notice was served.

Decisions on references by third parties.

100.—(1) A person who has required a case to be referred to the Tribunal may at any time before the conclusion of the proceedings before the Tribunal withdraw the reference.

Withdrawal of references.

(2) The Secretary of State may at any such time withdraw any reference made at the request of a person on whom a notice was served under any of the provisions mentioned in subsection (1)(*a*) of section 97 above if he—

(*a*) decides as mentioned in subsection (2)(*a*) or (3)(*a*)(i) or (*b*)(i) of that section ; and

(*b*) gives such a notice as is mentioned in subsection (2)(*b*) or (3)(*a*)(ii) or (*b*)(ii) of that section ;

but a reference shall not be withdrawn by virtue of such a decision and notice as are mentioned in paragraph (*b*) of subsection (3) unless the decision is made and the notice is given before the prohibition, requirement or variation has taken effect.

(3) Where a case is withdrawn from the Tribunal under this section the Tribunal shall not further investigate the case or make a report under section 98 or 99 above ; but where the reference is withdrawn otherwise than by the Secretary of State he may require the Tribunal to make a report to him on the results of its investigation up to the time when the reference was withdrawn.

(4) Where two or more persons have required a case to be referred to the Tribunal the withdrawal of the reference by one or more of them shall not affect the functions of the Tribunal as respects the case so far as relating to a person who has not withdrawn the reference.

(5) Where a person on whom a notice was served under section 29, 34 or 60 above withdraws a case from the Tribunal sub-

section (5) of each of those sections shall apply to him as if he had not required the case to be referred.

Reports.

101.—(1) In preparing its report on any case the Tribunal shall have regard to the need to exclude, so far as practicable, any matter which relates to the affairs of a particular person (not being a person who required or could have required the case to be referred to the Tribunal) where the publication of that matter would or might, in the opinion of the Tribunal, seriously and prejudicially affect the interests of that person.

(2) The Secretary of State may, in such cases as he thinks fit, publish the report of the Tribunal and offer copies of any such report for sale.

(3) The Secretary of State may, on request and on payment of the prescribed fee, supply a copy of a report of the Tribunal to any person whose conduct is referred to in the report or whose interests as a client or creditor are affected by the conduct of a person to whom the proceedings before the Tribunal related.

(4) If the Secretary of State is of opinion that there is good reason for not disclosing any part of a report he may cause that part to be omitted from the report as published under subsection (2) or from the copy of it supplied under subsection (3) above.

(5) A copy of a report of the Tribunal endorsed with a certificate signed by or on behalf of the Secretary of State stating that it is a true copy shall be admissible as evidence of the opinion of the Tribunal as to any matter referred to in the report ; and a certificate purporting to be signed as aforesaid shall be deemed to have been duly signed unless the contrary is shown.

CHAPTER X
INFORMATION

Register of
authorised
persons and
recognised
organisations
etc.

102.—(1) The Secretary of State shall keep a register containing an entry in respect of—

   (a) each person who is an authorised person by virtue of an authorisation granted by the Secretary of State ;

   (b) each other person who appears to him to be an authorised person by virtue of any provision of this Part of this Act ;

   (c) each recognised self-regulating organisation, recognised professional body, recognised investment exchange and recognised clearing house ;

(*d*) each authorised unit trust scheme and recognised scheme ;

(*e*) each person in respect of whom a direction under section 59 above is in force.

(2) The entry in respect of each authorised person shall consist of—

(*a*) a statement of the provision by virtue of which he is an authorised person ;

(*b*) in the case of a person who is an authorised person by virtue of membership of a recognised self-regulating organisation or certification by a recognised professional body, the name and address of the organisation or body ;

(*c*) in the case of a person who is an authorised person by virtue of section 25 or 31 above, information as to the services which that person holds himself out as able to provide ;

(*d*) in the case of a person who is an authorised person by virtue of section 31 above, the address notified to the Secretary of State under section 32 above ;

(*e*) in the case of a person who is an authorised person by virtue of any provision other than section 31 above, the date on which he became an authorised person by virtue of that provision ; and

(*f*) such other information as the Secretary of State may determine.

(3) The entry in respect of each such organisation, body, exchange or clearing house as is mentioned in subsection (1)(*c*) above shall consist of its name and address and such other information as the Secretary of State may determine.

(4) The entry in respect of each such scheme as is mentioned in subsection (1)(*d*) above shall consist of its name and, in the case of an authorised unit trust scheme, the name and address of the manager and trustee and, in the case of a recognised scheme, the name and address of the operator and of any representative of the operator in the United Kingdom and, in either case, such other information as the Secretary of State may determine.

(5) The entry in respect of each such person as is mentioned in subsection (1)(*e*) above shall include particulars of any consent for that person's employment given by the Secretary of State.

(6) Where it appears to the Secretary of State that any person in respect of whom there is an entry in the register by virtue of subsection (1) (*a*) or (*b*) above has ceased to be an authorised

person (whether by death, by withdrawal or other cessation of his authorisation, as a result of his ceasing to be a member of a recognised self-regulating organisation or otherwise) the Secretary of State shall make a note to that effect in the entry together with the reason why the person in question is no longer an authorised person.

(7) Where—

> (a) an organisation, body, exchange or clearing house in respect of which there is an entry in the register by virtue of paragraph (c) of subsection (1) above has ceased to be recognised or ceased to exist ;
>
> (b) an authorised unit trust scheme or recognised scheme in respect of which there is an entry in the register by virtue of paragraph (d) of that subsection has ceased to be authorised or recognised ; or
>
> (c) the direction applying to a person in respect of whom there is an entry in the register by virtue of paragraph (e) of that subsection has ceased to have effect,

the Secretary of State shall make a note to that effect in the entry.

(8) An entry in respect of which a note is made under subsection (6) or (7) above may be removed from the register at the end of such period as the Secretary of State thinks appropriate.

Inspection of register.

103.—(1) The information contained in the entries included in the register otherwise than by virtue of section 102(1)(e) above shall be open to inspection ; and the Secretary of State may publish the information contained in those entries in any form he thinks appropriate and may offer copies of any such information for sale.

(2) A person shall be entitled to ascertain whether there is an entry in the register by virtue of subsection (1)(e) of section 102 above (not being an entry in respect of which there is a note under subsection (7) of that section) in respect of a particular person specified by him and, if there is such an entry, to inspect it.

(3) Except as provided by subsection (2) above the information contained in the register by virtue of section 102(1)(e) above shall not be open to inspection by any person unless he satisfies the Secretary of State that he has a good reason for seeking the information.

(4) A person to whom information is made available by the

Secretary of State under subsection (3) above shall not, without
the consent of the Secretary of State or of the person to whom
the information relates, make use of it except for the purpose
for which it was made available.

(5) Information which by virtue of this section is open to
inspection shall be open to inspection free of charge but only
at such times and places as the Secretary of State may appoint;
and a person entitled to inspect any information may obtain a
certified copy of it from the Secretary of State on payment of
the prescribed fee.

(6) The register may be kept by the Secretary of State in such
form as he thinks appropriate with a view to facilitating inspection of the information which it contains.

104.—(1) The Secretary of State may by notice in writing
require a person who is authorised to carry on investment business by virtue of section 22, 24, 25 or 31 above to furnish him
with such information as he may reasonably require for the
exercise of his functions under this Act.

Power to call
for
information.

(2) The Secretary of State may by notice in writing require
a recognised self-regulating organisation, recognised professional
body, recognised investment exchange or recognised clearing
house to furnish him with such information as he may reasonably
require for the exercise of his functions under this Act.

(3) The Secretary of State may require any information which
he requires under this section to be furnished within such reasonable time and verified in such manner as he may specify.

(4) Sections 60, 61 and 62 above shall have effect in relation
to a contravention of a requirement imposed under subsection
(1) above as they have effect in relation to a contravention of the
provisions to which those sections apply.

105.—(1) The powers of the Secretary of State under this section shall be exercisable in any case in which it appears to him
that there is good reason to do so for the purpose of investigating
the affairs, or any aspect of the affairs, of any person so far as
relevant to any investment business which he is or was carrying
on or appears to the Secretary of State to be or to have been
carrying on.

Investigation
powers.

(2) Those powers shall not be exercisable for the purpose of
investigating the affairs of any exempted person unless he is an
appointed representative or the investigation is in respect of investment business in respect of which he is not an exempted person and shall not be exercisable for the purpose of investigating

the affairs of a member of a recognised self-regulating organisation or a person certified by a recognised professional body in respect of investment business in the carrying on of which he is subject to its rules unless—

(a) that organisation or body has requested the Secretary of State to investigate those affairs ; or

(b) it appears to him that the organisation or body is unable or unwilling to investigate them in a satisfactory manner.

(3) The Secretary of State may require the person whose affairs are to be investigated (" the person under investigation ") or any connected person to attend before the Secretary of State at a specified time and place and answer questions or otherwise furnish information with respect to any matter relevant to the investigation.

(4) The Secretary of State may require the person under investigation or any other person to produce at a specified time and place any specified documents which appear to the Secretary of State to relate to any matter relevant to the investigation ; and—

(a) if any such documents are produced, the Secretary of State may take copies or extracts from them or require the person producing them or any connected person to provide an explanation of any of them ;

(b) if any such documents are not produced, the Secretary of State may require the person who was required to produce them to state, to the best of his knowledge and belief, where they are.

(5) A statement by a person in compliance with a requirement imposed by virtue of this section may be used in evidence against him.

(6) A person shall not under this section be required to disclose any information or produce any document which he would be entitled to refuse to disclose or produce on grounds of legal professional privilege in proceedings in the High Court or on grounds of confidentiality as between client and professional legal adviser in proceedings in the Court of Session except that a lawyer may be required to furnish the name and address of his client.

1979 c. 37.

(7) The Secretary of State shall not require a recognised bank or licensed institution within the meaning of the Banking Act 1979 to disclose any information or produce any document relating to the affairs of a customer unless the Secretary of State considers it necessary to do so for the purpose of investigating any investment business carried on, or appearing to the Secretary

of State to be carried on or to have been carried on, by the bank, institution or customer or, if the customer is a related company of the person under investigation, by that person.

(8) Where a person claims a lien on a document its production under this section shall be without prejudice to the lien.

(9) In this section—

" connected person ", in relation to any other person means—

> (a) any person who is or was that other person's partner, employee, agent, appointed representative, banker, auditor or solicitor ; and

> (b) where the other person is a body corporate, any person who is or was a director, secretary or controller of that body corporate or of another body corporate of which it is or was a subsidiary ; and

> (c) where the other person is an unincorporated association, any person who is or was a member of the governing body or an officer or controller of the association ; and

> (d) where the other person is an appointed representative, any person who is or was his principal ; and

> (e) where the other person is the person under investigation (being a body corporate), any related company of that body corporate and any person who is a connected person in relation to that company ;

" documents " includes information recorded in any form and, in relation to information recorded otherwise than in legible form, references to its production include references to producing a copy of the information in legible form ;

" related company ", in relation to a person under investigation (being a body corporate), means any other body corporate which is or at any material time was—

> (a) a holding company or subsidiary of the person under investigation ;

> (b) a subsidiary of a holding company of that person ; or

> (c) a holding company of a subsidiary of that person,

and whose affairs it is in the Secretary of State's opinion necessary to investigate for the purpose of investigating the affairs of that person.

(10) Any person who without reasonable excuse fails to comply with a requirement imposed on him under this section shall

be guilty of an offence and liable on summary conviction to imprisonment for a term not exceeding six months or to a fine not exceeding the fifth level on the standard scale or to both.

Exercise of
investigation
powers by
officer etc.

106.—(1) The Secretary of State may authorise any officer of his or any other competent person to exercise on his behalf all or any of the powers conferred by section 105 above but no such authority shall be granted except for the purpose of investigating the affairs, or any aspects of the affairs, of a person specified in the authority.

(2) No person shall be bound to comply with any requirement imposed by a person exercising powers by virtue of an authority granted under this section unless he has, if required to do so, produced evidence of his authority.

(3) Where the Secretary of State authorises a person other than one of his officers to exercise any powers by virtue of this section that person shall make a report to the Secretary of State in such manner as he may require on the exercise of those powers and the results of exercising them.

CHAPTER XI

AUDITORS

Appointment
of auditors.

107.—(1) The Secretary of State may make rules requiring a person who is authorised to carry on investment business by virtue of section 25 or 31 above and who, apart from the rules, is not required by or under any enactment to appoint an auditor to appoint as an auditor a person satisfying such conditions as to qualifications and otherwise as may be specified in or imposed under the rules.

(2) Rules under this section may make provision—

(a) specifying the manner in which and the time within which an auditor is to be appointed ;

(b) requiring the Secretary of State to be notified of any such appointment and enabling the Secretary of State to make an appointment if no appointment is made or notified as required by the rules ;

(c) with respect to the remuneration of an auditor appointed under the rules ;

(d) with respect to the term of office, removal and resignation of any such auditor ;

(e) requiring any such auditor who is removed, resigns or is not reappointed to notify the Secretary of State whether there are any circumstances connected with his ceasing to hold office which he considers should be brought to the Secretary of State's attention.

(3) **An auditor appointed under the rules shall in accordance with the rules examine and report on the accounts of the authorised person in question and shall for that purpose have such duties and powers as are specified in the rules.**

108.—(1) If in any case it appears to the Secretary of State that there is good reason to do so he may direct any person who is authorised to carry on investment business by virtue of section 25 or 31 above to submit for further examination by a person approved by the Secretary of State—

Power to require second audit.

> (*a*) any accounts on which that person's auditor has reported or any information given under section 52 or 104 above which has been verified by that auditor ; or

> (*b*) such matters contained in any such accounts or information as are specified in the direction ;

and the person making the further examination shall report his conclusions to the Secretary of State.

(2) Any further examination and report required by a direction under this section shall be at the expense of the authorised person concerned and shall be carried out and made within such time as is specified in the direction or within such further time as the Secretary of State may allow.

(3) The person carrying out an examination under this section shall have all the powers that were available to the auditor ; and it shall be the duty of the auditor to afford him all such assistance as he may require.

(4) Where a report made under this section relates to accounts which under any enactment are required to be sent to or made available for inspection by any person or to be delivered for registration, the report, or any part of it (or a note that such a report has been made) may be similarly sent, made available or delivered by the Secretary of State.

109.—(1) No duty to which an auditor of an authorised person may be subject shall be regarded as contravened by reason of his communicating in good faith to the Secretary of State, whether or not in response to a request from him, any information or opinion on a matter of which the auditor has become aware in his capacity as auditor of that person and which is relevant to any functions of the Secretary of State under this Act.

Communication by auditor with supervisory authorities.

(2) If it appears to the Secretary of State that any auditor or class of auditor to whom subsection (1) above applies is not subject to satisfactory rules made or guidance issued by a professional body specifying circumstances in which matters are to be communicated to the Secretary of State as mentioned in that subsection the Secretary of State may himself make rules

applying to that auditor or that class of auditor and specifying such circumstances ; and it shall be the duty of an auditor to whom the rules made by the Secretary of State apply to communicate a matter to the Secretary of State in the circumstances specified by the rules.

(3) The matters to be communicated to the Secretary of State in accordance with any such rules or guidance may include matters relating to persons other than the authorised person.

(4) No such rules as are mentioned in subsection (2) above shall be made by the Secretary of State unless a draft of them has been laid before and approved by a resolution of each House of Parliament.

(5) This section applies to—

> (a) the communication by an auditor to a recognised self-regulating organisation or recognised professional body of matters relevant to its function of determining whether a person is a fit and proper person to carry on investment business ; and

> (b) the communication to such an organisation or body or any other authority or person of matters relevant to its or his function of determining whether a person is complying with the rules applicable to his conduct of investment business,

as it applies to the communication to the Secretary of State of matters relevant to his functions under this Act.

Overseas
business.

110.—(1) A person incorporated or having his head office outside the United Kingdom who is authorised as mentioned in subsection (1) of section 107 above may, whether or not he is required to appoint an auditor apart from the rules made under that subsection, appoint an auditor in accordance with those rules in respect of the investment business carried on by him in the United Kingdom and in that event that person shall be treated for the purposes of this Chapter as the auditor of that person.

(2) In the case of a person to be appointed as auditor of a person incorporated or having his head office outside the United Kingdom the conditions as to qualifications imposed by or under the rules made under that section may be regarded as satisfied by qualifications obtained outside the United Kingdom which appear to the Secretary of State to be equivalent.

(3) A person incorporated or having his head office outside the United Kingdom shall not be regarded for the purposes of section 25 above as a fit and proper person to carry on investment business unless—

(a) he has appointed an auditor in accordance with rules made under section 107 above in respect of the investment business carried on by him in the United Kingdom ; or

(b) he has an auditor having qualifications, powers and duties appearing to the Secretary of State to be equivalent to those applying to an auditor appointed in accordance with those rules,

and, in either case, the auditor is able and willing to communicate with the Secretary of State and other bodies and persons as mentioned in section 109 above.

111.—(1) Any authorised person and any officer, controller or manager of an authorised person, who knowingly or recklessly furnishes an auditor appointed under the rules made under section 107 or a person carrying out an examination under section 108 above with information which the auditor or that person requires or is entitled to require and which is false or misleading in a material particular shall be guilty of an offence and liable—

(a) on conviction on indictment, to imprisonment for a term not exceeding two years or to a fine or to both ;

(b) on summary conviction, to imprisonment for a term not exceeding six months or to a fine not exceeding the statutory maximum or to both.

(2) The duty of an auditor under section 108(3) above shall be enforceable by mandamus or, in Scotland, by an order for specific performance under section 91 of the Court of Session Act 1868.

(3) If it appears to the Secretary of State that an auditor has failed to comply with the duty mentioned in section 109(2) above, the Secretary of State may disqualify him from being the auditor of an authorised person or any class of authorised person ; but the Secretary of State may remove any disqualification imposed under this subsection if satisfied that the person in question will in future comply with that duty.

(4) An authorised person shall not appoint as auditor a person disqualified under subsection (3) above ; and a person who is an authorised person by virtue of membership of a recognised self-regulating organisation or certification by a recognised professional body who contravenes this subsection shall be treated as having contravened the rules of the organisation or body.

PART I
CHAPTER XII

Application fees.

CHAPTER XII

FEES

112.—(1) An applicant for a recognition order under Chapter III or IV of this Part of this Act shall pay such fees in respect of his application as may be required by a scheme made and published by the Secretary of State ; and no application for such an order shall be regarded as duly made unless this subsection is complied with.

(2) A scheme made for the purposes of subsection (1) above shall specify the time when the fees are to be paid and may—

(a) provide for the determination of the fees in accordance with a specified scale or other specified factors ;

(b) provide for the return or abatement of any fees where an application is refused or withdrawn ; and

(c) make different provision for different cases.

(3) Any scheme made for the purposes of subsection (1) above shall come into operation on such date as is specified in the scheme (not being earlier than the day on which it is first published) and shall apply to applications made on or after the date on which it comes into operation.

(4) The power to make a scheme for the purposes of subsection (1) above includes power to vary or revoke a previous scheme made under those provisions.

(5) Every application under section 26, 77 or 88 above shall be accompanied by the prescribed fee and every notice given to the Secretary of State under section 32, 86(2) or 87(3) above shall be accompanied by such fee as may be prescribed ; and no such application or notice shall be regarded as duly made or given unless this subsection is complied with.

Periodical fees.

113.—(1) Every recognised self-regulating organisation, recognised professional body, recognised investment exchange and recognised clearing house shall pay such periodical fees to the Secretary of State as may be prescribed.

(2) So long as a body is authorised under section 22 above to carry on insurance business which is investment business it shall pay to the Secretary of State such periodical fees as may be prescribed.

(3) So long as a society is authorised under section 23 above to carry on investment business it shall—

(a) if it is authorised by virtue of subsection (1) of that section, pay to the Chief Registrar of friendly societies such periodical fees as he may by regulations specify; and

(*b*) if it is authorised by virtue of subsection (2) of that section, pay to the Registrar of Friendly Societies for Northern Ireland such periodical fees as he may by regulations specify.

(4) A person who is an authorised person by virtue of section 25 or 31 above shall pay such periodical fees to the Secretary of State as may be prescribed.

(5) If a person fails to pay any fee which is payable by him under subsection (4) above the Secretary of State may serve on him a written notice requiring him to pay the fee within twenty-eight days of service of the notice; and if the fee is not paid within that period that person's authorisation shall cease to have effect unless the Secretary of State otherwise directs.

(6) A direction under subsection (5) above may be given so as to have retrospective effect; and the Secretary of State may under that subsection direct that the person in question shall continue to be an authorised person only for such period as is specified in the direction.

(7) Subsection (5) above is without prejudice to the recovery of any fee as a debt due to the Crown.

(8) The manager of each authorised unit trust scheme and the operator of each recognised scheme shall pay such periodical fees to the Secretary of State as may be prescribed.

CHAPTER XIII

TRANSFER OF FUNCTIONS TO DESIGNATED AGENCY

114.—(1) If it appears to the Secretary of State—

(*a*) that a body corporate has been established which is able and willing to discharge all or any of the functions to which this section applies; and

(*b*) that the requirements of Schedule 7 to this Act are satisfied in the case of that body,

he may, subject to the provisions of this section and Chapter XIV of this Part of this Act, make an order transferring all or any of those functions to that body.

Power to transfer functions to designated agency.

(2) The body to which functions are transferred by the first order made under subsection (1) above shall be the body known as The Securities and Investments Board Limited if it appears to the Secretary of State that it is able and willing to discharge them, that the requirements mentioned in paragraph (*b*) of that

subsection are satisfied in the case of that body and that he is not precluded from making the order by the subsequent provisions of this section or Chapter XIV of this Part of this Act.

(3) An order under subsection (1) above is in this Act referred to as " a delegation order " and a body to which functions are transferred by a delegation order is in this Act referred to as " a designated agency ".

(4) Subject to subsections (5) and (6) below, this section applies to any functions of the Secretary of State under Chapters II to XII of this Part of this Act and to his functions under paragraphs 23 and 25(2) of Schedule 1 and paragraphs 4, 5 and 15 of Schedule 15 to this Act.

(5) This section does not apply to any functions under—

(a) section 31(4) ;

(b) section 46 ;

(c) section 48(8) ;

(d) section 58(3) ;

(e) section 86(1) or 87(1) ;

(f) section 96 ;

(g) section 109(2) above.

(6) This section does not apply to the making or revocation of a recognition order in respect of an overseas investment exchange or overseas clearing house or the making of an application to the court under section 12 above in respect of any such exchange or clearing house.

(7) Any function may be transferred by a delegation order either wholly or in part.

(8) In the case of a function under section 6 or 72 or a function under section 61 which is exercisable by virtue of subsection (1)(a)(ii) or (iii) of that section, the transfer may be subject to a reservation that it is to be exercisable by the Secretary of State concurrently with the designated agency and any transfer of a function under section 94, 105 or 106 shall be subject to such a reservation.

(9) The Secretary of State shall not make a delegation order transferring any function of making rules or regulations to a designated agency unless—

(a) the agency has furnished him with a copy of the rules and regulations which it proposes to make in the exercise of those functions ; and

(b) he is satisfied that those rules and regulations will afford investors an adequate level of protection and,

in the case of such rules and regulations as are mentioned in Schedule 8 to this Act, comply with the
principles set out in that Schedule.

(10) The Secretary of State shall also before making a delegation order transferring any functions to a designated agency
require it to furnish him with a copy of any guidance intended
to have continuing effect which it proposes to issue in writing
or other legible form and the Secretary of State may take any
such guidance into account in determining whether he is satisfied
as mentioned in subsection (9)(*b*) above.

(11) No delegation order shall be made unless a draft of
it has been laid before and approved by a resolution of each
House of Parliament.

(12) In this Act references to guidance issued by a designated
agency are references to guidance issued or any recommendation
made by it which is issued or made to persons generally or to
any class of persons, being, in either case, persons who are or
may be subject to rules or regulations made by it, or who are
or may be recognised or authorised by it, in the exercise of its
functions under a delegation order.

115.—(1) The Secretary of State may at the request or with Resumption
the consent of a designated agency make an order resuming all of transferred
or any of the functions transferred to the agency by a delegation functions.
order.

(2) The Secretary of State may, in the circumstances mentioned in subsection (3), (4) or (5) below, make an order
resuming—

(*a*) all the functions transferred to a designated agency by
a delegation order ; or

(*b*) all, all legislative or all administrative functions transferred to a designated agency by a delegation order so
far as relating to investments or investment business
of any class.

(3) An order may be made under subsection (2) above if at
any time it appears to the Secretary of State that any of the
requirements of Schedule 7 to this Act are not satisfied in the
case of the agency.

(4) An order may be made under subsection (2) above as
respects functions relating to any class of investment or investment business if at any time it appears to the Secretary of State
that the agency is unable or unwilling to discharge all or any
of the transferred functions in respect of all or any investments
or investment business falling within that class.

(5) Where the transferred functions consist of or include any functions of making rules or regulations an order may be made under subsection (2) above if at any time it appears to the Secretary of State that the rules or regulations made by the agency do not satisfy the requirements of section 114(9)(*b*) above.

(6) An order under subsection (1) above shall be subject to annulment in pursuance of a resolution of either House of Parliament; and no other order shall be made under this section unless a draft of it has been laid before and approved by a resolution of each House of Parliament.

(7) In subsection (2)(*b*) above—

    (*a*) " legislative functions " means functions of making rules or regulations ;

    (*b*) " administrative functions " means functions other than legislative functions ;

but the resumption of legislative functions shall not deprive a designated agency of any function of prescribing fees to be paid or information to be furnished in connection with administrative functions retained by the agency ; and the resumption of administrative functions shall extend to the function of prescribing fees to be paid and information to be furnished in connection with those administrative functions.

Status and exercise of transferred functions.

116. Schedule 9 to this Act shall have effect as respects the status of a designated agency and the exercise of the functions transferred to it by a delegation order.

Reports and accounts.

117.—(1) A designated agency shall at least once in each year for which the delegation order is in force make a report to the Secretary of State on the discharge of the functions transferred to it by the order and on such other matters as the order may require.

(2) The Secretary of State shall lay before Parliament copies of each report received by him under this section.

(3) The Secretary of State may give directions to a designated agency with respect to its accounts and the audit of its accounts ; and it shall be the duty of the agency to comply with the directions.

1985 c. 6.

(4) Subsection (3) above shall not apply to a designated agency which is a company to which section 227 of the Companies Act 1985 applies ; but the Secretary of State may require any designated agency (whether or not such a company) to comply with any provisions of that Act which would not otherwise apply to it or direct that any provision of that Act shall apply to the agency with such modifications as are specified in the direction ;

and it shall be the duty of the agency to comply with any such
requirement or direction.

(5) In subsection (4) above the references to the Companies
Act 1985 and section 227 of that Act include references to the
corresponding Northern Ireland provisions.

118.—(1) A delegation order shall not affect anything pre- Transitional
viously done in the exercise of a function which is transferred and
by the order ; and any order resuming a function shall not affect supplementary
anything previously done by the designated agency in the exer- provisions.
cise of a function which is resumed.

(2) A delegation order and an order resuming any functions
transferred by a delegation order may contain, or the Secretary
of State may by a separate order under this section make, such
transitional and other supplementary provisions as he thinks
necessary or expedient in connection with the delegation order
or the order resuming the functions in question.

(3) The provisions that may be made under subsection (2)
above in connection with a delegation order include, in particular, provisions—

    (a) for modifying or excluding any provision of this Act in
        its application to any function transferred by the order ;

    (b) for applying to a designated agency, in connection with
        any such function, any provision applying to the Secre-
        tary of State which is contained in or made under any
        other enactment ;

    (c) for the transfer of any property, rights or liabilities from
        the Secretary of State to a designated agency ;

    (d) for the carrying on and completion by a designated
        agency of anything in process of being done by the
        Secretary of State when the order takes effect ; and

    (e) for the substitution of a designated agency for the Secre-
        tary of State in any instrument, contract or legal pro-
        ceedings.

(4) The provisions that may be made under subsection (2)
above in connection with an order resuming any functions include, in particular, provisions—

    (a) for the transfer of any property, rights or liabilities
        from the agency to the Secretary of State ;

    (b) for the carrying on and completion by the Secretary of
        State of anything in process of being done by the
        agency when the order takes effect ;

(c) for the substitution of the Secretary of State for the agency in any instrument, contract or legal proceedings ; and

(d) in a case where some functions remain with the agency, for modifying or excluding any provision of this Act in its application to any such functions.

(5) In a case where any function of a designated agency is resumed and is to be immediately transferred by a delegation order to another designated agency, the provisions that may be made under subsection (2) above may include provisions for any of the matters mentioned in paragraphs (a) to (c) of subsection (4) above, taking references to the Secretary of State as references to that other agency.

(6) Any order under this section shall be subject to annulment in pursuance of a resolution of either House of Parliament.

CHAPTER XIV

PREVENTION OF RESTRICTIVE PRACTICES

Examination of rules and practices

Recognised
self-regulating
organisations,
investment
exchanges and
clearing
houses.

119.—(1) The Secretary of State shall not make a recognition order in respect of a self-regulating organisation, investment exchange or clearing house unless he is satisfied that—

(a) the rules and any guidance of which copies are furnished with the application for the order ; and

(b) in the case of an investment exchange, any arrangements of which particulars are furnished with the application,

do not have, and are not intended or likely to have, to any significant extent the effect of restricting, distorting or preventing competition or, if they have or are intended or likely to have that effect to any significant extent, that the effect is not greater than is necessary for the protection of investors.

(2) The powers conferred by subsection (3) below shall be exercisable by the Secretary of State if at any time it appears to him that—

(a) any rules made or guidance issued by a recognised self-regulating organisation, investment exchange or clearing house or any clearing arrangements made by a recognised clearing house ;

(b) any practices of any such organisation, exchange or clearing house ; or

(*c*) any practices of persons who are members of, or otherwise subject to the rules made by, any such organisation, exchange or clearing house,

have, or are intended or likely to have, to a significant extent the
effect of restricting, distorting or preventing competition and that
that effect is greater than is necessary for the protection of
investors.

(3) The powers exercisable under this subsection are—

(*a*) to revoke the recognition order of the organisation, exchange or clearing house ;

(*b*) to direct it to take specified steps for the purpose of
securing that the rules, guidance, arrangements or practices in question do not have the effect mentioned in
subsection (2) above ;

(*c*) to make alterations in the rules for that purpose ;

and subsections (2) to (5), (7) and (9) of section 11 above shall
have effect in relation to the revocation of a recognition order
under this subsection as they have effect in relation to the revocation of such an order under subsection (1) of that section.

(4) Subsection (3)(*c*) above does not apply to an overseas
investment exchange or overseas clearing house.

(5) The practices referred to in paragraph (*b*) of subsection
(2) above are practices of the organisation, exchange or clearing house in its capacity as such, being, in the case of a clearing
house, practices in respect of its clearing arrangements ; and the
practices referred to in paragraph (*c*) of that subsection are
practices in relation to business in respect of which the persons
in question are subject to the rules of the organisation, exchange or clearing house and which are required or contemplated
by its rules or guidance or otherwise attributable to its conduct
in its capacity as such.

120.—(1) This section applies instead of section 119 above
where the function of making or revoking a recognition order in
respect of a self-regulating organisation, investment exchange or
clearing house is exercisable by a designated agency.

*Modification
of s. 119
where
recognition
function is
transferred.*

(2) The designated agency—

(*a*) shall send to the Secretary of State a copy of the rules
and of any guidance or arrangements of which copies
or particulars are furnished with any application made
to the agency for a recognition order together with any
other information supplied with or in connection with
the application ; and

(*b*) shall not make the recognition order without the leave of the Secretary of State ;

and he shall not give leave in any case in which he would (apart from the delegation order) have been precluded by section 119(1) above from making the recognition order.

(3) A designated agency shall send the Secretary of State a copy of any notice received by it under section 14(6) or 41(5) or (6) above.

(4) If at any time it appears to the Secretary of State in the case of a recognised self-regulating organisation, recognised investment exchange or recognised clearing house that there are circumstances such that (apart from the delegation order) he would have been able to exercise any of the powers conferred by subsection (3) of section 119 above he may, notwithstanding the delegation order, himself exercise the power conferred by paragraph (*a*) of that subsection or direct the designated agency to exercise the power conferred by paragraph (*b*) or (*c*) of that subsection in such manner as he may specify.

Designated
agencies.

121.—(1) The Secretary of State shall not make a delegation order transferring any function to a designated agency unless he is satisfied that any rules, regulations and guidance of which copies are furnished to him under section 114(9) or (10) above do not have, and are not intended or likely to have, to any significant extent the effect of restricting, distorting or preventing competition or, if they have or are intended or likely to have that effect to any significant extent, that the effect is not greater than is necessary for the protection of investors.

(2) The powers conferred by subsection (3) below shall be exercisable by the Secretary of State if at any time it appears to him that—

(*a*) any rules or regulations made by a designated agency in the exercise of functions transferred to it by a delegation order or any guidance issued by a designated agency ;

(*b*) any practices of a designated agency ; or

(*c*) any practices of persons who are subject to rules or regulations made by it in the exercise of those functions,

have, or are intended or are likely to have, to any significant extent the effect of restricting, distorting or preventing competition and that that effect is greater than is necessary for the protection of investors.

(3) The powers exercisable under this subsection are—

(*a*) to make an order in respect of the agency under section

115(2) above as if the circumstances were such as are
there mentioned ; or

(b) to direct the agency to take specified steps for the
purpose of securing that the rules, regulations, guidance or practices in question do not have the effect
mentioned in subsection (2) above.

(4) The practices referred to in paragraph (b) of subsection
(2) above are practices of the designated agency in its capacity
as such ; and the practices referred to in paragraph (c) of that
subsection are practices in relation to business in respect of
which the persons in question are subject to any such rules or
regulations as are mentioned in paragraph (a) of that subsection
and which are required or contemplated by those rules or regulations or by any such guidance as is there mentioned or are otherwise attributable to the conduct of the agency in its capacity
as such.

Consultation with Director General of Fair Trading

122.—(1) The Secretary of State shall before deciding—

(a) whether to refuse to make, or to refuse leave for the
making of, a recognition order in pursuance of section
119(1) or 120(2) above ; or

(b) whether he is precluded by section 121(1) above from
making a delegation order,

Reports by
Director
General of
Fair Trading.

send to the Director General of Fair Trading (in this Chapter
referred to as " the Director ") a copy of the rules and regulations
and of any guidance or arrangements which the Secretary of State
is required to consider in making that decision together with such
other information as the Secretary of State considers will assist
the Director in discharging his functions under subsection (2)
below.

(2) The Director shall report to the Secretary of State whether,
in his opinion, the rules, regulations, guidance or arrangements
of which copies are sent to him under subsection (1) above have,
or are intended or likely to have, to any significant extent the
effect of restricting, distorting, or preventing competition and, if
so, what that effect is likely to be ; and in making any such decision as is mentioned in that subsection the Secretary of State
shall have regard to the Director's report.

(3) The Secretary of State shall send the Director copies of
any notice received by him under section 14(6), 41(5) or (6) or
120(3) above or under paragraph 4 of Schedule 9 to this Act
together with such other information as the Secretary of State
considers will assist the Director in discharging his functions
under subsections (4) and (5) below.

(4) The Director shall keep under review—

    (*a*) the rules, guidance, arrangements and regulations mentioned in section 119(2) and 121(2) above ; and

    (*b*) the matters specified in the notices of which copies are sent to him under subsection (3) above ;

and if at any time he is of the opinion that any such rules, guidance, arrangements, regulations or matters, or any such rules, guidance, arrangements or regulations taken together with any such matters, have, or are intended or likely to have, to any significant extent the effect mentioned in subsection (2) above, he shall make a report to the Secretary of State stating his opinion and what that effect is or is likely to be.

(5) The Director may report to the Secretary of State his opinion that any such matter as is mentioned in subsection (4)(*b*) above does not in his opinion have, and is not intended or likely to have, to any significant extent the effect mentioned in subsection (2) above.

(6) The Director may from time to time consider whether any such practices as are mentioned in section 119(2) or 121(2) above have, or are intended or likely to have, to any significant extent the effect mentioned in subsection (2) above and, if so, what that effect is or is likely to be ; and if he is of that opinion he shall make a report to the Secretary of State stating his opinion and what the effect is or is likely to be.

(7) The Secretary of State shall not exercise his powers under section 119(3), 120(4) or 121(3) above except after receiving and considering a report from the Director under subsection (4) or (6) above.

(8) The Director may, if he thinks fit, publish any report made by him under this section but shall exclude from a published report, so far as practicable, any matter which relates to the affairs of a particular person (other than the self-regulating organisation, investment exchange, clearing house or designated agency concerned) the publication of which would or might in his opinion seriously and prejudicially affect the interests of that person.

Investigations
by Director
General of
Fair Trading.

123.—(1) For the purpose of investigating any matter with a view to its consideration under section 122 above the Director may by a notice in writing—

    (*a*) require any person to produce, at a time and place specified in the notice, to the Director or to any person appointed by him for the purpose, any documents which are specified or described in the notice and which are documents in his custody or under his control and relating to any matter relevant to the investigation ; or

(b) require any person carrying on any business to furnish to the Director such information as may be specified or described in the notice, and specify the time within which, and the manner and form in which, any such information is to be furnished.

(2) A person shall not under this section be required to produce any document or disclose any information which he would be entitled to refuse to produce or disclose on grounds of legal professional privilege in proceedings in the High Court or on grounds of confidentiality as between client and professional legal adviser in proceedings in the Court of Session.

(3) Subsections (5) to (8) of section 85 of the Fair Trading Act 1973 (enforcement provisions) shall apply in relation to a notice under this section as they apply in relation to a notice under subsection (1) of that section.

Consequential exemptions from competition law

124.—(1) For the purpose of determining whether a monopoly situation within the meaning of the Fair Trading Act 1973 exists by reason of the circumstances mentioned in section 7(1)(c) of that Act, no account shall be taken of—

(a) the rules made or guidance issued by a recognised self-regulating organisation, recognised investment exchange or recognised clearing house or any conduct constituting such a practice as is mentioned in section 119(2) above ;

(b) any clearing arrangements or any conduct required or contemplated by any such arrangements ; or

(c) the rules or regulations made or guidance issued by a designated agency in the exercise of functions transferred to it by a delegation order or any conduct constituting such a practice as is mentioned in section 121(2) above.

(2) Where a recognition order is revoked there shall be disregarded for the purpose mentioned in subsection (1) above any such conduct as is mentioned in that subsection which occurred while the order was in force.

(3) Where on a monopoly reference under section 50 or 51 of the said Act of 1973 falling within section 49 of that Act the Monopolies and Mergers Commission find that a monopoly situation within the meaning of that Act exists and—

(a) that the person (or, if more than one, any of the persons) in whose favour it exists is subject to the rules of a recognised self-regulating organisation, recognised investment exchange or recognised clearing house or to the rules or regulations made by a designated agency in the exercise of functions transferred to it by a delegation order; or

(b) that any such person's conduct in carrying on any business to which those rules or regulations relate is the subject of guidance issued by such an organisation, exchange, clearing house or agency ; or

(c) that any such person is a party to any clearing arrangements ; or

(d) that the person (or, if more than one, any of the persons) in whose favour the monopoly situation exists is such an organisation, exchange or clearing house as is mentioned in paragraph (a) above or a designated agency,

the Commission, in making their report on that reference, shall exclude from their consideration the question whether the rules, regulations, guidance or clearing arrangements or any acts or omissions of such an organisation, exchange, clearing house or agency as is mentioned in paragraph (d) above in its capacity as such operate, or may be expected to operate, against the public interest ; and section 54(3) of that Act shall have effect subject to the provisions of this subsection.

The Restrictive Trade Practices Act 1976.
1976 c. 34.

125.—(1) The Restrictive Trade Practices Act 1976 shall not apply to any agreement for the constitution of a recognised self-regulating organisation, recognised investment exchange or recognised clearing house, including any term deemed to be contained in it by virtue of section 8(2) or 16(3) of that Act.

(2) The said Act of 1976 shall not apply to any agreement the parties to which consist of or include—

(a) any such organisation, exchange or clearing house as is mentioned in subsection (1) above ; or

(b) a person who is subject to the rules of any such organisation, exchange or clearing house or to the rules or regulations made by a designated agency in the exercise of functions transferred to it by a delegation order,

by reason of any term the inclusion of which in the agreement is required or contemplated by the rules, regulations or guidance of that organisation, exchange, clearing house or agency.

(3) The said Act of 1976 shall not apply to any clearing arrangements or to any agreement between a recognised investment exchange and a recognised clearing house by reason

of any term the inclusion of which in the agreement is required
or contemplated by any clearing arrangements.

(4) Where the recognition order in respect of a self-regulating
organisation, investment exchange or clearing house is revoked
the foregoing provisions shall have effect as if the organisation,
exchange or clearing house had continued to be recognised until
the end of the period of six months beginning with the day on
which the revocation takes effect.

(5) Where an agreement ceases by virtue of this section to be
subject to registration—

    (*a*) the Director shall remove from the register maintained
        by him under the said Act of 1976 any particulars
        which are entered or filed in that register in respect of
        the agreement ; and

    (*b*) any proceedings in respect of the agreement which are
        pending before the Restrictive Practices Court shall
        be discontinued.

(6) Where an agreement which has been exempt from registration by virtue of this section ceases to be exempt in consequence of the revocation of a recognition order, the time within
which particulars of the agreement are to be furnished in accordance with section 24 of and Schedule 2 to the said Act of 1976
shall be the period of one month beginning with the day on
which the agreement ceased to be exempt from registration.

(7) Where in the case of an agreement registered under the
said Act of 1976 a term ceases to fall within subsection (2) or (3)
above in consequence of the revocation of a recognition order
and particulars of that term have not previously been furnished
to the Director under section 24 of that Act, those particulars
shall be furnished to him within the period of one month beginning with the day on which the term ceased to fall within
that subsection.

(8) The Restrictive Trade Practices (Stock Exchange) Act
1984 shall cease to have effect.

1984 c. 2.

126.—(1) No course of conduct constituting any such practice
as is mentioned in section 119(2) or 121(2) above shall constitute an anti-competitive practice for the purposes of the Competition Act 1980.

The
Competition
Act 1980.

1980 c. 21.

(2) Where a recognition order or delegation order is revoked,
there shall not be treated as an anti-competitive practice for
the purposes of that Act any such course of conduct as is
mentioned in subsection (1) above which occurred while the
order was in force.

PART I
CHAPTER XIV
Modification
of Restrictive
Trade Practices
Act 1976 in
relation to
recognised
professional
bodies.
1976 c. 34.

Recognised professional bodies

127.—(1) This section applies to—

(a) any agreement for the constitution of a recognised professional body, including any term deemed to be contained in it by virtue of section 16(3) of the Restrictive Trade Practices Act 1976 ; and

(b) any other agreement—

(i) the parties to which consist of or include such a body, a person certified by such a body or a member of such a body ; and

(ii) to which that Act applies by virtue of any term the inclusion of which in the agreement is required or contemplated by rules or guidance of that body relating to the carrying on of investment business by persons certified by it.

(2) If it appears to the Secretary of State that the restrictions in an agreement to which this section applies—

(a) do not have, and are not intended or likely to have, to any significant extent the effect of restricting, distorting or preventing competition ; or

(b) if all or any of them have, or are intended or likely to have, that effect to any significant extent, that the effect is not greater than is necessary for the protection of investors,

he may give a direction to the Director requiring him not to make an application to the Restrictive Practices Court under Part I of the said Act of 1976 in respect of the agreement.

(3) If it appears to the Secretary of State that one or more (but not all) of the restrictions in an agreement to which this section applies—

(a) do not have, and are not intended or likely to have, to any significant extent the effect mentioned in subsection (2) above ; or

(b) if they have, or are intended or likely to have, that effect to any significant extent that the effect is not greater than is necessary for the protection of investors,

he may make a declaration to that effect and give notice of it to the Director and the Restrictive Practices Court.

(4) The Restrictive Practices Court shall not in any proceedings begun by an application made after notice has been given to it of a declaration under this section make any finding or exercise any power under Part I of the said Act of 1976 in relation to a restriction in respect of which the declaration has effect.

(5) The Director shall not make any application to the Restrictive Practices Court under Part I of the said Act of 1976 in
respect of any agreement to which this section applies unless—

    (*a*) he has notified the Secretary of State of his intention to
        do so ; and

    (*b*) the Secretary of State has either notified him that he
        does not intend to give a direction or make a declara-
        tion under this section or has given him notice of a
        declaration in respect of it ;

and where the Director proposes to make any such application
he shall furnish the Secretary of State with particulars of the
agreement and the restrictions by virtue of which the said Act
of 1976 applies to it and such other information as he considers
will assist the Secretary of State in deciding whether to exercise
his powers under this section or as the Secretary of State may
request.

(6) The Secretary of State may—

    (*a*) revoke a direction or declaration under this section ;

    (*b*) vary any such declaration ; or

    (*c*) give a direction or make a declaration notwithstanding
        a previous notification to the Director that he did not
        intend to give a direction or make a declaration,

if he is satisfied that there has been a material change of circumstances such that the grounds for the direction or declaration
have ceased to exist, that there are grounds for a different declaration or that there are grounds for giving a direction or making a
declaration, as the case may be.

(7) The Secretary of State shall give notice to the Director of
the revocation of a direction and to the Director and the Restrictive Practices Court of the revocation or variation of a declaration ; and no such variation shall have effect so as to restrict
the powers of the Court in any proceedings begun by an application already made by the Director.

(8) A direction or declaration under this section shall cease to
have effect if the agreement in question ceases to be one to which
this section applies.

(9) This section applies to information provisions as it applies
to restrictions.

Supplemental

128.—(1) Before the Secretary of State exercises a power Supple-
under section 119(3)(*b*) or (*c*) above, his power to refuse leave mentary
under section 120(2) above or his power to give a direction under provisions.
section 120(4) above in respect of a self-regulating organisation.

investment exchange or clearing house, or his power under section 121(3)(*b*) above in respect of a designated agency, he shall—

> (*a*) give written notice of his intention to do so to the organisation, exchange, clearing house or agency and take such steps (whether by publication or otherwise) as he thinks appropriate for bringing the notice to the attention of any other person who in his opinion is likely to be affected by the exercise of the power ; and

> (*b*) have regard to any representation made within such time as he considers reasonable by the organisation, exchange, clearing house or agency or by any such other person.

(2) A notice under subsection (1) above shall give particulars of the manner in which the Secretary of State proposes to exercise the power in question and state the reasons for which he proposes to act ; and the statement of reasons may include matters contained in any report received by him under section 122 above.

(3) Any direction given under this Chapter shall, on the application of the person by whom it was given, be enforceable by mandamus or, in Scotland, by an order for specific performance under section 91 of the Court of Session Act 1868.

1868 c. 100.

(4) The fact that any rules or regulations made by a recognised self-regulating organisation, investment exchange or clearing house or by a designated agency have been altered by or pursuant to a direction given by the Secretary of State under this Chapter shall not preclude their subsequent alteration or revocation by that organisation, exchange, clearing house or agency.

(5) In determining under this Chapter whether any guidance has, or is likely to have, any particular effect the Secretary of State and the Director may assume that the persons to whom it is addressed will act in conformity with it.

PART II

INSURANCE BUSINESS

Application of investment business provisions to regulated insurance companies.
1982 c. 50.

129. Schedule 10 to this Act shall have effect with respect to the application of the foregoing provisions of this Act to regulated insurance companies, that is to say—

> (*a*) insurance companies to which Part II of the Insurance Companies Act 1982 applies ; and

> (*b*) insurance companies which are authorised persons by virtue of section 31 above.

130.—(1) Subject to subsections (2) and (3) below, no person shall—

    (*a*) issue or cause to be issued in the United Kingdom an advertisement—

        (i) inviting any person to enter or offer to enter into a contract of insurance rights under which constitute an investment for the purposes of this Act, or

        (ii) containing information calculated to lead directly or indirectly to any person doing so ; or

    (*b*) in the course of a business, advise or procure any person in the United Kingdom to enter into such a contract.

(2) Subsection (1) above does not apply where the contract of insurance referred to in that subsection is to be with—

    (*a*) a body authorised under section 3 or 4 of the Insurance Companies Act 1982 to effect and carry out such contracts of insurance ;

    (*b*) a body registered under the enactments relating to friendly societies ;

    (*c*) an insurance company the head office of which is in a member State other than the United Kingdom and which is entitled to carry on there insurance business of the relevant class ;

    (*d*) an insurance company which has a branch or agency in such a member State and is entitled under the law of that State to carry on there insurance business of the relevant class ;

and in this subsection " the relevant class " means the class of insurance business specified in Schedule 1 or 2 to the Insurance Companies Act 1982 into which the effecting and carrying out of the contract in question falls.

(3) Subsection (1) above also does not apply where—

    (*a*) the contract of insurance referred to in that subsection is to be with an insurance company authorised to effect or carry out such contracts of insurance in any country or territory which is for the time being designated for the purposes of this section by an order made by the Secretary of State ; and

    (*b*) any conditions imposed by the order designating the country or territory have been satisfied.

(4) The Secretary of State shall not make an order designating any country or territory for the purposes of this section unless he is satisfied that the law under which insurance companies are authorised and supervised in that country or territory affords

PART II   adequate protection to policy holders and potential policy holders against the risk that the companies may be unable to meet their liabilities ; and, if at any time it appears to him that the law of a country or territory which has been designated under this section does not satisfy that requirement, he may by a further order revoke the order designating that country or territory.

(5) An order under this section shall be subject to annulment in pursuance of a resolution of either House of Parliament.

(6) Subject to subsections (7) and (8) below, any person who contravenes this section shall be guilty of an offence and liable—

    (*a*) on conviction on indictment, to imprisonment for a term not exceeding two years or to a fine or to both ;

    (*b*) on summary conviction, to imprisonment for a term not exceeding six months or to a fine not exceeding the statutory maximum or to both.

(7) A person who in the ordinary course of a business other than investment business issues an advertisement to the order of another person shall not be guilty of an offence under this section if he proves that the matters contained in the advertisement were not (wholly or in part) devised or selected by him or by any person under his direction or control and that he believed on reasonable grounds after due enquiry that the person to whose order the advertisement was issued was an authorised person.

(8) A person other than the insurance company with which the contract of insurance is to be made shall not be guilty of an offence under this section if he proves that he believed on reasonable grounds after due enquiry that subsection (2) or (3) above applied in the case of the contravention in question.

Contracts
made after
contravention
of s. 130.

131.—(1) Where there has been a contravention of section 130 above, then, subject to subsections (3) and (4) below—

    (*a*) the insurance company shall not be entitled to enforce any contract of insurance with which the advertisement, advice or procurement was concerned and which was entered into after the contravention occurred ; and

    (*b*) the other party shall be entitled to recover any money or other property paid or transferred by him under the contract, together with compensation for any loss sustained by him as a result of having parted with it.

(2) The compensation recoverable under subsection (1) above shall be such as the parties may agree or as a court may, on the application of either party, determine.

(3) In a case where the contravention referred to in subsection (1) above was a contravention by the insurance company with

which the contract was made, the court may allow the contract
to be enforced or money or property paid or transferred under it
to be retained if it is satisfied—

(a) that the person against whom enforcement is sought or
who is seeking to recover the money or property was
not influenced, or not influenced to any material extent,
by the advertisement or, as the case may be, the advice
in making his decision to enter into the contract; or

(b) that the advertisement or, as the case may be, the
advice was not misleading as to the nature of the
company with which the contract was to be made or
the terms of the contract and fairly stated any risks
involved in entering into it.

(4) In a case where the contravention of section 130 above
referred to in subsection (1) above was a contravention by a
person other than the insurance company with which the contract was made the court may allow the contract to be enforced
or money or property paid or transferred under it to be retained
if it is satisfied that at the time the contract was made the
company had no reason to believe that any contravention of
section 130 above had taken place in relation to the contract.

(5) Where a person elects not to perform a contract which by
virtue of subsection (1) above is unenforceable against him or
by virtue of that subsection recovers money paid or other
property transferred by him under a contract he shall not be
entitled to any benefits under the contract and shall repay any
money and return any other property received by him under
the contract.

(6) Where any property transferred under a contract to which
this section applies has passed to a third party the references to
that property in this section shall be construed as references
to its value at the time of its transfer under the contract.

(7) A contravention of section 130 above by an authorised
person shall be actionable at the suit of any person who suffers
loss as a result of the contravention.

(8) Section 61 above shall have effect in relation to a contravention or proposed contravention of section 130 above as
it has effect in relation to a contravention or proposed contravention of section 57 above.

132.—(1) Subject to subsection (3) below, a contract of insur-   Insurance
ance (not being an agreement to which section 5(1) above   contracts
applies) which is entered into by a person in the course of carry-   effected in
ing on insurance business in contravention of section 2 of the   contravention
Insurance Companies Act 1982 shall be unenforceable against   Insurance
the other party; and that party shall be entitled to recover any   Companies
money or other property paid or transferred by him under the   Act 1982.
                                                          1982 c. 50.

contract, together with compensation for any loss sustained by him as a result of having parted with it.

(2) The compensation recoverable under subsection (1) above shall be such as the parties may agree or as a court may, on the application of either party, determine.

(3) A court may allow a contract to which subsection (1) above applies to be enforced or money or property paid or transferred under it to be retained if it is satisfied—

    (*a*) that the person carrying on insurance business reasonably believed that his entering into the contract did not constitute a contravention of section 2 of the said Act of 1982 ; and

    (*b*) that it is just and equitable for the contract to be enforced or, as the case may be, for the money or property paid or transferred under it to be retained.

(4) Where a person elects not to perform a contract which by virtue of this section is unenforceable against him or by virtue of this section recovers money or property paid or transferred under a contract he shall not be entitled to any benefits under the contract and shall repay any money and return any other property received by him under the contract.

(5) Where any property transferred under a contract to which this section applies has passed to a third party the references to that property in this section shall be construed as references to its value at the time of its transfer under the contract.

(6) A contravention of section 2 of the said Act of 1982 shall not make a contract of insurance illegal or invalid to any greater extent than is provided in this section ; and a contravention of that section in respect of a contract of insurance shall not affect the validity of any re-insurance contract entered into in respect of that contract.

Misleading statements as to insurance contracts.

133.—(1) Any person who—

    (*a*) makes a statement, promise or forecast which he knows to be misleading, false or deceptive or dishonestly conceals any material facts ; or

    (*b*) recklessly makes (dishonestly or otherwise) a statement, promise or forecast which is misleading, false or deceptive,

is guilty of an offence if he makes the statement, promise or forecast or conceals the facts for the purpose of inducing, or is reckless as to whether it may induce, another person (whether or not the person to whom the statement, promise or forecast is made or from whom the facts are concealed) to enter into or offer to enter into, or to refrain from entering or offering to enter into, a contract of insurance with an insurance company (not being an investment agreement) or to exercise, or refrain from exercising, any rights conferred by such a contract.

(2) Subsection (1) above does not apply unless—

(a) the statement, promise or forecast is made in or from, or the facts are concealed in or from, the United Kingdom;

(b) the person on whom the inducement is intended to or may have effect is in the United Kingdom; or

(c) the contract is or would be entered into or the rights are or would be exercisable in the United Kingdom.

(3) A person guilty of an offence under this section shall be liable—

(a) on conviction on indictment, to imprisonment for a term not exceeding seven years or to a fine or to both;

(b) on summary conviction, to imprisonment for a term not exceeding six months or to a fine not exceeding the statutory maximum or to both.

134. In section 7(4)(c)(ii) of the Insurance Companies Act 1982 (definition of controller by reference to exercise of not less than one-third of voting power) for the words " one-third " there shall be substituted the words " 15 per cent.".

Controllers of insurance companies.
1982 c. 50.

135.—(1) After section 21 of the Insurance Companies Act 1982 there shall be inserted—

Communication by auditor with Secretary of State.

" Communication by auditor with Secretary of State.

21A.—(1) No duty to which an auditor of an insurance company to which this Part of this Act applies may be subject shall be regarded as contravened by reason of his communicating in good faith to the Secretary of State, whether or not in response to a request from him, any information or opinion on a matter of which the auditor has become aware in his capacity as auditor of that company and which is relevant to any functions of the Secretary of State under this Act.

(2) If it appears to the Secretary of State that any auditor or class of auditor to whom subsection (1) above applies is not subject to satisfactory rules

made or guidance issued by a professional body specifying circumstances in which matters are to be communicated to the Secretary of State as mentioned in that subsection the Secretary of State may make regulations applying to that auditor or class of auditor and specifying such circumstances; and it shall be the duty of an auditor to whom the regulations made by the Secretary of State apply to communicate a matter to the Secretary of State in the circumstances specified by the regulations.

(3) The matters to be communicated to the Secretary of State in accordance with any such rules or guidance or regulations may include matters relating to persons other than the company.

(4) No regulations shall be made under subsection (2) above unless a draft of them has been laid before and approved by a resolution of each House of Parliament.

(5) If it appears to the Secretary of State that an auditor has failed to comply with the duty mentioned in subsection (2) above, the Secretary of State may disqualify him from being the auditor of an insurance company or any class of insurance company to which Part II of this Act applies; but the Secretary of State may remove any disqualification imposed under this subsection if satisfied that the person in question will in future comply with that duty.

(6) An insurance company to which this Part of this Act applies shall not appoint as auditor a person disqualified under subsection (5) above.".

(2) In section 71(7) of that Act (which lists the provisions of that Act default in complying with which is not an offence) after the words " section 16 " there shall be inserted the word " 21A ", and in section 97(4) of that Act (which provides that regulations under that Act are to be subject to annulment) after the word " Act " there shall be inserted the words ", except regulations under section 21A(3),".

Arrangements
to avoid
unfairness
between
separate
insurance
funds etc.
1982 c. 50.

136.—(1) After section 31 of the Insurance Companies Act 1982 there shall be inserted—

" Arrangements to avoid unfairness between separate insurance funds etc.

31A.—(1) An insurance company to which this Part of this Act applies which carries on long term business in the United Kingdom shall secure that adequate arrangements are in force for securing that transactions affecting assets of the company (other than transactions outside its control) do not operate unfairly between the section 28 fund or funds and the other assets of the company or, in a case where the company has more than one identified fund, between those funds.

(2) In this section—

" the section 28 fund or funds " means the assets representing the fund or funds maintained by the company under section 28(1) (*b*) above ; and

" identified fund ", in relation to a company, means assets representing the company's receipts from a particular part of its long term business which can be identified as such by virtue of accounting or other records maintained by the company."

(2) In section 71(7) of that Act (which lists the provisions of that Act default in complying with which is not an offence) before the word " or " there shall be inserted the word " 31A ".

137. In section 78(2) of the Insurance Companies Act 1982 (regulations in respect of linked long term policies) after paragraph (*a*) there shall be inserted— Regulations in respect of linked long term policies. 1982 c. 50.

" (*aa*) restricting the proportion of those benefits which may be determined by reference to property of a specified description or a specified index ; ".

138.—(1) Rules made under section 8 of the Insurance Brokers (Registration) Act 1977 may require an applicant for registration or enrolment to state whether he is an authorised person or exempted person under Part I of this Act and, if so, to give particulars of the authorisation or exemption ; and an individual shall be treated as satisfying the requirements of section 3(2)(*a*) of that Act (applicant for registration to satisfy Council as to his character and suitability) if he is an authorised person or a member of a partnership or unincorporated association which is an authorised person. Insurance brokers. 1977 c. 46.

(2) In drawing up any statement under section 10 of that Act or making any rules under section 11 or 12 of that Act after the coming into force of this section the Insurance Brokers Registration Council shall take proper account of any provisions applicable to, and powers exercisable in relation to, registered insurance brokers or enrolled bodies corporate under this Act.

(3) In section 12(1) and (2) of that Act (which requires the Council to make professional indemnity rules) for the words " The Council shall " there shall be substituted the words " The Council may ".

(4) In section 15 of that Act (erasure from register and list for unprofessional conduct etc.) after subsection (2) there shall be inserted—

" (2A) The Disciplinary Committee may, if they think fit, direct that the name of a registered insurance broker or enrolled body corporate shall be erased from the register or list if it appears to the Committee that any responsible person has concluded that the broker (or a related person) or the body corporate has contravened or failed to comply with—

(a) any provision of the Financial Services Act 1986 or any rule or regulation made under it to which he or it is or was subject at the time of the contravention or failure ; or

(b) any rule of any recognised self-regulating organisation or recognised professional body (within the meaning of that Act), to which he is or was subject at that time.

(2B) In subsection (2A) above—

(a) " responsible person " means a person responsible under the Financial Services Act 1986 or under the rules of any recognised self-regulating organisation or recognised professional body (within the meaning of that Act) for determining whether any contravention of any provision of that Act or rules or regulations made under it or any rules of that organisation or body has occurred ; and

(b) " related person " means a partnership or unincorporated association of which the broker in question is (or was at the time of the failure or contravention in question) a member or a body corporate of which he is (or was at that time) a director."

(5) The Insurance Brokers Registration Council shall co-operate, by the sharing of information and otherwise, with the Secretary of State and any other authority, body or person having responsibility for the supervision or regulation of investment business or other financial services.

(6) For the purposes of the said Act of 1977 " authorised insurers " shall include—

(a) an insurance company the head office of which is in a member State other than the United Kingdom and which is entitled to carry on there insurance business

corresponding to that mentioned in the definition of
" authorised insurers " in that Act ; and

(*b*) an insurance company which has a branch or agency in such a member State and is entitled under the law of that State to carry on there insurance business corresponding to that mentioned in that definition.

139.—(1) In section 5 of the Industrial Assurance Act 1923 Industrial (prohibition on issue of illegal policies) the references to policies assurance. which are illegal or not within the legal powers of a society 1923 c. 8. or company shall not be construed as applying to any policy issued—

(*a*) in the course of carrying on investment business in contravention of section 3 above ; or

(*b*) in the course of carrying on insurance business in contravention of section 2 of the Insurance Companies 1982 c. 50. Act 1982.

(2) In section 20(4) of the said Act of 1923 the reference to a person employed by a collecting society or industrial assurance company and in section 34 of that Act the references to a person in the regular employment of such a society or company shall include references to an appointed representative of such a society or company but as respects section 34 only if the contract in question is an investment agreement.

(3) Where it appears to the Industrial Assurance Commissioner that rules made by virtue of section 48(2)(*j*) (or corresponding rules made by a recognised self-regulating organisation) make arrangements for the settlement of a dispute referred to him under section 32 of the said Act of 1923 or that such rules relate to some of the matters in dispute he may, if he thinks fit, delegate his functions in respect of the dispute so as to enable it to be settled in accordance with the rules.

(4) If such rules provide that any dispute may be referred to the Industrial Assurance Commissioner he may deal with any dispute referred to him in pursuance of those rules as if it were 1974 c. 46. a dispute referred under section 77 of the Friendly Societies Act 1974 and may delegate his functions in respect of any such dispute to any other person.

(5) The foregoing provisions of this section shall apply to Northern Ireland with the substitution for the references to sections 5, 20(4), 32 and 34 of the said Act of 1923 and section 77 of the said Act of 1974 of references to Articles 20, 27(2), 36 and 38 of the Industrial Assurance (Northern Ireland) Order 1979/1574 1979 and section 65 of the Friendly Societies Act (Northern (N.I.13). 1970 c. 31. (N.I.).

PART II

Ireland) 1970 and for the references to the Industrial Assurance Commissioner of references to the Industrial Assurance Commissioner for Northern Ireland.

PART III

FRIENDLY SOCIETIES

Friendly societies.

140. Schedule 11 to this Act shall have effect as respects the regulation of friendly societies.

Indemnity schemes.

141.—(1) Any two or more registered friendly societies may, notwithstanding any provision to the contrary in their rules, enter into arrangements for the purpose of making funds available to meet losses incurred by any society which is a party to the arrangements or by the members of any such society by virtue of their membership of it.

(2) No such arrangements shall come into force unless they have been approved by the Chief Registrar of friendly societies or, as the case may be, the Registrar of Friendly Societies for Northern Ireland.

PART IV

OFFICIAL LISTING OF SECURITIES

Official listing

142.—(1) No investment to which this section applies shall be admitted to the Official List of The Stock Exchange except in accordance with the provisions of this Part of this Act.

(2) Subject to subsections (3) and (4) below, this section applies to any investment falling within paragraph 1, 2, 4 or 5 of Schedule 1 to this Act.

(3) In the application of those paragraphs for the purposes of subsection (2) above—

(*a*) paragraphs 1, 4 and 5 shall have effect as if paragraph 1 did not contain the exclusion relating to building societies, industrial and provident societies or credit unions ;

(*b*) paragraph 2 shall have effect as if it included any instrument falling within paragraph 3 issued otherwise than by the government of a member State or a local authority in a member State ; and

(*c*) paragraphs 4 and 5 shall have effect as if they referred only to investments falling within paragraph 1.

(4) The Secretary of State may by order direct that this section shall apply also to investments falling within paragraph 6 of Schedule 1 to this Act or to such investments of any class or description.

(5) An order under subsection (4) above shall be subject to annulment in pursuance of a resolution of either House of Parliament.

(6) In this Part of this Act " the competent authority " means, subject to section 157 below, the Council of The Stock Exchange ; and that authority may make rules (in this Act referred to as " listing rules ") for the purposes of any of the following provisions.

(7) In this Part of this Act—

     " issuer ", in relation to any securities, means the person by whom they have been or are to be issued except that in relation to a certificate or other instrument falling within paragraph 5 of Schedule 1 to this Act it means the person who issued or is to issue the securities to which the certificate or instrument relates ;

     " the Official List " means the Official List of The Stock Exchange ;

     " securities " means investments to which this section applies ;

and references to listing are references to inclusion in the Official List in pursuance of this Part of this Act.

(8) Any functions of the competent authority under this Part of this Act may be exercised by any committee, sub-committee, officer or servant of the authority except that listing rules—

     (*a*) shall be made only by the authority itself or by a committee or sub-committee of the authority ; and

     (*b*) if made by a committee or sub-committee, shall cease to have effect at the end of the period of twenty-eight days beginning with the day on which they are made (but without prejudice to anything done under them) unless before the end of that period they are confirmed by the authority.

(9) Nothing in this Part of this Act affects the powers of the Council of The Stock Exchange in respect of investments to which this section does not apply and such investments may be admitted to the Official List otherwise than in accordance with this Part of this Act.

143.—(1) An application for listing shall be made to the competent authority in such manner as the listing rules may require. Applications for listing.

(2) No application for the listing of any securities shall be made except by or with the consent of the issuer of the securities.

(3) No application for listing shall be made in respect of securities to be issued by a private company or by an old public company within the meaning of section 1 of the Companies Consolidation (Consequential Provisions) Act 1985 or the corresponding Northern Ireland provision.

144.—(1) The competent authority shall not admit any securities to the Official List except on an application duly made in accordance with section 143 above and unless satisfied that—

    (*a*) the requirements of the listing rules made by the authority for the purposes of this section and in force when the application is made ; and

    (*b*) any other requirements imposed by the authority in relation to that application,

are complied with.

(2) Without prejudice to the generality of the power of the competent authority to make listing rules for the purposes of this section, such rules may, in particular, require as a condition of the admission of any securities to the Official List—

    (*a*) the submission to, and approval by, the authority of a document (in this Act referred to as " listing particulars ") in such form and containing such information as may be specified in the rules ; and

    (*b*) the publication of that document ;

or, in such cases as may be specified by the rules, the publication of a document other than listing particulars.

(3) The competent authority may refuse an application—

    (*a*) if it considers that by reason of any matter relating to the issuer the admission of the securities would be detrimental to the interests of investors ; or

    (*b*) in the case of securities already officially listed in another member State, if the issuer has failed to comply with any obligations to which he is subject by virtue of that listing.

(4) The competent authority shall notify the applicant of its decision on the application within six months from the date on which the application is received or, if within that period the authority has required the applicant to furnish further information in connection with the application, from the date on which that information is furnished.

(5) If the competent authority does not notify the applicant of its decision within the time required by subsection (4) above it shall be taken to have refused the application.

(6) When any securities have been admitted to the Official List their admission shall not be called in question on the ground that any requirement or condition for their admission has not been complied with.

145.—(1) The competent authority may, in accordance with Discontinuance and the listing rules, discontinue the listing of any securities if satis-ance and fied that there are special circumstances which preclude normal suspension of listing. regular dealings in the securities.

(2) The competent authority may in accordance with the listing rules suspend the listing of any securities.

(3) Securities the listing of which is suspended under subsection (2) above shall nevertheless be regarded as listed for the purposes of sections 153 and 155 below.

(4) This section applies to securities included in the Official List at the coming into force of this Part of this Act as it applies to securities included by virtue of this Part.

146.—(1) In addition to the information specified by listing General rules or required by the competent authority as a condition of duty of the admission of any securities to the Official List any listing disclosure in particulars submitted to the competent authority under section particulars. 144 above shall contain all such information as investors and their professional advisers would reasonably require, and reasonably expect to find there, for the purpose of making an informed assessment of—

> (*a*) the assets and liabilities, financial position, profits and losses, and prospects of the issuer of the securities ; and

> (*b*) the rights attaching to those securities.

(2) The information to be included by virtue of this section shall be such information as is mentioned in subsection (1) above which is within the knowledge of any person responsible for the listing particulars or which it would be reasonable for him to obtain by making enquiries.

(3) In determining what information is required to be included in listing particulars by virtue of this section regard shall be had—

> (*a*) to the nature of the securities and of the issuer of the securities ;

(b) to the nature of the persons likely to consider their acquisition ;

(c) to the fact that certain matters may reasonably be expected to be within the knowledge of professional advisers of any kind which those persons may reasonably be expected to consult ; and

(d) to any information available to investors or their professional advisers by virtue of requirements imposed under section 153 below or by or under any other enactment or by virtue of requirements imposed by a recognised investment exchange for the purpose of complying with paragraph 2(2)(b) of Schedule 4 to this Act.

Supplementary listing particulars.

147.—(1) If at any time after the preparation of listing particulars for submission to the competent authority under section 144 above and before the commencement of dealings in the securities following their admission to the Official List—

(a) there is a significant change affecting any matter contained in those particulars whose inclusion was required by section 146 above or by listing rules or by the competent authority ; or

(b) a significant new matter arises the inclusion of information in respect of which would have been so required if it had arisen when the particulars were prepared,

the issuer of the securities shall, in accordance with listing rules made for the purposes of this section, submit to the competent authority for its approval and, if approved, publish supplementary listing particulars of the change or new matter.

(2) In subsection (1) above " significant " means significant for the purpose of making an informed assessment of the matters mentioned in section 146(1) above.

(3) Where the issuer of the securities is not aware of the change or new matter in question he shall not be under any duty to comply with subsection (1) above unless he is notified of it by a person responsible for the listing particulars ; but it shall be the duty of any person responsible for those particulars who is aware of such a matter to give notice of it to the issuer.

(4) Subsection (1) above applies also as respects matters contained in any supplementary listing particulars previously published under this section in respect of the securities in question.

148.—(1) The competent authority may authorise the omission from listing particulars or supplementary listing particulars
of any information the inclusion of which would otherwise be
required by section 146 above—

> (a) on the ground that its disclosure would be contrary to
> the public interest ;
>
> (b) subject to subsection (2) below, on the ground that its
> disclosure would be seriously detrimental to the issuer
> of the securities ; or
>
> (c) in the case of securities which fall within paragraph 2
> of Schedule 1 to this Act as modified by section 142
> (3)(b) above and are of any class specified by listing
> rules, on the ground that its disclosure is unnecessary
> for persons of the kind who may be expected norm-
> ally to buy or deal in the securities.

(2) No authority shall be granted under subsection (1)(b) above
in respect of, and no such authority shall be regarded as extending to, information the non-disclosure of which would be likely
to mislead a person considering the acquisition of the securities
as to any facts the knowledge of which it is essential for him to
have in order to make an informed assessment.

(3) The Secretary of State or the Treasury may issue a certificate to the effect that the disclosure of any information (including information that would otherwise have to be included in particulars for which they are themselves responsible) would be
contrary to the public interest and the competent authority shall
be entitled to act on any such certificate in exercising its powers
under subsection (1)(a) above.

(4) This section is without prejudice to any powers of the competent authority under rules made by virtue of section 156(2)
below.

149.—(1) On or before the date on which listing particulars
or supplementary listing particulars are published as required
by listing rules a copy of the particulars shall be delivered for
registration to the registrar of companies and a statement that a
copy has been delivered to him shall be included in the particulars.

(2) In subsection (1) above " the registrar of companies "
means—

> (a) if the securities in question are or are to be issued by
> a company incorporated in Great Britain, the registrar
> of companies in England and Wales or the registrar of
> companies in Scotland according to whether the com-
> pany's registered office is in England and Wales or in
> Scotland ;

(*b*) if the securities in question are or are to be issued by a company incorporated in Northern Ireland, the registrar of companies for Northern Ireland;

(*c*) in any other case, any of those registrars.

(3) If any particulars are published without a copy of them having been delivered as required by this section the issuer of the securities in question and any person who is knowingly a party to the publication shall be guilty of an offence and liable—

(*a*) on conviction on indictment, to a fine;

(*b*) on summary conviction, to a fine not exceeding the statutory maximum.

Compensation for false or misleading particulars.

150.—(1) Subject to section 151 below, the person or persons responsible for any listing particulars or supplementary listing particulars shall be liable to pay compensation to any person who has acquired any of the securities in question and suffered loss in respect of them as a result of any untrue or misleading statement in the particulars or the omission from them of any matter required to be included by section 146 or 147 above.

(2) Where listing rules require listing particulars to include information as to any particular matter on the basis that the particulars must include a statement either as to that matter or, if such is the case, that there is no such matter, the omission from the particulars of the information shall be treated for the purposes of subsection (1) above as a statement that there is no such matter.

(3) Subject to section 151 below, a person who fails to comply with section 147 above shall be liable to pay compensation to any person who has acquired any of the securities in question and suffered loss in respect of them as a result of the failure.

(4) This section does not affect any liability which any person may incur apart from this section.

(5) References in this section to the acquisition by any person of securities include references to his contracting to acquire them or an interest in them.

(6) No person shall by reason of being a promoter of a company or otherwise incur any liability for failing to disclose any information which he would not be required to disclose in listing particulars in respect of a company's securities if he were responsible for those particulars or, if he is responsible for them, which he is entitled to omit by virtue of section 148 above.

151.—(1) A person shall not incurr any liability under section PART IV
150(1) above for any loss in respect of securities caused by any Exemption
such statement or omission as is there mentioned if he satisfies from liability
the court that at the time when the particulars were submitted to pay
to the competent authority he reasonably believed, having made compensation.
such enquiries (if any) as were reasonable, that the statement
was true and not misleading or that the matter whose omission
caused the loss was properly omitted and—

> (a) that he continued in that belief until the time when the
> securities were acquired ; or

> (b) that they were acquired before it was reasonably practi-
> cable to bring a correction to the attention of persons
> likely to acquire the securities in question ; or

> (c) that before the securities were acquired he had taken all
> such steps as it was reasonable for him to have taken
> to secure that a correction was brought to the attention
> of those persons ; or

> (d) that he continued in that belief until after the com-
> mencement of dealings in the securities following their
> admission to the Official List and that the securities
> were acquired after such a lapse of time that he ought
> in the circumstances to be reasonably excused.

(2) A person shall not incur any liability under section 150(1)
above for any loss in respect of securities caused by a statement
purporting to be made by or on the authority of another person
as an expert which is, and is stated to be, included in the particulars with that other person's consent if he satisfies the court
that at the time when the particulars were submitted to the competent authority he believed on reasonable grounds that the other
person was competent to make or authorise the statement and
had consented to its inclusion in the form and context in which
it was included and—

> (a) that he continued in that belief until the time when the
> securities were acquired ; or

> (b) that they were acquired before it was reasonably prac-
> ticable to bring the fact that the expert was not com-
> petent or had not consented to the attention of persons
> likely to acquire the securities in question ; or

> (c) that before the securities were acquired he had taken
> all such steps as it was reasonable for him to have
> taken to secure that that fact was brought to the at-
> tention of those persons ; or

> (d) that he continued in that belief until after the commence-
> ment of dealings in the securities following their ad-
> mission to the Official List and that the securities were

acquired after such a lapse of time that he ought in the circumstances to be reasonably excused.

(3) Without prejudice to subsections (1) and (2) above, a person shall not incur any liability under section 150(1) above for any loss in respect of any securities caused by any such statement or omission as is there mentioned if he satisfies the court—

> (*a*) that before the securities were acquired a correction, or where the statement was such as is mentioned in subsection (2), the fact that the expert was not competent or had not consented had been published in a manner calculated to bring it to the attention of persons likely to acquire the securities in question ; or
>
> (*b*) that he took all such steps as it was reasonable for him to take to secure such publication and reasonably believed that it had taken place before the securities were acquired.

(4) A person shall not incur any liability under section 150(1) above for any loss resulting from a statement made by an official person or contained in a public official document which is included in the particulars if he satisfies the court that the statement is accurately and fairly reproduced.

(5) A person shall not incur any liability under section 150(1) or (3) above if he satisfies the court that the person suffering the loss acquired the securities in question with knowledge that the statement was false or misleading, of the omitted matter or of the change or new matter, as the case may be.

(6) A person shall not incur any liability under section 150(3) above if he satisfies the court that he reasonably believed that the change or new matter in question was not such as to call for supplementary listing particulars.

(7) In this section " expert " includes any engineer, valuer, accountant or other person whose profession, qualifications or experience give authority to a statement made by him ; and references to the acquisition of securities include references to contracting to acquire them or an interest in them.

Persons
responsible for
particulars.
    152.—(1) For the purposes of this Part of this Act the persons responsible for listing particulars or supplementary listing particulars are—

> (*a*) the issuer of the securities to which the particulars relate ;
>
> (*b*) where the issuer is a body corporate, each person who is a director of that body at the time when the particulars are submitted to the competent authority ;

(c) where the issuer is a body corporate, each person who
has authorised himself to be named, and is named, in
the particulars as a director or as having agreed to
become a director of that body either immediately or
at a future time ;

(d) each person who accepts, and is stated in the particulars
as accepting, responsibility for, or for any part of, the
particulars ;

(e) each person not falling within any of the foregoing paragraphs who has authorised the contents of, or any part
of, the particulars.

(2) A person is not responsible for any particulars by virtue of
subsection (1)(b) above if they are published without his knowledge or consent and on becoming aware of their publication
he forthwith gives reasonable public notice that they were
published without his knowledge or consent.

(3) Where a person has accepted responsibility for, or
authorised, only part of the contents of any particulars, he is
responsible under subsection (1)(d) or (e) above for only that
part and only if it is included in (or substantially in) the form
and context to which he has agreed.

(4) Where the particulars relate to securities which are to be
issued in connection with an offer by (or by a wholly-owned
subsidiary of), the issuer for, or an agreement for the acquistion
by (or by a wholly-owned subsidiary of) the issuer of, securities
issued by another person or in connection with any arrangement
whereby the whole of the undertaking of another person is to
become the undertaking of the issuer (of a wholly-owned subsidiary of the issuer or of a body corporate which will become
such a subsidiary by virtue of the arrangement) then if—

(a) that other person ; and

(b) where that other person is a body corporate, each person
who is a director of that body at the time when the
particulars are submitted to the competent authority
and each other person who has authorised himself to
be named, and is named, in the particulars as a director of that body,

is responsible by virtue of paragraph (d) of subsection (1) above
for any part of the particulars relating to that other person or
to the securities or undertaking to which the offer, agreement
or arrangement relates, no person shall be responsible for that
part under paragraph (a), (b) or (c) of that subsection but without
prejudice to his being responsible under paragraph (d).

(5) Neither paragraph (b) nor paragraph (c) of subsection (1)
above applies in the case of an issuer of international securities

PART IV   of a class specified by listing rules for the purposes of section 148(1)(c) above ; and neither of those paragraphs nor paragraph (b) of subsection (4) above applies in the case of any director certified by the competent authority as a person to whom that paragraph should not apply by reason of his having an interest, or of any other circumstances, making it inappropriate for him to be responsible by virtue of that paragraph.

(6) In subsection (5) above " international securities " means any investment falling within paragraph 2 of Schedule 1 to this Act as modified by section 142(3)(b) above which is of a kind likely to be dealt in by bodies incorporated in or persons resident in a country or territory outside the United Kingdom, is denominated in a currency other than sterling or is otherwise connected with such a country or territory.

(7) In this section " wholly-owned subsidiary ", in relation to a person other than a body corporate, means any body corporate that would be his wholly-owned subsidiary if he were a body corporate.

(8) Nothing in this section shall be construed as making a person responsible for any particulars by reason of giving advice as to their contents in a professional capacity.

(9) Where by virtue of this section the issuer of any shares pays or is liable to pay compensation under section 150 above for loss suffered in respect of shares for which a person has subscribed no account shall be taken of that liability or payment in determining any question as to the amount paid on subscription for those shares or as to the amount paid up or deemed to be paid up on them.

Obligations of issuers of listed securities.

153.—(1) Listing rules may specify requirements to be complied with by issuers of listed securities and make provision with respect to the action that may be taken by the competent authority in the event of non-compliance, including provision—

(a) authorising the authority to publish the fact that an issuer has contravened any provision of the rules ; and

(b) if the rules require an issuer to publish any information, authorising the authority to publish it in the event of his failure to do so.

(2) This section applies to the issuer of securities included in the Official List at the coming into force of this Part of this Act as it applies to the issuer of securities included by virtue of this Part.

154.—(1) Where listing particulars are or are to be published in connection with an application for the listing of any securities no advertisement or other information of a kind specified by listing rules shall be issued in the United Kingdom unless the contents of the advertisement or other information have been submitted to the competent authority and that authority has either—

(*a*) approved those contents ; or

(*b*) authorised the issue of the advertisement or information without such approval.

(2) An authorised person who contravenes this section shall be treated as having contravened rules made under Chapter V of Part I of this Act or, in the case of a person who is an authorised person by virtue of his membership of a recognised self-regulating organisation or certification by a recognised professional body, the rules of that organisation or body.

(3) Subject to subsection (4) below, a person other than an authorised person, who contravenes this section shall be guilty of an offence and liable—

(*a*) on conviction on indictment, to imprisonment for a term not exceeding two years or to a fine or to both ;

(*b*) on summary conviction, to a fine not exceeding the statutory maximum.

(4) A person who in the ordinary course of a business other than investment business issues an advertisement or other information to the order of another person shall not be guilty of an offence under this section if he proves that he believed on reasonable grounds that the advertisement or information had been approved or its issue authorised by the competent authority.

(5) Where information has been approved, or its issue has been authorised, under this section neither the person issuing it nor any person responsible for, or for any part of, the listing particulars shall incur any civil liability by reason of any statement in or omission from the information if that information and the listing particulars, taken together, would not be likely to mislead persons of the kind likely to consider the acquisition of the securities in question.

155. Listing rules may require the payment of fees to the competent authority in respect of applications for listing and the retention of securities in the Official List.

156.—(1) Listing rules may make different provision for differ-ent cases.

(2) Listing rules may authorise the competent authority to dispense with or modify the application of the rules in particular cases and by reference to any circumstances.

(3) Listing rules shall be made by an instrument in writing.

(4) Immediately after an instrument containing listing rules is made it shall be printed and made available to the public with or without payment.

(5) A person shall not be taken to have contravened any listing rule if he shows that at the time of the alleged contra-vention the instrument containing the rule had not been made available as required by subsection (4) above.

(6) The production of a printed copy of an instrument pur-porting to be made by the competent authority on which is endorsed a certificate signed by an officer of the authority auth-orised by it for that purpose and stating—

(a) that the instrument was made by the authority ;

(b) that the copy is a true copy of the instrument ; and

(c) that on a specified date the instrument was made avail-able to the public as required by subsection (4) above,

shall be prima facie evidence or, in Scotland, sufficient evidence of the facts stated in the certificate.

(7) Any certificate purporting to be signed as mentioned in subsection (6) above shall be deemed to have been duly signed unless the contrary is shown.

(8) Any person wishing in any legal proceedings to cite an instrument made by the competent authority may require the authority to cause a copy of it to be endorsed with such a certifi-cate as is mentioned in subsection (6) above.

Alteration of
competent
authority.
157.—(1) The Secretary of State may by order transfer the functions as competent authority of the Council of The Stock Exchange to another body or other bodies either at the request of the Council or if it appears to him—

(a) that the Council is exercising those functions in a man-ner which is unnecessary for the protection of investors and fails to take into account the proper interests of issuers and proposed issuers of securities ; or

(b) that it is necessary to do so for the protection of in-vestors.

(2) The Secretary of State may by order transfer all or any of the functions as competent authority from any body or

bodies to which they have been previously transferred under this
section to another body or bodies.

(3) Any order made under subsection (1) above at the request
of the Council shall be subject to annulment in pursuance of a
resolution of either House of Parliament; and no other order
shall be made under this section unless a draft of it has been
laid before and approved by a resolution of each House of
Parliament.

(4) An order under this section shall not affect anything
previously done by any body (" the previous authority ") in the
exercise of functions which are transferred by the order to another body (" the new authority ") and may contain such supplementary provisions as the Secretary of State thinks necessary or
expedient, including provisions—

   (a) for modifying or excluding any provision of this Part
      of this Act in its application to any such functions;

   (b) for the transfer of any property, rights or liabilities re-
      lating to any such functions from the previous authority
      to the new authority;

   (c) for the carrying on and completion by the new auth-
      ority of anything in process of being done by the pre-
      vious authority when the order takes effect; and

   (d) for the substitution of the new authority for the pre-
      vious authority in any instrument, contract or legal
      proceedings.

(5) If by virtue of this section the function of admission to or
discontinuance or suspension of listing is exercisable otherwise than by the Council of The Stock Exchange, references in
this Part of this Act to the competent authority admitting securities to the Official List or to discontinuing or suspending the listing of any securities shall be construed as references to the
giving of directions to the Council of The Stock Exchange to
admit the securities or to discontinue or suspend their listing;
and it shall be the duty of the Council to comply with any
such direction.

PART V

OFFERS OF UNLISTED SECURITIES

158.—(1) This Part of this Act applies to any investment—   Preliminary.

   (a) which is not listed, or the subject of an application for
      listing, in accordance with Part IV of this Act; and

   (b) falls within paragraph 1, 2, 4 or 5 of Schedule 1 to this
      Act.

(2) In the application of those paragraphs for the purposes of subsection (1) above—

(*a*) paragraphs 4 and 5 shall have effect with the omission of references to investments falling within paragraph 3 ; and

(*b*) paragraph 4 shall have effect as if it referred only to instruments issued by the person issuing the investment to be subscribed for.

(3) In this Part of this A⸱⸱—

" issuer ", in relation to any securities, means the person by whom they have been or are to be issued except that in relation to a certificate or other instrument falling within paragraph 5 of Schedule 1 to this Act it means the person who issued or is to issue the securities to which the certificate or instrument relates ;

" securities " means investments to which this section applies.

(4) For the purposes of this Part of this Act an advertisement offers securities if—

(*a*) it invites a person to enter into an agreement for or with a view to subscribing for or otherwise acquiring or underwriting any securities ; or

(*b*) it contains information calculated to lead directly or indirectly to a person entering into such an agreement.

(5) In this Part of this Act " the registrar of companies ", in relation to any securities, means—

(*a*) if the securities are or are to be issued by a company incorporated in Great Britain, the registrar of companies in England and Wales or the registrar of companies in Scotland according to whether the company's registered office is in England and Wales or in Scotland ;

(*b*) if the securities are or are to be issued by a company incorporated in Northern Ireland, the registrar of companies for Northern Ireland ;

(*c*) in any other case, any of those registrars.

(6) In this Part of this Act " approved exchange ", in relation to dealings in any securities, means a recognised investment exchange approved by the Secretary of State for the purposes of this Part of this Act either generally or in relation to such dealings, and the Secretary of State shall give notice in such manner as he thinks appropriate of the exchanges which are for the time being approved.

159.—(1) Subject to subsection (2) and section 161 below, no person shall issue or cause to be issued in the United King- dom an advertisement offering any securities on the occasion of their admission to dealings on an approved exchange or on terms that they will be issued if admitted to such dealings un- less—

    (*a*) a document (in this Part of this Act referred to as a " prospectus ") containing information about the securities has been submitted to and approved by the exchange and delivered for registration to the registrar of companies ; or

    (*b*) the advertisement is such that no agreement can be entered into in pursuance of it until such a prospectus has been submitted, approved and delivered as aforesaid.

(2) Subsection (1) above does not apply if a prospectus relating to the securities has been delivered for registration under this Part of this Act in the previous twelve months and the approved exchange certifies that it is satisfied that persons likely to consider acquiring the securities will have sufficient information to enable them to decide whether to do so from that prospectus and any information published in connection with the admission of the securities.

160.—(1) Subject to subsections (5) and (6) and section 161 below, no person shall issue or cause to be issued in the United Kingdom an advertisement offering any securities which is a primary or secondary offer within the meaning of this section unless—

    (*a*) he has delivered for registration to the registrar of companies a prospectus relating to the securities and expressed to be in respect of the offer ; or

    (*b*) the advertisement is such that no agreement can be entered into in pursuance of it until such a prospectus has been delivered by him as aforesaid.

(2) For the purposes of this section a primary offer is an advertisement issued otherwise than as mentioned in section 159(1) above inviting persons to enter into an agreement for or with a view to subscribing (whether or not in cash) for or underwriting the securities to which it relates or containing information calculated to lead directly or indirectly to their doing so.

(3) For the purposes of this section a secondary offer is any other advertisement issued otherwise than as mentioned in section 159(1) above inviting persons to enter into an agreement for or with a view to acquiring the securities to which it relates

PART V   or containing information calculated to lead directly or indirectly
to their doing so, being an advertisement issued or caused to
be issued by—

> (a) a person who has acquired the securities from the issuer
> with a view to issuing such an advertisement in respect
> of them ;
>
> (b) a person who, with a view to issuing such an advertise-
> ment in respect of them, has acquired the securities
> otherwise than from the issuer but without their
> having been admitted to dealings on an approved
> exchange or held by a person who acquired them as an
> investment and without any intention that such an
> advertisement should be issued in respect of them ; or
>
> (c) a person who is a controller of the issuer or has been
> such a controller in the previous twelve months and
> who is acting with the consent or participation of the
> issuer in issuing the advertisement.

(4) For the purposes of subsection (3)(a) above it shall be
presumed in the absence of evidence to the contrary that a person has acquired securities with a view to issuing an advertisement offering the securities if he issues it or causes it to be
issued—

> (a) within six months after the issue of the securities ; or
>
> (b) before the consideration due from him for their acquisi-
> tion is received by the person from whom he acquired
> them.

(5) Subsection (1) above does not apply to a secondary offer
if such a prospectus as is mentioned in that subsection has been
delivered in accordance with that subsection in respect of an
offer of the same securities made in the previous six months by a
person making a primary offer or a previous secondary offer.

(6) Subsection (1) above does not apply to an advertisement
issued in such circumstances as may be specified by an order
made by the Secretary of State for the purpose of exempting
from that subsection—

> (a) advertisements appearing to him to have a private char-
> acter, whether by reason of a connection between the
> person issuing them and those to whom they are
> addressed or otherwise ;
>
> (b) advertisements appearing to him to deal with investments
> only incidentally ;
>
> (c) advertisements issued to persons appearing to him to be
> sufficiently expert to understand any risks involved ; or
>
> (d) such other classes of advertisement as he thinks fit.

(7) Without prejudice to subsection (6)(*c*) above an order made by the Secretary of State may exempt from subsection (1) above an advertisement issued in whatever circumstances if it relates to securities appearing to him to be of a kind that can be expected normally to be bought or dealt in only by persons sufficiently expert to understand any risks involved.

(8) An order under subsection (6) or (7) above may require any person who by virtue of the order is authorised to issue an advertisement to comply with such requirements as are specified in the order.

(9) An order made by virtue of subsection (6)(*a*), (*b*) or (*c*) or by virtue of subsection (7) above shall be subject to annulment in pursuance of a resolution of either House of Parliament ; and no order shall be made by virtue of subsection (6)(*d*) above unless a draft of it has been laid before and approved by a resolution of each House of Parliament.

161.—(1) Sections 159 and 160 above do not apply to any Exceptions. advertisement offering securities if the offer is conditional on their admission to listing in accordance with Part IV of this Act and section 159 above does not apply to any advertisement offering securities if they have been listed in accordance with that Part in the previous twelve months and the approved exchange in question certifies that persons likely to consider acquiring them will have sufficient information to enable them to decide whether to do so.

(2) Neither of those sections applies to any such advertisement as is mentioned in section 58(2) above.

(3) Neither of those sections applies if other securities issued by the same person (whether or not securities of the same class as those to which the offer relates) are already dealt in on an approved exchange and the exchange certifies that persons likely to consider acquiring the securities to which the offer relates will have sufficient information to enable them to decide whether to do so having regard to the steps that have been taken to comply in respect of those other securities with the requirements imposed by the exchange for the purpose of complying with paragraph 2(2)(*b*) of Schedule 4 to this Act, to the nature of the securities to which the offer relates, to the circumstances of their issue and to the information about the issuer which is available to investors by virtue of any enactment.

(4) If it appears to the Secretary of State that the law of a country or territory outside the United Kingdom provides investors in the United Kingdom with protection at least equivalent to that provided by Part IV of this Act or this Part of this Act

PART V

in respect of securities dealt in on an exchange or exchanges in that country or territory he may by order specify circumstances in which those sections are not to apply to advertisements offering those securities.

(5) An order under subsection (4) above shall be subject to annulment in pursuance of a resolution of either House of Parliament.

Form and content of prospectus.

162.—(1) A prospectus shall contain such information and comply with such other requirements as may be prescribed by rules made by the Secretary of State for the purposes of this section.

(2) Rules under this section may make provision whereby compliance with any requirements imposed by or under the law of a country or territory outside the United Kingdom is treated as compliance with any requirements of the rules.

(3) If it appears to the Secretary of State that an approved exchange has rules in respect of prospectuses relating to securities dealt in on the exchange, and practices in exercising any powers conferred by the rules, which provide investors with protection at least equivalent to that provided by rules under this section he may direct that any such prospectus shall be subject to the rules of the exchange instead of the rules made under this section.

General duty of disclosure in prospectus.

163.—(1) In addition to the information required to be included in a prospectus by virtue of rules applying to it by virtue of section 162 above a prospectus shall contain all such information as investors and their professional advisers would reasonably require, and reasonably expect to find there, for the purpose of making an informed assessment of—

(a) the assets and liabilities, financial position, profits and losses, and prospects of the issuer of the securities ; and

(b) the rights attaching to those securities.

(2) The information to be included by virtue of this section shall be such information as is mentioned in subsection (1) above which is within the knowledge of any person responsible for the prospectus or which it would be reasonable for him to obtain by making enquiries.

(3) In determining what information is required to be included in a prospectus by virtue of this section regard shall be had—

(a) to the nature of the securities and of the issuer of the securities ;

(b) to the nature of the persons likely to consider their acquisition ;

(c) to the fact that certain matters may reasonably be
    expected to be within the knowledge of professional
    advisers of any kind which those persons may reason-
    ably be expected to consult ; and

(d) to any information available to investors or their profes-
    sional advisers by virtue of any enactment or by virtue
    of requirements imposed by a recognised investment
    exchange for the purpose of complying with paragraph
    2(2)(b) of Schedule 4 to this Act.

164.—(1) Where a prospectus has been registered under this   Supplemen-
Part of this Act in respect of an offer of securities and at any   tary
time while an agreement in respect of those securities can be   prospectus.
entered into in pursuance of that offer—

   (a) there is a significant change affecting any matter con-
       tained in the prospectus whose inclusion was required
       by rules applying to it by virtue of section 162 above
       or by section 163 above ; or

   (b) a significant new matter arises the inclusion of informa-
       tion in respect of which would have been so required if
       it had arisen when the prospectus was prepared,

the person who delivered the prospectus for registration to the
registrar of companies shall deliver to him for registration a
supplementary prospectus containing particulars of the change
or new matter.

(2) In subsection (1) above " significant " means significant for
the purpose of making an informed assessment of the matters
mentioned in section 163(1) above.

(3) Where the person who delivered the prospectus for registration is not aware of the change or new matter in question he
shall not be under any duty to comply with subsection (1) above
unless he is notified of it by a person responsible for the prospectus ; but any person responsible for the prospectus who is
aware of such a matter shall be under a duty to give him
notice of it.

(4) Subsection (1) above applies also as respects matters contained in a supplementary prospectus previously registered under
this section in respect of the securities in question.

165.—(1) If in the case of any approved exchange the Secre-   Exemptions
tary of State so directs, the exchange shall have power to   from
authorise the omission from a prospectus or supplementary pros-   disclosure.
pectus of any information the inclusion of which would otherwise be required by section 163 above—

   (a) on the ground that its disclosure would be contrary to
       the public interest ;

(*b*) subject to subsection (2) below, on the ground that its disclosure would be seriously detrimental to the issuer of the securities; or

(*c*) in the case of securities which fall within paragraph 2 of Schedule 1 to this Act and are of any class specified by the rules of the exchange, on the ground that its disclosure is unnecessary for persons of the kind who may be expected normally to buy or deal in the securities.

(2) No authority shall be granted under subsection (1)(*b*) above in respect of, and no such authority shall be regarded as extending to, information the non-disclosure of which would be likely to mislead a person considering the acquisition of the securities as to any facts the knowledge of which it is essential for him to have in order to make an informed assessment.

(3) The Secretary of State or the Treasury may issue a certificate to the effect that the disclosure of any information (including information that would otherwise have to be included in a prospectus or supplementary prospectus for which they are themselves responsible) would be contrary to the public interest and the exchange shall be entitled to act on any such certificate in exercising its powers under subsection (1)(*a*) above.

Compensation for false or misleading prospectus.   **166.**—(1) Subject to section 167 below, the person or persons responsible for a prospectus or supplementary prospectus shall be liable to pay compensation to any person who has acquired the securities to which the prospectus relates and suffered loss in respect of them as a result of any untrue or misleading statement in the prospectus or the omission from it of any matter required to be included by section 163 or 164 above.

(2) Where rules applicable to a prospectus by virtue of section 162 above require it to include information as to any particular matter on the basis that the prospectus must include a statement either as to that matter or, if such is the case, that there is no such matter, the omission from the prospectus of the information shall be treated for the purpose of subsection (1) above as a statement that there is no such matter.

(3) Subject to section 167 below, a person who fails to comply with section 164 above shall be liable to pay compensation to any person who has acquired any of the securities in question and suffered loss in respect of them as a result of the failure.

(4) This section does not affect any liability which any person may incur apart from this section.

(5) References in this section to the acquisition by any person of securities include references to his contracting to acquire them or an interest in them.

167.—(1) A person shall not incur any liability under section
166(1) above for any loss in respect of securities caused by any
such statement or omission as is there mentioned if he satisfies
the court that at the time when the prospectus or supplementary
prospectus was delivered for registration he reasonably believed,
having made such enquiries (if any) as were reasonable, that the
statement was true and not misleading or that the matter whose
omission caused the loss was properly omitted and—

    (a) that he continued in that belief until the time when the
        securities were acquired ; or

    (b) that they were acquired before it was reasonably practi-
        cable to bring a correction to the attention of persons
        likely to acquire the securities in question ; or

    (c) that before the securities were acquired he had taken
        all such steps as it was reasonable for him to have
        taken to secure that a correction was brought to the at-
        tention of those persons ; or

    (d) that the securities were acquired after such a lapse of
        time that he ought in the circumstances to be reason-
        ably excused ;

but paragraph (d) above does not apply where the securities
are dealt in on an approved exchange unless he satisfies the
court that he continued in that belief until after the commencement of dealings in the securities on that exchange.

(2) A person shall not incur any liability under section 166(1)
above for any loss in respect of securities caused by a statement
purporting to be made by or on the authority of another person
as an expert which is, and is stated to be, included in the prospectus or supplementary prospectus with that other person's
consent if he satisfies the court that at the time when the prospectus or supplementary prospectus was delivered for registration he believed on reasonable grounds that the other person
was competent to make or authorise the statement and had consented to its inclusion in the form and context in which it
was included and—

    (a) that he continued in that belief until the time when the
        securities were acquired ; or

    (b) that they were acquired before it was reasonably practi-
        cable to bring the fact that the expert was not com-
        petent or had not consented to the attention of persons
        likely to acquire the securities in question ; or

    (c) that before the securities were acquired he had taken
        all such steps as it was reasonable for him to have
        taken to secure that that fact was brought to the at-
        tention of those persons ; or

(*d*) that the securities were acquired after such a lapse of time that he ought in the circumstances to be reasonably excused ;

but paragraph (*d*) above does not apply where the securities are dealt in on an approved exchange unless he satisfies the court that he continued in that belief until after the commencement of dealings in the securities on that exchange.

(3) Without prejudice to subsections (1) and (2) above, a person shall not incur any liability under section 166(1) above for any loss in respect of any securities caused by any such statement or omission as is there mentioned if he satisfies the court—

(*a*) that before the securities were acquired a correction or, where the statement was such as is mentioned in subsection (2) above, the fact that the expert was not competent or had not consented had been published in a manner calculated to bring it to the attention of persons likely to acquire the securities in question ; or

(*b*) that he took all such steps as it was reasonable for him to take to secure such publication and reasonably believed that it had taken place before the securities were acquired.

(4) A person shall not incur any liability under section 166(1) above for any loss resulting from a statement made by an official person or contained in a public official document which is included in the prospectus or supplementary prospectus if he satisfies the court that the statement is accurately and fairly reproduced.

(5) A person shall not incur any liability under section 166(1) or (3) above if he satisfies the court that the person suffering the loss acquired the securities in question with knowledge that the statement was false or misleading, of the omitted matter or of the change or new matter, as the case may be.

(6) A person shall not incur any liability under section 166(3) above if he satisfies the court that he reasonably believed that the change or new matter in question was not such as to call for a supplementary prospectus.

(7) In this section " expert " includes any engineer, valuer, accountant or other person whose profession, qualifications or experience give authority to a statement made by him ; and references to the acquisition of securities include references to contracting to acquire them or an interest in them.

168.—(1) For the purposes of this Part of this Act the persons responsible for a propectus or supplementary prospectus are—

   (a) the issuer of the securities to which the prospectus or supplementary prospectus relates ;

   (b) where the issuer is a body corporate, each person who is a director of that body at the time when the prospectus or supplementary prospectus is delivered for registration ;

   (c) where the issuer is a body corporate, each person who has authorised himself to be named, and is named, in the prospectus or supplementary prospectus as a director or as having agreed to become a director of that body either immediately or at a future time ;

   (d) each person who accepts, and is stated in the prospectus or supplementary prospectus as accepting, responsibility for, or for any part of, the prospectus or supplementary prospectus ;

   (e) each person not falling within any of the foregoing paragraphs who has authorised the contents of, or of any part of, the prospectus or supplementary prospectus.

(2) A person is not responsible under subsection (1)(a), (b) or (c) above unless the issuer has made or authorised the offer in relation to which the prospectus or supplementary prospectus was delivered for registration ; and a person is not responsible for a prospectus or supplementary prospectus by virtue of subsection (1)(b) above if it is delivered for registration without his knowledge or consent and on becoming aware of its delivery he forthwith gives reasonable public notice that it was delivered without his knowledge or consent.

(3) Where a person has accepted responsibility for, or authorised, only part of the contents of any prospectus or supplementary prospectus he is responsible under subsection (1)(d) or (e) above for only that part and only if it is included in (or substantially in) the form and context to which he has agreed.

(4) Where a prospectus or supplementary prospectus relates to securities which are to be issued in connection with an offer by (or by a wholly-owned subsidiary of) the issuer for, or an agreement for the acquisition by (or by a wholly-owned subsidiary of) the issuer of, securities issued by another person or in connection with any arrangement whereby the whole of the undertaking of another person is to become the undertaking of the issuer (of a wholly-owned subsidiary of the issuer or of a body corporate which will become such a subsidiary by virtue of the arrangement) then if—

   (a) that other person ; and

(b) where that other person is a body corporate, each person who is a director of that body at the time when the prospectus or supplementary prospectus is delivered for registration and each other person who has authorised himself to be named, and is named, in the prospectus or supplementary prospectus as a director of that body,

is responsible by virtue of paragraph (d) of subsection (1) above for any part of the prospectus or supplementary prospectus relating to that other person or to the securities or undertaking to which the offer, agreement or arrangement relates, no person shall be responsible for that part under paragraph (a), (b) or (c) of that subsection but without prejudice to his being responsible under paragraph (d).

(5) Neither paragraph (b) nor paragraph (c) of subsection (1) above nor paragraph (b) of subsection (4) above applies in the case of any director if the prospectus or supplementary prospectus is subject to the rules of an approved exchange by virtue of section 162(3) above and he is certified by the exchange as a person to whom that paragraph should not apply by reason of his having an interest, or of any other circumstances, making it inappropriate for him to be responsible by virtue of that paragraph.

(6) In this section " wholly-owned subsidiary ", in relation to a person other than a body corporate, means any body corporate that would be his wholly-owned subsidiary if he were a body corporate.

(7) Nothing in this section shall be construed as making a person responsible for any prospectus or supplementary prospectus by reason only of giving advice as to its contents in a professional capacity.

(8) Where by virtue of this section the issuer of any shares pays or is liable to pay compensation under section 166 above for loss suffered in respect of shares for which a person has subscribed no account shall be taken of that liability or payment in determining any question as to the amount paid on subscription for those shares or as to the amount paid up or deemed to be paid up on them.

Terms and implementation of offer.

169.—(1) The Secretary of State may make rules—

(a) regulating the terms on which a person may offer securities by an advertisement to which this Part of this Act applies ; and

(b) otherwise regulating his conduct with a view to ensuring that the persons to whom the offer is addressed are treated equally and fairly.

(2) Rules under this section may, in particular, make provision with respect to the giving of priority as between persons to whom an offer is made and with respect to the payment of commissions.

(3) Section 162(2) above shall apply also to rules made under this section.

170.—(1) No private company and no old public company shall issue or cause to be issued in the United Kingdom any advertisement offering securities to be issued by that company.

Advertisements by private companies and old public companies.

(2) Subsection (1) above shall not apply to an advertisement issued in such circumstances as may be specified by an order made by the Secretary of State for the purpose of exempting from that subsection such advertisements as are mentioned in section 160(6)(*a*), (*b*) or (*c*) above.

(3) An order under subsection (2) above may require any person who by virtue of the order is authorised to issue an advertisement to comply with such requirements as are specified in the order.

(4) An order under subsection (2) above shall be subject to annulment in pursuance of a resolution of either House of Parliament.

(5) In this section " old public company " has the meaning given in section 1 of the Companies Consolidation (Consequential Provisions) Act 1985 or the corresponding Northern Ireland provision.

1985 c. 9.

171.—(1) An authorised person who—

Contraventions.

(*a*) contravenes section 159 or 160 above or rules made under section 169 above ;

(*b*) contravenes any requirement imposed by an order under section 160(6) or (7) or 170 above ; or

(*c*) on behalf of a company issues or causes to be issued an advertisement which that company is prohibited from issuing by section 170 above,

shall be treated as having contravened rules made under Chapter V of Part I of this Act or, in the case of a person who is an authorised person by virtue of his membership of a recognised self-regulating organisation or certification by a recognised professional body, the rules of that organisation or body.

(2) Section 57 above shall apply to a company which issues or causes to be issued an advertisement in contravention of section 170 above as it applies to a person who issues an advertisement in contravention of that section.

(3) A person, other than an authorised person, who contravenes section 159 or 160, the rules made under section 169 or any requirement imposed by an order under section 160(6) or (7) or 170 above shall be guilty of an offence and liable—

(*a*) on conviction on indictment, to imprisonment for a term not exceeding two years or to a fine or to both ;

(*b*) on summary conviction, to imprisonment for a term not exceeding six months or to a fine not exceeding the statutory maximum or to both.

(4) A person who in the ordinary course of a business other than investment business issues an advertisement to the order of another person shall not be guilty of an offence under subsection (3) above in respect of a contravention of section 159 or 160 above if he proves that he believed on reasonable grounds that neither section 159 nor section 160 above applied to the advertisement or that one of those sections had been complied with in respect of the advertisement.

(5) Without prejudice to any liability under section 166 above, a person shall not be regarded as having contravened section 159 or 160 above by reason only of a prospectus not having fully complied with the requirements of this Part of this Act as to its form and content.

(6) Any contravention to which this section applies shall be actionable at the suit of a person who suffers loss as a result of the contravention subject to the defences and other incidents applying to actions for breach of statutory duty.

PART VI

TAKEOVER OFFERS

Takeover offers.
1985 c. 6.

172.—(1) The provisions set out in Schedule 12 to this Act shall be substituted for sections 428, 429 and 430 of the Companies Act 1985.

(2) Subsection (1) above does not affect any case in which the offer in respect of the scheme or contract mentioned in section 428(1) was made before the coming into force of this section.

PART VII

INSIDER DEALING

Information obtained in official capacity: public bodies etc.
1985 c. 8.

173.—(1) In section 2 of the Company Securities (Insider Dealing) Act 1985 (abuse of information obtained by Crown servants in official capacity) for the word " Crown " wherever it occurs there shall be substituted the word " public ".

(2) At the end of that section there shall be added—

" (4) ' Public servant ' means—

(*a*) a Crown servant ;

(*b*) a member, officer or servant of a designated
agency, competent authority or transferee body
(within the meaning of the Financial Services Act
1986) ;

(*c*) an officer or servant of a recognised self-regulating
organisation, recognised investment exchange or
recognised clearing house (within the meaning of
that Act) ;

(*d*) any person declared by an order for the time being
in force under subsection (5) to be a public servant
for the purposes of this section.

(5) If it appears to the Secretary of State that the members, officers or employees of or persons otherwise connected
with any body appearing to him to exercise public functions
may have access to unpublished price sensitive information
relating to securities, he may by order declare that those
persons are to be public servants for the purposes of this
section.

(6) The power to make an order under subsection (5)
shall be exercisable by statutory instrument and an instrument containing such an order shall be subject to annulment
in pursuance of a resolution of either House of Parliament."

174.—(1) In subsection (1) of section 3 of the Company Securities (Insider Dealing) Act 1985 (actions not prohibited by sections 1 and 2 of that Act) at the end of paragraph (*c*) there shall
be inserted the words " ; or   Market makers, off market dealers etc. 1985 c. 8.

(*d*) doing any particular thing in relation to any particular
securities if the information—

     (i) was obtained by him in the course of a business of a market maker in those securities in which
he was engaged or employed, and

     (ii) was of a description which it would be reasonable to expect him to obtain in the ordinary course
of that business,

and he does that thing in good faith in the course of
that business.".

(2) At the end of that subsection there shall be inserted—

" ' Market maker ' means a person (whether an individual,
partnership or company) who—

     (*a*) holds himself out at all normal times in compliance with the rules of a recognised stock exchange
as willing to buy and sell securities at prices specified by him ; and

     (*b*) is recognised as doing so by that recognised
stock exchange.".

PART VII

(3) The existing provisions of section 4 of that Act (off-market deals in advertised securities) shall become subsection (1) of that section and after that subsection there shall be inserted—

"(2) In its application by virtue of this section the definition of "market maker" in section 3(1) shall have effect as if the references to a recognised stock exchange were references to a recognised investment exchange (other than an overseas investment exchange) within the meaning of the Financial Services Act 1986.".

(4) In section 13 of that Act—

(a) in subsection (1) (which defines dealing in securities and provides that references to dealing on a recognised stock exchange include dealing through an investment exchange) the words from "and references" onwards shall be omitted ; and

(b) for subsection (3) (definition of off-market dealer) there shall be substituted—

"(3) 'Off-market dealer' means a person who is an authorised person within the meaning of the Financial Services Act 1986.".

Price stabilisation.
1985 c. 8.

175. For section 6 of the Company Securities (Insider Dealing) Act 1985 (international bonds) there shall be substituted—

"Price stabilisation.   **6.**—(1) No provision of section 1, 2, 4 or 5 prohibits an individual from doing anything for the purpose of stabilising the price of securities if it is done in conformity with rules made under section 48 of the Financial Services Act 1986 and—

(a) in respect of securities which fall within any of paragraphs 1 to 5 of Schedule 1 to that Act and are specified by the rules ; and

(b) during such period before or after the issue of those securities as is specified by the rules.

(2) Any order under subsection (8) of section 48 of that Act shall apply also in relation to subsection (1) of this section.".

Contracts for differences by reference to securities.

176. After subsection (1) of section 13 of the Company Securities (Insider Dealing) Act 1985 (definition of dealing in securities), there shall be inserted—

"(1A) For the purposes of this Act a person who (whether as principal or agent) buys or sells or agrees to buy or sell investments within paragraph 9 of Schedule 1 to the Financial Services Act 1986 (contracts for differences etc.)

where the purpose or pretended purpose mentioned in that paragraph is to secure a profit or avoid a loss wholly or partly by reference to fluctuations in the value or price of securities shall be treated as if he were dealing in those securities.".

177.—(1) If it appears to the Secretary of State that there are circumstances suggesting that there may have been a contraven- into insider tion of section 1, 2, 4 or 5 of the Company Securities (Insider dealing. Dealing) Act 1985, he may appoint one or more competent 1985 c. 8. inspectors to carry out such investigations as are requisite to establish whether or not any such contravention has occurred and to report the results of their investigations to him.

(2) The appointment under this section of an inspector may limit the period during which he is to continue his investigation or confine it to particular matters.

(3) If the inspectors consider that any person is or may be able to give information concerning any such contravention they may require that person—

(*a*) to produce to them any documents in his possession or under his control relating to the company in relation to whose securities the contravention is suspected to have occurred or to its securities ;

(*b*) to attend before them ; and

(*c*) otherwise to give them all assistance in connection with the investigation which he is reasonably able to give ,

and it shall be the duty of that person to comply with that requirement.

(4) An inspector may examine on oath any person who he considers is or may be able to give information concerning any such contravention, and may administer an oath accordingly.

(5) The inspectors shall make such interim reports to the Secretary of State as they think fit or he may direct and on the conclusion of the investigation they shall make a final report to him.

(6) A statement made by a person in compliance with a requirement imposed by virtue of this section may be used in evidence against him.

(7) A person shall not under this section be required to disclose any information or produce any document which he would be entitled to refuse to disclose or produce on grounds of legal professional privilege in proceedings in the High Court or on grounds of confidentiality as between client and professional legal adviser in proceedings in the Court of Session.

PART VII   (8) Nothing in this section shall require a person carrying on the business of banking to disclose any information or produce any document relating to the affairs of a customer unless—

(a) the customer is a person who the inspectors have reason to believe may be able to give information concerning a suspected contravention ; and

(b) the Secretary of State is satisfied that the disclosure or production is necessary for the purposes of the investigation.

(9) Where a person claims a lien on a document its production under this section shall be without prejudice to his lien.

(10) In this section "document" includes information recorded in any form ; and in relation to information recorded otherwise than in legible form references to its production include references to producing a copy of the information in legible form.

Penalties for failure to co-operate with s. 177 investigations.

178.—(1) If any person—

(a) refuses to comply with any request under subsection (3) of section 177 above ; or

(b) refuses to answer any question put to him by the inspectors appointed under that section with respect to any matter relevant for establishing whether or not any suspected contravention has occurred,

the inspectors may certify that fact in writing to the court and the court may inquire into the case.

(2) If, after hearing any witness who may be produced against or on behalf of the alleged offender and any statement which may be offered in defence, the court is satisfied that he did without reasonable excuse refuse to comply with such a request or answer any such question, the court may—

(a) punish him in like manner as if he had been guilty of contempt of the court ; or

(b) direct that the Secretary of State may exercise his powers under this section in respect of him ;

and the court may give a direction under paragraph (b) above notwithstanding that the offender is not within the jurisdiction of the court if the court is satisfied that he was notified of his right to appear before the court and of the powers available under this section.

(3) Where the court gives a direction under subsection (2)(b) above in respect of an authorised person the Secretary of State may serve a notice on him—

(*a*) cancelling any authorisation of his to carry on invest-
     ment business after the expiry of a specified period
     after the service of the notice ;

(*b*) disqualifying him from becoming authorised to carry on
     investment business after the expiry of a specified
     period ;

(*c*) restricting any authorisation of his in respect of invest-
     ment business during a specified period to the perfor-
     mance of contracts entered into before the notice comes
     into force ;

(*d*) prohibiting him from entering into transactions of a
     specified kind or entering into them except in specified
     circumstances or to a specified extent ;

(*e*) prohibiting him from soliciting business from persons of
     a specified kind or otherwise than from such persons ;
     or

(*f*) prohibiting him from carrying on business in a specified
     manner or otherwise than in a specified manner.

(4) The period mentioned in paragraphs (*a*) and (*c*) of subsection (3) above shall be such period as appears to the Secretary
of State reasonable to enable the person on whom the notice is
served to complete the performance of any contracts entered into
before the notice comes into force and to terminate such of
them as are of a continuing nature.

(5) Where the court gives a direction under subsection (2)(*b*)
above in the case of an unauthorised person the Secretary of
State may direct that any authorised person who knowingly
transacts investment business of a specified kind, or in specified
circumstances or to a specified extent, with or on behalf of that
unauthorised person shall be treated as having contravened rules
made under Chapter V of Part I of this Act or, in the case of a
person who is an authorised person by virtue of his membership
of a recognised self-regulating organisation or certification by a
recognised professional body, the rules of that organisation or
body.

(6) A person shall not be treated for the purposes of subsection
(2) above as having a reasonable excuse for refusing to comply
with a request or answer a question in a case where the contravention or suspected contravention being investigated relates to
dealing by him on the instructions or for the account of another
person, by reason that at the time of the refusal—

(*a*) he did not know the identity of that other person ; or

(*b*) he was subject to the law of a country or territory out-
     side the United Kingdom which prohibited him from
     disclosing information relating to the dealing without

the consent of that other person, if he might have obtained that consent or obtained exemption from that law.

(7) A notice served on a person under subsection (3) above may be revoked at any time by the Secretary of State by serving a revocation notice on him ; and the Secretary of State shall revoke such a notice if it appears to him that he has agreed to comply with the relevant request or answer the relevant question.

(8) The revocation of such a notice as is mentioned in subsection (3)(*a*) above shall not have the effect of reviving the authorisation cancelled by the notice except where the person would (apart from the notice) at the time of the revocation be an authorised person by virtue of his membership of a recognised self-regulating organisation or certification by a recognised professional body ; but nothing in this subsection shall be construed as preventing any person who has been subject to such a notice from again becoming authorised after the revocation of the notice.

(9) If it appears to the Secretary of State—

(*a*) that a person on whom he serves a notice under subsection (3) above is an authorised person by virtue of an authorisation granted by a designated agency or by virtue of membership of a recognised self-regulating organisation or certification by a recognised professional body ; or

(*b*) that a person on whom he serves a revocation notice under subsection (7) above was such an authorised person at the time that the notice which is being revoked was served,

he shall serve a copy of the notice on that agency, organisation or body.

(10) The functions to which section 114 above applies shall include the functions of the Secretary of State under this section but any transfer of those functions shall be subject to a reservation that they are to be exercisable by him concurrently with the designated agency and so as to be exercisable by the agency subject to such conditions or restrictions as the Secretary of State may from time to time impose.

PART VIII

RESTRICTIONS ON DISCLOSURE OF INFORMATION

Restrictions
on disclosure
of
information.

179.—(1) Subject to section 180 below, information which is restricted information for the purposes of this section and relates to the business or other affairs of any person shall not be disclosed by a person mentioned in subsection (3) below (" the

primary recipient ") or any person obtaining the information PART VIII
directly or indirectly from him without the consent of the person
from whom the primary recipient obtained the information and
if different, the person to whom it relates.

(2) Subject to subsection (4) below, information is restricted
information for the purposees of this section if it was obtained
by the primary recipient for the purposes of, or in the discharge
of his functions under, this Act or any rules or regulations made
under this Act (whether or not by virtue of any requirement to
supply it made under those provisions).

(3) The persons mentioned in subsection (1) above are—
   (*a*) the Secretary of State ;
   (*b*) any designated agency, transferee body or body ad-
        ministering a scheme under section 54 above ;
   (*c*) the Director General of Fair Trading ;
   (*d*) the Chief Registrar of friendly societies ;
   (*e*) the Registrar of Friendly Societies for Northern Ireland ;
   (*f*) the Bank of England ;
   (*g*) any member of the Tribunal ;
   (*h*) any person appointed or authorised to exercise any
        powers under section 94, 106 or 177 above ; and
   (*i*) any officer or servant of any such person.

(4) Information shall not be treated as restricted information
for the purposes of this section if it has been made available to
the public by virtue of being disclosed in any circumstances
in which or for any purpose for which disclosure is not precluded by this section.

(5) Subject to section 180 below, information obtained by the
competent authority in the exercise of its functions under Part
IV of this Act or received by it pursuant to a Community obligation from any authority exercising corresponding functions in
another member State shall not be disclosed without the consent
of the person from whom the competent authority obtained the
information and, if different, the person to whom it relates.

(6) Any person who contravenes this section shall be guilty of
an offence and liable—
   (*a*) on conviction on indictment, to imprisonment for a
        term not exceeding two years or to a fine or to both ;
   (*b*) on summary conviction, to imprisonment for a term not
        exceeding three months or to a fine not exceeding the
        statutory maximum or to both.

PART VIII
Exceptions
from
restrictions on
disclosure.

180.—(1) Section 179 above shall not preclude the disclosure of information—

(a) with a view to the institution of or otherwise for the purposes of criminal proceedings ;

(b) with a view to the institution of or otherwise for the purposes of any civil proceedings arising under or by virtue of this Act or proceedings before the Tribunal ;

(c) for the purpose of enabling or assisting the Secretary of State to exercise any powers conferred on him by this Act or by the enactments relating to companies insurance companies or insolvency or for the purpose of enabling or assisting any inspector appointed by him under the enactments relating to companies to discharge his functions ;

(d) for the purpose of enabling or assisting the Department of Economic Development for Northern Ireland to exercise any powers conferred on it by the enactments relating to companies or insolvency or for the purpose of enabling or assisting any inspector appointed by it under the enactments relating to companies to discharge his functions ;

(e) for the purpose of enabling or assisting a designated agency or transferee body or the competent authority to discharge its functions under this Act or of enabling or assisting the body administering a scheme under section 54 above to discharge its functions under the scheme ;

1979 c. 37.

(f) for the purpose of enabling or assisting the Bank of England to discharge its functions under the Banking Act 1979 or any other functions ;

(g) for the purpose of enabling or assisting the Deposit Protection Board to discharge its functions under that Act ;

(h) for the purpose of enabling or assisting the Chief Registrar of friendly societies or the Registrar of Friendly Societies for Northern Ireland to discharge his functions under this Act or under the enactments relating to friendly societies or building societies ;

(i) for the purpose of enabling or assisting the Industrial Assurance Commissioner or the Industrial Assurance Commissioner for Northern Ireland to discharge his functions under the enactments relating to industrial assurance ;

1977 c. 46.

(j) for the purpose of enabling or assisting the Insurance Brokers Registration Council to discharge its functions under the Insurance Brokers (Registration) Act 1977 ;

(*k*) for the purpose of enabling or assisting an official receiver to discharge his functions under the enactments
relating to insolvency or for the purpose of enabling or
assisting a body which is for the time being a recognised professional body for the purposes of section 391
of the Insolvency Act 1986 to discharge its functions   1986 c. 45.
as such ;

(*l*) for the purpose of enabling or assisting the Building
Societies Commission to discharge its functions under
the Building Societies Act 1986 ;   1986 c. 53.

(*m*) for the purpose of enabling or assisting the Director
General of Fair Trading to discharge his functions
under this Act ;

(*n*) for the purpose of enabling or assisting a recognised
self-regulating organisation, recognised investment
exchange, recognised professional body, or recognised
clearing house to discharge its functions as such ;

(*o*) with a view to the institution of, or otherwise for the
purposes of, any disciplinary proceedings relating to the
exercise by a solicitor, auditor, accountant, valuer or
actuary of his professional duties ;

(*p*) for the purpose of enabling or assisting any person
appointed or authorised to exercise any powers under
section 94, 106 or 177 above to discharge his functions ;

(*q*) for the purpose of enabling or assisting an auditor of
an authorised person or a person approved under section 108 above to discharge his functions ;

(*r*) if the information is or has been available to the public
from other sources ;

(*s*) in a summary or collection of information framed in
such a way as not to enable the identity of any person
to whom the information relates to be ascertained ; or

(*t*) in pursuance of any Community obligation.

(2) Section 179 above shall not preclude the disclosure of
information to the Secretary of State or to the Treasury if the
disclosure is made in the interests of investors or in the public
interest.

(3) Subject to subsection (4) below, section 179 above shall
not preclude the disclosure of information for the purpose of
enabling or assisting any public or other authority for the time
being designated for the purposes of this section by an order
made by the Secretary of State to discharge any functions which
are specified in the order.

(4) An order under subsection (3) above designating an authority for the purposes of that subsection may—

    (a) impose conditions subject to which the disclosure of information is permitted by that subsection ; and

    (b) otherwise restrict the circumstances in which that subsection permits disclosure.

(5) Section 179 above shall not preclude the disclosure—

    (a) of any information contained in an unpublished report of the Tribunal which has been made available to any person under this Act, by the person to whom it was made available or by any person obtaining the information directly or indirectly from him ;

    (b) of any information contained in any notice or copy of a notice served under this Act, notice of the contents of which has not been given to the public, by the person on whom it was served or any person obtaining the information directly or indirectly from him ;

    (c) of any information contained in the register kept under section 102 above by virtue of subsection (1)(e) of that section, by a person who has inspected the register under section 103(2) or (3) above or any person obtaining the information directly or indirectly from him.

(6) Section 179 above shall not preclude the disclosure of information for the purpose of enabling or assisting an authority in a country or territory outside the United Kingdom to exercise functions corresponding to those of the Secretary of State under this Act or the Insurance Companies Act 1982 or to those of the Bank of England under the Banking Act 1979 or to those of the competent authority under this Act or any other functions in connection with rules of law corresponding to the provisions of the Company Securities (Insider Dealing) Act 1985 or Part VII of this Act.

1982 c. 50.
1979 c. 37.

1985 c. 8.

(7) Section 179 above shall not preclude the disclosure of information by the Director General of Fair Trading or any officer or servant of his or any person obtaining the information directly or indirectly from the Director or any such officer or servant if the information was obtained by the Director or any such officer or servant for the purposes of or in the discharge of his functions under this Act (whether or not he was the primary recipient of the information within the meaning of section 179 above) and the disclosure is made—

    (a) for the purpose of enabling or assisting the Director, the Secretary of State or any other Minister, the Monopolies and Mergers Commission or any Northern Ireland department to discharge any function conferred

on him or them by the Fair Trading Act 1973 (other PART VIII
than Part II or III of that Act), the Restrictive Trade 1973 c. 41.
Practices Act 1976 or the Competition Act 1980 ; or 1976 c. 34.

(*b*) for the purposes of any civil proceedings under any of 1980 c. 21.
those provisions ;

and information shall not be treated as restricted information
for the purposes of section 179 above if it has been made available to the public by virtue of this subsection.

(8) The Secretary of State may by order modify the application of any provision of this section so as—

(*a*) to prevent the disclosure by virtue of that provision ; or

(*b*) to restrict the extent to which disclosure is permitted by
virtue of that provision,

of information received by a person specified in the order
pursuant to a Community obligation from a person exercising
functions in relation to a collective investment scheme who is
also so specified.

(9) An order under subsection (3) or (8) above shall be subject
to annulment in pursuance of a resolution of either House of
Parliament.

181.—(1) If it appears to the Secretary of State to be in the Directions
public interest to do so, he may give a direction prohibiting the restricting
disclosure to any person in a country or territory outside the disclosure of
United Kingdom which is specified in the direction, or to such overseas.
persons in such a country or territory as may be so specified,
of such information to which this section applies as may be so
specified.

(2) A direction under subsection (1) above—

(*a*) may prohibit disclosure of the information to which it
applies by all persons or only by such persons or classes
of person as may be specified in it ; and

(*b*) may prohibit such disclosure absolutely or in such cases
or subject to such conditions as to consent or otherwise
as may be specified in it ;

and a direction prohibiting disclosure by all persons shall be
published by the Secretary of State in such manner as appears to
him to be appropriate.

(3) This section applies to any information relating to the
business or other affairs of any person which was obtained
(whether or not by virtue of any requirement to supply it) directly
or indirectly—

(*a*) by a designated agency, a transferee body, the competent authority or any person appointed or authorised to

exercise any powers under section 94, 106 or 177 above (or any officer or servant of any such body or person) for the purposes or in the discharge of any functions of that body or person under this Act or any rules or regulations made under this Act or of any monitoring agency functions ; or

(b) by a recognised self-regulating organisation, a recognised professional body, a recognised investment exchange or a recognised clearing house other than an overseas investment exchange or clearing house (or any officer or servant of such an organisation, body, investment exchange or clearing house) for the purposes or in the discharge of any of its functions as such or of any monitoring agency functions.

(4) In subsection (3) above " monitoring agency functions " means any functions exercisable on behalf of another body by virtue of arrangements made pursuant to paragraph 4(2) of Schedule 2, paragraph 4(6) of Schedule 3, paragraph 3(2) of Schedule 4 or paragraph 3(2) of Schedule 7 to this Act or of such arrangements as are mentioned in section 39(4)(b) above.

(5) A direction under this section shall not prohibit the disclosure by any person other than a person mentioned in subsection (3) above of—

(a) information relating only to the affairs of that person ; or

(b) information obtained by that person otherwise than directly or indirectly from a person mentioned in subsection (3) above.

(6) A direction under this section shall not prohibit the disclosure of information in pursuance of any Community obligation.

(7) A person who knowingly discloses information in contravention of a direction under this section shall be guilty of an offence and liable—

(a) on conviction on indictment, to imprisonment for a term not exceeding two years or to a fine or to both ;

(b) on summary conviction, to imprisonment for a term not exceeding three months or to a fine not exceeding the statutory maximum or to both.

(8) A person shall not be guilty of an offence under this section by virtue of anything done or omitted to be done by him outside the United Kingdom unless he is a British citizen, a British Dependent Territories citizen, a British Overseas citizen or a body corporate incorporated in the United Kingdom.

182. The enactments mentioned in Schedule 13 to this Act shall have effect with the amendments there specified (which relate to the circumstances in which information obtained under those enactments may be disclosed).

PART VIII
Disclosure of information under enactments relating to fair trading, banking, insurance and companies.

PART IX

RECIPROCITY

183.—(1) If it appears to the Secretary of State or the Treasury that by reason of—

Reciprocal facilities for financial business.

(a) the law of any country outside the United Kingdom ; or

(b) any action taken by or the practices of the government or any other authority or body in that country,

persons connected with the United Kingdom are unable to carry on investment, insurance or banking business in, or in relation to, that country on terms as favourable as those on which persons connected with that country are able to carry on any such business in, or in relation to, the United Kingdom, the Secretary of State or, as the case may be, the Treasury may serve a notice under this subsection on any person connected with that country who is carrying on or appears to them to intend to carry on any such business in, or in relation to, the United Kingdom.

(2) No notice shall be served under subsection (1) above unless the Secretary of State or, as the case may be, the Treasury consider it in the national interest to serve it ; and before doing so the Secretary of State or, as the case may be, the Treasury shall so far as they consider expedient consult such body or bodies as appear to them to represent the interests of persons likely to be affected.

(3) A notice under subsection (1) above shall state the grounds on which it is given (identifying the country in relation to which those grounds are considered to exist) ; and any such notice shall come into force on such date as may be specified in it.

(4) For the purposes of this section a person is connected with a country if it appears to the Secretary of State or, as the case may be, the Treasury—

(a) in the case of an individual, that he is a national of or resident in that country or carries on investment, insurance or banking business from a principal place of business there ;

(b) in the case of a body corporate, that it is incorporated or has a principal place of business in that country or is controlled by a person or persons connected with that country ;

(*c*) in the case of a partnership, that it has a principal place of business in that country or that any partner is connected with that country ;

(*d*) in the case of an unincorporated association which is not a partnership, that it is formed under the law of that country, has a principal place of business there or is controlled by a person or persons connected with that country.

(5) In this section " country " includes any territory or part of a country or territory ; and where it appears to the Secretary of State or, as the case may be, the Treasury that there are such grounds as are mentioned in subsection (1) above in the case of any part of a country or territory their powers under that subsection shall also be exercisable in respect of any person who is connected with that country or territory or any other part of it.

Investment and insurance business.

184.—(1) A notice under section 183 above relating to the carrying on of investment business or insurance business shall be served by the Secretary of State and such a notice may be a disqualification notice, a restriction notice or a partial restriction notice and may relate to the carrying on of business of both kinds.

(2) A disqualification notice as respects investment business or insurance business shall have the effect of—

(*a*) cancelling any authorisation of the person concerned to carry on that business after the expiry of such period after the service of the notice as may be specified in it ;

(*b*) disqualifying him from becoming authorised to carry on that business after the expiry of that period ; and

(*c*) restricting any authorisation of the person concerned in respect of that business during that period to the performance of contracts entered into before the notice comes into force ;

and the period specified in such a notice shall be such period as appears to the Secretary of State to be reasonable to enable the person on whom it is served to complete the performance of those contracts and to terminate such of them as are of a continuing nature.

(3) A restriction notice as respects investment business or insurance business shall have the effect of restricting any authorisation of the person concerned in respect of that business to the performance of contracts entered into before the notice comes into force.

(4) A partial restriction notice as respects investment business   PART IX
may prohibit the person concerned from—

    (*a*) entering into transactions of any specified kind or enter-
ing into them except in specified circumstances or to
a specified extent ;

    (*b*) soliciting business from persons of a specified kind or
otherwise than from such persons ;

    (*c*) carrying on business in a specified manner or otherwise
than in a specified manner.

(5) A partial restriction notice as respects insurance business
may direct that the person concerned shall cease to be authorised under section 3 or 4 of the Insurance Companies Act 1982   1982 c. 50.
to effect contracts of insurance of any description specified in
the notice.

(6) If it appears to the Secretary of State that a person on
whom he serves a notice under section 183 above as respects
investment business is an authorised person by virtue of an
authorisation granted by a designated agency or by virtue of
membership of a recognised self-regulating organisation or certification by a recognised professional body he shall serve a copy
of the notice on that agency, organisation or body.

(7) If it appears to the Secretary of State—

    (*a*) that any person on whom a partial restriction notice has
been served by him has contravened any provision of
that notice or, in the case of a notice under subsection
(5) above, effected a contract of insurance of a description specified in the notice ; and

    (*b*) that any such grounds as are mentioned in subsection
(1) of section 183 above still exist in the case of the
country concerned,

he may serve a disqualification notice or a restriction notice on
him under that section.

(8) Sections 28, 33, 60, 61 and 62 above shall have effect in
relation to a contravention of such a notice as is mentioned in
subsection (4) above as they have effect in relation to any such
contravention as is mentioned in those sections.

185.—(1) A notice under section 183 above relating to the Banking
carrying on of a deposit-taking business as a recognised bank business.
or licensed institution within the meaning of the Banking Act 1979 c. 37.
1979 shall be served by the Treasury and may be either a disqualification notice or a partial restriction notice.

(2) A disqualification notice relating to such business shall
have the effect of—

    (*a*) cancelling any recognition or licence granted to the
person concerned under the Banking Act 1979 ; and

(b) disqualifying him from becoming a recognised bank or licensed institution within the meaning of that Act.

(3) A partial restriction notice relating to such business may—

(a) prohibit the person concerned from dealing with or disposing of his assets in any manner specified in the direction ;

(b) impose limitations on the acceptance by him of deposits ;

(c) prohibit him from soliciting deposits either generally or from persons who are not already depositors ;

(d) prohibit him from entering into any other transaction or class of transactions ;

(e) require him to take certain steps, to pursue or refrain from pursuing a particular course of activities or to restrict the scope of his business in a particular way.

(4) The Treasury shall serve on the Bank of England a copy of any notice served by them under section 183 above.

(5) Any person who contravenes any provision of a partial restriction notice served on him by the Treasury under this section shall be guilty of an offence and liable—

(a) on conviction on indictment, to a fine ;

(b) on summary conviction, to a fine not exceeding the statutory maximum.

(6) Any such contravention shall be actionable at the suit of a person who suffers loss as a result of the contravention subject to the defences and other incidents applying to actions for breach of statutory duty, but no such contravention shall invalidate any transaction.

1979 c. 37.   (7) At the end of subsection (1) of section 8 of the Banking Act 1979 (power to give directions in connection with termination of deposit-taking authority) there shall be inserted—

" (d) at any time after a disqualification notice has been served on the institution by the Treasury under section 183 of the Financial Services Act 1986.".

Variation and revocation of notices.   **186.**—(1) The Secretary of State or the Treasury may vary a partial restriction notice served under section 183 above by a notice in writing served on the person concerned ; and any such notice shall come into force on such date as is specified in the notice.

(2) A notice under section 183 above may be revoked at any time by the Secretary of State or, as the case may be, the Treasury by serving a revocation notice on the person concerned ;

and the Secretary of State or, as the case may be, the Treasury shall revoke a notice if it appears to them that there are no longer any such grounds as are mentioned in subsection (1) of that section in the case of the country concerned.

(3) The revocation of a disqualification notice as respects investment business or insurance business shall not have the effect of reviving the authorisation which was cancelled by the notice except where the notice relates to investment business and the person concerned would (apart from the disqualification notice) at the time of the revocation be an authorised person as respects the investment business in question by virtue of his membership of a recognised self-regulating organisation or certification by a recognised professional body.

(4) The revocation of a disqualification notice as respects banking business shall not have the effect of reviving the recognition or licence which was cancelled by the notice.

(5) Nothing in subsection (3) or (4) above shall be construed as preventing any person who has been subject to a disqualification notice as respects any business from again becoming authorised or, as the case may be, becoming a recognised bank or licensed institution within the meaning of the Banking Act 1979 after the revocation of the notice. 1979 c. 37.

(6) If it appears to the Secretary of State that a person on whom he serves a notice under this section as respects investment business was an authorised person by virtue of an authorisation granted by a designated agency or by virtue of membership of a recognised self-regulating organisation or certification by a recognised professional body at the time that the notice which is being varied or revoked was served, he shall serve a copy of the notice on that agency, organisation or body.

(7) The Treasury shall serve on the Bank of England a copy of any notice served by them under this section.

PART X

MISCELLANEOUS AND SUPPLEMENTARY

187.—(1) Neither a recognised self-regulating organisation nor Exemption any of its officers or servants or members of its governing body from liability shall be liable in damages for anything done or omitted in the for damages. discharge or purported discharge of any functions to which this subsection applies unless the act or omission is shown to have been in bad faith.

F 2

(2) The functions to which subsection (1) above applies are the functions of the organisation so far as relating to, or to matters arising out of—

>   (a) the rules, practices, powers and arrangements of the organisation to which the requirements in paragraphs 1 to 6 of Schedule 2 to this Act apply ;

>   (b) the obligations with which paragraph 7 of that Schedule requires the organisation to comply ;

>   (c) any guidance issued by the organisation ;

>   (d) the powers of the organisation under section 53(2), 64(4), 72(5), 73(5) or 105(2)(a) above ; or

>   (e) the obligations to which the organisation is subject by virtue of this Act.

(3) No designated agency or transferee body nor any member, officer or servant of a designated agency or transferee body shall be liable in damages for anything done or omitted in the discharge or purported discharge of the functions exercisable by the agency by virtue of a delegation order or, as the case may be, the functions exercisable by the body by virtue of a transfer order unless the act or omission is shown to have been in bad faith.

(4) Neither the competent authority nor any member, officer, or servant of that authority shall be liable in damages for anything done or omitted in the discharge or purported discharge of any functions of the authority under Part IV of this Act unless the act or omission is shown to have been in bad faith.

(5) The functions to which subsections (1) and (3) above apply also include any functions exercisable by a recognised self-regulating organisation, designated agency or transferee body on behalf of another body by virtue of arrangements made pursuant to paragraph 4(2) of Schedule 2, paragraph 4(6) of Schedule 3, paragraph 3(2) of Schedule 4 or paragraph 3(2) of Schedule 7 to this Act or of such arrangements as are mentioned in section 39(4)(b) above.

(6) A recognised professional body may make it a condition of any certificate issued by it for the purposes of Part I of this Act that neither the body nor any of its officers or servants or members of its governing body is to be liable in damages for anything done or omitted in the discharge or purported discharge of any functions to which this subsection applies unless the act or omission is shown to have been in bad faith.

(7) The functions to which subsection (6) above applies are the functions of the body so far as relating to, or to matters arising out of—

>   (a) the rules, practices and arrangements of the body to which the requirements in paragraphs 2 to 5 of Schedule 3 to this Act apply ;

(b) the obligations with which paragraph 6 of that Schedule
requires the body to comply ;

(c) any guidance issued by the body in respect of any matters dealt with by such rules as are mentioned in paragraph (a) above ;

(d) the powers of the body under the provisions mentioned
in subsection (2)(d) above or under section 54(3) above ;
or

(e) the obligations to which the body is subject by virtue of
this Act.

PART X

188.—(1) Proceedings arising out of any act or omission (or
proposed act or omission) of a designated agency, transferee
body or the competent authority in the discharge or purported
discharge of any of its functions under this Act may be brought
in the High Court or the Court of Session.

Jurisdiction
as respects
actions
concerning
designated
agency etc.

(2) At the end of Schedule 5 to the Civil Jurisdiction and
Judgments Act 1982 (exclusion of certain proceedings from the
provisions of Schedule 4 to that Act which determine whether
the courts in each part of the United Kingdom have jurisdiction
in proceedings) there shall be inserted—

1982 c. 27.

" *Proceedings concerning financial services agencies*

10. Such proceedings as are mentioned in section 188 of
the Financial Services Act 1986.".

189.—(1) The Rehabilitation of Offenders Act 1974 shall
have effect subject to the provisions of this section in cases where
the spent conviction is for—

Restriction of
Rehabilitation
of Offenders
Act 1974.
1974 c. 53.

(a) an offence involving fraud or other dishonesty ; or

(b) an offence under legislation (whether or not of the
United Kingdom) relating to companies (including
insider dealing), building societies, industrial and provident societies, credit unions, friendly societies, insurance, banking or other financial services, insolvency,
consumer credit or consumer protection.

(2) Nothing in section 4(1) (restriction on evidence as to spent
convictions in proceedings) shall prevent the determination in
any proceedings specified in Part I of Schedule 14 to this Act of
any issue, or prevent the admission or requirement in any such
proceedings of any evidence, relating to a person's previous
convictions for any such offence as is mentioned in subsection
(1) above or to circumstances ancillary thereto.

(3) A conviction for any such offence as is mentioned in subsection (1) above shall not be regarded as spent for the purposes

PART X   of section 4(2) (questions relating to an individual's previous convictions) if—

(*a*) the question is put by or on behalf of a person specified in the first column of Part II of that Schedule and relates to an individual (whether or not the person questioned) specified in relation to the person putting the question in the second column of that Part ; and

(*b*) the person questioned is informed when the question is put that by virtue of this section convictions for any such offence are to be disclosed.

(4) Section 4(3)(*b*) (spent conviction not to be ground for excluding person from office, occupation etc.) shall not prevent a person specified in the first column of Part III of that Schedule from taking such action as is specified in relation to that person in the second column of that Part by reason, or partly by reason, of a spent conviction for any such offence as is mentioned in subsection (1) above of an individual who is—

(*a*) the person in respect of whom the action is taken ;

(*b*) as respects action within paragraph 1 or 4 of that Part, an associate of that person ; or

(*c*) as respects action within paragraph 1 of that Part consisting of a decision to refuse or revoke an order declaring a collective investment scheme to be an authorised unit trust scheme or a recognised scheme, the operator or trustee of the scheme or an associate of his,

or of any circumstances ancillary to such a conviction or of a failure (whether or not by that individual) to disclose such a conviction or any such circumstances.

(5) Parts I, II and III of that Schedule shall have effect subject to Part IV.

(6) In this section and that Schedule " associate " means—

(*a*) in relation to a body corporate, a director, manager or controller ;

(*b*) in relation to a partnership, a partner or manager ;

(*c*) in relation to a registered friendly society, a trustee, manager or member of the committee of the society ;

(*d*) in relation to an unincorporated association, a member of its governing body or an officer, manager or controller ;

(*e*) in relation to an individual, a manager.

(7) This section and that Schedule shall apply to Northern Ireland with the substitution for the references to the said Act of 1974 and section 4(1), (2) and (3)(*b*) of that Act of references to the Rehabilitation of Offenders (Northern Ireland) Order 1978 and Article 5(1), (2) and (3)(*b*) of that Order.

1978/1908
(N.I.27).

190. An order under section 30 of the Data Protection Act
1984 (exemption from subject access provisions of data held for
the purpose of discharging designated functions conferred by or
under enactments relating to the regulation of financial services
etc.) may designate for the purposes of that section as if they were
functions conferred by or under such an enactment as is there
mentioned—

> (a) any functions of a recognised self-regulating organisa-
> tion in connection with the admission or expulsion
> of members, the suspension of a person's membership
> or the supervision or regulation of persons carrying on
> investment business by virtue of membership of the
> organisation ;
>
> (b) any functions of a recognised professional body in con-
> nection with the issue of certificates for the purposes of
> Part I of this Act, the withdrawal or suspension of
> such certificates or the supervision or regulation of per-
> sons carrying on investment business by virtue of cer-
> tification by that body ;
>
> (c) any functions of a recognised self-regulating organisa-
> tion for friendly societies in connection with the super-
> vision or regulation of its member societies.

191.—(1) Subject to the provisions of this section, a person
who apart from this section would not be regarded as carrying
on investment business shall be treated as doing so if he engages
in the activity of management falling within paragraph 14 of
Schedule 1 to this Act in a case where the assets referred to in
that paragraph are held for the purposes of an occupational
pension scheme.

(2) Subsection (1) above does not apply where all decisions,
or all day to day decisions, in the carrying on of that activity
so far as relating to assets which are investments are taken on
behalf of the person concerned by—

> (a) an authorised person ;
>
> (b) an exempted person who in doing so is acting in the
> course of the business in respect of which he is ex-
> empt ; or
>
> (c) a person who does not require authorisation to manage
> the assets by virtue of Part IV of Schedule 1 to this
> Act.

(3) The Secretary of State may by order direct that a person
of such description as is specified in the order shall not by virtue
of this section be treated as carrying on investment business
where the assets are held for the purposes of an occupational
pension scheme of such description as is so specified, being a

F 4

PART X

scheme in the case of which it appears to the Secretary of State that management by an authorised or exempted person is unnecessary having regard to the size of the scheme and the control exercisable over its affairs by the members.

(4) An order under subsection (3) above shall be subject to annulment in pursuance of a resolution of either House of Parliament.

(5) For the purposes of subsection (1) above paragraph 14 of Schedule 1 to this Act shall be construed without reference to paragraph 22 of that Schedule.

International obligations.

192.—(1) If it appears to the Secretary of State—

(a) that any action proposed to be taken by a recognised self-regulating organisation, designated agency, transferee body or competent authority would be incompatible with Community obligations or any other international obligations of the United Kingdom ; or

(b) that any action which that organisation, agency, body or authority has power to take is required for the purpose of implementing any such obligations,

he may direct the organisation, agency, body or authority not to take or, as the case may be, to take the action in question.

(2) Subsection (1) above applies also to an approved exchange within the meaning of Part V of this Act in respect of any action which it proposes to take or has power to take in respect of rules applying to a prospectus by virtue of a direction under section 162(3) above.

(3) A direction under this section may include such supplementary or incidental requirements as the Secretary of State thinks necessary or expedient.

(4) Where the function of making or revoking a recognition order in respect of a self-regulating organisation is exercisable by a designated agency any direction under subsection (1) above in respect of that organisation shall be a direction requiring the agency to give the organisation such a direction as is specified in the direction given by the Secretary of State.

(5) Any direction under this section shall, on the application of the person by whom it was given, be enforceable by mandamus or, in Scotland, by an order for specific performance under section 91 of the Court of Session Act 1868.

1868 c. 100.

Exemption from Banking Act 1979.

1979 c. 37.

193.—(1) Section 1(1) of the Banking Act 1979 (control of deposit-taking) shall not apply to the acceptance of a deposit by an authorised or exempted person in the course or for the purpose of engaging in any activity falling within paragraph 12 of

Schedule 1 to this Act with or on behalf of the person by whom
or on whose behalf the deposit is made or any activity falling
within paragraph 13, 14 or 16 of that Schedule on behalf of
that person.

(2) Subsection (1) above applies to an exempted person only if
the activity is one in respect of which he is exempt; and for the
purposes of that subsection the paragraphs of Schedule 1 there
mentioned shall be construed without reference to Parts III and
IV of that Schedule.

(3) This section is without prejudice to any exemption from the
said Act of 1979 which applies to an authorised or exempted
person apart from this section.

194.—(1) In section 5 of the Stock Exchange (Completion of   Transfers
Bargains) Act 1976 (protection of trustees etc. in case of transfer   to or from
of shares etc. to or from a stock exchange nominee)—   recognised
clearing
    (a) for the words "a stock exchange nominee", in the first   houses.
       place where they occur, there shall be substituted the   1976 c. 47.
       words "a recognised clearing house or a nominee of a
       recognised clearing house or of a recognised invest-
       ment exchange";

    (b) for those words in the second place where they occur
       there shall be substituted the words "such a clearing
       house or nominee";

    (c) at the end there shall be added the words "; but no per-
       son shall be a nominee for the purposes of this section
       unless he is a person designated for the purposes of this
       section in the rules of the recognised investment ex-
       change in question".

(2) The provisions of that section as amended by subsection
(1) above shall become subsection (1) of that section and after
that subsection there shall be inserted—

    " (2) In this section " a recognised clearing house " means
    a recognised clearing house within the meaning of the
    Financial Services Act 1986 acting in relation to a recog-
    nised investment exchange within the meaning of that
    Act and " a recognised investment exchange " has the same
    meaning as in that Act."

(3) In Article 7 of the Stock Exchange (Completion of Bar-   S.I. 1977/1254
gains) (Northern Ireland) Order 1977 (protection of trustees etc.   (N.I.21).
in case of transfer of shares etc. to or from a stock exchange
nominee)—

    (a) for the words "a stock exchange nominee", in the first
       place where they occur, there shall be substituted the
       words "a recognised clearing house or a nominee of

a recognised clearing house or of a recognised investment exchange ";

> (b) for those words in the second place where they occur there shall be substituted the words " such a clearing house or nominee ";
>
> (c) at the end there shall be added the words " ; but no person shall be a nominee for the purposes of this Article unless he is a person designated for the purposes of this Article in the rules of the recognised investment exchange in question ".

(4) The provisions of that Article as amended by subsection (3) above shall become paragraph (1) of that Article and after that paragraph there shall be inserted—

> " (2) In this Article " a recognised clearing house " means a recognised clearing house within the meaning of the Financial Services Act 1986 acting in relation to a recognised investment exchange within the meaning of that Act and " a recognised investment exchange " has the same meaning as in that Act."

1985 c. 6.   (5) In subsection (4) of section 185 of the Companies Act 1985 (exemption from duty to issue certificates in respect of shares etc. in cases of allotment or transfer to a stock exchange nominee)—

> (a) for the words " a stock exchange nominee " in the first place where they occur there shall be substituted the words " a recognised clearing house or a nominee of a recognised clearing house or of a recognised investment exchange ";
>
> (b) for those words in the second place where they occur there shall be substituted the words " such a clearing house or nominee ";
>
> (c) at the end of the first paragraph in that subsection there shall be inserted the words " ; but no person shall be a nominee for the purposes of this section unless he is a person designated for the purposes of this section in the rules of the recognised investment exchange in question " ; and
>
> (d) for the second paragraph in that subsection there shall be substituted—
>
> > " ' Recognised clearing house ' means a recognised clearing house within the meaning of the Financial Services Act 1986 acting in relation to a recognised investment exchange and ' recognised investment exchange ' has the same meaning as in that Act.".

(6) In paragraph (4) of Article 195 of the Companies (Northern Part X Ireland) Order 1986 (duty to issue certificates in respect of shares S.I. 1986/1032 etc. in cases of allotment or transfer unless it is to a stock ex- (N.I.6). change nominee)—

 (*a*) for the words " a stock exchange nominee " in the first place where they occur there shall be substituted the words " a recognised clearing house or a nominee of a recognised clearing house or of a recognised investment exchange " ;

 (*b*) for those words in the second place where they occur there shall be substituted the words " such a clearing house or nominee " ;

 (*c*) at the end of the first sub-paragraph in that paragraph there shall be inserted the words " ; but no person shall be a nominee for the purposes of this Article unless he is a person designated for the purposes of this Article in the rules of the recognised investment exchange in question " ; and

 (*d*) for the second sub-paragraph in that paragraph there shall be substituted " ' recognised clearing house ' means a recognised clearing house within the meaning of the Financial Services Act 1986 acting in relation to a recognised investment exchange and ' recognised investment exchange ' has the same meaning as in that Act.".

195. As respects debentures which, under the terms of issue, Offers of must be repaid within less than one year of the date of issue— short-dated debentures.

 (*a*) section 79(2) of the Companies Act 1985 (offer of deben- 1985 c. 6. tures of oversea company deemed not to be an offer to the public if made to professional investor) shall apply for the purposes of Chapter I of Part III of that Act as well as for those of Chapter II of that Part ; and

 (*b*) Article 89(2) of the Companies (Northern Ireland) Order S.I. 1986/1032 1986 (corresponding provisions for Northern Ireland) (N.I.6). shall apply for the purposes of Chapter I of Part IV of that Order as well as for those of Chapter II of that Part.

196.—(1) Section 153 of the Companies Act 1985 (transactions Financial not prohibited by section 151) shall be amended as follows. assistance for employees' share schemes.

(2) After subsection (4)(*b*) there shall be inserted—

" (*bb*) without prejudice to paragraph (*b*), the provision 1985 c. 6. of financial assistance by a company or any of its subsidiaries for the purposes of or in connection with anything done by the company (or a company connected with it) for the purpose of enabling or facilitating transactions in shares in the first-mentioned company between, and involving the acquisition of beneficial ownership of those shares by, any of the following persons—

> (i) the bona fide employees or former employees of that company or of another company in the same group ; or
>
> (ii) the wives, husbands, widows, widowers, children or step-children under the age of eighteen of any such employees or former employees.".

(3) After subsection (4) there shall be inserted—

" (5) For the purposes of subsection (4)(*bb*) a company is connected with another company if—

> (*a*) they are in the same group ; or
>
> (*b*) one is entitled, either alone or with any other company in the same group, to exercise or control the exercise of a majority of the voting rights attributable to the share capital which are exercisable in all circumstances at any general meeting of the other company or of its holding company ;

and in this section " group ", in relation to a company, means that company, any other company which is its holding company or subsidiary and any other company which is a subsidiary of that holding company.".

(4) Article 163 of the Companies (Northern Ireland) Order 1986 (transactions not prohibited by Article 161) shall be amended as follows.

(5) After paragraph (4)(*b*) there shall be inserted—

" (*bb*) without prejudice to sub-paragraph (*b*), the provision of financial assistance by a company or any of its subsidiaries for the purposes of or in connection with anything done by the company (or a company connected with it) for the purpose of enabling or facilitating transactions in shares in the first-mentioned company between, and involving the acquisition of beneficial ownership of those shares by, any of the following persons—

> (i) the bona fide employees or former employees of that company or of another company in the same group ; or
>
> (ii) the wives, husbands, widows, widowers, children, step-children or adopted children under the age of eighteen of such employees or former employees."

(6) After paragraph (4) there shall be inserted—

" (5) For the purposes of paragraph (4)(*bb*) a company is connected with another company if—

> (*a*) they are in the same group ; or

> (*b*) one is entitled, either alone or with any other company in the same group, to exercise or control the exercise of a majority of the voting rights attributable to the share capital which are exercisable in all circumstances at any general meeting of the other company or of its holding company ;

and in this Article " group ", in relation to a company, means that company, any other company which is its holding company or subsidiary and any other company which is a subsidiary of that holding company.".

197.—(1) In section 209 of the Companies Act 1985 (interests to be disregarded for purposes of sections 198 to 202)—

> (*a*) in subsection (1)(*f*) after the word " jobber " there shall be inserted the words " or market maker " ;

> (*b*) after subsection (4) there shall be inserted—

> > " (4A) A person is a market maker for the purposes of subsection (1)(*f*) if—

> > > (*a*) he holds himself out at all normal times in compliance with the rules of a recognised investment exchange other than an overseas investment exchange (within the meaning of the Financial Services Act 1986) as willing to buy and sell securities at prices specified by him ; and

> > > (*b*) is recognised as doing so by that investment exchange ;

> > and an interest of such a person in shares is an exempt interest if he carries on business as a market maker in the United Kingdom, is subject to such rules in the carrying on of that business and holds the interest for the purposes of that business.".

(2) In Article 217 of the Companies (Northern Ireland) Order 1986 (interests to be disregarded for purposes of Articles 206 to 210 (disclosure of interests in shares))—

> (*a*) in paragraph (1)(*d*) after the word " jobber " there shall be inserted the words " or market maker " ;

> (*b*) after paragraph (4) there shall be inserted—

> > " (4A) A person is a market maker for the purposes of paragraph (1)(*d*) if—

> > > (*a*) he holds himself out at all normal times in

compliance with the rules of a recognised investment exchange other than an overseas investment exchange (within the meaning of the Financial Services Act 1986) as willing to buy and sell securities at prices specified by him ; and

(b) is recognised as doing so by that investment exchange,

and an interest of such a person in shares is an exempt interest if he carries on business as a market maker in the United Kingdom, is subject to such rules in the carrying on of that business and holds the interest for the purposes of that business.".

Power to petition for winding up etc. on information obtained under Act.

1985 c. 6.

1986 c. 46.

198.—(1) In section 440 of the Companies Act 1985—

(a) after the words " section 437 " there shall be inserted the words " above or section 94 of the Financial Services Act 1986 " ; and

(b) after the words " 448 below " there shall be inserted the words " or section 105 of that Act ".

(2) In section 8 of the Company Directors Disqualification Act 1986—

(a) after the words " the Companies Act " there shall be inserted the words " or section 94 or 177 of the Financial Services Act 1986 " ; and

(b) for the words " that Act " there shall be substituted the words " the Companies Act or section 105 of the Financial Services Act 1986 ".

S.I. 1986/1032 N.I .6).

(3) In Article 433 of the Companies (Northern Ireland) Order 1986—

(a) after the words " Article 430 " there shall be inserted the words " or section 94 of the Financial Services Act 1986 " ; and

(b) after the word " 441 " there shall be inserted the words " or section 105 of that Act ".

Powers of entry.

1985 c. 8.

199.—(1) A justice of the peace may issue a warrant under this section if satisfied on information on oath laid by or on behalf of the Secretary of State that there are reasonable grounds for believing—

(a) that an offence has been committed under section 4, 47, 57, 130, 133 or 171(2) or (3) above or section 1, 2, 4 or 5 of the Company Securities (Insider Dealing) Act 1985 and that there are on any premises docu-

ments relevant to the question whether that offence
has been committed ; or

(*b*) that there are on any premises owned or occupied by a
person whose affairs, or any aspect of whose affairs, are
being investigated under section 105 above documents
whose production has been required under that section
and which have not been produced in compliance with
that requirement ;

but paragraph (*b*) above applies only if the person there
mentioned is an authorised person, a person whose authorisation
has been suspended or who is the subject of a direction under
section 33(1)(*b*) above or an appointed representative of an
authorised person.

(2) A justice of the peace may issue a warrant under this
section if satisfied on information on oath laid by an inspector
appointed under section 94 above that there are reasonable
grounds for believing that there are on any premises owned or
occupied by—

(*a*) the manager, trustee or operator of any scheme the
affairs of which are being investigated under subsection
(1) of that section ; or

(*b*) a manager, trustee or operator whose affairs are being
investigated under that subsection,

any documents whose production has been required under that
section and which have not been produced in compliance with
that requirement.

(3) A warrant under this section shall authorise a constable,
together with any other person named in it and any other
constables—

(*a*) to enter the premises specified in the information, using
such force as is reasonably necessary for the purpose ;

(*b*) to search the premises and take possession of any documents appearing to be such documents as are mentioned in subsection (1)(*a*) or (*b*) or, as the case may
be, in subsection (2) above or to take, in relation to
any such documents, any other steps which may appear
to be necessary for preserving them or preventing
interference with them ;

(*c*) to take copies of any such documents ; and

(*d*) to require any person named in the warrant to provide
an explanation of them or to state where they may be
found.

(4) A warrant under this section shall continue in force until
the end of the period of one month beginning with the day on
which it is issued.

(5) Any documents of which possession is taken under this section may be retained—

(a) for a period of three months ; or

(b) if within that period proceedings to which the documents are relevant are commenced against any person for an offence under this Act or section 1, 2, 4 or 5 of the said Act of 1985, until the conclusion of those proceedings.

(6) Any person who obstructs the exercise of any rights conferred by a warrant issued under this section or fails without reasonable excuse to comply with any requirement imposed in accordance with subsection (3)(d) above shall be guilty of an offence and liable—

(a) on conviction on indictment, to a fine ;

(b) on summary conviction, to a fine not exceeding the statutory maximum.

(7) The functions to which section 114 above applies shall include the functions of the Secretary of State under this section ; but if any of those functions are transferred under that section the transfer may be subject to a reservation that they are to be exercisable by the Secretary of State concurrently with the designated agency and, in the case of functions exercisable by virtue of subsection (1)(a) above, so as to be exercisable by the agency subject to such conditions or restrictions as the Secretary of State may from time to time impose.

(8) In the application of this section to Scotland the references to a justice of the peace shall include references to a sheriff and for references to the laying of information on oath there shall be substituted references to furnishing evidence on oath ; and in the application of this section to Northern Ireland for references to the laying of information on oath there shall be substituted references to making a complaint on oath.

(9) In this section " documents " includes information recorded in any form and, in relation to information recorded otherwise than in legible form, references to its production include references to producing a copy of the information in legible form.

False and misleading statements.   **200.**—(1) A person commits an offence if—

(a) for the purposes of or in connection with any application under this Act ; or

(b) in purported compliance with any requirement imposed on him by or under this Act,

he furnishes information which he knows to be false or misleading in a material particular or recklessly furnishes information which is false or misleading in a material particular.

(2) A person commits an offence if, not being an authorised   PART X
person or exempted person, he—

   (*a*) describes himself as such a person ; or

   (*b*) so holds himself out as to indicate or be reasonably
         understood to indicate that he is such a person.

(3) A person commits an offence if, not having a status to
which this subsection applies, he—

   (*a*) describes himself as having that status, or

   (*b*) so holds himself out as to indicate or be reasonably
         understood to indicate that he has that status.

(4) Subsection (3) above applies to the status of recognised
self-regulating organisation, recognised professional body, recognised investment exchange or recognised clearing house.

(5) A person guilty of an offence under subsection (1) above
shall be liable—

   (*a*) on conviction on indictment, to imprisonment for a term
         not exceeding two years or to a fine or to both ;

   (*b*) on summary conviction, to imprisonment for a term not
         exceeding six months or to a fine not exceeding the
         statutory maximum or to both.

(6) A person guilty of an offence under subsection (2) or (3)
above shall be liable on summary conviction to imprisonment
for a term not exceeding six months or to a fine not exceeding the
fifth level on the standard scale or to both.

(7) Where a contravention of subsection (2) or (3) above
involves a public display of the offending description or other
matter the maximum fine that may be imposed under subsection
(6) above shall be an amount equal to the fifth level on the standard scale multiplied by the number of days for which the
display has continued.

(8) In proceedings brought against any person for an offence
under subsection (2) or (3) above it shall be a defence for him
to prove that he took all reasonable precautions and exercised
all due diligence to avoid the commission of the offence.

201.—(1) Proceedings in respect of an offence under any pro- Prosecutions.
vision of this Act other than section 133 or 185 shall not be
instituted—

   (*a*) in England and Wales, except by or with the consent
         of the Secretary of State or the Director of Public
         Prosecutions ; or

   (*b*) in Northern Ireland, except by or with the consent of
         the Secretary of State or the Director of Public Pro-
         secutions for Northern Ireland.

PART X

(2) Proceedings in respect of an offence under section 133 above shall not be instituted—

    (a) in England and Wales, except by or with the consent of the Secretary of State, the Industrial Assurance Commissioner or the Director of Public Prosecutions; or

    (b) in Northern Ireland, except by or with the consent of the Secretary of State or the Director of Public Prosecutions for Northern Ireland.

(3) Proceedings in respect of an offence under section 185 above shall not be instituted—

    (a) in England and Wales, except by or with the consent of the Treasury or the Director of Public Prosecutions; or

    (b) in Northern Ireland, except by or with the consent of the Treasury or the Director of Public Prosecutions for Northern Ireland.

(4) The functions to which section 114 above applies shall include the function of the Secretary of State under subsection (1) above to institute proceedings but any transfer of that function shall be subject to a reservation that it is to be exercisable by him concurrently with the designated agency and so as to be exercisable by the agency subject to such conditions or restrictions as the Secretary of State may from time to time impose.

Offences by bodies corporate, partnerships and unincorporated associations.

202.—(1) Where an offence under this Act committed by a body corporate is proved to have been committed with the consent or connivance of, or to be attributable to any neglect on the part of—

    (a) any director, manager, secretary or other similar officer of the body corporate, or any person who was purporting to act in any such capacity; or

    (b) a controller of the body corporate,

he, as well as the body corporate, shall be guilty of that offence and liable to be proceeded against and punished accordingly.

(2) Where the affairs of a body corporate are managed by the members subsection (1) above shall apply in relation to the acts and defaults of a member in connection with his functions of management as if he were a director of the body corporate.

(3) Where a partnership is guilty of an offence under this Act every partner, other than a partner who is proved to have been ignorant of or to have attempted to prevent the commission of the offence, shall also be guilty of that offence and be liable to be proceeded against and punished accordingly.

(4) Where an unincorporated association (other than a part-   PART X
nership) is guilty of an offence under this Act—

(a) every officer of the association who is bound to fulfil
any duty of which the breach is the offence ; or

(b) if there is no such officer, every member of the governing body other than a member who is proved to have
been ignorant of or to have attempted to prevent the
commission of the offence,

shall also be guilty of the offence and be liable to be proceeded
against and punished accordingly.

203.—(1) Summary proceedings for an offence under this Act Jurisdiction
may, without prejudice to any jurisdiction exercisable apart from and
this section, be taken against any body corporate or unincorpor- procedure
ated association at any place at which it has a place of business in respect of
and against an individual at any place where he is for the time offences.
being.

(2) Proceedings for an offence alleged to have been committed
under this Act by an unincorporated association shall be brought
in the name of the association (and not in that of any of its
members) and for the purposes of any such proceedings any rules
of court relating to the service of documents shall have effect as
if the association were a corporation.

(3) Section 33 of the Criminal Justice Act 1925 and Schedule 1925 c. 86.
3 to the Magistrates' Courts Act 1980 (procedure on charge of 1980 c. 43.
offence against a corporation) shall have effect in a case in which
an unincorporated association is charged in England and Wales
with an offence under this Act in like manner as they have
effect in the case of a corporation.

(4) In relation to any proceedings on indictment in Scotland
for an offence alleged to have been committed under this Act
by an unincorporated association, section 74 of the Criminal 1975 c. 21.
Procedure (Scotland) Act 1975 (proceedings on indictment against
bodies corporate) shall have effect as if the association were a
body corporate.

(5) Section 18 of the Criminal Justice Act (Northern Ireland) 1945 c. 15.
1945 and Schedule 4 to the Magistrates' Courts (Northern Ire- (N.I.).
land) Order 1981 (procedure on charge of offence against a cor- S.I. 1981/1675
poration) shall have effect in a case in which an unincorporated (N.I. 26).
association is charged in Northern Ireland with an offence under
this Act in like manner as they have effect in the case of a corporation.

(6) A fine imposed on an unincorporated association on its
conviction of an offence under this Act shall be paid out of the
funds of the association.

PART X
Service of
notices.

204.—(1) This section has effect in relation to any notice, direction or other document required or authorised by or under this Act to be given to or served on any person other than the Secretary of State, the Chief Registrar of friendly societies or the Registrar of Friendly Societies for Northern Ireland.

(2) Any such document may be given to or served on the person in question—

    (a) by delivering it to him ;

    (b) by leaving it at his proper address ; or

    (c) by sending it by post to him at that address.

(3) Any such document may—

    (a) in the case of a body corporate, be given to or served on the secretary or clerk of that body ;

    (b) in the case of a partnership, be given to or served on any partner ;

    (c) in the case of an unincorporated association other than a partnership, be given to or served on any member of the governing body of the association ;

    (d) in the case of an appointed representative, be given to or served on his principal.

1978 c. 30.

(4) For the purposes of this section and section 7 of the Interpretation Act 1978 (service of documents by post) in its application to this section, the proper address of any person is his last known address (whether of his residence or of a place where he carries on business or is employed) and also any address applicable in his case under the following provisions—

    (a) in the case of a member of a recognised self-regulating organisation or a person certified by a recognised professional body who does not have a place of business in the United Kingdom, the address of that organisation or body ;

    (b) in the case of a body corporate, its secretary or its clerk, the address of its registered or principal office in the United Kingdom ;

    (c) in the case of an unincorporated association (other than a partnership) or a member of its governing body, its principal office in the United Kingdom.

(5) Where a person has notified the Secretary of State of an address or a new address at which documents may be given to or served on him under this Act that address shall also be his proper address for the purposes mentioned in subsection (4) above or, as the case may be, his proper address for those purposes in substitution for that previously notified.

205.—(1) The Secretary of State may make regulations pre-   PART X
cribing anything which by this Act is authorised or required to   Regulations,
be prescribed.   rules and
orders.

(2) Subject to subsection (5) below, any power of the Secretary
of State to make regulations, rules or orders under this Act shall
be exercisable by statutory instrument.

(3) Subject to subsection (5) below, any regulations, rules or
orders made under this Act by the Secretary of State may make
different provision for different cases.

(4) Except as otherwise provided, a statutory instrument containing regulations or rules under this Act shall be subject to
annulment in pursuance of a resolution of either House of Parliament.

(5) Subsections (2) and (3) above do not apply to a recognition order, an order declaring a collective investment scheme to
be an authorised unit trust scheme or a recognised scheme or to
an order revoking any such order.

206.—(1) The Secretary of State may publish information or   Publication of
give advice, or arrange for the publication of information or the   information
giving of advice, in such form and manner as he considers   and advice.
appropriate with respect to—

> (a) the operation of this Act and the rules and regulations
> made under it, including in particular the rights of
> investors, the duties of authorised persons and the
> steps to be taken for enforcing those rights or comply-
> ing with those duties ;

> (b) any matters relating to the functions of the Secretary
> of State under this Act or any such rules or regula-
> tions ;

> (c) any other matters about which it appears to him to be
> desirable to publish information or give advice for the
> protection of investors or any class of investors.

(2) The Secretary of State may offer for sale copies of information published under this section and may, if he thinks fit,
make a reasonable charge for advice given under this section
at any person's request.

(3) This section shall not be construed as authorising the disclosure of restricted information within the meaning of section
179 above in any case in which it could not be disclosed apart
from the provisions of this section.

PART X   (4) The functions to which section 114 above applies shall include the functions of the Secretary of State under this section.

Interpretation.   **207.**—(1) In this Act, except where the context otherwise requires—

" appointed representative " has the meaning given in section 44 above ;

" authorised person " means a person authorised under Chapter III of Part I of this Act ;

" authorised unit trust scheme " means a unit trust scheme declared by an order of the Secretary of State for the time being in force to be an authorised unit trust scheme for the purposes of this Act ;

" body corporate " includes a body corporate constituted under the law of a country or territory outside the United Kingdom ;

" certified " and " certification " mean certified or certification by a recognised professional body for the purposes of Part I of this Act ;

" clearing arrangements " has the meaning given in section 38(2) above ;

" competent authority " means the competent authority for the purposes of Part IV of this Act ;

" collective investment scheme " has the meaning given in section 75 above ;

" delegation order " and " designated agency " have the meaning given in section 114(3) above ;

" director ", in relation to a body corporate, includes a person occupying in relation to it the position of a director (by whatever name called) and any person in accordance with whose directions or instructions (not being advice given in a professional capacity) the directors of that body are accustomed to act ;

" exempted person " means a person exempted under Chapter IV of Part I of this Act ;

" group ", in relation to a body corporate, means that body corporate, any other body corporate which is its holding company or subsidiary and any other body corporate which is a subsidiary of that holding company ;

" guidance ", in relation to a self-regulating organisation, professional body, investment exchange, clearing house or designated agency, has the meaning given in section 8(4), 16(4), 36(3), 38(3) or 114(12) above ;

" investment advertisement " has the meaning given in section 57(2) above ;

" investment agreement " has the meaning given in section 44(9) above ;

" listing particulars " has the meaning given in section 144(2) above ;

" member ", in relation to a self-regulating organisation or professional body, has the meaning given in section 8(2) or 16(2) above ;

" occupational pension scheme " means any scheme or arrangement which is comprised in one or more instruments or agreements and which has, or is capable of having, effect in relation to one or more descriptions or categories of employment so as to provide benefits, in the form of pensions or otherwise, payable on termination of service, or on death or retirement, to or in respect of earners with qualifying service in an employment of any such description or category ;

" operator ", in relation to a collective investment scheme, shall be construed in accordance with section 75(8) above ;

" open-ended investment company " has the meaning given in section 75(8) above ;

" overseas investment exchange " and " overseas clearing house " mean a recognised investment exchange or recognised clearing house in the case of which the recognition order was made by virtue of section 40 above ;

" participant " has the meaning given in section 75(2) above ;

" partnership " includes a partnership constituted under the law of a country or territory outside the United Kingdom ;

" prescribed " means prescribed by regulations made by the Secretary of State ;

" principal ", in relation to an appointed representative, has the meaning given in section 44 above ;

" private company " has the meaning given in section 1(3) of the Companies Act 1985 or the corresponding Northern Ireland provision ;   1985 c. 6.

" recognised clearing house " means a body declared by an order of the Secretary of State for the time being in force to be a recognised clearing house for the purposes of this Act ;

" recognised investment exchange " means a body declared by an order of the Secretary of State for the time being in force to be a recognised investment exchange for the purposes of this Act ;

" recognised professional body " means a body declared by an order of the Secretary of State for the time being in force to be a recognised professional body for the purposes of this Act ;

" recognised scheme " means a scheme recognised under section 86, 87 or 88 above ;

" recognised self-regulating organisation " means a body declared by an order of the Secretary of State for the time being in force to be a recognised self-regulating organisation for the purposes of this Act ;

" recognised self-regulating organisation for friendly societies " has the meaning given in paragraph 1 of Schedule 11 to this Act ;

" recognition order " means an order declaring a body to be a recognised self-regulating organisation, self-regulating organisation for friendly societies, professional body, investment exchange or clearing house ;

" registered friendly society " means—

1974 c. 46.
(a) a society which is a friendly society within the meaning of section 7(1)(a) of the Friendly Societies Act 1974 and is registered within the meaning of that Act ; or

1970 c. 31 (N.I.).
(b) a society which is a friendly society within the meaning of section 1(1)(a) of the Friendly Societies Act (Northern Ireland) 1970 and is registered or deemed to be registered under that Act ;

" rules ", in relation to a self-regulating organisation, professional body, investment exchange or clearing house, has the meaning given in section 8(3), 16(3), 36(2) or 38(2) above ;

" transfer order " and " transferee body " have the meaning given in paragraph 28(4) of Schedule 11 to this Act ;

" the Tribunal " means the Financial Services Tribunal ;

" trustee ", in relation to a collective investment scheme, has the meaning given in section 75(8) above ;

" unit trust scheme " and " units " have the meaning given in section 75(8) above.

(2) In this Act " advertisement " includes every form of advertising, whether in a publication, by the display of notices, signs, labels or showcards, by means of circulars, catalogues,

price lists or other documents, by an exhibition of pictures or
photographic or cinematographic films, by way of sound broadcasting or television, by the distribution of recordings, or in any
other manner ; and references to the issue of an advertisement
shall be construed accordingly.

(3) For the purposes of this Act an advertisement or other
information issued outside the United Kingdom shall be treated
as issued in the United Kingdom if it is directed to persons in
the United Kingdom or is made available to them otherwise
than in a newspaper, journal, magazine or other periodical
publication published and circulating principally outside the
United Kingdom or in a sound or television broadcast transmitted principally for reception outside the United Kingdom.

(4) The Independent Broadcasting Authority shall not be
regarded as contravening any provision of this Act by reason
of broadcasting an advertisement in accordance with the pro- 1981 c. 68.
visions of the Broadcasting Act 1981.

(5) In this Act " controller " means—

   (a) in relation to a body corporate, a person who, either
       alone or with any associate or associates, is entitled
       to exercise, or control the exercise of, 15 per cent. or
       more of the voting power at any general meeting of
       the body corporate or another body corporate of which
       it is a subsidiary ; and

   (b) in relation to an unincorporated association—

       (i) any person in accordance with whose direc-
       tions or instructions, either alone or with those of
       any associate or associates, the officers or members
       of the governing body of the association are accus-
       tomed to act (but disregarding advice given in a
       professional capacity) ; and

       (ii) any person who, either alone or with any
       associate or associates, is entitled to exercise, or con-
       trol the exercise of, 15 per cent. or more of the
       voting power at any general meeting of the associa-
       tion ;

and for the purposes of this subsection " associate ", in relation
to any person, means that person's wife, husband or minor child
or step-child, any body corporate of which that person is a
director, any person who is an employee or partner of that
person and, if that person is a body corporate, any subsidiary
of that body corporate and any employee of any such subsidiary.

(6) In this Act, except in relation to a unit trust scheme or a

Part X   registered friendly society, " manager " means an employee who—

> (a) under the immediate authority of his employer is responsible, either alone or jointly with one or more other persons, for the conduct of his employer's business ; or
>
> (b) under the immediate authority of his employer or of a person who is a manager by virtue of paragraph (a) above exercises managerial functions or is responsible for maintaining accounts or other records of his employer ;

and, where the employer is not an individual, references in this subsection to the authority of the employer are references to the authority, in the case of a body corporate, of the directors, in the case of a partnership, of the partners and, in the case of an unincorporated association, of its officers or the members of its governing body.

(7) In this Act " insurance business ", " insurance company " and " contract of insurance " have the same meanings as in the Insurance Companies Act 1982.

1982 c. 50.

1985 c. 6.   (8) Section 736 of the Companies Act 1985 (meaning of subsidiary and holding company) shall apply for the purposes of this Act.

(9) In the application of this Act to Scotland, references to a matter being actionable at the suit of a person shall be construed as references to the matter being actionable at the instance of that person.

(10) For the purposes of any provision of this Act authorising or requiring a person to do anything within a specified number of days no account shall be taken of any day which is a public holiday in any part of the United Kingdom.

(11) Nothing in Part I of this Act shall be construed as applying to investment business carried on by any person when acting as agent or otherwise on behalf of the Crown.

Gibraltar.   **208.**—(1) Subject to the provisions of this section, section 31, 58(1)(c), 86 and 130(2)(c) and (d) above shall apply as if Gibraltar were a member State.

(2) References in those provisions to a national of a member State shall, in relation to Gibraltar, be construed as references to a British Dependent Territories citizen or a body incorporated in Gibraltar.

(3) In the case of a collective investment scheme constituted in Gibraltar the reference in subsection (3)(a) of section 86 above

to a relevant Community instrument shall be taken as a reference to any Community instrument the object of which is the co-ordination or approximation of the laws, regulations or administrative provisions of member States relating to collective investment schemes of a kind which satisfy the requirements prescribed for the purposes of that section.

(4) The Secretary of State may by regulations make such provision as appears to him to be necessary or expedient to secure—

    (a) that he may give notice under subsection (2) of section 86 above on grounds relating to the law of Gibraltar ; and

    (b) that this Act applies as if a scheme which is constituted in a member State other than the United Kingdom and recognised in Gibraltar under provisions which appear to the Secretary of State to give effect to the provisions of a relevant Community instrument were a scheme recognised under that section.

209.—(1) This Act extends to Northern Ireland.

    Northern Ireland.

(2) Subject to any Order made after the passing of this Act by virtue of subsection (1)(a) of section 3 of the Northern Ireland Constitution Act 1973 the regulation of investment business, the official listing of securities and offers of unlisted securities shall not be transferred matters for the purposes of that Act but shall for the purposes of subsection (2) of that section be treated as specified in Schedule 3 to that Act.

    1973 c. 36.

210.—(1) Any expenses incurred by the Secretary of State under this Act shall be defrayed out of moneys provided by Parliament.

    Expenses and receipts.

(2) Any fees or other sums received by the Secretary of State under this Act shall be paid into the Consolidated Fund.

(3) Subsections (1) and (2) above apply also to expenses incurred and fees received under this Act by the Chief Registrar of friendly societies ; and any fees received under this Act by the Registrar of Friendly Societies for Northern Ireland shall be paid into the Consolidated Fund of Northern Ireland.

211.—(1) This Act shall come into force on such day as the Secretary of State may by order appoint and different days may be appointed for different provisions or different purposes.

    Commencement and transitional provisions.

(2) Subsection (1) above does not apply to section 195 which shall come into force when this Act is passed.

(3) Schedule 15 to this Act shall have effect with respect to the transitional matters there mentioned.

Short title, consequential amendments and repeals.

212.—(1) This Act may be cited as the Financial Services Act 1986.

(2) The enactments and instruments mentioned in Schedule 16 to this Act shall have effect with the amendments there specified, being amendments consequential on the provisions of this Act.

(3) The enactments mentioned in Part I of Schedule 17 to this Act and the instruments mentioned in Part II of that Schedule are hereby repealed or revoked to the extent specified in the third column of those Parts.

SCHEDULES

SCHEDULE 1

INVESTMENTS AND INVESTMENT BUSINESS

PART I

INVESTMENTS

Shares etc.

1. Shares and stock in the share capital of a company.

Note. In this paragraph "company" includes any body corporate and also any unincorporated body constituted under the law of a country or territory outside the United Kingdom but does not include an open-ended investment company or any body incorporated under the law of, or of any part of, the United Kingdom relating to building societies, industrial and provident societies or credit unions.

Debentures

2. Debentures, including debenture stock, loan stock, bonds, certificates of deposit and other instruments creating or acknowledging indebtedness, not being instruments falling within paragraph 3 below.

Note. This paragraph shall not be construed as applying—

(*a*) to any instrument acknowledging or creating indebtedness for, or for money borrowed to defray, the consideration payable under a contract for the supply of goods or services ;

(*b*) to a cheque or other bill of exchange, a banker's draft or a letter of credit ; or

(*c*) to a banknote, a statement showing a balance in a current, deposit or savings account or (by reason of any financial obligation contained in it) to a lease or other disposition of property, a heritable security or an insurance policy.

Government and public securities

3. Loan stock, bonds and other instruments creating or acknowledging indebtedness issued by or on behalf of a government, local authority or public authority.

Notes

(1) In this paragraph "government, local authority or public authority" means—

(*a*) the government of the United Kingdom, of Northern Ireland, or of any country or territory outside the United Kingdom ;

(*b*) a local authority in the United Kingdom or elsewhere ;

(*c*) any international organisation the members of which include the United Kingdom or another member State.

(2) The Note to paragraph 2 above shall, so far as applicable, apply also to this paragraph.

Instruments entitling to shares or securities

4. Warrants or other instruments entitling the holder to subscribe for investments falling within paragraph 1, 2 or 3 above.

Notes

(1) It is immaterial whether the investments are for the time being in existence or identifiable.

(2) An investment falling within this paragraph shall not be regarded as falling within paragraph 7, 8 or 9 below.

Certificates representing securities

5. Certificates or other instruments which confer—

(a) property rights in respect of any investment falling within paragraph 1, 2, 3 or 4 above ;

(b) any right to acquire, dispose of, underwrite or convert an investment, being a right to which the holder would be entitled if he held any such investment to which the certificate or instrument relates ; or

(c) a contractual right (other than an option) to acquire any such investment otherwise than by subscription.

Note. This paragraph does not apply to any instrument which confers rights in respect of two or more investments issued by different persons or in respect of two or more different investments falling within paragraph 3 above and issued by the same person.

Units in collective investment scheme

6. Units in a collective investment scheme, including shares in or securities of an open-ended investment company.

Options

7. Options to acquire or dispose of—

(a) an investment falling within any other paragraph of this Part of this Schedule ;

(b) currency of the United Kingdom or of any other country or territory ;

(c) gold or silver ; or

(d) an option to acquire or dispose of an investment falling within this paragraph by virtue of (a), (b) or (c) above.

Futures

8. Rights under a contract for the sale of a commodity or property of any other description under which delivery is to be made at a future date and at a price agreed upon when the contract is made.

Notes

(1) This paragraph does not apply if the contract is made for commercial and not investment purposes.

(2) A contract shall be regarded as made for investment purposes if it is made or traded on a recognised investment exchange or made otherwise than on a recognised investment exchange but expressed to be as traded on such an exchange or on the same terms as those on which an equivalent contract would be made on such an exchange.

(3) A contract not falling within Note (2) above shall be regarded as made for commercial purposes if under the terms of the contract delivery is to be made within seven days.

(4) The following are indications that any other contract is made for a commercial purpose and the absence of any of them is an indication that it is made for investment purposes—

    (*a*) either or each of the parties is a producer of the commodity or other property or uses it in his business ;

    (*b*) the seller delivers or intends to deliver the property or the purchaser takes or intends to take delivery of it.

(5) It is an indication that a contract is made for commercial purposes that the price, the lot, the delivery date or the other terms are determined by the parties for the purposes of the particular contract and not by reference to regularly published prices, to standard lots or delivery dates or to standard terms.

(6) The following are also indications that a contract is made for investment purposes—

    (*a*) it is expressed to be as traded on a market or on an exchange ;

    (*b*) performance of the contract is ensured by an investment exchange or a clearing house ;

    (*c*) there are arrangements for the payment or provision of margin.

(7) A price shall be taken to have been agreed upon when a contract is made—

    (*a*) notwithstanding that it is left to be determined by reference to the price at which a contract is to be entered into on a market or exchange or could be entered into at a time and place specified in the contract ; or

    (*b*) in a case where the contract is expressed to be by reference to a standard lot and quality, notwithstanding that provision is made for a variation in the price to take account of any variation in quantity or quality on delivery.

Contracts for differences etc.

9. Rights under a contract for differences or under any other contract the purpose or pretended purpose of which is to secure a profit or avoid a loss by reference to fluctuations in the value or price of property of any description or in an index or other factor designated for that purpose in the contract.

    Note. This paragraph does not apply where the parties intend that the profit is to be obtained or the loss avoided by taking delivery of any property to which the contract relates.

Long term insurance contracts

10. Rights under a contract the effecting and carrying out of which constitutes long term business within the meaning of the Insurance Companies Act 1982.

Notes

(1) This paragraph does not apply to rights under a contract of insurance if—

    (*a*) the benefits under the contract are payable only on death or in respect of incapacity due to injury, sickness or infirmity ;

    (*b*) no benefits are payable under the contract on a death (other than a death due to accident) unless it occurs within ten years of the date on which the life of the person in question was first insured under the contract or before that person attains a specified age not exceeding seventy years ;

    (*c*) the contract has no surrender value or the consideration consists of a single premium and the surrender value does not exceed that premium ; and

    (*d*) the contract does not make provision for its conversion or extension in a manner that would result in its ceasing to comply with paragraphs (*a*), (*b*) and (*c*) above.

(2) Where the provisions of a contract of insurance are such that the effecting and carrying out of the contract—

1982 c. 50.

    (*a*) constitutes both long term business within the meaning of the Insurance Companies Act 1982 and general business within the meaning of that Act ; or

    (*b*) by virtue of section 1(3) of that Act constitutes long term business notwithstanding the inclusion of subsidiary general business provisions,

references in this paragraph to rights and benefits under the contract are references only to such rights and benefits as are attributable to the provisions of the contract relating to long term business.

(3) This paragraph does not apply to rights under a re-insurance contract.

(4) Rights falling within this paragraph shall not be regarded as falling within paragraph 9 above.

Rights and interests in investments

11. Rights to and interests in anything which is an investment falling within any other paragraph of this Part of this Schedule.

Notes

(1) This paragraph does not apply to interests under the trusts of an occupational pension scheme.

(2) This paragraph does not apply to rights or interests which are investments by virtue of any other paragraph of this Part of this Schedule.

PART II

ACTIVITIES CONSTITUTING INVESTMENT BUSINESS

Dealing in investments

12. Buying, selling, subscribing for or underwriting investments or offering or agreeing to do so, either as principal or as an agent.

Arranging deals in investments

13. Making, or offering or agreeing to make—

(*a*) arrangements with a view to another person buying, selling, subscribing for or underwriting a particular investment ; or

(*b*) arrangements with a view to a person who participates in the arrangements buying, selling, subscribing for or underwriting investments.

Notes

(1) This paragraph does not apply to a person by reason of his making, or offering or agreeing to make, arrangements with a view to a transaction to which he will himself be a party as principal or which will be entered into by him as agent for one of the parties.

(2) The arrangements in (*a*) above are arrangements which bring about or would bring about the transaction in question.

Managing investments

14. Managing, or offering or agreeing to manage, assets belonging to another person if—

(*a*) those assets consist of or include investments ; or

(*b*) the arrangements for their management are such that those assets may consist of or include investments at the discretion of the person managing or offering or agreeing to manage them and either they have at any time since the date of the coming into force of section 3 of this Act done so or the arrangements have at any time (whether before or after that date) been held out as arrangements under which they would do so.

Investment advice

15. Giving, or offering or agreeing to give, to persons in their capacity as investors or potential investors advice on the merits of their purchasing, selling, subscribing for or underwriting an investment, or exercising any right conferred by an investment to acquire, dispose of, underwrite or convert an investment.

Establishing etc. collective investment schemes

16. Establishing, operating or winding up a collective investment scheme, including acting as trustee of an authorised unit trust scheme.

Part IV   G

PART III

EXCLUDED ACTIVITIES

Dealings as principal

17.—(1) Paragraph 12 above applies to a transaction which is or
is to be entered into by a person as principal only if—

  (*a*) he holds himself out as willing to enter into transactions
     of that kind at prices determined by him generally and con-
     tinuously rather than in respect of each particular trans-
     action ; or

  (*b*) he holds himself out as engaging in the business of buying
     investments with a view to selling them and those invest-
     ments are or include investments of the kind to which the
     transaction relates ; or

  (*c*) he regularly solicits members of the public for the purpose
     of inducing them to enter as principals or agents into trans-
     actions to which that paragraph applies and the transaction
     is or is to be entered into as a result of his having solicited
     members of the public in that manner.

(2) In sub-paragraph (1) above " buying " and " selling " means
buying and selling by transactions to which paragraph 12 above
applies and " members of the public ", in relation to the person
soliciting them (" the relevant person "), means any other persons
except—

  (*a*) authorised persons, exempted persons, or persons holding a
     permission under paragraph 23 below ;

  (*b*) members of the same group as the relevant person ;

  (*c*) persons who are, or propose to become, participators with
     the relevant person in a joint enterprise ;

  (*d*) any person who is solicited by the relevant person with a
     view to—

       (i) the acquisition by the relevant person of 20 per
       cent. or more of the voting shares in a body corporate
       (that is to say, shares carrying not less than that percent-
       age of the voting rights attributable to share capital which
       are exercisable in all circumstances at any general meet-
       ing of the body) ; or

       (ii) if the relevant person (either alone or with other
       members of the same group as himself) holds 20 per
       cent. or more of the voting shares in a body corporate,
       the acquisition by him of further shares in the body or
       the disposal by him of shares in that body to the person
       solicited or to a member of the same group as that
       person ; or

       (iii) if the person solicited (either alone or with other
       members of the same group as himself) holds 20 per
       cent. or more of the voting shares in a body corporate,
       the disposal by the relevant person of further shares in
       that body to the person solicited or to a member of the
       same group as that person ;

(*e*) any person whose head office is outside the United Kingdom, who is solicited by an approach made or directed to him at a place outside the United Kingdom and whose ordinary business involves him in engaging in activities which fall within Part II of this Schedule or would do so apart from this Part or Part IV.

(3) Sub-paragraph (1) above applies only if the investment to which the transaction relates or will relate falls within any of paragraphs 1 to 6 above or, so far as relevant to any of those paragraphs, paragraph 11 above.

(4) Paragraph 12 above does not apply to a transaction which relates or is to relate to any other investment and which is or is to be entered into by a person as principal if he is not an authorised person and the transaction is or is to be entered into by him—

(*a*) with or through an authorised person, an exempted person or a person holding a permission under paragraph 23 below ; or

(*b*) through an office outside the United Kingdom, maintained by a party to the transaction, and with or through a person whose head office is situated outside the United Kingdom and whose ordinary business is such as is mentioned in sub-paragraph (2)(*e*) above.

Groups and joint enterprises

18.—(1) Paragraph 12 above does not apply to any transaction which is or is to be entered into by a person as principal with another person if—

(*a*) they are bodies corporate in the same group ; or

(*b*) they are, or propose to become, participators in a joint enterprise and the transaction is or is to be entered into for the purposes of, or in connection with, that enterprise.

(2) Paragraph 12 above does not apply to any transaction which is or is to be entered into by any person as agent for another person in the circumstances mentioned in sub-paragraph (1)(*a*) or (*b*) above if—

(*a*) where the investment falls within any of paragraphs 1 to 6 above or, so far as relevant to any of those paragraphs, paragraph 11 above, the agent does not—

(i) hold himself out (otherwise than to other bodies corporate in the same group or persons who are or propose to become participators with him in a joint enterprise) as engaging in the business of buying investments with a view to selling them and those investments are or include investments of the kind to which the transaction relates ; or

(ii) regularly solicit members of the public for the purpose of inducing them to enter as principals or agents into transactions to which paragraph 12 above applies ;

and the transaction is not or is not to be entered into as a result of his having solicited members of the public in that manner ;

   (b) where the investment is not as mentioned in paragraph (a) above—

      (i) the agent enters into the transaction with or through an authorised person, an exempted person or a person holding a permission under paragraph 23 below ; or

      (ii) the transaction is effected through an office outside the United Kingdom, maintained by a party to the transaction, and with or through a person whose head office is situated outside the United Kingdom and whose ordinary business involves him in engaging in activities which fall within Part II of this Schedule or would do so apart from this Part or Part IV.

(3) Paragraph 13 above does not apply to arrangements which a person makes or offers or agrees to make if—

   (a) that person is a body corporate and the arrangements are with a view to another body corporate in the same group entering into a transaction of the kind mentioned in that paragraph ; or

   (b) that person is or proposes to become a participator in a joint enterprise and the arrangements are with a view to another person who is or proposes to become a participator in the enterprise entering into such a transaction for the purposes of or in connection with that enterprise.

(4) Paragraph 14 above does not apply to a person by reason of his managing or offering or agreeing to manage the investments of another person if—

   (a) they are bodies corporate in the same group ; or

   (b) they are, or propose to become, participators in a joint enterprise and the investments are or are to be managed for the purposes of, or in connection with, that enterprise.

(5) Paragraph 15 above does not apply to advice given by a person to another person if—

   (a) they are bodies corporate in the same group ; or

   (b) they are, or propose to become, participators in a joint enterprise and the advice is given for the purposes of, or in connection with, that enterprise.

(6) The definitions in paragraph 17(2) above shall apply also for the purposes of sub-paragraph (2)(a) above except that the relevant person referred to in paragraph 17(2)(d) shall be the person for whom the agent is acting.

Sale of goods and supply of services

19.—(1) This paragraph has effect where a person (" the supplier ") sells or offers or agrees to sell goods to another person (" the customer ") or supplies or offers or agrees to supply him with services.

and the supplier's main business is to supply goods or services and SCH. 1
not to engage in activities falling within Part II of this Schedule.

(2) Paragraph 12 above does not apply to any transaction which
is or is to be entered into by the supplier as principal if it is or is to
be entered into by him with the customer for the purposes of or in
connection with the sale or supply or a related sale or supply (that
is to say, a sale or supply to the customer otherwise than by the
supplier but for or in connection with the same purpose as the
first-mentioned sale or supply).

(3) Paragraph 12 above does not apply to any transaction which
is or is to be entered into by the supplier as agent for the customer
if it is or is to be entered into for the purposes of or in connection
with the sale or supply or a related sale or supply and—

(a) where the investment falls within any of paragraphs 1 to 6
above or, so far as relevant to any of those paragraphs,
paragraph 11 above, the supplier does not—

(i) hold himself out (otherwise than to the customer)
as engaging in the business of buying investments with a
view to selling them and those investments are or include investments of the kind to which the transaction
relates ; or

(ii) regularly solicit members of the public for the
purpose of inducing them to enter as principals or agents
into transactions to which paragraph 12 above applies ;
and the transaction is not or is not to be entered into as a
result of his having solicited members of the public in that
manner ;

(b) where the investment is not as mentioned in paragraph (a)
above, the supplier enters into the transaction—

(i) with or through an authorised person, an exempted
person or a person holding a permission under paragraph 23 below ; or

(ii) through an office outside the United Kingdom,
maintained by a party to the transaction, and with or
through a person whose head office is situated outside
the United Kingdom and whose ordinary business involves him in engaging in activities which fall within
Part II of this Schedule or would do so apart from this
Part or Part IV.

(4) Paragraph 13 above does not apply to arrangements which
the supplier makes or offers or agrees to make with a view to the
customer entering into a transaction for the purposes of or in connection with the sale or supply or a related sale or supply.

(5) Paragraph 14 above does not apply to the supplier by reason
of his managing or offering or agreeing to manage the investments
of the customer if they are or are to be managed for the purposes of
or in connection with the sale or supply or a related sale or supply.

(6) Paragraph 15 above does not apply to advice given by the
supplier to the customer for the purposes of or in connection with

G 3

the sale or supply or a related sale or supply or to a person with whom the customer proposes to enter into a transaction for the purposes of or in connection with the sale or supply or a related sale or supply.

(7) Where the supplier is a body corporate and a member of a group sub-paragraphs (2) to (6) above shall apply to any other member of the group as they apply to the supplier ; and where the customer is a body corporate and a member of a group references in those sub-paragraphs to the customer include references to any other member of the group.

(8) The definitions in paragraph 17(2) above shall apply also for the purposes of sub-paragraph (3)(*a*) above.

Employees' share schemes

20.—(1) Paragraphs 12 and 13 above do not apply to anything done by a body corporate, a body corporate connected with it or a relevant trustee for the purpose of enabling or facilitating trans-actions in shares in or debentures of the first-mentioned body between or for the benefit of any of the persons mentioned in sub-paragraph (2) below or the holding of such shares or debentures by or for the benefit of any such persons.

(2) The persons referred to in sub-paragraph (1) above are—

    (*a*) the bona fide employees or former employees of the body cor-porate or of another body corporate in the same group ; or

    (*b*) the wives, husbands, widows, widowers, or children or step-children under the age of eighteen of such employees or former employees.

(3) In this paragraph " a relevant trustee " means a person hold-ing shares in or debentures of a body corporate as trustee in pursu-ance of arrangements made for the purpose mentioned in sub-paragraph (1) above by, or by a body corporate connected with, that body corporate.

(4) In this paragraph " shares " and " debentures " include any investment falling within paragraph 1 or 2 above and also include any investment falling within paragraph 4 or 5 above so far as relat-ing to those paragraphs or any investment falling within paragraph 11 above so far as relating to paragraph 1, 2, 4 or 5.

(5) For the purposes of this paragraph a body corporate is connec-ted with another body corporate if—

    (*a*) they are in the same group ; or

    (*b*) one is entitled, either alone or with any other body cor-porate in the same group, to exercise or control the exer-cise of a majority of the voting rights attributable to the share capital which are exercisable in all circumstances at any general meeting of the other body corporate or of its holding company.

Sale of private company

21.—(1) Paragraphs 12 and 13 above do not apply to the acquisition or disposal of, or to anything done for the purposes of the acquisition or disposal of, shares in a private company, and paragraph 15 above does not apply to advice given in connection with the acquisition or disposal of such shares, if—

   (a) the shares consist of or include shares carrying 75 per cent. or more of the voting rights attributable to share capital which are exercisable in all circumstances at any general meeting of the company ; or

   (b) the shares, together with any already held by the person acquiring them, carry not less than that percentage of those voting rights ; and

   (c) in either case, the acquisition and disposal is, or is to be, between parties each of whom is a body corporate, a partnership, a single individual or a group of connected individuals.

(2) For the purposes of subsection (1)(c) above " a group of connected individuals ", in relation to the party disposing of the shares, means persons each of whom is, or is a close relative of, a director or manager of the company and, in relation to the party acquiring the shares, means persons each of whom is, or is a close relative of, a person who is to be a director or manager of the company.

(3) In this paragraph " private company " means a private company within the meaning of section 1(3) of the Companies Act 1985 or the corresponding Northern Ireland provision and " close relative " means a person's spouse, his children and step-children, his parents and step-parents, his brothers and sisters and his step-brothers and step-sisters. 1985 c. 6.

Trustees and personal representatives

22.—(1) Paragraph 12 above does not apply to a person by reason of his buying, selling or subscribing for an investment or offering or agreeing to do so if—

   (a) the investment is or, as the case may be, is to be held by him as bare trustee or, in Scotland, as nominee for another person ;

   (b) he is acting on that person's instructions ; and

   (c) he does not hold himself out as providing a service of buying and selling investments.

(2) Paragraph 13 above does not apply to anything done by a person as trustee or personal representative with a view to—

   (a) a fellow trustee or personal representative and himself engaging in their capacity as such in an activity falling within paragraph 12 above ; or

   (b) a beneficiary under the trust, will or intestacy engaging in any such activity,

unless that person is remunerated for what he does in addition to any remuneration he receives for discharging his duties as trustee or personal representative.

(3) Paragraph 14 above does not apply to anything done by a person as trustee or personal representative unless he holds himself out as offering investment management services or is remunerated for providing such services in addition to any remuneration he receives for discharging his duties as trustee or personal representative.

(4) Paragraph 15 above does not apply to advice given by a person as trustee or personal representative to—

(a) a fellow trustee or personal representative for the purposes of the trust or estate ; or

(b) a beneficiary under the trust, will or intestacy concerning his interest in the trust fund or estate,

unless that person is remunerated for doing so in addition to any remuneration he receives for discharging his duties as trustee or personal representative.

(5) Sub-paragraph (1) above has effect to the exclusion of paragraph 17 above as respects any transaction in respect of which the conditions in sub-paragraph (1)(a) and (b) are satisfied.

Dealings in course of non-investment business

23.—(1) Paragraph 12 above does not apply to anything done by a person—

(a) as principal ;

(b) if that person is a body corporate in a group, as agent for another member of the group ; or

(c) as agent for a person who is or proposes to become a participator with him in a joint enterprise and for the purposes of or in connection with that enterprise,

if it is done in accordance with the terms and conditions of a permission granted to him by the Secretary of State under this paragraph.

(2) Any application for permission under this paragraph shall be accompanied or supported by such information as the Secretary of State may require and shall not be regarded as duly made unless accompanied by the prescribed fee.

(3) The Secretary of State may grant a permission under this paragraph if it appears to him—

(a) that the applicant's main business, or if he is a member of a group the main business of the group, does not consist of activities for which a person is required to be authorised under this Act ;

(b) that the applicant's business is likely to involve such activities which fall within paragraph 12 above ; and

(c) that, having regard to the nature of the applicant's main business and, if he is a member of a group, the main business of the group taken as a whole, the manner in which, the persons with whom and the purposes for which the applicant proposes to engage in activities that would require him to be an authorised person and to any other relevant matters, it is inappropriate to require him to be subject to regulation as an authorised person.

(4) Any permission under this paragraph shall be granted by a notice in writing ; and the Secretary of State may by a further notice in writing withdraw any such permission if for any reason it appears to him that it is not appropriate for it to continue in force.

(5) The Secretary of State may make regulations requiring persons holding permissions under this paragraph to furnish him with information for the purpose of enabling him to determine whether those permissions should continue in force ; and such regulations may, in particular, require such persons—

(a) to give him notice forthwith of the occurrence of such events as are specified in the regulations and such information in respect of those events as is so specified ;

(b) to furnish him at such times or in respect of such periods as are specified in the regulations with such information as is so specified.

(6) Section 61 of this Act shall have effect in relation to a contravention of any condition imposed by a permission under this paragraph as it has effect in relation to any such contravention as is mentioned in subsection (1)(a) of that section.

(7) Section 104 of this Act shall apply to a person holding a permission under this paragraph as if he were authorised to carry on investment business as there mentioned ; and sections 105 and 106 of this Act shall have effect as if anything done by him in accordance with such permission constituted the carrying on of investment business.

Advice given in course of profession or non-investment business

24.—(1) Paragraph 15 above does not apply to advice—

(a) which is given in the course of the carrying on of any profession or of a business not otherwise constituting investment business ; and

(b) the giving of which is a necessary part of other advice or services given in the course of carrying on that profession or business.

(2) Advice shall not be regarded as falling within sub-paragraph (1)(b) above if it is remunerated separately from the other advice or services.

Newspapers

25.—(1) Paragraph 15 above does not apply to advice given in a newspaper, journal, magazine or other periodical publication if the principal purpose of the publication, taken as a whole and including any advertisements contained in it, is not to lead persons to invest in any particular investment.

(2) The Secretary of State may, on the application of the proprietor of any periodical publication, certify that it is of the nature described in sub-paragraph (1) above and revoke any such certificate if he considers that it is no longer justified.

(3) A certificate given under sub-paragraph (2) above and not revoked shall be conclusive evidence of the matters certified.

PART IV

ADDITIONAL EXCLUSIONS FOR PERSONS WITHOUT PERMANENT PLACE OF BUSINESS IN UNITED KINGDOM

Transactions with or through authorised or exempted persons

26.—(1) Paragraph 12 above does not apply to any transaction by a person not falling within section 1(3)(*a*) of this Act (" an overseas person ") with or through—

(*a*) an authorised person ; or

(*b*) an exempted person acting in the course of business in respect of which he is exempt.

(2) Paragraph 13 above does not apply if—

(*a*) the arrangements are made by an overseas person with, or the offer or agreement to make them is made by him to or with, an authorised person or an exempted person and, in the case of an exempted person, the arrangements are with a view to his entering into a transaction in respect of which he is exempt ; or

(*b*) the transactions with a view to which the arrangements are made are, as respects transactions in the United Kingdom, confined to transactions by authorised persons and transactions by exempted persons in respect of which they are exempt.

Unsolicited or legitimately solicited transactions etc. with or for other persons

27.—(1) Paragraph 12 above does not apply to any transaction entered into by an overseas person as principal with, or as agent for, a person in the United Kingdom, paragraphs 13, 14 and 15 above do not apply to any offer made by an overseas person to or agreement made by him with a person in the United Kingdom and paragraph 15 above does not apply to any advice given by an overseas person to a person in the United Kingdom if the transaction, offer, agreement or advice is the result of—

(*a*) an approach made to the overseas person by or on behalf of the person in the United Kingdom which either has not been in any way solicited by the overseas person or has been solicited by him in a way which has not contravened section 56 or 57 of this Act ; or

(*b*) an approach made by the overseas person which has not contravened either of those sections.

(2) Where the transaction is entered into by the overseas person as SCH. 1
agent for a person in the United Kingdom, sub-paragraph (1) above
applies only if—

(*a*) the other party is outside the United Kingdom ; or

(*b*) the other party is in the United Kingdom and the transaction
is the result of such an approach by the other party as is
mentioned in sub-paragraph (1)(*a*) above or of such an
approach as is mentioned in sub-paragraph (1)(*b*) above.

PART V
INTERPRETATION

28.—(1) In this Schedule—

(*a*) " property " includes currency of the United Kingdom or
any other country or territory ;

(*b*) references to an instrument include references to any record
whether or not in the form of a document ;

(*c*) references to an offer include references to an invitation to
treat ;

(*d*) references to buying and selling include references to any
acquisition or disposal for valuable consideration.

(2) In sub-paragraph (1)(*d*) above " disposal " includes—

(*a*) in the case of an investment consisting of rights under a
contract or other arrangements, assuming the corresponding
liabilities under the contract or arrangements ;

(*b*) in the case of any other investment, issuing or creating the
investment or granting the rights or interests of which it
consists ;

(*c*) in the case of an investment consisting of rights under a
contract, surrendering, assigning or converting those rights.

(3) A company shall not by reason of issuing its own shares or
share warrants, and a person shall not by reason of issuing his own
debentures or debenture warrants, be regarded for the purposes of
this Schedule as disposing of them or, by reason of anything done
for the purpose of issuing them, be regarded as making arrangements with a view to a person subscribing for or otherwise acquiring
them or underwriting them.

(4) In sub-paragraph (3) above " company " has the same meaning as in paragraph 1 above, " shares " and " debentures " include
any investments falling within paragraph 1 or 2 above and " share
warrants " and " debenture warrants " means any investment which
falls within paragraph 4 above and relates to shares in the company
concerned or, as the case may be, to debentures issued by the person
concerned.

29. For the purposes of this Schedule a transaction is entered
into through a person if he enters into it as agent or arranges for it
to be entered into by another person as principal or agent.

30. For the purposes of this Schedule a group shall be treated
as including any body corporate which is a related company within

the meaning of paragraph 92 of Schedule 4 to the Companies Act 1985 of any member of the group or would be such a related company if the member of the group were a company within the meaning of that Act.

31. In this Schedule "a joint enterprise" means an enterprise into which two or more persons ("the participators") enter for commercial reasons related to a business or businesses (other than investment business) carried on by them ; and where a participator is a body corporate and a member of a group each other member of the group shall also be regarded as a participator in the enterprise.

32. Where a person is an exempted person as respects only part of the investment business carried on by him anything done by him in carrying on that part shall be disregarded in determining whether any paragraph of Part III or IV of this Schedule applies to anything done by him in the course of business in respect of which he is not exempt.

33. In determining for the purposes of this Schedule whether anything constitutes an investment or the carrying on of investment business section 18 of the Gaming Act 1845, section 1 of the Gaming Act 1892, any corresponding provision in force in Northern Ireland and any rule of the law of Scotland whereby a contract by way of gaming or wagering is not legally enforceable shall be disregarded.

SCHEDULE 2

REQUIREMENTS FOR RECOGNITION OF SELF-REGULATING ORGANISATION

Members to be fit and proper persons

1.—(1) The rules and practices of the organisation must be such as to secure that its members are fit and proper persons to carry on investment business of the kind with which the organisation is concerned.

(2) Where the organisation is concerned with investment business of different kinds its rules and practices must be such as to secure that a member carrying on investment business of any of those kinds is a fit and proper person to carry on investment business of that kind.

(3) The matters which may be taken into account under the rules in determining whether a person is a fit and proper person must include those that the Secretary of State may take into account under section 27 above.

(4) This paragraph does not apply to a person who is not an authorised person by virtue of being a member of the organisation.

Admission, expulsion and discipline

2. The rules and practices of the organisation relating to—

(a) the admission and expulsion of members ; and

(b) the discipline it exercises over its members,

must be fair and reasonable and include adequate provision for appeals.

Safeguards for investors

3.—(1) The rules of the organisation governing the carrying on of investment business of any kind by its members must afford investors protection at least equivalent to that afforded in respect of investment business of that kind by the rules and regulations for the time being in force under Chapter V of Part I of this Act.

(2) The rules under that Chapter to be taken into account for the purposes of sub-paragraph (1) above include the rules made under section 49 and under sections 53 and 54 so far as not themselves applying to the members of the organisation.

(3) The organisation must, so far as practicable, have powers for purposes corresponding to those of Chapter VI of Part I of this Act.

(4) The rules of the organisation must enable it to prevent a member resigning from the organisation if the organisation considers that any matter affecting him should be investigated as a preliminary to a decision on the question whether he should be expelled or otherwise disciplined or if it considers that it is desirable that a prohibition or requirement should be imposed on him under the powers mentioned in sub-paragraph (3) above or that any prohibition or requirement imposed on him under those powers should continue in force.

Monitoring and enforcement

4.—(1) The organisation must have adequate arrangements and resources for the effective monitoring and enforcement of compliance with its rules and with any rules or regulations to which its members are subject under Chapter V of Part I of this Act in respect of investment business of a kind regulated by the organisation.

(2) The arrangements for monitoring may make provision for that function to be performed on behalf of the organisation (and without affecting its responsibility) by any other body or person who is able and willing to perform it.

The governing body

5.—(1) The arrangements of the organisation with respect to the appointment, removal from office and functions of the persons responsible for making or enforcing the rules of the organisation must be such as to secure a proper balance—

(a) between the interests of the different members of the organisation ; and

(b) between the interests of the organisation or its members and the interests of the public.

(2) The arrangements shall not be regarded as satisfying the requirements of this paragraph unless the persons responsible for those matters include a number of persons independent of the organisation and its members sufficient to secure the balance referred to in sub-paragraph (1)(b) above.

Investigation of complaints

6.—(1) The organisation must have effective arrangements for the investigation of complaints against the organisation or its members.

(2) The arrangements may make provision for the whole or part of that function to be performed by and to be the responsibility of a body or person independent of the organisation.

Promotion and maintenance of standards

7. The organisation must be able and willing to promote and maintain high standards of integrity and fair dealing in the carrying on of investment business and to co-operate, by the sharing of information and otherwise, with the Secretary of State and any other authority, body or person having responsibility for the supervision or regulation of investment business or other financial services.

SCHEDULE 3

REQUIREMENTS FOR RECOGNITION OF PROFESSIONAL BODY

Statutory status

1. The body must—

    (a) regulate the practice of a profession in the exercise of statutory powers ; or

    (b) be recognised (otherwise than under this Act) for a statutory purpose by a Minister of the Crown or by, or by the head of, a Northern Ireland department ; or

    (c) be specified in a provision contained in or made under an enactment as a body whose members are qualified to exercise functions or hold offices specified in that provision.

Certification

2.—(1) The body must have rules, practices and arrangements for securing that no person can be certified by the body for the purposes of Part I of this Act unless the following conditions are satisfied.

(2) The certified person must be either—

    (a) an individual who is a member of the body ; or

    (b) a person managed and controlled by one or more individuals each of whom is a member of a recognised professional body and at least one of whom is a member of the certifying body.

(3) Where the certified person is an individual his main business must be the practice of the profession regulated by the certifying body and he must be practising that profession otherwise than in partnership ; and where the certified person is not an individual that person's main business must be the practice of the profession or professions regulated by the recognised professional body or bodies of which the individual or individuals mentioned in sub-paragraph (2)(b) above are members.

(4) In the application of sub-paragraphs (2) and (3) above to a
certificate which is to be or has been issued to a partnership constituted under the law of England and Wales or Northern Ireland
or the law of any other country or territory under which a partnership is not a legal person, references to the certified person shall
be construed as references to the partnership.

Safeguards for investors

3.—(1) The body must have rules regulating the carrying on of
investment business by persons certified by it ; and those rules must
in respect of investment business of any kind regulated by them
afford to investors protection at least equivalent to that afforded in
respect of investment business of that kind by the rules and regulations for the time being in force under Chapter V of Part I of this
Act.

(2) The rules under that Chapter to be taken into account for
the purposes of this paragraph include the rules made under section
49 and under sections 53 and 54 so far as not themselves applying
to persons certified by the body.

Monitoring and enforcement

4.—(1) The body must have adequate arrangements and resources
for the effective monitoring of the continued compliance by persons
certified by it with the conditions mentioned in paragraph 2 above
and rules, practices and arrangements for the withdrawal or suspension of certification (subject to appropriate transitional provisions)
in the event of any of those conditions ceasing to be satisfied.

(2) The body must have adequate arrangements and resources for
the effective monitoring and enforcement of compliance by persons
certified by it with the rules of the body relating to the carrying on
of investment business and with any rules or regulations to which
those persons are subject under Chapter V of Part I of this Act in
respect of business of a kind regulated by the body.

(3) The arrangements for enforcement must include provision
for the withdrawal or suspension of certification and may include
provision for disciplining members of the body who manage or
control a certified person.

(4) The arrangements for enforcement may make provision for
the whole or part of that function to be performed by and to be the
responsibility of a body or person independent of the professional
body.

(5) The arrangements for enforcement must be such as to secure
a proper balance between the interests of persons certified by the
body and the interests of the public ; and the arrangements shall not
be regarded as satisfying that requirement unless the persons responsible for enforcement include a sufficient number of persons who are
independent of the body and its members and of persons certified
by it.

Sch. 3

(6) The arrangements for monitoring may make provision for that function to be performed on behalf of the body (and without affecting its responsibility) by any other body or person who is able and willing to perform it.

Investigation of complaints

5.—(1) The body must have effective arrangements for the investigation of complaints relating to—

(a) the carrying on by persons certified by it of investment business in respect of which they are subject to its rules ; and

(b) its regulation of investment business.

(2) Paragraph 4(4) above applies also to arrangements made pursuant to this paragraph.

Promotion and maintenance of standards

6. The body must be able and willing to promote and maintain high standards of integrity and fair dealing in the carrying on of investment business and to co-operate, by the sharing of information and otherwise, with the Secretary of State and any other authority, body or person having responsibility for the supervision or regulation of investment business or other financial services.

Sections 36 and 37.

SCHEDULE 4

REQUIREMENTS FOR RECOGNITION OF INVESTMENT EXCHANGE

Financial resources

1. The exchange must have financial resources sufficient for the proper performance of its functions.

Safeguards for investors

2.—(1) The rules and practices of the exchange must ensure that business conducted by means of its facilities is conducted in an orderly manner and so as to afford proper protection to investors.

(2) The exchange must—

(a) limit dealings on the exchange to investments in which there is a proper market ; and

(b) where relevant, require issuers of investments dealt in on the exchange to comply with such obligations as will, so far as possible, afford to persons dealing in the investments proper information for determining their current value.

(3) In the case of securities to which Part IV of this Act applies compliance by The Stock Exchange with the provisions of that Part shall be treated as compliance by it with sub-paragraph (2) above.

(4) The exchange must either have its own arrangements for ensuring the performance of transactions effected on the exchange

or ensure their performance by means of services provided under clearing arrangements made by it with a recognised clearing house.

(5) The exchange must either itself have or secure the provision on its behalf of satisfactory arrangements for recording the transactions effected on the exchange.

(6) Sub-paragraphs (2), (4) and (5) above are without prejudice to the generality of sub-paragraph (1) above.

Monitoring and enforcement

3.—(1) The exchange must have adequate arrangements and resources for the effective monitoring and enforcement of compliance with its rules and any clearing arrangements made by it.

(2) The arrangements for monitoring may make provision for that function to be performed on behalf of the exchange (and without affecting its responsibility) by any other body or person who is able and willing to perform it.

Investigation of complaints

4. The exchange must have effective arrangements for the investigation of complaints in respect of business transacted by means of its facilities.

Promotion and maintenance of standards

5. The exchange must be able and willing to promote and maintain high standards of integrity and fair dealing in the carrying on of investment business and to co-operate, by the sharing of information and otherwise, with the Secretary of State and any other authority, body or person having responsibility for the supervision or regulation of investment business or other financial services.

SCHEDULE 5

LISTED MONEY MARKET INSTITUTIONS

Section 43.

PART I

TRANSACTIONS NOT SUBJECT TO MONETARY LIMIT

1. This Part of this Schedule applies to any transaction entered into by the listed institution as principal (or as agent for another listed institution) with another listed institution or the Bank of England (whether acting as principal or agent) if the transaction falls within paragraph 2 or 3 below.

2.—(1) A transaction falls within this paragraph if it is in respect of an investment specified in sub-paragraph (2) below and—

    (a) in the case of an investment within any of paragraphs (a) to (d) of that sub-paragraph, the transaction is not regulated by the rules of a recognised investment exchange ; and

    (b) in the case of any other investment specified in that sub-paragraph, the transaction is not made on such an exchange or expressed to be as so made.

Sch. 5

1979 c. 37.

(2) The investments referred to above are—

(*a*) a debenture or other instrument falling within paragraph 2 of Schedule 1 to this Act which is issued—

(i) by a recognised bank or licensed institution within the meaning of the Banking Act 1979 or a building society incorporated in, or in any part of, the United Kingdom ; and

(ii) on terms requiring repayment not later than five years from the date of issue ;

(*b*) any other debenture or instrument falling within paragraph 2 of Schedule 1 to this Act which is issued on terms requiring repayment not later than one year from the date of issue ;

(*c*) loan stock, or any other instrument, falling within paragraph 3 of Schedule 1 to this Act which is issued on terms requiring repayment not later than one year or, if issued by a local authority in the United Kingdom, five years from the date of issue ;

(*d*) a warrant or other instrument falling within paragraph 4 of Schedule 1 to this Act which entitles the holder to subscribe for an investment within paragraph (*a*), (*b*) or (*c*) above ;

(*e*) any certificate or other instrument falling within paragraph 5 or 11 of Schedule 1 to this Act and relating to an investment within paragraph (*a*), (*b*) or (*c*) above ;

(*f*) an option falling within paragraph 7 of Schedule 1 to this Act and relating to—

(i) an investment within paragraph (*a*), (*b*) or (*c*) above ;

(ii) currency of the United Kingdom or of any other country or territory ; or

(iii) gold or silver ;

(*g*) rights under a contract falling within paragraph 8 of Schedule 1 to this Act for the sale of—

(i) an investment within paragraph (*a*), (*b*) or (*c*) above ;

(ii) currency of the United Kingdom or of any other country or territory ; or

(iii) gold or silver ;

(*h*) rights under a contract falling within paragraph 9 of Schedule 1 to this Act by reference to fluctuations in—

(i) the value or price of any investment falling within any of the foregoing paragraphs ; or

(ii) currency of the United Kingdom or of any other country or territory ; or

(iii) the rate of interest on loans in any such currency or any index of such rates ;

(*i*) an option to acquire or dispose of an investment within paragraph (*f*), (*g*) or (*h*) above.

3.—(1) A transaction falls within this paragraph if it is a transaction by which one of the parties agrees to sell or transfer an
investment falling within paragraph 2 or 3 of Schedule 1 to this Act
and by the same or a collateral agreement that party agrees, or
acquires an option, to buy back or re-acquire that investment or an
equivalent amount of a similar investment within twelve months of
the sale or transfer.

(2) For the purposes of this paragraph investments shall be
regarded as similar if they entitle their holders to the same rights
against the same persons as to capital and interest and the same
remedies for the enforcement of those rights.

Part II
Transactions Subject to Monetary Limit

4.—(1) This Part of this Schedule applies to any transaction
entered into by the listed institution—

  (a) as principal (or as agent for another listed institution) with
    an unlisted person (whether acting as principal or agent);

  (b) as agent for an unlisted person with a listed institution or
    the Bank of England (whether acting as principal or agent);
    or

  (c) as agent for an unlisted person with another unlisted per-
    son (whether acting as principal or agent),
if the transaction falls within paragraph 2 or 3 above and the conditions in paragraph 5 or, as the case may be, paragraph 7 below
are satisfied.

(2) In this Part of this Schedule and in Part III below " unlisted
person " means a person who is neither a listed institution nor the
Bank of England.

5.—(1) In the case of a transaction falling within paragraph 2
above the conditions referred to above are as follows but subject to
paragraph 6 below.

(2) The consideration for a transaction in respect of an investment falling within paragraph 2(2)(a), (b), (c) or (e) above must be
not less than £100,000.

(3) The consideration payable on subscription in the case of an
investment falling within paragraph 2(2)(d) must not be less than
£500,000.

(4) The value or price of the property in respect of which an
option within paragraph 2(2)(f) above is granted must not be less
than £500,000.

(5) The price payable under a contract within paragraph 2(2)(g)
above must be not less than £500,000.

(6) The value or price the fluctuation in which, or the amount
the fluctuation in the interest on which, is relevant for the purposes
of a contract within paragraph 2(2)(h) above must not be less than
£500,000.

(7) In the case of an option falling within paragraph 2(2)(*i*) above the condition in sub-paragraph (4), (5) or (6) above, as the case may be, must be satisfied in respect of the investment to which the option relates.

6. The conditions in paragraph 5 above do not apply to a transaction entered into by the listed institution as mentioned in paragraph (*a*), (*b*) or (*c*) of paragraph 4(1) above if—

> (*a*) the unlisted person mentioned in paragraph (*a*) or (*b*) or, as the case may be, each of the unlisted persons mentioned in paragraph (*c*) has in the previous eighteen months entered into another transaction in respect of an investment specified in paragraph 2(2) above ;

> (*b*) those conditions were satisfied in the case of that other transaction ; and

> (*c*) that other transaction was entered into by that person (whether acting as principal or agent) with the listed institution (whether acting as principal or agent) or was entered into by that person through the agency of that institution or was entered into by him (whether acting as principal or agent) as a result of arrangements made by that institution.

7. In the case of a transaction falling within paragraph 3 above the condition referred to in paragraph 4 above is that the consideration for the sale or transfer must be not less than £100,000.

8. The monetary limits mentioned in this Part of this Schedule refer to the time when the transaction is entered into ; and where the consideration, value, price or amount referred to above is not in sterling it shall be converted at the rate of exchange prevailing at that time.

Part III

Transactions arranged by Listed Institutions

9. Subject to paragraphs 10 and 11 below, this Part of this Schedule applies to any transaction arranged by the listed institution which—

> (*a*) is entered into by another listed institution as principal (or as agent for another listed institution) with another listed institution or the Bank of England (whether acting as principal or agent) ;

> (*b*) is entered into by another listed institution (whether acting as principal or agent) with an unlisted person (whether acting as principal or agent) ; or

> (*c*) is entered into between unlisted persons (whether acting as principal or agent),

if the transaction falls within paragraph 2 or 3 above.

10. In the case of a transaction falling within paragraph 2 above paragraph 9(*b*) and (*c*) above do not apply unless either the conditions in paragraph 5 above are satisfied or—

> (*a*) the unlisted person mentioned in paragraph (*b*) or, as the

case may be, each of the unlisted persons mentioned in
paragraph (c) has in the previous eighteen months entered
into another transaction in respect of an investment specified in paragraph 2(2) above ;

(b) those conditions were satisfied in the case of that other
transaction ; and

(c) that other transaction was entered into by that person
(whether acting as principal or agent) with the listed institution making the arrangements (whether acting as principal or agent) or through the agency of that institution or
was entered into by that person (whether acting as principal or agent) as a result of arrangements made by that
institution.

11. In the case of a transaction falling within paragraph 3 above
paragraph 9(b) and (c) above do not apply unless the condition in
paragraph 7 above is satisfied.

SCHEDULE 6

The Financial Services Tribunal

Term of office of members

1.—(1) A person appointed to the panel mentioned in section
96(2) of this Act shall hold and vacate his office in accordance with
the terms of his appointment and on ceasing to hold office shall be
eligible for re-appointment.

(2) A member of the panel appointed by the Lord Chancellor
may resign his office by notice in writing to the Lord Chancellor ;
and a member of the panel appointed by the Secretary of State may
resign his office by notice in writing to the Secretary of State.

Expenses

2. The Secretary of State shall pay to the persons serving as
members of the Tribunal such remuneration and allowances as he
may determine and shall defray such other expenses of the Tribunal
as he may approve.

Staff

3. The Secretary of State may provide the Tribunal with such
officers and servants as he thinks necessary for the proper discharge
of its functions.

Procedure

4.—(1) The Secretary of State may make rules for regulating the
procedure of the Tribunal, including provision for the holding of
any proceedings in private, for the awarding of costs (or, in Scotland, expenses) and for the payment of expenses to persons required
to attend before the Tribunal.

(2) The Tribunal may appoint counsel or a solicitor to assist
it in proceedings before the Tribunal.

Evidence

5.—(1) The Tribunal may by summons require any person to attend, at such time and place as is specified in the summons, to give evidence or to produce any document in his custody or under his control which the Tribunal considers it necessary to examine.

(2) The Tribunal may take evidence on oath and for that purpose administer oaths or may, instead of administering an oath, require the person examined to make and subscribe a declaration of the truth of the matters in respect of which he is examined.

(3) Any person who without reasonable excuse—

    (*a*) refuses or fails to attend in obedience to a summons issued by the Tribunal or to give evidence ; or

    (*b*) alters, suppresses, conceals or destroys or refuses to produce a document which he may be required to produce for the purposes of proceedings before the Tribunal,

shall be guilty of an offence.

(4) A person guilty of an offence under paragraph (*a*) of sub-paragraph (3) above shall be liable on summary conviction to a fine not exceeding the fifth level on the standard scale ; and a person guilty of an offence under paragraph (*b*) of that sub-paragraph shall be liable—

    (*a*) on conviction on indictment, to imprisonment for a term not exceeding two years or to a fine or to both ;

    (*b*) on summary conviction, to a fine not exceeding the statutory maximum.

(5) A person shall not under this paragraph be required to disclose any information or produce any document which he would be entitled to refuse to disclose or produce on grounds of legal professional privilege in proceedings in the High Court or on grounds of confidentiality as between client and professional legal adviser in proceedings in the Court of Session except that a lawyer may be required to furnish the name and address of his client.

(6) Any reference in this paragraph to the production of a document includes a reference to the production of a legible copy of information recorded otherwise than in legible form ; and the reference to suppressing a document includes a reference to destroying the means of reproducing information recorded otherwise than in legible form.

Appeals and supervision by Council on Tribunals

1971 c. 62.   6. The Tribunals and Inquiries Act 1971 shall be amended as follows—

    (*a*) in section 8(2) after " 6A " there shall be inserted " 6B " ;

    (*b*) in section 13(1) after " 6 " there shall be inserted " 6B " ;

    (*c*) in Schedule 1, after paragraph 6A there shall be inserted—

        " Financial services.   6B. The Financial Services Tribunal established by section 96 of the Financial Services Act 1986."

Parliamentary disqualification

7.—(1) In Part III of Schedule 1 to the House of Commons Dis- 1975 c. 24.
qualification Act 1975 (disqualifying offices) there shall be inserted
at the appropriate place " Any member of the Financial Services
Tribunal in receipt of remuneration ".

(2) A corresponding amendment shall be made in Part III of
Schedule 1 to the Northern Ireland Assembly Disqualification Act 1975 c. 25.
1975.

SCHEDULE 7

Section 114.

QUALIFICATIONS OF DESIGNATED AGENCY

Constitution

1.—(1) The constitution of the agency must provide for it to
have—

   (*a*) a chairman ; and

   (*b*) a governing body consisting of the chairman and other
        members ;

and the provisions of the constitution relating to the chairman and
the other members of the governing body must comply with the
following provisions of this paragraph.

(2) The chairman and other members of the governing body
must be persons appointed and liable to removal from office by the
Secretary of State and the Governor of the Bank of England acting
jointly.

(3) The members of the governing body must include—

   (*a*) persons with experience of investment business of a kind
        relevant to the functions or proposed functions of the
        agency ; and

   (*b*) other persons, including regular users on their own
        account or on behalf of others of services provided by per-
        sons carrying on investment business of any such kind ;

and the composition of that body must be such as to secure a proper
balance between the interests of persons carrying on investment
business and the interests of the public.

Arrangements for discharge of functions

2.—(1) The agency's arrangements for the discharge of its functions must comply with the following provisions of this paragraph.

(2) Any rules or regulations must be made by the governing body
of the agency.

(3) Any decision taken in the exercise of other functions must be
taken at a level appropriate to the importance of the decision.

(4) In the case of functions to be discharged by the governing
body, the members falling respectively within paragraphs (*a*) and (*b*)

of paragraph 1(3) above must, so far as practicable, have an opportunity to express their opinions.

(5) Subject to sub-paragraphs (2) to (4) above, the arrangements may enable any functions to be discharged by a committee, sub-committee, officer or servant of the agency.

Monitoring and enforcement

3.—(1) The agency must have a satisfactory system—
  (a) for enabling it to determine whether persons regulated by it are complying with the obligations which it is the responsibility of the agency to enforce ; and
  (b) for the discharge of the agency's responsibility for the enforcement of those obligations.

(2) The system may provide for the functions mentioned in sub-paragraph (1)(a) to be performed on its behalf (and without affecting its responsibility) by any other body or person who is able and willing to perform them.

Investigation of complaints

4.—(1) The agency must have effective arrangements for the investigation of complaints arising out of the conduct of investment business by authorised persons or against any recognised self-regulating organisation, professional body, investment exchange or clearing house.

(2) The arrangements must make provision for the investigation of complaints in respect of authorised persons to be carried out in appropriate cases independently of the agency and those persons.

Promotion and maintenance of standards

5. The agency must be able and willing to promote and maintain high standards of integrity and fair dealing in the carrying on of investment business and to co-operate, by the sharing of information and otherwise, with the Secretary of State and any other authority, body or person having responsibility for the supervision or regulation of investment business or other financial services.

Records

6. The agency must have satisfactory arrangements for recording decisions made in the exercise of its functions and for the safe-keeping of those records which ought to be preserved.

SCHEDULE 8

Principles applicable to Designated Agency's Rules and Regulations

Standards

1. The rules made under section 48 of this Act (in this Schedule referred to as " conduct of business rules ") and the other rules and

regulations made under Part I of this Act must promote high standards of integrity and fair dealing in the conduct of investment business.

2. The conduct of business rules must make proper provision for requiring an authorised person to act with due skill, care and diligence in providing any service which he provides or holds himself out as willing to provide.

3. The conduct of business rules must make proper provision for requiring an authorised person to subordinate his own interests to those of his clients and to act fairly between his clients.

4. The conduct of business rules must make proper provision for requiring an authorised person to ensure that, in anything done by him for the persons with whom he deals, due regard is had to their circumstances.

Disclosure

5. The conduct of business rules must make proper provision for the disclosure by an authorised person of interests in, and facts material to, transactions which are entered into by him in the course of carrying on investment business or in respect of which he gives advice in the course of carrying on such business, including information as to any commissions or other inducements received or receivable from a third party in connection with any such transaction.

6. The conduct of business rules must make proper provision for the disclosure by an authorised person of the capacity in which and the terms on which he enters into any such transaction.

7. The conduct of business rules, or those rules and rules under section 51 of this Act, must make proper provision for requiring an authorised person who in the course of carrying on investment business enters or offers to enter into a transaction in respect of an investment with any person, or gives any person advice about such a transaction, to give that person such information as to the nature of the investment and the financial implications of the transaction as will enable him to make an informed decision.

8. Rules made under section 48 of this Act regulating action for the purpose of stabilising the price of investments must make proper provision for ensuring that where action is or is to be taken in conformity with the rules adequate arrangements exist for making known that the price of the investments in respect of which the action is or is to be taken (and, where relevant, of any other investments) may be affected by that action and the period during which it may be affected; and where a transaction is or is to be entered into during a period when it is known that the price of the investment to which it relates may be affected by any such action the information referred to in paragraph 7 above includes information to that effect.

Protection

9. The conduct of business rules and any regulations made under section 55 of this Act must make proper provision for the protection of property for which an authorised person is liable to account to another person.

SCH. 8

10. Rules made under sections 53 and 54 of this Act must make the best provision that can reasonably be made under those sections.

Records

11. The conduct of business rules must require the keeping of proper records and make provision for their inspection in appropriate cases.

Classes of investors

12. The conduct of business rules and the other rules and regulations made under Chapter V of Part I of this Act must take proper account of the fact that provisions that are appropriate for regulating the conduct of business in relation to some classes of investors may not (by reason of their knowledge, experience or otherwise) be appropriate in relation to others.

Section 116.

SCHEDULE 9

DESIGNATED AGENCIES: STATUS AND EXERCISE OF TRANSFERRED FUNCTIONS

Status

1.—(1) A designated agency shall not be regarded as acting on behalf of the Crown and its members, officers and servants shall not be regarded as Crown servants.

1975 c. 24.

(2) In Part III of Schedule 1 to the House of Commons Disqualification Act 1975 (disqualifying offices) there shall be inserted at the appropriate place—

" Chairman of a designated agency within the meaning of the Financial Services Act 1986 if he is in receipt of remuneration ".

1975 c. 25.

(3) An amendment corresponding to that in sub-paragraph (2) above shall be made in Part III of Schedule 1 to the Northern Ireland Assembly Disqualification Act 1975.

Exemption from requirement of " limited " in name of designated agency

1985 c. 6.

2.—(1) A company is exempt from the requirements of the Companies Act 1985 relating to the use of " limited " as part of the company name if—

    (*a*) it is a designated agency ; and

    (*b*) its memorandum or articles comply with the requirements specified in paragraph (*b*) of subsection (3) of section 30 of that Act.

(2) In subsection (4) of that section (statutory declaration of compliance with requirements entitling company to exemption) the reference to the requirements of subsection (3) of that section shall include a reference to the requirements of sub-paragraph (1) above.

(3) In section 31 of that Act (provisions applicable to exempted companies) the reference to a company which is exempt under section 30 of that Act shall include a reference to a company that is exempt under this paragraph and, in relation to such a company, the power conferred by subsection (2) of that section (direction to include " limited " in company name) shall be exercisable on the ground that the company has ceased to be a designated agency instead of the ground mentioned in paragraph (*a*) of that subsection.

(4) In this paragraph references to the said Act of 1985 and sections 30 and 31 of that Act include references to the corresponding provisions in force in Northern Ireland.

The Tribunal

3.—(1) Where a case is referred to the Tribunal by a designated agency the Tribunal shall send the Secretary of State a copy of any report made by it to the agency in respect of that case.

(2) Where the powers which the Tribunal could, apart from any delegation order, require the Secretary of State to exercise are, by virtue of such an order or of an order resuming any function transferred by it, exercisable partly by the Secretary of State and partly by a designated agency or designated agencies the Tribunal may require any of them to exercise such of those powers as are exercisable by them respectively.

Legislative functions

4.—(1) A designated agency shall send the Secretary of State a copy of any rules or regulations made by it by virtue of functions transferred to it by a delegation order and give him written notice of any amendment or revocation of or addition to any such rules or regulations.

(2) A designated agency shall—

   (*a*) send the Secretary of State a copy of any guidance issued by the agency which is intended to have continuing effect and is issued in writing or other legible form ; and

   (*b*) give him written notice of any amendment, revocation of or addition to guidance issued by it ;

but notice need not be given of the revocation of guidance other than such as is mentioned in paragraph (*a*) above or of any amendment or addition which does not result in or consist of such guidance as is there mentioned.

5. Paragraphs 6 to 9 below shall have effect instead of section 205 (2) and (4) of this Act in relation to rules and regulations made by a designated agency in the exercise of functions transferred to it by a delegation order.

6. The rules and regulations shall be made by an instrument in writing.

7. The instrument shall specify the provision of this Act under which it is made.

8.—(1) Immediately after an instrument is made it shall be printed and made available to the public with or without payment.

(2) A person shall not be taken to have contravened any rule or regulation if he shows that at the time of the alleged contravention the instrument containing the rule or regulation had not been made available as required by this paragraph.

9.—(1) The production of a printed copy of an instrument purporting to be made by the agency on which is endorsed a certificate signed by an officer of the agency authorised by it for that purpose and stating—

(a) that the instrument was made by the agency ;

(b) that the copy is a true copy of the instrument ; and

(c) that on a specified date the instrument was made available to the public as required by paragraph 8 above,

shall be prima facie evidence or, in Scotland, sufficient evidence of the facts stated in the certificate.

(2) Any certificate purporting to be signed as mentioned in sub-paragraph (1) above shall be deemed to have been duly signed unless the contrary is shown.

(3) Any person wishing in any legal proceedings to cite an instrument made by the agency may require the agency to cause a copy of it to be endorsed with such a certificate as is mentioned in this paragraph.

Fees

10.—(1) A designated agency may retain any fees payable to it by virtue of the delegation order.

(2) Any such fees shall be applicable for meeting the expenses of the agency in discharging its functions under the order and for any purposes incidental thereto.

(3) Any fees payable to a designated agency by virtue of a delegation order made before the coming into force of section 3 of this Act may also be applied for repaying the principal of, and paying interest on, any money borrowed by the agency (or by any other person whose liabilities in respect of the money are assumed by the agency) which has been used for the purpose of defraying expenses incurred before the making of the order (whether before or after the passing of this Act) in making preparations for the agency becoming a designated agency.

11. If the function of prescribing the amount of any fee, or of making a scheme under section 112 above, is exercisable by a designated agency it may prescribe or make provision for such fees as will enable it to defray any such expenses as are mentioned in paragraph 10 above.

Consultation

12.—(1) Before making any rules or regulations by virtue of functions transferred to it by a delegation order a designated agency

shall, subject to sub-paragraphs (2) and (3) below, publish the proposed rules and regulations in such manner as appears to the agency
to be best calculated to bring them to the attention of the public,
together with a statement that representations in respect of the proposals can be made to the agency within a specified period ; and
before making the rules or regulations the agency shall have regard
to any representations duly made in accordance with that statement.

(2) Sub-paragraph (1) above does not apply in any case in which
the agency considers that the delay involved in complying with that
sub-paragraph would be prejudicial to the interests of investors.

(3) Sub-paragraph (1) above does not apply to the making of any
rule or regulation if it is in the same terms (or substantially the same
terms) as a proposed rule or regulation which was furnished by the
agency to the Secretary of State for the purposes of section 114(9)
of this Act.

Exchange of information

13.—(1) The Secretary of State may communicate to a designated
agency any information in his possession of which he could have
availed himself for the purpose of exercising any function which
by virtue of a delegation order is for the time being exercisable by
the agency.

(2) A designated agency may in the exercise of any function
which by virtue of a delegation order is for the time being exercisable by it communicate to any other person any information
which has been communicated to the agency by the Secretary of
State and which the Secretary of State could have communicated
to that person in the exercise of that function.

(3) No communication of information under sub-paragraph (1)
above shall constitute publication for the purposes of the law of
defamation.

SCHEDULE 10   Section 129.

Regulated Insurance Companies

Preliminary

1. In this Part of this Schedule " a regulated insurance company "
means any such company as is mentioned in section 129 of this
Act.

Authorisations for investment business and insurance business

2.—(1) An insurance company to which section 22 of this Act
applies shall not be an authorised person except by virtue of that
section.

(2) If an insurance company to which Part II of the Insurance 1982 c. 50.
Companies Act 1982 applies but to which section 22 of this Act does
not apply becomes an authorised person by virtue of any other
provision of this Act it shall be an authorised person only as respects
the management of the investments of any pension fund which is

established solely for the benefit of the officers or employees and their dependants of that company or of any other body corporate in the same group as that company.

(3) An insurance company to which section 31 of this Act applies shall not, so long as it is an authorised person by virtue of that section, be an authorised person by virtue of any other provision of this Act.

(4) None of the provisions of Part I of this Act shall be construed as authorising any person to carry on insurance business in any case in which he could not lawfully do so apart from those provisions.

Recognition of self-regulating organisation with insurance company members.

3.—(1) In the case of a self-regulating organisation whose members include or may include regulated insurance companies the requirements of Schedule 2 to this Act shall include a requirement that the rules of the organisation must take proper account of Part
II of the Insurance Companies Act 1982 or, as the case may be, of the provisions for corresponding purposes in the law of any member State in which such companies are established.

(2) Where the function of making or revoking a recognition order in respect of such a self-regulating organisation is exercisable by a designated agency it shall not regard that requirement as satisfied unless the Secretary of State has certified that he also regards it as satisfied.

(3) A delegation order—

    (a) may reserve to the Secretary of State the function of revoking a recognition order in respect of such a self-regulating organisation as is mentioned in sub-paragraph (1) above on the ground that the requirement there mentioned is not satisfied ; and

    (b) shall not transfer to a designated agency the function of revoking any such recognition order on the ground that the organisation has contravened sub-paragraphs (3) or (4) of paragraph 6 below as applied by sub-paragraph (5) of that paragraph.

(4) In the case of such a self-regulating organisation as is mentioned in sub-paragraph (1) above the requirements of Schedule 2 to this Act referred to in section 187(2)(a) of this Act shall include the requirement mentioned in that sub-paragraph.

Modification of provisions as to conduct of investment business

4.—(1) The rules under section 48 of this Act shall not apply to a regulated insurance company except so far as they make provision as respects the matters mentioned in sub-paragraph (2) below.

(2) The matters referred to in sub-paragraph (1) above are—

    (a) procuring proposals for policies the rights under which constitute an investment for the purposes of this Act and advising persons on such policies and the exercise of the rights conferred by them ;

(*b*) managing the investments of pension funds, procuring persons to enter into contracts for the management of such
investments and advising persons on such contracts and the
exercise of the rights conferred by them ;

(*c*) matters incidental to those mentioned in paragraph (*a*) and
(*b*) above.

(3) The rules under section 49 of this Act shall not apply to an
insurance company which is an authorised person by virtue of
section 31 of this Act.

(4) The rules under sections 53 and 54 of this Act shall not apply
to loss arising as a result of a regulated insurance company being
unable to meet its liabilities under a contract of insurance.

(5) A direction under section 59 of this Act shall not prohibit the
employment of a person by a regulated insurance company except
in connection with—

(*a*) the matters mentioned in sub-paragraph (2) above ; or

(*b*) investment business carried on in connection with or for
the purposes of those matters.

(6) The Secretary of State shall not make a delegation order transferring any functions of making rules or regulations under Chapter V
of Part I of this Act in relation to a regulated insurance company
unless he is satisfied that those rules and regulations will take proper
account of Part II of the Insurance Companies Act 1982 or, as the
case may be, of the provisions for corresponding purposes in the law
of the member State in which the company is established ; and in
section 115(5) of this Act the reference to the requirements of section
114(9)(*b*) shall include a reference to the requirements of this sub-
paragraph.

Restriction of provisions as to conduct of insurance business

5.—(1) Regulations under section 72 of the Insurance Companies
Act 1982 (insurance advertisements) shall not apply to so much of
any advertisement issued by an authorised person as relates to a contract of insurance the rights under which constitute an investment for
the purposes of this Act.

(2) No requirement imposed under section 74 of that Act (inter-
mediaries in insurance transactions) shall apply in respect of an
invitation issued by, or by an appointed representative of, an authorised person in relation to a contract of insurance the rights under
which constitute an investment for the purposes of this Act.

(3) Subject to sub-paragraph (4) below, sections 75 to 77 of that
Act (right to withdraw from long-term policies) shall not apply to
a regulated insurance company in respect of a contract of insurance
the rights under which constitute an investment for the purposes of
this Act.

(4) Sub-paragraph (3) above does not affect the operation of the
said sections 75 to 77 in a case in which the statutory notice required
by those sections has been or ought to have been served before
the coming into force of that sub-paragraph.

Exercise of powers of intervention etc.

6.—(1) The powers conferred by Chapter VI of Part I of this Act shall not be exercisable in relation to a regulated insurance company on the ground specified in section 64(1)(*a*) of this Act for reasons relating to the ability of the company to meet its liabilities to policy holders or potential policy holders.

(2) The powers conferred by sections 66 and 68 of this Act, and those conferred by section 67 of this Act so far as applicable to assets belonging to the authorised person, shall not be exercisable in relation to a regulated insurance company.

(3) A designated agency shall not in the case of a regulated insurance company impose any prohibition or requirement under section 65 or 67 of this Act, or vary any such prohibition or requirement, unless it has given reasonable notice of its intention to do so to the Secretary of State and informed him—

> (*a*) of the manner in which and the date on or after which it intends to exercise that power ; and

> (*b*) in the case of a proposal to impose a prohibition or requirement, on which of the grounds specified in section 64(1) of this Act it proposes to act and its reasons for considering that the ground in question exists and that it is necessary to impose the prohibition or requirement.

(4) A designated agency shall not exercise any power to which sub-paragraph (3) above applies if the Secretary of State has before the date specified in accordance with sub-paragraph (3), above served on it a notice in writing directing it not to do so ; and the Secretary of State may serve such a notice if he considers it desirable for protecting policy holders or potential policy holders of the company against the risk that it may be unable to meet its liabilities or to fulfil the reasonable expectations of its policy holders or potential policy holders.

(5) Sub-paragraphs (3) and (4) above shall, with the necessary modifications, apply also where a recognised self-regulating organisation proposes to exercise, in the case of a member who is a regulated insurance company, any powers of the organisation for purposes corresponding to those of Chapter VI of Part I of this Act.

(6) The powers conferred by sections 72 and 73 of this Act shall not be exercisable in relation to a regulated insurance company.

Withdrawal of insurance business authorisation

1982 c. 50.   7.—(1) At the end of section 11(2)(*a*) of the Insurance Companies Act 1982 (withdrawal of authorisation in respect of new business where insurance company has failed to satisfy an obligation to which it is subject by virtue of that Act) there shall be inserted the words " or the Financial Services Act 1986 or, if it is a member of a recognised self-regulating organisation within the meaning of that Act, an obligation to which it is subject by virtue of the rules of that organisation ".

(2) After subsection (2) of section 13 of that Act (final withdrawal of authorisation) there shall be inserted—

"(2A) The Secretary of State may direct that an insurance
company shall cease to be authorised to carry on business which
is insurance business by virtue of section 95(*c*)(ii) of this Act
if it appears to him that the company has failed to satisfy an
obligation to which it is subject by virtue of the Financial
Services Act 1986 or, if it is a member of a recognised self-
regulating organisation within the meaning of that Act, an
obligation to which it is subject by virtue of the rules of that
organisation.

(2B) Subsections (3), (5) and (6) of section 11 and subsections (1) and (5) to (8) of section 12 above shall apply to
a direction under subsection (2A) above as they apply to a
direction under section 11."

*Termination of investment business authorisation of
insurer established in other member State*

8.—(1) Sections 33(1)(*b*) and 34 of this Act shall not apply to
a regulated insurance company.

(2) A direction under section 33(1)(*a*) of this Act in respect of such
an insurance company may provide that the company shall cease
to be an authorised person except as respects investment business
of a kind specified in the direction and shall not make it unlawful
for the company to effect a contract of insurance in pursuance of
a subsisting contract of insurance.

(3) Where the Secretary of State proposes to give a direction
under section 33(1)(*a*) of this Act in respect of such an insurance
company he shall give it written notice of his intention to do so,
giving particulars of the grounds on which he proposes to act and
of the rights exercisable under sub-paragraph (4) below.

(4) An insurance company on which a notice is served under
sub-paragraph (3) above may within fourteen days after the date
of service make written representations to the Secretary of State
and, if desired, oral representations to a person appointed for
that purpose by the Secretary of State; and the Secretary of
State shall have regard to any representations made in accordance
with this sub-paragraph in determining whether to give the direction.

(5) After giving a direction under section 33(1)(*a*) of this Act in
respect of a regulated insurance company the Secretary of State shall
inform the company in writing of the reasons for giving the direction.

(6) A delegation order shall not transfer to a designated agency
the function of giving a direction under section 33(1)(*a*) of this Act
in respect of a regulated insurance company.

Powers of Tribunal

9. In the case of a regulated insurance company the provisions
mentioned in section 98(4) of this Act shall include sections 11 and
13(2A) of the Insurance Companies Act 1982 but where the Tribunal 1982 c. 50.

SCH. 10   reports that the appropriate decision would be to take action under either of those sections or under section 33(1)(*a*) of this Act the Secretary of State shall take the report into consideration but shall not be bound to act upon it.

Consultation with designated agencies

10.—(1) Where any functions under this Act are for the time being exercisable by a designated agency in relation to regulated insurance companies the Secretary of State shall, before issuing an authorisation under section 3 of the Insurance Companies Act 1982
1982 c. 50.   to an applicant who proposes to carry on in the United Kingdom insurance business which is investment business—

> (*a*) seek the advice of the designated agency with respect to any matters which are relevant to those functions of the agency and relate to the applicant, his proposed business or persons who will be associated with him in, or in connection with, that business ; and
>
> (*b*) take into account any advice on those matters given to him by the agency before the end of the period within which the application is required to be decided.

(2) The Secretary of State may for the purpose of obtaining the advice of a designated agency under sub-paragraph (1) above furnish it with any information obtained by him in connection with the application.

(3) If a designated agency by which any functions under this Act are for the time being exercisable in relation to regulated insurance companies has reasonable grounds for believing that any such insurance company has failed to comply with an obligation to which it is subject by virtue of this Act it shall forthwith give notice of that fact to the Secretary of State so that he can take it into consideration in deciding whether to give a direction in respect of the company under section 11 or 13(2A) of the said Act of 1982 or section 33 of this Act.

(4) A notice under sub-paragraph (3) above shall contain particulars of the obligation in question and of the agency's reasons for considering that the company has failed to satisfy that obligation.

(5) A designated agency need not give a notice under sub-paragraph (3) above in respect of any matter unless it considers that that matter (either alone or in conjunction with other matters) would justify the withdrawal of authorisation under section 28 of this Act in the case of a person to whom that section applies.

Section 140.   SCHEDULE 11

FRIENDLY SOCIETIES

PART I

PRELIMINARY

1. In this Schedule—
    " a regulated friendly society " means a society which is an

authorised person by virtue of section 23 of this Act as respects such investment business as is mentioned in that section ;

" regulated business ", in relation to a regulated friendly society, means investment business as respects which the society is authorised by virtue of that section ;

" a self-regulating organisation for friendly societies " means a self-regulating organisation which is permitted under its rules to admit regulated friendly societies as members and to regulate the carrying on by such societies of regulated business ;

" a recognised self-regulating organisation for friendly societies " means a body declared by an order of the Registrar for the time being in force to be a recognised self-regulating organisation for friendly societies for the purposes of this Schedule ;

" a member society " means a regulated friendly society which is a member of an appropriate recognised self-regulating organisation for friendly societies and is subject to its rules in carrying on all its regulated business and, for the purposes of this definition, " an appropriate recognised self-regulating organisation for friendly societies " means—

(a) in the case of any such society as is mentioned in section 23(1) of this Act, an organisation declared by an order of the Chief Registrar of friendly societies for the time being in force to be a recognised self-regulating organisation for friendly societies for the purposes of this Schedule ; and

(b) in the case of any such society as is mentioned in section 23(2) of this Act, an organisation declared by an order of the Registrar of Friendly Societies for Northern Ireland for the time being in force to be such an organisation ;

" the Registrar " means—

(a) in relation to any such society as is mentioned in section 23(1) of this Act, or to any self-regulating organisation for friendly societies which has applied for or been granted a recognition order made by him, the Chief Registrar of friendly societies ; and

(b) in relation to any such society as is mentioned in section 23(2) of this Act, or to any self-regulating organisation for friendly societies which has applied for or been granted a recognition order made by him, the Registrar of Friendly Societies for Northern Ireland.

PART II

SELF-REGULATING ORGANISATIONS FOR FRIENDLY SOCIETIES

Recognition

2.—(1) A self-regulating organisation for friendly societies may apply to the Chief Registrar of friendly societies or the Registrar of

H 2

Friendly Societies for Northern Ireland for an order declaring it to be a recognised self-regulating organisation for friendly societies for the purposes of this Schedule.

(2) An application under sub-paragraph (1) above—

(a) shall be made in such manner as the Registrar may direct; and

(b) shall be accompanied by such information as the Registrar may reasonably require for the purpose of determining the application.

(3) At any time after receiving an application and before determining it the Registrar may require the applicant to furnish additional information.

(4) The directions and requirements given or imposed under sub-paragraphs (2) and (3) above may differ as between different applications.

(5) Any information to be furnished to the Registrar under this paragraph shall, if he so requires, be in such form or verified in such manner as he may specify.

(6) Every application shall be accompanied by a copy of the applicant's rules and of any guidance issued by the applicant which is intended to have continuing effect and is issued in writing or other legible form.

3.—(1) If, on an application duly made in accordance with paragraph 2 above and after being furnished with all such information as he may require under that paragraph, it appears to the Registrar from that information and having regard to any other information in his possession that the requirements mentioned in paragraph 4 below are satisfied as respects that organisation, he may, with the consent of the Secretary of State and subject to sub-paragraph (2) below, make an order ("a recognition order") declaring the applicant to be a recognised self-regulating organisation for friendly societies.

(2) Where the Registrar proposes to grant an application for a recognition order he shall send to the Secretary of State a copy of the application together with a copy of the rules and any guidance accompanying the application and the Secretary of State shall not consent to the making of the recognition order unless he is satisfied that the rules and guidance of which copies have been sent to him under this sub-paragraph do not have, and are not intended or likely to have, to any significant extent the effect of restricting, distorting or preventing competition or, if they have or are intended or likely to have that effect to any significant extent, that the effect is not greater than is necessary for the protection of investors.

(3) Section 122 of this Act shall apply in relation to the decision whether to consent to the making of a recognition order under this paragraph as it applies to the decisions mentioned in subsection (1) of that section.

(4) Subsections (1) and (2) of section 128 of this Act shall apply for the purposes of this paragraph as if the powers there mentioned included the power of refusing consent to the making of

a recognition order under this paragraph and subsection (5) of that
section shall apply for that purpose as if the reference to Chapter
XIV of Part I included a reference to this paragraph.

(5) The Registrar may refuse to make a recognition order in
respect of an organisation if he considers that its recognition is
unnecessary having regard to the existence of one or more other
organisations which are concerned with such investment business
as is mentioned in section 23 of this Act and which have been or are
likely to be recognised under this paragraph.

(6) Where the Registrar refuses an application for a recognition
order he shall give the applicant a written notice to that effect
specifying a requirement which in the opinion of the Registrar is not
satisfied, stating that the application is refused on the ground mentioned in sub-paragraph (5) above or stating that the Secretary of
State has refused to consent to the making of the order.

(7) A recognition order shall state the date on which it takes effect.

4.—(1) The requirements referred to in paragraph 3 above are that
mentioned in sub-paragraph (2) below and those set out in paragraphs 2 to 7 of Schedule 2 to this Act as modified in sub-paragraphs
(3) to (5) below.

(2) The rules of the organisation must take proper account of the 1974 c. 46.
Friendly Societies Act 1974, or as the case may be, the Friendly 1970 c. 31
Societies Act (Northern Ireland) 1970. (N.I.).

(3) References in paragraphs 2, 3, 4 and 6 of Schedule 2 to
members are to members who are regulated friendly societies.

(4) In paragraph 3 of that Schedule—

  (a) in sub-paragraph (1) for the reference to Chapter V of Part
      I of this Act there shall be substituted a reference to para-
      graphs 14 to 22 below ; and

  (b) in sub-paragraph (2) the reference to section 49 of this
      Act shall be omitted and for the reference to sections 53
      and 54 there shall be substituted a reference to paragraphs
      17 and 18 below ; and

  (c) in sub-paragraph (3) for the reference to Chapter VI of that
      Part there shall be substituted a reference to the powers
      exercisable by the Registrar by virtue of paragraph 23
      below.

(5) In paragraph 4 of that Schedule for the reference to Chapter V
of Part I of this Act there shall be substituted references to paragraphs 14 to 22 below.

Revocation of recognition

5.—(1) A recognition order may be revoked by a further order
made by the Registrar if at any time it appears to him—

  (a) that any requirement mentioned in paragraph 4(1) above is
      not satisfied in the case of the organisation to which the
      recognition order relates (" the recognised organisation ") ;

H3

(*b*) that the recognised organisation has failed to comply with any obligation to which it is subject by virtue of this Act ; or

(*c*) that the continued recognition of the organisation is undesirable having regard to the existence of one or more other organisations which have been or are to be recognised under paragraph 3 above.

(2) Subsections (2) to (9) of section 11 of this Act shall have effect in relation to the revocation of a recognition order under this paragraph as they have effect in relation to the revocation of a recognition order under subsection (1) of that section but with the substitution—

(*a*) for references to the Secretary of State of references to the Registrar ;

(*b*) for the reference in subsection (3) to members of a reference to members of the organisation which are member societies in relation to it ; and

(*c*) for the reference in subsection (6) to investors of a reference to members of the societies which are member societies in relation to the organisation.

Compliance orders

6.—(1) If at any time it appears to the Registrar—

(*a*) that any requirement mentioned in paragraph 3 above is not satisfied in the case of a recognised self-regulating organisation for friendly societies ; or

(*b*) that such an organisation has failed to comply with any obligation to which it is subject by virtue of this Act,

he may, instead of revoking the recognition order under paragraph 5 above, make an application to the court under this paragraph.

(2) If on any such application the court decides that the requirement in question is not satisfied or, as the case may be, that the organisation has failed to comply with the obligation in question it may order the organisation concerned to take such steps as the court directs for securing that that requirement is satisfied or that that obligation is complied with.

(3) The jurisdiction conferred by this paragraph shall be exercisable by the High Court and the Court of Session.

7.—(1) If at any time it appears to the Registrar that the rules of a recognised self-regulating organisation for friendly societies do not satisfy the requirements of paragraph 3(1) of Schedule 2 to this Act as modified by paragraph 4(4) above he may, instead of revoking the recognition order or making an application under paragraph 6 above, direct the organisation to alter, or himself alter, its rules in such manner as he considers necessary for securing that the rules satisfy those requirements.

(2) Before giving a direction or making any alteration under this paragraph the Registrar shall consult the organisation concerned.

(3) Any direction given under sub-paragraph (1) above shall, on the application of the Registrar, be enforceable by mandamus or, in Scotland, by an order for specific performance under section 91 of the Court of Session Act 1868.

(4) A recognised self-regulating organisation for friendly societies whose rules have been altered by or pursuant to a direction given by the Registrar under sub-paragraph (1) above may apply to the court and if the court is satisfied—

> (*a*) that the rules without the alteration satisfied the requirements mentioned in that sub-paragraph ; or
>
> (*b*) that other alterations proposed by the organisation would result in the rules satisfying those requirements,

the court may set aside the alteration made by or pursuant to the direction given by the Registrar and, in a case within paragraph (*b*) above, order the organisation to make the alterations proposed by it ; but the setting aside of an alteration under this sub-paragraph shall not affect its previous operation.

(5) The jurisdiction conferred by sub-paragraph (4) above shall be exercisable by the High Court and the Court of Session.

(6) Subsections (2) to (7) and (9) of section 11 of this Act shall, with the modifications mentioned in paragraph 5(2) above and any other necessary modifications, have effect in relation to any direction given or alteration made by the Registrar under sub-paragraph (1) above as they have effect in relation to an order revoking a recognition order.

(7) The fact that the rules of an organisation have been altered by or pursuant to a direction given by the Registrar, or pursuant to an order made by the court, under this paragraph shall not preclude their subsequent alteration or revocation by that organisation.

8.—(1) The Registrar or the Secretary of State may make regulations requiring a recognised self-regulating organisation for friendly societies to give the Registrar or, as the case may be, the Secretary of State forthwith notice of the occurrence of such events relating to the organisation or its members as are specified in the regulations and such information in respect of those events as is so specified.

(2) The Registrar or the Secretary of State may make regulations requiring a recognised self-regulating organisation for friendly societies to furnish the Registrar or, as the case may be, the Secretary of State at such times or in respect of such periods as are specified in the regulations with such information relating to the organisation or its members as is so specified.

(3) The notices and information required to be given or furnished under the foregoing provisions of this paragraph shall be such as the Registrar or, as the case may be, the Secretary of State may reasonably require for the exercise of his functions under this Act.

(4) Regulations under the foregoing provisions of this paragraph may require information to be given in a specified form and to be verified in a specified manner.

(5) A notice or information required to be given or furnished under the foregoing provisions of this paragraph shall be given in writing or such other manner as the Registrar or, as the case may be, the Secretary of State may approve.

(6) Where a recognised self-regulating organisation for friendly societies amends, revokes or adds to its rules or guidance it shall within seven days give the Registrar written notice of the amendment, revocation or addition; but notice need not be given of the revocation of guidance other than such as is mentioned in paragraph 2(6) above or of any amendment of or addition to guidance which does not result in or consist of such guidance as is there mentioned.

(7) The Registrar shall send the Secretary of State a copy of any notice given to him under sub-paragraph (6) above.

(8) Contravention of or of regulations under this paragraph shall not be an offence.

9.—(1) A recognised self-regulating organisation for friendly societies shall not exercise any powers for purposes corresponding to those of the powers exercisable by the Registrar by virtue of paragraph 23 below in relation to a regulated friendly society unless it has given reasonable notice of its intention to do so to the Registrar and informed him—

(a) of the manner in which and the date on or after which it intends to exercise the power; and

(b) in the case of a proposal to impose a prohibition or requirement, of the reason why it proposes to act and its reasons for considering that that reason exists and that it is necessary to impose the prohibition or requirement.

(2) A recognised self-regulating organisation for friendly societies shall not exercise any power to which sub-paragraph (1)(a) above applies if before the date given in the notice in pursuance of that sub-paragraph the Registrar has served on it a notice in writing directing it not to do so; and the Registrar may serve such a notice if he considers it is desirable for protecting members or potential members of the society against the risk that it may be unable to meet its liabilities or to fulfil the reasonable expectations of its members or potential members.

Prevention of restrictive practices

10.—(1) The powers conferred by sub-paragraph (2) below shall be exercisable by the Secretary of State if at any time it appears to him that—

(a) any rules made or guidance issued by a recognised self-regulating organisation for friendly societies;

(b) any practices of any such organisation; or

(c) any practices of persons who are members of, or otherwise subject to the rules made by, any such organisation,

have, or are intended or likely to have, to a significant extent the effect of restricting, distorting or preventing competition and that that effect is greater than is necessary for the protection of investors.

(2) The powers exercisable under this sub-paragraph are to direct the Registrar—

    (*a*) to revoke the recognition order of the organisation ;

    (*b*) to direct the organisation to take specified steps for the purpose of securing that the rules, guidance or practices in question do not have the effect mentioned in sub-paragraph (1) above ;

    (*c*) to make alterations in the rules for that purpose ;

and subsections (2) to (5), (7) and (9) of section 11 of this Act, as applied by sub-paragraph (2) of paragraph 5 above, shall have effect in relation to the revocation of a recognition order by virtue of a direction under this sub-paragraph as they have effect in relation to the revocation of such an order under sub-paragraph (1) of that paragraph.

(3) The practices referred to in paragraph (*b*) of sub-paragraph (1) above are practices of the organisation in its capacity as such ; and the practices referred to in paragraph (*c*) of that sub-paragraph are practices in relation to business in respect of which the persons in question are subject to the rules of the organisation and which are required or contemplated by its rules or guidance or otherwise attributable to its conduct in its capacity as such.

(4) Subsections (3) to (8) of section 122 of this Act shall apply for the purposes of this paragraph as if—

    (*a*) the reference to a notice in subsection (3) included a notice received under paragraph 8(7) above or 33(4) below ;

    (*b*) the references to rules and guidance in subsection (4) included such rules and guidance as are mentioned in sub-paragraph (1) above ;

    (*c*) the reference to practices in subsection (6) included such practices as are mentioned in sub-paragraph (1) above ; and

    (*d*) the reference to the Secretary of State's powers in subsection (7) included his powers under sub-paragraph (2) above.

(6) Section 128 of this Act shall apply for the purposes of this paragraph as if—

    (*a*) the powers referred to in subsection (1) of that section included the powers conferred by sub-paragraph (2)(*b*) and (*c*) above ;

    (*b*) the references to Chapter XIV of Part I included references to this paragraph ; and

    (*c*) the reference to a recognised self-regulating organisation included a reference to a recognised self-regulating organisation for friendly societies.

Fees

11.—(1) An applicant for a recognition order under paragraph 3 above shall pay such fees in respect of his application as may be required by a scheme made and published by the Registrar ; and no application for such an order shall be regarded as duly made unless this sub-paragraph is complied with.

　　(2) Subsections (2) to (4) of section 112 of this Act apply to a scheme under sub-paragraph (1) above as they apply to a scheme under subsection (1) of that section.

(3) Every recognised self-regulating organisation for friendly societies shall pay such periodical fees to the Registrar as he may by regulations prescribe.

Application of provisions of this Act

12.—(1) Subject to the following provisions of this paragraph, sections 44(7), 102(1)(c), 124, 125, 126, 180(1)(n), 181, 187, 192 and 200(4) of this Act shall apply in relation to recognised self-regulating organisations for friendly societies as they apply in relation to recognised self-regulating organisations.

(2) In its application by virtue of sub-paragraph (1) above section 126(1) of this Act shall have effect as if the reference to section 119(2) were a reference to paragraph 10(1) above.

(3) In its application by virtue of sub-paragraph (1) above subsection (2) of section 187 of this Act shall have effect as if—

　　(a) the reference in paragraph (a) to paragraphs 1 to 6 of Schedule 2 were to paragraphs 2 to 6 of that Schedule (as they apply by virtue of paragraph 4 above) and to sub-paragraph (2) of paragraph 4 above ; and

　　(b) paragraph (d) referred to the powers of the organisation under paragraph 23(4) below.

(4) A direction under subsection (1) of section 192 of this Act as it applies by virtue of sub-paragraph (1) above shall direct the Registrar to direct the organisation not to take or, as the case may be, to take the action in question ; and where the function of making or revoking a recognition order in respect of a self-regulating organisation for friendly societies is exercisable by a transferee body any direction under that subsection as it applies as aforesaid shall be a direction requiring the Registrar to direct the transferee body to give the organisation such a direction as is specified in the direction given by the Secretary of State.

(5) Subsection (5) of that section shall not apply to a direction given to the Registrar by virtue of this paragraph.

PART III

REGISTRAR'S POWERS IN RELATION TO REGULATED FRIENDLY SOCIETIES

Special provisions for regulated friendly societies

13. Paragraphs 14 to 25 below shall have effect in connection with the exercise of powers for the regulation of regulated friendly societies in relation to regulated business, but nothing in this Part of this Schedule shall affect the exercise of any power conferred by this Act in relation to a regulated friendly society which is an authorised person by virtue of section 25 of this Act to the extent that the power relates to other investment business.

Conduct of investment business

14.—(1) The rules under section 48 of this Act shall not apply to a regulated friendly society but the Registrar may, with the consent of the Secretary of State, make such rules as may be made under that section regulating the conduct of any such society other than a member society as respects the matters mentioned in sub-paragraph (2) below.

(2) The matters referred to in sub-paragraph (1) above are—

(a) procuring persons to transact regulated business with it and advising persons as to the exercise of rights conferred by investments acquired from the society in the course of such business ;

(b) managing the investments of pension funds, procuring persons to enter into contracts for the management of such investments and advising persons on such contracts and the exercise of the rights conferred by them ;

(c) matters incidental to those mentioned in paragraphs (a) and (b) above.

(3) Section 50 of this Act shall apply in relation to rules under this paragraph as it applies in relation to rules under section 48 except that—

(a) for the reference to the Secretary of State there shall be substituted a reference to the Registrar ; and

(b) the Registrar shall not exercise the power under subsection (1) to alter the requirement of rules made under this paragraph without the consent of the Secretary of State.

15.—(1) The rules under section 51 of this Act shall not apply to any investment agreement which a person has entered or offered to enter into with a regulated friendly society if, as respects the society, entering into the agreement constitutes the carrying on of regulated business but the Registrar may, with the consent of the Secretary of State, make rules for enabling a person who has entered or offered to enter into such an agreement to rescind the agreement or withdraw the offer within such period and in such manner as may be specified in the rules.

(2) Subsection (2) of section 51 of this Act shall apply in relation to rules under this paragraph as it applies in relation to rules under that section but with the substitution for the reference to the Secretary of State of a reference to the Registrar.

16.—(1) Regulations under section 52 of this Act shall not apply to any regulated friendly society but the Registrar may, with the consent of the Secretary of State, make such regulations as may be made under that section imposing requirements on regulated friendly societies other than member societies.

(2) Any notice or information required to be given or furnished under this paragraph shall be given in writing or in such other manner as the Registrar may approve.

17.—(1) Rules under section 53 of this Act shall not apply to any regulated friendly society but the Registrar may, with the consent of the Secretary of State make rules concerning indemnity against any claim in respect of any description of civil liability incurred by a regulated friendly society in connection with any regulated business.

(2) Such rules shall not apply to a member society of a recognised self-regulating organisation for friendly societies unless that organisation has requested that such rules should apply to it; and any such request shall not be capable of being withdrawn after rules giving effect to it have been made but without prejudice to the power of the Registrar to revoke the rules if he and the Secretary of State think fit.

(3) Subsections (3) and (4) of section 53 of this Act shall apply in relation to such rules as they apply to rules under that section but with the substitution for references to the Secretary of State of references to the Registrar.

18.—(1) No scheme established by rules under section 54 shall apply in cases where persons who are or have been regulated friendly societies are unable, or likely to be unable, to satisfy claims in respect of any description of civil liability incurred by them in connection with any regulated business but the Registrar may, with the consent of the Secretary of State, by rules establish a scheme for compensating investors in such cases.

(2) Subject to sub-paragraph (3) below, subsections (2) to (4) and (6) of that section shall apply in relation to such rules as they apply to rules under that section but with the substitution for the references to the Secretary of State, authorised persons, members and a recognised self-regulating organisation of references respectively to the Registrar, regulated friendly societies, member societies and a recognised self-regulating organisation for friendly societies.

(3) Subsection (3) of that section shall have effect with the substitution for the words " the Secretary of State is satisfied " of the words " the Registrar and the Secretary of State are satisfied ".

(4) The references in section 179(3)(*b*) and 180(1)(*e*) of this Act to the body administering a scheme established under section 54 of this Act shall include the body administering a scheme established under this paragraph.

19.—(1) Regulations under section 55 of this Act shall not apply to money held by regulated friendly societies but the Registrar may, with the consent of the Secretary of State, make regulations with respect to money held by a regulated friendly society in such circumstances as may be specified in the regulations.

(2) Regulations under this paragraph shall not provide that money held by a regulated friendly society shall be held as mentioned in paragraph (*a*) of subsection (2) of that section but paragraphs (*b*) to (*f*) of that subsection and subsections (3) and (4) of that section shall apply in relation to regulations made under this paragraph as they apply in relation to regulations under that section (but with the

substitution for the reference in paragraphs (*b*) and (*e*) of subsection (2) to a member of a recognised self-regulating organisation of a reference to a member society of a recognised self-regulating organisation for friendly societies and for the reference in paragraph (*e*) of that subsection to the Secretary of State of a reference to the Registrar).

20. Regulations under section 56(1) of this Act shall not permit anything to be done by a regulated friendly society but that section shall not apply to anything done by such a society in the course of or in consequence of an unsolicited call which, as respects the society constitutes the carrying on of regulated business, if it is permitted to be done by the society in those circumstances—

> (*a*) in the case of a member society, by the rules of the recognised self-regulating organisation for friendly societies of which it is a member ; and

> (*b*) in any other case, by regulations made by the Registrar with the consent of the Secretary of State.

21.—(1) If it appears to the Registrar that a regulated friendly society other than a member society has contravened—

> (*a*) any provision of rules or regulations made under this Schedule or of section 56 or 59 of this Act ;

> (*b*) any condition imposed under section 50 of this Act as it applies by virtue of paragraph 14(3) above ;

> (*c*) any prohibition or requirement imposed under Chapter VI of Part I of this Act as it applies by virtue of paragraph 23 below ; or

> (*d*) any requirement imposed under paragraph 24 below ;

he may publish a statement to that effect.

(2) Subsections (2) to (5) of section 60 above shall apply in relation to the power under sub-paragraph (1) above as they apply in relation to the power in subsection (1) of that section but with the substitution for the references to the Secretary of State of references to the Registrar.

22.—(1) If on the application of the Registrar the court is satisfied—

> (*a*) that there is a reasonable likelihood that any regulated friendly society will contravene any provision of—

>> (i) any prohibition or requirement imposed under Chapter VI of Part I of this Act as it applies by virtue of paragraph 23 below ;

>> (ii) the rules or regulations made under this Schedule ;

>> (iii) any requirement imposed under paragraph 24 below ;

>> (iv) section 47, 56 or 59 of this Act ;

(v) the rules of a recognised self-regulating organisation for friendly societies in relation to which it is a member society,

or any condition imposed under section 50 of this Act as it applies by virtue of paragraph 14(3) above ;

(b) that any regulated friendly society has contravened any such provision or condition and that there is a reasonable likelihood that the contravention will continue or be repeated ; or

(c) that any person has contravened any such provision or condition and that there are steps that could be taken for remedying the contravention,

the court may grant an injunction restraining the contravention or, in Scotland, an interdict prohibiting the contravention or, as the case may be, make an order requiring the society and any other person who appears to the court to have been knowingly concerned in the contravention to take steps to remedy it.

(2) No application shall be made by the Registrar under sub-paragraph (1) above in respect of any such rules as are mentioned in paragraph (a)(v) of that sub-paragraph unless it appears to him that the organisation is unable or unwilling to take appropriate steps to restrain the contravention or to require the society concerned to take such steps as are mentioned in sub-paragraph (1) above.

(3) Subsections (3) to (9) of section 61 of this Act apply to such a contravention as is mentioned in sub-paragraph (1)(a) above as they apply to such a contravention as is mentioned in subsection (3) of that section, but with the substitution for the references to the Secretary of State of references to the Registrar.

(4) Without prejudice to the preceding provisions of this paragraph—

(a) a contravention of any rules or regulations made under this Schedule ;

(b) a contravention of any prohibition or requirement imposed under Chapter VI of Part I of this Act as it applies by virtue of paragraph 23 below ;

(c) a contravention of any requirement imposed under paragraph 24 below ;

(d) a contravention by a member society of any rules of the recognised self-regulating organisation for friendly societies of which it is a member relating to a matter in respect of which rules or regulations have been or could be made under this Schedule or of any requirement or prohibition imposed by the organisation in the exercise of powers for purposes corresponding to those of the said Chapter VI or paragraph 24 ;

shall be actionable at the suit of a person who suffers loss as a result of the contravention subject to the defences and other incidents applying to actions for breach of statutory duty, but no person shall be guilty of an offence by reason of any such contravention and no such contravention shall invalidate any transaction.

(5) This paragraph is without prejudice to any equitable remedy available in respect of property which by virtue of a requirement under section 67 of this Act as it applies by virtue of paragraph 23 below is subject to a trust.

Intervention, information and investigations

23.—(1) The powers conferred by Chapter VI of Part I of this Act shall not be exercisable in relation to a regulated friendly society or the appointed representative of such a society by the Secretary of State but instead shall be exercisable by the Registrar ; and accordingly references in that Chapter to the Secretary of State shall as respects the exercise of powers in relation to a regulated friendly society or such a representative be taken as references to the Registrar.

(2) Section 64 of this Act shall not apply to the exercise of those powers by virtue of sub-paragraph (1) above but those powers shall only be exercisable by the Registrar if it appears to him—

(a) that the exercise of the powers is desirable in the interests of members or potential members of the regulated friendly society ; or

(b) that the society is not a fit person to carry on regulated business of a particular kind or to the extent to which it is carrying it on or proposing to carry it on ; or

(c) that the society has contravened any provision of this Act or of any rules or regulations made under it or in purported compliance with any such provision has furnished him with false, inaccurate or misleading information or has contravened any prohibition or requirement imposed under this Act.

(3) For the purposes of sub-paragraph (2)(b) above the Registrar may take into account any matters that could be taken into account in deciding whether to withdraw or suspend an authorisation under Chapter III of Part I of this Act.

(4) The powers conferred by this paragraph shall not be exercisable in relation—

(a) to a member society which is subject to the rules of a recognised self-regulating organisation for friendly societies in carrying on all the investment business carried on by it ; or

(b) to an appointed representative of a member society if that member society, and each other member society which is his principal, is subject to the rules of such an organisation in carrying on the investment business in respect of which it has accepted responsibility for his activities ;

except that the powers conferred by virtue of section 67(1)(b) of this Act may on any of the grounds mentioned in sub-paragraph (2) above be exercised in relation to a member society or appointed representative at the request of the organisation in relation to which the society or, as the case may be, the society which is the representative's principal is a member society.

24.—(1) The Registrar may by notice in writing require any regulated friendly society (other than a member society) or any self-regulating organisation for friendly societies to furnish him with such information as he may reasonably require for the exercise of his functions under this Act.

(2) The Registrar may require any information which he requires under this paragraph to be furnished within such reasonable time and verified in such manner as he may specify.

25.—(1) Where a notice or copy of a notice is served on any person under section 60 or section 70 of this Act as they apply by virtue of paragraph 21(2) or 23 above, Chapter IX of Part I of this Act (other than section 96) shall, subject to sub-paragraph (2) below, have effect—

(a) with the substitution for the references to the Secretary of State of references to the Registrar ; and

(b) as if for the references in section 98(4) to sections 28, 33 and 60 of this Act there were substituted references to paragraphs 21, 23, 24, 26 and 27 of this Schedule.

(2) Where the friendly society in question is an authorised person by virtue of section 25 of this Act the provisions mentioned in sub-paragraph (1) above shall have effect as if the references substituted by that sub-paragraph had effect in addition to rather than in substitution for the references for which they are there substituted.

(3) Where the Tribunal reports that the appropriate decision is to take action under paragraph 26 or 27 of this Schedule the Registrar shall take the report into account but shall not be bound to act on it.

Exercise of powers under enactments relating to friendly societies

26.—(1) If it appears to the Chief Registrar of friendly societies that a regulated friendly society which is an authorised person by virtue of section 23(1) of this Act—

(a) has contravened any provision of—

(i) this Act or any rules or regulations made under it ;

(ii) any requirement imposed under paragraph 24 above ;

(iii) the rules of a recognised self-regulating organisation for friendly societies in relation to which it is a member society ; or

(b) in purported compliance with any such provision has furnished false, inaccurate or misleading information,

he may exercise any of the powers mentioned in sub-paragraph (2) below in relation to that society.

(2) The powers mentioned in sub-paragraph (1) above are those under subsection (1) of section 87 (inspection and winding up of registered friendly societies), subsection (1) of section 88 (suspension

of business of registered friendly societies), subsections (1) and (2)   Sch. 11
of section 89 (production of documents) and subsections (1) and (2)
of section 91 (cancellation and suspension of registration) of the
Friendly Societies Act 1974 ; and subject to sub-paragraph (3) below 1974 c. 46.
the remaining provisions of those sections shall apply in relation
to the exercise of those powers by virtue of this paragraph as they do
in relation to their exercise in the circumstances mentioned in those
sections.

(3) In its application by virtue of this paragraph—

(a) section 88 of the said Act of 1974 shall have effect with
the omission of subsections (3), (5) and (9) ; and

(b) section 89 of that Act shall have effect with the omission
of subsection (7).

27.—(1) If it appears to the Registrar of Friendly Societies for
Northern Ireland that a regulated friendly society which is an
authorised person by virtue of section 23(2) of this Act—

(a) has contravened any provision of—

(i) this Act or any rules or regulations made under it ;

(ii) any requirement imposed under paragraph 24
above ;

(iii) the rules of a recognised self-regulating organisation for friendly societies in relation to which it is a
member society ; or

(b) in purported compliance with any such provision has furnished false, inaccurate or misleading information,

he may exercise any of the powers mentioned in sub-paragraph
(2) below in relation to that society.

(2) The powers mentioned in sub-paragraph (1) above are those
under subsection (1) of section 77 (inspection and winding up of
registered friendly societies), subsection (1) of section 78 (suspension of business of registered friendly societies), subsections (1) and
(2) of section 79 (production of documents) and subsections (1) and
(2) of section 80 (cancellation and suspension of registration) of
the Friendly Societies Act (Northern Ireland) 1970 ; and subject to 1970 c. 31
sub-paragraph (3) below the remaining provisions of those sections (N.I.).
shall apply in relation to the exercise of those powers by virtue of
this paragraph as they do in relation to their exercise in the circumstances mentioned in those sections.

(3) In its application by virtue of this paragraph section 78 of
the said Act of 1970 shall have effect with the omission in subsection (2) of the words from " and such notice " onwards and of
subsection (4).

PART IV

TRANSFER OF REGISTRAR'S FUNCTIONS

28.—(1) If it appears to the Registrar—

(a) that a body corporate has been established which is able and
willing to discharge all or any of the functions to which
this paragraph applies ; and

(b) that the requirements of Schedule 7 to this Act (as it has effect by virtue of sub-paragraph (3) below) are satisfied in the case of that body,

he may, with the consent of the Secretary of State and subject to the following provisions of this paragraph and paragraphs 29 and 30 below, make an order transferring all or any of those functions to that body.

(2) The body to which functions are transferred by the first order made under sub-paragraph (1) above shall be the body known as The Securities and Investments Board Limited if the Secretary of State consents to the making of the order and it appears to the Registrar that that body is able and willing to discharge those functions, that the requirements mentioned in paragraph (b) of that sub-paragraph are satisfied in the case of that body and that he is not precluded from making the order by the following provisions of this paragraph or paragraph 29 or 30 below.

(3) For the purposes of sub-paragraph (1) above Schedule 7 shall have effect as if—

(a) for references to a designated agency there were substituted references to a transferee body ; and

(b) for the reference to complaints in paragraph 4 there were substituted a reference to complaints arising out of the conduct by regulated friendly societies of regulated business.

(4) An order under sub-paragraph (1) above is in this Act referred to as a transfer order and a body to which functions are transferred by a transfer order is in this Act referred to as a transferee body.

(5) Subject to sub-paragraphs (6) and (8) below, this paragraph applies to the functions of the Registrar under section 113(3) of this Act and paragraph 38 below and any functions conferred on him by virtue of paragraphs 2 to 25 above other than the powers under sections 66 and 68 of this Act and, so far as applicable to assets belonging to a regulated friendly society, the power under section 67 of this Act.

(6) If the Registrar transfers his functions under Chapter VI of Part I of this Act they shall not be exercisable by the transferee body if the only reasons by virtue of which it appears to the body as mentioned in paragraph 23(2) above relate to the sufficiency of the funds of the society to meet existing claims or of the rates of contribution to cover benefits assured.

(7) Any function may be transferred by an order under this paragraph either wholly or in part and a function may be transferred in respect of all societies or only in respect of such societies as are specified in the order.

(8) A transfer order—

(a) may reserve to the Registrar the function of revoking a recognition order in respect of a self-regulating organisation

for friendly societies on the ground that the requirement
mentioned in paragraph 4(2) above is not satisfied ; and

(*b*) shall not transfer to a transferee body the function of revoking any such recognition order on the ground that the organisation has contravened the provisions of paragraph 9 above.

(9) No transfer order shall be made unless a draft of it has been laid before and approved by a resolution of each House of Parliament.

29. The Registrar shall not make a transfer order transferring any function of making rules or regulations to a transferee body unless—

(*a*) the body has furnished him and the Secretary of State with a copy of the rules or regulations which it proposes to make in the exercise of those functions ; and

(*b*) they are both satisfied that those rules or regulations will—

(i) afford investors an adequate level of protection,

(ii) in the case of rules and regulations corresponding to those mentioned in Schedule 8 to this Act, comply with the principles set out in that Schedule, and

(iii) take proper account of the supervision of the friendly societies by the Registrar under the enactments relating to friendly societies.

30.—(1) The Registrar shall also before making a transfer order transferring any functions to a transferee body require it to furnish him and the Secretary of State with a copy of any guidance intended to have continuing effect which it proposes to issue in writing or other legible form and they may take such guidance into account in determining whether they are satisfied as mentioned in paragraph 29(*b*) above.

(2) In this Act references to guidance issued by a transferee body are references to guidance issued or any recommendation made by it which is issued or made to regulated friendly societies or self-regulating organisations for friendly societies generally or to any class of regulated friendly societies or self-regulating organisations for friendly societies, being societies which are or may be subject to rules or regulations made by it or organisations which are or may be recognised by it in the exercise of its functions under a transfer order.

31.—(1) Subject to the provisions of this paragraph, sections 115, 116, 117(3) to (5) and 118 of this Act shall apply in relation to the transfer of functions under paragraph 28 above as they apply in relation to the transfer of functions under section 114 of this Act.

(2) Subject to sub-paragraphs (5) and (6)(*b*) below, for references in those provisions to the Secretary of State, a designated agency and a delegation order there shall be substituted respectively references to the Registrar, a transferee body and a transfer order.

(3) The Registrar may not exercise the powers conferred by sub-sections (1) and (2) of section 115 except with the consent of the Secretary of State.

(4) In subsection (3) of section 115 for the reference to Schedule 7 to this Act there shall be substituted a reference to that Schedule as it has effect by virtue of paragraph 28(3) above and in subsection (5) of that section for the reference to section 114(9)(*b*) of this Act there shall be substituted a reference to paragraph 29(*b*) above.

(5) Section 118(3)(*b*) shall have effect as if the reference to any provision applying to the Secretary of State were a reference to any provision applying to the Secretary of State or the Registrar.

(6) In Schedule 9 to this Act—

(*a*) paragraph 1(2) and (3) shall be omitted ;

(*b*) paragraph 4 shall have effect as if the references to the Secretary of State were references to the Secretary of State and the Registrar ;

(*c*) paragraph 5 shall have effect as if the reference to section 205(2) were a reference to paragraph 45(1) below ;

(*d*) paragraph 12(3) shall have effect as if the reference to section 114(9) were a reference to paragraph 29 above.

(7) The power mentioned in paragraph 2(3) of Schedule 9 to this Act shall not be exercisable on the ground that the company has ceased to be a designated agency or, as the case may be, a trans-feree body if the company remains a transferee body or, as the case may be, a designated agency.

32. A transferee body shall at least once in each year for which the transfer order is in force make a report to the Registrar on the discharge of the functions transferred to it by the order and on such other matters as the order may require and the Registrar shall send a copy of each report received by him under this paragraph to the Secretary of State who shall lay copies of the report before Parliament.

33.—(1) This paragraph applies where the function of making or revoking a recognition order in respect of a self-regulating organisa-tion for friendly societies is exercisable by a transferee body.

(2) Paragraph 3(2) above shall have effect as if the first reference to the Secretary of State included a reference to the Registrar.

(3) The transferee body shall not regard the requirement men-tioned in paragraph 4(2) as satisfied unless the Registrar has certified that he also regards it as satisfied.

(4) A transferee body shall send the Registrar and the Secretary of State a copy of any notice received by it under paragraph 8(6) **above.**

(5) Where the Secretary of State exercises any of the powers con-   Sch. 11
ferred by paragraph 10(2) above in relation to an organisation the
Registrar shall direct the transferee body to take the appropriate
action in relation to that organisation and such a direction shall,
on the application of the Registrar, be enforceable by mandamus or,
in Scotland, by an order for specific performance under section 91
of the Court of Session Act 1868.   1868 c. 100.

34. A transferee body to which the Registrar has transferred any
function of making rules or regulations may make those rules or
regulations without the consent of the Secretary of State.

35.—(1) A transferee body shall not impose any prohibition or
requirement under section 65 or 67 of this Act on a regulated
friendly society or vary any such prohibition or requirement unless
it has given reasonable notice of its intention to do so to the
Registrar and informed him—

(*a*) of the manner in which and the date on or after which it
intends to exercise the power ; and

(*b*) in the case of a proposal to impose a prohibition or requirement, on which of the grounds specified in paragraph 23(2)
above it proposes to act and its reasons for considering
that the ground in question exists and that it is necessary
to impose the prohibition or requirement.

(2) A transferee body shall not exercise any power to which sub-
paragraph (1) above applies if before the date given in the notice in
pursuance of sub-paragraph (1)(*a*) above the Registrar has served on
it a notice in writing directing it not to do so ; and the Registrar
may serve such a notice if he considers it is desirable for protecting members or potential members of the regulated friendly society
against the risk that it may be unable to meet its liabilities or to
fulfil the reasonable expectations of its members or potential
members.

36.—(1) The Secretary of State shall not consent to the making
of an order by the Registrar under paragraph 28 above transferring
any functions to a transferee body unless he is satisfied that any
rules, regulations, guidance and recommendations of which copies
are furnished to him under paragraphs 29(*a*) and 30(1) above do
not have, and are not intended or likely to have, to any significant
extent the effect of restricting, distorting or preventing competition
or, if they have or are intended or likely to have that effect to any
significant extent, that the effect is not greater than is necessary for
the protection of investors.

(2) Section 121(2) and (4) and sections 122 to 128 above shall
have effect in relation to transferee bodies and transfer orders as
they have effect in relation to designated agencies and designation
orders but subject to the following modifications.

(3) Those provisions shall have effect as if the powers exercisable under section 121(3) were—

> (a) to make an order transferring back to the Registrar all or any of the functions transferred to the transferee body by a transfer order ; or
>
> (b) to direct the Registrar to direct the transferee body to take specified steps for the purpose of securing that the rules, regulations, guidance or practices in question do not have the effect mentioned in sub-paragraph (1) above.

(4) No order shall be made by virtue of sub-paragraph (3) above unless a draft of it has been laid before and approved by a resolution of each House of Parliament.

(5) For the decisions referred to in section 122(1) there shall be substituted a reference to the Secretary of State's decision whether he is precluded by sub-paragraph (1) above from giving his consent to the making of a transfer order.

(6) Section 128 shall apply as if—

> (a) the powers referred to in subsection (1) of that section included the power conferred by sub-paragraph (3)(b) above ; and
>
> (b) the references to Chapter XIV of Part I included references to this paragraph.

37.—(1) If a transferee body has reasonable grounds for believing that any regulated friendly society has failed to comply with an obligation to which it is subject by virtue of this Act it shall forthwith give notice of that fact to the Registrar so that he can take it into consideration in deciding whether to exercise in relation to the society any of the powers conferred on him by sections 87 to 89 and 91 of the Friendly Societies Act 1974 or, as the case may be, sections 77 to 80 of the Friendly Societies Act (Northern Ireland) 1970 (inspection, winding up, suspension of business and cancellation and suspension of registration).

1974 c. 46.
1970 c. 31
(N.I.).

(2) A notice under sub-paragraph (1) above shall contain particulars of the obligation in question and of the transferee body's reasons for considering that the society has failed to satisfy that obligation.

(3) A transferee body need not give a notice under sub-paragraph (1) above in respect of any matter unless it considers that that matter (either alone or in conjunction with other matters) would justify the withdrawal of authorisation under section 28 of this Act in the case of a person to whom that provision applies.

Part V
Miscellaneous and Supplemental

38.—(1) The Registrar may publish information or give advice, or arrange for the publication of information or the giving of advice, in such form and manner as he considers appropriate with respect to—

> (a) the operation of this Schedule and the rules and regulations made under it in relation to registered friendly societies,

including in particular the rights of their members, the
duties of such societies and the steps to be taken for
enforcing those rights or complying with those duties ;

(b) any matters relating to the functions of the Registrar under
   this Schedule or any such rules or regulations ;

(c) any other matters about which it appears to him to be
   desirable to publish information or give advice for the protection of those members or any class of them.

(2) The Registrar may offer for sale copies of information published under this paragraph and may, if he thinks fit, make reasonable charges for advice given under this paragraph at any person's
request.

(3) This paragraph shall not be construed as authorising the disclosure of restricted information within the meaning of section 179
of this Act in any case in which it could not be disclosed apart
from the provisions of this paragraph.

39. In the case of an application for authorisation under section 26
of this Act made by a society which is registered under the Friendly
Societies Act 1974 within the meaning of that Act or is registered or
deemed to be registered under the Friendly Societies Act (Northern 1974 c. 46.
Ireland) 1970 (" a registered society "), section 27(3)(c) of this Act 1970 c. 31 (N.I.).
shall have effect as if it referred only to any person who is a trustee,
manager or member of the committee of the society.

40. Where the other person mentioned in paragraph (c) of the
definition of " connected person " in section 105(9) of this Act is a
registered society that paragraph shall have effect with the substitution for the words from " member " onwards of the words " trustee,
manager or member of the committee of the society ".

41. In relation to any such document as is mentioned in subsection
(1) of section 204 of this Act which is required or authorised to be
given to or served on a registered society—

(a) subsection (3)(c) of that section shall have effect with the
   substitution for the words from " member " onwards of the
   words " trustee, manager or member of the committee of
   the society " ; and

(b) subsection (4)(c) of that section shall have effect as if for the
   words from " member " onwards there were substituted the
   words " trustee, manager or member of the committee of the
   society, the office which is its registered office in accordance
   with its rules ".

42. Rules under paragraphs 14, 15, 17 and 18 above and regulations under paragraphs 16, 19 and 20 above shall apply notwithstanding any provision to the contrary in the rules of any regulated
friendly society to which they apply.

SCH. 11   43.—(1) Where it appears to the Registrar, the assistant registrar
for Scotland, the Industrial Assurance Commissioner or the Industrial Assurance Commissioner for Northern Ireland that any such
rules as are mentioned in section 48(2)(*j*) of this Act which are made
by virtue of paragraph 14 above (or any corresponding rules made
by a self-regulating organisation for friendly societies) make arrangements for the settlement of a dispute referred to him under section
1974 c. 46.   77 of the Friendly Societies Act 1974, section 65 of the Friendly
1970 c. 31   Societies Act (Northern Ireland) 1970, section 32 of the Industrial
(N.I.).   Assurance Act 1923 or Article 36 of the Industrial Assurance (Nor-
1923 c. 8.   thern Ireland) Order 1979 or that such rules relate to some of the
S.I. 1979/1574   matters in dispute he may, if he thinks fit, delegate his functions in
(N.I.13).   respect of the dispute so as to enable it to be settled in accordance
with the rules.

(2) If such rules provide that any dispute may be referred to such
a person, that person may deal with any dispute referred to him in
pursuance of those rules as if it were a dispute referred to him as
aforesaid and may delegate his functions in respect of any such
dispute to any other person.

1975 c. 24.   44. —(1) In Part III of Schedule 1 to the House of Commons
Disqualification Act 1975 (disqualifying offices) there shall be inserted at the appropriate place—

    "Chairman of a transferee body within the meaning of
    Schedule 11 to the Financial Services Act 1986 if he is in
    receipt of remuneration."

1975 c. 25.   (2) A corresponding amendment shall be made in Part III of
Schedule 1 to the Northern Ireland Assembly Disqualification Act
1975.

45.—(1) Any power of the Chief Registrar of friendly societies to
make regulations, rules or orders which is exercisable by virtue of
1946 c. 36.   this Act shall be exercisable by statutory instrument and the Statutory Instruments Act 1946 shall apply to any such power as if the
Chief Registrar of friendly societies were a Minister of the Crown.

(2) Any such power of the Registrar of Friendly Societies for
Northern Ireland shall be exercisable by statutory rule for the pur-
S.I. 1979/1573   poses of the Statutory Rules (Northern Ireland) Order 1979.
(N.I.12).

(3) Any regulations, rules or orders made under this Schedule
by the Registrar may make different provision for different cases.

Section 172.   SCHEDULE 12
                            TAKEOVER OFFERS:
        PROVISIONS SUBSTITUTED FOR SECTIONS 428, 429 AND 430
                       OF COMPANIES ACT 1985

                            PART XIIIA
                          TAKEOVER OFFERS

"Takeover   428.—(1) In this Part of this Act "a takeover offer" means an
offers."   offer to acquire all the shares, or all the shares of any class or

classes, in a company (other than shares which at the date of the offer are already held by the offeror), being an offer on terms which are the same in relation to all the shares to which the offer relates or, where those shares include shares of different classes, in relation to all the shares of each class.

(2) In subsection (1) " shares " means shares which have been allotted on the date of the offer but a takeover offer may include among the shares to which it relates all or any shares that are subsequently allotted before a date specified in or determined in accordance with the terms of the offer.

(3) The terms offered in relation to any shares shall for the purposes of this section be treated as being the same in relation to all the shares or, as the case may be, all the shares of a class to which the offer relates notwithstanding any variation permitted by subsection (4).

(4) A variation is permitted by this subsection where—

  (a) the law of a country or territory outside the United Kingdom precludes an offer of consideration in the form or any of the forms specified in the terms in question or precludes it except after compliance by the offeror with conditions with which he is unable to comply or which he regards as unduly onerous ; and

  (b) the variation is such that the persons to whom an offer of consideration in that form is precluded are able to receive consideration otherwise than in that form but of substantially equivalent value.

(5) The reference in subsection (1) to shares already held by the offeror includes a reference to shares which he has contracted to acquire but that shall not be construed as including shares which are the subject of a contract binding the holder to accept the offer when it is made, being a contract entered into by the holder either for no consideration and under seal or for no consideration other than a promise by the offeror to make the offer.

(6) In the application of subsection (5) to Scotland, the words " and under seal " shall be omitted.

(7) Where the terms of an offer make provision for their revision and for acceptances on the previous terms to be treated as acceptances on the revised terms, the revision shall not be regarded for the purposes of this Part of this Act as the making of a fresh offer and references in this Part of this Act to the date of the offer shall accordingly be construed as references to the date on which the original offer was made.

(8) In this Part of this Act " the offeror " means, subject to section 430D, the person making a takeover offer and " the company " means the company whose shares are the subject of the offer.

429.—(1) If, in a case in which a takeover offer does not relate **Right of** to shares of different classes, the offeror has by virtue of acceptances **offeror to buy** of the offer acquired or contracted to acquire not less than nine- **out minority shareholders.**

tenths in value of the shares to which the offer relates he may give notice to the holder of any shares to which the offer relates which the offeror has not acquired or contracted to acquire that he desires to acquire those shares.

(2) If, in a case in which a takeover offer relates to shares of different classes, the offeror has by virtue of acceptances of the offer acquired or contracted to acquire not less than nine-tenths in value of the shares of any class to which the offer relates, he may give notice to the holder of any shares of that class which the offeror has not acquired or contracted to acquire that he desires to acquire those shares.

(3) No notice shall be given under subsection (1) or (2) unless the offeror has acquired or contracted to acquire the shares necessary to satisfy the minimum specified in that subsection before the end of the period of four months beginning with the date of the offer ; and no such notice shall be given after the end of the period of two months beginning with the date on which he has acquired or contracted to acquire shares which satisfy that minimum.

(4) Any notice under this section shall be given in the prescribed manner ; and when the offeror gives the first notice in relation to an offer he shall send a copy of it to the company together with a statutory declaration by him in the prescribed form stating that the conditions for the giving of the notice are satisfied.

(5) Where the offeror is a company (whether or not a company within the meaning of this Act) the statutory declaration shall be signed by a director.

(6) Any person who fails to send a copy of a notice or a statutory declaration as required by subsection (4) or makes such a declaration for the purposes of that subsection knowing it to be false or without having reasonable grounds for believing it to be true shall be liable to imprisonment or a fine, or both, and for continued failure to send the copy or declaration, to a daily default fine.

(7) If any person is charged with an offence for failing to send a copy of a notice as required by subsection (4) it is a defence for him to prove that he took reasonable steps for securing compliance with that subsection.

(8) Where during the period within which a takeover offer can be accepted the offeror acquires or contracts to acquire any of the shares to which the offer relates but otherwise than by virtue of acceptances of the offer, then, if—

> (a) the value of the consideration for which they are acquired or contracted to be acquired (" the acquisition consideration ") does not at that time exceed the value of the consideration specified in the terms of the offer ; or
>
> (b) those terms are subsequently revised so that when the revision is announced the value of the acquisition consideration, at the time mentioned in paragraph (a) above, no longer exceeds the value of the consideration specified in those terms,

the offeror shall be treated for the purposes of this section as having
acquired or contracted to acquire those shares by virtue of acceptances of the offer ; but in any other case those shares shall be treated
as excluded from those to which the offer relates.

430.—(1) The following provisions shall, subject to section 430C,
have effect where a notice is given in respect of any shares under
section 429.

(2) The offeror shall be entitled and bound to acquire those
shares on the terms of the offer.

(3) Where the terms of an offer are such as to give the holder of
any shares a choice of consideration the notice shall give particulars
of the choice and state—

    (*a*) that the holder of the shares may within six weeks from
        the date of the notice indicate his choice by a written
        communication sent to the offeror at an address specified in
        the notice ; and

    (*b*) which consideration specified in the offer is to be taken
        as applying in default of his indicating a choice as
        aforesaid ;

and the terms of the offer mentioned in subsection (2) shall be
determined accordingly.

(4) Subsection (3) applies whether or not any time-limit or other
conditions applicable to the choice under the terms of the offer
can still be complied with ; and if the consideration chosen by the
holder of the shares—

    (*a*) is not cash and the offeror is no longer able to provide it ;
        or

    (*b*) was to have been provided by a third party who is no
        longer bound or able to provide it,

the consideration shall be taken to consist of an amount of cash
payable by the offeror which at the date of the notice is equivalent
to the chosen consideration.

(5) At the end of six weeks from the date of the notice the offeror
shall forthwith—

    (*a*) send a copy of the notice to the company ; and

    (*b*) pay or transfer to the company the consideration for the
        shares to which the notice relates.

(6) If the shares to which the notice relates are registered the
copy of the notice sent to the company under subsection (5)(*a*) shall
be accompanied by an instrument of transfer executed on behalf
of the shareholder by a person appointed by the offeror ; and on
receipt of that instrument the company shall register the offeror as
the holder of those shares.

(7) If the shares to which the notice relates are transferable by
the delivery of warrants or other instruments the copy of the notice

sent to the company under subsection (5)(*a*) shall be accompanied by a statement to that effect ; and the company shall on receipt of the statement issue the offeror with warrants or other instruments in respect of the shares and those already in issue in respect of the shares shall become void.

(8) Where the consideration referred to in paragraph (*b*) of subsection (5) consists of shares or securities to be allotted by the offeror the reference in that paragraph to the transfer of the consideration shall be construed as a reference to the allotment of the shares or securities to the company.

(9) Any sum received by a company under paragraph (*b*) of subsection (5) and any other consideration received under that paragraph shall be held by the company on trust for the person entitled to the shares in respect of which the sum or other consideration was received.

(10) Any sum received by a company under paragraph (*b*) of subsection (5), and any dividend or other sum accruing from any other consideration received by a company under that paragraph, shall be paid into a separate bank account, being an account the balance on which bears interest at an appropriate rate and can be withdrawn by such notice (if any) as is appropriate.

(11) Where after reasonable enquiry made at such intervals as are reasonable the person entitled to any consideration held on trust by virtue of subsection (9) cannot be found and twelve years have elapsed since the consideration was received or the company is wound up the consideration (together with any interest, dividend or other benefit that has accrued from it) shall be paid into court.

(12) In relation to a company registered in Scotland, subsections (13) and (14) shall apply in place of subsection (11).

(13) Where after reasonable enquiry made at such intervals as are reasonable the person entitled to any consideration held on trust by virtue of subsection (9) cannot be found and twelve years have elapsed since the consideration was received or the company is wound up—

    (*a*) the trust shall terminate ;

    (*b*) the company or, as the case may be, the liquidator shall sell any consideration other than cash and any benefit other than cash that has accrued from the consideration ; and

    (*c*) a sum representing—

        (i) the consideration so far as it is cash ;

        (ii) the proceeds of any sale under paragraph (*b*) above ; and

        (iii) any interest, dividend or other benefit that has accrued from the consideration,

    shall be deposited in the name of the Accountant of Court in a bank account such as is referred to in subsection (10) and the receipt for the deposit shall be transmitted to the Accountant of Court.

(14) Section 58 of the Bankruptcy (Scotland) Act 1985 (so far as consistent with this Act) shall apply with any necessary modifications to sums deposited under subsection (13) as that section applies to sums deposited under section 57(1)(*a*) of that Act.

(15) The expenses of any such enquiry as is mentioned in subsection (11) or (13) may be defrayed out of the money or other property held on trust for the person or persons to whom the enquiry relates.

430A.—(1) If a takeover offer relates to all the shares in a company and at any time before the end of the period within which the offer can be accepted—

(*a*) the offeror has by virtue of acceptances of the offer acquired or contracted to acquire some (but not all) of the shares to which the offer relates ; and

(*b*) those shares, with or without any other shares in the company which he has acquired or contracted to acquire, amount to not less than nine-tenths in value of all the shares in the company,

the holder of any shares to which the offer relates who has not accepted the offer may by a written communication addressed to the offeror require him to acquire those shares.

(2) If a takeover offer relates to shares of any class or classes and at any time before the end of the period within which the offer can be accepted—

(*a*) the offeror has by virtue of acceptances of the offer acquired or contracted to acquire some (but not all) of the shares of any class to which the offer relates ; and

(*b*) those shares, with or without any other shares of that class which he has acquired or contracted to acquire, amount to not less than nine-tenths in value of all the shares of that class,

the holder of any shares of that class who has not accepted the offer may by a written communication addressed to the offeror require him to acquire those shares.

(3) Within one month of the time specified in subsection (1) or, as the case may be, subsection (2) the offeror shall give any shareholder who has not accepted the offer notice in the prescribed manner of the rights that are exercisable by him under that subsection ; and if the notice is given before the end of the period mentioned in that subsection it shall state that the offer is still open for acceptance.

(4) A notice under subsection (3) may specify a period for the exercise of the rights conferred by this section and in that event the rights shall not be exercisable after the end of that period ; but no such period shall end less than three months after the end of the period within which the offer can be accepted.

(5) Subsection (3) does not apply if the offeror has given the shareholder a notice in respect of the shares in question under section 429.

(6) If the offeror fails to comply with subsection (3) he and, if the offeror is a company, every officer of the company who is in default or to whose neglect the failure is attributable, shall be liable to a fine and, for continued contravention, to a daily default fine.

(7) If an offeror other than a company is charged with an offence for failing to comply with subsection (3) it is a defence for him to prove that he took all reasonable steps for securing compliance with that subsection.

430B.—(1) The following provisions shall, subject to section 430C, have effect where a shareholder exercises his rights in respect of any shares under section 430A.

(2) The offeror shall be entitled and bound to acquire those shares on the terms of the offer or on such other terms as may be agreed.

(3) Where the terms of an offer are such as to give the holder of shares a choice of consideration the holder of the shares may indicate his choice when requiring the offeror to acquire them and the notice given to the holder under section 430A(3)—

(a) shall give particulars of the choice and of the rights conferred by this subsection ; and

(b) may state which consideration specified in the offer is to be taken as applying in default of his indicating a choice ;

and the terms of the offer mentioned in subsection (2) shall be determined accordingly.

(4) Subsection (3) applies whether or not any time-limit or other conditions applicable to the choice under the terms of the offer can still be complied with ; and if the consideration chosen by the holder of the shares—

(a) is not cash and the offeror is no longer able to provide it ; or

(b) was to have been provided by a third party who is no longer bound or able to provide it,

the consideration shall be taken to consist of an amount of cash payable by the offeror which at the date when the holder of the shares requires the offeror to acquire them is equivalent to the chosen consideration.

430C.—(1) Where a notice is given under section 429 to the holder of any shares the court may, on an application made by him within six weeks from the date on which the notice was given—

(a) order that the offeror shall not be entitled and bound to acquire the shares ; or

(b) specify terms of acquisition different from those of the offer.

(2) If an application to the court under subsection (1) is pending at the end of the period mentioned in subsection (5) of section 430 that subsection shall not have effect until the application has been disposed of.

(3) Where the holder of any shares exercises his rights under section 430A the court may, on an application made by him or the offeror, order that the terms on which the offeror is entitled and bound to acquire the shares shall be such as the court thinks fit.

(4) No order for costs or expenses shall be made against a shareholder making an application under subsection (1) or (3) unless the court considers—

(a) that the application was unnecessary, improper or vexatious ; or

(b) that there has been unreasonable delay in making the application or unreasonable conduct on his part in conducting the proceedings on the application.

(5) Where a takeover offer has not been accepted to the extent necessary for entitling the offeror to give notices under subsection (1) or (2) of section 429 the court may, on the application of the offeror, make an order authorising him to give notices under that subsection if satisfied—

(a) that the offeror has after reasonable enquiry been unable to trace one or more of the persons holding shares to which the offer relates ;

(b) that the shares which the offeror has acquired or contracted to acquire by virtue of acceptances of the offer, together with the shares held by the person or persons mentioned in paragraph (a), amount to not less than the minimum specified in that subsection ; and

(c) that the consideration offered is fair and reasonable ;

but the court shall not make an order under this subsection unless it considers that it is just and equitable to do so having regard, in particular, to the number of shareholders who have been traced but who have not accepted the offer.

430D.—(1) A takeover offer may be made by two or more persons jointly and in that event this Part of this Act has effect with the following modifications.

Joint offers.

(2) The conditions for the exercise of the rights conferred by sections 429 and 430A shall be satisfied by the joint offerors acquiring or contracting to acquire the necessary shares jointly (as respects acquisitions by virtue of acceptances of the offer) and either jointly or separately (in other cases) ; and, subject to the following provisions, the rights and obligations of the offeror under those sections and sections 430 and 430B shall be respectively joint rights and joint and several obligations of the joint offerors.

(3) It shall be a sufficient compliance with any provision of those sections requiring or authorising a notice or other document to be given or sent by or to the joint offerors that it is given or sent by or to any of them ; but the statutory declaration required by section 429(4) shall be made by all of them and, in the case of a joint offeror being a company, signed by a director of that company.

(4) In sections 428, 430(8) and 430E references to the offeror shall be construed as references to the joint offerors or any of them.

SCH. 12

(5) In section 430(6) and (7) references to the offeror shall be construed as references to the joint offerors or such of them as they may determine.

(6) In sections 430(4)(*a*) and 430B(4)(*a*) references to the offeror being no longer able to provide the relevant consideration shall be construed as references to none of the joint offerors being able to do so.

(7) In section 430C references to the offeror shall be construed as references to the joint offerors except that any application under subsection (3) or (5) may be made by any of them and the reference in subsection (5)(*a*) to the offeror having been unable to trace one or more of the persons holding shares shall be construed as a reference to none of the offerors having been able to do so.

Associates.

430E.—(1) The requirement in section 428(1) that a takeover offer must extend to all the shares, or all the shares of any class or classes, in a company shall be regarded as satisfied notwithstanding that the offer does not extend to shares which associates of the offeror hold or have contracted to acquire ; but, subject to subsection (2), shares which any such associate holds or has contracted to acquire, whether at the time when the offer is made or subsequently, shall be disregarded for the purposes of any reference in this Part of this Act to the shares to which a takeover offer relates.

(2) Where during the period within which a takeover offer can be accepted any associate of the offeror acquires or contracts to acquire any of the shares to which the offer relates, then, if the condition specified in subsection (8)(*a*) or (*b*) of section 429 is satisfied as respects those shares they shall be treated for the purposes of that section as shares to which the offer relates.

(3) In section 430A(1)(*b*) and (2)(*b*) the reference to shares which the offeror has acquired or contracted to acquire shall include a reference to shares which any associate of his has acquired or contracted to acquire.

(4) In this section " associate ", in relation to an offeror means—

    (*a*) a nominee of the offeror ;

    (*b*) a holding company, subsidiary or fellow subsidiary of the offeror or a nominee of such a holding company, subsidiary or fellow subsidiary ;

    (*c*) a body corporate in which the offeror is substantially interested ; or

    (*d*) any person who is, or is a nominee of, a party to an agreement with the offeror for the acquisition of, or of an interest in, the shares which are the subject of the takeover offer, being an agreement which includes provisions imposing obligations or restrictions such as are mentioned in section 204 (2)(*a*).

(5) For the purposes of subsection (4)(*b*) a company is a fellow subsidiary of another body corporate if both are subsidiaries of the same body corporate but neither is a subsidiary of the other.

(6) For the purposes of subsection (4)(*c*) an offeror has a substantial interest in a body corporate if—

   (*a*) that body or its directors are accustomed to act in accordance with his directions or instructions ; or

   (*b*) he is entitled to exercise or control the exercise of one-third or more of the voting power at general meetings of that body.

(7) Subsections (5) and (6) of section 204 shall apply to subsection (4)(*d*) above as they apply to that section and subsections (3) and (4) of section 203 shall apply for the purposes of subsection (6) above as they apply for the purposes of subsection (2)(*b*) of that section.

(8) Where the offeror is an individual his associates shall also include his spouse and any minor child or step-child of his.

430F.—(1) For the purposes of this Part of this Act securities of a company shall be treated as shares in the company if they are convertible into or entitle the holder to subscribe for such shares ; and references to the holder of shares or a shareholder shall be construed accordingly. Convertible
securities.

(2) Subsection (1) shall not be construed as requiring any securities to be treated—

   (*a*) as shares of the same class as those into which they are convertible or for which the holder is entitled to subscribe ; or

   (*b*) as shares of the same class as other securities by reason only that the shares into which they are convertible or for which the holder is entitled to subscribe are of the same class.

SCHEDULE 13

DISCLOSURE OF INFORMATION

Section 182.

1. In section 133(2)(*a*) of the Fair Trading Act 1973 after the words " the Telecommunications Act 1984 " there shall be inserted the words " or Chapter XIV of Part I of the Financial Services Act 1986 ". 1973 c. 41.

2. In section 41(1)(*a*) of the Restrictive Trade Practices Act 1976 after the words " the Telecommunications Act 1984 " there shall be inserted the words " or Chapter XIV of Part I of the Financial Services Act 1986 ". 1976 c. 34.

3.—(1) In section 19 of the Banking Act 1979 after subsection (2) there shall be inserted— 1979 c. 37.

   " (2A) Nothing in subsection (1) above prohibits the disclosure of information by the Bank to any person specified in the first column of the following Table if the Bank considers—

(a) that the disclosure would enable or assist the Bank to discharge its functions under this Act ; or

(b) that it would enable or assist that person to discharge the functions specified in relation to him in the second column of that Table.

TABLE

Person	*Functions*
The Secretary of State.	Functions under the Insurance Companies Act 1982 or the Financial Services Act 1986.
The Chief Registrar of friendly societies or the Registrar of Friendly Societies for Northern Ireland.	Functions under the Financial Services Act 1986 or under the enactments relating to friendly societies.
A designated agency or transferee body or the competent authority (within the meaning of the Financial Services Act 1986).	Functions under the Financial Services Act 1986.
A recognised self-regulating organisation, recognised professional body, recognised investment exchange, recognised clearing house or recognised self-regulating organisation for friendly societies (within the meaning of the Financial Services Act 1986).	Functions in its capacity as an organisation, body, exchange or clearing house recognised under the Financial Services Act 1986.
A person appointed or authorised to exercise any powers under section 94, 106 or 177 of the Financial Services Act 1986.	Functions arising from his appointment or authorisation under that section.
The body administering a scheme under section 54 of or paragraph 18 of Schedule 11 to the Financial Services Act 1986.	Functions under the scheme.

(2B) Nothing in subsection (1) above prohibits the disclosure by a person specified in the first column of the Table in subsection (2A) above of information obtained by him by virtue of a disclosure authorised by that subsection if he makes the disclosure with the consent of the Bank and for the purpose of enabling or assisting himself to discharge any functions specified in relation to him in the second column of that Table ; and before deciding whether to give its consent to such a disclosure by any person the Bank shall take account of any representations made by him as to the desirability of or the necessity for the disclosure.".

(2) For subsection (6) of that section there shall be substituted—

" (6) Nothing in subsection (1) above prohibits the disclosure of information by or with the consent of the Bank for the purpose of enabling or assisting an authority in a country or territory outside the United Kingdom to exercise functions corresponding to those of the Bank under this Act, or to those of the Secretary of State under the Insurance Companies Act 1982 or the Financial Services Act 1986 or to those of the competent authority under the said Act of 1986 or any other functions in connection with rules of law corresponding to the provisions of the Company Securities (Insider Dealing) Act 1985 or Part VII of the said Act of 1986.".

4. In section 20(4) of that Act—

(*a*) for the words " in a country or territory outside the United Kingdom " there shall be substituted the words " in a member State other than the United Kingdom " ; and

(*b*) in paragraph (*b*) for the words " subsections (4) to (6) " there shall be substituted the words " subsections (2A), (2B) and (4) to (6) ".

5. At the end of section 19(3) of the Competition Act 1980 there shall be inserted—   1980 c. 21.

" (*h*) Chapter XIV of Part I of the Financial Services Act 1986 ".

6. For subsections (1) and (2) of section 47A of the Insurance Companies Act 1982 there shall be substituted—   1982 c. 50

" (1) Subject to the following provisions of this section, no information relating to the business or other affairs of any person which has been obtained under section 44(2) to (4) above shall be disclosed without the consent of the person from whom the information was obtained and, if different, the person to whom it relates.

(2) Subsection (1) above shall not preclude the disclosure of information to any person who is a competent authority for the purposes of section 449 of the Companies Act 1985.   1985 c. 6.

(2A) Subsection (1) above shall not preclude the disclosure of information as mentioned in any of the paragraphs except (*m*) of subsection (1) of section 180 of the Financial Services Act 1986 or in subsection (3) or (4) of that section or as mentioned in section 449(1) of the Companies Act 1985.

(2B) Subsection (1) above shall not preclude the disclosure of any such information as is mentioned in section 180(5) of the Financial Services Act 1986 by any person who by virtue of that section is not precluded by section 179 of that Act from disclosing it."

7. After subsection (1) of section 437 of the Companies Act 1985 there shall be inserted—

" (1A) Any persons who have been appointed under section

431 or 432 may at any time and, if the Secretary of State directs them to do so, shall inform him of any matters coming to their knowledge as a result of their investigations ." ;

and subsection (2) of section 433 of that Act shall be omitted.

8. In section 446 of that Act—

    (*a*) in subsection (3) for the words " to 436 " there shall be substituted the words " to 437 " ; and

    (*b*) subsection (5) shall be omitted.

9.—(1) In subsection (1) of section 449 of that Act—

    (*a*) for paragraphs (*a*) and (*b*) there shall be substituted—

        " (*a*) with a view to the institution of or otherwise for the purposes of criminal proceedings ; ".

    (*b*) for paragraph (*d*) there shall be substituted—

        " (*d*) for the purpose of enabling or assisting the Secretary of State to exercise any of his functions under this Act, the Insider Dealing Act, the Prevention of Fraud (Investments) Act 1958, the Insurance Companies Act 1982, the Insolvency Act 1986, the Company Directors Disqualification Act 1986 or the Financial Services Act 1986.

1958 c. 45.
1982 c. 50.
1986 c. 45.
1986 c. 46.

        (*dd*) for the purpose of enabling or assisting the Department of Economic Development for Northern Ireland to exercise any powers conferred on it by the enactments relating to companies or insolvency or for the purpose of enabling or assisting any inspector appointed by it under the enactments relating to companies to discharge his functions " ;

    (*c*) after paragraph (*e*) there shall be inserted—

        " (*f*) for the purpose of enabling or assisting the Bank of England to discharge its functions under the Banking Act 1979 or any other functions,

        (*g*) for the purpose of enabling or assisting the Deposit Protection Board to discharge its functions under that Act,

        (*h*) for any purpose mentioned in section 180(1)(*b*), (*e*), (*h*), (*n*) *or* (*p*) of the Financial Services Act 1986,

        (*i*) for the purpose of enabling or assisting the Industrial Assurance Commissioner or the Industrial Assurance Commissioner for Northern Ireland to discharge his functions under the enactments relating to industrial assurance,

        (*j*) for the purpose of enabling or assisting the Insurance Brokers Registration Council to discharge its functions under the Insurance Brokers (Registration) Act 1977,

1977 c. 46.

        (*k*) for the purpose of enabling or assisting an official receiver to discharge his functions under the enactments relating to insolvency or for the purpose of enabling or assisting a body which is for the time being a recognised professional body for the purposes of section 391 of the Insolvency Act 1986 to discharge its functions as such,

(*l*) with a view to the institution of, or otherwise for the purposes of, any disciplinary proceedings relating to the exercise by a solicitor, auditor, accountant, valuer or actuary of his professional duties,

(*m*) for the purpose of enabling or assisting an authority in a country or territory outside the United Kingdom to exercise corresponding supervisory functions.".

(2) After subsection (1) of that section there shall be inserted—

" (1A) In subsection (1) above ' corresponding supervisory functions ' means functions corresponding to those of the Secretary of State or the competent authority under the Financial Services Act 1986 or to those of the Secretary of State under the Insurance Companies Act 1982 or to those of the Bank of England under the Banking Act 1979 or any other functions in connection with rules of law corresponding to the provisions of the Insider Dealing Act or Part VII of the Financial Services Act 1986.

(1B) Subject to subsection (1C), subsection (1) shall not preclude publication or disclosure for the purpose of enabling or assisting any public or other authority for the time being designated for the purposes of this section by the Secretary of State by an order in a statutory instrument to discharge any functions which are specified in the order.

(1C) An order under subsection (1B) designating an authority for the purpose of that subsection may—

(*a*) impose conditions subject to which the publication or disclosure of any information or document is permitted by that subsection ; and

(*b*) otherwise restrict the circumstances in which that subsection permits publication or disclosure.

(1D) Subsection (1) shall not preclude the publication or disclosure of any such information as is mentioned in section 180(5) of the Financial Services Act 1986 by any person who by virtue of that section is not precluded by section 179 of that Act from disclosing it."

(3) For subsection (3) of that section (competent authorities) there shall be substituted—

" (3) For the purposes of this section each of the following is a competent authority—

(*a*) the Secretary of State,

(*b*) the Department of Economic Development for Northern Ireland and any officer of that Department,

(*c*) an inspector appointed under this Part by the Secretary of State,

(*d*) the Treasury and any officer of the Treasury,

(*e*) the Bank of England and any officer or servant of the Bank,

(*f*) the Lord Advocate,

(*g*) the Director of Public Prosecutions, and the Director of Public Prosecutions for Northern Ireland,

(*h*) any designated agency or transferee body within the meaning of the Financial Services Act 1986 and any officer or servant of such an agency or body,

(*i*) any person appointed or authorised to exercise any powers under section 94, 106 or 177 of the Financial Services Act 1986 and any officer or servant of such a person,

(*j*) the body administering a scheme under section 54 of or paragraph 18 of Schedule 11 to that Act and any officer or servant of such a body,

(*k*) the Chief Registrar of friendly societies and the Registrar of Friendly Societies for Northern Ireland and any officer or servant of either of them.

(*l*) the Industrial Assurance Commissioner and the Industrial Assurance Commissioner for Northern Ireland and any officer of either of them,

(*m*) any constable,

(*n*) any procurator fiscal.

(4) A statutory instrument containing an order under subsection (1B) is subject to annulment in pursuance of a resolution of either House of Parliament.".

10. After section 451 of that Act there shall be inserted—

" Disclosure of information by Secretary of State.   451A. The Secretary of State may, if he thinks fit, disclose any information obtained under this Part of this Act—

(*a*) to any person who is a competent authority for the purposes of section 449, or

(*b*) in any circumstances in which or for any purpose for which that section does not preclude the disclosure of the information to which it applies."

S.I. 1986/1032 (N.I.6).   11. After Article 430(1) of the Companies (Northern Ireland) Order 1986 there shall be inserted—

" (1A) Any persons who have been appointed under Article 424 or 425 may at any time and, if the Department directs them to do so shall, inform it of any matters coming to their knowledge as a result of their investigation. " ;

and Article 426(2) of that Order shall be omitted.

12. In Article 439 of that Order—

(*a*) in paragraph (3) for the words " to 429 " there shall be substituted the words " to 430 " ; and

(*b*) paragraph (5) shall be omitted.

13.—(1) In paragraph (1) of Article 442 of that Order—

(*a*) for sub-paragraphs (*a*) and (*b*) there shall be substituted—
"(*a*) with a view to the institution of or otherwise for the purposes of criminal proceedings ; " ;

(*b*) for sub-paragraph (*d*) there shall be substituted—
"(*d*) for the purpose of enabling or assisting the Department to exercise any of its functions under this Order, the Insider Dealing Order or the Prevention of Fraud (Investments) Act (Northern Ireland) 1940 ;

(*dd*) for the purpose of enabling or assisting the Secretary of State to exercise any functions conferred on him by the enactments relating to companies or insolvency, the Prevention of Fraud (Investments) Act 1958, the Insurance Companies Act 1982, or the Financial Services Act 1986, or for the purpose of enabling or assisting any inspector appointed by him under the enactments relating to companies to discharge his functions " ;

(*c*) after sub-paragraph (*e*) there shall be inserted—
"(*f*) for the purposes of enabling or assisting the Bank of England to discharge its functions under the Banking Act 1979 or any other functions ;

(*g*) for the purposes of enabling or assisting the Deposit Protection Board to discharge its functions under that Act ;

(*h*) for any purpose mentioned in section 180(1)(*b*), (*e*), (*h*), (*n*) or (*p*) of the Financial Services Act 1986 ;

(*i*) for the purpose of enabling or assisting the Industrial Assurance Commissioner for Northern Ireland or the Industrial Assurance Commissioner in Great Britain to discharge his functions under the enactments relating to industrial assurance ;

(*j*) for the purpose of enabling or assisting the Insurance Brokers Registration Council to discharge its functions under the Insurance Brokers (Registration) Act 1977 ;

(*k*) for the purpose of enabling or assisting the official assignee to discharge his functions under the enactments relating to companies or bankruptcy ;

(*l*) with a view to the institution of, or otherwise for the purposes of, any disciplinary proceedings relating to the exercise by a solicitor, auditor, accountant, valuer or actuary of his professional duties ;

(*m*) for the purpose of enabling or assisting an authority in a country or territory outside the United Kingdom to exercise corresponding supervisory functions.".

(2) After paragraph (1) of that Article there shall be inserted—
"(1A) In paragraph (1) "corresponding supervisory functions" means functions corresponding to those of the Secretary of State or the competent authority under the Financial Services

ſ 4

Act 1986 or to those of the Secretary of State under the Insurance Companies Act 1982 or to those of the Bank of England under the Banking Act 1979 or any other functions in connection with rules of law corresponding to the provisions of the Insider Dealing Order or Part VII of the Financial Services Act 1986.

(1B) Subject to paragraph (1C), paragraph (1) shall not preclude publication or disclosure for the purpose of enabling or assisting any public or other authority for the time being designated for the purposes of this Article by an order made by the Department to discharge any functions which are specified in the order.

(1C) An order under paragraph (1B) designating an authority for the purpose of that paragraph may—

   (a) impose conditions subject to which the publication or disclosure of any information or document is permitted by that paragraph ; and

   (b) otherwise restrict the circumstances in which that paragraph permits publication or disclosure.

(1D) Paragraph (1) shall not preclude the publication or disclosure of any such information as is mentioned in section 180(5) of the Financial Services Act 1986 by any person who by virtue of that section is not precluded by section 179 of that Act from disclosing it."

(3) For paragraph (3) of that Article (competent authorities) there shall be substituted—

" (3) For the purposes of this Article each of the following is a competent authority—

   (a) the Department and any officer of the Department,

   (b) the Secretary of State,

   (c) an inspector appointed under this Part by the Department,

   (d) the Department of Finance and Personnel and any officer of that Department ;

   (e) the Treasury and any officer of the Treasury,

   (f) the Bank of England and any officer or servant of the Bank,

   (g) the Lord Advocate,

   (h) the Director of Public Prosecutions for Northern Ireland and the Director of Public Prosecutions in England and Wales,

   (i) any designated agency or transferee body within the meaning of the Financial Services Act 1986 and any officer or servant of such an agency or body,

   (j) any person appointed or authorised to exercise any powers under section 94, 106 or 177 of the Financial Services Act 1986 and any officer or servant of such a person,

(*k*) the body administering a scheme under section 54 of
or paragraph 18 of Schedule 11 to that Act and any
officer or servant of such a body.

(*l*) the Registrar of Friendly Societies and the Chief Registrar of friendly societies in Great Britain and any
officer or servant of either of them,

(*m*) the Industrial Assurance Commissioner for Northern
Ireland and the Industrial Assurance Commissioner in
Great Britain and any officer of either of them,

(*n*) any constable,

(*o*) any procurator fiscal.

(4) An order under paragraph (1B) is subject to negative
resolution."

14. After Article 444 of that order there shall be inserted—

" *Disclosure of information by Department*

444A. The Department may, if it thinks fit, disclose any
information obtained under this Part—

(*a*) to any person who is a competent authority for the
purposes of Article 442, or

(*b*) in any circumstances in which or for any purpose for
which that Article does not preclude the disclosure of
the information to which it applies.".

SCHEDULE 14   Section 189.

RESTRICTION OF REHABILITATION OF OFFENDERS ACT 1974   1974 c. 53.

PART I

EXEMPTED PROCEEDINGS

1. Any proceedings with respect to a decision or proposed decision
of the Secretary of State or a designated agency—

(*a*) refusing, withdrawing or suspending an authorisation ;

(*b*) refusing an application under section 28(5) of this Act ;

(*c*) giving a direction under section 59 of this Act or refusing an
application for consent or for the variation of a consent
under that section ;

(*d*) exercising a power under Chapter VI of Part I of this Act
or refusing an application for the rescission or variation
of a prohibition or requirement imposed under that
Chapter ;

(*e*) refusing to make or revoking an order declaring a collective
investment scheme to be an authorised unit trust scheme
or a recognised scheme.

2. Any proceedings with respect to a decision or proposed decision
of a recognised self-regulating organisation—

(*a*) refusing or suspending a person's membership of the organisation ;

(b) expelling a member of the organisation ;

(c) exercising a power of the organisation for purposes corresponding to those of Chapter VI of Part I of this Act.

3.—(1) Any proceedings with respect to a decision or proposed decision of a recognised professional body—

(a) refusing or suspending a person's membership of the body ;

(b) expelling a member of the body.

(2) Any proceedings with respect to a decision or proposed decision of a recognised professional body or of any other body or person having functions in respect of the enforcement of the recognised professional body's rules relating to the carrying on of investment business—

(a) exercising a power for purposes corresponding to those of Chapter VI of Part I of this Act ;

(b) refusing, suspending or withdrawing a certificate issued for the purposes of Part I of this Act.

4. Any proceedings with respect to a decision or proposed decision of the competent authority under Part IV of this Act refusing an application for listing or to discontinue or suspend the listing of any securities.

5. Any proceedings with respect to a decision or proposed decision of the Chief Registrar of friendly societies, the Registrar of Friendly Societies for Northern Ireland or a transferee body, exercising a power exercisable by virtue of paragraph 23 of Schedule 11 to this Act or refusing an application for the rescission or variation of a prohibition or requirement imposed in the exercise of such a power.

6. Any proceedings with respect to a decision or proposed decision of a recognised self-regulating organisation for friendly societies—

(a) refusing or suspending a society's membership of the organisation ;

(b) expelling a member of the organisation ;

(c) exercising a power of the organisation for purposes corresponding to those for which powers are exercisable by the Registrar by virtue of paragraph 23 of Schedule 11 to this Act.

PART II

EXEMPTED QUESTIONS

Person putting question	*Individual to whom question relates*
1. The Secretary of State or a designated agency.	(a) An authorised person.
	(b) An applicant for authorisation under section 26 of this Act.

Person putting question	*Individual to whom question relates*	SCH. 14
	(c) A person whose authorisation is suspended.	
	(d) The operator or trustee of a recognised scheme or a collective investment scheme in respect of which a notice has been given by the operator under section 87(3) or an application made under section 88 of this Act.	
	(e) An individual who is an associate of a person (whether or not an individual) described in paragraph (a), (b), (c) or (d) above.	
2. A recognised self-regulating organisation or recognised professional body.	(a) A member of the organisation or body.	
	(b) An applicant for membership of the organisation or body.	
	(c) A person whose membership of the organisation or body is suspended.	
	(d) An individual who is an associate of a person (whether or not an individual) described in paragraph (a), (b) or (c) above.	
3. A recognised professional body.	(a) A person certified by the body.	
	(b) An applicant for certification by the body.	
	(c) A person whose certification by the body is suspended.	
	(d) An individual who is an associate of a person (whether or not an individual) described in paragraph (a), (b) or (c) above.	
4. A person (whether or not an individual) described in paragraph 1 (a), (b), (c) or (d), paragraph 2(a), (b) or (c) or paragraph 3(a), (b) or (c) above.	An individual who is or is seeking to become an associate of the person in column 1.	
5. The competent authority or any other person.	An individual from or in respect of whom information is sought in connection with an application for listing under Part IV of this Act.	

Person putting question	*Individual to whom question relates*
6. The competent authority.	An individual who is or is seeking to become an associate of the issuer of securities listed under Part IV of this Act and from or in respect of whom information is sought which the issuer of the securities is required to furnish under listing rules.
7. The Chief Registrar of friendly societies, the Registrar of Friendly Societies for Northern Ireland or a transferee body.	An individual who is an associate of a society which is authorised under section 23 of this Act.
8. A recognised self-regulating organisation for friendly societies.	An individual who is an associate of a member or an applicant for membership of the organisation or of a society whose membership of the organisation is suspended.

PART III

EXEMPTED ACTIONS

Person taking action	*Exempted action*
1. The Secretary of State, a designated agency, a recognised self-regulating organisation, a recognised professional body, any other body or person mentioned in paragraph 3(2) of Part I of this Schedule or the competent authority.	Any such decision or proposed decision as is mentioned in Part I of this Schedule.
2. A person (whether or not an individual) described in paragraph 1(*a*), (*b*), (*c*) or (*d*), paragraph 2(*a*), (*b*) or (*c*) or paragraph 3(*a*), (*b*) or (*c*) of Part II of this Schedule.	Dismissing or excluding an individual from being or becoming an associate of the person in column 1.
3. The issuer of securities listed or subject to an application for listing under Part IV of this Act.	Dismissing or excluding an individual from being or becoming an associate of the issuer.
4. The Chief Registrar of friendly societies, the Registrar of Friendly Societies for Northern Ireland, a transferee body or a recognised self-regulating organisation for friendly societies.	Any such decision or proposed decision as is mentioned in Part I of this Schedule.

SUPPLEMENTAL

1. In Part I of this Schedule " proceedings " includes any pro- 1974 c. 53.
ceedings within the meaning of section 4 of the Rehabilitation of
Offenders Act 1974.

2. In Parts II and III of this Schedule—

(*a*) references to an applicant for authorisation, membership or
certification are references to an applicant who has not yet
been informed of the decision on his application ;

(*b*) references to an application for listing under Part IV of this
Act are references to an application the decision on which
has not yet been communicated to the applicant and which
is not taken by virtue of section 144(5) of this Act to have
been refused.

3. Paragraph 1(*d*) of Part II of this Schedule and so much of paragraph 1(*e*) as relates to it—

(*a*) apply only if the question is put to elicit information for
the purpose of determining whether the operator or trustee
is a fit and proper person to act as operator or trustee of
the scheme in question ;

(*b*) apply in the case of a scheme in respect of which a notice
has been given under subsection (3) of section 87 only
until the end of the period within which the operator may
receive a notification from the Secretary of State under
that subsection or, if earlier, the receipt by him of such
a notification ;

(*c*) apply in the case of a scheme in respect of which an application has been made under section 88 only until the
applicant has been informed of the decision on the application.

SCHEDULE 15

Section 211(3).

TRANSITIONAL PROVISIONS

Interim authorisation

1.—(1) If before such day as is appointed for the purposes of this
paragraph by an order made by the Secretary of State a person
has applied—

(*a*) for membership of any body which on that day is a recognised self-regulating organisation ; or

(*b*) for authorisation by the Secretary of State,

and the application has not been determined before the day on which
section 3 of this Act comes into force, that person shall, subject to
sub-paragraphs (2), (3) and (4) below, be treated until the determination of the application as if he had been granted an authorisation by the Secretary of State.

(2) Sub-paragraph (1) above does not apply to a person who immediately before the day on which section 3 of this Act comes into force is prohibited by the Prevention of Fraud (Investments) Act 1958 (in this Schedule referred to as " the previous Act ") from carrying on the business of dealing in securities—

(a) by reason of the refusal or revocation at any time before that day of a licence under that Act; or

(b) by reason of the revocation at any time before that day of an order declaring him to be an exempted dealer.

(3) If a person who has made any such application as is mentioned in sub-paragraph (1) above has before the day on which section 3 of this Act comes into force been served with a notice under section 6 or 16(3) of the previous Act (proposed refusal or revocation of licence or proposed revocation of exemption order) but the refusal or revocation to which the notice relates has not taken place before that day—

(a) the provisions of that Act with respect to the refusal or revocation of a licence or the revocation of an order under section 16 of that Act shall continue to apply to him until the application mentioned in sub-paragraph (1) above is determined; and

(b) that sub-paragraph shall cease to apply to him if before the determination of the application mentioned in that sub-paragraph his application for a licence under that Act is refused, his licence under that Act is revoked or the order declaring him to be an exempted dealer under that Act is revoked.

(4) Notwithstanding sub-paragraph (1) above section 102(1)(a) of this Act shall not apply to a person entitled to carry on investment business by virtue of that sub-paragraph but the Secretary of State may make available for public inspection the information with respect to the holders of principal's licences mentioned in section 9 of the previous Act, any information in his possession by virtue of section 15(3) or (4) of that Act and the information mentioned in section 16(4) of that Act.

(5) Notwithstanding subsection (2) of section 3 of the previous Act a licence granted under that section before the day on which section 3 of this Act comes into force shall, unless revoked under section 6 of that Act, continue in force until that day.

Return of fees on pending applications

2. Any fee paid in respect of an application under section 3 of the previous Act which is pending on the day on which that Act is repealed shall be repaid to the applicant.

Deposits and undertakings

3. The repeal of section 4 of the previous Act shall not affect the operation of that section in a case where—

(a) a sum deposited in accordance with that section has become payable as provided in subsection (2) of that section before the date on which the repeal takes effect ; or

(b) a sum has become payable before that date in pursuance of an undertaking given under subsection (4) of that section,

but, subject as aforesaid, any sum deposited under that section may be withdrawn by the depositor on application to the Accountant General of the Supreme Court and any undertaking given under that section shall be discharged.

Interim recognition of professional bodies

4.—(1) If on an application made under section 17 of this Act it appears to the Secretary of State that any of the requirements of section 18(3) of this Act or paragraphs 2 to 6 of Schedule 3 to this Act are not satisfied he may in accordance with this paragraph make a recognition order under section 18 of this Act (" an interim recognition order ") notwithstanding that all or any of those requirements are not satisfied.

(2) The Secretary of State may, subject to sub-paragraphs (3) and (4) below, make an interim recognition order if he is satisfied—

(a) that the applicant proposes to adopt rules and practices and to make arrangements which will satisfy such of the requirements mentioned in sub-paragraph (1) above as are not satisfied ;

(b) that it is not practicable for those rules, practices and arrangements to be brought into effect before the date on which section 3 of this Act comes into force but that they will be brought into effect within a reasonable time thereafter ; and

(c) that in the meantime the applicant will enforce its existing rules in such a way, and issue such guidance, as will in respect of investment business of any kind carried on by persons certified by it (or by virtue of paragraph 5 below treated as certified by it) afford to investors protection as nearly as may be equivalent to that provided as respects investment business of that kind by the rules and regulations under Chapter V of Part I of this Act.

(3) Where the requirements which are not satisfied consist of or include those mentioned in paragraph 2 of Schedule 3 to this Act an application for an interim recognition order shall be accompanied by—

(a) a list of the persons to whom the applicant proposes to issue certificates for the purposes of Part I of this Act ; and

(b) particulars of the criteria adopted for determining the persons included in the list ;

and the Secretary of State shall not make the order unless it appears to him that those criteria conform as nearly as may be to the conditions mentioned in that paragraph and that the applicant will, until the requirements of that paragraph are satisfied, have arrangements for securing that no person is certified by it (or by virtue of paragraph 5 below treated as certified by it) except in accordance with those criteria and for the effective monitoring of continued compliance by those persons with those criteria.

(4) Where the requirements which are not satisfied consist of or include that mentioned in paragraph 6 of Schedule 3 to this Act, the Secretary of State shall not make an interim recognition order unless it appears to him that the applicant will, until that requirement is satisfied, take such steps for complying with it as are reasonably practicable.

(5) An application for an interim recognition order shall be accompanied by a copy of the rules and by particulars of the practices and arrangements referred to in sub-paragraph (2)(a) above.

(6) An interim recognition order shall not be revocable but shall cease to be in force at the end of such period as is specified in it ; and that period shall be such as will in the opinion of the Secretary of State allow a reasonable time for the rules, practices and arrangements mentioned in sub-paragraph (5) above to be brought into effect.

(7) The Secretary of State may on the application of the body to which an interim recognition order relates extend the period specified in it if that body satisfies him—

(a) that there are sufficient reasons why the rules, practices and arrangements mentioned in sub-paragraph (5) above cannot be brought into effect by the end of that period ; and

(b) that those rules, practices and arrangements, or other rules, practices and arrangements which satisfy the requirements mentioned in sub-paragraph (2)(a) above and of which copies or particulars are furnished to the Secretary of State, will be brought into effect within a reasonable time thereafter ;

but not more than one application shall be made by a body under this sub-paragraph.

(8) A recognition order under section 18 of this Act shall cease to be an interim recognition order if before it ceases to be in force—

(a) the rules, practices and arrangements of which copies or particulars were furnished to the Secretary of State under sub-paragraph (5) or (7)(b) above are brought into effect ; or

(b) the Secretary of State certifies that other rules, practices and arrangements which have been brought into effect comply with the requirements mentioned in sub-paragraph (1) above.

(9) In this paragraph references to the adoption of rules or the making of arrangements include references to taking such other steps as may be necessary for bringing them into effect.

Interim authorisation by recognised professional bodies

5.—(1) If at the time when an interim recognition order is made in respect of a professional body that body is unable to issue certificates for the purposes of this Act, any person who at that time is included in the list furnished by that body to the Secretary of State in accordance with paragraph 4(3)(*a*) above shall be treated for the purposes of this Act as a person certified by that body.

(2) If at any time while an interim recognition order is in force in respect of a professional body and before the body is able to issue certificates as mentioned in sub-paragraph (1) above the body notifies the Secretary of State that a person not included in that list satisfies the criteria of which particulars were furnished by the body in accordance with paragraph 4(3)(*b*) above, that person shall, on receipt of the notification by the Secretary of State, be treated for the purposes of this Act as a person certified by that body.

(3) If at any time while an interim recognition order is in force in respect of a professional body it appears to the body—

(*a*) that a person treated by virtue of sub-paragraph (1) or (2) above as certified by it has ceased (after the expiration of such transitional period, if any, as appears to the body to be appropriate) to satisfy the criteria mentioned in sub-paragraph (2) above ; or

(*b*) that any such person should for any other reason cease to be treated as certified by it,

it shall forthwith give notice of that fact to the Secretary of State and the person in question shall, on receipt of that notification by the Secretary of State, cease to be treated as certified by that body.

(4) Where by virtue of this paragraph a partnership is treated as certified by a recognised professional body section 15(3) of this Act shall apply as it applies where a certificate has in fact been issued to a partnership.

(5) Where by virtue of this paragraph any persons are treated as certified by a recognised professional body the requirements of paragraph 2 of Schedule 3 to this Act so far as relating to the retention by a person of a certificate issued by that body and the requirements of paragraph 4 of that Schedule shall apply to the body as if the references to persons certified by it included references to persons treated as certified.

Power of recognised professional body to make rules required by this Act.

6.—(1) Where a recognised professional body regulates the practice of a profession in the exercise of statutory powers the matters in respect of which rules can be made in the exercise of those powers shall, if they would not otherwise do so, include any matter in respect of which rules are required to be made—

(*a*) so that the recognition order in respect of that body can cease to be an interim recognition order ; or

(*b*) where the recognition order was not, or has ceased to be, an interim recognition order, so that the body can continue to be a recognised professional body.

(2) Rules made by virtue of this paragraph may in particular make provision for the issue, withdrawal and suspension of certifi-

SCH. 15   cates for the purposes of this Act and the making of charges in respect of their issue and may accordingly apply to persons who are, or are to be, certified or treated as certified by the body in question whether or not they are persons in relation to whom rules could be made apart from this paragraph.

(3) Rules made by virtue of this paragraph may make different provision for different cases.

(4) The Secretary of State may at the request of a recognised professional body by order extend, modify or exclude any statutory provision relating to the regulation of the conduct, practice, or discipline of members of that body to such extent as he thinks necessary or expedient in consequence of the provisions of this paragraph ; and any order made by virtue of this sub-paragraph shall be subject to annulment in pursuance of a resolution of either House of Parliament.

Notice of commencement of business

7. In the case of a person who is carrying on investment business in the United Kingdom on the day on which section 31 of this Act comes into force, section 32 of this Act shall have effect as if it required him to give the notice referred to in that section forthwith.

Advertisements

1985 c. 6.   8.—(1) So long as Part III of the Companies Act 1985 remains in force section 57 of this Act shall not apply—

> (a) in relation to any distribution of a prospectus to which section 56 of that Act applies or would apply if not excluded by subsection (5)(b) of that section or to which section 72 of that Act applies or would apply if not excluded by subsection (6)(b) of that section or by section 76 of that Act, or in relation to any distribution of a document relating to securities of a corporation incorporated in Great Britain which is not a registered company, being a document which—
>
>> (i) would, if the corporation were a registered company, be a prospectus to which section 56 of that Act applies or would apply if not excluded as aforesaid, and
>>
>> (ii) contains all the matters and is issued with the consents which, by virtue of sections 72 to 75 of that Act, it would have to contain and be issued with if the corporation were a company incorporated outside Great Britain and the document were a prospectus issued by that company ;
>
> (b) in relation to any issue of a form of application for shares in, or debentures of, a corporation, together with—
>
>> (i) a prospectus which complies with the requirements of section 56 of that Act or is not required to comply with them because excluded by subsection (5)(b) of that section, or complies with the requirements of Chapter II

of Part III of that Act relating to prospectuses and is not issued in contravention of sections 74 and 75 of that Act, or

(ii) in the case of a corporation incorporated in Great Britain which is not a registered company, a document containing all the matters and issued with the consents mentioned in sub-paragraph (*a*)(ii) of this paragraph, or in connection with a bona fide invitation to a person to enter into an underwriting agreement with respect to the shares or debentures.

(2) The provisions of this paragraph shall apply to Northern Ireland with the substitution for the references to Part III and Chapter II of Part III of the Companies Act 1985 of references to 1985 c. 6. Part IV and Chapter II of Part IV of the Companies (Northern S.I. 1986/1032 Ireland) Order 1986, for the references to sections 56, 56(5)(*b*), 72, (N.I.6). 72(6)(*b*), 74, 76 and 72 to 75 of the Companies Act 1985 of references to Articles 66, 66(5)(*b*), 82, 82(6)(*b*), 84, 86 and 82 to 85 of the Companies (Northern Ireland) Order 1986, for the references to a corporation incorporated in Great Britain of references to a corporation incorporated in Northern Ireland and for the reference to a company incorporated outside Great Britain of a reference to a company incorporated outside the United Kingdom.

Authorised unit trust schemes

9.—(1) Where an order under section 17 of the previous Act (authorisation of unit trust schemes) is in force in respect of a unit trust scheme immediately before the coming into force of Chapter VIII of Part I of this Act the scheme shall be treated as an authorised unit trust scheme under that Part and the order as an order under section 78 of this Act.

(2) In relation to any such authorised unit trust scheme the reference in section 79(1)(*a*) of this Act to the requirements for the making of the order shall be construed as a reference to the requirements for the making of an order under section 78, but the scheme shall not be regarded as failing to comply with those requirements by reason of the manager or trustee not being an authorised person if he is treated as such a person by virtue of paragraph 1 above.

(3) If before the day on which Chapter VIII of Part I comes into force a notice in respect of a scheme has been served under subsection (2) of section 17 of the previous Act (proposed revocation of authorisation of unit trust scheme) but the revocation has not taken place before that day, the provisions of that subsection shall continue to apply in relation to the scheme and sub-paragraph (1) above shall cease to apply to it if the authorisation is revoked under that subsection.

Recognised collective investment schemes

10.—(1) If at any time before the coming into force of section 86 of this Act it appears to the Secretary of State that the law of a member State other than the United Kingdom confers rights on the

SCH. 15   managers and trustees of authorised unit trust schemes entitling them to carry on in that State on terms equivalent to those of that section—

(a) investment business which consists in operating or acting as trustee in relation to such schemes ; and

(b) any investment business which is carried on by them in connection with or for the purposes of such schemes,

he may by order direct that schemes constituted in that State which satisfy such requirements as are specified in the order shall be recognised schemes for the purposes of this Act.

(2) Subsections (2) to (9) of section 86 of this Act shall have effect in relation to any scheme recognised by virtue of this paragraph ; and the references in section 24 and 207(1) of this Act to a scheme recognised under section 86, and in section 76(1) of this Act to a scheme recognised under Chapter VIII of Part I of this Act, shall include references to any scheme recognised by virtue of this paragraph.

(3) In section 86(3)(a) as applied by sub-paragraph (2) above the reference to the rights conferred by any relevant Community instrument shall be construed as a reference to the rights conferred by virtue of an order made under this paragraph.

11.—(1) Subsection (7) of section 88 of this Act shall not apply to a scheme which is in existence on the date on which this Act is passed if—

(a) the units under the scheme are included in the Official List of The Stock Exchange and have been so included throughout the period of five years ending on the date on which this paragraph comes into force ;

(b) the law of the country or territory in which the scheme is established precludes the participants being entitled or the operator being required as mentioned in that subsection ; and

(c) throughout the period of five years ending on the date on which the application is made under that section, units under the scheme have in fact been regularly redeemed as mentioned in that subsection or the operator has in fact regularly ensured that participants were able to sell their units as there mentioned.

(2) The grounds for revoking an order made under section 88 of this Act by virtue of this paragraph shall include the ground that it appears to the Secretary of State that since the making of the order units under the scheme have ceased to be regularly redeemed or the operator has ceased regularly to ensure their sale as mentioned in sub-paragraph (1)(c) above.

Delegation orders

12.—(1) A delegation order may transfer a function notwithstanding that the provision conferring it has not yet come into force but no such function shall be exercisable by virtue of the order until the coming into force of that provision.

(2) Sub-paragraph (1) above applies also to a transfer order under   SCH. 15
paragraph 28(1) of Schedule 11 to this Act.

Disclosure of information

13. In determining for the purposes of section 180(6) of this Act
and the enactments amended by paragraphs 3(2), 9(2) and 13(2) of
Schedule 13 to this Act whether the functions of an authority in a
country or territory outside the United Kingdom correspond to
functions conferred by any of the provisions of this Act regard shall
be had to those provisions whether or not they have already come
into force.

Temporary exemptions for friendly societies

14.—(1) A registered friendly society which transacts no investment business after the date on which section 3 of this Act comes
into force except for the purpose of making or carrying out relevant
existing members' contracts shall be treated for the purposes of
that section as if it were an exempted person under Chapter IV of
Part I of this Act.

(2) Subject to sub-paragraph (3) below, for the purposes of this
paragraph " relevant existing members' contracts ", in relation to any
society, means—

    (a) contracts made by the society before that date ; and

    (b) in the case of a small income society—

        (i) during the period of three years beginning with
that date, tax exempt investment agreements made by it
with persons who were members of the society before
that date ; and

        (ii) after the expiry of that period, tax exempt in-
vestment agreements made by it with such persons before
the expiry of that period.

(3) Paragraph (b) of sub-paragraph (2) above shall not apply to
a registered friendly society after the expiry of the period of two
years beginning with that date unless before the expiry of that period
it has by special resolution (within the meaning of the Friendly 1974 c. 46.
Societies Act 1974 or, as the case may be, the Friendly Societies Act 1970 c. 31 (N.I.)
(Northern Ireland) 1970) determined—

    (a) to transact no further investment business except for the
purpose of carrying out contracts entered into before the
expiry of the said period of three years ; or

    (b) to take such action as is necessary to procure the transfer
of its engagements to another such society or a company
or the amalgamation of the society with another such
society under section 82 of the said Act of 1974 or, as the
case may be, section 70 of the said Act of 1970,

and a copy of that resolution has been registered in accordance
with section 86 of the said Act of 1974 or, as the case may be,
section 75 of the said Act of 1970.

(4) For the purpose of sub-paragraph (2) above a society is a small income society if its income in 1985 from members' contributions did not exceed £50,000.

(5) For the purposes of sub-paragraph (2) above an investment agreement is a tax exempt investment agreement if the society by which it is made may obtain exemption from income and corporation tax on the profits from it under section 332 of the Income and
Corporation Taxes Act 1970.

(6) A society to which sub-paragraph (1) or (2) above applies shall not be an authorised person for the purposes of this Act nor a regulated friendly society for the purposes of the provisions of Schedule 11 to this Act.

Dealings in course of non-investment business

15. If before the day on which section 3 of this Act comes into force a person has applied for permission under paragraph 23 of Schedule 1 to this Act and the application has not been determined before that day, that person shall, until the determination of the application and subject to his complying with such requirements as the Secretary of State may impose, be treated as if he had been granted a permission under that paragraph.

Northern Ireland

16. The foregoing provisions shall apply to Northern Ireland with the substitution for references to the previous Act or any provision of
that Act of references to the Prevention of Fraud (Investments) Act (Northern Ireland) 1940 and the corresponding provision of that Act.

SCHEDULE 16

CONSEQUENTIAL AMENDMENTS

1. In section 22 of the Charities Act 1960—

   (a) subsection (10) shall be omitted ; and

   (b) in subsection (11) for the words "Subsections (9) and (10)" there shall be substituted the words "Subsection (9)".

2. In the Trustee Investments Act 1961—

   (a) in section 11(3) for the words "the Prevention of Fraud (Investments) Act 1958 or the Prevention of Fraud (Investments) Act (Northern Ireland) 1940" there shall be substituted the words "the Financial Services Act 1986";

   (b) for paragraph 3 of Part III of Schedule 1 there shall be substituted—

      "3. In any units of an authorised unit trust scheme within the meaning of the Financial Services Act 1986";

   (c) in paragraph 2(a) of Part IV of Schedule 1 for the words from " a recognised stock exchange " onwards there shall

be substituted the words " a recognised investment exchange SCH. 16
within the meaning of the Financial Services Act 1986 " ;

(*d*) in the definition of " securities " in paragraph 4 of Part IV
of that Schedule after the word " debentures " there shall be
inserted the words " units within paragraph 3 of Part III of
this Schedule ".

3. In section 32 of the Clergy Pensions Measure 1961 No. 3—

(*a*) for paragraph (*t*) of subsection (1) there shall be substituted—
    "(*t*) in any units in any authorised unit trust scheme
    or a recognised scheme within the meaning of the Finan-
    cial Services Act 1986"; and

(*b*) in subsection (5)(*a*) for the words from "a recognised stock
exchange" onwards there shall be substituted the words "a
recognised investment exchange within the meaning of the
Financial Services Act 1986.".

4. In the Stock Transfer Act 1963—   1963 c. 18.

(*a*) for paragraph (*e*) of section 1(4) there shall be substituted—
    "(*e*) units of an authorised unit trust scheme or a
    recognised scheme within the meaning of the Financial
    Services Act 1986"; and

(*b*) in the definition of " securities " in section 4(1) for the words
from "unit trust scheme" to "scheme" there shall be substituted the words "collective investment scheme within the
meaning of the Financial Services Act 1986".

5. In the Stock Transfer Act (Northern Ireland) 1963—   1963 c. 24.
                                                            (N.I.).
(*a*) for paragraph (*e*) of section 1(4) there shall be substituted—
    "(*e*) units of an authorised unit trust scheme or a
    recognised scheme within the meaning of the Financial
    Services Act 1986"; and

(*b*) in the definition of "securities" in section 4(1) for the words
from "unit trust scheme" to "scheme" there shall be substituted the words "collective investment scheme within the
meaning of the Financial Services Act 1986".

6. In section 25 of the Charities Act (Northern Ireland) 1964— 1964 c. 33
                                                               (N.I.).
(*a*) subsection (16) shall be omitted ; and

(*b*) in subsection (17) for the words " Subsections (15) and (16) "
there shall be substituted the words ' Subsection (15) ".

7. In the Local Authorities' Mutual Investment Trust Act 1968— 1968 c. 25.

(*a*) in section 1(2) for the words " recognised stock exchange
within the meaning of the Prevention of Fraud (Investments)
Act 1958 " there shall be substituted the words " recognised
investment exchange within the meaning of the Financial
Services Act 1986" ; and

(*b*) in the definition of " unit trust scheme " in section 2 for
the words " Prevention of Fraud (Investments) Act 1958 "

there shall be substituted the words "Financial Services Act 1986".

8. In the Local Government Act 1972—

(*a*) in section 98(1) for the words from "and" onwards there shall be substituted the words "means—

    (*a*) investments falling within any of paragraphs 1 to 6 of Schedule 1 to the Financial Services Act 1986 or, so far as relevant to any of those paragraphs, paragraph 11 of that Schedule ; or

    (*b*) rights (whether actual or contingent) in respect of money lent to, or deposited with, any society registered under the Industrial and Provident Societies Act 1965 or any building society within the meaning of the Building Societies Act 1986." ; and

(*b*) for the definition of "securities" in section 146(2) there shall be substituted—

    " "securities" has the meaning given in section 98(1) above ".

9. For subsection (1) of section 42 of the Local Government (Scotland) Act 1973 there shall be substituted—

    "(1) In sections 39 and 41 of this Act "securities" means—

    (*a*) investments falling within any of paragraphs 1 to 6 of Schedule 1 to the Financial Services Act 1986 or, so far as relevant to any of those paragraphs, paragraph 11 of that Schedule ; or

    (*b*) rights (whether actual or contingent) in respect of money lent to, or deposited with, any society registered under the Industrial and Provident Societies Act 1965 or any building society within the meaning of the Building Societies Act 1986."

10. For paragraph 20 of Schedule 1 to the Industry Act 1975 there shall be substituted—

    "20. Section 57 of the Financial Services Act 1986 (restrictions on advertising) shall not apply to any investment advertisement within the meaning of that section which the Board issue or cause to be issued in the discharge of their functions."

11. For paragraph 20 of Schedule 1 to the Scottish Development Agency Act 1975 there shall be substituted—

    "20. Section 57 of the Financial Services Act 1986 (restrictions on advertising) shall not apply to any investment advertisement within the meaning of that section which the Agency issue or cause to be issued in the discharge of their functions."

12. For paragraph 21 of Schedule 1 to the Welsh Development Agency Act 1975 there shall be substituted—

    "21. Section 57 of the Financial Services Act 1986 (restrictions on advertising) shall not apply to any investment advertisement within the meaning of that section which the Agency issue or cause to be issued in the discharge of their functions.".

13. In section 3(5) of the Aircraft and Shipbuilding Industries Act Sch. 16
1977 the words "Sections 428 to 430 of the Companies Act 1985 1977 c. 3.
and" shall be omitted and for the words "those sections" there
shall be substituted the words "that section".

14. In paragraph 10(1)(c) of Part II of Schedule 10 to the Finance 1980 c. 48.
Act 1980 for the words "sections 428 to 430" there shall be substituted the words "sections 428 to 430F".

15. For the definition of "securities" in section 3(6) of the 1981 c. 28.
Licensing (Alcohol Education and Research) Act 1981 there shall
be substituted—

> ""securities" means any investments falling within any of
> paragraphs 1 to 6 of Schedule 1 to the Financial Services Act
> 1986 or, so far as relevant to any of those paragraphs, para-
> graph 11 of that Schedule".

16. In section 97 of the Companies Act 1985— 1985 c. 6.

> (a) in subsection (1) after the word "conditions" there shall
> be inserted the words "and any conditions which apply in
> respect of any such payment by virtue of rules made under
> section 169(2) of the Financial Services Act 1986"; and
>
> (b) in subsection (2)(a) for the words from "10 per cent." on-
> wards there shall be substituted the words—
>
>> "(i) any limit imposed on it by those rules or, if none
>> is so imposed, 10 per cent, of the price at which the
>> shares are issued; or
>>
>> (ii) the amount or rate authorised by the articles,
>> whichever is the less".

17. In section 163 of the Companies Act 1985—

> (a) for the words "a recognised stock exchange" in each place
> where they occur there shall be substituted the words "a
> recognised investment exchange";
>
> (b) for the words "that stock exchange" in subsection (1) there
> shall be substituted the words "that investment exchange";
>
> (c) in subsection (2) in paragraph (a) for the words "on that
> stock exchange" there shall be substituted the words
> "under Part IV of the Financial Services Act 1986" and
> in paragraph (b) for the words "that stock exchange" in
> both places where they occur there shall be substituted the
> words "that investment exchange";
>
> (d) after subsection (3) of that section there shall be inserted—
>
>> "(4) In this section "recognised investment ex-
>> change" means a recognised investment exchange other
>> than an overseas investment exchange within the meaning
>> of the Financial Services Act 1986."

18. In section 209(1)(c) of the Companies Act 1985 for the words
"the Prevention of Fraud (Investments) Act 1958" there shall be
substituted the words "the Financial Services Act 1986".

19. In section 265(4)(*a*) of the Companies Act 1985 for the words " recognised stock exchange " there shall be substituted the words " recognised investment exchange other than an overseas investment exchange within the meaning of the Financial Services Act 1986 ".

20. In section 329(1) of the Companies Act 1985 for the words " recognised stock exchange ", " that stock exchange " and " the stock exchange " there shall be substituted respectively the words " recognised investment exchange other than an overseas investment exchange within the meaning of the Financial Services Act 1986 ", " that investment exchange " and " the investment exchange ".

21. For paragraphs (*a*) to (*c*) of section 446(4) of the Companies Act 1985 there shall be substituted—

" (*a*) to any individual who is an authorised person within the meaning of the Financial Services Act 1986 ;

(*b*) to any individual who holds a permission granted under paragraph 23 of Schedule 1 to that Act ;

(*c*) to any officer (whether past or present) of a body corporate which is such an authorised person or holds such a permission ;

(*d*) to any partner (whether past or present) in a partnership which is such an authorised person or holds such a permission ;

(*e*) to any member of the governing body or officer (in either case whether past or present) of an unincorporated association which is such an authorised person or holds such a permission ".

22. At the end of sections 716(2) and 717(1) of the Companies Act 1985 there shall be inserted the words—

" and in this subsection ' recognised stock exchange ' means The Stock Exchange and any other stock exchange which is declared to be a recognised stock exchange for the purposes of this section by an order in a statutory instrument made by the Secretary of State which is for the time being in force ; ".

23. In Schedule 4 to the Companies Act 1985—

(*a*) in paragraph 45 for the words " recognised stock exchange " there shall be substituted the words " recognised investment exchange other than an overseas investment exchange within the meaning of the Financial Services Act 1986 " ; and

(*b*) in paragraph 84 for the words from " on a recognised stock exchange " onwards there shall be substituted the words " on a recognised investment exchange other than an overseas investment exchange within the meaning of the Financial Services Act 1986 or on any stock exchange of repute outside Great Britain ".

24. In Schedule 9 to the Companies Act 1985 in paragraphs 10(3) and 33 for the words " recognised stock exchange " there shall be substituted the words " recognised investment exchange other than

an overseas investment exchange within the meaning of the Financial   Sch. 16
Services Act 1986 ".

25. In paragraph 11 of Schedule 13 to the Companies Act 1985 1985 c. 6.
for paragraph (*a*) there shall be substituted—

(*a*) any unit trust scheme which is an authorised unit trust
scheme within the meaning of the Financial Services Act
1986 ".

26. In Schedule 22 to the Companies Act 1985, in the second
column of the entry relating to section 185(4) for the words " stock
exchange " there shall be substituted the words " clearing house or ".

27. In Schedule 24 to the Companies Act 1985—

(*a*) in the second column of the entry relating to section 329(3)
for the words " stock exchange " there shall be substituted
the words " investment exchange " ; and

(*b*) after the entry relating to section 427(5) there shall be
inserted—

| " 429(6) | Offeror failing to send copy of notice or making statutory declaration knowing it to be false, etc. | 1. On indictment. 2. Summary. | 2 years or a fine; or both. 6 months or the statutory maximum; or both. | One-fiftieth of the statutory maximum. |
| 430A(6) | Offeror failing to give notice of rights to minority shareholder. | 1. On indictment. 2. Summary. | A fine. The statutory maximum. | One fiftieth of the statutory maximum." |

28. In section 16 of the Company Securities (Insider Dealing) Act 1985 c. 8.
1985—

(*a*) in subsection (1) for the definition of " recognised stock
exchange " there shall be substituted—

" ' recognised stock exchange ' means The Stock Exchange and any other investment exchange which is
declared by an order of the Secretary of State for the
time being in force to be a recognised stock exchange for
the purposes of this Act ; " ; and

(*b*) after that subsection there shall be inserted—

" (1A) The power to make an order under subsection
(1) above shall be exercisable by statutory instrument." ;

(*c*) in subsection (2) for the word " 15 " there shall be substituted the word " 14 ".

29. For paragraph (*c*) of section 10(1) of the Bankruptcy (Scotland) 1985 c. 66.
Act 1985 there shall be substituted—

" (*c*) a petition is before a court for the winding up of the
debtor under Part IV or V of the Insolvency Act 1986 or
section 72 of the Financial Services Act 1986 ;".

30. In section 101 of the Building Societies Act 1986—   1986 c. 53.

(*a*) for paragraph (1)(*a*) there shall be substituted—

" (*a*) offer for sale or invite subscription for any shares
in or debentures of the company or allot or agree to
allot any such shares or debentures with a view to their
being offered for sale ;":

(*b*) in subsection (1) after the words " the effect of the offer " there shall be inserted the words " the invitation " ; and

(*c*) in subsection (2) for the words " the public " there shall be substituted the words ", invite subscription for,".

31. In Article 107 of the Companies (Northern Ireland) Order 1986—

(*a*) in paragraph (1) after the word " conditions " there shall be inserted the words " and any conditions which apply in respect of any such payment by virtue of rules made under section 169(2) of the Financial Services Act 1986 "·

(*b*) in sub-paragraph (2)(*a*) for the words from " 10 per cent." onwards there shall be substituted the words—

" (i) any limit imposed on it by those rules or, if none is so imposed, 10 per cent. of the price at which the shares are issued ; or

(ii) the amount or rate authorised by the articles, whichever is the less ".

32. In Article 173 of the Companies (Northern Ireland) Order 1986—

(*a*) for the words " a recognised stock exchange ", in each place where they occur, there shall be substituted the words " a recognised investment exchange ";

(*b*) for the words " that stock exchange " in paragraph (1) there shall be substituted the words " that investment exchange ";

(*c*) in paragraph (2), in sub-paragraph (*a*) for the words " on that stock exchange " there shall be substituted the words " under Part IV of the Financial Services Act 1986 " and in sub-paragraph (*b*) for the words " that stock exchange " in both places where they occur there shall be substituted the words " that investment exchange ";

(*d*) after paragraph (3) there shall be inserted—

" (4) In this Article " recognised investment exchange " means a recognised investment exchange other than an overseas investment exchange within the meaning of the Financial Services Act 1986."

33. In Article 217(1) (*b*) of the Companies (Northern Ireland) Order 1986 for the words " the Prevention of Fraud (Investments) Act (Northern Ireland) 1940 or of the Prevention of Fraud (Investments) Act 1958 " there shall be substituted the words " the Financial Services Act 1986 ".

34. In Article 273(4)(*a*) of the Companies (Northern Ireland) Order 1986 for the words " recognised stock exchange " there shall be substituted the words " recognised investment exchange other than an overseas investment exchange within the meaning of the Financial Services Act 1986 ".

35. In Article 337(1) of the Companies (Northern Ireland) Order 1986 for the words " recognised stock exchange ", " that stock

exchange" and "the stock exchange" there shall be substituted
respectively the words "recognised investment exchange", "that
investment exchange" and "the investment exchange".

36. For sub-paragraphs (*a*) to (*c*) of Article 439(4) of the Companies (Northern Ireland) Order 1986 there shall be substituted—

" (*a*) to any individual who is an authorised person within the
   meaning of the Financial Services Act 1986 ;

(*b*) to any individual who holds a permission granted under
   paragraph 23 of Schedule 1 to that Act ;

(*c*) to an officer (whether past or present) of a body corporate
   which is such an authorised person or holds such a permission ;

(*d*) to any partner (whether past or present) in a partnership
   which is such an authorised person or holds such a permission ;

(*e*) to any member of the governing body or officer (in either
   case whether past or present) of an unincorporated association which is such an authorised person or holds such a
   permission ".

37. At the end of Article 665(2) and 666(1) of the Companies
(Northern Ireland) Order 1986 there shall be inserted the words—

" and in this paragraph 'recognised stock exchange' means
   The Stock Exchange and any other stock exchange which
   is declared by an order of the Department for the time
   being in force to be a recognised stock exchange for the
   purposes of this Article ; ".

38. In Schedule 4 to the Companies (Northern Ireland) Order
1986—

(*a*) in paragraph 45 for the words " recognised stock exchange "
   there shall be substituted the words " recognised investment
   exchange other than an overseas investment exchange within the meaning of the Financial Services Act 1986 "

(*b*) in paragraph 83 for the words from " on a recognised stock
   exchange " onwards there shall be substituted the words
   " on a recognised investment exchange other than an overseas investment exchange within the meaning of the
   Financial Services Act 1986 or on any stock exchange of
   repute outside Northern Ireland ".

39. In Schedule 9 to the Companies (Northern Ireland) Order
1986, in paragraph 10(3) and 33 for the words " recognised stock
exchange " there shall be substituted the words " recognised investment exchange other than an overseas investment exchange within
the meaning of the Financial Services Act 1986. "

40. In paragraph 11 of Schedule 13 to the Companies (Northern
Ireland) Order 1986 for paragraph (*a*) there shall be substituted—

(*a*) any unit trust scheme which is an authorised **unit trust** scheme within the meaning of the Financial Services Act 1986 ".

41. In Schedule 21 to the Companies (Northern Ireland) Order 1986 in the second column of the entry relating to Article 195(4) for the words " stock exchange " there shall be substituted the words " clearing house or ".

42. In Schedule 23 to the Companies (Northern Ireland) Order 1986 in the second column of the entry relating to Article 337(3) for the words " stock exchange " there shall be substituted the words " investment exchange ".

43. In Article 2(1) of the Company Securities (Insider Dealing) (Northern Ireland) Order 1986, for the definition of " recognised stock exchange " there shall be substituted—

" ' recognised stock exchange ' means The Stock Exchange and any other investment exchange which is declared by an order of the Department for the time being in force to be a recognised stock exchange for the purposes of this Order ; ".

SCHEDULE 17

REPEALS AND REVOCATIONS

PART I

ENACTMENTS

Chapter	Short title	Extent of repeal
4 & 5 Geo. 6. c. 9 (N.I.).	The Prevention of Fraud (Investments) Act (Northern Ireland) 1940.	The whole Act.
6 & 7 Eliz. 2. c. 45.	The Prevention of Fraud (Investments) Act 1958.	The whole Act.
8&9 Eliz.2 c. 58.	The Charities Act 1960.	Section 22(10).
10 & 11 Eliz. 2. c. 23.	The South Africa Act 1962.	In Schedule 4, the entry relating to the Prevention of Fraud (Investments) Act 1958.
1964 c. 33 (N.I.).	The Charities Act (Northern Ireland) 1964.	Section 25(16).
1965 c. 2.	The Administration of Justice Act 1965.	Section 14(1)(*e*) and (5)(*e*). In Schedule 1, the entry relating to the Prevention of Fraud (Investments) Act 1958.
1971 c. 62.	The Tribunals and Inquiries Act 1971.	In Part I of Schedule 1, the entry relating to the tribunal constituted under section 6 of the Prevention of Fraud (Investments) Act 1958.
1972 c. 71.	The Criminal Justice Act 1972.	In Schedule 5, the entry relating to the Prevention of Fraud (Investments) Act 1958.
1975 c. 24.	The House of Commons Disqualification Act 1975.	In Part II of Schedule 1 the words " The Tribunal established under the Prevention of Fraud (Investments) Act 1958.
1975 c. 68.	The Industry Act 1975.	In Schedule 1, paragraph 19.
1975 c. 69.	The Scottish Development Agency Act 1975.	In Schedule 1, paragraph 19.
1975 c. 70.	The Welsh Development Agency Act 1975.	In Schedule 1, paragraph 22.
1976 c. 47.	The Stock Exchange (Completion of Bargains) Act 1976.	Section 7(2).
1977 c. 3.	The Aircraft and Shipbuilding Industries Act 1977.	In section 3(5), the words " Sections 428 to 430 of the Companies Act 1985 and ".
1978 c. 23.	The Judicature (Northern Ireland) Act 1978.	Section 84(3)(*c*).
1979 c. 37.	The Banking Act 1979.	Section 20(1) to (3). In Schedule 1, paragraph 9. In Schedule 6, paragraphs 4 and 5.
1982 c. 50.	The Insurance Companies Act 1982.	Section 73. Section 79.
1982 c. 53.	The Administration of Justice Act 1982.	Section 42(8).
1984 c. 2.	The Restrictive Trade Practices (Stock Exchange) Act 1984.	The whole Act.

Chapter	Short title	Extent of repeal
1985 c. 6.	The Companies Act 1985.	Part III. Sections 81 to 83. In section 84(1) the words from " This " onwards. In section 85(1) the words " 83 or ". Sections 86 and 87. In section 97, subsection (2)(*b*) together with the word "and" immediately preceding it and subsections (3) and (4). Section 433(2). Section 446(5) and (6). In section 449(1)(*d*), the words " the Prevention of Fraud (Investments) Act 1958 ". In section 693, paragraph (*a*) and in paragraph (*d*) the words " in every such prospectus as above-mentioned and ". Section 709(2) and (3). In section 744, the definitions of " recognised stock exchange " and " prospectus issued generally ". Schedule 3. In Schedule 22, the entries relating to Parts III and IV. In Schedule 24, the entries relating to sections 56(4), 61, 64(5), 70(1), 78(1), 81(2), 82(5), 86(6), 87(4) and 97(4).
1985 c. 8.	The Company Securities (Insider Dealing) Act 1985.	In section 3(1), the word " or " immediately preceding paragraph (*c*). In section 13, in subsection (1), the words from " and references " onwards and subsection (2). Section 15.
1985 c. 9.	The Companies Consolidation (Consequential Provisions) Act 1985.	Section 7. In Schedule 2, the entries relating to the Prevention of Fraud (Investments) Act 1958, paragraph 19 of Schedule 1 to the Scottish Development Agency Act 1975, paragraph 22 of Schedule 1 to the Welsh Development Agency Act 1975, the Stock Exchange (Completion of Bargains) Act 1976, section 3(5) of the Aircraft and Shipbuilding Industries Act 1977 and section 20 of the Banking Act 1979
1986 c. 31.	The Airports Act 1986.	Section 10.
1986 c. 44.	The Gas Act 1986.	Section 58.
1986 c. 60.	The Financial Services Act 1986.	Section 195

PART II

INSTRUMENTS

Number	Title	Extent of revocation
S.I. 1977/1254 (6 N.I. 21).	The Stock Exchange (Completion of Bargains (Northern Ireland) Order 1977.	Article 2(2).
S.I. 1986/1032 (N.I. 6).	The Companies (Northern Ireland) Order 1986.	In Article 2(1), the definitions of " prospectus issued generally" and " recognised stock exchange ". Part IV. Articles 91 to 93. In Article 94(1) the words from " This " onwards. In Article 95(1) the words " 93 or ". Articles 96 and 97. In Article 107, paragraph (2)(*b*) together with the word " and" immediately preceding it and paragraphs (3) and (4). Article 426(2). Article 439(5) and (6). In Article 442(1)(*d*), the words " the Prevention of Fraud (Investments) Act (Northern Ireland) 1940 ". In Article 643(1), sub-paragraph (*a*) and in sub-paragraph (*d*) the words " in every such prospectus as is mentioned in sub-paragraph (*a*) and ". Article 658(2) and (3). Schedule 3. In Schedule 21, the entries relating to Parts IV and V. In Schedule 23, the entries relating to Articles 66(4), 71, 74(5), 80(1), 88(1), 91(2), 92(5), 96(6), 97(4) and 107(4).
S.I. 1986/1035 (N.I. 9).	The Companies (Consequential Provisions) (Northern Ireland Order 1986.	In Schedule 2, the entries relating to the Prevention of of Fraud (Investments) Act (Northern Ireland) 1940 and section 20 of the Banking Act 1979.
S.I. 1984/716.	The Stock Exchange (Listing) Regulations 1984.	The whole Regulations.

Education (No. 2) Act 1986

1986 CHAPTER 61

An Act to amend the law relating to education.

[7th November 1986]

BE IT ENACTED by the Queen's most Excellent Majesty, by and with the advice and consent of the Lords Spiritual and Temporal, and Commons, in this present Parliament assembled, and by the authority of the same, as follows:—

PART I

INTRODUCTORY

1.—(1) For every county, voluntary and maintained special school there shall be—

Instruments of government and articles of government.

(a) an instrument providing for the constitution of a governing body of the school (to be known as the instrument of government); and

(b) an instrument in accordance with which the school is to be conducted (to be known as the articles of government).

(2) The instrument of government and articles of government shall be made by order of the local education authority.

(3) The instrument of government shall contain such provisions as are required either by Part II of this Act (which is concerned, among other things, with the size and composition of governing bodies and the procedures for electing members and filling vacancies) or by any other enactment.

K 2

PART I
(4) The articles of government shall contain such provisions as are required either by Part III of this Act (which is concerned, among other things, with the manner in which schools are to be conducted and the allocation of functions between the local education authority, the governing body and the head teacher) or by any other enactment.

(5) The instrument of government and articles of government shall—

(a) contain no provision which is inconsistent with any provision made by or under this Act or any other enactment ; and

(b) comply with any trust deed relating to the school.

(6) This section is subject to the following provisions of this Act—

(a) section 9 (which provides for two or more schools to be grouped under a single governing body in certain circumstances) ; and

(b) section 12 (which provides for certain existing, or proposed, schools to have temporary governing bodies pending the constitution of governing bodies under instruments of government).

Procedure in relation to making etc. of instruments and articles.
2.—(1) Before making any order under section 1 of this Act, a local education authority shall consult the governing body and the head teacher of the school concerned.

(2) Before making any such order in respect of a voluntary school, a local education authority shall—

(a) secure the agreement of the governing body to the terms of the proposed order ;

(b) if it embodies or varies an instrument of government, secure the agreement of the foundation governors to any provisions which are of particular concern to those governors ; and

(c) have regard to the way in which the school has been conducted.

(3) Where the governing body of any county, voluntary or maintained special school make a proposal to the local education authority for the alteration of the provision made by the instrument of government, or articles of government, for the school, it shall be the duty of the authority to consider their proposal.

(4) Where—

(a) the foundation governors of a voluntary school make a proposal to the local education authority for the alteration of the provision made by the instrument of government for the school ; and

(b) the proposal relates solely to one or more matters which are of particular concern to those governors ;

it shall be the duty of the authority to consider their proposal.

(5) Where a local education authority—

(a) propose to make an order under section 1 but cannot secure any agreement required by subsection (2) above ; or

(b) refuse, in the case of a voluntary school, to make such an order in response to a proposal of a kind mentioned in subsection (3) or (4) above ;

the authority or (as the case may be) the governing body or foundation governors may refer the matter to the Secretary of State.

(6) On any reference to him under subsection (5) above, the Secretary of State shall give such direction as he thinks fit having regard, in particular, to the status of the school as a controlled, aided or (as the case may be) special agreement school.

(7) Where it appears to the Secretary of State—

(a) that an order, or proposed order, under section 1 is in any respect inconsistent with the provisions of any trust deed relating to the school ; and

(b) that it is expedient in the interests of the school that the provisions of the trust deed should be modified for the purpose of removing the inconsistency ;

he may by order make such modifications in the trust deed as appear to him to be just and expedient for that purpose.

PART II

SCHOOL GOVERNMENT

Governing bodies

3.—(1) This section applies in relation to any county, controlled or maintained special school.

(2) The instrument of government for such a school which has less than 100 registered pupils shall, subject to section 7 of

Governing bodies for county, controlled and maintained special schools.

K 3

this Act, provide for the governing body to consist of the following (and no others)—

> (a) two parent governors ;
>
> (b) two governors appointed by the local education authority ;
>
> (c) one teacher governor ;
>
> (d) the head teacher, unless he chooses not to be a governor ; and
>
> (e) either—
>
> > (i) two foundation governors and one co-opted governor, in the case of a controlled school ; or
> >
> > (ii) three co-opted governors, in any other case.

(3) The instrument of government for such a school which has more than 99, but less than 300, registered pupils shall, subject to section 7, provide for the governing body to consist of the following (and no others)—

> (a) three parent governors ;
>
> (b) three governors appointed by the local education authority ;
>
> (c) one teacher governor ;
>
> (d) the head teacher, unless he chooses not to be a governor ; and
>
> (e) either—
>
> > (i) three foundation governors and one co-opted governor, in the case of a controlled school ; or
> >
> > (ii) four co-opted governors, in any other case.

(4) The instrument of government for such a school which has more than 299, but less than 600, registered pupils shall, subject to section 7, provide for the governing body to consist of the following (and no others)—

> (a) four parent governors ;
>
> (b) four governors appointed by the local education authority ;
>
> (c) two teacher governors ;
>
> (d) the head teacher, unless he chooses not to be a governor ; and
>
> (e) either—
>
> > (i) four foundation governors and one co-opted governor, in the case of a controlled school ; or
> >
> > (ii) five co-opted governors, in any other case.

(5) The instrument of government for such a school which has more than 599 registered pupils shall, subject to section 7,

provide for the governing body to consist of the following (and no others)—

- (a) five parent governors ;
- (b) five governors appointed by the local education authority ;
- (c) two teacher governors ;
- (d) the head teacher, unless he chooses not to be a governor ; and
- (e) either—
  - (i) four foundation governors and two co-opted governors, in the case of a controlled school ; or
  - (ii) six co-opted governors, in any other case.

(6) Where the instrument of government so provides, a school to which subsection (5) above would otherwise apply shall be treated for the purposes of this section as one to which subsection (4) above applies.

(7) Where the head teacher is a governor he shall be treated for all purposes as being an ex officio governor.

4.—(1) This section applies in relation to any aided or special agreement school.

(2) The instrument of government for such a school shall provide for the governing body to include—

- (a) at least one governor appointed by the local education authority ;
- (b) in the case of a school which is a primary school serving an area in which there is a minor authority, at least one governor appointed by the authority ;
- (c) foundation governors ;
- (d) at least one parent governor ;
- (e) in the case of a school which has less than 300 registered pupils, at least one teacher governor ;
- (f) in the case of a school which has 300 or more registered pupils, at least two teacher governors ; and
- (g) the head teacher, unless he chooses not to be a governor.

(3) The instrument of government for such a school shall provide—

- (a) for such number of foundation governors as will lead to their outnumbering the other governors—
  - (i) by two, if the governing body of the school will consist of eighteen or fewer governors ; and

K 4

(ii) by three, if it will consist of more than eighteen governors ; and

(b) for at least one of the foundation governors to be (at the time of his appointment) a parent of a registered pupil at the school.

(4) Where the head teacher of such a school has chosen not to be a governor, he shall nevertheless be counted as one for the purposes of calculating the required number of foundation governors.

(5) Subject to subsection (3) above, nothing in this section shall be taken to prevent the instrument of government for such a school from providing for the governing body to include governors in addition to those required by virtue of this section.

(6) Where the head teacher is a governor he shall be treated for all purposes as being an ex officio governor.

Governors

Appointment of parent governors by governing body.

5.—(1) The instrument of government for any county or controlled school, or for any maintained special school which is not established in a hospital, may provide that if at the time when the instrument is made, or at any later time when there is a vacancy for a parent governor—

(a) at least fifty per cent. of the registered pupils at the school are boarders ; and

(b) it would, in the opinion of the local education authority, be impracticable for there to be an election of parent governors ;

the parent governors, or (as the case may be) the parent governor required to fill that vacancy, shall be appointed by the other members of the governing body.

(2) The instrument of government for every county, controlled and maintained special school at which parent governors are to be, or may be, elected shall provide for the required number of parent governors to be made up by parent governors appointed by the other members of the governing body if—

(a) one or more vacancies for parent governors are required to be filled by election ; and

(b) the number of parents standing for election as parent governors is less than the number of vacancies.

(3) Where, in the opinion of the local education authority, it is likely to be impracticable for there to be elections of parent governors at any maintained special school which is established in a hospital, the instrument of government for that school may

provide for the parent governors to be appointed by the other   PART II
members of the governing body.

(4) The instrument of government for any school to which
this section applies shall provide for it to be the duty of governors—

    (*a*) in appointing any parent governor under any provision
made by virtue of this section—

        (i) to appoint a person who is the parent of a registered pupil at the school, where it is reasonably
practicable to do so ; and

        (ii) where it is not, to appoint a person who is the
parent of one or more children of compulsory school
age ;

    (*b*) not to appoint any person as a parent governor, under
any such provision, if that person is—

        (i) an elected member of the local education authority ;

        (ii) an employee of the authority or of the governing body of any aided school maintained by the authority ; or

        (iii) a co-opted member of any education committee of the authority.

6. The instrument of government for any county, controlled   Connection
or maintained special school shall provide for it to be the duty   with local
of the governors concerned, in co-opting any person to be a   business
member of the governing body (otherwise than as a foundation   community.
governor)—

    (*a*) to have regard—

        (i) to the extent to which they and the other governors are members of the local business community ;
and

        (ii) to any representations made to the governing
body as to the desirability of increasing the connection between the governing body and that community ; and

    (*b*) where it appears to them that no governor of the school
is a member of the local business community, or that
it is desirable to increase the number of governors who
are, to co-opt a person who appears to them to be a
member of that community.

PART II
Appointment
of
representative
governors in
place of
co-opted
governors.

7.—(1) The instrument of government for every primary school which is a county or controlled school serving an area in which there is a minor authority shall provide for one governor to be appointed by that authority.

(2) The instrument of government for every maintained special school which is established in a hospital shall provide for one governor to be appointed by the district health authority.

(3) The instrument of government for every maintained special school (other than one established in a hospital) shall, if the school has less than 100 registered pupils, provide for one governor to be appointed—

(*a*) by a voluntary organisation designated by the local education authority, in relation to the school, as the appropriate voluntary organisation concerned with matters in respect of which the school is specially organised; or

(*b*) jointly by two or more voluntary organisations so designated;

and shall, if it has more than 99 registered pupils, provide for two governors to be so appointed.

(4) Where, by virtue of subsection (3) above, an instrument of government is required to provide for the appointment of two governors, it may make different provision in relation to the appointment of one governor to that made in relation to the appointment of the other.

(5) Where a local education authority are satisfied, in relation to any special school, that there is no voluntary organisation which it would be appropriate to designate for the purposes of subsection (3) above, that subsection shall not apply to its instrument of government.

(6) Where the instrument of government for any school is required by this section to provide for the appointment of any governor, the instrument—

(*a*) shall name the person or persons by whom the governor is to be appointed;

(*b*) shall not provide for a co-opted governor if the school is a controlled school with less than 600 registered pupils or is treated as such a school for the purposes of section 3 of this Act by virtue of subsection (6) of that section; and

(*c*) in any other case, shall provide for one or (as the case may be) two fewer co-opted governors than would otherwise be provided for.

(7) In subsection (6) above, references to co-opted governors are to governors required to be co-opted by virtue of section 3

of this Act and do not include references to co-opted foundation governors.

8.—(1) The proceedings of the governing body of any county, voluntary or maintained special school shall not be invalidated by—

   (a) any vacancy among their number ; or

   (b) any defect in the election or appointment of any governor.

(2) The instrument of government for every county, controlled and maintained special school shall provide for each governor, other than one who is an ex officio governor, to hold office for a term of four years.

(3) Subsection (2) above shall not be taken to prevent a governor from being elected or appointed for a further term, or from being disqualified, by virtue of regulations made under subsection (6) below, for continuing to hold office.

(4) Any governor of a county, voluntary or maintained special school may at any time resign his office.

(5) Any foundation governor of a voluntary school, or governor of a county, voluntary or maintained special school appointed otherwise than by being co-opted, may be removed from office by the person or persons who appointed him.

For the purposes of this subsection, a governor appointed in accordance with any provision made by virtue of section 5 of this Act shall be treated as having been co-opted.

(6) The Secretary of State may by regulations make provision as to the meetings and proceedings of the governing bodies of county, voluntary and maintained special schools (including provision modifying that made by subsection (1) above) and the circumstances in which persons are to be disqualified for holding office as governors of such schools.

(7) The regulations may, in particular, provide—

   (a) for the election by the governors of any such school of one of their number to be chairman, and one to be vice-chairman, of the school's governing body for such period as may be prescribed ;

   (b) for the chairman of the governing body of any such school, or such other member of that body as may be prescribed, to have power in prescribed circumstances to discharge any of the functions of that body as a matter of urgency ; and

   (c) as to the quorum required for the purposes of making appointments in accordance with any provision made by virtue of section 5 of this Act or when business is transacted by governors of a particular category.

(8) The minutes of the proceedings of the governing body of any county, voluntary or maintained special school shall be open to inspection by the local education authority.

(9) The instrument of government for every county, voluntary and maintained special school may make provision with respect to the matters mentioned in subsections (6) and (7) above.

(10) Any provision made by the instrument of government for any such school which relates to a matter dealt with by regulations under subsection (6) above (including any provision made by virtue of subsection (2) above) shall have effect subject to the regulations.

(11) No decision of a kind mentioned in subsection (12) below which is taken at a meeting of the governing body of any aided or special agreement school shall have effect unless it is confirmed at a second meeting of the governing body held not less than twenty-eight days after the first.

(12) The decisions are—

    (*a*) any decision that would result in the submission of proposals under section 13 of the 1980 Act (establishment and alteration of voluntary schools);

    (*b*) any decision to serve a notice under section 14(1) of the 1944 Act (discontinuance of school);

    (*c*) any decision that would result in an application under section 15(4) of the 1944 Act (revocation of order whereby school is an aided or special agreement school);

    (*d*) any decision to request the making of an order under subsection (2) of section 16 of the 1944 Act (discontinuance of school for which another school is substituted) or as to the submissions to be made to the Secretary of State in any consultations under subsection (3) of that section;

    (*e*) any decision to make an agreement under Schedule 2 to the 1944 Act (agreement for transfer of interest in school to local education authority).

Grouping of schools

Grouping
of schools
under single
governing
body.

9.—(1) Subject to the requirements as to consent imposed by section 10 of this Act, a local education authority may resolve that any two or more schools maintained by them shall be grouped for the purposes of this Part of this Act.

(2) Where any schools are so grouped, they shall (subject to the following provisions of this section)—

(a) be treated for the purposes of this Part as a single school ; and

(b) have a single governing body constituted under a single instrument of government

(3) For the purposes of this Part of this Act, a group shall be treated—

(a) as an aided school, if it contains at least one such school ;

(b) as a special agreement school, if it contains at least one such school and paragraph (a) above does not apply ;

(c) as a controlled school, if it contains at least one such school and neither paragraph (a) nor paragraph (b) above applies ;

(d) as a maintained special school, if it consists only of such schools ; and

(e) as a county school, if none of the preceding paragraphs apply.

(4) Where any proposal or alteration of a kind mentioned in subsection (5) below relates to any school which is grouped with one or more other schools under this section, it shall be the duty of the local education authority—

(a) to review the grouping of those schools and to consider whether or not it should be brought to an end ; and

(b) where the Secretary of State's consent to the grouping, or continued grouping, was at any time required by section 10 of this Act and the authority consider that the grouping should be continued—

(i) to report to him on the results of their review ; and

(ii) to provide him with such information as he may reasonably require with a view to enabling him to consider whether or not the grouping should be brought to an end.

(5) The proposals and alterations referred to in subsection (4) above are—

(a) any proposal under—

(i) section 16 of the 1944 Act (transfer of schools to new sites and substitution of new for old schools) ;

(ii) sections 12 to 15 of the 1980 Act (establishment, discontinuance and alteration of schools) ; or

(iii) section 54 of this Act ;

(b) any alteration made to arrangements approved by the Secretary of State in accordance with regulations made under section 12 of the 1981 Act (approval of special schools) ; and

(c) any alteration in the status of an aided or special agreement school effected by an order of the Secretary of State under section 15(4) of the 1944 Act (revocation of order by virtue of which school is an aided or special agreement school).

(6) The Secretary of State may by order bring to an end any grouping under this section in respect of which his consent was at any time required by section 10 of this Act.

(7) Any grouping under this section may also be brought to an end—

(a) if the group does not include any voluntary school, by resolution of the local education authority ; and

(b) if it does include any such school—

(i) by resolution of the authority made with the agreement of the school's governing body ; or

(ii) by one year's notice given either by the authority to the governing body or by the governing body to the authority.

(8) Any order under section 1 of this Act embodying an instrument of government for two or more schools which are grouped under this section shall be deemed to have been revoked—

(a) in the case of a group which was established for a specified period, at the end of that period ; or

(b) on the bringing to an end of the group in accordance with subsection (6) or (7) above.

(9) Schedule 1 to this Act shall have effect for the purpose of making further provision in relation to schools grouped under this section.

Requirements as to consent to grouping.

10.—(1) Before resolving to group any schools under section 9 of this Act, a local education authority shall obtain the consent of the Secretary of State to the proposed grouping unless—

(a) the group will consist only of two primary schools both of which serve substantially the same area ;

(b) neither of the schools is a special school ; and

(c) where they are in Wales, there is no significant difference between them in their use of the Welsh language.

(2) The Secretary of State's consent may be given subject to such conditions as he sees fit to impose with respect to the duration of the grouping to which his consent is given.

(3) Where two primary schools have been grouped under PART II
section 9 in circumstances in which the Secretary of State's consent was not required under subsection (1) above, his consent to
their continuing to be so grouped shall be required if a change
of circumstances occurs such that a proposal to group those
schools under section 9 made after that change would require
his consent under that subsection.

(4) Where the Secretary of State's consent is required to the
grouping or continued grouping of any schools under section 9,
sections 3 to 7 of this Act shall apply in relation to the group
subject to such modifications (if any) as he may direct.

(5) No local education authority may pass a resolution under
section 9 applying to any voluntary school without first obtaining
the consent of its governing body.

(6) No local education authority may pass a resolution under
section 9 applying to any county or maintained special school
without first consulting its governing body.

(7) Any dispute as to whether, for the purposes of this section—

    (*a*) two primary schools are to be regarded as serving sub-
        stantially the same area ; or

    (*b*) there is any significant difference between two primary
        schools in their use of the Welsh language ;

shall be determined by the Secretary of State.

Reviews

11.—(1) The constitution of the governing body of every Review of
county, controlled and maintained special school shall be re- constitution of
viewed in accordance with the provisions of this section on, or governing
as soon as is reasonably practicable after, the occurrence of any bodies of
event which is a relevant event in relation to the school. county,
controlled and
maintained
(2) In this section " relevant event ", in relation to any school, special
means any of the following— schools.

    (*a*) the implementation of any proposal under—

        (i) section 16(1) of the 1944 Act (transfer of schools
        to new sites) ;

        (ii) section 12(1)(*d*) of the 1980 Act (alteration of
        county schools) ; or

        (iii) section 13(1)(*b*) of the 1980 Act (alteration of
        voluntary schools) ;

        which provides for an increase in the number of regis-
        tered pupils at the school ;

(b) in the case of a maintained special school, the implementation of any proposal to change approved arrangements which provides for an increase in the number of registered pupils at the school ;

(c) where no relevant event of a kind mentioned in paragraph (a) or (b) above has occurred in relation to the school before the fourth anniversary of the date on which the current instrument of government for the school was made, that anniversary ;

(d) where any relevant event has previously occurred in relation to the school, the fourth anniversary of the latest such event.

(3) Any review which is required by virtue of the occurrence of a relevant event of a kind mentioned in paragraph (a)(i), (ii) or (b) of subsection (2) above shall be carried out by the local education authority and any other review which is required by this section shall be carried out by the governing body.

(4) Whenever the local education authority or governing body of a school are required to carry out a review under this section they shall consider whether—

(a) the governing body are properly constituted ;

(b) the provision made by the instrument of government for the school is in any respect different from that which a new instrument of government would be required to make.

(5) Where the governing body of a school have carried out a review under this section and have established that the provision made by the instrument of government for the school is in one or more respects different from that which a new instrument of government for the school would be required to make, they shall report the fact to the local education authority.

(6) Where a relevant event of a kind mentioned in paragraph (a)(i), (ii) or (b) of subsection (2) above has occurred in relation to any school, the local education authority shall determine the date on which, for the purposes of this section, that event is to be taken to have occurred, and shall notify the governing body accordingly.

(7) In this section " approved arrangements " means arrangements approved by the Secretary of State in accordance with regulations made under section 12 of the 1981 Act (approval of special schools).

Temporary governing bodies

12.—(1) Where—

(*a*) the Secretary of State has approved, under section 12 or 13 of the 1980 Act, any proposal of a kind mentioned in subsection (2) below ; or

(*b*) a local education authority making any such proposal have determined, under section 12(7) of that Act, that it should be implemented ;

the local education authority shall make an arrangement for the constitution of a temporary governing body for the school (or proposed school) pending the constitution of its governing body under an instrument of government.

(2) The proposals referred to in subsection (1) above are—

(*a*) any proposal made by a local education authority—

　　(i) to establish a new county school ; or

　　(ii) to maintain as a county school any school which is neither a county school nor a voluntary school ; and

(*b*) any proposal that a relevant school should be maintained by a local education authority as a voluntary school.

(3) Where a local education authority propose to establish a new special school, they shall make an arrangement for the constitution of a temporary governing body for the school—

(*a*) at least one year before the date on which the first pupils are expected to be admitted ; or

(*b*) on the day on which their resolution to establish the school is passed.

(4) Where a proposal of a kind mentioned in subsection (2) above has been duly published, the local education authority may make an arrangement for the constitution of a temporary governing body in anticipation of the approval of the proposal by the Secretary of State or (as the case may be) of the determination by the authority that it should be implemented.

(5) Where any proposal that a relevant school should be maintained by a local education authority as a controlled school has been duly published, the authority shall consult the promoters—

(*a*) as to whether the power given to the authority by subsection (4) above should be exercised ; and

(*b*) if the authority propose to exercise it, as to the date on which it should be exercised.

(6) Where any proposal that a relevant school should be maintained by a local education authority as an aided school has been duly published, the authority and the promoters shall consider—

    (a) whether the power given to the authority by subsection (4) above should be exercised ; and

    (b) where they agree that it should, on what date the authority should exercise it.

(7) Where, in a case falling within subsection (6) above, the authority and the promoters fail to agree on the question mentioned in paragraph (a) or on that mentioned in paragraph (b), either of them may refer the matter to the Secretary of State.

(8) On any reference under subsection (7) above, the Secretary of State shall give such direction as he thinks fit.

(9) In this section " relevant school ", in relation to any proposal, means a school which—

    (a) was established by those making the proposal, or by persons whom they represent, and which is not a voluntary school ; or

    (b) is proposed to be so established.

(10) Schedule 2 to this Act shall have effect for the purpose of supplementing this section.

Miscellaneous and supplemental

Effect of change of circumstances on instrument of government.

13.—(1) Any instrument of government to which this Act applies shall (subject to subsection (2) below and paragraph 3(2) of Schedule 2 to this Act) make such provision as is appropriate having regard to all the circumstances of the school as at the date on which the instrument is made.

(2) Where a proposal of a kind mentioned in section 11(2)(a) or (b) of this Act has been implemented in relation to any school, the number of registered pupils at the school shall, for the purposes of subsection (1) above and until the number of registered pupils at the school reaches the maximum number of pupils provided for by the proposal, be deemed to be that maximum number.

(3) Where subsection (2) applies in relation to any school, the local education authority or (in the case of a proposal under section 13(1)(b) of the 1980 Act) the governing body may determine that it shall cease to apply (but without prejudice to its operation in relation to the implementation of any further proposal).

(4) Where the effect of any subsequent change in the cir- cumstances of a school is that the provision made by the instrument of government for the school differs in any respect from the provision which a new instrument of government would be required to make, it shall be the duty of the local education authority (subject to subsection (7) below): —

    (*a*) to vary the instrument of government in such manner as is required to remove any such difference ; or

    (*b*) to make a new instrument of government.

(5) Any instrument of government to which this Act applies may make provision which would be appropriate in the event of such a change in the circumstances of the school as is anticipated by that provision (including in particular a change in the number of registered pupils at the school).

(6) No provision made by any such instrument in anticipation of a change in the number of registered pupils at the school shall have effect before it is established, by a review under section 11 of this Act, that a new instrument of government for the school in question would be required to make that provision.

(7) For the purposes of subsection (4) above, any change in the number of registered pupils at a school occurring after the instrument of government for the school is made, or (as the case may be) varied, may be disregarded until a review under section 11 of this Act establishes that the provision made by the instrument differs in any respect from the provision which a new instrument of government for the school would be required to make.

(8) Where subsection (2) above has applied in relation to any school but the local education authority or (as the case may be) governing body have subsequently determined that it should cease to apply, subsections (4) and (7) above shall have effect as if a change in the number of registered pupils at the school had occurred at the time when that determination was made.

(9) Subsections (6) and (7) above do not apply to aided or special agreement schools.

14.—(1) Where—

    (*a*) any county, controlled or maintained special school has more governors of a particular category than are provided for by the instrument of government for the school ; and

    (*b*) the excess is not eliminated by the required number of governors of that category resigning ;

such number of governors of that category as is required to eliminate the excess shall cease to hold office.

(2) The governors who are to cease to hold office shall be selected on the basis of seniority, the longest serving governor being the first to be selected, and so on.

(3) Where it is necessary for the purpose of subsection (2) above to select one or more governors from a group of equal seniority, it shall be done by drawing lots.

(4) Subsections (2) and (3) above do not apply in relation to foundation governors.

(5) The instrument of government for every controlled school shall make provision for the procedure to be adopted whenever subsection (1) above requires any foundation governor to cease to hold office.

Miscellaneous.   **15.**—(1) Where a school to which section 3 or 4 of this Act applies has more than one head teacher (whether or not as a result of two or more schools being grouped under section 9 of this Act), each of them shall be a governor unless he chooses not to be.

(2) It shall be for the local education authority, in the case of a county, controlled or maintained special school, and for the governing body, in the case of an aided or special agreement school—

> (a) to determine, for the purposes of an election of parent governors or teacher governors to the governing body, any question whether a person is—
>> (i) a parent of a registered pupil at the school ; or
>> (ii) a teacher at the school ; and
> (b) to make all necessary arrangements for, and to determine all other matters relating to, any such election.

(3) The power conferred by subsection (2)(b) above includes power to make provision as to qualifying dates but does not include power to impose any requirement as to the minimum number of votes required to be cast for a candidate to be elected.

(4) Any such election which is contested must be held by secret ballot.

(5) The arrangements made under subsection (2)(b) above shall, in the case of any election of a parent governor, provide for every person who is entitled to vote in the election to have an opportunity to do so by post or, if he so prefers, by having his ballot paper returned to the school by a registered pupil at the school.

(6) Where a vacancy for a parent governor of any county, voluntary or maintained special school is required to be filled by

election, it shall be the duty of the appropriate authority to take
such steps as are reasonably practicable to secure that every
person who is known to them to be a parent of a registered
pupil at the school is—

    (a) informed of the vacancy and that it is required to be
        filled by election ;

    (b) informed that he is entitled to stand as a candidate, and
        vote, at the election ; and

    (c) given an opportunity to do so.

(7) The instrument of government for every voluntary school
shall name the person or persons (if any) who are entitled to
appoint any foundation governor.

(8) The instrument of government for any voluntary school
may provide for any foundation governorship to be held ex
officio by the holder of an office named in the instrument.

(9) The qualification of any person for election or appointment
as a governor, of a particular category, of any county, voluntary
or maintained special school, shall not have the effect of disqualifying him for election or appointment as a governor, of
any other category, of that school.

(10) No person shall at any time hold more than one governorship of the same county, voluntary or maintained special
school.

(11) Where the instrument of government for any county,
voluntary or maintained special school provides for one or more
governors to be appointed by persons acting jointly, any such
appointment shall be made, in the event of failure on the part
of those persons to make an agreed appointment—

    (a) by the Secretary of State ; or

    (b) in accordance with any direction given by him.

(12) No instrument of government for any county, voluntary
or maintained special school which provides for one or more persons to be co-opted, by governors, as members of the governing
body of the school shall make any provision (otherwise than by
virtue of section 6 of this Act) which has the effect of restricting
those governors in their choice of person to co-opt.

(13) In subsection (12) above, references to co-opted governors are to governors required to be co-opted by virtue of section
3 of this Act and do not include references to co-opted foundation governors.

(14) No person shall be qualified for membership of the governing body of any county, voluntary or maintained special school
unless he is aged eighteen or over, at the date of his election or
appointment.

(15) In subsection (6) above, " appropriate authority " means—

    (a) the local education authority, in the case of a county, controlled or maintained special school ; and

    (b) the governing body, in the case of an aided or special agreement school.

PART III

ORGANISATION AND FUNCTIONS

General

General
responsibility
for conduct of
certain schools.

16.—(1) The articles of government for every county, voluntary and maintained special school shall provide for the conduct of the school to be under the direction of the governing body, but subject to any provision of the articles conferring specific functions on any person other than the governing body, and to the provision made (otherwise than in the articles) by or under this Act or any other enactment.

(2) The Secretary of State may by regulations make provision as to the circumstances in which, in any case where—

    (a) any provision of, or made under, this Act requires the governing body of a school to be consulted before a particular step is taken by the local education authority or the head teacher ; and

    (b) the authority or head teacher require to take that step as a matter of urgency but are unable to contact the chairman or vice-chairman of the governing body ;

the authority or (as the case may be) the head teacher may proceed without consulting the governing body.

(3) Where a county, voluntary or maintained special school is organised in two or more separate departments, each with a head teacher, any provision made by or under this Act which confers functions on, or in relation to, the head teacher of the school shall, except where the articles of government provide otherwise, have effect as if each department were a separate school.

School curriculum

Duty of local
education
authority to
state policy.

17.—(1) It shall be the duty of every local education authority—

    (a) to determine, and keep under review, their policy in relation to the secular curriculum for the county, voluntary and special schools maintained by them ;

    (b) to make, and keep up to date, a written statement of that policy ; and

(c) to furnish the governing body and head teacher of every
such school with a copy of the statement and publish it
in such other manner as the authority consider appropriate.

(2) In discharging their duty under subsection (1) above, an
authority shall consider, in particular—

(a) the range of the secular curriculum ; and

(b) the balance between its different components.

(3) In carrying out their functions under this Act or any
other enactment, a local education authority shall have regard
to their policy in relation to the secular curriculum for their
schools, as expressed in their statement.

(4) Every head teacher to whom any copy of a statement is
furnished under this section shall make it available, at all reasonable times, to persons wishing to inspect it.

18.—(1) The articles of government for every county, con-   County,
trolled and maintained special school shall provide for it to be   controlled and
the duty of the governing body to consider—   maintained
    special schools.

(a) the policy of the local education authority as to the
secular curriculum for the authority's schools, as expressed in the statement made by the authority under section 17 of this Act ;

(b) what, in their opinion, should be the aims of the secular
curriculum for the school ; and

(c) how (if at all) the authority's policy with regard to
matters other than sex education should in their
opinion be modified in relation to the school ;

and to make, and keep up to date, a written statement of their
conclusions.

(2) The articles of government for every such school shall
provide for it to be the duty of the governing body—

(a) to consider separately (while having regard to the local
education authority's statement under section 17 of this
Act) the question whether sex education should form
part of the secular curriculum for the school ; and

(b) to make, and keep up to date, a separate written statement—

(i) of their policy with regard to the content and
organisation of the relevant part of the curriculum ;
or

(ii) where they conclude that sex education should
not form part of the secular curriculum, of that conclusion.

(3) The articles of government for every such school shall provide for it to be the duty of the governing body—

(*a*) when considering the matters mentioned in subsections (1) and (2) above, to do so in consultation with the head teacher and to have regard—

(i) to any representations which are made to them, with regard to any of those matters, by any persons connected with the community served by the school; and

(ii) to any such representations which are made to them by the chief officer of police and which are connected with his responsibilities;

(*b*) to consult the authority before making or varying any statement under subsection (1) above; and

(*c*) to furnish the authority and head teacher with an up to date copy of any statement under this section.

(4) The articles of government for every such school shall provide for it to be the duty of the head teacher to make any statement furnished to him under this section available at all reasonable times, to persons wishing to inspect it.

(5) The articles of government for every such school shall provide for the determination and organisation of the secular curriculum for the school to be the responsibility of the head teacher and for it to be his duty to secure that that curriculum is followed within the school.

(6) The articles of government for every such school shall provide for it to be the duty of the head teacher, in discharging his duties in relation to the secular curriculum for the school—

(*a*) to consider the statement of the local education authority under section 17 of this Act and those of the governing body under this section;

(*b*) to have regard—

(i) to any representations which are made to him, with regard to the determination or organisation of the secular curriculum, by any persons connected with the community served by the school; and

(ii) to any such representations which are made to him by the chief officer of police and which are connected with that officer's responsibilities; and

(*c*) to ensure that that curriculum—

(i) so far as it relates to sex education, is compatible with the governing body's policy (as expressed in their statement under subsection (2) above) except where that policy is incompatible with any part of the syllabus for a course which forms part of that curriculum and leads to a public examination ;

(ii) so far as it relates to other matters, is compatible with the authority's policy (as expressed in their statement) or, to the extent to which it is incompatible, is compatible with that policy as modified by the governing body's statement under subsection (1) above ; and

(iii) is compatible with the enactments relating to education (including, in particular, those relating to children with special educational needs).

(7) The articles of government for every such school shall provide for the governing body to have power to review their conclusions about the matters mentioned in subsections (1) and (2) above whenever they think fit, and for it to be their duty to do so immediately following—

(*a*) the implementation of any proposal under—

(i) section 16 of the 1944 Act (transfer of schools to new sites) ;

(ii) section 12 or 13 of the 1980 Act (establishment, alteration and discontinuance of schools) ; or

(iii) section 15 of the 1980 Act (reduction of school places) ;

which materially affects the school ; or

(*b*) in the case of a maintained special school, any change in any of the arrangements made for pupils at the school and their special educational needs which must be complied with (by virtue of regulations made under section 12 of the 1981 Act) for the school to be approved as a maintained special school under section 9(5) of the 1944 Act.

(8) The article of government for every such school shall provide for it to be the duty of the governing body, where—

(*a*) they have completed such a review ; and

(*b*) they consider it appropriate to make a fresh written statement of their conclusions ;

to do so and to furnish the local education authority and the head teacher with a copy of it.

19.—(1) The articles of government for every aided and special agreement school shall provide—

Aided and special agreement schools.

(*a*) for the content of the secular curriculum for the school to be under the control of the governing body ;

(*b*) for the governing body to have regard to the policy of the local education authority as to the curriculum for the authority's schools, as expressed in the statement made by the authority under section 17 of this Act ; and

(c) for the head teacher to be allocated by the governing body such functions as will, subject to the resources available, enable him to determine and organise the curriculum and secure that it is followed within the school.

(2) The articles of government for every such school shall provide for it to be the duty of the governing body, when considering the content of the secular curriculum for the school, to have regard—

(a) to any representations which are made to them, with regard to that curriculum, by any persons connected with the community served by the school ; and

(b) to any such representations which—

(i) are made to them by the chief officer of police ; and

(ii) are connected with his responsibilities.

(3) Where the governing body of any such school make any statement in writing of their policy as to the secular curriculum for the school they shall furnish a copy of it to the head teacher ; and the head teacher shall make it available, at all reasonable times, to persons wishing to inspect it.

Information for parents.

20. The Secretary of State shall make regulations requiring the governing body of every county, voluntary and maintained special school to make available to parents of registered pupils at the school, in such form and manner and at such times as may be prescribed—

(a) such information as to any syllabuses to be followed by those pupils ; and

(b) such other information as to the educational provision made for them by the school ;

as may be prescribed.

School terms etc.

Terms, sessions and holidays.

21.—(1) The articles of government for every county, controlled and maintained special school shall provide for it to be the duty of the local education authority to determine—

(a) the times at which the school session is to begin and end on any day ; and

(b) the dates and times at which the school terms and holidays are to begin and end.

(2) The articles of government for every such school shall provide for the local education authority to have power to require pupils in attendance at the school to attend at any place outside the school premises for the purpose of receiving any instruction or training included in the secular curriculum for the school.

(3) The articles of government for every aided and special agreement school shall make the same provision as is required by subsections (1) and (2) above, but in relation to the governing body in place of the local education authority.

Discipline

22. The articles of government for every county, voluntary and maintained special school shall provide—

Discipline: general duties.

> (*a*) for it to be the duty of the head teacher to determine measures (which may include the making of rules and provision for enforcing them) to be taken with a view to—

>> (i) promoting, among pupils, self-discipline and proper regard for authority ;

>> (ii) encouraging good behaviour on the part of pupils ;

>> (iii) securing that the standard of behaviour of pupils is acceptable ; and

>> (iv) otherwise regulating the conduct of pupils ;

> (*b*) for it to be the duty of the head teacher, in determining any such measures—

>> (i) to act in accordance with any written statement of general principles provided for him by the governing body ; and

>> (ii) to have regard to any guidance that they may offer in relation to particular matters ;

> (*c*) for it to be the duty of the head teacher to make any such measures generally known within the school ;

> (*d*) for the standard of behaviour which is to be regarded as acceptable at the school to be determined by the head teacher, so far as it is not determined by the governing body ;

> (*e*) for it to be the duty of the governing body and the head teacher to consult the local education authority, before determining any such measures, on any matter

    arising from the proposed measures which can reasonably be expected—

        (i) to lead to increased expenditure by the authority ; or

        (ii) to affect the responsibilities of the authority as an employer ;

    (*f*) for the power to exclude a pupil from the school (whether by suspension, expulsion or otherwise) to be exercisable only by the head teacher.

Exclusion of
pupils: duty
to inform
parents etc.

23. The articles of government for every county, voluntary and maintained special school shall provide—

    (*a*) for it to be the duty of the head teacher—

        (i) where he excludes from the school a pupil who is under eighteen, to take (without delay) reasonable steps to inform a parent of the pupil of the period of the exclusion and the reasons for it ;

        (ii) where he decides that any exclusion of such a pupil from the school which was originally for a fixed or indefinite period should be made permanent, to take (without delay) reasonable steps to inform a parent of the pupil of his decision and of the reasons for it ; and

        (iii) where he excludes any pupil from the school to take (without delay) reasonable steps to inform the pupil, if he is aged eighteen or over, or a parent of his, if he is under eighteen, that the pupil or (as the case may be) parent may make representations about the exclusion to the governing body and the local education authority ;

    (*b*) for it to be the duty of the head teacher, where he excludes a pupil from the school—

        (i) for more than five school days (in the aggregate) in any one term ; or

        (ii) in circumstances in which the pupil would, as a result of his exclusion from the school, lose an opportunity to take any public examination ;

    to inform the local education authority and the governing body (without delay) of the period of the exclusion and of the reasons for it and where he decides that any exclusion of a pupil from the school which was originally for a fixed or indefinite period should be made permanent, to inform them (without delay) of his decision and of the reasons for it.

24. The articles of government for every county, controlled and maintained special school shall provide—

PART III
Reinstatement of excluded pupils: county, controlled and maintained special schools.

(*a*) for it to be the duty of the local education authority, where they have been informed of the permanent exclusion of a pupil from the school—

    (i) to consider, after consulting the governing body, whether he should be reinstated immediately, reinstated by a particular date or not reinstated ;

    (ii) where they consider that he should be reinstated, to give the appropriate direction to the head teacher ; and

    (iii) where they consider that he should not be reinstated, to inform the pupil (if he is aged eighteen or over) or a parent of his (if he is under eighteen) of their decision ;

(*b*) for it to be the duty of the head teacher, where he has excluded a pupil from the school—

    (i) for more than five school days (in the aggregate) in any one term ; or

    (ii) in circumstances in which the pupil would, as a result of his exclusion from the school, lose an opportunity to take any public examination ;

to comply with any direction for the reinstatement of the pupil given by the governing body or the local education authority, in the case of an exclusion for a fixed period, or by the governing body, in the case of an exclusion which is for an indefinite period or is permanent ;

(*c*) for it to be the duty of the local education authority, where they have been informed of the indefinite exclusion of a pupil from the school, to consult the governing body and, where the governing body do not intend to direct the head teacher to reinstate the pupil or the authority consider that he should be reinstated by a date which is earlier than that determined by the governing body as the date by which he is to be reinstated—

    (i) to direct that he be reinstated immediately ; or

    (ii) to direct that he be reinstated within such period as may be specified in the direction ;

(*d*) for it to be the duty of the local education authority where—

    (i) they have been informed of the exclusion of a pupil from the school for a fixed period ; and

PART III

           (ii) they propose to give a direction for his reinstatement;

to consult the governing body before doing so;

(e) for any direction given by virtue of paragraph (c) above to cease to have effect (without prejudice to any subsequent direction given by virtue of any other provision made by the articles in accordance with this section) if the head teacher decides that the exclusion of the pupil concerned should be made permanent;

(f) for it to be the duty of the head teacher to comply with any direction given in exercise of the duty imposed on the local education authority by virtue of paragraph (a) or (c) above;

(g) for it to be the duty of the head teacher, where conflicting directions for the reinstatement of a pupil are given by the governing body and the local education authority, to comply with that direction which will lead to the earlier reinstatement of the pupil; and

(h) for it to be the duty of the governing body and the local education authority to inform each other and—

           (i) the pupil concerned, if he is aged eighteen or over; or

           (ii) a parent of his, if he is under eighteen;

of any direction, of a kind mentioned in this section, which is given by them.

Reinstatement of excluded pupils: aided and special agreement schools.

25. The articles of government for every aided and special agreement school shall provide—

(a) for it to be the duty of the governing body, where they have been informed of the permanent exclusion of a pupil from the school—

           (i) to consider whether he should be reinstated immediately, reinstated by a particular date or not reinstated;

           (ii) where they consider that he should be reinstated, to give the appropriate direction to the head teacher; and

           (iii) where they consider that he should not be reinstated, to inform (without delay) the local education authority and either the pupil, if he is aged eighteen or over, or a parent of his, if he is under eighteen, of their decision;

(*b*) for it to be the duty of the head teacher where he has
excluded a pupil from the school—

    (i) for more than five school days (in the aggregate) in any one term ; or

    (ii) in circumstances in which the pupil would, as a result of his exclusion from the school, lose an opportunity to take any public examination ;

to comply with any direction for the reinstatement of the pupil given by the governing body or, in the case of an exclusion for a fixed period, by the governing body or the local education authority ;

(*c*) for it to be the duty of the local education authority to consult the governing body before giving any direction by virtue of paragraph (*b*) above ;

(*d*) for it to be the duty of the local education authority, where they have been informed of the indefinite exclusion of a pupil from the school, to consult the governing body and, where the governing body do not intend to direct the head teacher to reinstate the pupil or the authority consider that he should be reinstated by a date which is earlier than that determined by the governing body as the date by which he is to be reinstated—

    (i) to direct that he be reinstated immediately ; or

    (ii) to direct that he be reinstated within such period as may be specified in the direction ;

(*e*) for any direction given by virtue of paragraph (*d*) above to cease to have effect (without prejudice to any direction given by virtue of any other provision made by the articles in accordance with this section) if the head teacher decides that the exclusion of the pupil concerned should be made permanent ;

(*f*) for it to be the duty of the head teacher to comply with any direction given in exercise of the duty imposed on the local education authority by virtue of paragraph (*d*) above ;

(*g*) for it to be the duty of the head teacher, where conflicting directions for the reinstatement of a pupil are given by the governing body and the local education authority, to comply with that direction which will lead to the earlier reinstatement of the pupil ; and

(*h*) for it to be the duty of the governing body and the local education authority to inform each other and—

    (i) the pupil concerned, if he is aged eighteen or over ; or

(ii) a parent of his, if he is under eighteen ;

of any direction, of a kind mentioned in this section, which is given by them.

Appeals.

26.—(1) Every local education authority shall make arrangements for enabling—

(a) a registered pupil at a county, controlled or maintained special school who is aged eighteen or over, or a parent of his, in the case of a pupil at such a school who is under eighteen, to appeal against any decision not to reinstate the pupil following his permanent exclusion from the school ; and

(b) any governing body of such a school, the head teacher of which has been directed by the authority to reinstate any registered pupil at the school who has been permanently excluded, to appeal against the direction.

(2) The governing body of every aided or special agreement school shall make arrangements for enabling a registered pupil at the school who is aged eighteen or over, or a parent of a pupil at such a school who is under eighteen to appeal against any decision not to reinstate the pupil following his permanent exclusion from the school.

(3) Joint arrangements may be made under subsection (2) above by the governing bodies of two or more aided or special agreement schools maintained by the same local education authority.

(4) Any appeal by virtue of this section shall be to an appeal committee constituted in accordance with Part I of Schedule 2 to the 1980 Act ; and Schedule 3 to this Act shall have effect, in place of Part II of Schedule 2 to the 1980 Act, in relation to any such appeal.

(5) The decision of an appeal committee on any such appeal shall be binding on the persons concerned ; and where the committee determines that the pupil in question should be reinstated it shall direct that he be reinstated immediately or direct that he be reinstated by such date as is specified in the direction.

Exclusion: additional provision for appeals.

27. Where the articles of government for any county, voluntary or maintained special school provide—

(a) for the parents of any pupil who is excluded from the school in circumstances in which no right of appeal is given by section 26 of this Act to have the right to appeal against his exclusion to a person specified by the articles ; and (*b*) for the procedure to be followed on such an appeal ;   any decision on such an appeal that the pupil should be reinstated, or that he should be reinstated earlier than would otherwise be the case, shall be binding on the head teacher.

28.—(1) Every local education authority shall have power, in the circumstances mentioned in subsection (3) below, to take such steps in relation to any county, controlled or special school maintained by them as they consider are required to prevent the breakdown, or continuing breakdown, of discipline at the school.

(2) The governing body and the head teacher of every aided and special agreement school shall, in the circumstances mentioned in subsection (3) below, consider any representations made to them by the local education authority.

(3) The circumstances are that—

 (*a*) in the opinion of the authority—

   (i) the behaviour of registered pupils at the school ; or

   (ii) any action taken by such pupils or their parents ;

  is such that the education of any such pupils is, or is likely in the immediate future to become, severely prejudiced ; and

 (*b*) the governing body have been informed in writing of the authority's opinion.

(4) Steps taken by an authority under subsection (1) above may include the giving of any direction to the governing body or head teacher.

Finance

29.—(1) The articles of government for every county, volun- tary and maintained special school shall provide—

 (*a*) for it to be the duty of the local education authority (with a view to assisting the governing body to judge whether expenditure in relation to their school represents the economic, efficient and effective use of resources) to furnish the governing body, once in every year, with a statement of—

   (i) expenditure incurred or proposed to be incurred by the authority in meeting the day to day cost of running the school (itemised as the authority think appropriate) ; and

   (ii) such expenditure of a capital nature, incurred or proposed to be incurred by the authority, as they consider appropriate ;

(*b*) for it to be the duty of the local education authority to make available, in every year, a sum of money which the governing body are to be entitled to spend at their discretion (but subject to paragraph (*c*) below) on books, equipment, stationery and such other heads of expenditure (if any) as may be specified by the authority or prescribed by the Secretary of State ;

(*c*) for it to be the duty of the governing body, in spending any such sum, to comply with such reasonable conditions as the authority think fit to impose ;

(*d*) for the governing body to have power to delegate to the head teacher, to such extent as they may specify, their powers in relation to the sum so made available ; and

(*e*) for it to be the duty of the governing body not to incur any expenditure under any of the heads of expenditure mentioned in paragraph (*b*) above which, in the opinion of the head teacher, would be inappropriate in relation to the curriculum for the school.

(2) Before making any regulations under subsection (1)(*b*) above, the Secretary of State shall consult such associations of local authorities as appear to him to be concerned and any local authority with whom consultation appears to him to be desirable.

Reports and meetings

Governors' annual report to parents.

30.—(1) The articles of government for every county, voluntary and maintained special school shall provide for it to be the duty of the governing body to prepare, once in every school year, a report (" the governors' report ") containing—

(*a*) a summary of the steps taken by the governing body in the discharge of their functions during the period since their last report ; and

(*b*) such other information as the articles may require.

(2) The articles of government for every such school shall, in particular, require the governors' report—

(*a*) to be as brief as is reasonably consistent with the requirements as to its contents ;

(*b*) where there is an obligation on the governing body (by virtue of section 31 of this Act) to hold an annual parents' meeting—

(i) to give details of the date, time and place for the next such meeting and its agenda ;

(ii) to indicate that the purpose of that meeting will be to discuss both the governors' report and the discharge by the governing body, the head teacher and the local education authority of their functions in relation to the school ; and

(iii) to report on the consideration which has been given to any resolutions passed at the previous such meeting;

(c) to give the name of each governor and indicate whether he is a parent, teacher or foundation governor or was co-opted or otherwise appointed as a governor or is an ex officio governor;

(d) to say, in the case of an appointed governor, by whom he was appointed;

(e) to give, in relation to each governor who is not an ex officio governor, the date on which his term of office comes to an end;

(f) to name, and give the address of, the chairman of the governing body and their clerk;

(g) to give such information as is available to the governing body about arrangements for the next election of parent governors;

(h) to contain a financial statement—

(i) reproducing or summarising the latest financial statement provided for the governing body by the local education authority (by virtue of paragraph (a) of section 29(1) of this Act);

(ii) indicating, in general terms, how any sum made available to the governing body by the authority (by virtue of paragraph (b) of that section), in the period covered by the report, was used; and

(iii) giving details of the application of any gifts made to the school in that period;

(i) to give, in the case of a secondary school, such information in relation to public examinations as is required to be published by virtue of section 8(5) of the 1980 Act;

(j) to describe what steps have been taken by the governing body to develop or strengthen the school's links with the community (including links with the police); and

(k) to draw attention to the information made available by the governing body in accordance with the regulations made under section 20 of this Act.

(3) The articles of government for every such school shall—

(a) enable the governing body to produce their report in such language or languages (in addition to English) as they consider appropriate; and

(b) require them to produce it in such language or languages (in addition to English and any other language in which the governing body propose to produce it) as the local education authority may direct.

(4) The articles of government for every such school shall provide for it to be the duty of the governing body of any such school to take such steps as are reasonably practicable to secure that—

    (a) the parents of all registered pupils at the school and all persons employed at the school are given (free of charge) a copy of the governors' report;

    (b) copies of the report are available for inspection (at all reasonable times and free of charge) at the school; and

    (c) where there is an obligation on the governing body (by virtue of section 31 of this Act) to hold an annual parents' meeting, copies of the report to be considered at that meeting are given to parents not less than two weeks before that meeting.

Annual
parents'
meetings.

31.—(1) Subject to subsections (7) and (8) below, the articles of government for every county, voluntary and maintained special school shall provide for it to be the duty of the governing body to hold a meeting once in every school year (" the annual parents' meeting ") which is open to—

    (a) all parents of registered pupils at the school;

    (b) the head teacher; and

    (c) such other persons as the governing body may invite.

(2) The purpose of the meeting shall be to provide an opportunity for discussion of—

    (a) the governors' report; and

    (b) the discharge by the governing body, the head teacher and the local education authority of their functions in relation to the school.

(3) No person who is not a parent of a registered pupil at the school may vote on any question put to the meeting.

(4) The articles of government for every such school shall provide—

    (a) for the proceedings at any annual parents' meeting to be under the control of the governing body;

    (b) for any annual parents' meeting, at which the required number of parents of registered pupils at the school are present, to be entitled to pass (by a simple majority) resolutions on any matters which may properly be discussed at the meeting;

    (c) for it to be the duty of the governing body—

        (i) to consider any resolution which is duly passed at such a meeting and which they consider is a matter for them;

(ii) to send to the head teacher a copy of any such resolution which they consider is a matter for him ; and

(iii) to send to the local education authority a copy of any such resolution which they consider is a matter for the authority ; and

(*d*) for it to be the duty of the head teacher, and of the local education authority, to consider any such resolution a copy of which has been sent to him, or them, by the governing body and to provide the governing body with a brief comment on it (in writing) for inclusion in their next governors' report.

(5) The articles of government for every county, controlled and maintained special school shall provide for any question whether any person is to be treated as the parent of a registered pupil at the school, for the purposes of any provision of the articles relating to the annual parents' meeting, to be determined by the local education authority.

(6) The articles of government for every aided or special agreement school shall provide for any such question to be determined by the governing body.

(7) The articles of government for every special school established in a hospital shall provide that where the governing body are of the opinion that it would be impracticable to hold an annual parents' meeting in a particular school year they may refrain from holding such a meeting in that year.

(8) The articles of government for every county, voluntary and maintained special school (other than a special school established in a hospital), the proportion of registered pupils at which who are boarders is, or is likely to be, at least fifty per cent., shall provide that where—

(*a*) the governing body are of the opinion that it would be impracticable to hold an annual parents' meeting in a particular school year ; and

(*b*) at least fifty per cent. of the registered pupils at the school are boarders at the time when the governing body form that opinion ;

they may refrain from holding such a meeting in that year.

(9) In subsection (4)(*b*) above " the required number ", in relation to any school, means any number equal to at least twenty per cent. of the number of registered pupils at the school.

PART III
Reports by
governing body
and head
teacher.

32.—(1) The articles of government for every county, voluntary and maintained special school shall provide—

(a) for the governing body to furnish to the local education authority such reports in connection with the discharge of their functions as the authority may require (either on a regular basis or from time to time) ; and

(b) for the head teacher to furnish to the governing body or (as the case may be) local education authority such reports in connection with the discharge of his functions as the governing body or authority may so require.

(2) The articles of government for every aided school shall provide—

(a) for the local education authority to notify the governing body of any requirement of a kind mentioned in subsection (1)(b) above which is imposed by them on the head teacher ; and

(b) for the head teacher to furnish the governing body with a copy of any report which he makes in complying with the requirement.

Admissions

Admissions.

33.—(1) Where the governing body of any county or voluntary school are responsible for determining the arrangements for admitting pupils to the school, they shall—

(a) at least once in every school year, consult the local education authority as to whether those arrangements are satisfactory ; and

(b) consult the authority before determining, or varying, any of them.

(2) Where the local education authority are responsible for determining the arrangements for admitting pupils to any such school they shall—

(a) at least once in every school year, consult the governing body as to whether those arrangements are satisfactory ; and

(b) consult the governing body before determining, or varying, any of them.

Appointment and dismissal of staff

Determination
of staff
complement
for schools.

34.—(1) Every county, controlled, special agreement and maintained special school shall have a complement of teaching and non-teaching posts determined by the local education authority.

(2) The complement for any such school shall include—

(*a*) all full-time teaching posts ; and

(*b*) all part-time teaching posts which are to be filled by persons whose only employment with the authority will be at the school.

(3) The complement for any such school shall not include any staff employed by the authority solely in connection with either or both of the following—

(*a*) the provision of meals ;

(*b*) the supervision of pupils at midday.

35.—(1) The appointment and dismissal of staff (including teachers) at every county, controlled, special agreement and maintained special school shall be under the control of the local education authority, but— Appointment and dismissal of staff: introductory.

(*a*) the appointment of a head teacher shall be subject to the provision made by the articles of government for the school in accordance with section 37 of this Act ;

(*b*) the appointment of a deputy head teacher shall be subject to the provision made by the articles in accordance with section 39 of this Act ;

(*c*) the appointment and dismissal of the clerk to the governing body shall be subject to section 40 of this Act and to any provision made by the articles in accordance with that section ;

(*d*) the appointment of any other staff (including any teacher), to a post which is part of the school's complement, shall be subject to the provision made by the articles in accordance with section 38 of this Act ;

(*e*) the dismissal of staff shall be subject to the provision made by the articles in accordance with section 41 of this Act ;

(*f*) the appointment and dismissal of staff at any school for which there is a temporary governing body shall be subject to the provisions of Schedule 2 to this Act ; and

(*g*) this section is subject to the provisions of sections 27 and 28 of the 1944 Act (which relate to religious education).

(2) The articles of government for every such school shall provide for it to be the duty of the local education authority to consult the governing body and the head teacher before appointing any person to work solely at the school otherwise than—

(*a*) in a teaching post ;

(*b*) in a non-teaching post which is part of the complement of the school ; or (*c*) solely in connection with either or both of the following—

>   (i) the provision of meals;

>   (ii) the supervision of pupils at midday.

The selection
panel.

36.—(1) The articles of government for every county, controlled, special agreement and maintained special school shall provide—

(*a*) for the constitution of a selection panel whenever such a panel is required, by virtue of section 37 or 39 of this Act, in relation to the appointment of a head teacher or deputy head teacher;

(*b*) for the selection panel to consist of a specified number of persons appointed to it by the local education authority and a specified number of governors appointed to it by the governing body, the number so specified being—

>   (i) in each case, not less than three; and

>   (ii) in relation to appointments made by the governing body, not less than the number specified in relation to appointments made by the authority; and

(*c*) for the governing body and the authority to have power to replace, at any time, any member of the selection panel whom they have appointed.

(2) The Secretary of State may by regulations make provision as to the meetings and proceedings of selection panels.

Appointment
of head
teacher.

37.—(1) The articles of government for every county, controlled, special agreement and maintained special school shall provide—

(*a*) for it to be the duty of the local education authority not to appoint a person to be the head teacher of the school unless his appointment has been recommended by a selection panel constituted in accordance with the articles;

(*b*) for it to be the duty of the authority, in the event of the post of head teacher being vacant, to appoint an acting head teacher after consulting the governing body;

(*c*) for it to be the duty of the authority, before appointing a head teacher, to advertise the vacancy in such publications circulating throughout England and Wales as they consider appropriate;

(*d*) for it to be the duty of the selection panel constituted
in relation to the appointment of a head teacher to
interview such applicants for the post as they think
fit;

(*e*) in the event of a failure of the panel to agree on the
applicants whom they wish to interview—

(i) for those members of the panel appointed by
the governing body to have the right to nominate not
more than two applicants to be interviewed by the
panel; and

(ii) for the other members of the panel to have
the right to nominate not more than two other
applicants to be so interviewed;

(*f*) for it to be the duty of the panel, where they consider
that it is appropriate to do so, to recommend to the
authority for appointment as head teacher one of the
applicants interviewed by them;

(*g*) for it to be the duty of the panel, where they are unable
to agree on a person to recommend to the authority—

(i) to repeat (with a view to reaching agreement)
such of the steps which they are required to take by
virtue of paragraphs (*d*) to (*f*) above as they think
fit;

(ii) where they have repeated any of those steps
and remain unable to agree, or have decided that
it is not appropriate to repeat any of them, to require the authority to re-advertise the vacancy; and

(iii) where the vacancy is re-advertised, to repeat
all of those steps;

(*h*) for it to be the duty of the panel, where the authority
decline to appoint a person recommended by them—

(i) where there are applicants for the post whom
they have not interviewed, to interview such of
those applicants (if any) as they think fit;

(ii) to recommend another of the applicants interviewed by them, if they think fit;

(iii) to ask the authority to re-advertise the
vacancy, if they consider that it should be re-
advertised; and

(iv) where the vacancy is re-advertised, to repeat
the steps which they are required to take by virtue
of paragraphs (*d*) to (*f*);

(*i*) for it to be the duty of the authority to re-advertise the
post of head teacher where they are required to do so

by the panel; and for the authority to have power to do so, where—

(i) the post has been duly advertised;

(ii) the selection panel have failed to make either a recommendation which is acceptable to the authority or a request that the post be re-advertised; and

(iii) the authority are of the opinion that the panel have had sufficient time in which to carry out their functions; and

(*j*) for the chief education officer of the authority, or a member of his department nominated by him, to have the right to attend all proceedings of the panel (including interviews) for the purpose of giving advice to members of the panel.

(2) In this section " head teacher " does not include an acting head teacher.

Appointment of certain other staff.
38.—(1) The articles of government for every county, controlled, special agreement and maintained special school shall provide for it to be the duty of the local education authority, where there is a vacancy in any post which is part of the complement of the school—

(*a*) to decide whether, in the case of a post which is not a new one, it should be retained;

(*b*) to advertise the vacancy, and fill it in accordance with the procedure laid down by virtue of subsection (3) below, unless they have the intention mentioned in paragraph (*c*) below; and

(*c*) to fill the vacancy in accordance with the procedure laid down by virtue of subsection (4) below, if they intend to appoint a person who, at the time when they form that intention, is an employee of theirs or has been appointed to take up employment with them at a future date.

(2) This section does not apply in relation to the appointment of a head teacher or deputy head teacher or to any temporary appointment made pending—

(*a*) the return to work of the holder of the post in question; or

(*b*) the taking of any steps required by the articles of government in relation to the vacancy in question.

(3) The articles of government for every such school shall provide—

(*a*) for it to be the duty of the authority, where they decide to advertise the vacancy, to do so in a manner likely in their opinion to bring it to the notice of persons (including employees of theirs) who are qualified to fill the post ;

(b) for it to be the duty of the governing body, where the vacancy is advertised—

(i) to interview such applicants for the post as they think fit ; and

(ii) where they consider that it is appropriate to do so, to recommend to the authority for appointment to the post one of the applicants interviewed by them ;

(c) for it to be the duty of the governing body, where they are unable to agree on a person to recommend to the authority—

(i) to repeat the steps which they are required to take by virtue of paragraph (b) above, if they consider that to do so might lead to their reaching agreement ;

(ii) where they have repeated those steps and remain unable to agree, or have decided that it is not appropriate to repeat them, to ask the authority to re-advertise the vacancy ; and

(iii) where the vacancy is re-advertised, to repeat those steps ;

(d) for it to be the duty of the governing body, where the authority decline to appoint a person recommended by them—

(i) where there are applicants for the post whom they have not interviewed, to interview such of those applicants (if any) as they think fit ;

(ii) to recommend another of the applicants interviewed by them, if they think fit ;

(iii) to ask the authority to re-advertise the vacancy, if they consider that it should be re-advertised ; and

(iv) where the vacancy is re-advertised, to repeat the steps which they are required to take by virtue of paragraph (b) above ;

(e) for it to be the duty of the authority, where they are asked by the governing body to re-advertise the vacancy, to do so unless they decide—

(i) that the post is to be removed from the complement of the school ; or

(ii) to appoint a person who, at the time when that decision is made, is an employee of theirs or has been appointed to take up employment with them at a future date ; and

(f) for—

    (i) the head teacher, where he would not otherwise be entitled to be present ; and

    (ii) such person (if any) as the authority appoint to represent them,

to be entitled to be present, for the purpose of giving advice, whenever governors meet to discuss the appointment or an applicant is interviewed.

(4) The articles of government for every such school shall provide—

    (a) in the event of the vacancy not being advertised, for the governing body to be entitled to determine a specification for the post in consultation with the head teacher ;

    (b) where the governing body have determined such a specification, for it to be their duty to send a copy of it to the authority ;

    (c) for it to be the duty of the authority—

        (i) to have regard to the specification, and consult the governing body and the head teacher, when considering whom to appoint to the post ; and

        (ii) if they make an appointment to a teaching post with which the governing body disagree, to report the fact to the next meeting of their appropriate education committee.

(5) No local education authority shall appoint a person to a post which they have advertised in accordance with requirements imposed by virtue of subsection (3) above unless—

    (a) his appointment has been recommended in accordance with those requirements ; or

    (b) the authority decide to appoint a person who, at the time when that decision is made, is an employee of theirs or has been appointed to take up employment with them at a future date.

(6) The articles of government for every such school shall provide—

    (a) for the governing body to have power to delegate any of the functions which are theirs by virtue of this section, in relation to the filling of a particular vacancy or a vacancy of a kind specified by them, to—

        (i) one or more governors ;

        (ii) the head teacher ; or

        (iii) one or more governors and the head teacher acting together ; and

(*b*) for the provision made in the articles by virtue of sub-   Part III
section (3)(*e*) or (4)(*c*)(ii) to apply in such a case with
the substitution of references to the person or persons
to whom the functions are delegated for references to
the governing body.

39.—(1) The articles of government for every county, con-   Appointment
trolled, special agreement and maintained special school shall, of deputy
in relation to the appointment of a deputy head teacher for the head teacher.
school, make—

(*a*) the same provision, modified in accordance with subsections (2) and (3) below, as that made by the articles
(in accordance with section 37 of this Act) in relation
to the appointment of a head teacher for the school ; or

(*b*) the same provision as that made by the articles (in
accordance with section 38 of this Act) in relation to
the appointment of other teachers at the school.

(2) Articles of government which, in accordance with subsection (1) above, provide for the appointment of a deputy head
teacher for the school to be on the recommendation of a
selection panel shall provide for the head teacher, where he is
not a member of the panel—

(*a*) to be entitled to be present, for the purpose of giving
advice, at any proceedings of the panel (including
interviews) ; and

(*b*) whether or not he attends any such proceedings, to
be consulted by the panel before it makes any recommendation to the local education authority.

(3) No provision shall be required in the articles of government
similar to that mentioned in section 37(1)(*b*) of this Act.

(4) In subsection (1) above " head teacher " does not include
an acting head teacher.

40.—(1) The articles of government for every county and Appointment
maintained special school shall provide for the clerk to the and dismissal
governing body to be appointed by the local education auth- of clerk to
ority in accordance with arrangements to be determined by governing
them in consultation with the governing body. body.

(2) The clerk to the governing body of any controlled or
special agreement school shall be appointed—

(*a*) where the articles of government make provision in
relation to his appointment, in accordance with that
provision ;

(*b*) in every other case, by the authority in accordance with arrangements determined by them in consultation with the governing body.

(3) Arrangements determined in respect of any school under subsections (1) or (2)(*b*) above may be varied by the authority in consultation with the governing body.

(4) The articles of government for every county and maintained special school shall provide for it to be the duty of the authority not to dismiss the clerk except in accordance with arrangements determined by them in consultation with the governing body.

(5) The articles of government for every county, controlled, special agreement and maintained special school shall provide for the governing body to have power, where the clerk fails to attend any meeting of theirs, to appoint one of their number to act as clerk for the purposes of that meeting, but without prejudice to his position as a governor.

(6) The clerk to the governing body of any controlled or special agreement schools may not be dismissed except—

(*a*) where the articles of government make provision in relation to his dismissal, in accordance with that provision ; or

(*b*) in any other case, in accordance with arrangements determined by the local education authority in consultation with the governing body.

(7) The articles of government for every county, controlled, special agreement and maintained special school shall provide for it to be the duty of the local education authority to consider any representations made to them by the governing body as to the dismissal of their clerk.

Dismissal, etc. of staff.

41.—(1) The articles of government for every county, controlled, special agreement and maintained special school shall provide—

(*a*) for it to be the duty of the local education authority to consult the governing body and the head teacher (except where he is the person concerned) before—

(i) dismissing (otherwise than under section 27(5) or 28(4) of the 1944 Act, which allow foundation governors to require the authority to dismiss a reserved teacher) any person to whom subsection (3) below applies ;

(ii) otherwise requiring any such person to cease to work at the school ; or

(iii) permitting any such person to retire in circumstances in which he would be entitled to compensation for premature retirement;

(*b*) for it to be the duty of the local education authority, where a teacher at the school is required to complete an initial period of probation, to consult the governing body and the head teacher before—

(i) extending his period of probation; or

(ii) deciding whether he has completed it successfully;

(*c*) for it to be the duty of the local education authority, where the governing body recommend to them that a person should cease to work at the school, to consider their recommendation;

(*d*) for both the governing body and the head teacher to have power to suspend any person employed to work at the school where, in the opinion of the governing body or (as the case may be) the head teacher, his exclusion from the school is required; and

(*e*) for it to be the duty of the governing body, or head teacher, when exercising that power—

(i) to inform the local education authority and the head teacher or (as the case may be) governing body forthwith; and

(ii) to end the suspension if directed to do so by the authority.

(2) In this section " suspend " means suspend without loss of emoluments.

(3) This subsection applies to any person who is employed—

(*a*) in a post which is part of the complement of the school in question; or

(*b*) to work solely at the school in any other post, otherwise than solely in connection with either or both of the following—

(i) the provision of meals;

(ii) the supervision of pupils at midday.

School premises

42. The articles of government for every county and maintained special school shall provide—

(*a*) for the use of the school premises at all times other than during any school session, or break between sessions on the same day, to be under the control of the governing body;

School premises.

    (*b*) for the governing body to exercise control subject to any direction given to them by the local education authority and in so doing to have regard to the desirability of the premises being made available (when not required by or in connection with the school) for use by members of the community served by the school.

Part IV
Miscellaneous

Freedom of
speech in
universities,
polytechnics
and colleges.

43.—(1) Every individual and body of persons concerned in the government of any establishment to which this section applies shall take such steps as are reasonably practicable to ensure that freedom of speech within the law is secured for members, students and employees of the establishment and for visiting speakers.

(2) The duty imposed by subsection (1) above includes (in particular) the duty to ensure, so far as is reasonably practicable, that the use of any premises of the establishment is not denied to any individual or body of persons on any ground connected with—

    (*a*) the beliefs or views of that individual or of any member of that body ; or

    (*b*) the policy or objectives of that body.

(3) The governing body of every such establishment shall, with a view to facilitating the discharge of the duty imposed by subsection (1) above in relation to that establishment, issue and keep up to date a code of practice setting out—

    (*a*) the procedures to be followed by members, students and employees of the establishment in connection with the organisation—

        (i) of meetings which are to be held on premises of the establishment and which fall within any class of meeting specified in the code ; and

        (ii) of other activities which are to take place on those premises and which fall within any class of activity so specified ; and

    (*b*) the conduct required of such persons in connection with any such meeting or activity ;

and dealing with such other matters as the governing body consider appropriate.

(4) Every individual and body of persons concerned in the government of any such establishment shall take such steps as are reasonably practicable (including where appropriate the initiation of disciplinary measures) to secure that the requirements of the code of practice for that establishment, issued under subsection (3) above, are complied with.

(5) The establishments to which this section applies are—

   (a) any university ;

   (b) any establishment which is maintained by a local education authority and for which section 1 of the 1968 (No. 2) Act (government and conduct of colleges of education and other institutions providing further education) requires there to be an instrument of government ; and

   (c) any establishment of further education designated by or under regulations made under section 27 of the 1980 Act as an establishment substantially dependent for its maintenance on assistance from local education authorities or on grants under section 100(1)(b) of the 1944 Act.

(6) In this section—

   " governing body ", in relation to any university, means the executive governing body which has responsibility for the management and administration of its revenue and property and the conduct of its affairs (that is to say the body commonly called the council of the university) ;

   " university " includes a university college and any college, or institution in the nature of a college, in a university.

(7) Where any establishment—

   (a) falls within subsection (5)(b) above ; or

   (b) falls within subsection (5)(c) above by virtue of being substantially dependent for its maintenance on assistance from local education authorities ;

the local education authority or authorities maintaining or (as the case may be) assisting the establishment shall, for the purposes of this section, be taken to be concerned in its government.

(8) Where a students' union occupies premises which are not premises of the establishment in connection with which the union is constituted, any reference in this section to the premises of the establishment shall be taken to include a reference to the premises occupied by the students' union.

44.—(1) The local education authority by whom any county, Political voluntary or special school is maintained, and the governing indoctrination. body and head teacher of the school shall forbid—

   (a) the pursuit of partisan political activities by any of those registered pupils at the school who are junior pupils ; and

PART IV

    (b) the promotion of partisan political views in the teaching of any subject in the school.

(2) In the case of activities which take place otherwise than on the premises of the school concerned, subsection (1)(a) above applies only where arrangements for junior pupils to take part in the activities are made by any member of the staff of the school (in his capacity as such) or by anyone acting on his, or the school's behalf.

Duty to secure balanced treatment of political issues.

45. The local education authority by whom any county, voluntary or special school is maintained, and the governing body and head teacher of the school, shall take such steps as are reasonably practicable to secure that where political issues are brought to the attention of pupils while they are—

    (a) at the school ; or

    (b) taking part in extra-curricular activities which are provided or organised for registered pupils at the school by or on behalf of the school ;

they are offered a balanced presentation of opposing views.

Sex education.

46. The local education authority by whom any county, voluntary or special school is maintained, and the governing body and head teacher of the school, shall take such steps as are reasonably practicable to secure that where sex education is given to any registered pupils at the school it is given in such a manner as to encourage those pupils to have due regard to moral considerations and the value of family life.

Abolition of corporal punishment.

47.—(1) Where, in any proceedings, it is shown that corporal punishment has been given to a pupil by or on the authority of a member of the staff, giving the punishment cannot be justified on the ground that it was done in pursuance of a right exercisable by the member of the staff by virtue of his position as such.

(2) Subject to subsection (3) below, references in this section to giving corporal punishment are references to doing anything for the purposes of punishing the pupil concerned (whether or not there are also other reasons for doing it) which, apart from any justification, would constitute battery.

(3) A person is not to be taken for the purposes of this section as giving corporal punishment by virtue of anything done for reasons that include averting an immediate danger of personal injury to, or an immediate danger to the property of, any person (including the pupil concerned).

(4) A person does not commit an offence by reason of any PART IV conduct relating to a pupil which would, apart from this section, be justified on the ground that it is done in pursuance of a right exercisable by a member of the staff by virtue of his position as such.

(5) In this section " pupil " means a person—

    (a) for whom education is provided—

        (i) at a school maintained by a local education authority ;

        (ii) at a special school not so maintained ; or

        (iii) at an independent school which is maintained or assisted by a Minister of the Crown (including a school of which a government department is the proprietor) or assisted by a local education authority and which falls within a prescribed class ;

    (b) for whom primary or secondary education, or education which would be primary or secondary education if it were provided full-time, is provided by a local education authority otherwise than at a school ; or

    (c) to whom subsection (6) below applies and for whom education is provided at an independent school which does not fall within paragraph (a)(iii) above ;

but does not include any person who is aged eighteen or over.

(6) This subsection applies to a person if—

    (a) he holds an assisted place under a scheme operated by the Secretary of State under section 17 of the 1980 Act ;

    (b) any of the fees or expenses payable in respect of his attendance at school are paid by the Secretary of State under section 100 of the 1944 Act or by a local education authority under section 6 of the Education (Mis- 1953 c. 33. cellaneous Provisions) Act 1953 ;

    (c) any of the fees payable in respect of his attendance at school are paid by a local education authority under section 81 of the 1944 Act ; or

    (d) he falls within a prescribed category of persons.

(7) The Secretary of State may prescribe, for the purposes of subsection (6)(d) above, one or more categories of persons who appear to him to be persons in respect of whom any fees are paid out of public funds.

(8) A person shall not be debarred from receiving education (whether by refusing him admission to a school, suspending his attendance or otherwise) by reason of the fact that this section applies in relation to him, or if he were admitted might so apply.

PART IV

(9) The power conferred on the Secretary of State by paragraph 4 of Schedule 4 to the 1980 Act to terminate a participation agreement under section 17 of that Act if he is not satisfied that appropriate educational standards are being maintained includes power to do so if he is not satisfied that subsection (8) above is being complied with.

(10) In this section " member of the staff " means—

(a) in relation to a person who is a pupil by reason of the provision of education for him at any school, any teacher who works at the school and any other person who has lawful control or charge of the pupil and works there ; and

(b) in relation to a person who is a pupil by reason of the provision of education for him by a local education authority at a place other than a school, any teacher employed by the authority who works at that place and any other person employed by the authority who has lawful control or charge of the pupil and works there.

1974 c. 28.

(11) An Order in Council under paragraph 1(1)(b) of Schedule 1 to the Northern Ireland Act 1974 (legislation for Northern Ireland in the interim period) which states that it is made only for the purposes corresponding to those of this section—

(a) shall not be subject to paragraph 1(4) and (5) of that Schedule (affirmative resolution of both Houses of Parliament) ; but

(b) shall be subject to annulment in pursuance of a resolution of either House.

Abolition of corporal punishment: Scotland.

48. After section 48 of the Education Act (Scotland) 1980, there shall be inserted the following new section—

" *Corporal Punishment*

1980 c. 44.

Abolition of corporal punishment of pupils.

48A.—(1) Where, in any proceedings, it is shown that corporal punishment has been given to a pupil by or on the authority of a member of the staff, giving the punishment cannot be justified on the ground that it was done in pursuance of a right exercisable by the member of the staff by virtue of his position as such.

(2) Subject to subsection (3) below, references in this section to giving corporal punishment are references to doing anything for the purposes of punishing the pupil concerned (whether or not there are also other reasons for doing it) which, apart from any justification, would constitute physical assault upon the person.

(3) A person is not to be taken for the purposes of this section as giving corporal punishment by virtue of anything done for reasons which include averting an immediate danger of personal injury to, or an immediate danger to the property of, any person (including the pupil concerned).

(4) A person does not commit an offence by reason of any conduct relating to a pupil which would, apart from this section, be justified on the ground that it was done in pursuance of a right exercisable by a member of the staff by virtue of his position as such.

(5) In this section ' pupil ' means a person—

   (*a*) for whom education is provided—

      (i) at a public school,

      (ii) at a grant-aided school, or

      (iii) at an independent school, maintained or assisted by a Minister of the Crown, which is a school prescribed by regulations made under this section or falls within a category of schools so prescribed.

   (*b*) for whom school education is provided by an education authority otherwise than at a school, or

   (*c*) to whom subsection (6) below applies and for whom education is provided at an independent school which does not fall within paragraph (*a*)(iii) above.

(6) This subsection applies to a person if—

   (*a*) he holds an assisted place under a scheme operated by the Secretary of State under section 75A of this Act.

   (*b*) any of the fees or expenses payable in respect of his attendance at school are paid by the Secretary of State under section 73(*f*) of this Act.

   (*c*) any of the fees payable in respect of his attendance at school are paid by an education authority under section 24(1)(*c*), 49 (2)(*b*), 50(1) or 64(3) of this Act, or

   (*d*) he falls within a category, prescribed by regulations made under this section, of persons appearing to the Secretary of State to be persons in respect of whom any fees are paid out of public funds.

(7) In this section ' member of the staff ' means—

    (a) in relation to a person who is a pupil by reason of the provision of education for him at any school, any teacher who works at the school and any other person who has lawful control or charge of the pupil and works there, and

    (b) in relation to a person who is a pupil by reason of the provision of school education for him by an education authority at a place other than a school, any teacher employed by the authority who works at that place and any other person employed by the authority who has lawful control or charge of the pupil and works there.

(8) The Secretary of State may, by order made by statutory instrument, prescribe—

    (a) schools or categories of school for the purposes of subsection (5)(a)(iii) above ; and

    (b) categories of persons for the purposes of subsection (6)(d) above.

(9) A person shall not be debarred from receiving education (whether by refusing him admission to, or excluding him from, a school or otherwise) by reason of the fact that this section applies in relation to him, or if he were admitted might so apply.

(10) The power conferred on the Secretary of State by paragraph 4 of Schedule 1A to this Act to revoke a determination under section 75A of this Act if he is not satisfied that appropriate educational standards are being maintained includes power to do so if he is not satisfied that subsection (9) above is being complied with.".

Appraisal of
performance
of teachers.

49.—(1) The Secretary of State may by regulations make provision requiring local education authorities, or such other persons as may be prescribed, to secure that the performance of teachers to whom the regulations apply—

    (a) in discharging their duties ; and

    (b) in engaging in other activities connected with the establishments at which they are employed ;

is regularly appraised in accordance with such requirements as may be prescribed.

(2) The regulations may, in particular, make provision—

(a) requiring the governing bodies of such categories of schools or other establishments as may be prescribed—

(i) to secure, so far as it is reasonably practicable for them to do so, that any arrangements made in accordance with the regulations are complied with in relation to their establishments ; and

(ii) to provide such assistance to the local education authority as the authority may reasonably require in connection with their obligations under the regulations ;

(b) with respect to the disclosure to teachers of the results of appraisals and the provision of opportunities for them to make representations with respect to those results ; and

(c) requiring local education authorities to have regard to the results of appraisals in the exercise of such of their functions as may be prescribed.

(3) The regulations may be expressed to apply to any of the following categories of teacher, that is to say teachers employed—

(a) at any school maintained by a local education authority ;

(b) at any special school (whether or not so maintained) ;

(c) at any further education establishment provided by a local education authority ;

(d) at any further education establishment designated by regulations made under section 27 of the 1980 Act as an establishment substantially dependent for its maintenance—

(i) on assistance from local education authorities ; or

(ii) on grants under section 100(1)(b) of the 1944 Act ;

(e) at any school or other establishment which falls within any prescribed class of school, or other establishment, of a kind mentioned in any of paragraphs (a) to (d) above ; or

(f) by a local education authority otherwise than at a school or further education establishment.

(4) Before making any regulations under subsection (1) above, the Secretary of State shall consult—

(a) such associations of local authorities, and representatives of teachers, as appear to him to be concerned ; and

(b) any other person with whom consultation appears to him to be desirable.

50.—(1) The Secretary of State may by regulations make provision for the payment by him to local education authorities and other persons of grants to facilitate and encourage the training of—

(a) teachers ;

(b) youth and community workers ;

(c) education welfare officers ;

(d) educational psychologists ;

(e) local education authority inspectors ;

(f) education advisers employed by such authorities ; and

(g) such other classes of person, employed in connection with the discharge of any of the functions of such authorities, as may be prescribed.

(2) For the purposes of this section " training " includes—

(a) further training, whether or not the person undergoing it is already qualified ;

(b) the provision of experience (whether or not within education) which is likely to benefit a person in his capacity as an employee of the kind in question ;

(c) training a person with a view to his continuing to be employed in education but in a different capacity ; and

(d) the study of matters connected with, or relevant to, education.

(3) Regulations under this section may, in particular—

(a) provide for grants to be payable only in respect of training approved by the Secretary of State for the purposes of the regulations ;

(b) make provision whereby the making of payments by the Secretary of State in pursuance of the regulations is dependent on the fulfilment of such conditions as may be prescribed or otherwise determined by the Secretary of State ; and

(c) make provision requiring local education authorities, and other persons, to whom payments have been made in pursuance of the regulations to comply with such requests as may be prescribed or so determined.

(4) In this section—

"education welfare officer" means any person who is employed by a local education authority, or employed by any other authority in connection with education, and whose duties include securing the regular attendance at school of pupils of compulsory school age ;

" leisure-time facilities " means facilities of a kind which local education authorities are under the duty imposed by sections 41(*b*) and 53(1) of the 1944 Act (provision of facilities for leisure-time occupation, recreation and social and physical training) to secure are provided within their areas ; and

" youth and community worker " means any person who is employed (whether or not by a local education authority) in such category of employment connected with leisure-time facilities as may be prescribed.

51.—(1) Subject to subsection (2) below, where any provision Recoupment. for primary, secondary or further education is made by a local education authority in respect of a pupil who belongs to the area of another such authority, the providing authority shall, on making a claim within the prescribed period, be entitled to be paid by the other authority—

    (*a*) such amount as the authorities may agree ; or

    (*b*) failing agreement, such amount as may be determined in accordance with a direction given by the Secretary of State under this subsection.

(2) Subsection (1) above does not apply to provision for—

    (*a*) primary education made (otherwise than in a hospital) in respect of a pupil who has not attained the age of five years ; or

    (*b*) further education made in respect of pupils who do not fall within a prescribed category ;

unless it is made with the consent of the authority from whom payment is claimed.

(3) Any direction under subsection (1) above may—

    (*a*) be a general direction applying to all cases to which it is expressed to apply or a direction applying to a particular case ;

    (*b*) be designed to provide for the amounts payable by one authority to another to reflect average costs incurred by local education authorities in the provision of education (whether in England and Wales as a whole or in any particular area or areas) ; and

    (*c*) be based on figures for average costs determined by such body or bodies representing local education authorities, or on such other figures relating to costs so incurred, as the Secretary of State considers appropriate.

PART IV

(4) A direction applying to a particular case may be given notwithstanding that a general direction would otherwise apply to that case.

(5) It shall not be a ground for refusing to admit a pupil to or excluding a pupil from, a further education establishment that he does not belong to the area of a local education authority maintaining or assisting that establishment (" a responsible authority ").

(6) Subsection (5) above does not apply—

(a) in relation to pupils who do not fall into a prescribed category ; or

(b) to any refusal to admit a pupil to a further education establishment where his admission would cause a pupil belonging to the area of a responsible authority to be refused admission to that establishment.

(7) References in this section to provision for education include references to provision of any benefits or services for which provision is made by or under the enactments relating to education.

1980 c. 65.

(8) References in subsections (1) to (6) above to further education do not include references to further education of a kind such that expenditure on its provision would fall within paragraph 6 of Schedule 10 to the Local Government Planning and Land Act 1980.

(9) A local education authority may make a payment to another such authority under subsection (1) above notwithstanding that no claim has been made by the other authority under that subsection.

(10) For the purposes of this section any question whether a pupil belongs, or does not belong, to the area of a particular local education authority shall be decided, as it would for the purposes of the 1980 Act, in accordance with section 38(5) of that Act and the regulations made under that section.

(11) Any dispute between local education authorities as to whether one of them is entitled to be paid any amount by another under this section shall be determined by the Secretary of State.

1963 c. 33.

(12) Section 31(8) of the London Government Act 1963 (obligations in relation to pupils from outside the area of local education authority) shall cease to have effect.

Recoupment: cross-border provisions.

52.—(1) The Secretary of State may make regulations requiring or authorising payments of amounts determined by or under the regulations to be made by one authority to another where—

    (*a*) the authority receiving the payment makes, in such cases or circumstances as may be specified in the regulations, provision for education in respect of a pupil having such connection with the area of the paying authority as may be so specified ; and

    (*b*) one of the authorities is a local education authority and the other an education authority in Scotland.

(2) The basis on which amounts payable under the regulations are to be determined shall be such as the Secretary of State sees fit to specify in the regulations and may, in particular, be similar to that adopted by him in relation to directions given under section 51(1) of this Act.

(3) Any question concerning the connection of any pupil with the area of a particular local education authority or education authority shall be decided in accordance with the provisions of the regulations.

(4) The reference in subsection (1) above to provision for education includes a reference to provision of any benefits or services for which provision is made by or under the enactments relating to education.

53. In section 55 of the 1944 Act (provision of transport and School other facilities), the following subsection shall be added at the transport. end—

    " (3) In considering whether or not they are required by subsection (1) above to make arrangements in relation to a particular pupil, the local education authority shall have regard (amongst other things) to the age of the pupil and the nature of the route, or alternative routes, which he could reasonably be expected to take."

54.—(1) On an application duly made to him by the govern- Change of ing body of any controlled school, the Secretary of State may status of by order direct that as from the date specified in the order controlled the school shall be an aided school. school to aided school.

(2) The Secretary of State shall not make an order under this section unless he is satisfied that the governing body will be able and willing—

    (*a*) with the assistance of any maintenance contribution payable by him under the 1944 Act, to defray the expenses which would fall to be borne by them under section 15(3)(*a*) of that Act ; and

(b) to pay to the local education authority any compensation payable by the governing body under section 55 of this Act.

(3) Where the governing body of a controlled school propose to apply for an order under this section they shall, after consulting the local education authority—

    (a) publish their proposals in such manner as may be required by regulations made by the Secretary of State;

    (b) submit a copy of the published proposals to him; and

    (c) provide him with such information as he may reasonably require in order to enable him to give proper consideration to the proposals.

(4) The published proposals shall be accompanied by a statement which explains the effect of subsection (5) below and specifies the date on which the proposals are intended to be implemented.

(5) Before the end of the period of two months beginning with the day on which the proposals are first published, any of the following may submit objections to the proposals to the Secretary of State—

    (a) any ten or more local government electors for the area;

    (b) the governing body of any voluntary school affected by the proposals;

    (c) any local education authority concerned.

(6) Where, in consequence of an order made under this section, an amount will be payable by a governing body by way of compensation under section 55 of this Act, the order—

    (a) shall specify the amount so payable and the date by which it must be paid; and

    (b) may impose such conditions in relation to its payment as the Secretary of State thinks fit.

(7) Where the Secretary of State proposes, in making an order under this section, to specify as the date from which the school is to be an aided school a different date to that proposed by the governing body, he shall first consult both that body and the local education authority as to the date which it would be appropriate to specify in the order.

(8) On the application of the local education authority or of the foundation governors of the school any such order may be varied, by order made by the Secretary of State, so as to specify—

(*a*) a different date to that specified under subsection (1) above ; or

(*b*) a different amount to that specified under subsection (6) above.

(9) Before applying to the Secretary of State under subsection (8) above for the variation of an order, the foundation governors of the school shall consult the other governors.

(10) Before making any variation under subsection (8) above the Secretary of State shall consult—

(*a*) the local education authority, in the case of an application for variation made by foundation governors ; and

(*b*) the foundation governors of the school, in the case of any application for variation made by the local education authority.

(11) Where foundation governors are consulted by the Secretary of State under subsection (10)(*b*) above, they shall, before giving him their views, consult the other governors of the school.

(12) Any order under this section may make such provision (including the modification of any provision made by or under this Act) as the Secretary of State considers appropriate in connection with the transition of the school in question from controlled to aided status and may, in particular, make provision—

(*a*) as to the circumstances in which, and purposes for which, the school is to be treated, before the specified date, as if it were an aided school ;

(*b*) as to the time by which the new instrument of government and articles of government (appropriate for an aided school) are to be made for the school and the consent and consultation which is to be required before they are made ;

(*c*) where the local education authority propose to pass a resolution (under section 9 of this Act) to group the school when it becomes an aided school, as to the consent required before that resolution is passed ;

(*d*) as to the appointment and dismissal of staff for the school ;

(*e*) as to the arrangements to be made in relation to the admission of pupils to the school ;

(*f*) for the governing body of the school to continue, for such purposes as may be specified in the order, to act as the governing body after the school has become an aided school but before a new governing body has been constituted ; and

(*g*) as to functions exercisable by, or in relation to, the

PART IV

governing body or the governors of any category so specified.

Compensation payable by governing body on change from controlled to aided status.

55.—(1) Where a controlled school becomes an aided school by virtue of an order made under section 54 of this Act, the governing body shall pay to the local education authority (in accordance with the order) such sum, by way of compensation for capital expenditure on the school—

(a) as may be agreed by that body and the authority; or

(b) failing such agreement, as the Secretary of State thinks fit having regard to the current value of the property in question.

(2) In subsection (1) above " capital expenditure " means any expenditure incurred by the local education authority, or by any predecessor of theirs, in respect of the school under—

1953 c. 33.

(a) section 2 of the Education (Miscellaneous Provisions) Act 1953 (power of Secretary of State, in certain circumstances, to require local education authority to defray expenses of establishing a controlled school);

1946 c. 50.

(b) section 1 of the Education Act 1946 (power of Secretary of State, in certain circumstances, to require expenses incurred in enlarging controlled school to be paid by local education authority); or

(c) paragraph 1 of Schedule 1 to the Act of 1946 (provision of buildings etc. for voluntary schools);

other than expenditure which could have been so incurred in respect of the school if it had always been an aided school.

(3) The Secretary of State may, for the purpose of assisting him in any determination which he is required to make under subsection (1) above, appoint such person as he thinks competent to advise him on the valuation of property.

(4) No contribution, grant or loan shall be paid, or other payment made, by the Secretary of State to the governing body of any controlled school in respect of any compensation payable by them under this section.

Reports to Secretary of State.

56. The governing body of every—

(a) county, voluntary and maintained special school; and

(b) establishment which is maintained by a local education authority and for which section 1 of the 1968 (No. 2) Act (government and conduct of colleges of education and other institutions providing further education) requires there to be an instrument of government;

shall make such reports and returns, and give such information,

to the Secretary of State as he may require for the purpose
of the exercise of his functions in relation to education.

57. Every local education authority shall secure—   Information
    (*a*) that every governor of a county, voluntary or special   and training
    school maintained by them is provided (free of charge)   for governors.
    with—
        (i) a copy of the instrument of government, and of
        the articles of government, for the school ; and
        (ii) such other information as they consider appro-
        priate in connection with the discharge of his func-
        tions as a governor ; and
    (*b*) that there is made available to every such governor
    (free of charge) such training as the authority consider
    necessary for the effective discharge of those func-
    tions.

58.—(1) A local education authority may, in accordance with   Travelling
the provisions of a scheme made by them for the purposes of   and subsistence
this section, pay travelling and subsistence allowances to gov-   allowances for
ernors of—   governors of
    schools and
    (*a*) county, voluntary and maintained special schools ; and   establishments
    (*b*) any establishment which is maintained by a local educa-   of further
    tion authority and for which section 1 of the 1968   education.
    (No. 2) Act (government and conduct of colleges of
    education and other institutions providing further edu-
    cation) requires there to be an instrument of govern-
    ment.

(2) Such a scheme may make different provision in relation to
schools or other establishments of different categories (including provision for allowances not to be paid in respect of certain
categories) but shall not make different provision in relation to
different categories of governor of the same school or
establishment.

(3) A local education authority shall not make any payment
towards the cost of travelling or subsistence allowances for any
governor of a designated establishment of further education if—
    (*a*) the authority have not made any scheme under subsec-
    tion (1) above ; or
    (*b*) the arrangements under which the allowance would
    otherwise be payable—
        (i) provide for allowances which are to any extent
        more generous than the most generous payable by
        the authority under any such scheme ; or

(ii) contain any provision which the authority would not have power to include in any such scheme.

(4) In this section " designated establishment of further education " means an establishment of further education designated by or under regulations made under section 27 of the 1980 Act as an establishment substantially dependent for its maintenance on assistance from local education authorities or on grants under section 100(1)(*b*) of the 1944 Act.

(5) Subject to subsection (6) below, a local education authority may pay travelling and subsistence allowances to persons appointed to represent them on the governing bodies of—

(*a*) establishments of further education which are not maintained or assisted by them ; or

(*b*) any independent school or special school which is not maintained by them.

(6) A local education authority shall not pay any allowance under subsection (5) above for expenses in respect of which the person incurring them is entitled to reimbursement by any person other than the authority or if—

(*a*) the authority have not made any scheme under subsection (1) above ; or

(*b*) the arrangements under which the allowance would otherwise be payable—

(i) provide for allowances which are to any extent more generous than the most generous payable by the authority under any such scheme ; or

(ii) contain any provision which the authority would not have power to include in any such scheme.

(7) No allowance may be paid to any governor of a school or establishment of a kind mentioned in subsection (1) above in respect of the discharge of his functions as such a governor, otherwise than under this section.

Repeal of section 4 of 1944 Act.   **59.** Section 4 of the 1944 Act (which makes provision in relation to the two central advisory councils for education) shall cease to have effect.

Discontinuance of Secretary of State's duty to make annual reports.   **60.**—(1) Section 5 of the 1944 Act (which requires the Secretary of State to make an annual report to Parliament) shall cease to have effect.

(2) The Secretary of State's report under that section for the year 1985 shall be the last such report that he is required to make.

61.—(1) No person shall be qualified for membership of the governing body of any institution—

    (*a*) which is maintained by a local education authority ; and

    (*b*) for which section 1 of the 1968 (No. 2) Act (government and conduct of colleges of education and other institutions providing further education) requires there to be an instrument of government ;

unless he is a student of the institution or is aged eighteen or over at the date of his election or appointment.

(2) The Secretary of State may by regulations make provision restricting—

    (*a*) in relation to such matters or classes of matter as may be prescribed ;

    (*b*) in such circumstances as may be prescribed ; and

    (*c*) to such extent as may be prescribed ;

the participation of any student of such an institution who is a member of its governing body in the proceedings of that body.

(3) The instrument of government for any such institution may make such provision in relation to restricting the participation of any such student in the proceedings of its governing body (in addition to that made by the regulations) as the regulations may authorise.

62.—(1) The Secretary of State may make regulations requiring the governing body—

    (*a*) of every county, voluntary and maintained special school ; and

    (*b*) of every institution of a kind mentioned in section 61 of this Act ;

to make available, to such persons or classes of person as may be prescribed, such documents and information relating to the meetings and proceedings of the governing body as may be prescribed.

Access to papers etc. of governing bodies.

(2) Documents and information required by the regulations to be made available shall be made available in such form and manner, and at such times, as may be prescribed.

PART V

SUPPLEMENTAL

63.—(1) Any power of the Secretary of State to make orders or regulations under this Act (other than under section 2(7), 9(6) or 54) shall be exercised by statutory instrument.

Orders and regulations.

(2) Any such statutory instrument (other than one made under section 66, shall be subject to annulment in pursuance of a resolution of either House of Parliament.

(3) Regulations and orders under this Act may make different provision for different cases or different circumstances and may contain such incidental, supplemental or transitional provisions as the Secretary of State thinks fit.

(4) Without prejudice to subsection (3) above, regulations under this Act may make in relation to Wales provision different from that made in relation to England.

Expenses.

64. There shall be defrayed out of money provided by Parliament—

    (*a*) any expenses incurred by the Secretary of State under this Act ; and

    (*b*) any increase attributable to this Act in the sums payable out of such money under any other Act.

Interpretation.

65.—(1) In this Act—

1944 c. 31.   " the 1944 Act " means the Education Act 1944 ;

1968 c. 37.   " the 1968 (No. 2) Act " means the Education (No. 2) Act 1968 ;

1980 c. 20.   " the 1980 Act " means the Education Act 1980 ;

1981 c. 60.   " the 1981 Act " means the Education Act 1981 ;

    " boarder " includes a pupil who boards during the week but not at weekends ;

    " co-opted governor ", in relation to any school, means a person who is appointed to be a member of the governing body of the school by being co-opted by those governors of the school who have not themselves been so appointed but does not include a governor appointed in accordance with any provision made by virtue of section 5 of this Act ;

    " exclude ", in relation to the exclusion of any pupil from a school, means exclude on disciplinary grounds ;

    " head teacher ", except where provision to the contrary is made, includes an acting head teacher ;

    " maintained special school " means a special school which is maintained by a local education authority ;

    " parent governor ", in relation to any school, means (subject to section 5 of and Schedule 1 to this Act) a person who is elected as a member of the governing body of the school by parents of registered pupils at the school and who is himself such a parent at the time when he is elected ;

" promoters ", in relation to any intended new school, or school which it is proposed should be maintained by a local education authority, means the persons who intend to establish the school or (as the case may be) who established the school which it is proposed should be so maintained, or their representatives ;

" school day ", in relation to any school, means any day on which at that school there is a school session ; and

" teacher governor ", in relation to any school, means (subject to Schedule 1 to this Act) a person who is elected as a member of the governing body of the school by teachers at the school and who is himself such a teacher at the time when he is elected.

(2) Except where otherwise provided, in this Act " governing body " and " governor " do not include a temporary governing body or any member of such a body.

66.—(1) Sections 60 and 63 to 65, this section and section 67(1) to (3) and (7) of this Act shall come into force on the passing of this Act.

Commence-ment.

(2) Section 49 and 59 of this Act shall come into force at the end of the period of two months beginning with the day on which this Act is passed.

(3) The other provisions shall come into force on such date as the Secretary of State may by order appoint.

(4) Different dates may be appointed for different provisions or different purposes including, in particular, for the purpose of bringing particular provisions into force only in relation to particular schools or categories of school.

(5) Any order under this section may make such transitional provision as appears to the Secretary of State to be necessary or expedient in connection with the provisions brought into force by the order.

(6) Any such order may include such adaptations of the provisions which it brings into force, or of any other provisions of this Act then in force, as appear to him to be necessary or expedient for the purpose or in consequence of the operation of any provision of this Act (including, in particular, the provisions which the order brings into force) before the coming into force of any other provision.

67.—(1) This Act may be cited as the Education (No. 2) Act 1986.

Short title etc.

(2) This Act and the Education Acts 1944 to 1985 and the Education Act 1986 may be cited as the Education Acts 1944 to 1986.

(3) This Act shall be construed as one with the 1944 Act.

(4) Schedule 4 to this Act (which makes consequential amendments) shall have effect.

(5) This Act shall have effect subject to the transitional provisions set out in Schedule 5 to this Act.

(6) The enactments and instruments mentioned in Schedule 6 to this Act are hereby repealed or (as the case may be) revoked to the extent specified in the third column of that Schedule.

(7) In this Act—

   (*a*) sections 48, 52, 63(1) to (3) and 66(3) to (6), this section and so much of Schedule 6 as relates to any enactment which extends to Scotland, extend to Scotland; and

   (*b*) section 47(11) and this section extend to Northern Ireland;

but otherwise this Act extends only to England and Wales.

SCHEDULES

SCHEDULE 1

GROUPED SCHOOLS

General

1.—(1) In this Schedule—

"group" means two or more schools grouped under section 9 of this Act ; and

"grouped school" means a school which forms part of a group.

(2) Any reference in any enactment to the governing body or governors of a school shall be construed, in relation to any grouped school, as a reference to the governing body or governors of the group.

Procedure in relation to making etc. of instrument of government

2.—(1) Before making an order under section 1 of this Act embodying the first instrument of government for any group ; the local education authority shall consult the governing body and head teacher of each school within the group and, where the group contains one or more voluntary schools, shall—

(*a*) secure the agreement of the governing body of each such school to the terms of the proposed order ;

(*b*) secure the agreement of the foundation governors of each such school to any provisions which will be of particular concern to the foundation governors of the group ; and

(*c*) have regard to the way in which those schools have been conducted.

(2) Where such an order has been made, subsections (1) to (6) of section 2 of this Act shall apply in relation to any subsequent order embodying or varying the instrument of government for the group, or any proposal for the making of such an order—

(*a*) as if, in the case of a group which contains one or more voluntary schools, it were a single voluntary school ; and

(*b*) as if, in any other case, it were a single county school.

(3) For the purposes of subsection (5) of section 2, any agreement required by sub-paragraph (1) above shall be deemed to have been required by subsection (2) of that section.

Election of parent and teacher governors

3. The instrument of government for any group—

(*a*) may provide for the local education authority to have power to determine, in relation to every election of parent or teacher governors, the school or schools within the group the parents of registered pupils at which, or (as the case may be) the teachers at which, are to be entitled to stand and vote at the election ; and

M 3

(*b*) shall, where it does so, provide for it to be the duty of the
authority to ensure that the position after any such election
will be that there is no school within the group which will
not have had an opportunity to have so participated in the
election of at least one of the parent or (as the case may
be) teacher governors of the group.

Governors' annual report to parents

4.—(1) In discharging their duty to prepare governors' reports ;
the governing body for a group shall prepare separate reports in
relation to each of the schools within the group unless they decide
to hold a joint annual parents' meeting, under paragraph 5 below.

(2) Where the governing body for a group prepare a single report
covering all schools within the group, it shall be their duty to secure
that any matters which they propose to report on and which are likely
to be mainly of interest to the parents of registered pupils at a
particular school within the group are treated separately in the report.

Annual parents' meeting

5.—(1) In discharging their duty to hold an annual parents' meeting for any grouped school the governing body for the group may,
if they think fit, hold a joint meeting for all of the schools within
the group.

(2) Where—

(*a*) a joint meeting is held ; and

(*b*) the governing body have prepared separate governors' reports in relation to each of the schools within the group ;

the governing body shall, when discharging the duty imposed on
them by virtue of section 30(4) of this Act, attach to the report
prepared in relation to any one school in the group copies of the
reports prepared for each of the other schools within the group.

(3) Where at any joint meeting the question is put on any proposed
resolution which concerns one or more, but not all, of the schools
within the group—

(*a*) only parents of registered pupils at the school or schools
which the proposed resolution concerns may vote on the
question ; and

(*b*) the registered pupils at the other schools shall be disregarded for the purposes of section 31(4)(*b*) of this Act as it
applies in relation to the proposed resolution.

(4) Where at any joint meeting there is any disagreement as to
which schools within the group a proposed resolution concerns, the
matter shall be decided by the chairman of the governing body.

SCHEDULE 2

NEW SCHOOLS

PART I

GENERAL

1. In this Schedule—

"arrangement" means (except in paragraph 2(2)(*b*) or 19) an arrangement made under section 12 of this Act for the constitution of a temporary governing body for a new school ;

"new school" means any school, or proposed school, which is required to have a temporary governing body or in respect of which the local education authority have power to make an arrangement under section 12(4) ;

"relevant proposal" means the proposal (of a kind mentioned in section 12) by reference to which the school in question is a new school ; and

"temporary governor" means any member of a temporary governing body.

Constitution of temporary governing body

2.—(1) Subject to the provisions of this Schedule, every temporary governing body shall be constituted—

(*a*) in accordance with the provisions of sections 3 and 7 of this Act, in the case of a school whose governing body will be required to be constituted in accordance with those provisions; and

(*b*) in accordance with the provisions of section 4 of this Act, in the case of a school whose governing body will be required to be constituted in accordance with those provisions.

(2) For the purpose of the application of section 3, 4 or 7 of this Act in relation to the constitution of its temporary governing body, a new school shall be treated as having as registered pupils the maximum number of pupils referred to—

(*a*) in the relevant proposal ; or

(*b*) in the case of a new school which will be a special school; in the arrangements for the school approved by the Secretary of State in accordance with regulations made under section 12 of the 1981 Act (approval of special schools).

(3) In co-opting any person (otherwise than as a temporary foundation or teacher governor) to be a member of a temporary governing body of a new school which will be a county, controlled or maintained special school, the temporary governors concerned shall—

(*a*) have regard—

(i) to the extent to which they and the other temporary

governors are members of the local business community ; and

(ii) to any representations made to the temporary governing body as to the desirability of increasing the connection between the temporary governing body and that community ; and

(b) where it appears to them that no temporary governor of the new school is a member of the local business community, or that it is desirable to increase the number of temporary governors who are, co-opt a person who appears to them to be a member of that community.

(4) The first meeting of any temporary governing body shall be called—

(a) by their clerk ; or

(b) where he fails to call it within such period as the local education authority consider reasonable, by the authority.

PART II

SCHOOL GOVERNMENT

Transition from temporary governing body to governing body

3.—(1) The requirement for there to be an instrument of government for a school to which section 1 of this Act applies shall take effect in relation to a new school from the date on which the relevant proposal is implemented.

(2) When that requirement takes effect, paragraph 2(2) above shall apply in relation to the governing body of the school as it applied in relation to its temporary governing body and shall continue to apply, for the purposes of determining (at any time after the governing body is first constituted) what provision would be required to be made by a new instrument of government for the school, until such time as—

(a) the number of registered pupils at the school reaches the maximum referred to in paragraph 2(2) ; or

(b) the local education authority exercise the power conferred on them by virtue of sub-paragraph (3) below.

(3) The instrument of government for every school to which paragraph 2(2) above applies at the time when it is made shall provide for the local education authority to have power to direct that that paragraph shall cease to apply in relation to the school.

(4) The local education authority shall secure that the governing body of any new school is constituted—

(a) as soon as is reasonably practicable after the requirement for there to be an instrument of government for the school takes effect ; and

(b) in any event not later than the last day of the term in which pupils first attend the new school or (as the case may be) first attend the school after it becomes a maintained school.

(5) Where the requirement for there to be an instrument of government for a new school has taken effect, the temporary governing body of the school shall, until such time as the governing body is constituted—

> (*a*) continue in existence (notwithstanding that the arrangement under which they were constituted has come to an end by virtue of paragraph 5 below) ; and
>
> (*b*) be treated as if they were the governing body.

(6) Where a new school is grouped under section 9 of this Act, with effect from the time when an instrument of government is required for the school, any consent given by, or consultation with, the temporary governing body shall be treated for the purposes of section 10(5) and (6) of this Act as having been given by, or (as the case may be) held with, the governing body.

(7) Where any question arises as to the date which is to be taken to be the implementation date of any such proposal for the purposes of this paragraph, it shall be determined by the Secretary of State.

4.—(1) Before making any order under section 1 of this Act in respect of a new school, the local education authority shall consult the temporary governing body and head teacher.

(2) Before making any such order in respect of a new school which will be a voluntary school, the authority shall—

> (*a*) secure the agreement of the temporary governing body to the terms of the proposed order ; and
>
> (*b*) if it embodies or varies an instrument of government, secure the agreement of the temporary foundation governors to any provisions which are of particular concern to those governors.

(3) Where a local education authority propose to make any such order in respect of a new school but cannot secure any agreement required by this paragraph, they or (as the case may be) the temporary governing body or temporary foundation governors may refer the matter to the Secretary of State.

(4) On any reference to him under this paragraph the Secretary of State shall give such direction as he thinks fit.

Duration of arrangement for temporary governing body

5.—(1) Every arrangement shall (if it has not been brought to an end under sub-paragraph (2) below) come to an end when the requirement for there to be an instrument of government for the new school first has effect.

(2) Where an arrangement has been made by virtue of section 12(3) or (4) of this Act and

> (*a*) the proposal in question is withdrawn ;
>
> (*b*) the Secretary of State has decided not to approve that proposal or (as the case may be) not to approve the school as a special school ; or

(*c*) the local education authority have, under section 12(7) of
the 1980 Act, determined not to implement that proposal;
the occurrence of that event shall bring the arrangement to an end.

Composition of temporary governing body

6.—(1) No local education authority shall make an arrangement in
respect of a new school which will be a controlled school without
the agreement of the promoters as to the provision which will be
made in relation to the temporary foundation governors; and in the
event of any disagreement between the authority and the promoters
in respect of that provision, either of them may refer the matter
to the Secretary of State.

(2) No local education authority shall make an arrangement in
respect of a new school which will be an aided school without the
agreement of the promoters as to the composition of the temporary
governing body; and in the event of any disagreement between the
authority and the promoters as to the composition of that body,
either of them may refer the matter to the Secretary of State.

(3) On any reference under this paragraph, the Secretary of State
shall give such direction as he thinks fit.

Appointment of temporary parent and teacher governors

7.—(1) The temporary parent governors for a new school shall,
subject to sub-paragraph (2) below, be appointed—

   (*a*) where the school will be a county, controlled or maintained
special school, by the local education authority; and

   (*b*) where it will be an aided school, by the promoters.

(2) Where—

   (*a*) two or more schools have been, or are to be, discontinued (" the discontinued schools "); and

   (*b*) the registered pupils at those schools, or a substantial number
of those pupils, are expected to transfer to a new school;

the local education authority may (subject to sub-paragraph (3)
below) provide for any of the governing bodies of the discontinued
schools to appoint some or all of the temporary parent or teacher
governors of the new school.

(3) No provision may be made under sub-paragraph (2) above
for the appointment of temporary parent or teacher governors of a
new school which will be an aided school without the agreement of
the promoters; and in the event of any disagreement between the
authority and the promoters as to whether any such provision
should be made, either of them may refer the matter to the Secretary
of State.

(4) On any reference under sub-paragraph (3) above, the Secretary of State shall give such direction as he thinks fit.

(5) Before making any provision under sub-paragraph (2) above
for the appointment of temporary parent or teacher governors of a

new school which will be a controlled school, the local education
authority shall consult the promoters.

(6) No person shall be appointed under sub-paragraph (1) or (2) above as a temporary parent governor of a new school unless—

(a) he is the parent of a child who is likely to become a registered pupil at the school ; or

(b) where it is not reasonably practicable to appoint such a person, he is the parent of a child of compulsory school age.

(7) No person shall be appointed under sub-paragraph (1) as a temporary parent governor of a new school if he is—

(a) an elected member of the authority ;

(b) an employee of the authority or of the governing body of any aided school maintained by the authority ; or

(c) a co-opted member of any education committee of the authority.

Temporary teacher governors

8.—(1) Subject to paragraph 7(2) above, the temporary teacher governors of a new school shall be co-opted by a resolution passed at a meeting of those temporary governors who have not themselves been co-opted.

(2) No person shall be appointed as a temporary teacher governor of a new school unless he is employed as a teacher in a school maintained by a local education authority.

Duty to appoint suitably experienced members

9.—(1) Any person appointing a person as a temporary governor of a new school shall have regard to the desirability of that person being suitably experienced.

(2) For the purposes of this paragraph, a person is suitably experienced if he has served as a governor or temporary governor of a school and, in particular (in a case where registered pupils at another school which has been, or is to be, discontinued are expected to transfer to the new school), if he has served as a governor or temporary governor of that other school.

Proceedings etc.

10.—(1) The proceedings of a temporary governing body shall not be invalidated by—

(a) any vacancy among their number ; or

(b) any defect in the appointment of any temporary governor.

(2) Any member of a temporary governing body may at any time resign his office, or be removed from office, in the same way as a member of a governing body constituted under an instrument of government.

(3) The minutes of the proceedings of any temporary governing body shall be open to inspection by the local education authority.

(4) The Secretary of State may by regulations make similar provision in relation to temporary governing bodies and their members as may be made in relation to governing bodies and their members under section 8 of this Act.

Miscellaneous

11.—(1) The qualification of any person for appointment as a temporary governor, of a particular category, of any new school shall not have the effect of disqualifying him for appointment as a temporary governor, of any other category, of that school.

(2) No person shall at any time hold more than one temporary governorship of the same school.

(3) Where any temporary governor is to be appointed by persons acting jointly, the appointment shall be made, in the event of failure on the part of those persons to make an agreed appointment—

(a) by the Secretary of State ; or

(b) in accordance with any direction given by him.

(4) Subject to paragraph 2(3) above, where temporary governors are required to co-opt one or more persons to be temporary governors, the arrangement under which the temporary governing body are constituted shall not make any provision which has the effect of restricting those governors in their choice of person to co-opt.

(5) Sub-paragraph (4) above does not apply in relation to foundation governors.

(6) No person shall be qualified for membership of any temporary governing body unless he is aged eighteen or over at the date of his appointment.

PART III

ORGANISATION AND FUNCTIONS

General

12.—(1) The requirement for there to be articles of government for certain schools, which is imposed by section 1 of this Act, shall not apply in relation to a new school until such time as it is required to have an instrument of government (in accordance with section 1 as read with paragraph 3 of this Schedule).

(2) The determination of those matters relating to the conduct of any new school which require to be determined before a governing body is constituted for the school under an instrument of government shall be under the direction of the temporary governing body, but subject to any provision made by or under this Act (including, in particular, this Schedule) or any other enactment.

(3) The Secretary of State may by regulations make similar provision in relation to consultation with temporary governing bodies as he has power to make in relation to consultation with governing bodies under section 16(2) of this Act.

Reports and information to be provided by temporary governing body

13.—(1) Every temporary governing body shall furnish to the local education authority such reports in connection with the discharge of their functions as the authority may require (either on a regular basis or from time to time).

(2) Every temporary governing body shall make such reports and returns, and give such information, to the Secretary of State as he may require for the purpose of the exercise of his functions in relation to education.

(3) Every temporary governing body shall prepare—

    (a) immediately before the arrangement under which they are constituted comes to an end ; and

    (b) for the purpose of assisting the governing body who will succeed them ;

a brief report of the action which they have taken in the discharge of their functions ; and shall recommend (with reasons) persons who belong to the community served by the new school and who are, in the opinion of the temporary governing body, suitable for appointment as co-opted members of the governing body.

(4) Before making any recommendations under sub-paragraph (3) above, a temporary governing body shall consult representatives of the local business community.

(5) All minutes and papers of any temporary governing body, including the report prepared under sub-paragraph (3) above, shall be made available to their successors.

Head teacher's reports

14.—(1) The head teacher of any new school for which a temporary governing body have been constituted shall furnish that body, or (as the case may be) the local education authority, with such reports in connection with the discharge of his functions as that body or authority may require (either on a regular basis or from time to time).

(2) Where, under sub-paragraph (1) above, any requirement is imposed by a local education authority on the head teacher of a new school which will be an aided school, the authority shall notify the temporary governing body of that requirement ; and the head teacher of any such school shall furnish that body with a copy of any report which he makes in complying with any such requirement.

Preparation of curriculum

15.—(1) The head teacher of any new school for which a temporary governing body have been constituted shall, in preparing to discharge his functions in relation to the curriculum for the school, consult that body and the local education authority.

(2) Any authority who have been consulted under this paragraph shall inform the head teacher of the resources which are likely to be made available to the school ; and the head teacher shall have regard to any information so given to him.

School terms etc.

16. Pending the coming into force of the articles of government for a new school, the times at which the school session is to begin and end on any day and the dates and times at which the school terms and holidays are to begin and end shall be determined—

(*a*) by the temporary governing body, in the case of a school which will be an aided school ; and

(*b*) by the local education authority, in any other case.

Discipline

17. Pending the coming into force of the articles of government for a new school which will be a county, voluntary or maintained special school, the head teacher and the temporary governing body shall be under the same duties as will be required to be imposed on him and the governing body by virtue of section 22(*a*) to (*e*) of this Act.

Finance

18. Where a temporary governing body have been constituted for any new school, the local education authority shall consult that body and the head teacher on their proposed expenditure on books, equipment and stationery for the school.

Admission of pupils

19.—(1) The initial arrangements for the admission of pupils to a new school shall be made—

(*a*) where the school will be a county or controlled school, by the local education authority ; and

(*b*) where it will be an aided school, by the temporary governing body or, where that body have not been constituted and the promoters consider that it is expedient for the arrangements to be determined without delay, by the promoters.

(2) Any person making any initial arrangements under this paragraph shall have regard to the arrangements in force for the admission of pupils to comparable schools in the area of the local education authority.

(3) Before making any such initial arrangements for a new school which will be a county school, the authority shall consult the temporary governing body unless—

(*a*) that body have not been constituted ; and

(*b*) the authority consider that it is expedient for the initial arrangements to be determined without delay.

(4) Before making any such initial arrangements for a new school which will be a controlled school, the authority shall consult—

    (*a*) the temporary governing body ; or

    (*b*) where that body have not been constituted, the promoters.

(5) Before making any such initial arrangements for a new school which will be an aided school, the temporary governing body or (as the case may be) the promoters shall consult the authority.

(6) Sections 6 to 8 of the 1980 Act (admission to schools) shall have effect, in relation to any new school, as if the references to governors included references to the person responsible for the admission of pupils under the initial arrangements for that school.

Appointment of staff etc. at new aided schools

20.—(1) For the purposes of the appointment and dismissal of staff at any new school which will be an aided school, the local education authority and the temporary governing body shall (subject to sub-paragraph (2) below) have the same powers, and be under the same duties, as would the authority and the governing body for an aided school whose articles of government provided for—

    (*a*) staff employed solely in connection with the provision of school meals to be appointed by the authority ; and

    (*b*) other staff employed at the school to be appointed by the governing body.

(2) The first appointment of a clerk to the temporary governing body of any such school shall be made by the promoters.

(3) Where the arrangement for the constitution of a temporary governing body of any such school comes to an end, the person who was the clerk to that body shall act as clerk to the governing body who succeed them, pending the appointment of their clerk.

(4) The authority shall, with a view to enabling staff to be appointed in good time, notify the temporary governing body of every such school of the steps (if any) which they intend to take in respect of the school under sections 22(4) and 24(2) of the 1944 Act (powers of authority in relation to certain staff).

(5) Paragraphs 21 to 25 and 26 (1) and (2) below shall not apply in relation to any such school.

Determination of staff complement

21.—(1) Where a temporary governing body have been constituted for a new school, the complement of teaching and non-teaching posts for the school shall be determined by the local education authority.

(2) Section 34(2) and (3) of this Act shall apply in relation to any complement determined under this paragraph.

The selection panel

22.—(1) Whenever a selection panel is required by virtue of paragraph 23 or 25 below, it shall be constituted in accordance with this paragraph.

(2) A selection panel shall consist of such number of persons appointed to it by the local education authority, and such number of temporary governors appointed to it by the temporary governing body, as the authority shall determine.

(3) The number so determined shall—

(*a*) in each case, be not less than three ; and

(*b*) in relation to appointments made by the temporary governing body, be not less than the number determined in relation to appointments made by the authority.

(4) The temporary governing body and the authority shall have power to replace, at any time, any member of a selection panel whom they have appointed.

(5) The Secretary of State may by regulations make provision, for the purposes of this paragraph, as to the meetings and proceedings of selection panels.

Appointment of head teacher and acting head teacher

23.—(1) Subject to sub-paragraphs (2) and (3) below, the same provision shall apply in relation to the appointment of a head teacher for a new school for which a temporary governing body have been constituted as is required to be made in relation to the appointment of a head teacher by the articles of government of a school to which section 37 of this Act applies.

(2) Where—

(*a*) two or more schools are to be discontinued (" the discontinued schools ") ; and

(*b*) the registered pupils at those schools, or a substantial number of those pupils, are expected to transfer to a new school ;

the local education authority may, in consultation with the temporary governing body, appoint one of the head teachers of the discontinued schools as the first head teacher for the new school, instead of following the procedure mentioned in sub-paragraph (1) above.

(3) In the event of the post of head teacher for the new school being vacant, the authority may, if they think fit, appoint an acting head teacher after consulting the temporary governing body.

Appointment of certain other staff

24.—(1) Subject to sub-paragraph (3) below, the same provision shall apply in relation to the appointment of any person to a post which is part of the complement of a new school for which a temporary governing body have been constituted as is required to be made in relation to the appointment of any person to such a post by the articles of government of a school to which section 38 of this Act applies.

(2) The local education authority shall consult the temporary
governing body and the head teacher before appointing any person
to work solely at the school otherwise than—

    (*a*) in a teaching post ;

    (*b*) in a non-teaching post which is part of the complement of
        the school ; or

    (*c*) solely in connection with either or both of the following—

          (i) the provision of meals ;

          (ii) the supervision of pupils at midday.

(3) This paragraph does not apply in relation to the appointment
of a head teacher or deputy head teacher or to any temporary appointment pending—

    (*a*) the return to work of the holder of the post in question ; or

    (*b*) the taking of any steps required by this Schedule in relation
        to the vacancy in question.

Appointment of deputy head teacher

25. Where a temporary governing body have been constituted for
a new school, the provision which is to apply in relation to the
appointment of a deputy head teacher of the school shall be—

    (*a*) the same as that which may be made in the articles of
        government of a school to which section 39 of this Act
        applies by virtue of subsection (1)(*a*) of that section ; or

    (*b*) where the local education authority so decide, the same as
        that which may be made in the articles of government of
        such a school by virtue of subsection (1)(*b*) of section 39.

Appointment of clerk to temporary governing body

26.—(1) Where a temporary governing body have been constituted
for a new school, the clerk to the temporary governing body shall
be appointed by the local education authority.

(2) Where the arrangement for the constitution of a temporary
governing body of any new school comes to an end, the person who
was the clerk to that body shall act as clerk to the governing body
who succeed them, pending the appointment of a clerk under section
40 of this Act.

(3) Where the clerk to a temporary governing body fails to attend
any meeting of theirs, they may appoint one of their number to act
as clerk for the purposes of that meeting, but without prejudice to
his position as a temporary governor.

Part IV

Miscellaneous

Travelling and subsistence allowances etc.

27. Section 58 of this Act shall apply in relation to the members
of temporary governing bodies as it applies in relation to the
members of governing bodies of county, voluntary and maintained
special schools.

Expenses of temporary governing bodies, etc.

28. Where a temporary governing body are constituted for a new school, the local education authority shall be under the same duty to defray the expenses incurred in relation to the temporary governing body, and the staff appointed in accordance with the provisions of this Schedule, as they would be if the relevant proposal had been implemented and the temporary governing body were the governing body of the school.

Powers of Secretary of State

29. For the purposes of the following provisions of the 1944 Act—
    (a) section 67(1) (determination of disputes) ;
    (b) section 68 (prevention of unreasonable exercise of functions) ; and
    (c) section 99(1) and (2) (default) ;
a temporary governing body shall be treated as if they were the governing body of the school in question.

Provision of information for temporary governing bodies

30.—(1) Every local education authority shall secure that the temporary governing body of each of the new schools which will be maintained by them are, on being constituted, provided (free of charge) with such explanatory and other information as the authority consider is required to enable that body to discharge their functions effectively.

(2) Where a new school will be a county, controlled or maintained special school, the authority shall, in discharging their duty under sub-paragraph (1) above, inform the temporary governing body, in particular—
    (a) of the number of members of any selection panel required by virtue of paragraph 23 or 25 above who are to be appointed by the authority and the number who are to be appointed by the temporary governing body ;
    (b) where the authority intend to exercise the power conferred on them by paragraph 23(2) above, of their intention to do so ;
    (c) of the provision which is to apply in relation to the appointment of the deputy head teacher of the school ;
    (d) of the complement of staff for the school ; and
    (e) of the authority's proposals with regard to the appointment of staff for the school and the timing of appointments.

(3) Where a new school will be an aided school, the authority shall, in discharging their duty under sub-paragraph (1) above, inform the temporary governing body, in particular, of their proposals with regard to the appointment of staff for the school and the timing of appointments.

SCHEDULE 3

EXCLUSION ON DISCIPLINE GROUNDS: APPEALS

General

1. The articles of government for every county, controlled and maintained special school shall provide for it to be the duty of the local education authority, when (following the consideration which they are required to give to the case by virtue of section 24(*a*) of this Act) they inform a pupil, or a parent of his, of their decision that he should not be reinstated, to inform the pupil or (as the case may be) parent of his right to appeal against the decision.

2. The articles of government for every aided and special agreement school shall provide for it to be the duty of the governing body, when (following the consideration which they are required to give to the case by virtue of section 25(*a*) of this Act) they inform a pupil, or a parent of his, of their decision that he should not be reinstated, to inform the pupil or (as the case may be) parent of his right to appeal against the decision.

3.—(1) Where, in accordance with any provision of the articles of government of any school made by virtue of section 24(*a*) of this Act, the local education authority give a direction to the head teacher of the school for the reinstatement of any pupil who has been excluded, the direction shall not have effect for a period of seven days beginning with the day on which the governing body are informed of the direction by the authority unless, within that period, the governing body inform the authority that they do not intend to appeal against the direction.

(2) Where, before the end of that period, the governing body lodge an appeal against the direction in accordance with the relevant arrangements—

(*a*) the local education authority shall inform the pupil (if he is aged eighteen or over) or his parent (if he is under eighteen) of his right to make representations to the appeal committee ; and

(*b*) the direction shall not have effect unless it is confirmed by the appeal committee or the appeal is withdrawn.

(3) No appeal against such a direction may be made by the governing body after the direction has taken effect.

4. Part I of Schedule 2 of the 1980 Act (constitution of appeal committees) shall have effect in relation to appeals with the necessary modifications.

5. The Secretary of State may by order amend this Schedule.

Procedure

6. An appeal shall be by notice in writing setting out the grounds on which it is made.

SCH. 3   7. On an appeal by a pupil or parent, the appeal committee—

(a) shall afford the appellant an opportunity of appearing and making oral representations ;

(b) may allow him to be accompanied by a friend or to be represented ; and

(c) shall allow—

(i) the local eduction authority and the governing body to make written representations to the committee ; or

(ii) an officer of the authority nominated by the authority, and a governor nominated by the governing body, to appear and make oral representations.

8. On an appeal by a governing body, the appeal committee—

(a) shall afford a governor nominated by the governing body an opportunity of appearing and making oral representations ;

(b) shall afford the governing body an opportunity to be represented ;

(c) shall allow the pupil, if he is aged eighteen or over, or a parent of his, if he is under eighteen, to make written representations to the committee or to appear and make oral representations ; and

(d) shall allow the local education authority to make written representations or an officer of the authority nominated by them to appear and make oral representations.

9. The body responsible for making any arrangements under section 26 of this Act shall, in setting any time limits in connection with appeals, have regard to the desirability of securing that appeals are disposed of without delay.

10. In considering any appeal, the appeal committee shall take into account (amongst other things) any representations made to it by any of the persons whom it is required to afford an opportunity to make representations.

11. In the event of a disagreement between the members of an appeal committee the appeal under consideration shall be decided by a simple majority of the votes cast and in the case of an equality of votes the chairman of the committee shall have a second or casting vote.

12. The decision of an appeal committee and the grounds on which it is made shall be communicated by the committee in writing to the pupil (if he is aged eighteen or over) or a parent of his (if he is under eighteen) and to the local education authority and governing body.

13. All appeals shall be heard in private except when otherwise directed by the authority or governing body by whom the arrangements are made but, without prejudice to any of the provisions of this Schedule—

(a) a member of the local education authority may attend any hearing of an appeal by an appeal committee, as an observer ; and

(*b*) any member of the Council on Tribunals may attend any   Sch. 3
meeting of any appeal committee at which an appeal is
considered, as an observer.

14. Two or more appeals may be combined and dealt with in the
same proceedings if the appeal committee consider that it is expedient to do so because the issues raised by the appeals are the
same or connected.

15. Subject to the preceding provisions of this Schedule, all
matters relating to the procedure on appeals, including the time
within which they are to be brought, shall be determined by the
authority or governing body by whom the arrangements are made ;
and neither section 106 of the Local Government Act 1972 nor 1972 c. 70
paragraph 44 of Schedule 12 to that Act (procedure of committees
of local authorities) shall apply to an appeal committee constituted
in accordance with Part I of Schedule 2 to the Act of 1980.

16. In this Schedule references to appeals are to appeals under
section 26 of this Act.

SCHEDULE 4   Section 67(4).

Consequential Amendments

The Education Act 1944 (c.31)

1. In section 15(2) of the Education Act 1944 (change of status of
voluntary school), in the proviso—

   (*a*) the words " under this section " shall be inserted after " any
   application " ; and

   (*b*) the words " or section 54 of the Education (No. 2) Act
   1986 " shall be inserted after " this section ", where they
   last occur.

2. In section 22 of that Act, for subsection (4) (appointment and
dismissal of certain staff) there shall be substituted—

   " (4) The local education authority may give directions to the
   governors of any aided school as to the number and conditions
   of service of persons employed at the school for the purposes
   of the care and maintenance of the school premises.".

The Education Act 1962 (c.12)

3. In section 4(5) of the Education Act 1962 (meaning of " training " in relation to grants for training of teachers) for " sections 2
and 3 " there shall be substituted " section 2 ".

The Education (No.. 2) Act 1968 (c.37)

4. In section 3(3) of the Education (No. 2) Act 1968 (application
of enactment to certain establishments)—

   (*a*) after the word " applies " there shall be inserted the words
   " and special schools maintained by local education authorities " ; and

SCH. 4   (b) after the word "establishments", in the second place where it occurs, there shall be inserted the words "and schools".

The Local Government Act 1974 (c.7)

5. In paragraph 5 of Schedule 5 to the Local Government Act 1974 (matters not subject to investigation by Local Commissioner) after the words "Act 1944" there shall be inserted the words "or sections 17 to 19 of the Education (No. 2) Act 1986".

The Sex Discrimination Act 1975 (c.65)

6. In section 51 of the Sex Discrimination Act 1975 (acts done under statutory authority) the following subsection shall be added at the end—

"(3) This section shall apply in relation to instruments of government and articles of government for schools made under the Education (No. 2) Act 1986 as it applies in relation to instruments of government and articles of government for schools made by or under any Act passed before this Act.".

The Local Government, Planning and Land Act 1980 (c.65)

7. In paragraph 3(4) of Schedule 10 to the Local Government Planning and Land Act 1980 (interpretation), for the words "31 of the Education Act 1980" there shall be substituted the words "51 of the Education (No. 2) Act 1986".

Section 67(5).   SCHEDULE 5

TRANSITIONAL PROVISIONS

Instruments of government for certain existing schools

1.—(1) Section 1 of this Act shall not require the making of an instrument of government for any aided or special agreement school in respect of which there is in force, at the time when that section comes into force, and continues in force, an instrument under which its governing body is constituted ; but this paragraph shall cease to apply to any such school if it is grouped with another school under section 9 of this Act.

(2) Any such instrument shall, after the commencement of section 1, be treated for the purposes of this Act as having been made by order under that section.

Grouping

2. Where a local education authority propose to group two or more schools which are subject to an arrangement under section 3 of the 1980 Act (the "section 3 schools"), the references in subsections (5) and (6) of section 10 of this Act to the governing body of each of the schools concerned shall be construed as references to the persons deemed to be governors of the section 3 schools by section 3(7) of the 1980 Act.

Recommendations by outgoing governing bodies

3.—(1) The governing body for any county, controlled or maintained special school which is constituted under an instrument of government or arrangement in force immediately before section 1 of this Act comes into force shall recommend (with reasons) to any governing body who will succeed them persons who belong to the community served by the school and who are, in their opinion, suitable for appointment as co-opted members of their successor.

(2) Before making any recommendations under sub-paragraph (1) above, a governing body shall consult representatives of the local business community.

SCHEDULE 6

Section 67(6).

REPEALS AND REVOCATIONS

PART I

ENACTMENTS REPEALED

Chapter	Short title	Extent of repeal
7 & 8 Geo. 6. c. 31.	The Education Act 1944.	Section 4. Section 5. Sections 17 to 21. Section 23. Section 24(1). In section 27(3), from " but before " to end. In section 67(2), the words from " or whether " to " another ".
1962 c. 12.	The Education Act 1962.	In section 3, paragraph (*a*) and from " in the case of " to " this section ". In section 4(3), " (*a*) or ".
1963 c. 33.	The London Government Act 1963.	In section 31, subsections (7)(*a*) and (8).
1966 c. 42.	The Local Government Act 1966.	In Schedule 5, paragraph 6.
1968 c. 37.	The Education (No. 2) Act 1968.	Section 2. In section 3(2), the words " or subsection (4) of section 2 ".
1980 c. 20.	The Education Act 1980.	Section 2. Section 3. Section 4. Sections 31 and 32. In section 35(1), the words from " (other " to " (*b*)) ". Schedule 6.
1980 c. 44.	The Education (Scotland) Act 1980.	Section 23(5) to (7).
1980 c. 65.	The Local Government, Planning and Land Act 1980.	Section 68(5).

PART II

INSTRUMENTS REVOKED

Number	Name of instrument	Extent of revocation
S.I.1970/1 536.	The Transfer of Functions (Wales) Order 1970.	Article 4.

Salmon Act 1986

1986 CHAPTER 62

An Act to make fresh provision for the administration of
salmon fisheries in Scotland; to provide as to the
licensing and regulation of salmon dealing in Scotland
and in England and Wales; to provide for, and as
respects, certain offences in the law of Scotland and
in the law of England and Wales in connection with
salmon; to amend the Salmon and Freshwater Fisheries
Act 1975, section 5 of the Sea Fisheries Regulation Act
1966 and section 9 of the Diseases of Fish Act 1983; to
provide for the review of salmon fishing by means of
nets; and for connected purposes. [7th November 1986]

B E IT ENACTED by the Queen's most Excellent Majesty, by and
with the advice and consent of the Lords Spiritual and
Temporal, and Commons, in this present Parliament
assembled, and by the authority of the same, as follows:—

PART I

ADMINISTRATION OF SALMON FISHERIES IN SCOTLAND

Salmon fishery districts

1.—(1) A salmon fishery district shall be the area within the Salmon
coastal limits of a district (within the meaning of the Salmon fishery
Fisheries (Scotland) Acts 1862 to 1868) and extending— districts.

    (*a*) seaward for three miles from mean low water springs;
       and

    (*b*) landward to include the catchment area of each river
       which flows directly or indirectly into the sea within
       these limits

but excluding any area designated as a salmon fishery district by an order made under subsection (2) below.

(2) Notwithstanding subsection (1) above, the Secretary of State may, in accordance with section 2 of this Act, by order designate any area as a salmon fishery district, whether or not it includes all or part of a salmon fishery district—

    (*a*) established by subsection (1) above ; or

    (*b*) already designated as such by an order made under this subsection ;

and such an order is referred to in this Act as a " designation order ".

(3) Districts within the meaning of the Salmon Fisheries (Scotland) Acts 1862 to 1868 shall cease to exist and, subject to subsection (6) below—

    (*a*) any reference in any enactment to a particular district within that meaning shall be construed as a reference to the salmon fishery district established by subsection (1) above which has the same coastal limits as that district ; and

    (*b*) for references in any enactment, excluding this Act, to such districts in general there shall be substituted references to salmon fishery districts

and a salmon fishery district which has the same coastal limits as a district within the meaning of these Acts shall have the same name as that district.

(4) After consulting such persons as he thinks fit, the Secretary of State may, by order made by statutory instrument—

    (*a*) where an island or part of an island is not within the area of a salmon fishery district by virtue of subsections (1) or (2) above, include in the area of a salmon fishery district—

        (i) that island or that part ; and

        (ii) the sea within three miles from mean low water springs on that island or that part ;

    (*b*) where there is doubt as to whether a particular place is in a particular salmon fishery district, make provision for the purpose of removing that doubt ; or

    (*c*) change a reference used in describing a salmon fishery district where the suitability of that reference for that purpose has lessened or ceased

but such an order shall not create a salmon fishery district.

(5) The River Tweed shall not be a salmon fishery district except as otherwise provided in this Act.

(6) References in the Salmon and Freshwater Fisheries (Protection) (Scotland) Act 1951 and in any other enactment as amended by that Act to a district shall be construed as including references to the River Tweed.

2.—(1) A designation order shall provide for the abolition of such salmon fishery districts as are superseded by the district so designated.

(2) A designation order shall provide for the application to the district so designated of such regulations—

  (*a*) made under section 3 of this Act ; or

  (*b*) made under the Salmon Fisheries (Scotland) Acts 1862 to 1868 as respects the matters specified in section 6(6) of the Salmon Fisheries (Scotland) Act 1862

as the Secretary of State specifies in the order and he may, in such an order, amend regulations made under section 3(2)(*d*) of this Act or under section 6(6) of that Act in their application under this subsection.

(3) Subject to section 6(1) of this Act, a designation order shall specify for the district so designated the annual close time and the periods within that time when it is permitted to fish for and take salmon by rod and line ; and the order may make different provision for different parts of the district.

(4) The power under section 1(2) of this Act to make a designation order shall not extend to the River Tweed.

(5) Schedule 1 shall have effect as to the procedure in the making of a designation order.

(6) The Secretary of State may by order vary the provisions of Schedule 1 to this Act.

(7) An order under subsection (6) above shall be made by statutory instrument which shall be subject to annulment in pursuance of a resolution of either House of Parliament.

General regulation of salmon fisheries

3.—(1) Subject to subsection (4) below, regulations made under the Salmon Fisheries (Scotland) Acts 1862 to 1868 as respects the matters specified in section 6(6) of the Salmon Fisheries (Scotland) Act 1862 shall have effect in relation to a salmon fishery district as they had effect, immediately before the commencement of this section, in relation to the part of that salmon fishery district which was a district within the meaning of these Acts and which had the same coastal limits as that salmon fishery district.

(2) The Secretary of State shall have power, after consulting such persons as he considers appropriate, to make regulations with respect to—

(a) the due observance of the weekly close time ;

(b) the construction and use of cruives ;

(c) the construction and alteration of dams, including mill dams, or lades or water wheels so as to afford a reasonable means for the passage of salmon ;

(d) the meshes, materials and dimensions of nets used in fishing for or taking salmon ;

(e) obstructions in rivers or estuaries to the passage of salmon ;

(f) the construction, alteration and use for the control of the passage of salmon of—

(i) screens in off-takes from inland waters ; and

(ii) structures associated with such screens.

(3) The Secretary of State shall have power, after consulting such persons as he considers appropriate, to make regulations amending section 13 of the Salmon and Freshwater Fisheries (Protection) (Scotland) Act 1951 (extent of the weekly close time and the period within which rod and line fishing is permitted) ; provided always that such regulations shall not shorten the periods specified in the said section 13.

1951 c. 26.

(4) The power to make regulations under subsection (2) above includes power to revoke any regulations as described in subsection (1) above ; and such regulations shall be treated as revoked insofar as they are inconsistent with the provisions of regulations made under this section.

(5) The power to make regulations under paragraphs (c) or (f) of subsection (2) above includes power to except from the application of a regulation or part of a regulation any works or any category of works ; and section 11 of the Salmon Fisheries (Scotland) Act 1868 shall apply to regulations so made.

1868 c. 123.

(6) The power to make regulations under subsection (2)(d) above includes power—

(a) to make different provision for different districts or different parts of a district ;

(b) to except from the application of a regulation or part of a regulation a district or part of a district specified in the regulations.

(7) References in any enactment, other than in this Act or in section 36 of the Salmon Fisheries (Scotland) Act 1868, to—

(a) byelaws or regulations made under the Salmon Fisheries (Scotland) Acts 1862 to 1868 as respects the matters

specified in section 6(6) of the Salmon Fisheries (Scot-   PART I
land) Act 1862 ; or   1862 c. 97.

(*b*) the provisions of any of the Schedules to that Act of
1868 relating to such matters

shall be construed as including references to regulations made
under subsection (2) above.

(8) Regulations under this section shall be made by statutory
instrument which shall be subject to annulment in pursuance of
a resolution of either House of Parliament.

4.—(1) In subsection (2) of section 5 of the Electricity (Scot- Private
land) Act 1979 (formation of Fisheries Committee), after the generating
words " Secretary of State " where they first occur there shall stations.
be inserted the words " , to a body or person who wishes to 1979 c. 11.
establish or extend a private generating station under section
35 ".

(2) After subsection (1) of section 35 (control of private hydro-
electric generating stations), there shall be inserted the following subsections—

" (1A) A person or body wishing to establish or extend
any such station shall prepare proposals with a view to
the execution of the necessary works and paragraphs 2, 3
and 6 of Schedule 4 to this Act shall have effect in relation
to such proposals as if they were constructional schemes
proposed under section 10 of this Act and, for the purposes
of this subsection, references in that Schedule to the Boards
shall be construed as references to such a person or body.

(1B) The Secretary of State may make his consent under
subsection (1) above conditional on the acceptance by the
person or body of any recommendation made under paragraph 3 of Schedule 4 to this Act relating to the proposed establishment or extension ; and such person or
body shall be bound to implement such recommendation in
executing the proposed works.".

(3) In paragraph 1 of Schedule 4 (constitution and functions
of Fisheries Committee), after the words " Secretary of State "
where they secondly occur there shall be inserted the words " ,
to a body or person who wishes to establish or extend a private
generating station under section 35 ".

5.—(1) In section 15 of the Salmon Fisheries (Scotland) Act Enforcement
1868 (offences related to regulations)—   of regulations.

(*a*) for the words from the beginning to " following offences " 1868 c. 123.
there shall be substituted the words " Any person " ;

(*b*) paragraph (7) shall be omitted ; and

(c) for the words from " shall for every such offence " to the end there shall be substituted the words " shall be guilty of an offence ; and section 19 of the Salmon and Freshwater Fisheries (Protection) (Scotland) Act 1951 (forfeiture of fish, instruments, articles, vehicles or boats) shall apply in relation to persons convicted of an offence under this section as it applies to those convicted of an offence under Part I or section 13 of that Act ".

(2) Without prejudice to the generality of section 3(7) of this Act, in section 15 of that Act, " byelaw "—

(a) in paragraph (8), shall include regulations made under section 3(2) of this Act and the offence specified in that paragraph shall, as respects such regulations, extend to so much of the River Tweed as is situated outwith Scotland ; and

(b) in paragraphs (2), (3) and (4), shall include such regulations except to the extent that they extend to the River Tweed.

Annual close time.

6.—(1) The annual close time for a salmon fishery district shall be a continuous period of not less than 168 days and shall apply to every mode of fishing for and taking salmon except to the extent that provision is made for periods within that time during which it is permitted to fish for and take salmon by rod and line.

(2) Subject to subsection (3) below, the dates of the annual close time and the periods within that time when it is permitted to fish for and take salmon by rod and line shall be, in the case of any particular district—

(a) the dates and periods specified in the designation order made in respect of that district ; or

(b) where no designation order has been made in respect of that district, the dates and periods which were determined under section 6(5) of the Salmon Fisheries (Scotland) Act 1862, subject to any variation made under section 9 of the Salmon Fisheries (Scotland) Act 1868, which, immediately before the commencement of this section, were in force as respects the district within the meaning of the Salmon Fisheries (Scotland) Acts 1862 to 1868 which had the same coastal limits as that salmon fishery district.

(3) Notwithstanding subsection (2) above, the Secretary of State may, subject to subsection (1) above, by order prescribe for any district the dates of the annual close time and the periods within that time when it is permitted to fish for and take salmon by rod and line and he may make different provision for different

parts of a district; and such an order is referred to in this Act as an " annual close time order ".

(4) The Secretary of State may make an annual close time order in respect of a salmon fishery district only on application to him by—

(a) the district salmon fishery board for that district; or

(b) where there is no such board, two proprietors of salmon fisheries in that district.

(5) An application under subsection (4) above shall be accompanied by the applicant's written proposals which shall state—

(a) the proposed dates of the anual close time and the periods within that time when it shall be permitted to fish for and take salmon by rod and line in the district; and

(b) the general effect of the proposals

and the proposals may include different dates and periods for different parts of the district.

(6) Paragraphs 3 to 9 of Schedule 1 to this Act shall apply to the making of an annual close time order as they apply to the making of a designation order, and for this purpose—

(a) references to a designation order shall be construed as references to an annual close time order; and

(b) references to an applicant, and to an application, under paragraph 1 shall be construed respectively as references to an applicant, and to an application, under subsection (4) above.

(7) References in any enactment, other than in this Act, to—

(a) regulations or byelaws made under the Salmon Fisheries (Scotland) Acts 1862 to 1868 as respects the matters specified in section 6(5) of the Salmon Fisheries (Scotland) Act 1862; or 1862 c. 97.

(b) the provisions of Schedule C to the Salmon Fisheries (Scotland) Act 1868 relating to such matters 1868 c. 123.

shall be construed as including references to an annual close time order or to such part of a designation order as provides for the annual close time for a salmon fishery district.

7.—(1) Subject to subsection (2) below, the estuary limits of a river shall be the limits fixed by judicial decision or fixed and defined under section 6(1) of the Salmon Fisheries (Scotland) Act 1862. Estuary limits.

(2) Whether or not a river has estuary limits as described in subsection (1) above, the Secretary of State may, by order, prescribe limits or, as the case may be, different limits which shall

PART I   be the estuary limits for that river ; and such an order is referred
to in this Act as an " estuary limits order ".

(3) The Secretary of State may make an estuary limits order
only on application to him by—

(a) the district salmon fishery board for the district in which
the river is situated ; or

(b) where there is no such board, two proprietors of salmon
fisheries in that district.

(4) An application under subsection (3) above shall be accompanied by the applicant's written proposals which shall state—

(a) the proposed estuary limits ; and

(b) the general effect of the proposals.

(5) Paragraphs 3 to 9 of Schedule 1 to this Act shall apply to
the making of an estuary limits order as they apply to the making of a designation order, and for this purpose—

(a) references to a designation order shall be construed as
references to an estuary limits order ; and

(b) references to an applicant, and to an application, under
paragraph 1 shall be construed respectively as references to an applicant, and to an application, under subsection (3) above.

(6) For the purposes of this section—

" estuary limits " means limits which divide each river including its mouth or estuary from the sea ; and

" river " does not include the River Tweed.

(7) References in any enactment, other than in this Act or in
1868 c. 123.   section 36 of the Salmon Fisheries (Scotland) Act 1868, to—

(a) byelaws or regulations made under the Salmon Fisheries
(Scotland) Acts 1862 to 1868 as respects the matters
1862 c. 97.   specified in section 6(1) of the Salmon Fisheries (Scotland) Act 1862 ; or

(b) the provisions of Schedule B to the Salmon Fisheries
(Scotland) Act 1868 relating to such matters

shall be construed as including references to an estuary limits
order.

Use of baits   **8.**—(1) The Secretary of State may, subject to the provisions
and lures.   of this section, make regulations specifying baits and lures for
the purposes of the definition of " rod and line " in section 24
1951 c. 26.   of the Salmon and Freshwater Fisheries (Protection) (Scotland)
Act 1951.

(2) The Secretary of State may make regulations under this section only on—

(a) application to him by a district salmon fishery board ; or

(b) a joint application to him by more than one such board, and regulations made in respect of such application shall be made only in respect of the district of the applicant.

(3) Regulations under this section shall specify, subject to such exceptions as may be provided therein, all or any, or a combination of, the following—

(a) baits and lures or classes of baits and lures ;

(b) times when the regulations apply ;

(c) areas to which the regulations apply.

(4) An application under subsection (2) above shall be accompanied by the applicant's written proposals which shall state—

(a) the baits and lures which it is proposed should be specified ;

(b) the places to which and the times during which the proposed regulations should apply ; and

(c) the reasons for the proposals.

(5) Paragraphs 3 to 9 of Schedule 1 to this Act shall apply to the making of regulations under this section as they apply to the making of a designation order, and for this purpose—

(a) references to a designation order shall be construed as references to regulations under this section ; and

(b) references to an applicant, and to an application, under paragraph 1 shall be construed respectively as references to an applicant, and to an application, under subsection (2) above.

(6) In section 24(1) of the Salmon and Freshwater Fisheries 1951 c. 26. (Protection) (Scotland) Act 1951, at the end of the definition of " rod and line " there shall be inserted the following—" and, in the case of fishing for salmon in an area to which and at a time during which regulations made under section 8 of the Salmon Act 1986 apply, is not specified in such regulations in respect of that area and time ".

9. References in any enactment to the limits of the Solway Limits of the Firth shall be construed as references to the limits which were Solway Firth. fixed under section 6(2) of the Salmon Fisheries (Scotland) Act 1862 c. 97. 1862.

10.—(1) The byelaw enacted by section 10 of the Salmon Fish- Application of eries (Scotland) Act 1868 as Schedule G to that Act, as amended regulations and by any other enactment, and so much of section 15 of that Act annual close as relates thereto shall continue to have effect in relation to the time orders to the River Tweed 1868 c. 123.

River Tweed as it had effect before the commencement of this section.

(2) Regulations made under section 3 of this Act shall have effect in relation to the River Tweed but the power to make regulations under subsection (2)(*d*) of that section includes power to except the River Tweed from the application of any such regulation.

(3) Where such regulations have effect in relation to the River Tweed—

> (*a*) references to a salmon fishery district shall include references to the River Tweed ; and

> (*b*) references to a district salmon fishery board shall include references to the River Tweed Council

unless the contrary intention appears.

(4) Subsections (3), (4)(*a*), (5) and (6) of section 6 and section 8 of this Act shall have effect in relation to the River Tweed with the following modifications—

> (*a*) references to a salmon fishery district shall include references to the River Tweed ;

> (*b*) references to a district salmon fishery board shall include references to the River Tweed Council

and Schedule 1 to this Act shall, for the purposes of this subsection, be construed accordingly.

(5) In making an annual close time order in respect of the River Tweed, the Secretary of State may prescribe an annual close time, being a continuous period of not less than 153 days.

(6) The power to make regulations under—

> (*a*) section 3(2)(*a*) of this Act includes power to amend section 12 of the Tweed Fisheries Amendment Act 1859 ;

1859 c. lxx.

> (*b*) section 3(2)(*d*) of this Act includes power to amend sections 12 and 13 of that Act of 1859 ; and

> (*c*) section 3(2)(*e*) of this Act includes power to amend section 57 of the Tweed Fisheries Act 1857 ; and

1857 c. cxlviii.

> (*d*) section 8 of this Act includes power to amend section 6 of the Tweed Fisheries Amendment Act 1859

and the power to make an annual close time order in respect of the River Tweed includes power to amend section 6, 10 and 11 of that Act of 1859.

(7) This section extends to so much of the River Tweed as is situated outwith Scotland.

Proprietors

11.—(1) A qualified proprietor shall be, for the purposes of this Act, a proprietor of a salmon fishery entered in the valuation roll.

(2) Where any salmon fishery is not entered or not entered separately in the valuation roll, the assessor shall, on the request of—

(a) the clerk to the district salmon fishery board for the district in which the fishery is situated ; or

(b) where there is no such board for the district, the proprietor of that fishery,

value that fishery and enter it in the valuation roll.

(3) If a salmon fishery is situated in more than one salmon fishery district the assessor shall, on the request of—

(a) the clerk to the district salmon fishery board for either or any of these districts ; or

(b) where there is no such board, the proprietor of that fishery

value that fishery and enter it in the valuation roll according to its value in each district.

(4) A qualified proprietor shall be an upper proprietor or a lower proprietor for the purposes of this Act according to whether his salmon fishery is, respectively, upstream or down‧ stream of a division of a river as defined in subsection (7) below and, in this Act, " upper proprietor " and " lower proprietor " each mean a qualified proprietor.

(5) A qualified proprietor shall be both an upper proprietor and a lower proprietor if he is a qualified proprietor of one salmon fishery situated above and another situated below a division referred to in subsection (4) above, whether or not both fisheries are on the same river in the district, and he may act in either capacity or in both capacities in accordance with the provisions of this Act.

(6) Subject to subsection (5) above, a qualified proprietor in a salmon fishery district shall not be eligible for election, co-option or appointment to the district salmon fishery board for that district in respect of more than one salmon fishery.

(7) The division referred to in subsection (4) above shall be—

(a) a line across the river between points on either bank prescribed by the Secretary of State under subsection (8) below ; or

　　　(b) where the Secretary of State has not prescribed such points but a point of division has been fixed in accordance with section 6(4) of the Salmon Fisheries (Scotland) Act 1862, that point of division ; or

1862 c. 97.　　　(c) where no division has been effected under paragraphs (a) or (b) above, the normal tidal limit.

(8) When requested to do so by the district salmon fishery board for the district in which a river is situated, the Secretary of State may, by order made by statutory instrument, prescribe a point on each bank of the river to which the request relates.

(9) The clerk to a district salmon fishery board shall maintain a roll showing—

　　　(a) the upper and lower proprietors in the district ; and

　　　(b) the values of their fisheries as entered in the valuation roll ;

and the board may, if they are satisfied that a name should be added or removed, add or remove it.

1907 c. 51.　　　(10) Subject to section 5 of the Sheriff Courts (Scotland) Act 1907 (jurisdiction as regards heritable property), the sheriff may, on summary application made to him by a person whose request to the board to add or remove a name has not been met, order the board to add or remove that name.

Sole proprietor in a salmon fishery district.　　　**12.**—(1) Where, after the commencement of this section, there is in a salmon fishery district only one proprietor of salmon fisheries, for references in this Act, except under paragraph 1 of Schedule 2 to this Act, to two proprietors of salmon fisheries in a salmon fishery district for which there is no board there shall be substituted references to that sole proprietor.

(2) Where, immediately before the commencement of this section, there is a sole proprietor in a district within the meaning of the Salmon Fisheries (Scotland) Acts 1862 to 1868, the powers of a district board conferred on him by section 19 of the Salmon Fisheries (Scotland) Act 1862 shall, on the commencement of this Act, cease to be exercisable by him.

(3) A person appointed as a water bailiff by a sole proprietor mentioned in subsection (2) above shall, on the commencement of this section, cease to have the powers and duties of a water bailiff conferred on him by or under any enactment to the extent that such powers and duties relate to that appointment.

Mandatories.　　　**13.**—(1) A qualified proprietor or an elected member or chairman of a district salmon fishery board may at any time authorise a person to act for him ; and such a person is referred to in this Act as a " mandatory ".

(2) A mandatory may as such be elected under Schedule 2 to this Act as a representative of qualified proprietors or as chairman but a person may not authorise another to act as a co-opted member under this Act nor shall a mandatory be co-opted under section 16(2) of this Act.

(3) A person who is both an upper and a lower proprietor by virtue of section 11(5) of this Act may authorise a person in accordance with this section in either or both of his capacities or may do so in each capacity.

District salmon fishery boards

14.—(1) If proprietors of salmon fisheries in a salmon fishery district—

District salmon fishery boards.

    (a) form an association for the purpose of the protection or improvement of the fisheries within their district; and

    (b) elect, in accordance with Schedule 2 to this Act, a committee to act for them,

that committee shall be the district salmon fishery board for that district; and the purpose of such a board shall be the purpose specified above in respect of the association.

(2) A district salmon fishery board shall have the powers and duties conferred—

    (a) on them under this Act; and

    (b) by any other enactment on a district board within the meaning of the Salmon Fisheries (Scotland) Acts 1862 to 1868;

and references in any enactment, other than in this Act, to a district board within the meaning of the Salmon Fisheries (Scotland) Acts 1862 to 1868 shall be construed as references to a district salmon fishery board.

(3) Subject to subsection (4) below, a committee mentioned in subsection (1) above shall cease to be the district salmon fishery board for a district on the expiry of a period of three years from the date of the last meeting of proprietors which elected, in accordance with Part I of Schedule 2 to this Act, such members as require to be elected under Part II of that Schedule.

(4) On the coming into force of a designation order—

    (a) the transitional district board for; or

    (b) the committee within the meaning of this section in respect of

a district superseded by the district so designated, as the case may be, shall cease to be a district salmon fishery board; and

N3

PART I   the committee within the meaning of this section which has been constituted in accordance with Schedule 2 to this Act in anticipation of the order and in respect of the district designated by the order shall be the district salmon fishery board for that district.

(5) If a committee ceases to be a district salmon fishery board, the assets and liabilities of that board shall be the assets and liabilities of the members of the association for which the committee acts; but, for the purposes of the winding-up of such an association, any assets of the former board remaining after the settlement of the liabilities of the former board shall be distributed amongst all the proprietors in the district who were liable to the fishery assessment immediately before the date on which the committee ceased to be such a board, according to the valuation of each fishery as entered in the valuation roll at that date.

(6) A district salmon fishery board shall not be bound by any direction given to them by the association for which the elected members of the board act as a committee.

(7) Nothing in this section shall affect the powers and duties of the River Tweed Council.

(8) The powers and duties under any enactment of district boards constituted in accordance with the Salmon Fisheries (Scotland) Acts 1862 to 1868 shall cease to have effect in relation to such boards and Schedule 3 to this Act shall have effect as respects such a board which was in office immediately before the commencement of this section; and such a board is referred to in this Act as a " transitional district board ".

(9) There may be a district salmon fishery board for a district whether or not there are salmon in the waters of that district.

(10) The Secretary of State may by order vary the provisions of Schedule 2 or Schedule 3 to this Act.

(11) An order under subsection (10) above shall be made by statutory instrument which shall be subject to annulment in pursuance of a resolution of either House of Parliament.

Financial   **15.**—(1) Each year, a district salmon fishery board shall pre-
powers and   pare—
duties of
district   (a) a report; and
salmon fishery   (b) a statement of accounts, which shall be audited,
boards.
relating to the activities of the board; and the clerk of the board shall call an annual meeting of qualified proprietors in the district for the purposes of considering the report and the audited accounts.

(2) A district salmon fishery board shall have power to impose an assessment, to be known as the fishery assessment, on each salmon fishery in their district.

(3) The fishery assessment shall be assessed at such uniform   PART I
rate or rates as are determined for all fisheries in the district by
the board and shall be exigible according to the valuation of a
fishery as entered in the valuation roll.

(4) Subsections (2) and (3) of section 11 of this Act shall
apply for the purposes of this section as they apply for the purposes of that section.

(5) Arrears of fishery assessment may be recovered by—

    (a) the district salmon fishery board which imposed the
        assessment ; or

    (b) the district salmon fishery board for a district created by
        a designation order in respect of an assessment imposed
        by a district salmon fishery board for a district super-
        seded by that order ; or

    (c) the district salmon fishery board which replaced a tran-
        sitional district board in respect of an assessment im-
        posed by the transitional district board,

as the case may be, by action for payment of money.

(6) Any of the boards mentioned in subsection (5) above may
recover arrears of fishery assesment which were due immediately
before the commencement of this section under section 23 of
the Salmon Fisheries (Scotland) Act 1862 in respect of any part   1862 c. 97
of their district.

(7) The powers under subsections (5) and (6) above to recover
arrears of fishery assessment include power to recover interest,
chargeable at such rate as the Secretary of State shall, with the
consent of the Treasury, determine, on such arrears from—

    (a) in the case of recovery of arrears under subsection (5)
        above which have been outstanding for at least three
        months from the date of issue of a notice of assess-
        ment, that date ; or

    (b) in the case of recovery of arrears under subsection (6)
        above which have been outstanding for at least three
        months from the date of the coming into force of this
        section, that date,

until payment or the commencement of an action for payment,
whichever is the earlier.

(8) A board may, in carrying out its purpose under this Act,
borrow—

    (a) an amount not exceeding twice the amount of the fishery
        assessment collected within the twelve month period
        immediately prior to the date of the decision to bor-
        row ; or

(b) such higher sum as is approved by the proprietors of fisheries which together amount to four fifths of the total value of fisheries in the district as entered in the valuation roll.

(9) In subsection (8)(a) above, " collected " means collected in—

(a) the district for which that board is the district salmon fishery board ; and

(b) if that district has been designated in an order made under section 1(2) of this Act within that twelve month period, all the districts superseded by that order.

(10) In carrying out its purpose, a district salmon fishery board may authorise expenditure, including expenditure for the acquisition of heritable property, out of sums accruing to it from—

(a) the fishery assessment ;

(b) the exercise of the power, under subsection (8) above, to borrow ; or

(c) any other source ;

but it shall not pay to any member of that board any salary or fees for his acting in any way as a member of or under that board.

General powers and duties of district salmon fishery boards.

16.—(1) A district salmon fishery board may do such acts, execute such works and incur such expenses as may appear to them expedient for—

(a) the protection or improvement of the fisheries within their district ;

(b) the increase of salmon ; or

(c) the stocking of the waters of the district with salmon.

(2) The elected members of a district salmon fishery board shall, in accordance with Part II of Schedule 2 to this Act, co-opt representatives of salmon anglers and tenant netsmen.

(3) On such terms and conditions as the board think fit, a district salmon fishery board—

(a) shall appoint a person to act as clerk to the board ; and

(b) may appoint persons to act as water bailiffs, or in such other capacity as the board see fit.

(4) A district salmon fishery board may sue or be sued in the name of their clerk.

(5) References in any enactment to water bailiffs shall include references to waterbailiffs appointed under this section.

17.—(1) The first meeting of a district salmon fishery board
shall be at the date, time and place determined by the members
of the board who were elected at the meeting of qualified proprietors called under paragraph 1 of Schedule 2 to this Act but
in any case shall be no later than 21 days after that meeting.

(2) A district salmon fishery board shall determine the quorum
for their meetings.

(3) At any meeting of the board, each member shall have
one vote, subject to the following exceptions—

   (*a*) the chairman, in his capacity as such, shall have both
      a casting and a deliberative vote ; and

   (*b*) a person who is both an upper proprietor and a lower
      proprietor by virtue of section 11(5) of this Act shall
      have a vote in either capacity or in both capacities
      according to the capacity or capacities in which he has
      been elected or co-opted.

(4) No act or proceeding of a district salmon fishery board
shall be questioned on account of any vacancy in their membership and no defect in the qualification or appointment of any
person acting as a member shall vitiate any proceedings of the
board in which that member has taken part.

(5) The minutes of proceedings of district salmon fishery
boards shall be signed by the chairman and shall be conclusive
evidence of the proceedings ; and a meeting so minuted shall be
presumed to have been duly convened and held and all members thereof to have been duly qualified.

(6) On the written request of any two members of the board,
the chairman shall be bound to convene a meeting of the board
within fourteen days of receiving the request and the clerk shall
give notice to each member of the date, time and place of and
the agenda for that meeting.

18.—(1) Before the expiry of a period of three years from—

   (*a*) the first election of the members of the board ; or

   (*b*) the last meeting of qualified proprietors called under
      this section

the clerk to that board shall call a meeting of qualified proprietors in that district for the purpose of electing or re-electing, in
accordance with Part I of Schedule 2 to this Act, such members
as require to be elected under Part II of that Schedule ; and at
that meeting each member of the board shall resign.

(2) The provisions of Schedule 2 to this Act, apart from paragraph 1, shall apply to further elections as they apply to the
first election of the members.

PART I   (3) Without prejudice to subsection (1) above, a member of
a district salmon fishery board may resign at any time and where
a person ceases to meet the requirements of this Act for membership of a district salmon fishery board he shall cease to be a
member of that board.

(4) Where a person is both an upper and a lower proprietor
by virtue of section 11(5) of this Act, subsection (3) above shall
have effect as respects either or each such capacity.

(5) Where a vacancy in their number occurs, the board shall,
so far and as soon as is reasonably practicable, fill that vacancy
by—

(a) the electing by the elected members from amongst themselves of a new chairman ;

(b) the appointing by the elected members of a qualified
proprietor in the district as a representative of qualified
proprietors according to the rules in Schedule 2 to this
Act regarding the balance between upper and lower
proprietors ; and

(c) the co-opting by the board of a representative of salmon
anglers or of tenant netsmen in accordance with that
Schedule,

as the case may be, and a person appointed under paragraph (b)
above shall be an elected representative of qualified proprietors
for the purposes of this Act.

Application to the Esk

Application of   **19.** The provisions of Part I of this Act shall not apply to
Part I to the   so much of the River Esk, including its banks and tributary
River Esk.   streams, as is situated in Scotland.

PART II

OTHER PROVISIONS APPLYING TO SCOTLAND

Additional   **20.**—(1) Without prejudice to the generality of section 44 of
powers in   the Civic Government (Scotland) Act 1982 (power to designate
respect of   additional activities as subject to licensing and regulation) an
licensing and   order as respects dealing in salmon made under that section
regulation of   may—
salmon
dealing.   (a) define dealing in salmon and so define it as to—
1982 c. 45.
                  (i) include such acts preparatory to or connected
with dealing in salmon ;

(ii) exclude dealing in such class or classes of
salmon

as may be specified in the order ;

(*b*) provide that the offence under section 7(1) of that Act   PART II
(doing anything for which a licence is required without having one) shall be punishable—

    (i) on summary conviction, by imprisonment for a term not exceeding three months, or a fine not exceeding the statutory maximum or both ;

    (ii) on conviction on indictment, by imprisonment for a term not exceeding two years, or a fine or both ;

(*c*) provide that it shall be an offence for any person, other than a person holding a salmon dealer's licence, to buy salmon from or sell salmon to a person not having such a licence ;

(*d*) provide that the offences under the said section 7(1) and any provision under paragraph (*c*) above shall be subject to such exceptions as may be specified in the order ;

(*e*) provide that a licence shall be required only for such class or classes of dealing in salmon and dealing in such class or classes of salmon as may be specified in the order ;

(*f*) provide as to the exercise of powers of entry and search by water bailiffs and persons appointed by the Secretary of State under section 10(5) of the Salmon and   1951 c. 26. Freshwater Fisheries (Protection) (Scotland) Act 1951

but not so as to enable these powers to be exercised in any dwelling house or any yard, garden, outhouses and pertinents belonging thereto or usually enjoyed therewith.

(2) The Secretary of State shall have power, by order to prescribe, or to prescribe the maximum amounts of, the fees which the licensing authority may determine and charge under sub-paragraph (1) of paragraph 15 of Schedule 1 to the said Act of 1982 in respect of the licensing of dealing in salmon ; and in that respect the licensing authority's powers under that paragraph shall be subject to the provisions of any such order.

(3) An order made under subsection (2) above shall be made by statutory instrument which shall be subject to annulment in pursuance of a resolution of either House of Parliament.

21. In section 2 of the Salmon and Freshwater Fisheries   Permitted (Protection) (Scotland) Act 1951 (methods of fishing)—   methods of
    (*a*) after subsection (1) there shall be inserted the following   fishing for salmon. subsection—

        " (1A) No person shall fish for or take salmon in any waters in a salmon fishery district other than inland waters, except by rod and line, net and coble or bag net, fly net or other stake net."

(*b*) after subsection (2) there shall be inserted the following subsections—

" (2A) After consulting such persons as he considers appropriate, the Secretary of State may, for the purposes of this section, by regulations define fishing for or taking salmon by—

    (*a*) net and coble ;

    (*b*) bag net, fly net or other stake net,

whether by reference to anything used for the purpose, or to the circumstances in which or method by which it is so used, or to any combination thereof ; and, in relation to net and coble, may make different provision as respects inland waters from that made as respects other waters.

(2B) The power to make regulations under this section includes power to amend or repeal section 62 of the Tweed Fisheries Act 1857 and section 12 and 13 of the Tweed Fisheries Amendment Act 1859.

1857 c. cxlviii.
1859 c. lxx.

(2C) Regulations made under this section shall be made by statutory instrument which shall be subject to annulment in pursuance of a resolution of either House of Parliament.".

Offence of possessing salmon which have been illegally taken, killed or landed.

1951 c. 26.

22.—(1) After section 7 of the Salmon and Freshwater Fisheries (Protection) (Scotland) Act 1951 there shall be inserted the following section—

" Offence of possessing salmon which have been illegally taken, killed or landed.

    7A.—(1) A person who—

    (*a*) is in possession of salmon and believes ; or

    (*b*) is in possession of salmon in circumstances in which it would be reasonable for him to suspect

that a relevant offence has at any time been committed in relation to the salmon shall be guilty of an offence and liable—

    (i) on summary conviction to imprisonment for a term not exceeding three months, or to a fine not exceeding the statutory maximum or both ;

(ii) on conviction on indictment to imprisonment for a term not exceeding two years, or
to a fine or both.

(2) It shall be a defence in proceedings for an
offence under this section to show that no relevant
offence had in fact been committed in relation to the
salmon.

(3) It shall be lawful to convict a person charged
under this section on the evidence of one witness.

(4) For the purposes of this section an offence is
a relevant offence in relation to a salmon if—

(a) it is committed by taking, killing or landing
that salmon, either in Scotland or in England and Wales ; or

(b) that salmon is taken, killed or landed, either
in Scotland or in England and Wales in the
course of the commission of the offence.

(5) In subsection (4) above, " offence ", in relation
to the taking, killing or landing of salmon either in
Scotland or in England or Wales, means an offence
under the law applicable to the place where the
salmon is taken, killed or landed.

(6) A person shall not be guilty of an offence under
this section in respect of conduct which constitutes
a relevant offence in relation to any salmon or in
respect of anything done in good faith for purposes
connected with the prevention or detection of crime
or the investigation or treatment of disease.

(7) Where an offence under this Act committed by
a body corporate is proved to have been committed
with the consent or connivance of, or to be attributable to any neglect on the part of, any director,
manager, secretary or other similar officer of the body
corporate, or any person who was purporting to act
in any such capacity, he as well as the body corporate shall be guilty of the offence and shall be liable
to be proceeded against and punished accordingly.

(8) Where the affairs of a body corporate are
managed by its members, subsection (7) above shall
apply in relation to the acts and defaults of a member in connection with his functions of management
as if he were a director of the body corporate.".

PART II   (2) In section 11 of that Act (power of search)—

(a) in each of subsections (1) and (3) for the words " three and four" there shall be substituted " 1 to 4, 7 and 7A ";

(b) after the said subsection (3) there shall be inserted the following subsection—

" (3A) Where a constable has reasonable grounds for suspecting that an offence against section 7A of this Act is being committed and that evidence of the commission of the offence is to be found in any premises (other than a dwelling-house or any yard, garden, outhouses and pertinents belonging thereto or usually enjoyed therewith) but by reason of urgency or other good cause it is impracticable to apply for a warrant to search such premises, he may search them without warrant." ;

(c) in subsection (4)—

(i) for the words " section three or section four " there shall be substituted " any of the provisions of sections 1 to 4, 7 and 7A ";

(ii) after the word " thereon " there shall be inserted the words—

" or in any stationary vehicle on—

1984 c. 54.   (a) a road within the meaning of the Roads (Scotland) Act 1984 ; or

1980 c. 66.   (b) a highway within the meaning of the High-ways Act 1980

adjoining such water or such land,".

Power of court in trial of one offence to convict of another.   23. If, upon a trial for an offence under—

(a) section 10 of the Tweed Fisheries Amendment Act 1859 (having or selling salmon taken from the River Tweed during annual close time) ;

1859 c. cxlviii.   (b) section 21 of the Salmon Fisheries (Scotland) Act 1868 (buying or selling salmon in close time) ;
1868 c. 123.

(c) section 7 of the Salmon and Freshwater Fisheries (Pro-
1951 c. 26.   tection) (Scotland) Act 1951 (possessing illegally taken salmon or trout) ;

(d) section 7A of the said Act of 1951 (possessing illegally taken salmon) ; or

(e) any rule of law relating to reset ;

the court is not satisfied that the accused is guilty of the offence charged but is satisfied that he is guilty of another of these offen-ces, it may acquit him of the offence charged but find him guilty of the other offence and he shall then be liable to the same punishment as for that other offence.

24.—(1) A person who intentionally introduces any salmon or salmon eggs into inland waters in a salmon fishery district for which there is a district salmon fishery board shall be guilty of an offence and liable on summary conviction to a fine not exceeding level 2 on the standard scale.

PART II
Unauthorised
introduction
of salmon or
salmon eggs
into certain
waters.

(2) A person shall not be guilty of an offence under this section in respect of an introduction of salmon or salmon eggs into such waters if—

(a) he has the previous written consent of the district salmon fishery board for the salmon fishery district in which these waters are situated ; or

(b) the waters constitute or are included in a fish farm within the meaning of the Diseases of Fish Act 1937.

1937 c. 33.

25. After section 7 of the Salmon and Freshwater Fisheries (Protection) (Scotland) Act 1951, there shall be inserted the following section—

Fixed engines
in the Solway.
1951 c. 26.

"Fixed
engines in
the Solway.

7B.—(1) Any person who, for the purpose of taking or obstructing the free passage of salmon, places or uses an uncertificated fixed engine within the limits of the Solway Firth in Scotland shall be guilty of an offence and liable on summary conviction to a fine not exceeding level 4 on the standard scale.

(2) In subsection (1) above—
' fixed engine ' includes any net or other implement for taking fish which is fixed to the soil or made stationary in any other way ; and
' uncertificated ' means not having been certified as privileged under section 5 of the Solway Salmon Fisheries Commissioners (Scotland) Act 1877."

1877 c. ccxl

26.—(1) Section 21 of the Salmon and Freshwater Fisheries (Protection) (Scotland) Act 1951, (non-application of that Act to the River Esk in Scotland) shall be renumbered as subsection (1) of that section and—

Poaching in
the Esk.

(a) at the beginning of that subsection there shall be inserted the words " Subject to subsection (2) below," ; and

(b) after that subsection there shall be added the following subsection—
" (2) Section 1 of this Act and sections 3 and 18 to 20 so far as relating to an offence under that section shall apply to so much of the River Esk, including its banks and tributary streams, as is situated in Scotland.".

PART II
1975 c. 51. (2) In section 39 of the Salmon and Freshwater Fisheries Act 1975 (application of that Act to certain Border waters including the River Esk) there shall be inserted after subsection (1) the following subsection—

> " (1A) In the application of this Act, under subsection (1)(*b*) above, to the River Esk in Scotland, references to this Act in sections 31 to 33 and section 36 shall be construed as including references to sections 1, 3 and 18 to 20 of the Salmon and Freshwater Fisheries (Protection) (Scotland) Act 1951 as applied to that River by section 21 of that Act.".

1951 c. 26.

(3) In section 43(3) of the said Act of 1975 (Scottish extent) after the words " 39(1) " there shall be inserted the word " , (1A) ".

(4) Section 9 of the Solway Act 1804 shall, so far as relating to salmon, cease to have effect in relation to so much of the River Esk, including its banks and tributary streams, as is situated in Scotland.

Exemption from certain offences in respect of certain acts.

27.—(1) A person shall not, in respect of any act or omission relating to fishing for or taking salmon, be guilty of a contravention of an enactment prohibiting or regulating that act or omission if the act or omission has been exempted by the Secretary of State.

(2) The Secretary of State may exempt an act or omission under subsection (1) above only if he is satisfied that—

(*a*) the proprietor of every affected salmon fishery in the salmon fishery district in which the act or omission is to take place, being a salmon fishery entered in the valuation roll ; and

(*b*) if there is one, the district salmon fishery board for that district

have previously consented to it ; and, in this subsection, " salmon fishery district " includes the River Tweed and, in relation to that river, " district salmon fishery board " means the River Tweed Council.

(3) In subsection (2) above, " affected " means appearing to the Secretary of State to be likely to be affected by the exemption.

(4) An exemption under this subsection—

(*a*) may relate only to such person as may be specified in it ;

(*b*) may be subject to such conditions as may be so specified ;

(*c*) shall be in writing ;

(*d*) shall specify—
(i) the limits of the waters to which it relates ;
(ii) its duration ; and
(iii) the enactment to which it relates.

PART II

(5) In this section, "enactment" includes any instrument
made after the passing of this Act under any enactment.

28.—(1) A person shall not, in respect of any act or omission relating to salmon or salmon roe or eggs, be guilty of a contravention of an enactment prohibiting or regulating that act or
omission if—

Exemption
from certain
offences in
respect of acts
done for
scientific etc.
purposes.

(*a*) the act or omission is for—
(i) some scientific purpose ;
(ii) the purpose of protecting, improving or de-
veloping stocks of fish ; or
(iii) the purpose of conserving any creature or
other living thing ; and
(*b*) he has obtained the previous permission in writing—
(i) if the act or omission is one to which this sub-
paragraph applies, of the district salmon fishery
board for the salmon fishery district in which it
takes place or of the Secretary of State ; and
(ii) in any other case, of the Secretary of State
for the act or omission.

(2) Sub-paragraph (i) of subsection (1) (*b*) above applies if the
act or omission referred to in that sub-paragraph—

(*a*) takes place in a salmon fishery district for which there
is a district salmon fishery board ; and
(*b*) is a contravention of—
(i) section 45 of the Tweed Fisheries Act 1857 ;　1857 c. cxlviii.
(ii) section 6 of the Tweed Fisheries Amendment　1859 c. lxx.
Act 1859 ;
(iii) section 18, 19 or 20 of the Salmon Fisheries　1868 c. 123.
(Scotland) Act 1868 ; or
(iv) section 2 or 4(*c*) of the Salmon and Fresh-　1951 c. 26.
water Fisheries (Protection) (Scotland) Act 1951.

(3) A permission under subsection (1) above shall specify the
act or omission permitted and the enactment to which the permission relates.

(4) In this section—
(*a*) references to a salmon fishery district and to a district
salmon fishery board include respectively references to
the River Tweed and to the River Tweed Council ;

PART II

(*b*) " enactment " includes any instrument made after the passing of this Act under any enactment.

Application of sections 24 and 25 to River Esk and River Tweed.

29.—(1) Sections 27 and 28 of this Act, as respects any enactment—

(*a*) which does not apply to so much of the River Esk, including its banks and tributary streams, as is situated in Scotland but otherwise extends to Scotland, shall likewise not apply to that part of that River ;

(*b*) which applies to so much of the River Esk, with its banks and tributary streams up to their source, as is situated in Scotland but otherwise does not extend to Scotland, shall not apply to that part of that River ;

(*c*) which extends to Scotland only but also applies to so much of the River Tweed as is situated outwith Scotland, shall likewise apply to that part of that River.

(2) In this section, " enactment " includes any instrument made after the passing of this Act under any enactment.

Prosecution of offences under the Act of 1868.

1868 c. 123.

30.—(1) Section 30 and sections 38 to 40 of the Salmon Fisheries (Scotland) Act 1868 (prosecution of offences at the instance of the clerk to a district board or of any other person) shall cease to have effect but any proceedings begun before the commencement of this section shall proceed as if this section had not been passed.

(2) A person who commits an offence under section 15 or sections 18 to 24 of that Act may be convicted on the evidence of one witness.

PART III

PROVISIONS APPLYING TO ENGLAND AND WALES

Dealer licensing in England and Wales.

31.—(1) The Minister of Agriculture, Fisheries and Food and the Secretary of State may by order made by statutory instrument make provision for the purpose of prohibiting persons, in such cases as may be specified in the order, from—

(*a*) dealing in salmon otherwise than under and in accordance with a licence issued in pursuance of the order by such person as may be so specified ; or

(*b*) buying salmon from a person who is not licensed to deal in salmon.

(2) Without prejudice to the generality of subsection (1) above, an order under this section may—

(*a*) prescribe the manner and form of an application for a licence to deal in salmon and the sum, or maximum sum, to be paid on the making of such an application ;

(*b*) specify the circumstances in which such an application is to be granted or refused and the conditions that may be incorporated in such a licence ;

(*c*) authorise the amendment, revocation or suspension of such a licence ;

(*d*) create criminal offences consisting in the contravention of, or failure to comply with, provisions made under this section ;

(*e*) provide for matters to be determined for the purposes of any such provision by a person authorised by any such provision to issue a licence ; and

(*f*) make provision, whether by applying provisions of the Salmon and Freshwater Fisheries Act 1975 or otherwise, 1975 c. 51. for the purpose of facilitating the enforcement of any provision made under this section.

(3) An order under this section may—

(*a*) make different provision for different cases ; and

(*b*) contain such incidental, supplemental and transitional provision as appears to the Minister of Agriculture, Fisheries and Food and the Secretary of State to be necessary or expedient.

(4) Except in the case of an order to which subsection (5) below applies, no order shall be made under this section unless a draft of the order has been laid before, and approved by a resolution of, each House of Parliament.

(5) A statutory instrument containing an order under this section which relates exclusively to the sum, or maximum sum, to be paid on the making of an application for a licence to deal in salmon shall be subject to annulment in pursuance of a resolution of either House of Parliament.

(6) In this section " deal ", in relation to salmon, includes selling any quantity of salmon, whether by way of business or otherwise, and acting on behalf of a buyer or seller of salmon.

32.—(1) Subject to subsections (3) and (4) below, a person Handling shall be guilty of an offence if, at a time when he believes or it salmon in would be reasonable for him to suspect that a relevant offence has suspicious at any time been committed in relation to any salmon, he circumstances. receives the salmon, or undertakes or assists in its retention, removal or disposal by or for the benefit of another person, or if he arranges to do so.

(2) For the purposes of this section an offence is a relevant offence in relation to a salmon if—

(*a*) it is committed by taking, killing or landing that salmon, either in England and Wales or in Scotland ; or

PART III   (b) that salmon is taken, killed or landed, either in England and Wales or in Scotland, in the course of the commission of the offence.

(3) It shall be immaterial for the purposes of subsection (1) above that a person's belief or the grounds for suspicion relate neither specifically to a particular offence that has been committed nor exclusively to a relevant offence or to relevant offences ; but it shall be a defence in proceedings for an offence under this section to show that no relevant offence had in fact been committed in relation to the salmon in question.

(4) A person shall not be guilty of an offence under this section in respect of conduct which constitutes a relevant offence in relation to any salmon or in respect of anything done in good faith for purposes connected with the prevention or detection of crime or the investigation or treatment of disease.

(5) A person guilty of an offence under this section shall be liable—

(a) on summary conviction, to imprisonment for a term not exceeding three months or to a fine not exceeding the statutory maximum or to both ;

(b) on conviction on indictment, to imprisonment for a term not exceeding two years or to a fine or to both.

1975 c. 51.   (6) The Salmon and Freshwater Fisheries Act 1975 shall have effect as if—

(a) in section 31(1)(b) and (c) (powers of search of water bailiffs), the references to a fish taken in contravention of that Act included references to a salmon in relation to which a relevant offence has been committed ; and

(b) in sections 33(2) (warrants to enter suspected premises), 36(1) (water bailiffs to be constables for the purpose of enforcing Act) and 39(1) (border rivers) and in paragraph 39(1)(a) of Schedule 3 (prosecution by water authorities) and Part II of Schedule 4 (procedure on prosecutions), the references to that Act included references to this section.

(7) In this section " offence ", in relation to the taking, killing or landing of a salmon either in England and Wales or in Scotland, means an offence under the law applicable to the place where the salmon is taken, killed or landed.

Placing and use of fixed engines.   33.—(1) For subsection (1) of section 6 of the Salmon and Freshwater Fisheries Act 1975 (under which it is an offence to place a fixed engine in any inland or tidal waters or to use an

unauthorised fixed engine for specified purposes) there shall be   PART III
substituted the following subsection—

"(1) Any person who places or uses an unauthorised
fixed engine in any inland or tidal waters shall be guilty of
an offence ".

(2) In subsection (3) of the said section 6 (definition of unauthorised fixed engine), at the end of paragraph (*b*) there shall
be inserted " ; or

> (*c*) a fixed engine the placing and use of which is auth-
> orised by byelaws made by a water authority under
> this Act or by byelaws made by a local fisheries
> committee by virtue of section 37(2) of the Salmon
> Act 1986."

(3) In Part II of Schedule 3 to the said Act of 1975 (byelaws),
after paragraph 21 there shall be inserted the following paragraph—

> "21A. Authorising the placing and use of fixed engines
> at such places in the water authority area (not being places
> within the sea fisheries district of a local fisheries committee),
> at such times and in such manner as may be prescribed by
> the byelaws and imposing requirements as to the construc-
> tion, design, material and dimensions of such engines, in-
> cluding in the case of nets the size of mesh.".

34. In section 30 of the Salmon and Freshwater Fisheries Act   Introduction
1975 (prohibition of introduction of fish into inland waters with-   of fish into
out the consent of the water authority), at the end there shall be   fish farms
added the words " or the inland water is one which consists   without
exclusively of, or of part of, a fish farm and which, if it dis-   consent.
charges into another inland water, does so only through a con-   1975 c. 51.
duit constructed or adapted for the purpose.

In this section " fish farm " has the same meaning as in the   1937 c. 33.
Diseases of Fish Act 1937.".

35.—(1) In the Table in Part I of Schedule 4 to the Salmon   Removal of
and Freshwater Fisheries Act 1975 (mode of prosecution and   differential
punishment for offences), for the entries relating to sections 1   penalties under
and 27 (being entries which make different provision according   Salmon and
to whether the offender acted with another and do not provide   Freshwater
for imprisonment on summary conviction) there shall be sub-   Fisheries
stituted the following entries, respectively—   Act 1975.

PART III

Provision of Act creating the offence (1)	Description of offence (2)	Mode of prosecution (3)	Punishment (4)
" Section 1...	Fishing with certain instruments for salmon, trout or freshwater fish and possessing certain instruments for fishing for such fish.	(a) Summarily ... ... (b) On indictment	Three months or the statutory maximum or both. Two years or a fine or both.

Section 27 ...	Fishing for fish otherwise than under the authority of a licence and possessing an unlicensed instrument with intent to use it for fishing.	(a) If the instrument in question, or each of the instruments in question, is a rod and line, summarily.
		(b) In any other case—
		  (i) summarily ... ...
		
		  (ii) on indictment ... ...
			Level 4 on the standard scale.
			
			three months or the statutory maximum or both;
			two years or a fine or both.".

(2) Subsection (1) above shall not affect any proceedings in respect of, or the punishment for, an offence committed before that subsection comes into force.

Servants and agents authorised by fishing licences.

1975 c. 51.

36.—(1) For paragraph 9 of Schedule 2 to the Salmon and Freshwater Fisheries Act 1975 (persons treated as servants and agents of licensee for the purpose of being entitled to use an instrument under the authority of the licence) there shall be substituted the following paragraph—

" 9.—(1) A person who uses an instrument of any description for fishing in an area in relation to which an order under section 26 above limiting the number of licences for fishing with instruments of that description is in force shall not be treated for the purposes of section 25(3) above as the duly authorised servant or agent of any holder of a licence to use an instrument of that description unless, at the time that person uses the instrument—

(a) his name and address are entered on the licence in accordance with the following provisions of this Schedule ; and

(b) he is not himself the holder of a licence to use an instrument of that description in that area ; and

(c) he is accompanied by the licensee or has the consent of the water authority to his use of the instrument in the absence of the licensee.

(2) A person who uses an instrument of any description for fishing in an area in which no such order as is mentioned in sub-paragraph (1) above is in force shall not be treated for the purposes of section 25(3) above as the duly authorised servant or agent of any holder of a licence to use an instrument of that description unless, at the time that person uses the instrument—

(a) his name and address are entered on the licence in accordance with the following provisions of this Schedule ; or (*b*) he is accompanied by the licensee ; or

(*c*) he has the consent of the water authority to his use of the instrument otherwise than where there is compliance with paragraph (*a*) or (*b*) above.

(3) The consent of a water authority shall not be given under this paragraph except—

(*a*) in the case of a consent for the purposes of sub-paragraph (1) (*c*) above, in relation to a period which appears to the water authority to be a period throughout which the licensee will be unable through illness or injury to accompany his servant or agent ;

(*b*) in the case of a consent for the purposes of sub-paragraph (2)(*c*) above, where the giving of the consent appears to the water authority to be required by the special circumstances of the case."

(2) Accordingly, in section 25(3) of that Act, for the words from " not exceeding " onwards there shall be substituted the words " subject to the provisions of paragraphs 9 to 13 of Schedule 2 to this Act ".

37.—(1) Subject to subsection (3) below, the power of a local fisheries committee to make byelaws under section 5 of the Sea Fisheries Regulation Act 1966 shall be exercisable for the purposes of protecting salmon and of preventing any interference with their migration and shall be so exercisable as if the references in that section to sea fish included references to salmon.

(2) Subject to subsection (3) below, the power of a local fisheries committee to make byelaws under the said section 5 shall also include power to make byelaws which for the purposes of section 6 of the Salmon and Freshwater Fisheries Act 1975 authorise the placing and use of fixed engines at such places in their sea fisheries district, at such times and in such manner as may be prescribed by the byelaws and impose requirements as to the construction, design, material and dimensions of such engines, including in the case of nets the size of mesh.

(3) A local fisheries committee shall not make byelaws for any purpose mentioned in subsection (1) or (2) above unless the water authority whose area for the purposes of functions relating to fisheries includes the whole or any part of the committee's sea fisheries district have consented to byelaws being made by the committee for that purpose.

(4) For the purposes of any byelaws made by virtue of this section the references to sea fish in sections 10(2)(*c*) and 12 of the

PART III   said Act of 1966 (which include provision with respect to the seizure of, and searches for, sea fish taken in contravention of byelaws) shall be deemed to include references to salmon.

(5) In this section—

" fixed engine " has the same meaning as in the Salmon and Freshwater Fisheries Act 1975 ; and

" salmon " means fish of the salmon species and trout which migrate to and from the sea.

Disclosure of
information
furnished
under the
Diseases of
Fish Act 1983.
1983 c. 30.

38. In subsection (1) of section 9 of the Diseases of Fish Act 1983 (disclosure of information obtained in pursuance of section 7 of that Act), after paragraph (c) there shall be inserted the words " or

(d) for the purpose of enabling a water authority to carry out any of their functions under the 1937 Act ".

PART IV

MISCELLANEOUS

Review of
certain salmon
net fishing.

39.—(1) The Minister of Agriculture, Fisheries and Food and the Secretary of State shall, as soon as practicable after the end of the period of three years beginning with the passing of this Act, prepare a report which, in the context of the need to ensure—

(a) that sufficient salmon return to spawn in the rivers wholly or partly situated in the areas and districts specified in subsection (3) below ; and

(b) that fishing for salmon by means of nets is properly managed in those areas and districts,

reviews the nature and extent of all such fishing in those areas and districts.

(2) A copy of the report prepared under subsection (1) above shall be laid before each House of Parliament.

(3) The areas and districts referred to in subsection (1) above are the areas of the Yorkshire and Northumbrian water authorities and the salmon fishery districts from the River Forth to the River Ugie, the River Tweed being deemed for the purposes of this section to be included in those areas and districts.

Interpretation.

40.—(1) In this Act, unless the context otherwise requires—

" annual close time order " has the meaning ascribed to it in section 6 (3) of this Act ;

" assessor " means the assessor or depute assessor for a valuation area appointed under section 116 of the Local Government (Scotland) Act 1973 ;

1973 c. 65.

" board " and " district salmon fishery board " mean—

    (*a*) the committee of an association of proprietors of salmon fisheries within the meaning of section 14 of this Act ; or

    (*b*) a transitional district board within the meaning of section 14(8) of this Act ;

" coastal limits " means the limits of seacoast fixed for a district under section 6(3) of the Salmon Fisheries 1862 c. 97. (Scotland) Act 1862 ;

" designation order " has the meaning ascribed to it in section 1(2) of this Act ;

" district " and " salmon fishery district " mean an area described in section 1(1) of this Act or designated as such by a designation order ;

" enactment " includes any Act of Parliament, whether public, general, local or private, and any instrument made under any enactment ;

" fishery assessment " has the meaning ascribed to it in section 15(2) of this Act ;

" fishery " and " salmon fishery " means a salmon fishery in any river or estuary or in the sea ;

" inland waters " has the same meaning as in the Salmon and Freshwater Fisheries (Protection) (Scotland) Act 1951 c. 26. 1951 ;

" proprietor " means, subject to subsection (3) below, any person, partnership, company or corporation which is the proprietor of a salmon fishery or which receives or is entitled to receive the rents of such fishery on its own account or as trustee, guardian or factor for any person, company or corporation ;

" river " includes tributaries and any loch from or through which any river flows ;

" River Tweed " means " the River " as defined by the Tweed Fisheries Amendment Act 1859, as amended by 1859 c. lxx. the byelaw made under section 4 of the Salmon Fisher- 1863 c. 50. ies (Scotland) Act 1863 ;

" River Tweed Council " means the council constituted under section 6 of the Tweed Fisheries Act 1969 :   1969 c. xxiv.

" salmon " means all migratory fish of the species *Salmo salar* and *Salmo trutta* and commonly known as salmon and sea trout respectively or any part of any such fish ;

" tenant netsman " means a person in possession of a right, under a lease or sub-lease, of fishing for salmon with nets ; and

PART IV
1975 c. 30.

" valuation roll " means a roll made up under section 1 of the Local Government (Scotland) Act 1975.

(2) In Part I of this Act, " the Salmon Fisheries (Scotland) Acts 1862 to 1868 " means—

1862 c. 97.   the Salmon Fisheries (Scotland) Act 1862 ;

1864 c. 118.   the Salmon Fisheries (Scotland) Act 1864 ; and

1868 c. 123.   the Salmon Fisheries (Scotland) Act 1868.

(3) In this Act, " proprietor " includes not more than one person authorised by—

    (a) in the case of a fishery in which more than one person has a *pro indiviso* share, such persons ; or

    (b) in the case of a fishery in which the rights to that fishery are shared by more than one person in any other way, such persons,

but in neither case does it include, except by virtue of this subsection, a person whose right to that fishery is so shared.

Amendments and repeals.

41.—(1) The enactments mentioned in Schedule 4 to this Act shall have effect subject to the amendments there specified (being minor amendments or amendments consequential on the preceding provisions of this Act).

(2) Subject to subsections (3) and (4) below, the enactments mentioned in Schedule 5 to this Act are hereby repealed to the extent specified in the third column of that Schedule.

1868 c. 123.

(3) The repeal specified in Schedule 5 to this Act relating to section 13 of the Salmon Fisheries (Scotland) Act 1868 shall not extend to the River Tweed.

1863 c. 50.

(4) Notwithstanding the repeal specified in Schedule 5 to this Act relating to the Salmon Fisheries (Scotland) Act 1863, the byelaw made under section 4 of that Act in respect of the limits of the River Tweed shall continue to have effect ; and the repeal of that section shall not affect the legality of any mode of fishing for or taking salmon at any place.

Crown application.

42.—(1) Part I of this Act shall apply to land an interest in which belongs to Her Majesty in right of the Crown and land an interest in which belongs to a government department or is held in trust for Her Majesty for the purposes of a government department, but otherwise this Act shall not bind the Crown.

(2) In this section, " land " includes salmon fisheries.

Citation, commencement and extent.

43.—(1) This Act, which may be cited as the Salmon Act 1986, shall, with the exception of the provision mentioned in

subsection (2) below, come into force on the expiry of the period PART IV
of two months beginning with the date on which it is passed.

(2) Section 21 of this Act shall come into force on such date
as the Secretary of State may by order made by statutory instrument appoint, and such an order may include such transitional
or saving provisions as appear to the Secretary of State to be
necessary or expedient in connection with the provision brought
into force by the order.

(3) The provisions of this Act modifying or repealing other
enactments except section 38 have respectively the same extent as
those other enactments.

(4) Subject to the application of section 39(1) of the Salmon 1975 c. 51.
and Freshwater Fisheries Act 1975 (border rivers) in relation
to section 32 of this Act and the enactments amended by sections 33 to 36 of this Act, sections 31 to 38 of this Act extend to
England and Wales only.

(5) Except as this Act otherwise provides, Parts I and II
and section 42 of this Act extend to Scotland only.

SCHEDULES

Sections 2, 6, 7, 8 and 10.

SCHEDULE 1

PROVISIONS AS RESPECTS THE MAKING OF DESIGNATION ORDERS

Proposals for a designation order

1. The Secretary of State may make a designation order only on the application to him by—

    (a) a district salmon fishery board for a district which would be affected by the proposed order ;

    (b) where there is no such board, two proprietors of salmon fisheries in the area which would be affected by the proposed order ; or

    (c) any number of or combination of such boards or such proprietors in the area which would be affected by the proposed order

but the Secretary of State may act under this Schedule notwithstanding that the applicants do not represent the whole area which would be affected by the proposed order.

2. An application under paragraph 1 above shall be accompanied by the applicant's written proposals which shall state—

    (a) the area which it is proposed should be designated as a salmon fishery district ;

    (b) the salmon fishery district or districts which are, at the time of the application, contained wholly or partly within that area ;

    (c) the reasons for the creation of the proposed salmon fishery district ;

    (d) the proposed dates of the annual close time and the periods within which it shall be permitted to fish for and take salmon by rod and line in the proposed district ; and

    (e) the general effect of the proposals.

Consultation and publication

3. On receiving an application under paragraph 1 above, the Secretary of State shall consult such persons as he considers appropriate and may—

    (a) request from the applicant such additional information as he thinks fit ;

    (b) dismiss the application ;

    (c) proceed in accordance with the remaining provisions of this Schedule.

4.—(1) Before making a designation order, the Secretary of State shall direct that notice of the general effect of the proposals shall be given, specifying the time (not being less than 28 days from the date of the first publication of the notice) within which, and the manner in which, representations or objections with respect to the proposals may be made.

(2) Notice shall be given at least once in each of two successive weeks by advertising in a newspaper circulating in the district or districts affected by the proposals.

(3) The cost of giving notice shall be met by the applicant under paragraph 1 above.

5. At any time, the Secretary of State may alter the proposals in such way as he thinks fit and shall consider whether such alterations are sufficient to require—

(*a*) further consultation as mentioned in paragraph 3 above ; and

(*b*) further notice to be given under paragraph 4 above.

Making of order

6. If no representations or objections are duly made, or if all so made are withdrawn, the Secretary of State may make a designation order.

7.—(1) If any representation or objection duly made is not withdrawn, the Secretary of State may, after considering the same—

(*a*) make a designation order ;

(*b*) dismiss the application ; or

(*c*) cause a local inquiry to be held.

(2) The Secretary of State shall appoint a person to hold the inquiry and to report thereon to him.

(3) Notification of the time when and the place where the inquiry is to be held shall be sent to any person who has duly made and has not withdrawn representations about or objections to the proposals, and shall be published at least once in each of two successive weeks in a newspaper circulating in the district or districts affected by the proposals.

(4) The person appointed to hold the inquiry may administer oaths and examine witnesses on oath and may accept, in lieu of evidence on oath by any person, a statement in writing by that person.

(5) The Secretary of State may make orders as to the expenses incurred by him in relation to the inquiry (including such reasonable sum as he may determine for the services of the person appointed to hold the inquiry) and as to the expenses incurred by the parties to the inquiry and as to the parties by whom such expenses shall be paid.

(6) Any order of the Secretary of State under sub-paragraph (5) above requiring any party to pay expenses may be enforced in like manner as a recorded decree arbitral.

8. After considering the report of the person appointed to hold the inquiry in pursuance of paragraph 7 above and any representations or objections which were duly made, the Secretary of State may make a designation order.

9. The power to make a designation order shall be exercisable by statutory instrument.

SCHEDULE 2

ELECTION AND CO-OPTION OF MEMBERS OF DISTRICT SALMON FISHERY BOARDS

PART I

MEETING OF QUALIFIED PROPRIETORS

Calling of meeting

1.—(1) Where there is no district salmon fishery board or transitional district board for a district, the sheriff shall, on the application of two qualified proprietors of salmon fisheries in the district,—

(a) make up a roll of upper and lower proprietors in the district to which the application relates ;

(b) call a meeting of these proprietors, at such time and place as he may direct, for the purpose of forming an association of proprietors of salmon fisheries for that district and electing a committee to become the district salmon fishery board for that district ; and

(c) give notice at least once in each of two successive weeks by advertising in a newspaper circulating in the district of the date, time and place of that meeting.

(2) Where proposals for a designation order have been considered by the Secretary of State, in accordance with Schedule 1 to this Act, and he considers that a designation order should be made—

(a) the clerk or, acting jointly, the clerks to the district salmon fishery boards or transitional district boards for any district or districts which would be superseded by the proposed designation order shall perform, in respect of the proposed district, the duties specified in sub-paragraph (1) above ; or

(b) where there is no district salmon fishery board for any district which would be superseded by the proposed designation order, the sheriff shall perform the duties specified in sub-paragraph (1) above on the application of two proprietors of salmon fisheries in the proposed district

and the following provisions of this Schedule shall have effect in respect of the proposed district as if it had been designated.

(3) Where the salmon fishery district lies in more than one sheriffdom, the sheriff in whose jurisdiction lies the major part of that district may, for the purposes of this Schedule, perform the duties specified in sub-paragraph (1) above in an adjacent sheriffdom.

(4) The sheriff may recover from the committee formed in accordance with this Schedule all expenses incurred by him in the performance of his duties under this paragraph, whether or not that committee becomes a district salmon fishery board, but if it does become such a board, these expenses may be met out of the fishery assessment.

2.—(1) At a meeting of proprietors called—

(a) by the sheriff under paragraph 1 above ;

(*b*) by the clerk to a board in accordance with section 18(1) of
    this Act ; or

(*c*) by the clerk to a transitional district board in accordance
    with paragraph 7(*a*) of Schedule 3 to this Act,

the proprietors present shall elect or, as the case may be, re-elect
a committee to act on behalf of the association.

(2) If—

(*a*) the membership of that committee is in accordance with
    Part II of this Schedule ; and

(*b*) the requirements of this Part as respects eligibility are met

that committee shall be or continue to be the district salmon fishery
board for that district.

(3) Membership of such a committee, whether or not it is a
district salmon fishery board, shall not affect eligibility for membership of any other such committee or board.

Election of members

3.—(1) The meeting shall elect from amongst the qualified proprietors present a person to be chairman of the committee.

(2) In accordance with the following provisions of this Part of
this Schedule, representatives of qualified proprietors shall then be
elected by—

(*a*) the upper proprietors from amongst themselves ; and

(*b*) the lower proprietors from amongst themselves

but an election under this sub-paragraph shall not be held invalid
for the sole reason that there was only one upper or, as the case
may be, lower proprietor present.

(3) A qualified proprietor shall have, in respect of each fishery
he owns within the district, one vote in an election under this paragraph and shall have one additional vote for each £5,000 or part
thereof by which the value of that fishery as entered in the valuation
roll exceeds £5,000 but, subject to sub-paragraph (5) below, no proprietor shall have more than four votes in total as respects each
fishery.

(4) A proprietor of a salmon fishery in the district which has
been neither entered nor entered separately in the valuation roll
shall, notwithstanding anything to the contrary, have one vote at the
meeting and shall be eligible for election.

(5) A person who is both an upper and a lower proprietor by
virtue of section 11(5) of this Act shall count as both an upper and
as a lower proprietor for the purposes of this paragraph and he
may both vote and be elected in each capacity.

Balance between upper and lower proprietors

4.—(1) In the election of representatives of qualified proprietors,
not more than three may be elected by upper proprietors and not
more than three may be elected by lower proprietors.

SCH. 2   (2) Where there are less than three proprietors in the district
qualified as upper proprietors or less than three qualified as lower
proprietors, the number elected from either category shall not exceed
the number eligible for election in the other category.

(3) If the person elected as chairman is—

(a) an upper proprietor and there are less than four upper
proprietors in that district ; or

(b) a lower proprietor and there are less than four lower proprietors in that district,

he shall also be eligible for election as a representative of qualified
proprietors and, if elected, may act as such in addition to acting
as chairman.

(4) In calculating the numbers of upper and lower proprietors, a
person who is both an upper and a lower proprietor by virtue of
section 11(5) of this Act shall be counted in each capacity in which
he has been elected.

Co-optees

5.—(1) In the co-opting of representatives of salmon anglers and
of tenant netsmen under Part II below, the number of representatives
of salmon anglers shall equal the number of representatives of tenant
netsmen but that number shall be no more than three and shall not
exceed—

(a) the number of proprietors in the district qualified as upper
proprietors ; or

(b) the number of proprietors in the district qualified as lower
proprietors,

whichever is the smaller number of qualified proprietors.

(2) A person who is both an upper and a lower proprietor by
virtue of section 11(5) of this Act shall be counted in each capacity
for the purposes of sub-paragraph (1) above.

(3) A representative of salmon anglers shall be a person whom
the board consider to be representative of persons angling for salmon
in the district but who is not himself an upper proprietor in that
district.

(4) Before co-opting a person as a representative of salmon
anglers, the board shall consult such organisations representing
salmon anglers in the district as they think fit ; but this requirement shall not apply to the filling of a vacancy in accordance with
section 18(5) of this Act.

(5) A representative of tenant netsmen shall be—

(a) a tenant netsman in the district who is not a lower proprietor
in that district ;

(b) a tenant netsman in the district who is a lower proprietor in
that district if—

(i) there are insufficient tenant netsmen who are qualified or willing to be co-opted and who are not also lower
proprietors in that district ; and

(ii) he has not been elected to the board of that district as a representative of lower proprietors or as chairman ; or

(c) a lower proprietor in the district who is not a tenant netsman in that district if—

(i) there are insufficient tenant netsmen qualified or willing to be co-opted, whether or not they are also lower proprietors in that district ; and

(ii) he has not been elected to the board of that district as a representative of lower proprietors or as chairman,

but a person shall not be disqualified under this sub-paragraph solely because he is an upper proprietor in that district or has been elected to the board of that district as a representative of upper proprietors.

PART II

MEMBERSHIP

6.—(1) The members of the committee shall be members of a district salmon fishery board if the committee consists of the following persons—

(a) an elected chairman ; and

(b) in addition to the chairman, not more than six elected representatives of qualified proprietors in the district

and a person who is both an upper proprietor and a lower proprietor by virtue of section 11(5) of this Act may be elected in either capacity or in both capacities.

(2) As soon after the meeting of proprietors referred to in Part I above as is practicable, the chairman and the elected representatives of qualified proprietors shall, in accordance with the provisions of this Schedule co-opt representatives of salmon anglers and tenant netsmen in the district as required by section 16(2) of this Act.

(3) The members of a district salmon fishery board shall be—

(a) the persons mentioned in sub-paragraph (1) above ;

(b) not more than three co-opted representatives of salmon anglers in the district ; and

(c) not more than three co-opted representatives of tenant netsmen in the district

but a committee shall not fail to be a district salmon fishery board only by reason that no persons or not enough persons have been co-opted in accordance with this paragraph if—

(i) there has been insufficient time to co-opt such persons ; or

(ii) no persons or not enough persons are willing to be co-opted.

SCHEDULE 3   Section 14(8).

TRANSITIONAL DISTRICT BOARDS

1. Subject to the provisions of this Schedule, a transitional district board within the meaning of section 14(8) of this Act shall be

Part IV   O

Sch. 3

deemed to be a district salmon fishery board and have the powers and duties of such a board and references to a district salmon fishery board shall, unless the context otherwise requires, include references to a transitional district board.

2.—(1) Sections 16(2) and 18 of this Act shall not apply to a transitional district board, which may retain the membership which it had at the commencement of section 14 of this Act.

(2) Subject to paragraph 3 below, vacancies on that board may be filled by the board by an upper or, as the case may be, lower proprietor within the meaning of this Act.

(3) The chairman or a member of a transitional district board may authorise a person to act for him as chairman or as such a member.

3. The chairman of a transitional district board shall be the proprietor whose salmon fishery or, taken together, fisheries in that district has or have the greatest value entered in the valuation roll.

4. The clerk to a transitional district board shall prepare a new roll of upper and lower proprietors in that district in accordance with section 11 of this Act so as to include in the roll any proprietors who were not proprietors of salmon fisheries in that district immediately before the commencement of section 14 of this Act.

5.—(1) A transitional district board may continue to collect the whole or any outstanding part of the fishery assessment imposed under section 23 of the Salmon Fisheries (Scotland) Act 1862 from proprietors of fisheries on which that assessment had been imposed before the commencement of section 14 of this Act.

1862 c. 97.

(2) On the expiry of the period of the fishery assessment mentioned above, the board may levy a fishery assessment under section 15 of this Act but only in respect of fisheries in the district on which that assessment had been imposed before the commencement of section 14 of this Act.

(3) The board may recover arrears of fishery assessment, whether due before or after the commencement of section 14 of this Act, by action for payment of money.

(4) The power under subparagraph (3) above to recover arrears of fishery assessment includes power to recover interest, chargeable at such rate as the Secretary of State shall, with the consent of the Treasury, determine, on such arrears from—

    (a) in the case of recovery of arrears due before the date of the coming into force of section 14 of this Act which have been outstanding for at least three months from that date, that date ; or

    (b) in the case of recovery of arrears due in respect of an assessment imposed by a transitional district board which have been outstanding for at least three months from the date of issue of a notice of assessment, that date

until payment or the commencement of an action for payment, which-   Sch. 3
ever is the earlier.

6. A transitional district board shall cease to be deemed a district
salmon fishery board and shall cease to have such powers and duties
on the expiry of—

(*a*) three years from the date of the last meeting of proprietors
within the meaning of sections 18 or 24 of the Salmon
Fisheries (Scotland) Act 1862 or section 3 of the Salmon   1862 c. 97.
Fisheries (Scotland) Act 1868 ; or   1868 c. 123.

(*b*) six months from the date of the commencement of section
14 of this Act,

whichever is later.

7. At any time within the periods specified in paragraph 6 above,
the clerk to a transitional district board shall, on the instructions of
the board,—

(*a*) call a meeting of the upper and lower proprietors of the
district, at such time and place as the board may direct, for
the purpose of forming an association of proprietors of
salmon fisheries for that district and electing a committee
to become the district salmon fishery board for that district ;
and

(*b*) give notice at least once in two successive weeks by advertising in a newspaper circulating in the district of the date,
time and place of that meeting.

8. Notwithstanding paragraph 6 above, a transitional district board
shall cease to be deemed a district salmon fishery board and shall
cease to have the powers and duties of a transitional district board
on the election in accordance with Schedule 2 to this Act of a committee of an association of proprietors within the meaning of section
14 of this Act.

9. The assets and liabilities of a district board within the meaning
of the Salmon Fisheries (Scotland) Acts 1862 to 1868 shall be transferred to the transitional district board for that district and, likewise,
the assets and liabilities of a transitional district board shall be transferred to the district salmon fishery board for that district whenever
such a board is elected.

SCHEDULE 4   Section 41.

Minor and Consequential Amendments

Salmon Fisheries (Scotland) Act 1868 (c. 123.)

1. After section 1 of the Salmon Fisheries (Scotland) Act 1868
there shall be inserted the following section—

"Expressions   1A. In this Act, unless the context otherwise requires
used in this   the expressions " board " or " district salmon fishery
Act.   board ", " district " or " salmon fishery district ", " fishery ", " proprietor ", " salmon " and " river " shall have
the meanings ascribed to them in section 40(1) of the
Salmon Act 1986 (interpretation).".

O 2

SCH. 4   2. In section 11 of that Act (application to streams not frequented by salmon), for the words " mill dams " there shall be substituted the words " dams, including mill dams ".

3.—(1) In section 18 of that Act (offence of buying, selling, possessing etc. of salmon roe), the words from " uses " to " purposes, or " shall be omitted.

(2) In section 19 (offences in relation to young salmon, salmon spawn, spawning beds etc.), the words from " for the purpose " in the second place where they occur to " purpose, or " shall be omitted.

(3) In section 20 (offences in relation to unclean or unseasonable salmon), the words from " or to any person " onwards shall be omitted.

4. In the said section 19, for the word " wilfully " there shall be substituted the word "knowingly ".

5. In section 41 of that Act (extent), the words from " and Schedule G " to " Schedule " shall be omitted.

Diseases of Fish Act 1937 (c.33)

6. In subsection (3) of section 8 of the Diseases of Fish Act 1937 (penalties and legal proceedings) for the words after " be " there shall be substituted the words " proceeded against and punished in Scotland ".

Salmon and Freshwater Fisheries (Protection) (Scotland) Act 1951 (c. 26)

7. In section 1 of the Salmon and Freshwater Fisheries (Protection) (Scotland) Act 1951 (prohibition of poaching), for the words " low water mark " there shall be substituted the words " mean low water springs ".

8. Section 9 of that Act (saving for acts done for scientific and other purposes) shall be renumbered as subsection (1) of that section and—

(*a*) in that subsection the words from " or ", where fourthly occurring, onwards shall cease to have effect ; and

(*b*) after that subsection there shall be added the following subsection

    " (2) This section does not apply to an act relating to salmon.".

9. In section 15(1)(*c*) of that Act (power of Secretary of State to conduct inquiries and to obtain information), the words from " so as to show " to the end of that subsection shall be omitted.

10. In section 19(2) of that Act (forfeitures) the words " on indictment " shall be omitted.

11. In section 22 of that Act (provisions as to River Tweed), for the reference to the Board of Commissioners of the River Tweed there shall be substituted a reference to the council constituted under section 6 of the Tweed Fisheries Act 1969.

1969 c. xxiv.

12. In section 24 of that Act (interpretation), for the entries relating to " District " and " District Board " there shall be substituted the following entries—

" " District " and " Salmon Fishery District " shall be deemed to Sch. 4
include the River Tweed ;

" District Board " and " District Salmon Fishery Board " shall
include the council constituted under section 6 of the Tweed 1969 c. xxiv.
Fisheries Act 1969 ; ".

Salmon and Freshwater Fisheries Act 1975 (c. 51)

13. In section 39 of the Salmon and Freshwater Fisheries Act
1975 (Border rivers and Solway Firth), after subsection (4) there
shall be added the following subsection—

" (5) Nothing in this section shall authorise a water authority
to take legal proceedings in Scotland in respect of an offence
against this Act.".

14. In section 43(3) of that Act (Scottish extent), for the words
" and (4) " there shall be substituted the words " (4) and (5) ".

Freshwater and Salmon Fisheries (Scotland) Act 1976 (c. 22)

15.—(1) In section 7(5) of the Freshwater and Salmon Fisheries
(Scotland) Act 1976 (fish farmers to be exempted from certain
offences)—

(*a*) the word " 4 " shall be omitted ; and

(*b*) after the word " 8 " there shall be inserted the words " , 8A ".

(2) In Part I of Schedule 3 to that Act (offences from which fish
farmers are to be exempted)—

(*a*) paragraph 4 shall be omitted ; and

(*b*) after paragraph 8 there shall be inserted the following paragraph—

" (8A) In the Salmon Act 1986, regulations made under
section 3(2)(*a*) or (*d*) (general regulations).".

SCHEDULE 5

REPEALS

Chapter	Short title	Extent of repeal
1696 c. 35 (S.).	Salmon Act 1696.	The whole Act.
25 & 26 Vict. c. 97.	Salmon Fisheries (Scotland) Act 1862.	The whole Act.
26 & 27 Vict. c. 10.	Salmon Acts Amendment Act 1863.	The whole Act.
26 & 27 Vict. c. 50.	Salmon Fisheries (Scotland) Act 1863.	The whole Act.
27 & 28 Vict. c. 118.	Salmon Fisheries (Scotland) Act 1864.	The whole Act.
31 & 32 Vict. c. 123.	Salmon Fisheries (Scotland) Act 1868.	The whole Act except sections 1, 11, 15, 18 to 24, 26, 27, 29, 31 to 36 and 41.
33 & 34 Vict. c. 33.	Salmon Acts Amendment Act 1870.	The whole Act.
45 & 46 Vict. c. 78.	Fishery Board (Scotland) Act 1882.	The whole Act.
14 & 15 Geo. 6. c. 26.	Salmon and Freshwater Fisheries (Protection) (Scotland) Act 1951.	Section 14. In section 19(2) the words "on indictment,".

Housing and Planning Act 1986

1986 CHAPTER 63

An Act to make further provision with respect to housing, planning and local inquiries; to provide financial assistance for the regeneration of urban areas; and for connected purposes. [7th November, 1986]

BE IT ENACTED by the Queen's most Excellent Majesty, by and with the advice and consent of the Lords Spiritual and Temporal, and Commons, in this present Parliament assembled, and by the authority of the same, as follows:—

PART I

HOUSING

The right to buy

1. In Schedule 5 to the Housing Act 1985 (exceptions to the right to buy: certain dwelling-houses for persons of pensionable age), there shall be substituted for paragraph 11—

" **11.**—(1) The right to buy does not arise if the dwelling-house—

(*a*) is particularly suitable for occupation by persons of pensionable age, having regard—

(i) to its location, and

Exception to the right to buy with respect to dwelling-houses for persons of pensionable age.

1985 c. 68.

O4

(ii) to its size, design, heating system and other major features so far as those have been provided by the landlord, a predecessor of the tenant or a person qualified to succeed the tenant by virtue of Part IV of the Housing Act 1985,

(b) was let to the tenant or a predecessor in title of his for occupation by a person of pensionable age or a physically disabled person (whether the tenant or predecessor or another person).

(2) In determining whether a dwelling is particularly suitable, regard shall be had as to whether the dwelling—

(a) is easily accessible on foot ;

(b) is on one level ;

(c) being a flat located above ground floor, access by lift is available ;

(d) has no more than two bedrooms ;

(e) has a heating system serving the living room and at least one bedroom.".

Discount on
right to buy
and similar
sales.
1985 c. 68.

2.—(1) In section 129 of the Housing Act 1985 (discount on exercise of right to buy), for subsections (1) and (2) substitute—

" (1) Subject to the following provisions of this Part, a person exercising the right to buy is entitled to a discount of a percentage calculated by reference to the period which is to be taken into account in accordance with Schedule 4 (qualifying period for right to buy and discount).

(2) The discount is, subject to any order under subsection (2A)—

(a) in the case of a house, 32 per cent. plus one per cent. for each complete year by which the qualifying period exceeds two years, up to a maximum of 60 per cent. ;

(b) in the case of a flat, 44 per cent. plus two per cent. for each complete year by which the qualifying period exceeds two years, up to a maximum of 70 per cent.

(2A) The Secretary of State may by order made with the consent of the Treasury provide that, in such cases as may be specified in the order—

(a) the minimum percentage discount,

(b) the percentage increase for each complete year of the qualifying period after the first two, or (*c*) the maximum percentage discount,

shall be such percentage, higher than that specified in sub-section (2), as may be specified in the order.

(2B) An order—

(*a*) may make different provision with respect to different cases or descriptions of case,

(*b*) may contain such incidental, supplementary or transitional provisions as appear to the Secretary of State to be necessary or expedient, and

(*c*) shall be made by statutory instrument and shall not be made unless a draft of it has been laid before and approved by resolution of each House of Parliament.".

(2) The amendment made by subsection (1) does not apply where—

(*a*) the tenant's notice claiming to exercise the right to buy or, as the case may be, to acquire an additional share under a shared ownership lease was served before the commencement of that subsection, and

(*b*) the landlord has before commencement served its notice as to the terms of exercise of that right, that is, its notice under section 125 of, or paragraph 1(3) of Schedule 8 to, the Housing Act 1985,

1985 c. 68.

but without prejudice to the tenant's right to withdraw the notice served before commencement and serve a new notice.

(3) In the following provisions (which in the case of disposals at a discount require a covenant for repayment of a proportion of the discount if the dwelling-house is disposed of within five years)—

section 35(2) of the Housing Act 1985 (voluntary disposals by local authorities),

section 155(2) of that Act (disposals in pursuance of the right to buy),

section 155(3) of that Act (disposals in pursuance of the right to be granted a shared ownership lease), and

paragraph 1(2) of Schedule 2 to the Housing Associations Act 1985 (voluntary disposals by registered housing associations),

1985 c. 69.

for " five years " substitute " three years " and for " 20 per cent." substitute " one-third ".

(4) A conveyance or lease containing the covenant required by any of the provisions mentioned in subsection (3) which was executed before the amendments made by that subsection came

PART I

into force shall, provided no amount was then or had previously been payable under the covenant, have effect with such modifications as may be necessary to bring it into conformity with the amendments.

Discount on
exercise of
right to
purchase in
Scotland.
1980 c. 52.

3.—(1) In section 1 (secure tenant's right to purchase) of the Tenants' Rights, Etc. (Scotland) Act 1980, in subsection (5), after " (*b*) " insert—

" subject to an order under subsection (5B) below,".

(2) After subsection (5A) of the said section 1 insert—

" (5B) The Secretary of State may by order made with the consent of the Treasury provide that, in such cases as may be specified in the order—

(*a*) the minimum percentage discount,

(*b*) the percentage increase for each complete year of the qualifying period after the first two, or

(*c*) the maximum percentage discount,

shall be such percentage, higher than that specified in subsection (5)(*b*), as may be specified in the order.

(5C) An order—

(*a*) may make different provision with respect to different cases or descriptions of case,

(*b*) may contain such incidental, supplementary or transitional provisions, including such amendments to the provisions of section 9A (application of Part I when dwelling-house is repurchased as defective) below, as appear to the Secretary of State to be necessary or expedient, and

(*c*) shall be made by statutory instrument and shall not be made unless a draft of it has been laid before and approved by resolution of each House of Parliament.".

Service
charges
and other
contributions
payable after
exercise of
right to buy.
1985 c. 68.

4.—(1) In section 125 of the Housing Act 1985 (landlord's notice of purchase price and other matters), for subsection (4) (notice to include estimate of amount of service charges) substitute—

" (4) Where the notice states provisions which would enable the landlord to recover from the tenant—

(*a*) service charges, or

(*b*) improvement contributions,

the notice shall also contain the estimates and other information required by section 125A (service charges) or 125B (improvement contributions).".

(2) After that section insert—

"Estimates and information about service charges.

125A.—(1) A landlord's notice under section 125 shall state as regards service charges (excluding, in the case of a flat, charges to which subsection (2) applies)—

> (*a*) the landlord's estimate of the average annual amount (at current prices) which would be payable in respect of each head of charge in the reference period, and
>
> (*b*) the aggregate of those estimated amounts,

and shall contain a statement of the reference period adopted for the purpose of the estimates.

(2) A landlord's notice under section 125 given in respect of a flat shall, as regards service charges in respect of repairs (including works for the making good of structural defects), contain—

> (*a*) the estimates required by subsection (3), together with a statement of the reference period adopted for the purpose of the estimates, and
>
> (*b*) a statement of the effect of—
>
> > paragraph 16B of Schedule 6 (which restricts by reference to the estimates the amounts payable by the tenant), and
> >
> > section 450A and the regulations made under that section (right to a loan in respect of certain service charges).

(3) The following estimates are required for works in respect of which the landlord considers that costs may be incurred in the reference period—

> (*a*) for works itemised in the notice, estimates of the amount (at current prices) of the likely cost of, and of the tenant's likely contribution in respect of, each item, and the aggregate amounts of those estimated costs and contributions, and
>
> (*b*) for works not so itemised, an estimate of the average annual amount (at current prices) which the landlord considers is likely to be payable by the tenant.

Estimates and information about improvement contributions.

125B.—(1) A landlord's notice under section 125 given in respect of a flat shall, as regards improvement contributions, contain—

> (*a*) the estimates required by this section, together with a statement of the reference

period adopted for the purpose of the estimates, and

(*b*) a statement of the effect of paragraph 16C
of Schedule 6 (which restricts by reference
to the estimates the amounts payable by
the tenant).

(2) Estimates are required for works in respect of
which the landlord considers that costs may be incurred in the reference period.

(3) The works to which the estimates relate shall
be itemised and the estimates shall show—

(*a*) the amount (at current prices) of the likely
cost of, and of the tenant's likely contribution in respect of, each item, and

(*b*) the aggregate amounts of those estimated
costs and contributions.

Reference
period for
purposes of
ss. 125A
and 125B.

125C.—(1) The reference period for the purposes
of the estimates required by section 125A or 125B
is the period—

(*a*) beginning on such date not more than six
months after the notice is given as the landlord may reasonably specify as being a date
by which the conveyance will have been
made or the lease granted, and

(*b*) ending five years after that date or, where
the notice states that the conveyance or
lease will provide for a service charge or
improvement contribution to be calculated
by reference to a specified annual period,
with the end of the fifth such period beginning after that date.

(2) For the purpose of the estimates it shall be
assumed that the conveyance will be made or the
lease granted at the beginning of the reference
period on the terms stated in the notice.".

1985 c. 68.

(3) In section 127 of the Housing Act 1985 (valuation of
dwelling-house for purposes of right to buy) in subsection (1)
(basis of valuation), after paragraph (*b*) insert—

", and

(*c*) on the assumption that any service charges or improvement contributions payable will not be less than the
amounts to be expected in accordance with the estimates contained in the landlord's notice under section
125.".

(4) In Part III of Schedule 6 to the Housing Act 1985 (terms   PART I
of lease granted in pursuance of right to buy), after paragraph 1985 c. 68.
16 insert—

"Service charges and other contributions payable by the tenant

16A.—(1) The lease may require the tenant to bear a
reasonable part of the costs incurred by the landlord—

(a) in discharging or insuring against the obligations
imposed by the covenants implied by virtue of
paragraph 14(2) (repairs, making good structural
defects, provision of services, etc.), or

(b) in insuring against the obligations imposed by the
covenant implied by virtue of paragraph 14(3)
(rebuilding or reinstatement, etc.),

and to the extent that by virtue of paragraph 15(3) (effect
of provision of superior lease) such obligations are not
imposed on the landlord, to bear a reasonable part of the
costs incurred by the landlord in contributing to costs
incurred by a superior landlord or other person in discharging or, as the case may be, insuring against obligations
to the like effect.

(2) Where the lease requires the tenant to contribute to
the costs of insurance, it shall provide that the tenant is
entitled to inspect the relevant policy at such reasonable
times as may be specified in the lease.

(3) Where the landlord does not insure against the obligations imposed by the covenant implied by virtue of paragraph 14(3), or, as the case may be, the superior landlord
or other person does not insure against his obligations to
the like effect, the lease may require the tenant to pay
a reasonable sum in place of the contribution he could be
required to make if there were insurance.

(4) Where in any case the obligations imposed by the
covenants implied by virtue of paragraph 14(2) or (3) are
modified in accordance with paragraph 14(4) (power of
county court to authorise modification), the references in
this paragraph are to the obligations as so modified.

(5) This paragraph has effect subject to paragraph 16B
(restrictions in certain cases as regards costs incurred in
the initial period of the lease).

16B.—(1) Where a lease of a flat requires the tenant
to pay service charges in respect of repairs (including works
for the making good of structural defects), his liability in
respect of costs incurred in the initial period of the lease
is restricted as follows.

(2) He is not required to pay in respect of works itemised in the estimates contained in the landlord's notice under section 125 any more than the amount shown as his estimated contribution in respect of that item, together with an inflation allowance.

(3) He is not required to pay in respect of works not so itemised at a rate exceeding—

(*a*) as regards parts of the initial period falling within the reference period for the purposes of the estimates contained in the landlord's notice under section 125, the estimated annual average amount shown in the estimates;

(*b*) as regards parts of the initial period not falling within that reference period, the average rate produced by averaging over the reference period all works for which estimates are contained in the notice;

together, in each case, with an inflation allowance.

(4) The initial period of the lease for the purposes of this paragraph begins with the grant of the lease and ends five years after the grant, except that—

(*a*) if the lease includes provision for service charges to be payable in respect of costs incurred in a period before the grant of the lease, the initial period begins with the beginning of that period;

(*b*) if the lease provides for service charges to be calculated by reference to a specified annual period, the initial period continues until the end of the fifth such period beginning after the grant of the lease; and

(*c*) if the tenant served notice under section 142 deferring completion, the initial period ends on the date on which it would have ended if the lease had been granted on the date on which the notice was served.

16C.—(1) Where a lease of a flat requires the tenant to pay improvement contributions, his liability in respect of costs incurred in the initial period of the lease is restricted as follows.

(2) He is not required to make any payment in respect of works for which no estimate was given in the landlord's notice under section 125.

(3) He is not required to pay in respect of works for which an estimate was given in that notice any more than the amount shown as his estimated contribution in respect of that item, together with an inflation allowance.

(4) The initial period of the lease for the purposes of this PART I paragraph begins with the grant of the lease and ends five years after the grant, except that—

(a) if the lease includes provision for improvement contributions to be payable in respect of costs incurred in a period before the grant of the lease, the initial period begins with the beginning of that period ;

(b) if the lease provides for improvement contributions to be calculated by reference to a specified annual period, the initial period continues until the end of the fifth such period beginning after the grant of the lease ; and

(c) if the tenant served notice under section 142 deferring completion, the initial period ends on the date on which it would have ended if the lease had been granted on the date on which the notice was served.

16D.—(1) The Secretary of State may by order prescribe—

(a) the method by which inflation allowances for the purposes of paragraph 16B or 16C are to be calculated by reference to published statistics ; and

(b) the information to be given to a tenant when he is asked to pay a service charge or improvement contribution to which the provisions of paragraph 16B or 16C are or may be relevant.

(2) An order—

(a) may make different provision for different cases or descriptions of case, including different provision for different areas ;

(b) may contain such incidental, supplementary or transitional provisions as the Secretary of State thinks appropriate ; and

(c) shall be made by statutory instrument which shall be subject to annulment in pursuance of a resolution of either House of Parliament.".

(5) For paragraph 18 of Schedule 6 to the Housing Act 1985 1985 c. 68. (avoidance of certain provisions relating to service charges) substitute—

" 18. Where the dwelling-house is a flat, a provision of the lease or of an agreement collateral to it is void in so far as it purports—

(a) to authorise the recovery of such a charge as is mentioned in paragraph 16A (contributions in respect of repairs, etc.) otherwise than in accordance with that paragraph and paragraph 16B (restrictions in initial period of lease) ; or

(b) to authorise the recovery of any charge in respect of costs incurred by the landlord—

(i) in discharging the obligations imposed by the covenant implied by paragraph 14(3) (rebuilding or reinstatement, &c.), or those obligations as modified in accordance with paragraph 14(4), or

(ii) in contributing to costs incurred by a superior landlord or other person in discharging obligations to the like effect ; or

(c) to authorise the recovery of an improvement contribution otherwise than in accordance with paragraph 16C (restrictions in initial period of lease).".

(6) The amendments in this section do not apply where—

(a) the tenant's notice claiming to exercise the right to buy was served before the commencement of this section, and

1985 c. 68.

(b) the landlord has before commencement served his notice under section 125 of the Housing Act 1985 (notice of terms of exercise of right) ;

but without prejudice to the tenant's right to withdraw the notice served before commencement and serve a new notice.

Loans in respect of service charges.

5. In Part XIV of the Housing Act 1985 (loans for acquisition or improvement of housing), after section 450 insert—

" *Loans in respect of service charges*

Right to a loan in certain cases after exercise of right to buy.

450A.—(1) The Secretary of State may by regulations provide that where—

(a) a lease of a flat has been granted in pursuance of Part V (the right to buy), and

(b) the landlord is the housing authority who granted the lease or another housing authority,

the tenant has, in such circumstances as may be prescribed, a right to a loan in respect of service charges to which this section applies.

(2) This section applies to service charges in respect of repairs (whether to the flat, the building in

which it is situated or any other building or land)
which are payable in the period beginning with the
grant of the lease and ending with the tenth anniversary of the grant or, where the lease provides for
service charges to be payable by reference to a specified annual period, with the end of the tenth such
period beginning after the grant of the lease.

(3) The regulations may provide that the right—

    (*a*) arises only in respect of so much of a ser-
       vice charge as exceeds a minimum quali-
       fying amount and does not exceed a
       maximum qualifying amount, and

    (*b*) does not arise unless the amount thus
       qualifying for a loan itself exceeds a mini-
       mum amount,

the amounts being either prescribed or ascertained
in a prescribed manner.

(4) The regulations shall provide that the right
is—

    (*a*) where the landlord is a housing association,
       a right to an advance from the Housing
       Corporation, and

    (*b*) in any other case, a right to leave the whole
       or part of the service charge outstanding.

(5) The regulations may, as regards the procedure
for exercising the right, provide—

    (*a*) that a demand for service charges in res-
       pect of repairs shall inform the tenant
       whether, in the landlord's opinion, he is
       entitled to a loan and, if he is, what he
       must do to claim it ;

    (*b*) that the right must be claimed within a pre-
       scribed period of the demand ; and

    (*c*) that on the right being claimed the lender
       shall inform the tenant of the terms of the
       loan and of the prescribed period within
       which the tenant may accept the offer.

(6) In this section—

    " housing authority " includes any housing
       association within section 80 (the land-
       lord condition for secure tenancies) ; and

    " repairs " includes works for making good a
       structural defect.

PART I

Power to make loans in other cases.

450B.—(1) The Secretary of State may by regulations provide that where—

(a) a housing authority is the landlord of a flat under a long lease granted or assigned by the authority or by another housing authority, and

(b) the tenant is liable under the terms of the lease to pay service charges in respect of repairs (whether to the flat, the building in which it is situated or any other building or land),

the landlord or, where the landlord is a housing association, the Housing Corporation may, in such circumstances as may be prescribed, make a loan to the tenant in respect of the service charges.

(2) The regulations shall provide that the power is—

(a) where the landlord is a housing association, a power of the Housing Corporation to make an advance, and

(b) in any other case, a power of the landlord to leave the whole or part of the service charge outstanding.

(3) Where the tenant is entitled to a loan in pursuance of regulations under section 450A, the power conferred by regulations under this section may be exercised in respect of any part of the service charge which does not qualify for a loan under that section.

(4) In this section—

" housing authority " includes any housing association within section 80 (the landlord condition for secure tenancies) ; and

" repairs " includes works for making good a structural defect.

(5) This section does not affect any other power of the landlord, or the Housing Corporation, to make loans.

Supplementary provisions as to regulations under s. 450A or 450B.

450C.(1) This section applies to regulatinos under section 450A or 450B (regulations conferring right to loan, or power to make loan, in respect of service charges).

(2) The regulations may provide that the right or, as the case may be, the power does not arise in the case of any prescribed description of landlord.

(3) The regulations shall provide that the loan—

(a) in the case of a loan made in pursuance of regulations under section 450A (the right to a loan), shall be on such terms as may be prescribed, and

(b) in the case of a loan made by virtue of regulations under section 450B (power to make loan), shall be on such terms as the lender may determine subject to any provision made by the regulations ;

and shall, in either case, be secured by a mortgage of the flat in question, but may be made whether or not the flat is adequate security for the loan.

(4) The regulations may—

(a) as regards the rate of interest payable on the loan, either prescribe the rate or provide that the rate shall be such reasonable rate as may be determined by the lender or, where the lender is a local authority, provide that Schedule 16 applies (local authority mortgage interest rates) ;

(b) as regards administrative expenses of the lender in connection with a loan, provide that the lender may charge such expenses to the borrower, to the extent that they do not exceed such amount as may be prescribed, and that the expenses so charged may, at the option of the borrower in the case of a loan under section 450A and at the option of the lender in the case of a loan under section 450B, be added to the amount of the loan.

(5) The regulations may apply whenever the lease in question was granted or assigned and whenever the service charge in question became payable.

(6) The regulations—

(a) may make different provision for different cases or descriptions of case, including different provision for different areas ;

(b) may contain such incidental, supplementary and transitional provisions as the Secretary of State considers appropriate ; and

(c) shall be made by statutory instrument which shall be subject to annulment in pursuance of a resolution of either House of Parliament.".

PART I

Consultation
before
disposal to
private sector
landlord.
1985 c. 68.

Other provisions with respect to public sector housing

6.—(1) In Part IV of the Housing Act 1985 (secure tenancies and rights of secure tenants), after section 106 insert—

"Consultation before disposal to private sector landlord.

106A.—(1) The provisions of Schedule 3A have effect with respect to the duties of—

> (*a*) a local authority proposing to dispose of dwelling-houses subject to secure tenancies, and

> (*b*) the Secretary of State in considering whether to give his consent to such a disposal,

to have regard to the views of tenants liable as a result of the disposal to cease to be secure tenants.

(2) In relation to a disposal to which that Schedule applies, the provisions of that Schedule apply in place of the provisions of section 105 (consultation on matters of housing management).".

(2) After Schedule 3 to the Housing Act 1985 insert as Schedule 3A the Schedule set out in Schedule 1 to this Act (consultation before disposal to private sector landlord).

(3) The amendments made by this section apply to disposals after the commencement of this section.

Certificate of
fair rent with
a view to
disposal by
public sector
body.
1977 c. 42.

7.—(1) In section 69 of the Rent Act 1977 (certificates of fair rent), after subsection (1) insert—

" (1A) A public sector body to which this subsection applies may, with a view to the disposal of an interest in a dwelling-house, apply to the rent officer for a certificate specifying a rent which in the opinion of the rent officer would be a fair rent under a regulated tenancy of the dwelling-house—

> (*a*) in its present condition, or

> (*b*) after the completion of works of improvement, conversion or repair.

(1B) In subsection (1A) " public sector body " means an authority or body within section 80(1) of the Housing Act 1985 (the landlord condition for secure tenancies) other than the Housing Corporation, a housing association or a housing trust which is a charity.

In this subsection " housing association ", " housing trust " and " charity " have the same meaning as in Part IV of the Housing Act 1985.

(1C) A certificate under subsection (1) or (1A) shall be known as a certificate of fair rent.".

(2) In section 69(1) of the Rent Act 1977—

    (a) after " improvements ", in both places where it occurs, insert " or repairs ", and

    (b) at the end, add—

    " No application shall be made under this subsection if an application could be made under subsection (1A) below.".

8.—(1) In Part V of the Housing Act 1985 (the right to buy), after section 171 insert—

    "Preservation of right to buy on disposal to private sector landlord

Cases in which right to buy is preserved.
    171A.—(1) The provisions of this Part continue to apply where a person ceases to be a secure tenant of a dwelling-house by reason of the disposal by the landlord of an interest in the dwelling-house to a person who is not an authority or body within section 80 (the landlord condition for secure tenancies).

    (2) In the following provisions of this Part—

        (a) references to the preservation of the right to buy and to a person having the preserved right to buy are to the continued application of the provisions of this Part by virtue of this section and to a person in relation to whom those provisions so apply ;

        (b) " qualifying disposal " means a disposal in relation to which this section applies, and

        (c) the " former secure tenant " and the " former landlord " are the persons mentioned in subsection (1).

    (3) This section does not apply—

        (a) where the former landlord was a person against whom the right to buy could not be exercised by virtue of paragraph 1, 2 or 3 of Schedule 5 (charities and certain housing associations), or

        (b) in such other cases as may be excepted from the operation of this section by order of the Secretary of State.

    (4) Orders under subsection (3)(b)—

        (a) may relate to particular disposals and may make different provision with respect to different cases or descriptions of case, including different provision for different areas, and (*b*) shall be made by statutory instrument which shall be subject to annulment in pursuance of a resolution of either House of Parliament.

Extent of preserved right: qualifying persons and dwelling-houses.

171B.—(1) A person to whom this section applies has the preserved right to buy so long as he occupies the relevant dwelling-house as his only or principal home, subject to the following provisions of this Part.

(2) References in this Part to a " qualifying person " and " qualifying dwelling-house ", in relation to the preserved right to buy, are to a person who has that right and to a dwelling-house in relation to which a person has that right.

(3) The following are the persons to whom this section applies—

    (*a*) the former secure tenant, or in the case of a joint tenancy, each of them ;

    (*b*) a qualifying successor as defined in subsection (4) ; and

    (*c*) a person to whom a tenancy of a dwelling-house is granted jointly with a person who has the preserved right to buy in relation to that dwelling-house.

(4) The following are qualifying successors for this purpose—

    (*a*) where the former secure tenancy was not a joint tenancy, a person who, on the death of the former secure tenant, becomes by virtue of paragraph 2 or 3 of Part I of Schedule 1 to the Rent Act 1977 (surviving spouse or member of deceased tenant's family) the statutory tenant of a dwelling-house in relation to which the former secure tenant had the preserved right to buy immediately before his death ;

    (*b*) a person who becomes the tenant of a dwelling-house in pursuance of—

        (i) a property adjustment order under section 24 of the Matrimonial Causes Act 1973, or

        (ii) an order under Schedule 1 to the Matrimonial Homes Act 1983 transferring the tenancy,

    in place of a person who had the preserved right to buy in relation to that dwelling-house.

(5) The relevant dwelling-house is in the first instance—

(a) in relation to a person within paragraph (a) of subsection (3), the dwelling-house which was the subject of the qualifying disposal ;

(b) in relation to a person within paragraph (b) of that subsection, the dwelling-house of which he became the statutory tenant or tenant as mentioned in subsection (4)(a) or (b) ;

(c) in relation to a person within paragraph (c) of subsection (3), the dwelling-house of which he became a joint tenant as mentioned in that paragraph.

(6) If a person having the preserved right to buy becomes the tenant of another dwelling-house in place of the relevant dwelling-house (whether the new dwelling-house is entirely different or partly or substantially the same as the previous dwelling-house) and the landlord is the same person as the landlord of the previous dwelling-house or, where that landlord was a company, is a connected company, the new dwelling-house becomes the relevant dwelling-house for the purposes of the preserved right to buy.

For this purpose " connected company " means a subsidiary or holding company within the meaning of section 736 of the Companies Act 1985.

Modifications of this Part in relation to preserved right.

171C.—(1) Where the right to buy is preserved, the provisions of this Part have effect subject to such exceptions, adaptations and other modifications as may be prescribed by regulations made by the Secretary of State.

(2) The regulations may in particular provide—

(a) that paragraphs 5 to 11 of Schedule 5 (certain exceptions to the right to buy) do not apply ;

(b) that the right to a mortgage is exercisable against the former landlord or, if the former landlord was a housing association, against the Housing Corporation ;

(c) that the provisions of this Part relating to the right to be granted a shared ownership lease do not apply ; and (*d*) that the landlord is not required to but may include a covenant for the repayment of discount, provided its terms are no more onerous than those of the covenant provided for in section 155.

(3) The prescribed exceptions, adaptations and other modifications shall take the form of textual amendments of the provisions of this Part as they apply in cases where the right to buy is preserved; and the first regulations, and any subsequent consolidating regulations, shall set out the provisions of this Part as they so apply.

(4) The regulations—

(*a*) may make different provision for different cases or descriptions of case, including different provision for different areas,

(*b*) may contain such incidental, supplementary and transitional provisions as the Secretary of State considers appropriate, and

(*c*) shall be made by statutory instrument which shall be subject to annulment in pursuance of a resolution of either House of Parliament.

Subsequent dealings: disposal of landlord's interest in qualifying dwelling-house.

171D.—(1) The disposal by the landlord of an interest in the qualifying dwelling-house, whether his whole interest or a lesser interest, does not affect the preserved right to buy, unless—

(*a*) as a result of the disposal an authority or body within section 80(1) (the landlord condition for secure tenancies) becomes the landlord of the qualifying person or persons, or

(*b*) paragraph 6 of Schedule 9A applies (effect of failure to register entry protecting preserved right to buy),

in which case the right to buy ceases to be preserved.

(2) The disposal by the landlord of a qualifying dwelling-house of less than his whole interest as landlord of the dwelling-house, or in part of it, requires the consent of the Secretary of State, unless the disposal is to the qualifying person or persons.

(3) Consent may be given in relation to a particular disposal or generally in relation to disposals of a particular description and may, in either case, be given subject to conditions.

(4) A disposal made without the consent required by subsection (2) is void, except in a case where, by reason of a failure to make the entries on the land register or land charges register required by Schedule 9A, the preserved right to buy does not bind the person to whom the disposal is made.

Subsequent dealings: termination of landlord's interest in qualifying dwelling-house.

171E.—(1) On the termination of the landlord's interest in the qualifying dwelling-house—

(a) on the occurrence of an event determining his estate or interest, or by re-entry on a breach of condition or forfeiture, or

(b) where the interest is a leasehold interest, by notice given by him or a superior landlord, on the expiry or surrender of the term, or otherwise (subject to subsection (2)),

the right to buy ceases to be preserved.

(2) The termination of the landlord's interest by merger on his acquiring a superior interest, or on the acquisition by another person of the landlord's interest together with a superior interest, does not affect the preserved right to buy, unless—

(a) as a result of the acquisition an authority or body within section 80(1) (the landlord condition for secure tenancies) becomes the landlord of the qualifying person or persons, or

(b) paragraph 6 of Schedule 9A applies (effect of failure to register entry protecting preserved right to buy),

in which case the right to buy ceases to be preserved.

(3) Where the termination of the landlord's interest as mentioned in subsection (1) is caused by the act or omission of the landlord, a qualifying person who is thereby deprived of the preserved right to buy is entitled to be compensated by him.

Subsequent dealings: transfer of qualifying person to alternative accommodation.

171F. The court shall not order a qualifying person to give up possession of the qualifying dwelling-house in pursuance of section 98(1)(a) of the Rent Act 1977 (suitable alternative accommodation) unless the court is satisfied—

(a) that the preserved right to buy will, by virtue of section 171B(6) (accommodation with same landlord or connected company), continue to be exercisable in relation to the dwelling-house offered by way of alternative accommodation and that the interest of the landlord in the new dwelling-house will be—

    (i) where the new dwelling-house is a house, not less than the interest of the landlord in the existing dwelling-house, or

    (ii) where the new dwelling-house is a flat, not less than the interest of the landlord in the existing dwelling-house or a term of years of which 80 years or more remain unexpired, whichever is the less; or

(b) that the landlord of the new dwelling-house will be an authority or body within section 80(1) (the landlord condition for secure tenancies).

Land registration and related matters.

171G. Schedule 9A has effect with respect to registration of title and related matters arising in connection with the preservation of the right to buy.

Disposal after notice claiming to exercise right to buy, etc.

171H.—(1) Where notice has been given in respect of a dwelling-house claiming to exercise the right to buy or the right to a mortgage and before the completion of the exercise of that right the dwelling-house is the subject of—

(a) a qualifying disposal, or

(b) a disposal to which section 171D(1)(a) or 171E(2)(a) applies (disposal to authority or body satisfying landlord condition for secure tenancies),

all parties shall, subject to subsection (2), be in the same position as if the disponee had become the landlord before the notice was given and had been given that notice and any further notice given by the tenant to the landlord and had taken all steps which the landlord had taken.

(2) If the circumstances after the disposal differ in any material respect, as for example where—

(a) the interest of the disponee in the dwelling-house after the disposal differs from that of the disponor before the disposal, or

(b) the right to a mortgage becomes exercisable against the Housing Corporation rather than the former landlord, or *vice versa*, or

(c) any of the provisions of Schedule 5 (exceptions to the right to buy) becomes or ceases
to be applicable,

all those concerned shall, as soon as practicable after
the disposal, take all such steps (whether by way of
amending or withdrawing and re-serving any notice or
extending any period or otherwise) as may be requisite for the purpose of securing that all parties
are, as nearly as may be, in the same position as
they would have been if those circumstances had
obtained before the disposal.".

(2) After Schedule 9 to the Housing Act 1985 insert as 1985 c. 68.
Schedule 9A the Schedule set out in Schedule 2 to this Act
(land registration and related matters where right to buy preserved).

(3) The amendments made by this section apply to qualifying
disposals on or after the commencement of this section.

9.—(1) In Schedule 2 to the Housing Act 1985 (grounds for Redevelop-
possession of dwelling-houses let under secure tenancies), in ment of
Part II (grounds on which court may order possession if suit- dwelling-house
able alternative accommodation is available), after ground 10 subject to
(redevelopment by landlord) insert— secure
tenancy.

" Ground 10A

The dwelling-house is in an area which is the subject
of a redevelopment scheme approved by the Secretary of
State or the Housing Corporation in accordance with Part
V of this Schedule and the landlord intends within a
reasonable time of obtaining possession to dispose of the
dwelling-house in accordance with the scheme.

or

Part of the dwelling-house is in such an area and the
landlord intends within a reasonable time of obtaining
possession to dispose of that part in accordance with the
scheme and for that purpose reasonably requires possession of the dwelling-house.".

(2) At the end of that Schedule insert—

" PART V

APPROVAL OF REDEVELOPMENT SCHEMES FOR PURPOSES OF
GROUND 10A

1.—(1) The Secretary of State may, on the application
of the landlord, approve for the purposes of ground 10A in
Part II of this Schedule a scheme for the disposal and redevelopment of an area of land consisting of or including
the whole or part of one or more dwelling-houses.

(2) For this purpose—

    (*a*) " disposal " means a disposal of any interest in the land (including the grant of an option), and

    (*b*) " redevelopment " means the demolition or reconstruction of buildings or the carrying out of other works to buildings or land ;

and it is immaterial whether the disposal is to precede or follow the redevelopment.

(3) The Secretary of State may on the application of the landlord approve a variation of a scheme previously approved by him and may, in particular, approve a variation adding land to the area subject to the scheme.

2.—(1) Where a landlord proposes to apply to the Secretary of State for the approval of a scheme or variation it shall serve a notice in writing on any secure tenant of a dwelling-house affected by the proposal stating—

    (*a*) the main features of the proposed scheme or, as the case may be, the scheme as proposed to be varied,

    (*b*) that the landlord proposes to apply to the Secretary of State for approval of the scheme or variation, and

    (*c*) the effect of such approval, by virtue of section 84 and ground 10A in Part II of this Schedule, in relation to proceedings for possession of the dwelling-house,

and informing the tenant that he may, within such period as the landlord may allow (which shall be at least 28 days from service of the notice), make representations to the landlord about the proposal.

(2) The landlord shall not apply to the Secretary of State until it has considered any representations made to it within that period.

(3) In the case of a landlord to which section 105 applies (consultation on matters of housing management) the provisions of this paragraph apply in place of the provisions of that section in relation to the approval or variation of a redevelopment scheme.

3.—(1) In considering whether to give his approval to a scheme or variation the Secretary of State shall take into account, in particular—

    (*a*) the effect of the scheme on the extent and character of housing accommodation in the neighbourhood,

(*b*) over what period of time it is proposed that the
disposal and redevelopment will take place in
accordance with the scheme, and

(*c*) to what extent the scheme includes provision for
housing provided under the scheme to be sold or
let to existing tenants or persons nominated by the
landlord ;

and he shall take into account any representations made
to him and, so far as they are brought to his notice, any
representations made to the landlord.

(2) The landlord shall give to the Secretary of State such
information as to the representations made to it, and other
relevant matters, as the Secretary of State may require.

4. The Secretary of State shall not approve a scheme
or variation so as to include in the area subject to the
scheme—

(*a*) part only of one or more dwelling-houses, or

(*b*) one or more dwelling-houses not themselves affected
by the works involved in redevelopment but which
are proposed to be disposed of along with other
land which is so affected,

unless he is satisfied that the inclusion is justified in the
circumstances.

5.—(1) Approval may be given subject to conditions
and may be expressed to expire after a specified period.

(2) The Secretary of State, on the application of the landlord or otherwise, may vary an approval so as to—

(*a*) add, remove or vary conditions to which the
approval is subject ; or

(*b*) extend or restrict the period after which the
approval is to expire.

(3) Where approval is given subject to conditions, the
landlord may serve a notice under section 83 (notice of
proceedings for possession) specifying ground 10A notwithstanding that the conditions are not yet fulfilled but
the court shall not make an order for possession on that
ground unless satisfied that they are or will be fulfilled.

6. Where the landlord is a registered housing association,
the Housing Corporation, and not the Secretary of State,
has the functions conferred by this Part of this Schedule.

PART I   7. In this Part of this Schedule references to the landlord
of a dwelling-house include any authority or body within
section 80 (the landlord condition for secure tenancies) having an interest of any description in the dwelling-house.".

1973 c. 26.   (3) Section 29 of the Land Compensation Act 1973 (home loss
payments) is amended as follows—

    (a) in subsection (1) (circumstances in which, and persons
        by whom, payment to be made) after paragraph (d)
        insert—

           " (e) the making of an order for possession on
           ground 10 or 10A in Part II of Schedule 2 to the
           Housing Act 1985 ; "; and

    (b) in the same subsection, after paragraph (iv) insert—

           " (v) where paragraph (e) applies, the landlord." ;
        and

    (c) in subsection (4) (interests and rights to which the section
        applies), after paragraph (d) insert—

           " (e) a right to occupy the dwelling under a licence
           to which Part IV of the Housing Act 1985 (secure
           tenancies) applies.".

(4) In section 32 of the Land Compensation Act 1973 (supplementary provisions about home loss payments), after subsection
(7A) insert—

    " (7B) Where a landlord obtains possession by agreement
of a dwelling subject to a secure tenancy within the meaning of Part IV of the Housing Act 1985 and—

    (a) notice of proceedings for possession of the dwelling
        has been served, or might have been served, speci-
        fying ground 10 or 10A in Part II of Schedule 2
        to that Act, or

    (b) the landlord has applied, or could apply, to the
        Secretary of State or the Housing Corporation for
        approval for the purposes of ground 10A of a
        redevelopment scheme including the dwelling, or
        part of it,

the landlord may make to the person giving up possession
a payment corresponding to any home loss payment which
they would be required to make to him if an order for
possession had been made on either of those grounds.".

10. For section 27 of the Housing Act 1985 (agreements with
housing co-operatives), and the heading preceding it, substitute—

" *Management agreements*

Management
agreements.

27.—(1) A local housing authority may, with the approval of the Secretary of State, agree that another person shall exercise as agent of the authority in relation to—

> (*a*) such of the authority's houses as are specified in the agreement, and
>
> (*b*) any other land so specified which is held for a related purpose,

such of the authority's management functions as are so specified.

(2) In this Act " management agreement " and " manager ", in relation to such an agreement, mean an agreement under this section and the person with whom the agreement is made.

(3) A management agreement shall set out the terms on which the authority's functions are exercisable by the manager.

(4) A management agreement may, where the manager is a body or association, provide that the manager's functions under the agreement may be performed by a committee or sub-committee, or by an officer, of the body or association.

(5) The Secretary of State's approval (which may be given unconditionally or subject to conditions) is required both for the terms of the agreement and the identity of the manager.

(6) References in this section to the management functions of a local housing authority in relation to houses or land include—

> (*a*) functions conferred by any statutory provision, and
>
> (*b*) the powers and duties of the authority as holder of an estate or interest in the houses or land in question.

Consultation
required
before
management agreement can
be
approved.

27A.—(1) A local housing authority who propose to enter into a management agreement shall serve notice in writing on the tenant of each house to which the proposal relates informing him of—

> (*a*) such details of their proposal as the authority consider appropriate, but including the

identity of the person who is to be the manager under the agreement,

(b) the likely consequences of the agreement for the tenant, and

(c) the effect of the provisions of this section,

and informing him that he may, within such reasonable period as may be specified in the notice, make representations to the authority.

(2) The authority shall consider any representations made to them within that period and shall serve a further written notice on the tenant informing him—

(a) of any significant changes in their proposal, and

(b) that he may within such period as is specified (which must be at least 28 days after the service of the notice) communicate to the Secretary of State his objection to the proposal,

and informing him of the effect of subsection (5) (approval to be withheld if majority of tenants are opposed).

(3) The Secretary of State shall not entertain an application for approval of a management agreement unless the local housing authority certify that the requirements of subsections (1) and (2) as to consultation have been complied with; and the certificate shall be accompanied by a copy of the notices given by the authority in accordance with those subsections.

(4) The Secretary of State may require the authority to carry out such further consultation with their tenants, and to give him such information as to the results of that consultation, as he may direct.

(5) The Secretary of State shall not give his approval if it appears to him that a majority of the tenants of the houses to which the agreement relates do not wish the proposal to proceed; but this does not affect his general discretion to withhold his approval on grounds relating to whether the proposal has the support of the tenants or on any other ground.

(6) In making his decision the Secretary of State may have regard to any information available to him; and the local housing authority shall give him

such information as to the representations made to them by tenants and others, and other relevant matters, as he may require.

(7) A management agreement made with the approval of the Secretary of State is not invalidated by a failure on his part or that of the local housing authority to comply with the requirements of this section.

(8) In the case of secure tenants the provisions of this section apply in place of the provisions of section 105 (consultation on matters of housing management) in relation to the making of a management agreement.

27B.—(1) In this section " housing co-operative " means a society, company or body of trustees with which a housing co-operative agreement was made, that is to say—

> (a) an agreement to which paragraph 9 of Schedule 1 to the Housing Rents and Subsidies Act 1975 or Schedule 20 to the Housing Act 1980 applied or,
>
> (b) an agreement made under section 27 above before the commencement of section 10 of the Housing and Planning Act 1986 (which substituted the present section 27).

(2) A housing co-operative agreement made with a local housing authority which is in force immediately before the commencement of section 10 of the Housing and Planning Act 1986 has effect as if made under the present section 27, so that, in particular, any terms of the agreement providing for the letting of land to the housing co-operative no longer have effect except in relation to lettings made before commencement.

(3) A housing co-operative agreement made with a new town corporation or the Development Board for Rural Wales which is in force immediately before the commencement of section 10 of the Housing and Planning Act 1986 remains in force notwithstanding that the present section 27 does not apply to such authorities.

(4) In this Act (except in section 27) the expressions " management agreement " and " manager ", in relation to such an agreement, include a housing co-operative agreement to which subsection (2) or (3) applies and the housing co-operative with whom the agreement is made.".

PART I

Agreements with housing co-operatives under superseded provisions.

PART I
Proposals
for
co-operative
management
or ownership.
1985 c. 68.

11. In Part II of the Housing Act 1985, after the provisions inserted by section 10 above insert—

" *Proposals for co-operative management or ownership*

27C.—(1) If a qualifying tenants' association serves written notice on the local housing authority—

    (*a*) proposing that the authority should enter into a management agreement with the association with respect to houses and other land specified in the notice, or

    (*b*) proposing that the association should acquire from the authority houses and other land specified in the notice at a specified price,

the authority shall take the proposal into consideration.

(2) If the authority have not, by the end of the period of six months after service of the notice, accepted the proposal in principle, they shall give the association a written statement of the reasons why they have not done so.

(3) A tenants' association is a qualifying association for the purposes of this section if—

    (*a*) it is a housing association of which at least half the members are tenants of houses specified in the notice,

    (*b*) it has at least 50 such members or is registered under the Industrial and Provident Societies Act 1965, and

    (*c*) at least half the tenants of the specified houses are members of the association.".

Assured tenancies

Extension of
assured
tenancies
scheme to
cases where
works have
been carried
out.
1980 c. 51.

12.—(1) In section 56(1) of the Housing Act 1980 (tenancies which are assured tenancies), for paragraphs (*a*) and (*b*) substitute—

    " (*a*) the conditions described in section 56A or 56B are satisfied,

    (*b*) the interest of the landlord has, since the creation of the tenancy, belonged to an approved body, and

    (*c*) the tenancy would, when created, have been a protected tenancy or, as the case may be, a housing association tenancy but for this section.".

(2) After that section insert—

"Conditions for assured tenancy: newly erected buildings.

56A. The first set of conditions referred to in section 56(1)(a) above is that—

(a) the dwelling-house is, or forms part of, a building which was erected (and on which construction work first began) on or after 8th August 1980, and

(b) before the tenant first occupied the dwelling-house under the tenancy, no part of it had been occupied by any person as his residence except under an assured tenancy.

Conditions for assured tenancy: buildings to which works have been carried out.

56B.—(1) The second set of conditions referred to in section 56(1)(a) above is that—

(a) qualifying works have been carried out (whether before or after the commencement of this section),

(b) the dwelling-house is (or was) fit for human habitation at the relevant date, and

(c) since the qualifying works were carried out no part of the dwelling-house has been occupied by any person as his residence except under an assured tenancy,

and, in the case of the first relevant tenancy, that the person (or persons) to whom the tenancy is granted is not (or do not include) a person who was a secure occupier of the dwelling-house before the works were carried out.

(2) Qualifying works means works involving expenditure attributable to the dwelling-house of not less than the prescribed amount which are carried out within the period of two years preceding the relevant date at a time when the premises constituting the dwelling-house at the relevant date either were not a dwelling-house or no part of them was occupied by a person as his residence.

(3) Expenditure is attributable to a dwelling-house if it is incurred on works carried out to the premises constituting the dwelling-house at the relevant date or to other land or buildings let with the dwelling-house under the first relevant tenancy.

(4) Where the dwelling-house is a flat, there is also attributable to the dwelling-house a proportion of any expenditure incurred on works carried out to the structure, exterior or common parts of, or to common

P 2

facilities in, the building of which the dwelling-house forms part.

(5) The proportion so attributable shall be taken to be the amount produced by dividing the total amount of such expenditure by the number of units of occupation in the building at the relevant date.

(6) In this section—

' flat ' means a separate set of premises, whether or not on the same floor, which—

    (a) forms part of a building, and

    (b) is divided horizontally from some other part of the building ;

' the first relevant tenancy ' means the first tenancy after the carrying out of the qualifying works under which a person is entitled to occupy the dwelling-house as his residence ;

' the prescribed amount ' means the amount which at the relevant date is prescribed for the purposes of this section by order of the Secretary of State ;

' the relevant date ' means the date of grant of the first relevant tenancy ;

' secure occupier ' means a person who, whether alone or jointly with others, occupied or was entitled to occupy the dwelling-house as—

    (a) a protected or statutory tenant within the meaning of the Rent Act 1977,

    (b) a secure tenant within the meaning of Part IV of the Housing Act 1985, or

    (c) a protected occupier or statutory tenant within the meaning of the Rent (Agriculture) Act 1976.

Certification of fitness for purposes of s. 56B.

56C.—(1) An approved body having an interest in a dwelling-house which it proposes to let on an assured tenancy may—

    (a) apply in writing to the local housing authority for a certificate that the dwelling-house is fit for human habitation, or

    (b) submit to the local housing authority a list of works which it proposes to carry out to the dwelling-house with a request in writing for the authority's opinion whether the dwelling-house would, after the execution of the works, be fit for human habitation ;

and the authority shall as soon as may be after receiving the application or request, and upon payment of such reasonable fee as they may determine, take the matter into consideration.

(2) If the authority are of opinion that the dwelling-house is fit for human habitation, they shall give the approved body a certificate to that effect.

(3) If the authority are of opinion that the dwelling-house will be fit for human habitation after the execution of the proposed works, they shall inform the approved body that they are of that opinion.

(4) In any other case, the authority shall give the approved body a list of the works which in their opinion are required to make the dwelling-house fit for human habitation.

(5) Where the authority have responded in accordance with subsection (3) or (4) and the works in question have been executed to their satisfaction, they shall, if the approved body applies in writing, and upon payment of such reasonable fee as the authority may determine, give the body a certificate that the dwelling-house is fit for human habitation.

(6) For the purpose of determining whether the condition in section 56B(1)(*b*) was satisfied in any case (fitness of dwelling-house on relevant date), but not for any other purpose, a certificate given under this section is conclusive evidence that the dwelling-house was fit for human habitation on the date on which the certificate was given.

(7) In this section ' the local housing authority ' has the same meaning as in the Housing Act 1985.

Fitness for human habitation.

56D. In determining for any of the purposes of section 56B or 56C whether a dwelling-house is, or would be, fit for human habitation, regard shall be had to its condition in respect of the following matters—

    repair,
    stability,
    freedom from damp,
    internal arrangement,
    natural lighting,
    ventilation,
    water supply,
    drainage and sanitary conveniences,

PART I

facilities for the preparation and cooking of food and the disposal of waste water ; and the dwelling-house shall be deemed to be unfit only if it is, or would be, so far defective in one or more of those matters as to be not reasonably suitable for occupation in that condition.".

1980 c. 51.

(3) In section 57 of the Housing Act 1980 (effect of interest of landlord ceasing to belong to approved body), in subsections (1) and (2) for " section 56(3)(*a*) " substitute " section 56(1)(*b*) ".

Other amendments relating to assured tenancies.

1977 c. 42.

13.—(1) In section 19(5) of the Rent Act 1977 (contracts which are not restricted contracts), after paragraph (*e*) insert—

" , or

(*f*) it creates an assured tenancy within the meaning of section 56 of the Housing Act 1980 ; ".

(2) In Schedule 15 to the Rent Act 1977 (grounds for possession), in Part IV (definition of suitable alternative accommodation), renumber paragraph 4 as sub-paragraph (1) of that paragraph and after it insert—

" (2) For the purposes of sub-paragraph (1)(*b*) the terms of a tenancy shall not be treated as affording the required security by reason only of the fact that the tenancy is an assured tenancy within the meaning of section 56 of the Housing Act 1980.".

1976 c. 80.

(3) In Schedule 4 to the Rent (Agriculture) Act 1976 (grounds for possession), in Case I (alternative accommodation not provided or arranged by housing authority), renumber paragraph 2 as sub-paragraph (1) of that paragraph and after it insert—

" (2) For the purposes of sub-paragraph (1)(*b*) the terms of a tenancy shall not be treated as affording the required security by reason only of the fact that the tenancy is an assured tenancy within the meaning of section 56 of the Housing Act 1980.".

1954 c. 56.

(4) In section 37 of the Landlord and Tenant Act 1954 (compensation where an order for new tenancy precluded on certain grounds), in subsection (2) (computation of compensation) as set out in paragraph 7 of Schedule 5 to the Housing Act 1980 (application of 1954 Act to assured tenancies), after " be " insert " the product of the appropriate multiplier and ".

The above amendment applies notwithstanding that the application to the court under section 24 of the Landlord and Tenant Act 1954 was made before the commencement of this section, unless the application has been finally disposed of within the meaning of section 64(2) of that Act before commencement.

(5) In section 58 of the Housing Act 1980 (application of Landlord and Tenant Act 1954 to assured tenancies), at the end add—

" (3) In sections 56 to 58 of this Act ' tenancy ' has the
same meaning as in the Landlord and Tenant Act 1954 and
references to the granting of a tenancy shall be construed
accordingly.".

(6) In Schedule 5 to the Housing Act 1980 (application of
Landlord and Tenant Act 1954 to assured tenancies), for paragraph 8 (modification of provisions relating to contracting out)
substitute—

" 8. Section 38 applies as if the following provisions were
omitted—

   (*a*) in subsection (1), the words " (except as provided by
      subsection (4) of this section) " ;

   (*b*) in subsection (2), the words from the beginning to the
      end of paragraph (*b*) ;

   (*c*) subsections (3) and (4)."

The above amendment, so far as it relates to section 38(4) of
the Landlord and Tenant Act 1954, does not apply to an agreement both approved by the court under that provision and
entered into before the commencement of this section.

Miscellaneous

14.—(1) The Housing Act 1985 shall be amended in accordance with the following provisions.

(2) In section 58 (definition of homelessness) after subsection
(2) there shall be inserted the following subsections—

" (2A) A person shall not be treated as having accommodation unless it is accommodation which it would be reasonable for him to continue to occupy.

(2B) Regard may be had, in determining whether it would
be reasonable for a person to continue to occupy accommodation, to the general circumstances prevailing in relation to housing in the district of the local housing authority
to whom he has applied for accommodation or for assistance in obtaining accommodation.".

(3) For section 69(1) (provisions supplementary to ss. 63, 65
and 68) there shall be substituted the following subsection—

" (1) A local housing authority may perform any duty
under section 65 or 68 (duties to persons found to be homeless) to secure that accommodation becomes available for
the occupation of a person—

   (*a*) by making available suitable accommodation held
      by them under Part II (provision of housing) or
      any enactment, or

    (*b*) by securing that he obtains suitable accommodation from some other person, or

    (*c*) by giving him such advice and assistance as will secure that he obtains suitable accommodation from some other person,

and in determining whether accommodation is suitable they shall have regard to Part IX (slum clearance), X (overcrowding) and XI (houses in multiple occupation) of this Act.".

Grants for improvement or repair of common parts.
1985 c. 68.

  15. Part XV of the Housing Act 1985 (grants for works of improvement, repair and conversion) is amended in accordance with Schedule 3 so as to provide for a new form of grant towards the costs of works required for the improvement or repair of the common parts of a building containing one or more flats.

Housing management: financial assistance etc.

  16. In Part XIII of the Housing Act 1985 (general financial provisions), after section 429 insert—

 "Housing management: financial assistance etc.

  429A.—(1) The Secretary of State may, with the consent of the Treasury, give financial assistance—

    (*a*) to persons managing public sector or former public sector housing, and

    (*b*) to persons seeking to facilitate or encourage improvements in, or providing services in connection with, the management of such housing ;

and may, with the like consent, make payments otherwise than by way of financial assistance in pursuance of arrangements made with any such person.

  (2) For this purpose—

    (*a*) " public sector housing " means housing accommodation in which an authority or body within section 80 (the landlord condition for secure tenancies) has an interest by virtue of which it receives a rack-rent, or would do so if the premises were let at a rack-rent ; and

    (*b*) " former public sector housing " means housing accommodation in which such an authority, or a predecessor of such an authority or an authority abolished by the Local Government Act 1985 formerly had such an interest.

  (3) The Secretary of State may, with the consent of the Treasury, give financial assistance—

    (*a*) to persons providing educational or training courses in housing management,

(*b*) to persons providing services for those providing such courses, and

(*c*) to persons providing financial or other assistance for those attending such courses ;

and may, with the like consent, make payments
otherwise than by way of financial assistance in pursuance of arrangements made with any such person.

(4) Financial assistance given by the Secretary of
State under subsection (1) or (3) may be given in
any form, and may in particular be given by way
of grants, loans or guarantees or by incurring expenditure for the benefit of the person assisted ; but
the Secretary of State shall not in giving such assistance purchase loan or share capital in a company.

(5) Financial assistance may be given and other
payments made on such terms as the Secretary of
State, with the consent of the Treasury, considers
appropriate ; and the terms may, in particular, include provision as to the circumstances in which
the assistance or other payment must be repaid or
otherwise made good to the Secretary of State and
the manner in which that is to be done.

(6) A person receiving financial assistance under
this section shall comply with the terms on which
it is given and compliance may be enforced by the
Secretary of State.".

17.—(1) Section 70 of the Rent Act 1977 (determination of   Matters to be
fair rent) is amended as follows.   taken into
account in
(2) In subsection (1) (matters to be taken into account), omit   determining
the word " and " before paragraph (*b*) and after that paragraph   fair rent.
insert—   1977 c. 42.

" , and

(*c*) any premium, or sum in the nature of a premium, which
has been or may be lawfully required or received on
the grant, renewal, continuance or assignment of the
tenancy.".

(3) After subsection (4) insert—

"(4A) In this section " premium " has the same meaning
as in Part IX of this Act, and " sum in the nature of a
premium " means—

(*a*) any such loan as is mentioned in section 119 or 120
of this Act,

(*b*) any such excess over the reasonable price of furniture as is mentioned in section 123 of this Act, and

(*c*) any such advance payment of rent as is mentioned in section 126 of this Act.".

(4) The above amendments apply to every decision made by a rent officer or rent assessment committee after the commencement of this section, notwithstanding that the application was made before commencement or, in the case of a decision of a rent assessment committee, that the rent officer's decision was made before commencement.

Further provisions with respect to shared ownership leases.

1977 c. 42.
1976 c. 80.
1967 c. 88.

18. The provisions of Schedule 4 have effect to exclude certain shared ownership leases from the operation of the provisions of—

(*a*) the Rent Act 1977 and the Rent (Agriculture) Act 1976, and

(*b*) Part I of the Leasehold Reform Act 1967 (right of long leaseholder to enfranchisement or extension of lease).

Extension of permitted objects of registered housing associations.

1985 c. 69.

19. In section 4 of the Housing Associations Act 1985 (eligibility for registration), in subsection (3) (permissible additional purposes or objects of association), after paragraph (*d*) insert—

" (*dd*) providing services of any description for owners or occupiers of houses in arranging or carrying out works of maintenance, repair or improvement, or encouraging or facilitating the carrying out of such works ; ".

Disposal of dwellings in new towns.

1981 c. 64.

20.—(1) Part III of the New Towns Act 1981 (transfer of new town housing to district councils), is amended as follows.

(2) After section 57 insert—

" Savings for other powers of disposal.　57A. The provisions of this Part as to the transfer of dwellings in a new town to a district council shall not be construed as restricting—

(*a*) the power of the Commission under section 36 above,

(*b*) the power of a development corporation under section 64 below, or

(*c*) the power of the Development Board for Rural Wales under section 4 of the Development of Rural Wales Act 1976,

to dispose of such dwellings to any person.".

(3) The following provisions (which relate to the initiation of consultations with a view to the transfer of new town housing to a district council) are repealed—

section 43(3) and (4),

section 49(*b*) and (*c*).

21.—(1) In Part VIII of the Housing Act 1985 (area improvement) before section 260, under the heading "*Supplementary provisions*" insert—

"Effect of resolutions relating to housing action area or general improvement area.

259A.—(1) A resolution of a local housing authority passed after the commencement of this section—

(a) declaring an area to be a housing action area, excluding land from a housing action area or declaring that an area shall cease to be a housing action area, or

(b) declaring an area to be a general improvement area, excluding land from a general improvement area or declaring that an area shall cease to be a general improvement area,

has effect, subject to subsection (2), from the day on which the resolution is passed.

(2) A resolution declaring an area to be a general improvement area may be expressed to have effect from a future date, not later than four weeks after the passing of the resolution, on which the whole or part of that area will cease to be, or be included in, a housing action area.

Effect of certain resolutions passed before commencement of s. 259A.

259B.—(1) Where before the commencement of section 259A a local housing authority passed a resolution of any of the descriptions mentioned in the section expressed to have effect from a date after that on which it was passed—

(a) anything done before the commencement of this section in reliance on the view that the resolution was invalid shall have effect as if the resolution had not been passed, but

(b) otherwise, the resolution shall be taken for all purposes, both before and after the commencement of this section, to have been validly passed and to have had effect from the date on which it was expressed to have had effect ;

subject to the following provisions.

(2) A person shall not be proceeded against in respect of anything done or omitted before the commencement of this section which would not have been an offence if the resolution had not been passed.

(3) Where the resolution declared a housing action area or general improvement area and, before the commencement of this section, the local housing authority passed a further resolution making the like declaration in relation to the whole or part of the area to which the first resolution then related—

   (*a*) both resolutions are effective, notwithstanding that they relate in whole or in part to the same area ;

   (*b*) the area covered by both resolutions is a housing action area or general improvement area by virtue of the joint effect of the two resolutions, and in the case of a housing action area shall continue to be such an area (subject to the provisions of this Part) until the end of the period of five years beginning with the date on which the second resolution was passed ;

   (*c*) it is immaterial whether steps taken before the commencement of this section were taken in reliance on the first resolution or the second, but steps taken in reliance on the first shall not be proceeded with to the extent that they have been superseded by, or are inconsistent with, steps taken in reliance on the second ; and

   (*d*) the areas declared by the two resolutions may be treated as one for the purposes of section 245(3) or 259(3) (limit on aggregate expenditure qualifying for contributions by Secretary of State).

(4) The provisions of subsection (3) do not affect the powers of the Secretary of State under section 241(2)(*a*) and (*b*) (power to overrule declaration of housing action area or exclude land from area) and, so far as they relate to the duration of a housing action area, have effect subject to section 241(4) (effect of Secretary of State's decision in such a case).".

(2) In consequence of the above amendment, Part VIII of the Housing Act 1985 is further amended as follows—

   (*a*) in section 239(4) (duration of housing action area), omit " beginning with the date on which the resolution is passed " ;

   (*b*) in section 240(1) (steps to be taken after declaration of housing action area) omit " passing a resolution " ;

(c) in section 242(2) (incorporation into housing action area
of land comprised in general improvement area), for
" the resolution is passed declaring such an area "
substitute " the area is declared " ;

(d) in section 250(1) (exclusion of land from, or termination
of, housing action area), omit " on the date on which
the resolution is passed " ;

(e) in section 257 (duty to publish information) for " have
declared " substitute " have passed a resolution declaring " and for " assistance available " substitute
" assistance which is or will be available " ;

(f) in section 258(1)(b) (resolution terminating general improvement area), for " an area to be no longer " substitute " that an area shall cease to be " ;

(g) in section 258(2) (effect of resolution excluding land
from or terminating general improvement area) for
" the date on which the resolution takes effect " substitute " the date on which the exclusion or cessation
takes effect " and for " the exclusion or cessation "
substitute " the resolution ".

22.—(1) Section 16 of the Consumer Credit Act 1974 (exempt   Agreements
agreements) is amended as follows.   with certain
                                                                  housing bodies
(2) In subsection (1) (which enables orders to be made exempt-   exempt from
ing agreements with certain descriptions of creditor), after para-   Consumer
graph (f) insert—   Credit Act
                                                                  1974.
" (ff) a body corporate named or specifically referred to in   1974 c. 37.
an order made under—

section 156(4), 444(1) or 447(2)(a) of the Housing
Act 1985,

section 2 of the Home Purchase Assistance and
Housing Corporation Guarantee Act 1978 or section
31 of the Tenants' Rights, &c. (Scotland) Act 1980,
or

Article 154(1)(a) or 156AA of the Housing (Northern Ireland) Order 1981 or Article 10(6A) of the
Housing (Northern Ireland) Order 1983 ; or " ;

and in subsection (3) (requirements as to consultation), in paragraph (d) (consultation with responsible Minister), for " or (f) "
substitute ", (f) or (ff) ".

(3) After subsection (6) insert—

" (6A) This Act does not regulate a consumer credit
agreement where the creditor is a housing authority and the
agreement is secured by a land mortgage of a dwelling.

(6B) In subsection (6A) " housing authority " means—

PART I

    (a) as regards England and Wales, an authority or body within section 80(1) of the Housing Act 1985 (the landlord condition for secure tenancies), other than a housing association or a housing trust which is a charity;

    (b) as regards Scotland, a development corporation established under an order made, or having effect as if made under the New Towns (Scotland) Act 1968, the Scottish Special Housing Association or the Housing Corporation;

    (c) as regards Northern Ireland, the Northern Ireland Housing Executive.".

(4) The above amendments apply to agreements made after the commencement of this section.

Determination of price for leasehold enfranchisement.

1967 c. 88.

23.—(1) In section 9(1A) of the Leasehold Reform Act 1967 (determination of price payable for enfranchisement of higher value houses), in paragraph (a) (assumption that vendor is selling subject to existing tenancy) after " no right to acquire the freehold " insert " or an extended lease and, where the tenancy has been extended under this Part of this Act, that the tenancy will terminate on the original term date.".

(2) In section 23(5) of the Leasehold Reform Act 1967 (provisions as to tenancy granted in satisfaction of tenant's rights under Part I), in paragraph (b) (provisions which apply as if the tenancy were granted by way of extension) at the beginning insert " section 9(1) and (1A) above,".

(3) The above amendments do not apply—

    (a) where the price for enfranchisement has been determined, by agreement or otherwise, before the commencement of this section; or

    (b) where the notice under section 8 of the Leasehold Reform Act 1967 (notice of desire to have the freehold) was given before the passing of this Act; or

    (c) where notice under section 14 of that Act (notice of desire to have extended lease) was given before 5th March 1986.

Minor and consequential amendments; repeals.

1985 c. 68.

24.—(1) The enactments relating to housing are amended in accordance with Part I of Schedule 5 with respect to the following matters—

    (a) the effect of a covenant for repayment of discount given on the disposal of a dwelling-house;

    (b) the acquistion by an authority or body within section 80 of the Housing Act 1985 (the landlord condition

for secure tenancies) of a dwelling-house subject to a   PART I
statutory tenancy;

(c) the contents of a landlord's notice under section 125 of
that Act (notice of terms of exercise of right to buy);

(d) the steps to be taken where there is a change of landlord in the course of exercise of the right to buy;

(e) the deferment of completion in pursuance of the right
to buy;

(f) the maximum penalty for voting in contravention of
section 618(3) of the Housing Act 1985 (member of 1985 c. 68.
Common Council or committee voting on matter in
which he is interested);

(g) the withholding of consent to the assignment by way
of exchange of a secure tenancy of a dwelling-house
managed by a certain description of housing association;

(h) grants for affording tax relief to housing associations;

(i) the recovery of service charges in respect of the cost of
grant-aided works;

(j) miscellaneous corrections.

(2) Part II of Schedule 5 contains amendments consequential
on the provisions of this Part.

(3) The enactments specified in Part I of Schedule 12 are repealed to the extent specified.

PART II

SIMPLIFIED PLANNING ZONES

England and Wales

25.—(1) In Part III of the Town and Country Planning Act Simplified
1971 (general planning control), after section 24 insert—   planning
zones in
England
" *Simplified planning zone schemes*   and Wales.

Simplified   24A.—(1) A simplified planning zone is an area 1971 c. 78.
planning   in respect of which a simplified planning zone
zones.   scheme is in force.

(2) The adoption or approval of a simplified
planning zone scheme has effect to grant in relation
to the zone, or any part of it specified in the scheme,
planning permission for development specified in the
scheme or for development of any class so specified.

(3) Planning permission under a simplified planning zone scheme may be unconditional or subject

to such conditions, limitations or exceptions as may be specified in the scheme.

(4) Every local planning authority—

(a) shall consider, as soon as practicable after this section comes into operation, the question for which part or parts of their area a simplified planning zone scheme is desirable, and shall thereafter keep that question under review ; and

(b) shall prepare a scheme for any such part for which they decide, as a result of their original consideration or of any such review, that it is desirable to do so.

(5) The provisions of Schedule 8A to this Act have effect with respect to the making and alteration of simplified planning zone schemes and other related matters.

(6) The functions of local planning authorities under the provisions of this Act relating to simplified planning zone schemes shall be performed in non-metropolitan counties by the district planning authorities.

Simplified planning zone schemes: conditions and limitations on planning permission.

24B.—(1) The conditions and limitations on planning permission which may be specified in a simplified planning zone scheme may include—

(a) conditions or limitations in respect of all development permitted by the scheme or in respect of particular descriptions of development so permitted, and

(b) conditions or limitations requiring the consent, agreement or approval of the local planning authority in relation to particular descriptions of permitted development ;

and different conditions or limitations may be specified for different cases or classes of case.

(2) Nothing in a simplified planning zone scheme shall affect the right of any person—

(a) to do anything not amounting to development, or

(b) to carry out development for which planning permission is not required or for which permission has been granted otherwise than by the scheme ;

and no limitation or restriction subject to which permission has been granted otherwise than under the scheme shall affect the right of any person to carry out development for which permission has been granted under the scheme.

Duration of simplified planning zone scheme.

24C.—(1) A simplified planning zone scheme shall take effect on the date of its adoption or approval and shall cease to have effect at the end of the period of ten years beginning with that date.

(2) Upon the scheme's ceasing to have effect planning permission under the scheme shall also cease to have effect except in a case where the development authorised by it has been begun.

(3) The provisions of section 44(2) to (6) of this Act (which provide for the termination of planning permission if the completion of development is unreasonably delayed) apply to planning permission under a simplified planning zone scheme where development has been begun but not completed by the time the area ceased to be a simplified planning zone.

(4) The provisions of section 43(1) to (3) of this Act apply in determining for the purposes of this section when development shall be taken to be begun.

Alteration of simplified planning zone scheme.

24D.—(1) The adoption or approval of alterations to a simplified planning zone scheme has effect as follows.

(2) The adoption or approval of alterations providing for the inclusion of land in the simplified planning zone has effect to grant in relation to that land or such part of it as is specified in the scheme planning permission for development so specified or of any class so specified.

(3) The adoption or approval of alterations providing for the grant of planning permission has effect to grant such permission in relation to the simplified planning zone, or such part of it as is specified in the scheme, for development so specified or development of any class so specified.

(4) The adoption or approval of alterations providing for the withdrawal or relaxation of conditions, limitations or restrictions to which planning permission under the scheme is subject has effect to with-

draw or relax the conditions, limitations or restrictions forthwith.

(5) The adoption or approval of alterations providing for—

 (a) the exclusion of land from the simplified planning zone,

 (b) the withdrawal of planning permission, or

 (c) the imposition of new or more stringent conditions, limitations or restrictions to which planning permission under the scheme is subject,

has effect to withdraw permission, or to impose the conditions, limitations or restrictions, with effect from the end of the period of twelve months beginning with the date of the adoption or approval.

(6) The adoption or approval of alterations to a scheme does not affect planning permission under the scheme in any case where the development authorised by it has been begun.

The provisions of section 43(1) to (3) of this Act apply in determining for the purposes of this subsection when development shall be taken to be begun.

Exclusion of certain descriptions of land or development.

24E.—(1) The following descriptions of land may not be included in a simplified planning zone—

 (a) land in a National Park ;

 (b) land in a conservation area ;

 (c) land in an area designated under section 87 of the National Parks and Access to the Countryside Act 1949 as an area of outstanding natural beauty ;

 (d) land identified in the development plan for the district as part of a green belt ;

 (e) land in respect of which a notification or order is in force under section 28 or 29 of the Wildlife and Countryside Act 1981 (areas of special scientific interest).

(2) Where land included in a simplified planning zone becomes land of such a description, subsection (1) does not have effect to exclude it from the zone.

(3) The Secretary of State may by order provide that no simplified planning zone scheme shall have effect to grant planning permission—

(*a*) in relation to an area of land specified in
the order or to areas of land of a description so specified, or

(*b*) for development of a description specified
in the order.

(4) An order under subsection (3) has effect to
withdraw such planning permission under a simplified planning zone scheme already in force with
effect from the date on which the order comes into
force, except in a case where the development
authorised by the permission has been begun.

The provisions of section 43(1) to (3) of this Act
apply in determining for the purposes of this subsection when development shall be taken to be begun.".

(2) After Schedule 8 to the Town and Country Planning Act
1971 insert as Schedule 8A the Schedule set out in Part I of
Schedule 6 to this Act which contains provision with respect to
the making and alteration of simplified planning zone schemes
and other related matters.

(3) The Town and Country Planning Act 1971 also has effect
subject to the consequential amendments specified in Part II of
Schedule 6 to this Act.

Scotland

26.—(1) In Part III of the Town and Country Planning (Scot- Simplified
land) Act 1972 (general planning control), after section 21 in- planning
sert— zones in
Scotland.
1972 c. 52.

" *Simplified planning zone schemes*

21A.—(1) A simplified planning zone is an area
in respect of which a simplified planning zone scheme
is in force.

(2) The adoption or approval of a simplified planning zone scheme has effect to grant in relation to
the zone, or any part of it specified in the scheme,
planning permission for development specified in the
scheme or for development of any class so specified.

(3) Planning permission under a simplified planning zone scheme may be unconditional or subject
to such conditions, limitations or exceptions as may
be specified in the scheme.

(4) Every planning authority—

(*a*) shall consider, as soon as practicable after
this section comes into operation, the question for which part or parts of their district

a simplified planning zone scheme is desirable, and shall thereafter keep that question under review ; and

(b) shall prepare a scheme for any such part for which they decide, as a result of their original consideration or of any such review, that it is desirable to do so.

(5) The provisions of Schedule 6A to this Act have effect with respect to the making and alteration of simplified planning zone schemes and other related matters.

Simplified planning zone schemes: conditions and limitations on planning permission.

21B.—(1) The conditions and limitations on planning permission which may be specified in a simplified planning zone scheme may include—

(a) conditions or limitations in respect of all development permitted by the scheme or in respect of particular descriptions of development so permitted, and

(b) conditions or limitations requiring the consent, agreement or approval of the planning authority in relation to particular descriptions of permitted development ;

and different conditions or limitations may be specified for different cases or classes of case.

(2) Nothing in a simplified planning zone scheme shall affect the right of any person—

(a) to do anything not amounting to development, or

(b) to carry out development for which planning permission is not required or for which permission has been granted otherwise than by the scheme ;

and no limitation or restriction subject to which permission has been granted otherwise than under the scheme shall affect the right of any person to carry out development for which permission has been granted under the scheme.

Duration of simplified planning zone scheme.

21C.—(1) A simplified planning zone scheme shall take effect on the date of its adoption or approval and shall cease to have effect at the end of the period of ten years beginning with that date.

(2) Upon the scheme's ceasing to have effect planning permission under the scheme shall also cease to have effect except in a case where the development authorised by it has been begun.

(3) The provisions of section 41(2) to (6) of this   PART II
Act (which provide for the termination of planning
permission if the completion of development is unreasonably delayed) apply to planning permission
under a simplified planning zone scheme where
development has been begun but not completed by
the time the area ceases to be a simplified planning
zone.

(4) The provisions of section 40(1) to (3) of this
Act apply in determining for the purposes of this
section when development shall be taken to be
begun.

Alteration
of simplified
planning
scheme.

21D.—(1) The adoption or approval of alterations
to a simplified planning zone scheme has effect as
follows.

(2) The adoption or approval of alterations providing for the inclusion of land in the simplified
planning zone has effect to grant in relation to that
land or such part of it as is specified in the scheme
planning permission for development so specified
or of any class so specified.

(3) The adoption or approval of alterations providing for the grant of planning permission has effect
to grant such permission in relation to the simplified
planning zone, or such part of it as is specified in
the scheme, for development so specified or development of any class so specified.

(4) The adoption or approval of alterations providing for the withdrawal or relaxation of conditions,
limitations or restrictions to which planning permission under the scheme is subject has effect to withdraw or relax the conditions, limitations or restrictions forthwith.

(5) The adoption or approval of alterations providing for—

   (a) the exclusion of land from the simplified
       planning zone,

   (b) the withdrawal of planning permission, or

   (c) the imposition of new or more stringent
       conditions, limitations or restrictions to
       which planning permission under the
       scheme is subject,

PART II

has effect to withdraw permission, or to impose the conditions, limitations or restrictions, with effect from the end of the period of twelve months beginning with the date of the adoption or approval.

(6) The adoption or approval of alterations to a scheme does not affect planning permission under the scheme in any case where the development authorised by it has been begun.

The provisions of section 40(1) to (3) of this Act apply in determining for the purposes of this subsection when development shall be taken to be begun.

Exclusion of certain descriptions of land or development.

21E.—(1) The following descriptions of land may not be included in a simplified planning zone—

(a) land in a conservation area ;

(b) land in a National Scenic Area ;

(c) land identified in the development plan for the area as part of a green belt ;

(d) land in respect of which a notification or order is in force under section 28 or 29 of the Wildlife and Countryside Act 1981 (areas of special scientific interest).

1981 c. 69.

(2) Where land included in a simplified planning zone becomes land of such a description, subsection (1) does not have effect to exclude it from the zone.

(3) The Secretary of State may by order provide that no simplified planning zone scheme shall have effect to grant planning permission—

(a) in relation to an area of land specified in the order or to areas of land of a description so specified, or

(b) for development of a description specified in the order.

(4) An order under subsection (3) has effect to withdraw such planning permission under a simplified planning zone scheme already in force with effect from the date on which the order comes into force, except in a case where the development authorised by the permission has been begun.

The provisions of section 40(1) to (3) of this Act apply in determining for the purposes of this subsection when development shall be taken to be begun.".

1972 c. 52.

(2) After Schedule 6 to the Town and Country Planning

(Scotland) Act 1972 insert as Schedule 6A the Schedule set out in   PART II
Part III of Schedule 6 to this Act which contains provision with
respect to the making and alteration of simplified planning zone
schemes and other related matters.

(3) The Town and Country Planning (Scotland) Act 1972 also   1972 c. 52.
has effect subject to the consequential amendments specified in
Part IV of Schedule 6 to this Act.

PART III
FINANCIAL ASSISTANCE FOR URBAN REGENERATION

27.—(1) The Secretary of State may, with the consent of the   Power to
Treasury, give financial assistance to any person in respect of   give
qualifying expenditure incurred in connection with activities   assistance.
contributing to the regeneration of an urban area by bringing
land and buildings into effective use, creating an attractive environment, providing employment for people who live in the area
or ensuring that housing and social facilities are available to encourage people to live and work in the area.

(2) Expenditure incurred in connection with any of the following qualifies for assistance—

(a) the acquisition of land or buildings ;

(b) the reclamation, improvement or refurbishment of land
or buildings ;

(c) the development or redevelopment of land, including
the conversion or demolition of existing buildings ;

(d) the equipment or fitting out of buildings or land ;

(e) the provision of means of access, services or other facilities for buildings or land ;

(f) environmental improvements.

28.—(1) Financial assistance under section 27 may be given   Forms of
in any form.   assistance.

(2) Assistance may, in particular, be given by way of—

(a) grants,

(b) loans,

(c) guarantees, or

(d) incurring expenditure for the benefit of the person assisted.

(3) The Secretary of State shall not in giving financial assistance under section 27 purchase loan or share capital in a company.

29.—(1) Financial assistance under section 27 may be given   Terms on
on such terms as the Secretary of State, with the consent of the   which
Treasury, considers appropriate.   assistance
                                                               is given.

(2) The terms may, in particular, include provision as to—

(a) circumstances in which the assistance must be repaid, or otherwise made good, to the Secretary of State, and the manner in which that is to be done ; or

(b) circumstances in which the Secretary of State is entitled to recover the proceeds or part of the proceeds of any disposal of land or buildings in respect of which assistance was provided.

(3) The person receiving assistance shall comply with the terms on which it is given and compliance may be enforced by the Secretary of State.

PART IV

HAZARDOUS SUBSTANCES

England and Wales

Hazardous
substances
authorities.
1971 c. 78.

30. The following sections shall be inserted after section 1 of the Town and Country Planning Act 1971—

" Hazardous
substances
authorities—
general.

1A.—(1) Subject to subsections (2) to (4) below, in this Act " hazardous substances authority ", in relation to any land other than land to which section 1B below applies, means the council of the district or London borough in which it is situated.

(2) Subject to subsection (3) below, the county council are the hazardous substances authority if the land is in a non-metropolitan county and—

(a) is situated in a National Park ;

(b) is used for the winning and working of minerals (including their extraction from a mineral-working deposit) ; or

(c) is situated in England and used for the disposal of refuse or waste materials.

(3) A joint planning board or special planning board for a National Park are the hazardous substances authority for the Park.

(4) An urban development corporation are the hazardous substances authority for their area, if they are the local planning authority in relation to all kinds of development.

Hazardous
substances
authorities—
statutory
undertakers.

1B.—(1) In this Act " hazardous substances authority ", in relation to land to which this section applies, means the appropriate Minister.

(2) This section applies—

> (*a*) to operational land of statutory undertakers ;

> (*b*) to land in which statutory undertakers hold, or propose to acquire, an interest with a view to the land being used as operational land.

(3) For the purposes of this section any land to which this subsection applies but which is not operational land of statutory undertakers authorised to carry on a harbour shall be treated as if it were such operational land.

(4) Subsection (3) above applies—

> (*a*) to a wharf ; and

> (*b*) to harbour land,

as defined in the Harbours Act 1964.

1964 c. 40.

(5) Any question whether subsection (3) above applies to land shall be determined by the Secretary of State and the Minister who is the appropriate Minister in relation to operational land of statutory undertakers who are authorised to carry on harbour undertakings.".

31. The following shall be inserted after section 58A of the Town and Country Planning Act 1971—

Hazardous
substances.
1971 c. 78.

" *Hazardous substances*

Requirement
of hazardous
substances
consent.

58B.—(1) Subject to the provisions of this Part of this Act, the presence of a hazardous substance on, over or under land requires the consent of the hazardous substances authority (in this Act referred to as " hazardous substances consent ") unless the aggregate quantity of the substance—

> (*a*) on, under or over the land ;

> (*b*) on, under or over other land which is within 500 metres of it and controlled by the same person ; or

> (*c*) in or on a structure controlled by the same person any part of which is within 500 metres of it,

is less than the controlled quantity.

(2) The temporary presence of a hazardous substance while it is being transported from one place to another is not to be taken into account unless it is unloaded.

(3) The Secretary of State—

(a) shall by regulations specify—

(i) the substances that are hazardous substances for the purposes of this Act;

(ii) the quantity which is to be the controlled quantity of any such substance;

(b) may by regulations provide that hazardous substances consent is not required or is only required—

(i) in relation to land of prescribed descriptions;

(ii) by reason of the presence of hazardous substances in prescribed circumstances;

(c) may by regulations provide that, except in such circumstances as may be prescribed, all hazardous substances falling within a group specified in the regulations are to be treated as a single substance for the purposes of this Act.

(4) Regulations which—

(a) are made by virtue of sub-paragraph (i) of subsection (3)(a) above; or

(b) are made by virtue of sub-paragraph (ii) of that paragraph and reduce the controlled quantity of a substance,

may make such transitional provision as appears to the Secretary of State to be appropriate.

(5) The power to make such transitional provision includes, without prejudice to its generality, power to apply section 23 of the Housing and Planning Act 1986 subject to such modifications as appear to the Secretary of State to be appropriate.

(6) Regulations under this section may make different provisions for different cases or descriptions of cases.

(7) Bodies corporate which are inter-connected for the purposes of the Fair Trading Act 1973 are to be

1973 c. 41.

treated as being one person for the purposes of this section and sections 58C to 58K and 101B below.

Applications for hazardous substances consent.

58C.—(1) Provision may be made by regulations with respect to—

(a) the form and manner in which applications for hazardous substances consent are to be made ;

(b) the particulars which they are to contain and the evidence by which they are to be verified ;

(c) the manner in which they are to be advertised ; and

(d) the time within which they are to be dealt with.

(2) Regulations may provide that an application for hazardous substances consent, or an appeal against the refusal of such an application or against the imposition of a condition on such a consent, shall not be entertained unless it is accompanied by a certificate in the prescribed form and corresponding to one or other of those described in section 27(1)(a) to (d) of this Act ; and any such regulations may—

(a) include requirements corresponding to sections 27(2) and (4) and 29(3) of this Act ; and

(b) make provision as to who is to be treated as the owner of land for the purposes of any provision of the regulations.

(3) If any person issues a certificate which purports to comply with the requirements of regulations made by virtue of subsection (2) above and which contains a statement which he knows to be false or misleading in a material particular, or recklessly issues a certificate which purports to comply with those requirements and which contains a statement which is false or misleading in a material particular, he shall be guilty of an offence and liable on summary conviction to a fine of an amount not exceeding level 3 on the standard scale.

(4) Regulations—

(a) may require an applicant for hazardous substances consent or the hazardous substances authority or both to give publicity

to an application for hazardous substances
consent in such manner as may be prescribed ;

(*b*) may require hazardous substances authorities to conduct appropriate consultations
before determining applications for hazardous substances consent ;

(*c*) may provide for the manner in which such
a consultation is to be carried out and the
time within which—

(i) such a consultation ;

(ii) any stage in such a consultation,
is to be completed ;

(*d*) may require hazardous substances authorities to determine applications for hazardous substances consent within such time
as may be prescribed ;

(*e*) may require hazardous substances authorities to give prescribed persons or bodies
prescribed information about applications
for hazardous substances consent, including information as to the manner in which
such applications have been dealt with.

(5) In subsection (4) above " appropriate consultations " means—

(*a*) consultations—

(i) in the case of a hazardous substances
authority other than the appropriate Minister, with the Health and Safety Executive ; and

(ii) in the case of the appropriate Minister, with the Health and Safety Commission ; and

(*b*) consultations with such persons or bodies as
may be prescribed.

(6) Regulations under this section may make different provision for different cases or descriptions of
cases.

Deter-
mination of
applications
for
hazardous
substances
consent.

58D.—(1) Subject to the following provisions of
this Act, where an application is made to a hazardous substances authority for hazardous substances
consent, that authority, in dealing with the application, shall have regard to any material considerations,
and—

(a) may grant hazardous substances consent,
either unconditionally or subject to such
conditions as they think fit ; or

(b) may refuse hazardous substances consent.

(2) Without prejudice to the generality of subsection (1) above, in dealing with an application the
authority shall have regard—

(a) to any current or contemplated use of the
land to which the application relates ;

(b) to the way in which land in the vicinity is
being used or is likely to be used ;

(c) to any planning permission that has been
granted for development of land in the
vicinity ;

(d) to the provisions of the development plan ;
and

(e) to any advice which the Health and Safety
Executive or Health and Safety Commission have given following consultations in
pursuance of regulations under section
58C(4) above.

(3) If an application relates to more than one
hazardous substance, the authority may make different determinations in relation to each.

(4) It shall be the duty of a hazardous substances
authority, when granting hazardous substances consent, to include in that consent—

(a) a description of the land to which the consent relates ;

(b) a description of the hazardous substance or
substances to which it relates ; and

(c) in respect of each hazardous substance to
which it relates, a statement of the maximum quantity permitted by the consent to
be present at any one time and of all conditions relating to that substance subject
to which the consent is granted.

(5) Without prejudice to the generality of subsection (1) above, a hazardous substances authority
may grant hazardous substances consent subject to
conditions with respect to any of the following—

(*a*) how and where any hazardous substance to which the consent relates is to be kept or used ;

(*b*) times between which any such substance may be present ;

(*c*) the permanent removal of any such substance—

(i) on or before a date specified in the consent ; or

(ii) before the end of a period specified in it and commencing on the date on which it is granted ;

(*d*) the consent being conditional on the commencement or partial or complete execution of development on the land which is authorised by a specified planning permission ;

but an authority who are a hazardous substances authority by virtue of section 1A above may only grant consent subject to conditions as to how a hazardous substance is to be kept or used if the conditions are conditions to which the Health and Safety Executive have advised the authority that any consent they might grant should be subject.

References to Secretary of State and appeals.

58E.—(1) Subject to subsections (2) and (3) below, sections 35 to 37 of this Act shall have effect in relation to applications for hazardous substances consent and to decisions on such applications as though they were applications for planning permission.

(2) In the application of sections 35 to 37 of this Act to hazardous substances consent—

(*a*) references to the local planning authority shall be construed as references to the hazardous substances authority ;

(*b*) section 35(4) and section 36(5) and (7) shall be omitted ;

(*c*) the words " and in such manner as may be prescribed " shall be substituted for the words in section 36(2) following " time " ;

(*d*) in section 37, the words " by the development order " shall be omitted from both places where they occur.

(3) Subsections (1) and (2) above do not have effect in relation to applications for hazardous substances consent relating to land to which section 1B of this Act applies or to decisions on such applications.

Deemed hazardous substances consent by virtue of authorisation of government department.

58F.—(1) Where—

    (a) the authorisation of a government department is required by virtue of an enactment in respect of development to be carried out by a local authority, or by statutory undertakers not being a local authority ; and

    (b) the development would involve the presence of a hazardous substance in circumstances requiring hazardous substances consent,

the department may, on granting that authorisation, also direct that hazardous substances consent shall be deemed to be granted subject to such conditions (if any) as may be specified in the directions.

(2) The department shall consult the Health and Safety Commission before issuing any such directions.

(3) The provisions of this Act (except Parts VII and XII) shall apply in relation to any hazardous substances consent deemed to be granted by virtue of directions under this section as if it had been granted by the Secretary of State on an application referred to him under section 35 of this Act, as applied by section 58E of this Act.

(4) The reference in subsection (1) above to the authorisation of a government department is to be construed in accordance with section 40(3) of this Act.

Grants of hazardous substances consent without compliance with conditions previously attached.

58G.—(1) This section applies to an application for hazardous substances consent without a condition subject to which a previous hazardous substances consent was granted.

(2) On such an application the hazardous substances authority shall consider only the question of the conditions subject to which hazardous substances consent should be granted, and—

    (a) if they determine that hazardous substances consent should be granted subject to conditions differing from those subject to which the previous consent was granted, or that it should be granted unconditionally, they shall grant hazardous substances consent accordingly; and

(b) if they determine that hazardous substances consent should be granted subject to the same conditions as those subject to which the previous consent was granted, they shall refuse the application.

(3) Where—

(a) hazardous substances consent has been granted or is deemed to have been granted for the presence on, over or under land of more than one hazardous substance; and

(b) an application under this section does not relate to all the substances,

the hazardous substances authority shall only have regard to any condition relating to a substance to which the application does not relate to the extent that it has implications for a substance to which the application does relate.

(4) Where—

(a) more than one hazardous substances consent has been granted or is deemed to have been granted in respect of the same land; and

(b) an application under this section does not relate to all the consents,

the hazardous substances authority shall only have regard to any consent to which the application does not relate to the extent that it has implications for consent to which the application does relate.

(5) Regulations may make provision in relation to applications under this section corresponding to any provision that may be made by regulations under section 58C above in relation to applications for hazardous substances consent.

Power to revoke or modify hazardous substances consent.

58H.—(1) If it appears to the hazardous substances authority that—

(a) there has been a material change of use of land to which a hazardous substances consent relates; or

(*b*) planning permission has been granted for
development the carrying out of which
would involve a material change of use of
such land and the development to which
the permission relates has been commenced,

they may by order—

(i) if the consent relates only to one substance,
revoke it ;

(ii) if it relates to more than one, revoke it or
revoke it so far as it relates to a specified
substance.

(2) The hazardous substances authority may by
order—

(*a*) revoke a hazardous substances consent
which relates to only one substance if it
appears to them that that substance has not
for at least 5 years been present on, under
or over the land to which the consent
relates in a quantity equal to or exceeding
the controlled quantity ; and

(*b*) revoke a hazardous substances consent
which relates to a number of substances if
it appears to them that none of those substances has for at least 5 years been so
present.

(3) The hazardous substances authority may by
order revoke a hazardous substances consent or
modify it to such extent as they consider expedient
if it appears to them, having regard to any material
consideration, that it is expedient to revoke or modify
it.

(4) An order under this section shall specify the
grounds on which it is made.

(5) An order under this section, other than an
order relating to land to which section 1B of this
Act applies, shall not take effect unless it is confirmed by the Secretary of State, and the Secretary
of State may confirm any such order submitted to
him either without modification or subject to such
modification as he considers expedient.

(6) Where a hazardous substances authority submit an order under this section to the Secretary of

State for his confirmation under this section, the authority shall serve notice of the order—

(a) on any person who is an owner of the whole or any part of the land to which the order relates;

(b) on any person other than an owner who appears to them to be in control of the whole or any part of that land;

(c) on any other person who in their opinion will be affected by the order;

and if within the period specified in that behalf in the notice (not being less than 28 days from the service thereof) any person on whom the notice is served so requires, the Secretary of State, before confirming the order, shall afford to that person and to the hazardous substances authority an opportunity of appearing before, and being heard by, a person appointed by the Secretary of State for that purpose.

(7) Where an order under this section has been confirmed by the Secretary of State, the hazardous substances authority shall serve a copy of the order on every person who was entitled to be served with notice under subsection (6) above.

(8) Section 170 of this Act shall have effect where a hazardous substances consent is revoked or modified by an order made in the exercise of the power conferred by subsection (3) above as it has effect where an order is made under section 51 of this Act, but as if any reference in it to the local planning authority were a reference to the hazardous substances authority.

Provisions as to effect of hazardous substances consent and change of control of land.

58J.—(1) Without prejudice to the provisions of this Part of this Act, any hazardous substances consent shall (except in so far as it otherwise provides) enure for the benefit of the land to which it relates and of all persons for the time being interested in the land.

(2) A hazardous substances consent is revoked if there is a change in the person in control of part of the land to which it relates, unless an application for the continuation of the consent has previously been made to the hazardous substances authority.

(3) Regulations may make provision in relation to applications under subsection (2) above corresponding to any provision that may be made by

regulations under section 58C of this Act in relation to applications for hazardous substances consent.

(4) When such an application is made, the authority, having regard to any material consideration—

> (a) may modify the consent in any way they
> consider appropriate ; or
>
> (b) may revoke it.

(5) Without prejudice to the generality of subsection (4) above, in dealing with an application the
authority shall have regard—

> (a) to the matters to which a hazardous sub-
> stances authority are required to have re-
> gard by section 58D(2)(a) to (d) above ;
> and
>
> (b) to any advice which the Health and Safety
> Executive or Health and Safety Commis-
> sion have given following consultations in
> pursuance of regulations under subsection
> (3) above.

(6) If an application relates to more than one
consent, the authority may make different determinations in relation to each.

(7) If a consent relates to more than one hazardous substance, the authority may make different
determinations in relation to each.

(8) It shall be the duty of a hazardous substances
authority, when continuing hazardous substances
consent, to attach to the consent one of the following—

> (a) a statement that it is unchanged in relation
> to the matters included in it by virtue of
> section 58D(4) above ;
>
> (b) a statement of any change in respect of
> those matters.

(9) The modifications which a hazardous substances authority may make by virtue of subsection
(4)(a) above include, without prejudice to the generality of that paragraph, the making of the consent
subject to conditions with respect to any of the
matters mentioned in section 58D(5) above.

(10) Subject to subsection (11) below, sections 35
to 37 of this Act shall have effect in relation to

applications under subsection (2) above and to decisions on such applications as though they were applications for planning permission.

(11) In the application of sections 35 to 37 of this Act by virtue of subsection (10) above—

(a) references to the local planning authority shall be construed as references to the hazardous substances authority;

(b) section 35(4) and section 36(5) and (7) shall be omitted;

(c) the words " and in such manner as may be prescribed " shall be substituted for the words in section 36(2) following " time ";

(d) in section 37—

(i) the words " by the development order " shall be omitted from the first place where they occur; and

(ii) the words " the application shall be deemed to have been granted " shall be substituted for the words following paragraph (b).

(12) Where the authority modify or revoke the consent, they shall pay to the person in control of the whole of the land before the change compensation in respect of any loss or damage sustained by him and directly attributable to the modification or revocation.

Offences.   58K.—(1) Subject to this Part of this Act, if there is a contravention of hazardous substances control, the appropriate person shall be guilty of an offence.

(2) There is a contravention of hazardous substances control—

(a) if a quantity of a hazardous substance equal to or exceeding the controlled quantity is or has been present on, under or over land and either—

(i) there is no hazardous substances consent for the presence of the substance; or

(ii) there is hazardous substances consent for its presence but the quantity present exceeds the maximum quantity permitted by the consent:

(b) if there is or has been a failure to comply with a condition subject to which a hazardous substances consent was granted.

(3) In subsection (1) above " the appropriate person " means—

(a) in relation to a contravention falling within paragraph (a) of subsection (2) above—

(i) any person knowingly causing the substance to be present on, over or under the land ;

(ii) any person allowing it to be so present ; and

(b) in relation to a contravention falling within paragraph (a) or (b) of that subsection, the person in control of the land.

(4) A person guilty of an offence under this section shall be liable—

(a) on summary conviction, to a fine not exceeding the statutory maximum ; or

(b) on conviction on indictment, to a fine,

and if the contravention is continued after the conviction he shall be guilty of a further offence and liable on summary conviction to a fine not exceeding £200 for each day on which it continues, or on conviction on indictment to a fine.

(5) In any proceedings for an offence under this section it shall be a defence for the accused to prove—

(a) that he took all reasonable precautions and exercised all due diligence to avoid commission of the offence, or

(b) that commission of the offence could be avoided only by the taking of action amounting to a breach of a statutory duty.

(6) In any proceedings for an offence consisting of a contravention falling within subsection (2)(a) above, it shall be a defence for the accused to prove that at the time of the alleged commission of the offence he did not know, and had no reason to believe,—

(a) if the case falls within paragraph (a)(i)—

(i) that the substance was present ; or

(ii) that it was present in a quantity equal to or exceeding the controlled quantity ;

(b) if the case falls within paragraph (a)(ii),

that the substance was present in a quantity exceeding the maximum quantity permitted by the consent.

(7) In any proceedings for an offence consisting of a contravention falling within subsection (2)(b) above, it shall be a defence for the accused to prove that he did not know, and had no reason to believe, that there was a failure to comply with a condition subject to which hazardous substances consent had been granted.

Emergencies.   58L.—(1) If it appears to the Secretary of State—

(a) either—

(i) that the community or part of it is being or is likely to be deprived of an essential service or commodity ; or

(ii) that there is or is likely to be a shortage of such a service or commodity affecting the community or part of it ; and

(b) that the presence of a hazardous substance on, over or under land specified in the direction in circumstances such that hazardous substances consent would be required, is necessary for the effective provision of that service or commodity,

he may direct that, subject to such conditions or exceptions as he thinks fit, the presence of the substance on, over or under the land is not to constitute a contravention of hazardous substances control so long as the direction remains in force.

(2) A direction under this section—

(a) may be withdrawn at any time ;

(b) shall in any case cease to have effect at the end of the period of three months beginning with the day on which it was given, but without prejudice to the Secretary of State's power to give a further direction.

(3) Subject to subsection (4) below, the Secretary of State shall send a copy of any such direction to the authority which are the hazardous substances authority in relation to the land.

(4) Where the land is land to which section 1B of this Act applies, the Secretary of State shall send the copy to the authority which would be the hazardous substances authority in relation to the land but for that section.

Registers, **58M.**—(1) Every authority which is a hazardous
etc. substances authority by virtue of section 1A of this
Act shall keep, in such manner as may be prescribed,
a register containing such information as may be
prescribed with respect—

> (*a*) to applications for hazardous substances con-
> sent—
>> (i) made to that authority ; or
>> (ii) made to the appropriate Minister
>> with respect to land in relation to which,
>> but for section 1B of this Act, that auth-
>> ority would be the hazardous substances
>> authority ;
>
> and including information as to the manner
> in which such applications have been dealt
> with ;
> (*b*) to hazardous substances consent deemed to
> be granted under section 23 of the Housing
> and Planning Act 1986 with respect to land
> in relation to which that authority is, or
> but for section 1B of this Act would be,
> the hazardous substances authority ;
> (*c*) to revocations or modifications of hazardous
> substances consent granted with respect to
> such land ; and
> (*d*) to directions under section 58L of this Act
> sent to the authority by the Secretary of
> State.

(2) Where with respect to any land the appropriate Minister exercises any of the functions of a
hazardous substances authority, he shall send to the
authority which but for section 1B of this Act would
be the hazardous substances authority in relation to
the land any such information as appears to him to
be required by them for the purposes of maintaining
a register under this section.

(3) Every register kept under this section shall be
available for inspection by the public at all reasonable hours.

Health and **58N.**—(1) Nothing in—
safety
require- > (*a*) any hazardous substances consent granted or
ments. > deemed to be granted under—
>> (i) the preceding provisions of this Act ;
>> or

Q 4

(ii) section 34 of the Housing and Planning Act 1986 ; or

(b) any hazardous substances contravention notice issued under section 101B of this Act,

shall require or allow anything to be done in contravention of any of the relevant statutory provisions or any prohibition notice or improvement notice served under or by virtue of any of those provisions ; and to the extent that such a consent or notice purports to require or allow any such thing to be done, it shall be void.

(2) Where it appears to a hazardous substances authority who have granted, or are deemed to have granted, a hazardous substances consent or who have issued a hazardous substances contravention notice that the consent or notice or part of it is rendered void by subsection (1) above, the authority shall, as soon as is reasonably practicable, consult the appropriate body with regard to the matter.

(3) If the appropriate body advise the authority that the consent or notice is rendered wholly void, the authority shall revoke it.

(4) If they advise that part of the consent or notice is rendered void, the authority shall so modify it as to render it wholly operative.

(5) In this section—

" the appropriate body " means—

(a) in relation to a hazardous substances authority other than the appropriate Minister, the Health and Safety Executive ; and

(b) in relation to the appropriate Minister, the Health and Safety Commission ; and

" relevant statutory provisions ", " improvement notice " and " prohibition notice " have the same meanings as in Part I of the Health and Safety at Work etc. Act 1974.".

1974 c 37.

32. The following shall be inserted after section 101A of the Town and Country Planning Act 1971—

PART IV

Hazardous substances contravention notices.

1971 c. 78.

" *Hazardous substances*

Power to issue hazardous substances contravention notice.

101B.—(1) Subject to subsection (2) below, where it appears to the hazardous substances authority that there is or has been a contravention of hazardous substances control, they may issue a hazardous substances contravention notice if they consider it expedient to do so having regard to any material consideration.

(2) A hazardous substances authority shall not issue a hazardous substances contravention notice where it appears to them that a contravention of hazardous substances control can be avoided only by the taking of action amounting to a breach of a statutory duty.

(3) In this Act " hazardous substances contravention notice " means a notice—

(a) specifying an alleged contravention of hazardous substances control ; and

(b) requiring such steps as may be specified in the notice to be taken to remedy the contravention.

(4) A copy of a hazardous substances contravention notice shall be served—

(a) on the owner of the land to which it relates ;

(b) on any person other than the owner who appears to the hazardous substances authority to be in control of that land ; and

(c) on such other persons as may be prescribed.

(5) A hazardous substances contravention notice shall also specify—

(a) a date not less than 28 days from the date of service of copies of the notice as the date on which it is to take effect ;

(b) in respect of each of the steps required to be taken to remedy the contravention of hazardous substances control, the period from the notice taking effect within which the step is to be taken.

(6) Where a hazardous substances authority issue a hazardous substances contravention notice the steps required by the notice may, without prejudice to the generality of subsection (3)(b) above, if the

authority think it expedient, include a requirement that the hazardous substance be removed from the land.

(7) Where a notice includes such a requirement, it may also contain a direction that at the end of such period as may be specified in the notice any hazardous substances consent for the presence of the substance shall cease to have effect or, if it relates to more than one substance, shall cease to have effect so far as it relates to the substance which is required to be removed.

(8) The hazardous substances authority may withdraw a hazardous substances contravention notice (without prejudice to their power to issue another) at any time before it takes effect.

(9) If they do so, they shall forthwith give notice of the withdrawal to every person who was served with a copy of the notice.

(10) The Secretary of State may by regulations—

(*a*) specify matters which are to be included in hazardous substances contravention notices, in addition to those which are required to be included in them by this section;

(*b*) provide—

(i) for appeals to him against hazardous substances contravention notices;

(ii) for the persons by whom, grounds upon which and time within which such an appeal may be brought;

(iii) for the procedure to be followed on such appeals;

(iv) for the directions that may be given on such an appeal;

(v) for the application to such appeals, subject to such modifications as the regulations may specify, of any of the provisions of sections 88 to 88B, 243 and 246 of this Act;

(*c*) direct that any of the provisions of sections 89 to 93 of this Act shall have effect in relation to hazardous substances contravention notices subject to such modifications as he may specify in the regulations;

(*d*) make such other provision as he considers necessary or expedient in relation to hazardous substances contravention notices.

(11) If any person appeals against a hazardous substances contravention notice, the notice shall be of no effect pending the final determination or the withdrawal of the appeal.

(12) Regulations under this section may make different provision for different cases or descriptions of cases.".

33. The enactments mentioned in Part I of Schedule 7 to Consequential this Act shall have effect with the amendments there specified, amendments. being amendments consequential on the provisions of this Part of this Act.

34.—(1) Until the end of the transitional period— Transitional.

    (*a*) no offence is committed under section 58K of the Town 1971 c. 78. and Country Planning Act 1971 ; and

    (*b*) no hazardous substances contravention notice may be issued, in relation to a hazardous substance which is on, under or over any land,

if the substance was present on, under or over the land at any time within the establishment period and—

    (i) in a case in which at the commencement date notification in respect of the substance was required by any of the Notification Regulations, both the conditions specified in subsection (2) below were satisfied ; and

    (ii) in a case in which at that date such notification was not so required, the condition specified in paragraph (*b*) of that subsection is satisfied.

(2) The conditions mentioned in subsection (1) above are—

    (*a*) that notification required by the Notification Regulations was given before the commencement date ; and

    (*b*) that the substance has not been present during the transitional period in a quantity greater in aggregate than the established quantity.

(3) Where a hazardous substance was present on, under or over any land at any time within the establishment period, hazardous substances consent may be claimed in respect of its presence.

(4) A claim shall be made in the prescribed form before the end of the transitional period and shall contain the prescribed information as to the presence of the substance during the establishment period and as to how and where it was kept and used immediately before the commencement date.

(5) Subject to subsections (6) to (8) below, the hazardous substances authority shall be deemed to have granted any hazardous substances consent which is claimed under subsection (3) above.

(6) If at the commencement date notification in respect of the substance was required by regulation 3 or 5 of the Notification Regulations, hazardous substances consent is only to be deemed to be granted under this section if notification in respect of the substance was given before that date in accordance with those regulations.

(7) If at the commencement date such notification was not so required, hazardous substances consent is only to be deemed to be granted under this section if an aggregate quantity of the substance not less than the controlled quantity was present at any one time within the establishment period.

(8) If it appears to the hazardous substances authority that a claim for hazardous substances consent does not comply with subsection (4) above, it shall be their duty, before the end of the period of two weeks from their receipt of the claim,—

> (a) to notify the claimant that in their opinion the claim is invalid ; and
>
> (b) to give him their reasons for that opinion.

(9) Hazardous substances consent which is deemed to be granted under this section is subject to the conditions that—

> (a) the maximum aggregate quantity of the substance that may be present—
>
>> (i) on, under or over the land to which the claim relates ;
>>
>> (ii) on, under or over other land which is within 500 metres of it and controlled by the same person ; or
>>
>> (iii) in or on a structure controlled by the same person any part of which is within 500 metres of it,
>
> at any one time shall not exceed the established quantity ; and
>
> (b) the substance shall be kept and used in the place and manner in which information supplied in pursuance of regulations made by virtue of subsection (4) above shows that it was kept and used immediately before the commencement date, and
>
> (c) none of the substance shall be kept or used in a container greater in capacity than the container, or the largest of the containers, in which the substance was kept or used immediately before the commencement date.

(10) In this section—

" commencement date " means the date on which this Part of this Act comes into force ;

" the establishment period " means the period of 12 months immediately preceding the commencement date ;

" established quantity " means, in relation to any land—

(a) where before the commencement date there has been a notification in respect of a substance in accordance with any of the Notification Regulations—

(i) the quantity notified or last notified before the commencement date ; or

(ii) a quantity equal to twice the quantity which was so notified or last notified before the start of the establishment period,

whichever is the greater ;

(b) where a notification was not required before that date by any of those regulations, a quantity exceeding by 50 per cent, the maximum quantity which was present on, under or over the land at any one time within the establishment period ;

" Notification Regulations " means the Notification of Installations Handling Hazardous Substances Regulations 1982 ;

S.I. 1982/1357.

" the transitional period " means the period of 6 months beginning with the commencement date ;

and other expressions have the same meanings as in the Town and Country Planning Act 1971.

1971 c. 78.

Scotland

35. The following shall be inserted after section 56AA of the Town and Country Planning (Scotland) Act 1972—

Hazardous substances—Scotland.

1972 c. 52.

" *Hazardous substances*

Hazardous substances.

56A.—(1) Subject to subsection (2) of this section and to section 56B below, it shall be the duty of the planning authority to control hazardous substances in accordance with the provisions of this Act.

(2) An urban development corporation shall control hazardous substances in their area if they are

the planning authority in relation to all kinds of development.

Hazardous substances—statutory undertakers.

56B.—(1) The appropriate Minister shall be the planning authority in respect of hazardous substances in relation to land to which this section applies.

(2) This section applies—

(a) to operational land of statutory undertakers ;

(b) to land in which statutory undertakers hold, or propose to acquire, an interest with a view to the land being used as operational land.

(3) For the purposes of this section any land to which this subsection applies but which is not operational land of statutory undertakers authorised to carry on a harbour shall be treated as if it were such operational land.

(4) Subsection (3) above applies—

(a) to a wharf ; and

(b) to harbour land,

1964 c. 40.

as defined in the Harbours Act 1964.

(5) Any question whether subsection (3) above applies to land shall be determined by the Secretary of State and the Minister who is the appropriate Minister in relation to operational land of statutory undertakers who are authorised to carry on harbour undertakings.

Requirement of hazardous substances consent.

56C.—(1) Subject to the provisions of this Part of this Act, the presence of a hazardous substance on, over or under land requires the consent of the planning authority (in this Act referred to as " hazardous substances consent ") unless the aggregate quantity of the substance—

(a) on, under or over the land ;

(b) on, under or over other land which is within 500 metres of it and controlled by the same person ; or

(c) in or on a structure controlled by the same person any part of which is within 500 metres of it,

is less than the controlled quantity.

(2) The temporary presence of a hazardous sub-

stance while it is being transported from one place
to another is not to be taken into account unless it
is unloaded.

(3) The Secretary of State—

(*a*) shall by regulations specify—

(i) the substances that are hazardous
substances for the purposes of this Act ;

(ii) the quantity which is to be the controlled quantity of any such substance ;

(*b*) may by regulations provide that hazardous
substances consent is not required or is
only required—

(i) in relation to land of prescribed
descriptions ;

(ii) by reason of the presence of
hazardous substances in prescribed circumstances ;

(*c*) may by regulations provide that, except in
such circumstances as may be prescribed,
all hazardous substances falling within a
group specified in the regulations are to be
treated as a single substance for the purposes of this Act.

(4) Regulations which—

(*a*) are made by virtue of sub-paragraph (i) of
subsection (3)(*a*) above ; or

(*b*) are made by virtue of sub-paragraph (ii) of
that paragraph and reduce the controlled
quantity of a substance,

may make such transitional provision as appears to
the Secretary of State to be appropriate.

(5) The power to make such transitional provision
includes, without prejudice to its generality, power
to apply section 38 of the Housing and Planning
Act 1986 subject to such modifications as appear to
the Secretary of State to be appropriate.

(6) Regulations under this section may make different provision for different cases or descriptions of
cases.

(7) Bodies corporate which are inter-connected for
the purposes of the Fair Trading Act 1973 are to be   1973 c. 41.
treated as being one person for the purposes of this
section and sections 56D to 56L and 97B below.

Applications for hazardous substances consent.

56D.—(1) Provision may be made by regulations with respect to—

> (a) the form and manner in which applications for hazardous substances consent are to be made :
>
> (b) the particulars which they are to contain and the evidence by which they are to be verified ;
>
> (c) the manner in which they are to be advertised ; and
>
> (d) the time within which they are to be dealt with.

(2) Regulations may provide that an application for hazardous substances consent, or an appeal against the refusal of such an application or against the imposition of a condition on such a consent, shall not be entertained unless it is accompanied by a certificate in the prescribed form and corresponding to one or other of those described in section 24(1)(a) to (d) of this Act and any such regulations may—

> (a) include requirements corresponding to those mentioned in sections 23(1), 24(2) and (4) and 26(3) of this Act ; and
>
> (b) make provision as to who is to be treated as the owner of land for the purposes of any provision of the regulations.

(3) If any person issues a certificate which purports to comply with the requirements of regulations made by virtue of subsection (2) above and which contains a statement which he knows to be false or misleading in a material particular, or recklessly issues a certificate which purports to comply with those requirements and which contains a statement which is false or misleading in a material particular, he shall be guilty of an offence and liable on summary conviction to a fine not exceeding level 3 on the standard scale.

(4) Regulations—

> (a) may require an applicant for hazardous substances consent or the planning authority or both to give publicity to an application for hazardous substances consent in such manner as may be prescribed ;

(b) may require the planning authority to con-
duct appropriate consultations before determining applications for hazardous substances consent ;

(c) may provide for the manner in which such
a consultation is to be carried out and the
time within which—
    (i) such a consultation ;
    (ii) any stage in such a consultation,
is to be completed ;

(d) may require the planning authority to
determine applications for hazardous substances consent within such time as may be
prescribed ;

(e) may require the planning authority to give
prescribed persons or bodies prescribed
information about applications for hazardous substances consent including information as to the manner in which such
applications have been dealt with.

(5) In subsection (4) above " appropriate consultations " means—
    (a) consultations—
       (i) in the case of a planning authority
       other than the appropriate Minister, with
       the Health and Safety Executive ; and
       (ii) in the case of the appropriate Min-
       ister, with the Health and Safety Com-
       mission ; and

    (b) consultations with such persons or bodies
    as may be prescribed.

(6) Regulations under this section may make different provision for different cases or descriptions of
cases.

Determina-
tion of
applications
for hazardous
substances
consent.   56E.—(1) Subject to the following provisions of
this Act, where an application is made to a planning
authority for hazardous substances consent, that
authority, in dealing with the application, shall have
regard to any material considerations, and—

    (a) may grant hazardous substances consent,
either unconditionally or subject to such
conditions as they think fit ; or

(b) may refuse hazardous substances consent.

(2) Without prejudice to the generality of sub-section (1) above, in dealing with an application the authority shall have regard—

(a) to any current or contemplated use of the land to which the application relates ;

(b) to the way in which land in the vicinity is being used or is likely to be used ;

(c) to any planning permission that has been granted for development of land in the vicinity ;

(d) to the provisions of the development plan ; and

(e) to any advice which the Health and Safety Executive or Health and Safety Commission have given following consultations in pursuance of regulations under section 56D(4) above.

(3) If an application relates to more than one hazardous substance, the authority may make different determinations in relation to each.

(4) It shall be the duty of a planning authority, when granting hazardous substances consent, to include in that consent—

(a) a description of the land to which the consent relates ;

(b) a description of the hazardous substance or substances to which it relates ; and

(c) in respect of each hazardous substance to which it relates, a statement of the maximum amount permitted by the consent to be present at any one time and of all conditions relating to that substance subject to which the consent is granted.

(5) Without prejudice to the generality of sub-section (1) above, a planning authority may grant hazardous substances consent subject to conditions with respect to any of the following—

(a) how and where any hazardous substance to which the consent relates is to be kept or used ;

(*b*) times between which any such substance may be present ;

(*c*) the permanent removal of any such substance—

(i) on or before a date specified in the consent ; or

(ii) before the end of a period specified in it and commencing on the date on which it is granted ;

(*d*) the consent being conditional on the commencement or partial or complete execution of development on the land which is authorised by a specified planning permission,

but a planning authority other than the appropriate Minister may only grant consent subject to conditions as to how a hazardous substance is to be kept or used if the conditions are conditions to which the Health and Safety Executive have advised the authority that any consent they might grant should be subject.

References to regional planning authority and Secretary of State and appeals.

56F.—(1) Subject to subsections (2) and (3) below, sections 32 to 34 of this Act and section 179 (reference of applications to regional planning authority) of the Local Government (Scotland) Act 1973 shall have effect in relation to applications for hazardous substances consent and to decisions on such applications as though they were applications for planning permission.

1973 c. 65.

(2) In the application of sections 32 to 34 of this Act to hazardous substances consent—

(*a*) section 32(4) and section 33(5) and (7) shall be omitted ;

(*b*) the words " and in such manner as may be prescribed " shall be substituted for the words in section 33(2) following " time " ;

(*c*) in section 34, the words " by the development order " shall be omitted from both places where they occur.

(3) Subsections (1) and (2) above do not have effect in relation to applications for hazardous substances consent relating to land to which section 56B of this Act applies or to decisions on such applications.

PART IV

Deemed hazardous substances consent by virtue of authorisation of government department.

56G.—(1) Where—

(a) the authorisation of a government department is required by virtue of an enactment in respect of development to be carried out by a local authority, or by statutory undertakers not being a local authority; and

(b) the development would involve the presence of a hazardous substance in circumstances requiring hazardous substances consent,

the department may, on granting that authorisation, also direct that hazardous substances consent for that development shall be deemed to be granted subject to such conditions (if any) as may be specified in the directions.

(2) The department shall consult the Health and Safety Commission before issuing any such directions.

(3) The provisions of this Act (except Parts VII and XII) shall apply in relation to any hazardous substances consent deemed to be granted by virtue of directions under this section as if it had been granted by the Secretary of State on an application referred to him under section 32 of this Act, as applied by section 56F of this Act.

(4) The reference in subsection (1) above to the authorisation of a government department is to be construed in accordance with section 37(3) of this Act.

Grants of hazardous substances consent without compliance with conditions previously attached.

56H.—(1) This section applies to an application for hazardous substances consent without a condition subject to which a previous hazardous substances consent was granted or is deemed to have been granted.

(2) On such an application the planning authority shall consider only the question of the conditions subject to which hazardous substances consent should be granted, and—

(a) if they determine that hazardous substances consent should be granted subject to conditions differing from those subject to which the previous consent was granted, or that it should be granted unconditionally, they shall grant hazardous substances consent accordingly; and

(b) if they determine that hazardous substances

consent should be granted subject to the
same conditions as those subject to which
the previous consent was granted, they shall
refuse the application.

(3) Where—

(*a*) hazardous substances consent has been
granted or is deemed to have been granted
for the presence on, over or under land of
more than one hazardous substance ; and

(*b*) an application under this section does not
relate to all the substances,

the planning authority shall only have regard to any
condition relating to a substance to which the application does not relate to the extent that it has implications for a substance to which the application does
relate.

(4) Where—

(*a*) more than one hazardous substances consent
has been granted or is deemed to have been
granted in respect of the same land ; and

(*b*) an application under this section does not
relate to all the consents,

the planning authority shall only have regard to any
consent to which the application does not relate
to the extent that it has implications for a consent to
which the application does relate.

(5) Regulations may make provision in relation to
applications under this section corresponding to any
provision that may be made by regulations under
section 56D of this Act in relation to applications for
hazardous substances consent.

Power to
revoke or
modify
hazardous
substance
consent.

56J.—(1) If it appears to the planning authority
that—

(*a*) there has been a material change of use of
land to which a hazardous substances consent relates ; or

(*b*) planning permission has been granted for
development the carrying out of which
would involve a material change of use of
such land and the development to which
the permission relates has been commenced,

they may by order—

(i) if the consent relates only to one substance,
revoke it ;

(ii) if it relates to more than one, revoke it or revoke it so far as it relates to a specified substance.

(2) The planning authority may by order—

(a) revoke a hazardous substances consent which relates to only one substance if it appears to them that that substance has not for at least 5 years been present on, under or over the land to which the consent relates in a quantity equal to or exceeding the controlled quantity ; and

(b) revoke a hazardous substances consent which relates to a number of substances if it appears to them that none of those substances has for at least 5 years been so present.

(3) The planning authority may by order revoke a hazardous substances consent or modify it to such extent as they consider expedient if it appears to them, having regard to any material consideration, that it is expedient to revoke or modify it.

(4) An order under this section shall specify the grounds on which it is being made.

(5) An order under this section, other than an order relating to land to which section 56B of this Act applies, shall not take effect unless it is confirmed by the Secretary of State, and the Secretary of State may confirm any such order submitted to him either without modification or subject to such modification as he considers expedient.

(6) Where a planning authority submit an order under this section to the Secretary of State for his confirmation under this section, the authority shall serve notice of the order on—

(a) any person who is an owner, occupier or lessee of the whole or any part of the land to which the order relates ; and

(b) any other person who in their opinion will be affected by the order ;

and if within the period specified in that behalf in the notice (not being less than 28 days from the service thereof) any person on whom the notice is served so requires, the Secretary of State, before confirming the order, shall afford to that person and to the planning authority an opportunity of appearing before, and being heard by, a person appointed by the Secretary of State for that purpose.

(7) Where an order under this section has been confirmed by the Secretary of State, the planning authority shall serve a copy of the order on every person who was entitled to be served with notice under subsection (6) of this section.

(8) Section 159 of this Act shall have effect where a hazardous substances consent is revoked or modified by an order made in the exercise of the power conferred by subsection (3) of this section as it has effect where an order is made under section 49 of this Act.

Provisions
as to effect
of hazardous
substances
consent and
change of
control
of land.

56K.—(1) Without prejudice to the provisions of this Part of this Act, any hazardous substances consent shall (except in so far as it otherwise provides) enure for the benefit of the land to which it relates and of all persons for the time being interested in the land.

(2) A hazardous substances consent is revoked if there is a change in the person in control of part of the land to which it relates unless an application for the continuation of the consent has previously been made to the planning authority.

(3) Regulations may make provision in relation to applications under subsection (2) above corresponding to any provision that may be made by regulations under section 56D of this Act in relation to applications for hazardous substances consent.

(4) When such application is made, the authority, having regard to any material consideration—

(a) may modify the consent in any way they consider appropriate ; or

(b) may revoke it.

(5) Without prejudice to the generality of subsection (4) above, in dealing with an application the authority shall have regard—

(a) to the matters to which a planning authority are required to have regard by section 56E(2)(a) to (d) above ; and

(b) to any advice which the Health and Safety Executive or Health and Safety Commission have given following consultations in pursuance of regulations under subsection (3) above.

(6) If an application relates to more than one consent, the authority may make different determinations in relation to each.

(7) If a consent relates to more than one hazardous substance, the authority may make different determinations in relation to each.

(8) It shall be the duty of a planning authority, when continuing hazardous substances consent, to attach to the consent one of the following—

(a) a statement that is unchanged in relation to the matters included in it by virtue of section 56E(4) above ;

(b) a statement of any change in respect of those matters.

(9) The modifications which a planning authority may make by virtue of subsection (4)(a) above include, without prejudice to the generality of that paragraph, the making of the consent subject to conditions with respect to any of the matters mentioned in section 56E(5) above.

(10) Subject to subsection (11) below, sections 32 to 34 of this Act and section 179 of the Local Government (Scotland) Act 1973 shall have effect in relation to applications under subsection (2) above and to decisions on such applications as though they were applications for planning permission.

(11) In the application of sections 32 to 34 of this Act by virtue of subsection (10) above—

(a) section 32(4) and section 33(5) and (7) shall be omitted ;

(b) the words " and in such manner as may be prescribed " shall be substituted for the words in section 33(2) following " time " ;

(c) in section 34—

(i) the words " by the development order " shall be omitted from the first place where they occur ; and

(ii) the words " the application shall be PART IV
deemed to have been granted " shall be
substituted for the words following paragraph (*b*).

(12) Where the authority modify or revoke the
consent, they shall pay to the person in control of
the whole of the land before the change compensation in respect of any loss or damage sustained by
him and directly attributable to the modification
or revocation.

Offences.   56L.—(1) Subject to this Part of this Act, if there
is a contravention of hazardous substances control,
the appropriate person shall be guilty of an offence.

(2) There is a contravention of hazardous substances control—

(*a*) if a quantity of a hazardous substance equal
to or exceeding the controlled quantity is
or has been present on, under or over land
and either—

(i) there is no hazardous substances
consent for the presence of the substance ; or

(ii) there is hazardous substances consent for its presence but the quantity
present exceeds the maximum quantity
permitted by the consent ;

(*b*) if there is or has been a failure to comply
with a condition subject to which a hazardous substances consent was granted.

(3) In subsection (1) above " the appropriate person " means—

(*a*) in relation to a contravention falling within
paragraph (*a*) of subsection (2) above—

(i) any person knowingly causing the
substance to be present on, over or under
the land ;

(ii) any person allowing it to be so
present ; and

(*b*) in relation to a contravention falling within
paragraph (*a*) or (*b*) of that subsection, the
occupier of the land.

(4) A person guilty of an offence under this section shall be liable—

(a) on summary conviction, to a fine not exceeding the statutory maximum ; or

(b) on conviction on indictment, to a fine,

and if the contravention is continued after the conviction he shall be guilty of a further offence and liable on summary conviction to a fine not exceeding £200 for each day on which it continues or on conviction on indictment to a fine.

(5) In any proceedings for an offence under this section it shall be a defence for the accused to prove—

(a) that he took all reasonable precautions and exercised all due diligence to avoid commission of the offence ; or

(b) that commission of the offence could be avoided only by the taking of action amounting to a breach of a statutory duty.

(6) In any proceedings for an offence consisting of a contravention falling within subsection (2)(a) above, it shall be a defence for the accused to prove that at the time of the alleged commission of the offence he did not know, and had no reason to believe—

(a) if the case falls within paragraph (a)(i)—

(i) that the substance was present ; or

(ii) that it was present in a quantity equal to or exceeding the controlled quantity ;

(b) if the case falls within paragraph (a)(ii), that the substance was present in a quantity exceeding the maximum quantity permitted by the consent.

(7) In any proceedings for an offence consisting of a contravention falling within subsection (2)(b) above, it shall be a defence for the accused to prove that he did not know, and had no reason to believe, that he was failing to comply with a condition subject to which hazardous substances consent had been granted.

Emergencies.   56M.—(1) If it appears to the Secretary of State—

    (a) either—

        (i) that the community or part of it is being or is likely to be deprived of an essential service or commodity ; or

        (ii) that there is or is likely to be a shortage of such a service or commodity affecting the community or part of it ; and

    (b) that the presence of a hazardous substance on, over or under land specified in the direction in circumstances such that hazardous substances consent would be required, is necessary for the effective provision of that service or commodity,

he may direct that, subject to such conditions or exceptions as he thinks fit, the presence of the substance on, over or under the land is not to constitute a contravention of hazardous substances control so long as the direction remains in force.

(2) A direction under this section—

    (a) may be withdrawn at any time ;

    (b) shall in any case cease to have effect at the end of the period of three months beginning with the day on which it was given, but without prejudice to the Secretary of State's power to give a further direction.

(3) Subject to subsection (4) below, the Secretary of State shall send a copy of any such direction to the planning authority in relation to the land.

(4) Where the land is land to which section 56B of this Act applies, the Secretary of State shall send the copy to the authority which would be the planning authority in relation to that land but for that section.

Registers, etc.   56N.—(1) Every planning authority shall keep, in such manner as may be prescribed, a register containing such information as may be so prescribed with respect—

    (a) to applications for hazardous substances consent—

        (i) made to that authority, or

        (ii) made to the appropriate Minister with respect to land in relation to which,

PART IV

but for section 56B of this Act, that authority would be the planning authority;

and including information as to the manner in which such applications have been dealt with;

(b) to hazardous substances consent deemed to be granted under section 38 of the Housing and Planning Act 1986 with respect to land in relation to which that authority is or but for section 56B of this Act would be, the planning authority;

(c) to revocations or modifications of hazardous substances consent granted with respect to such land; and

(d) to directions under section 56M above sent to the authority by the Secretary of State.

(2) Where with respect to any land the appropriate Minister exercises any of the functions of a planning authority for the purposes of hazardous substances control he shall send to the authority which, but for section 56B of this Act, would be the planning authority for those purposes in relation to that land any such information as appears to him to be required by them for the purposes of mantaining a register under this section.

(3) Every register kept under this section shall be available for inspection by the public at all reasonable hours.

Health and safety requirements.

56O.—(1) Nothing in—

(a) any hazardous substances consent granted or deemed to be granted under—

    (i) the preceding provisions of this Act; or

    (ii) section 38 of the Housing and Planning Act 1986; or

(b) any hazardous substances contravention notice issued under section 97B of this Act,

shall require or allow anything to be done in contravention of any of the relevant statutory provisions or any prohibition notice or improvement notice served under or by virtue of any of those provisions; and to the extent that such a consent or notice purports to require or allow any such thing to be done, it shall be void.

(2) Where it appears to a planning authority who   PART IV
have granted or are deemed to have granted a
hazardous substances consent or who have issued a
hazardous substances contravention notice that the
consent or notice or part of it is rendered void by
subsection (1) above, the authority shall, as soon as is
reasonably practicable, consult the appropriate body
with regard to the matter.

(3) If the appropriate body advise the authority
that the consent or notice is rendered wholly void,
the authority shall revoke it.

(4) If they advise that part of the consent or
notice is rendered void, the authority shall so modify
it as to render it wholly operative.

(5) In this section—
    " the appropriate body " means—

        (a) in relation to a planning authority
        other than the appropriate Minister, the
        Health and Safety Executive ; and

        (b) in relation to the appropriate Min-
        ister, the Health and Safety Commission ;
        and

    " relevant statutory provisions ", " improve-
        ment notice " and " prohibition notice "
        have the same meanings as in Part I of the
        Health and Safety at Work etc. Act 1974.". 1974 c. 37.

36. The following shall be inserted after section 97A of the Hazardous
Town and Country Planning (Scotland) Act 1972—   substances
                                                     contravention
                                                     notices.
                " Hazardous substances
Power to   97B.—(1) Subject to subsection (2) below, where   1972 c. 52.
issue   it appears to the planning authority that there is or
hazardous   has been a contravention of hazardous substances
substances   control they may issue a hazardous substances con-
contravention travention notice if they consider it expedient to do
notice.   so having regard to any material consideration.

(2) A planning authority shall not issue a hazardous
substances contravention notice where it appears to
them that a contravention of hazardous substances
control can be avoided only by the taking of action
amounting to a breach of a statutory duty.

(3) In this Act " hazardous substances contravention notice " means a notice—

  (a) specifying an alleged contravention of hazardous substances control ; and

  (b) requiring such steps as may be specified in the notice to be taken to remedy the contravention.

(4) A copy of a hazardous substances contravention notice shall be served—

  (a) on the owner, the lessee and the occupier of the land to which it relates ; and

  (b) on such other persons as may be prescribed.

(5) A hazardous substances contravention notice shall also specify—

  (a) a date not less than 28 days from the date of service of copies of the notice as the date on which it is to take effect ;

  (b) in respect of each of the steps required to be taken to remedy the contravention of hazardous substances control, the period from the notice taking effect within which the step is to be taken.

(6) Where a planning authority issue a hazardous substances contravention notice the steps required by the notice may, without prejudice to the generality of subsection (3)(b) above, if the authority think it expedient, include a requirement that the hazardous substance be removed from the land.

(7) Where a notice includes such a requirement, it may also contain a direction that at the end of such period as may be specified in the notice any hazardous substances consent for the presence of the substance shall cease to have effect or, if it relates to more than one substance, shall cease to have effect so far as it relates to the substance which is required to be removed.

(8) The planning authority may withdraw a hazardous substances contravention notice (without prejudice to their power to issue another) at any time before it takes effect.

(9) If they do so, they shall forthwith give notice of the withdrawal to every person who was served with a copy of the notice.

(10) The Secretary of State may by regulations—   PART IV

> (a) specify matters which are to be included in hazardous substances contravention notices, in addition to those which are required to be included in them by this section;
>
> (b) provide—
>
>> (i) for appeals to him against hazardous substances contravention notices;
>>
>> (ii) for the persons by whom, grounds upon which and time within which such an appeal may be brought;
>>
>> (iii) for the procedure to be followed on such appeals;
>>
>> (iv) for the directions that may be given on such an appeal;
>>
>> (v) for the application to such appeals, subject to such modifications as the regulations may specify, of any of the provisions of sections 85, 231(3) and 233 of this Act;
>
> (c) direct that any of the provisions of sections 86 to 89A of this Act shall have effect in relation to hazardous substances contravention notices subject to such modifications as he may specify in the regulations;
>
> (d) make such other provision as he considers necessary or expedient in relation to hazardous substances contravention notices.

(11) If any person appeals against a hazardous substances contravention notice, the notice shall be of no effect pending the final determination or the withdrawal of the appeal.

(12) Regulations under this section may make different provisions for different cases or descriptions of cases.".

37. The enactments mentioned in Part II of Schedule 7 to this Act shall have effect with the amendments there specified, being amendments consequential on the provisions of this Part of this Act.   Consequential amendments.

38.—(1) Until the end of the transitional period—   Transitional (Scotland).

> (a) no offence is committed under section 56L of the Town and Country Planning (Scotland) Act 1972; and   1972 c. 52.

(b) no hazardous substances contravention notice may be issued, in relation to a hazardous substance which is on, under or over any land,

if the substance was present on, under or over the land at any time within the establishment period and—

    (i) in a case in which at the commencement date notification in respect of the substance was required by any of the Notification Regulations, both the conditions specified in subsection (2) below were satisfied ; and

    (ii) in a case in which at that date such notification was not so required, the condition specified in paragraph (b) of that subsection is satisfied.

(2) The conditions mentioned in subsection (1) above are—

    (a) that notification required by the Notification Regulations was given before the commencement date ; and

    (b) that the substance has not been present during the transitional period in a quantity greater in aggregate than the established quantity.

(3) Where a hazardous substance was present on, under or over any land at any time within the establishment period, hazardous substances consent may be claimed in respect of its presence.

(4) A claim shall be made in the prescribed form before the end of the transitional period and shall contain the prescribed information as to the presence of the substance during the establishment period and as to how and where it was kept and used immediately before the commencement date.

(5) Subject to subsections (6) to (8) below, the planning authority shall be deemed to have granted any hazardous substances consent which is claimed under subsection (2) above.

(6) If at the commencement date notification in respect of the substance was required by regulation 3 or 5 of the Notification Regulations, hazardous substances consent is only to be deemed to be granted under this section if notification in respect of the substance was given before that date in accordance with those regulations.

(7) If at the commencement date such notification was not so required, hazardous substances consent is only to be deemed to be granted under this section if an aggregate quantity of the substance not less than the controlled quantity was present at any one time within the establishment period.

(8) If it appears to the planning authority that a claim for hazardous substances consent does not comply with subsection

(4) above, it shall be their duty, before the end of the period of two weeks from their receipt of the claim,—

　(*a*) to notify the claimant that in their opinion the claim is invalid ; and

　(*b*) to give him their reasons for that opinion.

(9) Hazardous substances consent which is deemed to be granted under this section is subject to the conditions that—

　(*a*) the maximum aggregate quantity of the substance that may be present—

　　　(i) on, under or over the land to which the claim relates ;

　　　(ii) on, under or over other land which is within 500 metres of it and controlled by the same person ; or

　　　(iii) in or on a structure controlled by the same person any part of which is within 500 metres of it, at any one time shall not exceed the established quantity ; and

　(*b*) the substance shall be kept and used in the place and manner in which information supplied in pursuance of regulations made by virtue of subsection (4) above shows that it was kept and used immediately before the commencement date ; and

　(*c*) none of the substance shall be kept or used in a vessel or container greater in capacity than the container, or the largest of the containers, in which the substance was kept or used immediately before the commencement date.

(10) In this section—

" commencement date " means the date on which this Part of this Act comes into force ;

" the establishment period " means the period of 12 months immediately preceding the commencement date ;

" established quantity " means, in relation to any land—

　　　(*a*) where before the commencement date there has been a notification in respect of a substance in accordance with any of the Notification Regulations—

　　　　　(i) the quantity notified or last notified before the commencement date ; or

　　　　　(ii) a quantity equal to twice the quantity which was so notified or last notified before the start of the establishment period,

　　　whichever is the greater ;

(*b*) where a notification was not required before that date by any of those regulations, a quantity exceeding by 50 per cent. the maximum quantity which was present on, under or over the land at any one time within the establishment period ;

S.I. 1982/1357.   " Notification Regulations " means the Notification of Installations Handling Hazardous Substances Regulations 1982 ;

" the transitional period " means the period of 6 months beginning with the commencement date ;

1972 c. 52.   and other expressions have the same meaning as in the Town and Country Planning (Scotland) Act 1972.

PART V

Opencast Coal

Abolition of Secretary of State's power to authorise opencast working, &c.
1958 c. 69.

39.—(1) The following provisions of the Opencast Coal Act 1958 (" the 1958 Act ") shall cease to have effect—

(*a*) sections 1 and 2 (authorisation by Secretary of State of opencast working of coal and associated provisions) ; and

(*b*) section 9(2) (buildings on land comprised in a compulsory rights order),

but this subsection does not affect a direction given under section 2 of the 1958 Act before the day on which the repeal of that section by paragraph (*a*) above comes into operation, and any repeal by this Act of an enactment which relates to directions under section 2 of the 1958 Act shall have no effect in relation to directions whose effect is continued by this subsection.

(2) The repeal of section 2(4) of the 1958 Act shall not prevent the felling of a tree that could not have been felled but for paragraph (*a*) of that subsection (which negatived tree preservation orders).

(3) The 1958 Act shall have effect with the amendments specified in Part I of Schedule 8 to this Act and section 29 of the Acquisition of Land Act 1981 shall have effect with the amendments specified in Part II of that Schedule.

1981 c. 67.

(4) The enactments specified in Part II of Schedule 12 to this Act (which include enactments already obsolete or unnecessary) are repealed to the extent specified in the third column of that Schedule.

PART VI

MISCELLANEOUS PROVISIONS

England and Wales

40. The enactments relating to listed buildings and conserva- Listed
tion areas are amended in accordance with Part I of Schedule 9 buildings and
with respect to the following matters— conservation
areas.

(a) the treatment of free-standing objects and structures
within the curtilage of a listed building ;

(b) the scope of the exception for urgent works to a listed
building ;

(c) the grant of listed building consent subject to the
subsequent approval of detail ;

(d) applications for the variation or discharge of conditions
attached to listed building consent ;

(e) the extent of the exemption accorded to ecclesiastical
buildings ;

(f) dangerous structure orders in respect of listed buildings ;

(g) the power of a local authority, the Secretary of State
or the Historic Buildings and Monuments Commission
for England to carry out urgent works for the preservation of a building ;

(h) the control of demolition in a conservation area ;

(i) the form of an application for listed building consent ;
and

(j) the powers of the Secretary of State with respect to
applications for listed building consent.

41.—(1) In Part II of the Town and Country Planning Act Local plans
1971 (development plans), the sections set out in Part I of and unitary
Schedule 10 are substituted, except as to Greater London, for development
sections 10C to 15B (local plans), the main changes being— plans.
1971 c. 78.

(a) to provide for the co-ordination by county planning
authorities, in conjunction with the district planning
authorities, of the process of making, altering, repealing or replacing local plans ;

(b) to provide a short procedure for altering a local plan
where the issues are not of sufficient importance to
warrant the full procedure : and

(c) to enable the Secretary of State to direct a local planning
authority to reconsider proposals for making, altering,
repealing or replacing a local plan ; and

(d) to omit provisions which are spent in consequence of
the approval of structure plans for the whole of
England and Wales.

(2) The substituted sections have effect in relation to metropolitan counties until the coming into force of Part I of Schedule 1 to the Local Government Act 1985 (unitary development plans), but subject to the provisions of Part II of that Schedule.

(3) Part I of Schedule 1 to the Local Government Act 1985 (unitary development plans) is amended in accordance with Part II of Schedule 10 to this Act, so as to—

(*a*) provide a short procedure for altering a unitary development plan where the issues are not of sufficient importance to warrant the full procedure ; and

(*b*) enable the Secretary of State to direct a local planning authority to reconsider proposals for making, altering or replacing a unitary development plan.

Recovery of
Minister's
costs in
connection
with
inquiries.

1972 c. 70.

1976 c. 70.

1984 c. 27.

1985 c. 68.

42.—(1) The following provisions of this section apply where a Minister is authorised under or by virtue of any of the following statutory provisions to recover costs incurred by him in relation to an inquiry—

(*a*) section 250(4) of the Local Government Act 1972 (general provision as to costs of inquiries),

(*b*) section 96(5) of the Land Drainage Act 1976 (cost of inquiry under that Act),

(c) section 129(1)(*d*) of the Road Traffic Regulation Act 1984 (costs of inquiry under that Act),

(*d*) paragraph 9(2) of Schedule 22 to the Housing Act 1985 (costs of inquiry in connection with acquisition of land for clearance),

(*e*) any other statutory provision to which this section is applied by order of the Minister.

(2) What may be recovered by the Minister is the entire administrative cost of the inquiry, so that, in particular—

(*a*) there shall be treated as costs incurred in relation to the inquiry such reasonable sum as the Minister may determine in respect of the general staff costs and overheads of his department, and

(*b*) there shall be treated as costs incurred by the Minister holding the inquiry any costs incurred in relation to the inquiry by any other Minister or government department and, where appropriate, such reasonable sum as that Minister or department may determine in respect of general staff costs and overheads.

(3) The cost of an inquiry which does not take place may be recovered by the Minister from any person who would have been a party to the inquiry to the same extent, and in the same way, as the cost of an inquiry which does take place.

(4) The Minister may by regulations prescribe for any description of inquiry a standard daily amount and where an inquiry of that description does take place what may be recovered is—

> (a) the prescribed standard amount in respect of each day (or an appropriate proportion of that amount in respect of a part of a day) on which the inquiry sits or the person appointed to hold the inquiry is otherwise engaged on work connected with the inquiry,
>
> (b) costs actually incurred in connection with the inquiry on travelling or subsistence allowances or the provision of accomodation or other facilities for the inquiry,
>
> (c) any costs attributable to the appointment of an assessor to assist the person appointed to hold the inquiry, and
>
> (d) any legal costs or disbursements incurred or made by or on behalf of the Minister in connection with the inquiry.

(5) An order or regulations under this section shall be made by statutory instrument which shall be subject to annulment in pursuance of a resolution of either House of Parliament.

(6) An order applying this section to a statutory provision may provide for the consequential repeal of so much of that provision, or any other provision, as restricts the sum recoverable by the Minister in respect of the services of any officer engaged in the inquiry or is otherwise inconsistent with the application of the provisions of this section.

43. For section 125 of the Local Government Act 1972 (compulsory acquisition of land on behalf of parish or community councils) substitute—

> " Compulsory acquisition of land on behalf of parish or community councils.

Compulsory acquisition of land on behalf of parish or community councils.
1972 c. 70.

> 125.—(1) If a parish or community council are unable to acquire by agreement under section 124 above and on reasonable terms suitable land for a purpose for which they are authorised to acquire land other than—
>
> > (a) the purpose specified in section 124(1)(b) above, or
> >
> > (b) a purpose in relation to which the power of acquisition is by an enactment expressly limited to acquisition by agreement,
>
> they may represent the case to the council of the district in which the parish or community is situated.
>
> (2) If the district council are satisfied that suitable land for the purpose cannot be acquired on reasonable terms by agreement, they may be authorised by the Secretary of State to purchase compulsorily the land or part of it ; and the Acquisition of Land Act 1981 shall apply in relation to the purchase.

(3) The district council in making and the Secretary of State in confirming an order for the purposes of this section shall have regard to the extent of land held in the neighbourhood by an owner and to the convenience of other property belonging to the same owner and shall, as far as practicable, avoid taking an undue or inconvenient quantity of land from any one owner.

(4) The order shall be carried into effect by the district council but the land when acquired shall be conveyed to the parish or community council; and accordingly in construing for the purposes of this section and of the order any enactment applying in relation to the compulsory acquisition, the parish or community council or the district council, or the two councils jointly, shall, as the case may require, be treated as the acquiring authority.

(5) The district council may recover from the parish or community council the expenses incurred by them in connection with the acquisition of land under this section.

(6) If a parish or community council make representations to a district council with a view to the making of an order under this section and the district council—

    (a) refuse to make an order, or

    (b) do not make an order within 8 weeks from the making of the representations or such longer period as may be agreed between the two councils,

the parish or community council may petition the Secretary of State who may make the order, and this section and the provisions of the Acquisition of Land Act 1981 shall apply as if the order had been made by the district council and confirmed by the Secretary of State.

(7) In the application of this section to a parish or community council for a group of parishes or communities—

    (a) references to the parish or community shall be construed as references to the area of the group, and

    (b) if different parts of the area of the group lie in different districts, references to the council of the district in which the parish or community is situated shall be construed as references to the councils of each of the districts acting jointly."

44.—(1) For section 21 of the Electricity (Supply) Act 1919 (overhead wires) substitute—

"Overhead wires.

21.—(1) The Secretary of State shall before giving consent or authorisation for the placing of an electric line above ground give the local planning authority an opportunity of being heard.

(2) In subsection (1) "local planning authority" has the same meaning as in the Town and Country Planning Act 1971, except that in relation to a non-metropolitan county it includes the county planning authority only—

(a) where the line is to be placed in a National Park ; or

(b) where the line is a high voltage line, that is, a line for conveying or transmitting electricity at or above a voltage of 132,000 volts.".

(2) In section 34 of the Electricity Act 1957 (public inquiries), after subsection (1) (inquiry to be held if local planning authority object) insert—

" (1A) In subsection (1) " local planning authority "—

(a) in relation to an application for consent or authorisation under section 10(b) of the Schedule to the Act of 1899, means a local planning authority required to be given an opportunity of being heard under section 21 of the Electricity (Supply) Act 1919 ;

(b) in relation to an application for consent under section 2 of the Electric Lighting Act 1909, means a local planning authority required to be given an opportunity of stating an objection under that section.".

(3) Section 149(3)(a) of the Local Government, Planning and Land Act 1980 (power of Secretary of State to confer functions of local planning authority on urban development corporation) has effect in relation to—

section 21 of the Electricity (Supply) Act 1919, and

section 34 of the Electricity Act 1957, so far as applying to an application for consent or authorisation under section 10(b) of the Schedule to the Electric Lighting (Clauses) Act 1899,

as it has effect in relation to the provisions listed in Part I of Schedule 29 to the 1980 Act.

PART VI
Control of
advertise-
ments:
experimental
areas.
1971 c. 78.

45. In section 63 of the Town and Country Planning Act 1971 (control of advertisements), for subsection (3) (power to make different provision for different areas) substitute—

" (3) Regulations made for the purposes of this section may make different provision with respect to different areas, and in particular may make special provision—

(a) with respect to conservation areas.

(b) with respect to areas defined for the purposes of the regulations as experimental areas, and

(c) with respect to areas defined for the purposes of the regulations as areas of special control.

(3A) An area may be defined as an experimental area for a prescribed period for the purpose of assessing the effect on amenity or public safety of advertisements of a prescribed description.

(3B) An area may be defined as an area of special control if it is—

(a) a rural area, or

(b) an area which appears to the Secretary of State to require special protection on grounds of amenity ;

and, without prejudice to the generality of subsection (3), the regulations may prohibit the display in an area of special control of all advertisements except advertisements of such classes (if any) as may be prescribed.".

Land
adversely
affecting
amenity of
neighbour-
hood.

46. For section 65 of the Town and Country Planning Act 1971 (proper maintenance of waste land), and the heading preceding it, substitute—

" *Land adversely affecting amenity of neighbourhood*

Power to
require
proper
maintenance
of land.

65.—(1) If it appears to the local planning authority that the amenity of a part of their area, or of an adjoining area, is adversely affected by the condition of land in their area, they may serve on the owner and occupier of the land a notice under this section.

(2) The notice shall require such steps for remedying the condition of the land as may be specified in the notice to be taken within such period as may be so specified.

(3) Subject to the provisions of Part V of this Act, the notice shall take effect at the end of such period (not being less than 28 days after the service of the notice) as may be specified in the notice.

(4) In non-metropolitan counties the functions of the local planning authority under this section are exercisable by the district planning authorities.".

47. In section 134 of the Local Government, Planning and Land Act 1980 (power to designate urban development areas), omit subsection (2) (which restricts the power to land in metropolitan districts and certain land in or adjacent to inner London).

Areas which may be designated urban development areas.
1980 c. 65.

48.—(1) The following enactments are repealed—

(*a*) section 52 of the Requisitioned Land and War Works Act 1945 and paragraph 10 of the Schedule to the Requisitioned Land and War Works Act 1948 (reimbursement of expense of restoring land affected by war works, &c.);

(*b*) sections 66 to 72 of the Town and Country Planning Act 1971 (special control over industrial development);

(*c*) sections 250 to 252 of that Act (grants to local authorities for development of land, &c.).

Repeal of unnecessary enactments.
1945 c. 43.
1948 c. 17.
1971 c. 78.

(2) The repeal does not affect the operation—

(*a*) of section 52 of the Requisitioned Land and War Works Act 1945 or paragraph 10 of the Schedule to the Requisitioned Land and War Works Act 1948 in relation to undertakings given before the repeal;

(*b*) of sections 250 to 252 of the 1971 Act in relation to land for which approval for the purposes of regulations under section 250 was sought before 1st April 1986.

49.—(1) The Town and Country Planning Act 1971, and certain related enactments, are amended in accordance with Part I of Schedule 11 with respect to the following matters—

Minor and consequential amendments; repeals.

(*a*) the operation of the Use Classes Order on the subdivision of the planning unit;

(*b*) the provision which may be made by development orders;

(*c*) the construction of references to certain documents relating to access for the disabled;

(*d*) applications to vary or revoke conditions attached to planning permission;

(*e*) the procedure on appeals and applications disposed of without a local inquiry or hearing;

(*f*) purchase notices;

(*g*) local inquiries;

(*h*) the determination of appeals by inspectors ; and

(*i*) daily penalties for offences ;

and that Part also contains amendments consequential on the provisions of this Part.

(2) The enactments specified in Part III of Schedule 12 are repealed to the extent specified.

Scotland

Listed buildings and conservation areas.

50. The enactments relating to listed buildings and conservation areas are amended in accordance with Part II of Schedule 9 with respect to the following matters—

(*a*) the treatment of free-standing objects and structures within the curtilage of a listed building ;

(*b*) late applications for listed building consent ;

(*c*) defence to proceedings under section 53 ;

(*d*) the grant of listed building consent subject to subsequent approval of detail ;

(*e*) applications for the variation or discharge of conditions attached to listed building consent ;

(*f*) the extent of the exemption accorded to ecclesiastical buildings ;

(*g*) the effect of a listed building enforcement notice ;

(*h*) the power of a local authority or the Secretary of State to carry out urgent works for the preservation of a building ;

(*i*) the control of demolition in a conservation area ;

(*j*) the form of an application for listed building consent ;

(*k*) the calling in of applications for listed building consent ; and

(*l*) the application to planning authorities of provisions relating to listed buildings.

Grants for repair of buildings in town schemes.
1972 c. 42.

51. After section 10B of the Town and Country Planning (Amendment) Act 1972 there shall be inserted the following section—

" Grants for repair of buildings in town schemes.

10C.—(1) The Secretary of State may make grants for the purpose of defraying in whole or in part any expenditure incurred or to be incurred in the repair of a building which—

(*a*) is comprised in a town scheme ; and

(*b*) appears to him to be of architectural or historic interest.

(2) For the purposes of this section a building is comprised in a town scheme if—

  (*a*) it is in an area—

      (i) designated as a conservation area under section 262 of the Act of 1972 ; and

      (ii) appearing to the Secretary of State to be of outstanding architectural or historic interest ; and

  (*b*) it is included in a town scheme list or shown on a town scheme map.

(3) In subsection (2) above—

  " town scheme list ", means a list, compiled, after consultation with the Historic Buildings Council for Scotland, by the Secretary of State and one or more local authorities, of buildings which are to be the subject of a repair grant agreement ; and

  " town scheme map " means a map, prepared after such consultation by the Secretary of State and one or more local authorities, showing buildings which are to be the subject of such an agreement.

(4) In subsection (3) above—

  " repair grant agreement " means an agreement between the Secretary of State and any authority who have participated in the compilation of a town scheme list or the preparation of a town scheme map under which the Secretary of State and the authority or authorities who have so participated have agreed that a specified sum of money shall be set aside for a specified period of years for the purpose of making grants for the repair of the buildings included in the town scheme list or shown on the town scheme map.

(5) A grant under this section may be made subject to conditions imposed by the Secretary of State for such purposes as he may think fit.

PART VI

(6) Subject to subsection (7) below, before making any grant under this section the Secretary of State may consult with the Council, both as to the making of the grant and as to the conditions subject to which it should be made.

(7) Subsection (6) above shall not apply where the making of a grant appears to the Secretary of State to be a matter of immediate urgency.

(8) The Secretary of State may pay any grant under this section to an authority participating in a town scheme and may make arrangements with any such authority for the way in which the scheme is to be administered.

(9) Arrangements under subsection (8) above may include such arrangements for the offer and payment of grants under this section as may be agreed between the Secretary of State and any authority or authorities participating in a town scheme.

1962 c. 36.

(10) Section 2 of the Local Authorities (Historic Buildings) Act 1962 (recovery of grants made by local authorities on disposal of property within three years) shall apply to a grant made by the Secretary of State under this section as it applies to a grant for the repair of property made by a local authority under that Act ; and any reference to a local authority in that section shall accordingly be construed, in relation to a grant under this section, as a reference to the Secretary of State.

(11) In this section " local authority " means a regional, islands or district council.".

Termination of grants for redevelopment etc.

1972 c. 52.
1957 c. 38.

1966 c. 51.

52.—(1) No payment of grant under—

(a) sections 237 to 239 of the Town and Country Planning (Scotland) Act 1972,

(b) section 14 of the Housing and Town Development (Scotland) Act 1957, and

(c) section 9 of the Local Government (Scotland) Act 1966

shall be made for the financial year 1986-87 or for any subsequent financial year.

(2) No claim for grant under the enactments mentioned in subsection (1)(a) and (b) above in respect of financial years prior to 1986-87 shall be entertained by the Secretary of State unless—

(a) it is received by him before this Act is passed, and

(*b*) any information reasonably required by him in relation   PART VI
to any such claim is received by him before the expiry
of the period of two months after this Act is passed.

53.—(1) The Town and Country Planning (Scotland) Act   Minor and
1972, the Local Government (Scotland) Act 1973 and certain   consequential
related enactments are amended in accordance with Part II of   amendments;
Schedule 11 with respect to the following matters—   repeals.

1972 c. 52.
(*a*) directions as to modifications of local plans ;   1973 c. 65.

(*b*) the operation of the Use Classes Order on the subdivision of the planning unit ;

(*c*) the provision that may be made by development orders ;

(*d*) applications to vary or revoke conditions attached to
planning permission ;

(*e*) land adversely affecting the amenity of the neighbourhood ;

(*f*) purchase notices ;

(*g*) National Scenic Areas ;

(*h*) local inquiries ;

(*i*) procedure on applications and appeals disposed of without an inquiry or hearing ;

(*j*) the determination of appeals by appointed persons ;

(*k*) daily penalties for offences ;

and that Part also contains other minor amendments and amendments consequential on the provisions of this Part.

(2) The enactments mentioned in Part IV of Schedule 12 to
this Act are repealed to the extent specified.

Provisions common to England and Wales and Scotland   Effect of
modification
54.—(1) In Schedule 32 to the Local Government, Planning   or termination
and Land Act 1980 (enterprise zones), for paragraphs 21 and   of enterprise
22 (effect of modification or termination of scheme on planning   zone scheme.
permission) substitute—   1980 c. 65.

" *Effect on planning permission of modification or termination*
of scheme

21. Modifications to a scheme do not affect planning
permission under the scheme in any case where the development authorised by it has been begun before the modifications take effect.

PART VI

22.—(1) Upon an area ceasing to be an enterprise zone planning permission under the scheme shall cease to have effect except in a case where the development authorised by it has been begun.

(2) The following provisions (which provide for the termination of planning permission if the completion of development is unreasonably delayed) apply to planning permission under the scheme where development has been begun but not completed by the time the area ceases to be an enterprise zone—

> (a) in England and Wales, subsections (2) to (6) of section 44 of the 1971 Act;
>
> (b) in Scotland, subsections (2) to (6) of section 41 of the 1972 Act.".

(2) In paragraph 26 of that Schedule (interpretation of Part III of the Schedule), after sub-paragraph (1) insert—

> " (1A) The following provisions apply in determining for the purposes of this Schedule when development shall be taken to be begun—
>
> (a) in England and Wales, subsections (1) to (3) of section 43 of the 1971 Act;
>
> (b) in Scotland, subsections (1) to (3) of section 40 of the 1972 Act.".

Discrimination in exercise of planning functions.

1976 c. 74.

55.—In Part III of the Race Relations Act 1976 (discrimination in fields other than employment), after section 19 insert—

" *Planning*

Discrimination by planning authorities.

19A.—(1) It is unlawful for a planning authority to discriminate against a person in carrying out their planning functions.

(2) In this section " planning authority " means—

> (a) in England and Wales, a county, district or London borough council, a joint planning board, a special planning board or a National Park Committee, and
>
> (b) in Scotland, a planning authority or regional planning authority,

and includes an urban development corporation and a body having functions (whether as an enterprise zone authority or a body invited to prepare a scheme) under Schedule 32 to the Local Government, Planning and Land Act 1980.

(3) In this section " planning functions " means—

> (a) in England and Wales, functions under the Town and Country Planning Act 1971, and

such other functions as may be prescribed, PART VI
and

(b) in Scotland, functions under the Town and Country Planning (Scotland) Act 1972 or Part IX of the Local Government (Scotland) Act 1973, and such other functions as may be prescribed,

and includes, in relation to an urban development corporation, planning functions under Part XVI of the Local Government, Planning and Land Act 1980 and, in relation to an enterprise zone authority or body invited to prepare an enterprise zone scheme, functions under Part XVIII of that Act.".

PART VII

GENERAL PROVISIONS

56.—(1) There shall be paid out of money provided by Par-Financial liament any expenses of the Secretary of State under this Act provisions. and any increase attributable to this Act in the sums so payable under any other enactment.

(2) Any sums received by the Secretary of State under this Act shall be paid into the Consolidated Fund.

(3) There shall be paid out of or into the Consolidated Fund or the National Loans Fund any increase attributable to this Act in the sums so payable under any other enactment.

57.—(1) The following provisions of this Act come into force Commence- on the day this Act is passed— ment.

section 21 (effect of resolutions relating to housing action area or general improvement area) ;

section 24(1)(j), paragraphs 10 to 13 of Schedule 5, the repeals specified in the first part of Part I of Schedule 12 and section 24(3) so far as relating to those repeals (miscellaneous corrections) ;

section 52 (termination of grants for redevelopment in Scotland) ;

this Part.

(2) The other provisions of this Act come into force on such day as may be appointed by the Secretary of State by order made by statutory instrument and—

(a) different days may be appointed for different provisions or different purposes ; and

(b) an order may make such transitional provision as the Secretary of State thinks appropriate.

(3) For the purpose of any transitional provision in this Act or an order which refers to the date of service of a notice under

PART VII
1985 c. 68.

the Housing Act 1985, no account shall be taken of any steps taken under section 177 of that Act (amendment or withdrawal and re-service of notice to correct mistakes).

Extent.

58.—(1) The following provisions of this Act extend to England and Wales—

> Part I (housing), except section 3, paragraphs 10(7), 14 and 17 of Schedule 5 and the associated repeals in Part I of Schedule 12 ;
>
> in Part II (simplified planning zones), section 25 and Parts I and II of Schedule 6 ;
>
> Part III (financial assistance for urban regeneration) ;
>
> in Part IV (hazardous substances), sections 30 to 34 and Part I of Schedule 7 ;
>
> Part V (opencast coal) ;
>
> in Part VI (miscellaneous provisions), sections 40 to 49, 54 and 55, Part I of Schedule 9, Schedule 10, Part I of Schedule 11 and Part III of Schedule 12 ;
>
> this Part.

(2) The following provisions of this Act extend to Scotland—

> in Part I (housing), sections 3, 19 and 22, paragraphs 8, 10(7), 13, 14, 17, 18 and 42 of Schedule 5 and the associated repeals in Part I of Schedule 12 ;
>
> in Part II (simplified planning zones), section 26 and Parts III and IV of Schedule 6 ;
>
> Part III (financial assistance for urban regeneration) ;
>
> in Part IV (hazardous substances), sections 35 to 38 and Part II of Schedule 7 ;
>
> Part V (opencast coal), except so far as it repeals enactments which extend to England and Wales only ;
>
> in Part VI (miscellaneous provisions), sections 50 to 55, Part II of Schedule 9, Part II of Schedule 11 and Part IV of Schedule 12 ;
>
> this Part.

(3) The following provisions of this Act extend to Northern Ireland—

> section 22 (amendments of Consumer Credit Act 1974),
>
> paragraph 18 of Schedule 5 (amendment relating to stamp duty),
>
> this Part.

Short title.

59. This Act may be cited as the Housing and Planning Act 1986.

SCHEDULES

SCHEDULE 1

SCHEDULE TO BE INSERTED IN THE HOUSING ACT 1985

SCHEDULE 3A

CONSULTATION BEFORE DISPOSAL TO PRIVATE SECTOR LANDLORD

Disposals to which this Schedule applies

1.—(1) This Schedule applies to the disposal by a local authority of an interest in land as a result of which a secure tenant of the authority will become the tenant of a private sector landlord.

(2) For the purposes of this Schedule the grant of an option which if exercised would result in a secure tenant of a local authority becoming the tenant of a private sector landlord shall be treated as a disposal of the interest which is the subject of the option.

(3) Where a disposal of land by a local authority is in part a disposal to which this Schedule applies, the provisions of this Schedule apply to that part as to a separate disposal.

(4) In this paragraph " private sector landlord " means a person other than an authority or body within section 80 (the landlord condition for secure tenancies).

Application for Secretary of State's consent

2.—(1) The Secretary of State shall not entertain an application for his consent to a disposal to which this Schedule applies unless the authority certify either—

    (a) that the requirements of paragraph 3 as to consultation have been complied with, or

    (b) that the requirements of that paragraph as to consultation have been complied with except in relation to tenants expected to have vacated the dwelling-house in question before the disposal ;

and the certificate shall be accompanied by a copy of the notices given by the authority in accordance with that paragraph.

(2) Where the certificate is in the latter form, the Secretary of State shall not determine the application until the authority certify as regards the tenants not originally consulted—

    (a) that they have vacated the dwelling-house in question, or

    (b) that the requirements of paragraph 3 as to consultation have been complied with ;

and a certificate under sub-paragraph (b) shall be accompanied by a copy of the notices given by the authority in accordance with paragraph 3.

(3) References in this Schedule to the Secretary of State's consent to a disposal are to the consent required by section 32 or 43 (general requirement of consent for disposal of houses or land held for housing purposes).

Requirements as to consultation

3.—(1) The requirements as to consultation referred to above are as follows.

(2) The authority shall serve notice in writing on the tenant informing him of—

>   (a) such details of their proposal as the authority consider appropriate, but including the identity of the person to whom the disposal is to be made,
>
>   (b) the likely consequences of the disposal for the tenant, and
>
>   (c) the effect of the provisions of this Schedule and of sections 171A to 171H (preservation of right to buy on disposal to private sector landlord),

and informing him that he may, within such reasonable period as may be specified in the notice, make representations to the authority.

(3) The authority shall consider any representations made to them within that period and shall serve a further written notice on the tenant informing him—

>   (a) of any significant changes in their proposal, and
>
>   (b) that he may within such period as is specified (which must be at least 28 days after the service of the notice) communicate to the Secretary of State his objection to the proposal,

and informing him of the effect of paragraph 5 (consent to be withheld if majority of tenants are opposed).

Power to require further consultation

4. The Secretary of State may require the authority to carry out such further consultation with their tenants, and to give him such information as to the results of that consultation, as he may direct.

Consent to be withheld if majority of tenants are opposed

5.—(1) The Secretary of State shall not give his consent if it appears to him that a majority of the tenants of the dwelling-houses to which the application relates do not wish the disposal to proceed ; but this does not affect his general discretion to refuse consent on grounds relating to whether a disposal has the support of the tenants or on any other ground.

(2) In making his decision the Secretary of State may have regard to any information available to him ; and the local authority shall give him such information as to the representations made to them by tenants and others, and other relevant matters, as he may require.

Protection of purchasers

6. The Secretary of State's consent to a disposal is not invalidated by a failure on his part or that of the local authority to comply with the requirements of this Schedule.

SCHEDULE 2

SCHEDULE TO BE INSERTED IN THE HOUSING ACT 1985

SCHEDULE 9A

LAND REGISTRATION AND RELATED MATTERS WHERE RIGHT TO BUY
PRESERVED

*Statement to be contained in instrument effecting
qualifying disposal*

1. On a qualifying disposal, the disponor shall secure that the
instrument effecting the disposal—

(*a*) states that the disposal is, so far as it relates to dwelling-
houses occupied by secure tenants, a disposal to which
section 171A applies (preservation of right to buy on disposal to private landlord), and

(*b*) lists, to the best of the disponor's knowledge and belief, the
dwelling-houses to which the disposal relates which are
occupied by secure tenants.

Registration of title on qualifying disposal

2.—(1) Where on a qualifying disposal the disponor's title to
the dwelling-house is not registered, section 123 of the Land Regis- 1925 c. 21.
tration Act 1925 (compulsory registration of title) applies—

(*a*) whether or not the dwelling-house is in an area in which
an Order in Council under section 120 of that Act (areas
of compulsory registration) is in force, and

(*b*) whether or not, where the disposal takes the form of the
grant or assignment of a lease, the lease is granted for a
term of more than 21 years or, as the case may be, is a
lease for a term of which more than 21 years are unexpired.

(2) In such a case the disponor shall give the disponee a certificate stating that the disponor is entitled to effect the disposal subject
only to such incumbrances, rights and interests as are stated in the
instrument effecting the disposal or summarised in the certificate.

(3) Where the disponor's interest in the dwelling-house is a lease,
the certificate shall also state particulars of the lease and, with respect
to each superior title—

(*a*) where it is registered, the title number ;

(*b*) where it is not registered, whether it was investigated in the
usual way on the grant of the disponor's lease.

(4) The certificate shall be—

(*a*) in a form approved by the Chief Land Registrar, and

(*b*) signed by such officer of the disponor or such other person
as may be approved by the Chief Land Registrar,

and the Chief Registrar shall, for the purpose of registration of

SCH. 2

title, accept the certificate as sufficient evidence of the facts stated in it.

1925 c. 21.

3. Where a qualifying disposal takes the form of the grant or assignment of a lease, sections 8 and 22 of the Land Registration Act 1925 (application for registration of leasehold land and registration of dispositions of leasehold) apply notwithstanding that it is a lease for a term of which not more than 21 years are unexpired or, as the case may be, a lease granted for a term not exceeding 21 years; and accordingly section 70(1)(k) of that Act (leases which are overriding interests) does not apply.

Entries on register protecting preserved right to buy

4. The Chief Land Registrar on application being made for registration of a disposition of registered land or, as the case may be, of the disponee's title under a disposition of unregistered land, shall, if the instrument effecting the disposal contains the statement required by paragraph 1, enter in the register—

    (*a*) a notice protecting the rights of qualifying persons under this Part in relation to dwelling-houses comprised in the disposal, and

    (*b*) a restriction stating the requirement of consent under section 171D(2) for certain subsequent disposals of the landlord's interest.

Change of qualifying dwelling-house

5.—(1) This paragraph applies where by virtue of section 171B(6) a new dwelling-house becomes the qualifying dwelling-house which—

    (*a*) is entirely different from the previous qualifying dwelling-house, or

    (*b*) includes new land,

and applies to the new dwelling-house or the new land, as the case may be.

(2) If the landlord's title is registered, the landlord shall apply for the entry on the register of—

    (*a*) a notice protecting the rights of the qualifying person or persons under the provisions of this Part, and

    (*b*) a restriction stating the requirement of consent under section 171D(2) for certain disposals of the landlord's interest.

(3) A qualifying person may apply for the entry of such a notice and restriction and section 64(1) of the Land Registration Act 1925 (production of land certificate) does not apply to the entry of a notice or restriction on such an application; but without prejudice to the power of the Chief Land Registrar to call for the production of the certificate by the landlord.

(4) If the landlord's title is not registered, the rights of the qualifying person or persons under the provisions of this Part are registrable under the Land Charges Act 1972 in the same way as an estate contract and the landlord shall, and a qualifying person may, apply for such registration.

1972 c. 61.

Effect of non-registration

6.—(1) The rights of a qualifying person under this Part in relation to the qualifying dwelling-house—

(a) shall be treated as interests to which sections 20 and 23 of the Land Registration Act 1925 apply (under which the 1925 c. 21. transferee or grantee under a registered disposition takes free from estates and interests which are not protected on the register and are not overriding interests), and

(b) shall not be treated as overriding interests for the purposes of that Act, notwithstanding that the qualifying person is in actual occupation of the land.

(2) Where by virtue of paragraph 5(4) the rights of a qualifying person under this Part in relation to the qualifying dwelling-house are registrable under the Land Charges Act 1972 in the same way 1972 c. 61. as an estate contract, section 4(6) of that Act (under which such a contract may be void against a purchaser unless registered) applies accordingly, with the substitution for the reference to the contract being void of a reference to the right to buy ceasing to be preserved.

Statement required on certain disposals on which right to buy ceases to be preserved

7.—(1) A conveyance of the freehold or grant of a lease of the qualifying dwelling-house to a qualifying person in pursuance of the right to buy shall state that it is made in pursuance of the provisions of this Part as they apply by virtue of section 171A (preservation of the right to buy).

(2) Where on a conveyance of the freehold or grant of a lease of the qualifying dwelling-house to a qualifying person otherwise than in pursuance of the right to buy the dwelling-house ceases to be subject to any rights arising under this Part, the conveyance or grant shall contain a statement to that effect.

(3) Where on a disposal of an interest in a qualifying dwelling-house the dwelling-house ceases to be subject to the rights of a qualifying person under this Part by virtue of section 171D(1)(a) or 171E(2)(a) (qualifying person becoming tenant of authority or body satisfying landlord condition for secure tenancies), the instrument by which the disposal is effected shall state that the dwelling-house ceases as a result of the disposal to be subject to any rights arising by virtue of section 171A (preservation of the right to buy).

Removal of entries on land register

8. Where the registered title to land contains an entry made by virtue of this Schedule, the Chief Land Registrar shall, for the purpose of removing or amending the entry, accept as sufficient evidence of the facts stated in it a certificate by the registered proprietor that the whole or a specified part of the land is not subject to any rights of a qualifying person under this Part.

Liability to compensate or indemnify

9.—(1) An action for breach of statutory duty lies where—

(a) the disponor on a qualifying disposal fails to comply with paragraph 1 (duty to secure inclusion of statement in instrument effecting disposal), or

(b) the landlord on a change of the qualifying dwelling-house fails to comply with paragraph 5(2) or (4) (duty to apply for registration protecting preserved right to buy),

and a qualifying person is deprived of the preserved right to buy by reason of the non-registration of the matters which would have been registered if that duty had been complied with.

(2) If the Chief Land Registrar has to meet a claim under the Land Registration Acts 1925 to 1986 as a result of acting upon—

(a) a certificate given in pursuance of paragraph 2 (certificate of title on first registration),

(b) a statement made in pursuance of paragraph 7 (statements required on disposal on which right to buy ceases to be preserved), or

(c) a certificate given in pursuance of paragraph 8 (certificate that dwelling-house has ceased to be subject to rights under this Part),

the person who gave the certificate or made the statement shall indemnify him.

Meaning of " disposal " and " instrument effecting disposal "

10. References in this Schedule to a disposal or to the instrument effecting a disposal are to the conveyance, transfer, grant or assignment, as the case may be.

SCHEDULE 3

COMMON PARTS GRANTS

PART I

AMENDMENTS OF PART XV OF THE HOUSING ACT 1985

1.—(1) Section 460 of the Housing Act 1985 (general description of main grants) is amended as follows.

(2) In subsection (1) omit the word " and " after the reference to special grants and after the reference to repairs grants insert " common parts grants (sections 498A to 498G) ".

(3) In subsection (2) for paragraphs (b) and (c) substitute—

" (b) the improvement or repair of dwellings,

(c) the improvement or repair of the common parts of a building including one or more flats, and ".

2. In section 462(1) of the Housing Act 1985 (preliminary condition for grants: the age of the property), after paragraph (b) insert " , or (c) a common parts grant in respect of a building which was erected after 2nd October 1961,".

3. In section 463(1) of the Housing Act 1985 (preliminary condition for eligibility for grant: the interest of the applicant in the property) for " may entertain an application for a grant only if " substitute " shall not entertain an application for a grant, other than an application for a common parts grant, unless ".

4. After section 464 of the Housing Act 1985 insert—

" Pre-
liminary
conditions
for
application
for common
parts grant.

464A.—(1) A local housing authority shall not entertain an application for a common parts grant unless they are satisfied as regards the relevant works that the applicant either—

(a) has a duty to carry them out, or

(b) has power to carry them out and has a qualifying interest in the building or in a dwelling in the building,

and that, at the date of the application, at least the required proportion of the dwellings in the building is occupied by tenants.

(2) The following are qualifying interests for the purposes of subsection (1)(b)—

(a) an estate in fee simple absolute in possession ;

(b) a term of years absolute of which not less than five years remains unexpired at the date of the application ;

(c) a tenancy to which section 1 of the Landlord and Tenant Act 1954 applies (long tenancies at low rents) ;

(d) a protected tenancy, a secure tenancy, a protected occupancy or a statutory tenancy ;

(e) a tenancy which satisfies such conditions as may be prescribed by order of the Secretary of State.

(3) The required proportion mentioned in subsection (1) is three-quarters or such other proportion as may be—

(a) prescribed for the purposes of this section by order of the Secretary of State, or

(b) approved by him, in relation to a particular case or description of case, on application by the local housing authority ;

and " tenant " for the purposes of that requirement means a person who has an interest within any of paragraphs (b) to (e) of subsection (2) by virtue of which he occupies a dwelling in the building as his only or main residence.

SCH. 3

(4) An order under this section—

(*a*) may make different provision with respect to different cases or descriptions of case, including different provision for different areas, and

(*b*) shall be made by statutory instrument which shall be subject to annulment in pursuance of a resolution of either House of Parliament.

(5) This section has effect subject to section 513 (parsonages, applications by charities, &c.).".

1985 c. 68.

5. In section 466(1) of the Housing Act 1985 (grants requiring consent of the Secretary of State) for " or intermediate grant " substitute " , intermediate grant or common parts grant ".

6. After section 498 of the Housing Act 1985 insert—

" *Common parts grant*

Works for which common parts grants may be given.

498A.—(1) The works for which a common parts grant may be given are works required for the improvement or repair of the common parts of a building in which there are one or more flats, other than works for the provision of a dwelling.

(2) For this purpose—

(*a*) " flat " means a dwelling which is a separate set of premises, whether or not on the same floor, divided horizontally from some other part of the building, and

(*b*) " common parts " includes the structure and exterior of the building and common facilities provided, whether in the building or elsewhere, for persons who include the occupiers of one or more dwellings in the building.

Standard of repair to be attained.

498B.—(1) The local housing authority shall not, without the consent of the Secretary of State, approve an application for a common parts grant in respect of a building unless they are satisfied that on completion of the relevant works the common parts of the building will be in reasonable repair.

(2) The Secretary of State's consent to the approval of applications where that standard will not be attained may be given in particular cases or in relation to descriptions of case.

(3) If in the opinion of the authority the relevant works are more extensive than is necessary for the purpose of securing that the common parts of the building will attain that standard, the authority may, with the consent of the applicant, treat the application as varied so that the relevant works include only such works as seem to the authority necessary for that purpose ; and they may then approve the application as so varied.

Rateable value limit.

498C.—(1) The local housing authority shall not approve an application for a common parts grant in respect of a building if, on the date of the application, the average rateable value of the dwellings in the building exceeds the limit specified for the purposes of this section by order of the Secretary of State.

Sch. 3

(2) The consent of the Treasury is required for the making of an order.

(3) An order—

(a) may make different provision with respect to different cases or descriptions of case, including different provision for different areas, and

(b) shall be made by statutory instrument which shall be subject to annulment in pursuance of a resolution of either House of Parliament.

(4) For the purposes of this section—

(a) where a dwelling is a hereditament for which a rateable value is shown in the valuation list, the rateable value is the value shown ;

(b) where a dwelling forms part only of such a hereditament, or consists of or forms part of more than one such hereditament, the rateable value is such value as the local housing authority, after consultation with the applicant as to an appropriate apportionment or aggregation, shall determine.

(5) This section does not apply to buildings in housing action areas.

Common parts grants are discretionary.

498D.—(1) A local housing authority may approve an application for a common parts grant in such circumstances as they think fit.

(2) Subsection (1) has effect subject to the following provisions (which restrict the cases in which applications may be approved)—

section 465 (works already begun),

section 466 (cases in which consent of Secretary of State is required),

section 498B (standard of repair to be attained), and

section 498C (rateable value limit).

Common parts grants: estimated expense of works.

498E.—(1) Where a local housing authority approve an application for a common parts grant, they shall determine the amount of the expenses which in their opinion are proper to be incurred for the execution of the relevant works and shall notify the applicant of that amount.

(2) If, after an application for a grant has been approved, the authority are satisfied that owing to circumstances beyond the control of the applicant the relevant

works will not be carried out on the basis of the estimate contained in the application, they may, on receiving a further estimate, redetermine the estimated expense in relation to the grant.

(3) If the applicant satisfies the authority that—

(a) the relevant works cannot be, or could not have been, carried out without carrying out additional works, and

(b) this could not have been reasonably foreseen at the time the application was made,

the authority may determine a higher amount under subsection (1).

Common parts grant: limit on expense eligible for grant.

498F.—(1) Except in a case or description of case in respect of which the Secretary of State approves a higher eligible expense, the eligible expense for the purposes of a common parts grant is so much of the estimated expense as does not exceed the prescribed amount.

(2) In subsection (1) "the prescribed amount" means an amount prescribed, or ascertained in a manner prescribed, by order of the Secretary of State.

(3) An order—

(a) may make different provision with respect to different cases or descriptions of case, including different provision for different areas, and

(b) shall be made by statutory instrument which shall be subject to annulment in pursuance of a resolution of the House of Commons.

Common parts grants: determination of amount.

498G.—(1) The amount of a common parts grant shall be fixed by the local housing authority when they approve the application, and shall not exceed the appropriate percentage of the eligible expense.

(2) The authority shall notify the applicant of the amount of the grant together with the notification under section 498E(1) (notification of estimated expense of relevant works).

(3) Where the authority redetermine the amount of the estimated expense under section 498E(2) (new estimate where works cannot be carried out in accordance with original estimate), they shall make such other adjustments relating to the amount of the grant as appear to them to be appropriate ; but the amount of the grant shall not be increased beyond the amount which could have been notified when the application was approved if the estimate contained in the application had been of the same amount as the further estimate.

(4) Where the authority redetermine the amount of the estimated expense under section 498E(3) (redetermination where additional works prove necessary), the eligible expense under section 498F shall be recalculated and if

on the recalculation the amount of the eligible expense   SCH. 3
is greater than it was at the time when the application
was approved, the amount of the grant shall be increased
and the applicant notified accordingly.".

7. In section 499(3) of the Housing Act 1985 for "this Part" 1985 c. 68.
substitute "the following provisions of this Part down to section
507".

8. In section 511 of the Housing Act 1985 (payment of grants:
general), in subsection (3)(*b*) for "or repairs grant" substitute ", repairs grant or common parts grant".

9. In section 513 of the Housing Act 1985 (special cases: parsonages, applications by charities, &c.), in subsection (2) (provisions
disapplied) after the reference to section 464 omit the word "and"
and insert—

" so much of section 464A(1)(*b*) (preliminary conditions for
application for common parts grant) as requires the applicant to
have a qualifying interest in the premises, and ".

10.—(1) Section 514 of the Housing Act 1985 (power of local
housing authority to carry out works with agreement of person by
whom application for grant might be made) is amended as follows.

(2) For subsection (2) (definition of "requisite interest") substitute—

" (2) The reference in subsection (1) to a person having
the requisite interest is, except in the case of a common
parts grant, to a person who has an owner's interest in
every parcel of land on which the relevant works are to
be carried out ; and in this subsection " owner's interest "
has the same meaning as in section 463(1)(*a*).

(2A) The reference in subsection (1) to a person having
the requisite interest is in the case of a common parts
grant to a person who as regards the relevant works
either—

(*a*) has a duty to carry them out, or

(*b*) has power to carry them out and has a qualifying interest in the building or in a dwelling in
the building ;

and in this subsection ' qualifying interest ' has the same
meaning as in section 464A(1)(*b*).".

11. In section 515 of the Housing Act 1985, for subsections (2) and
(3) (effect on grant of disposal by applicant of his interest in the
property) substitute—

" (2) Where an application for a grant is approved but
before the certified date the applicant ceases to be a
person entitled to apply for a grant of that description—

(*a*) in the case of an improvement grant, intermediate
grant, special grant or repairs grant, no grant

shall be paid or, as the case may be, no further instalments shall be paid, and

(b) in the case of a common parts grant, the local housing authority may refuse to pay the grant or any further instalment,

and the authority may demand that any instalment of the grant which has been paid be repaid forthwith, together with interest from the date on which it was paid until repayment at such reasonable rate as the authority may determine.

(3) In subsection (2) ' the certified date ' means the date certified by the local housing authority as the date on which the dwelling, house or, as the case may be, the common parts of the building, first become fit for occupation or use after the completion of the relevant works to the satisfaction of the authority.

(4) For the purposes of subsection (2) an applicant ceases to be a person entitled to apply for a grant, other than a common parts grant, if he—

(a) ceases to have an owner's interest in every parcel of land on which the relevant works are to be or have been carried out, or

(b) ceases to be a tenant of the dwelling ;

and in this subsection ' owner's interest ' and ' tenant ' have the same meaning as in section 463(1)(a) and (b).

(5) For the purposes of subsection (2) an applicant ceases to be a person entitled to apply for a common parts grant if he—

(a) ceases to have a duty to carry out the relevant works, or

(b) ceases to have power to carry them out or to have a qualifying interest in the building or in a dwelling in the building ;

and in this subsection ' qualifying interest ' has the same meaning as in section 464A(1)(b).".

1985 c. 68.   12. In section 518 of the Housing Act 1985 (meaning of " dwelling for a disabled occupant " and related expressions), for subsection (3) substitute—

" (3) In this Part ' improvement '—

(a) in relation to a dwelling for a disabled occupant, includes the doing of works required for making the dwelling suitable for his accommodation, welfare or employment, and

(b) in relation to the common parts of a building which includes such a dwelling, includes the doing of works required for making the common parts suitable for use by a disabled occupant of a dwelling.".

13. Renumber section 519 of the Housing Act 1985 (meaning of "reasonable repair") as subsection (1) of that section and after it insert—

> "(2) In determining what is 'reasonable repair' in relation to the common parts of a building, a local housing authority shall have regard to—
>
> > (a) the age and character of the building and the locality in which it is situated, and
> >
> > (b) the character of the dwellings in the building and the period during which they are likely to be available for use as dwellings,
>
> and shall disregard the state of internal decorative repair of the building and the dwellings in it.".

14.—(1) Section 526 of the Housing Act 1985 (the index to Part XV) is amended as follows.

(2) At the appropriate places insert—

" common parts (for the purposes of common parts grant)	section 498A(2)(b) "
" common parts grant	sections 460 and 498A "
" flat (for the purposes of common parts grant)	section 498A(2)(a) ".

(3) In the second column of the entry relating to the expression "eligible expense" for "and 497" substitute ", 497 and 498F ".

PART II

AMENDMENTS OF OTHER ENACTMENTS

15. In section 116 of the Rent Act 1977 (consent of tenant to carrying out of works), in subsection (3) (cases in which county court may empower landlord to enter in absence of consent), for "improvement or intermediate grant" substitute "improvement grant, intermediate grant or common parts grant".

16.—(1) Part IV of the Housing Act 1985 (secure tenancies and rights of secure tenants) is amended as follows.

(2) In section 100 (power to reimburse cost of improvements carried out by tenant), in subsection (2) (cost to be net of grant), for " or repairs grant " substitute ", repairs grant or common parts grant ".

(3) In section 101 (rent not to be increased on account of improvements carried out by tenant), in the second part of subsection (1) (application of provision where improvement grant-aided), for " or repairs grant " substitute ", repairs grant or common parts grant ".

17. In section 244 of the Housing Act 1985 (powers of local housing authority with respect to environmental work in housing

SCH. 3   action area), in subsection (3) (no assistance for grant-aided works), for " or repairs grant " substitute ", repairs grant or common parts grant ".

1985 c. 68.   18. In section 255 of the Housing Act 1985 (powers of local housing authority in general improvement area), in subsection (2) (*b*) (no assistance for grant-aided works) for " or repairs grant " substitute ", repairs grant or common parts grant ".

19. In section 535 of the Housing Act 1985 (exclusion of assistance under Part XVI (defective housing) where grant application pending under Part XV), in subsection (1)(*a*) for " or repairs grant " substitute, " repairs grant or common parts grant ".

Section 18.

SCHEDULE 4
FURTHER PROVISIONS WITH RESPECT TO SHARED OWNERSHIP LEASES

The Rent Act 1977 (c.42)

1.—(1) Part I of the Rent Act 1977 (preliminary provisions) is amended as follows.

(2) After section 5 insert—

" Certain shared ownership leases.

   5A.—(1) A tenancy is not a protected tenancy if it is a qualifying shared ownership lease, that is—

     (*a*) a lease granted in pursuance of the right to be granted a shared ownership lease under Part V of the Housing Act 1985, or

     (*b*) a lease granted by a housing association and which complies with the conditions set out in subsection (2) below.

   (2) The conditions referred to in subsection (1)(*b*) above are that the lease—

     (*a*) was granted for a term of 99 years or more and is not (and cannot become) terminable except in pursuance of a provision for re-entry or forfeiture ;

     (*b*) was granted at a premium, calculated by reference to the value of the dwelling-house or the cost of providing it, of not less than 25 per cent., or such other percentage as may be prescribed, of the figure by reference to which it was calculated ;

     (*c*) provides for the tenant to acquire additional shares in the dwelling-house on terms specified in the lease and complying with such requirements as may be prescribed ;

     (*d*) does not restrict the tenant's powers to assign, mortgage or charge his interest in the dwelling-house ;

(e) if it enables the landlord to require payment for outstanding shares in the dwelling-house, does so only in such circumstances as may be prescribed ;

(f) provides, in the case of a house, for the tenant to acquire the landlord's interest on terms specified in the lease and complying with such requirements as may be prescribed ; and

(g) states the landlord's opinion that by virtue of this section the lease is excluded from the operation of this Act.

(3) The Secretary of State may by regulations prescribe anything requiring to be prescribed for the purposes of subsection (2) above.

(4) The regulations may—

(a) make different provision for different cases or descriptions of case, including different provision for different areas, and

(b) contain such incidental, supplementary or transitional provisions as the Secretary of State considers appropriate,

and shall be made by statutory instrument which shall be subject to annulment in pursuance of a resolution of either House of Parliament.

(5) In any proceedings the court may, if of opinion that it is just and equitable to do so, treat a lease as a qualifying shared ownership lease notwithstanding that the condition specified in subsection (2)(g) above is not satisfied.

(6) In this section—

" house " has the same meaning as in Part I of the Leasehold Reform Act 1967 ;

" housing association " has the same meaning as in the Housing Associations Act 1985 ; and

" lease " includes an agreement for a lease, and references to the grant of a lease shall be construed accordingly.".

(3) In section 19(5) (contracts which are not restricted contracts), after paragraph (c) insert—

" (cc) it creates a qualifying shared ownership lease within the meaning of section 5A of this Act ; or ".

The Rent (Agriculture) Act 1976 (c.80)

2. In Schedule 2 to the Rent (Agriculture) Act 1976 (licences and tenancies giving rise to protected occupancy), in paragraph 3

Sch. 4　(adaptation of provisions of Rent Act 1977 as they apply for the purposes of the 1976 Act), after sub-paragraph (2) insert—

"(2A) In section 5A (exclusion of certain shared ownership leases), in subsection (2)(g) (condition that lease states landlord's opinion that 1977 Act does not apply) for the reference to the 1977 Act substitute a reference to this Act.".

Part 1 of the Leasehold Reform Act 1967 (*c.88*)

3. In section 1 of the Leasehold Reform Act 1967 (tenants entitled to enfranchisement or extension), after subsection (1) insert—

"(1A) The references in subsection (1)(a) and (b) to a long tenancy at a low rent do not include a tenancy excluded from the operation of this Part by section 33A of and Schedule 4A to this Act.".

4. In section 3(2) of the Leasehold Reform Act 1967 after "long tenancy at a low rent" insert "(other than a lease excluded from the operation of this Part by section 33A of and Schedule 4A to this Act)".

5. After section 33 of the Leasehold Reform Act 1967 insert—

"Exclusion of certain shared ownership leases.　　33A. The provisions of Schedule 4A to this Act shall have effect to exclude certain shared ownership leases from the operation of this Part of this Act.".

6. After Schedule 4 to the Leasehold Reform Act 1967 insert—

"SCHEDULE 4A

Exclusion of Certain Shared Ownership Leases

*Leases granted in pursuance of right to be
granted a shared ownership lease*

1. A lease granted in pursuance of the right to be granted a shared ownership lease under Part V of the Housing Act 1985 is excluded from the operation of this Part of this Act.

*Certain leases granted by certain public
authorities*

2.—(1) A lease which—

　(a) was granted at a premium by a body mentioned in sub-paragraph (2), and

　(b) complies with the conditions set out in sub-paragraph (3),

is excluded from the operation of this Part at any time when the interest of the landlord belongs to such a body.

(2) The bodies are—

　(a) a county, district or London borough council, the Common Council of the City of London or the Council of the Isles of Scilly ;

(b) the Inner London Education Authority or a joint authority established by Part IV of the Local Government Act 1985 ;

(c) the Commission for the New Towns or a development corporation established by an order made, or having effect as made, under the New Towns Act 1981 ;

(d) an urban development corporation within the meaning of Part XVI of the Local Government, Planning and Land Act 1980 ;

(e) the Development Board for Rural Wales ;

(3) The conditions are that the lease—

(a) provides for the tenant to acquire the freehold for a consideration which is to be calculated in accordance with the lease and which is reasonable, having regard to the premium or premiums paid by the tenant under the lease, and

(b) states the landlord's opinion that by virtue of this paragraph the tenancy will be excluded from the operation of this Part of this Act at any time when the interest of the landlord belongs to a body mentioned in sub-paragraph (2) above.

(4) If, in proceedings in which it falls to be determined whether a lease complies with the condition in sub-paragraph (3)(a), the question arises whether the consideration payable by the tenant on acquiring the freehold is reasonable, it is for the landlord to show that it is.

Certain leases granted by housing associations

3.—(1) A lease granted by a housing association and which complies with the conditions set out in sub-paragraph (2) is excluded from the operation of this Part of this Act, whether or not the interest of the landlord still belongs to such an association.

(2) The conditions are that the lease—

(a) was granted for a term of 99 years or more and is not (and cannot become) terminable except in pursuance of a provision for re-entry or forfeiture ;

(b) was granted at a premium, calculated by reference to the value of the house or the cost of providing it, of not less than 25 per cent., or such other percentage as may be prescribed, of the figure by reference to which it was calculated ;

(c) provides for the tenant to acquire additional shares in the house on terms specified in the lease and complying with such requirements as may be prescribed ;

(d) does not restrict the tenant's powers to assign, mortgage or charge his interest in the house ;

  (e) if it enables the landlord to require payment for outstanding shares in the house, does so only in such
circumstances as may be prescribed ;

  (f) provides for the tenant to acquire the landlord's interest
on terms specified in the lease and complying with
such requirements as may be prescribed ; and

  (g) states the landlord's opinion that by virtue of this paragraph the lease is excluded from the operation of this
Part of this Act.

(3) In any proceedings the court may, if of the opinion that it
is just and equitable to do so, treat a lease as satisfying the
conditions in sub-paragraph (2) notwithstanding that the condition specified in paragraph (g) of that sub-paragraph is not
satisfied.

(4) In this paragraph " housing association " has the same
meaning as in the Housing Associations Act 1985.

4.—(1) A lease for the elderly granted by a registered housing
association and which complies with the conditions set out in
sub-paragraph (2) is excluded from the operation of this Part of
this Act at any time when the interest of the landlord belongs to
such an association.

(2) The conditions are that the lease—

  (a) is granted at a premium which is calculated by reference to a percentage of the value of the house or of the
cost of providing it,

  (b) complies, at the time when it is granted, with such
requirements as may be prescribed, and

  (c) states the landlord's opinion that by virtue of this paragraph the lease will be excluded from the operation
of this Part of this Act at any time when the interest
of the landlord belongs to a registered housing association.

(3) In this paragraph—

  " lease for the elderly " has such meaning as may be prescribed ; and

  " registered housing association " has the same meaning
as in the Housing Associations Act 1985.

Power to prescribe matters by regulations

5.—(1) The Secretary of State may by regulations prescribe
anything requiring to be prescribed for the purposes of this
Schedule.

(2) The regulations may—

  (a) make different provision for different cases or descriptions of case, including different provision for different
areas, and

(*b*) contain such incidental, supplementary or transitional provisions as the Secretary of State considers appropriate,

and shall be made by statutory instrument which shall be subject to annulment in pursuance of a resolution of either House of Parliament.

Interpretation

6. In this Schedule " lease " means a lease at law or in equity, and references to the grant of a lease shall be construed accordingly.".

Consequential amendments and repeals

7. In the Housing Act 1980, omit section 140.

8. In the Local Government, Planning and Land Act 1980, omit section 156(3).

9.—(1) The Local Government Act 1985 is amended as follows.

(2) In Schedule 13 (application of local authority provisions to residuary bodies), in paragraph 14, after sub-paragraph (*a*) insert—

" (*aa*) paragraph 2 of Schedule 4A to the Leasehold Reform Act 1967 ; ".

and at the end of sub-paragraph (*b*) insert " and " and omit sub-paragraph (*d*) and the word " and " preceding it.

(3) In Schedule 14, omit paragraph 58(*e*).

10. In Part IV of the Housing Act 1985 (secure tenancies), in section 115 (meaning of " long tenancy "), in subsection (2)(*c*) after " 1980 " insert " or paragraph 3(2)(*b*) of Schedule 4A to the Leasehold Reform Act 1967 ".

Transitional provisions and savings

11.—(1) The amendments made by this Schedule apply only in relation to leases granted after the commencement of this Schedule.

(2) This Schedule does not affect the operation of section 140 of the Housing Act 1980, the enactments applying that section and regulations made under it, in relation to leases granted before the commencement of this Schedule.

SCHEDULE 5

HOUSING: MINOR AND CONSEQUENTIAL AMENDMENTS

PART I

MINOR AMENDMENTS

Effect of covenant for repayment of discount

1985 c. 68.   1.—(1) In section 36 of the Housing Act 1985 (charge to secure repayment of discount given on voluntary disposal), after subsection (3) insert—

"(3A) The covenant required by section 35 (covenant for repayment of discount) does not, by virtue of its binding successors in title of the purchaser, bind a person exercising rights under a charge having priority over the charge taking effect by virtue of this section, or a person deriving title under him ; and a provision of the conveyance, grant or assignment, or of a collateral agreement, is void in so far as it purports to authorise a forfeiture, or to impose a penalty or disability, in the event of any such person failing to comply with the covenant.".

(2) In section 156 of the Housing Act 1985 (charge to secure repayment of discount given on exercise of right to buy), after subsection (3) insert—

"(3A) The covenant required by section 155 (covenant for repayment of discount) does not, by virtue of its binding successors in title of the tenant, bind a person exercising rights under a charge having priority over the charge taking effect by virtue of this section, or a person deriving title under him ; and a provision of the conveyance or grant, or of a collateral agreement, is void in so far as it purports to authorise a forfeiture, or to impose a penalty or disability, in the event of any such person failing to comply with that covenant.".

(3) In section 158 of the Housing Act 1985 (consideration for reconveyance or surrender of dwelling-house in National Park, etc. acquired in pursuance of right to buy) in subsection (3) (reduction of consideration where discount to be repaid or outstanding share to be paid for) after " shall be reduced " insert ", subject to subsection (4),", and after that subsection insert—

"(4) Where there is a charge on the dwelling-house having priority over the charge to secure payment of the sum due under the covenant mentioned in subsection (2), the consideration shall not be reduced under subsection (3) below the amount necessary to discharge the outstanding sum secured by the first-mentioned charge at the date of the offer to reconvey or surrender.".

1985 c. 69.   (4) In paragraph 2 of Schedule 2 to the Housing Associations Act 1985 (charge to secure repayment of discount given on voluntary disposal by housing association), after sub-paragraph (3) insert—

"(3A) The covenant required by paragraph 1 (covenant for repayment of discount) does not, by virtue of its binding successors in title of the purchaser, bind a person exercising rights under a charge having priority over the charge taking effect by

virtue of this paragraph, or a person deriving title under him ;   Sch. 5
and a provision of the conveyance, grant or assignment, or of a
collateral agreement, is void in so far as it purports to authorise
a forfeiture, or to impose a penalty or disability, in the event
of any such person failing to comply with that covenant.".

(5) The above amendments apply to covenants entered into before
as well as after the commencement of this paragraph.

Acquisition of dwelling-house subject to statutory tenancy

2. In Part IV of the Housing Act 1985 (secure tenancies), before 1985 c. 68.
section 110 under the heading "*Supplementary provisions*" insert—

"Acquisition   109A. Where an authority or body within section 80
of dwelling-   (the landlord condition for secure tenancies) becomes the
house subject   landlord of a dwelling-house subject to a statutory ten-
to statutory   ancy, the tenancy shall be treated for all purposes as if
tenancy.   it were a contractual tenancy on the same terms, and the
provisions of this Part apply accordingly.".

Landlord's notice to mention any structural defect

3. In section 125 of the Housing Act 1985 (exercise of right to
buy: landlord's notice of purchase price and certain other matters),
after subsection (4) insert—

"(4A) The notice shall contain a description of any structural
defect known to the landlord affecting the dwelling-house or the
building in which it is situated or any other building over which
the tenant will have rights under the conveyance or lease.".

*Re-service of notices, etc. on change of landlord in course of exercise
of right to buy*

4.—(1) Section 137 of the Housing Act 1985 (change of landlord
after notice claiming right to buy or right to a mortgage) is amended
as follows.

(2) Make the existing provision subsection (1) and in it after "all
parties shall" insert ", subject to subsection (2),".

(3) After that subsection insert—

"(2) If the circumstances after the disposal differ in any
material respect, as for example where—

(a) the interest of the disponee in the dwelling-house after
the disposal differs from that of the disponor before the
disposal, or

(b) the right to a mortgage becomes exercisable against the
Housing Corporation rather than the landlord, or *vice
versa*, or

(c) any of the provisions of Schedule 5 (exceptions to the
right to buy) becomes or ceases to be applicable,

all those concerned shall, as soon as practicable after the disposal, take all such steps (whether by way or amending or
withdrawing and re-serving any notice or extending any period
or otherwise) as may be requisite for the purpose of securing

S 3

SCH. 5   that all parties are, as nearly as may be, in the same position as they would have been if those circumstances had obtained before the disposal.".

Deferment of completion in pursuance of right to buy

1985 c. 68.   5.—(1) In sections 140(3)(*c*) and 152(3) of the Housing Act 1985 (period before notice to complete can be served where tenant entitled to defer completion) for "two years" substitute "three years ".

(2) In sections 142(1)(*c*), (2) and (5) and 151(3) of that Act for " £100 " (the amount which the tenant must deposit in order to be entitled to defer completion) substitute " £150 ".

(3) The above amendments apply where notice under section 142(1) of that Act claiming to be entitled to defer completion is served after the commencement of this paragraph.

(4) The above amendments to sections 140(3)(*c*), 142(5), 151(3) and 152(3) also apply where notice under section 142(1) of that Act claiming to be entitled to defer completion was served before the commencement of this paragraph if the tenant—

(*a*) serves a further notice on the landlord claiming the benefit of the longer period, and

(*b*) at the same time deposits with the landlord an additional £50 ;

and section 142(5) applies to the sum so deposited as if it had been deposited in pursuance of a notice under that section.

(5) No such further notice may be served if the landlord has already served a notice under section 140 or 152 of the Housing Act 1985 (landlord's first notice to complete).

(6) The following provisions of the Housing Act 1985 apply, as to provisions of Part V of that Act, to the provisions of this paragraph relating to a further notice or deposit—

section 170 (assistance in connection with legal proceedings),

section 176 (form and service of notices),

section 177 (errors and omissions in notices),

section 180 (statutory declarations),

section 181 (jurisdiction of county court).

Penalty for voting on certain housing matters

6.—(1) In section 618(4) of the Housing Act 1985 (penalty for member of Common Council or committee voting on housing matter relating to land in which he is interested), for "level 2 on the standard scale " substitute " level 4 on the standard scale ".

(2) The above amendment does not apply to offences committed before the commencement of this paragraph.

Grounds for withholding consent to assignment of secure tenancy   Sch. 5

7. In Schedule 3 to the Housing Act 1985 (grounds for with-   1985 c. 68.
holding consent to assignment by way of exchange), after Ground 9
add—

" Ground 10
The dwelling-house is the subject of a management agreement
under which the manager is a housing association of which at
least half the members are tenants of dwelling-houses subject to
the agreement, at least half the tenants of the dwelling-houses
are members of the association and the proposed assignee is
not, and is not willing to become, a member of the association.".

Grants for affording tax relief to housing associations.   1985 c. 69.

8.—(1) In section 62 of the Housing Associations Act 1985 (grants
for affording relief from tax), after subsection (1) insert—

" (1A) In subsection (1)(*a*) ' letting ' includes—

   (*a*) in England and Wales, the grant of a shared ownership
   lease ;

   (*b*) in Scotland, disposal under a shared ownership
   agreement.".

(2) In section 73 of the Housing Associations Act 1985 (the index
to Part II), at the appropriate place insert—

" shared ownership   Section 106 "
     agreement (in Scotland)

Service charges in respect of the cost of grant-aided works

9.—(1) In the Landlord and Tenant Act 1985, after section 20   1985 c. 70.
insert—

" Limitation   " 20A. Where relevant costs are incurred or to be in-
of service   curred on the carrying out of works in respect of which
charges: a grant has been or is to be paid under Part XV of the
grant-aided   Housing Act 1985 (grants for works of improvement,
works.   repair or conversion), the amount of the grant shall be
                  deducted from the costs and the amount of the service
                  charge payable shall be reduced accordingly.".

(2) In section 21 of the Landlord and Tenant Act 1985 (request
for summary of relevant costs), in subsection (5) (contents of summary) after " shall " insert " state whether any of the costs relate
to works in respect of which a grant has been or is to be paid
under Part XV of the Housing Act 1985 (grants for works of improvement, repair or conversion) and ".

(3) In section 47 of the Housing Act 1985 (limitation on service
charges payable after disposal of house by public sector authority),
after subsection (3) add—

   " (4) Where relevant costs are incurred or to be incurred on
   the carrying out of works in respect of which a grant has been

S 4

Sch. 5

or is to be paid under Part XV (grants for works of improvement, repair or conversion), the amount of the grant shall be deducted from the costs and the amount of the service charge payable shall be reduced accordingly.".

1985 c. 68.

(4) In section 48 of the Housing Act 1985 (request for summary of relevant costs), after subsection (3) (contents of summary) insert—

" (3A) The summary shall also state whether any of the costs relate to works in respect of which a grant has been or is to be paid under Part XV (grants for works of improvement, repair or conversion).".

Miscellaneous corrections

1973 c. 26.

10.—(1) In section 73(5) of the Land Compensation Act 1973—

(a) in paragraph (a) for " Part I of Schedule 24 to the Housing Act 1985 " substitute " Schedule 23 to the Housing Act 1985 ";

(b) in paragraph (b) for " Part II of that Schedule " substitute " Schedule 24 to that Act "; and

(c) in the closing words for " that Schedule " substitute " those Schedules ".

(2) In sections 207 and 322 of the Housing Act 1985, in the definition of " person having control " for " house " substitute " premises ".

(3) In section 251(5)(b) of the Housing Act 1985 after " housing action " insert " area ".

(4) In section 256(4)(b) of the Housing Act 1985 for " to the local planning authority " substitute " of the local planning authority ".

(5) In paragraph 1(2)(c) of Part I of Schedule 24 to the Housing Act 1985 for " demolished in pursuance of an undertaking given in accordance with section 264 " substitute " vacated in pursuance of an undertaking for its demolition ".

1985 c. 69.

(6) In section 10(2)(b) of the Housing Associations Act 1985, for " Schedule 3 to the Housing Act 1985 " substitute " Schedule 1 to the Housing Act 1985 ".

1985 c. 71.

(7) In paragraph 27 of Schedule 2 to the Housing (Consequential Provisions) Act 1985 for " (4) ", in both places where it occurs, substitute " (6) ".

(8) In Schedule 3 to the Housing (Consequential Provisions) Act 1985, after paragraph 2 insert—

" 2A. Any order made under section 115(11) of the Housing Act 1974 (form of notice of compensation where land in clearance area deemed appropriated for provision of housing) which was in force immediately before the repeal of that section by this Act may be revoked or amended by regulations under section 614 of the Housing Act 1985 (general power to prescribe forms, etc. by regulations).".

(9) The above amendments have effect from 1st April 1986.

11.—(1) In sections 80(1)(*a*) and 81(1)(*a*), (3)(*b*) and (4)(*b*) of the
Building Act 1984 (service of notices in respect of proposed demo- 1984 c. 55.
lition), after "demolition order" insert "or obstructive building
order".

(2) The above amendment to section 80 of the Building Act 1984
has effect from 1st April 1986.

12. In paragraph 14(2) of Schedule 11 and paragraph 8(2) of
Schedule 22 to the Housing Act 1985 (procedure after compulsory 1985 c. 68.
purchase order has become operative), for "a copy of the notice"
substitute "a copy of the order".

13. In Part II of the Housing Associations Act 1985 (housing as- 1985 c. 69.
sociation finance)—

> (*a*) in section 67(1) (loans by Public Works Loan Commis-
> sioners: England and Wales), and
>
> (*b*) in section 68(1) (loans by Public Works Loan Commis-
> sioners: Scotland),

for "housing association" substitute "registered housing association".

PART II

CONSEQUENTIAL AMENDMENTS

Housing Rents and Subsidies (Scotland) Act 1975

14. In section 5 of the Housing Rents and Subsidies (Scotland) 1975 c. 28.
Act 1975 (agreements for exercise by housing co-operatives of
certain local authority housing functions), omit subsection (6).

Rent Act 1977

15. In section 16 of the Rent Act 1977 (tenancy not protected 1977 c. 42.
if interest of landlord belongs to housing co-operative) for the words
from "within the meaning of section 27" to the end substitute
"within the meaning of section 27B of the Housing Act 1985
(agreements with housing co-operatives under certain superseded
provisions) and the dwelling-house is comprised in a housing co-
operative agreement within the meaning of that section".

16.—(1) Schedule 12 to the Rent Act 1977 (procedure on application for certificate of fair rent) is amended as follows.

(2) In paragraph (1)(*c*)—

> (*a*) after "section 69(1)(*a*)" insert "or (1A)(*b*)";
>
> (*b*) after "improvement" insert "or repair";
>
> (*c*) after "regulated" insert "or secure".

(3) In paragraph 3, after "If," insert—

> "in the case of—
>
> (*a*) an application under section 69(1) of this Act where the

dwelling-house is not subject to a regulated tenancy, or

   (*b*) an application under section 69(1A) of this Act where the dwelling-house is not subject to a secure tenancy," ;

and omit " unless the dwelling-house is subject to a regulated tenancy ".

(4) In paragraph 4, for the words from " an application " to " regulated tenancy " substitute "—

   (*a*) an application under section 69(1) of this Act where the dwelling-house is not subject to a regulated tenancy and which does not fall within paragraph 3 above, or

   (*b*) an application under section 69(1A) of this Act and which does not fall within paragraph 3 above and where the dwelling-house is not subject to a secure tenancy,".

(5) In paragraph 5(1), for " Where the dwelling-house is subject to a regulated tenancy " substitute " In the case of—

   (*a*) an application under section 69(1) of this Act where the dwelling-house is subject to a regulated tenancy, or

   (*b*) an application under section 69(1A) of this Act where the dwelling-house is subject to a secure tenancy,".

(6) In paragraphs 8(2) and 11, after " regulated " insert " or secure ".

(7) After paragraph 11 add—

   " 12. In this Schedule ' secure tenancy ' has the same meaning as in Part IV of the Housing Act 1985, but does not include such a tenancy where the landlord is the Housing Corporation, a housing association or a housing trust which is a charity.

   In this paragraph ' housing association ', ' housing trust ' and ' charity ' have the same meaning as in Part IV of the Housing Act 1985.".

Tenants' Rights, &c. (Scotland) Act 1980

1980 c. 52.   17. In section 1(10) of the Tenants' Rights, &c. (Scotland) Act 1980 (landlords relevant to qualifying period for right to purchase and discount) in paragraph (*e*) for " section 27 of the Housing Act 1985 " substitute " section 27B of the Housing Act 1985 ".

Finance Act 1981

1981 c. 35.   18. In section 107 of the Finance Act 1981 (stamp duty payable on disposal of dwelling-house at a discount by certain authorities), after subsection (3A) insert—

   " (3B) This section also applies to a conveyance or transfer on sale (including the grant of a lease) by a person against whom the right to buy under Part V of the Housing Act 1985 is exercisable by virtue of section 171A of that Act (preservation

of right to buy on disposal to private sector landlord) to a   Sch. 5
person who is the qualifying person for the purposes of the
preserved right to buy and in relation to whom that dwelling-
house is the qualifying dwelling-house."

Local Government Act 1985

19. In paragraph 22 of Schedule 13 to the Local Government Act 1985 c. 51.
1985 (provisions of Housing Act 1985 applying to residuary bodies)
after " 444," insert 450A to 450C,".

Housing Act 1985

20. In section 4(e) of the Housing Act 1985 (general definition of 1985 c. 68.
" local authority " for the Act) for " 444(4), 452(2), 453(2) " substitute " 458 ".

21. In section 20 of the Housing Act 1985 (houses of local authority
to which management provisions apply), for " down to section 26 "
substitute " down to section 27B ".

22. In section 21 of the Housing Act 1985 (management powers to
be exercised by local housing authority), in subsection (2) (general
proposition subject to section 27), for " (agreements for exercise of
housing management functions by co-operative) " substitute " (management agreements) ".

23. In section 30 of the Housing Act 1985 (application of housing
management provisions to new town corporations and the Development Board for Rural Wales), omit subsection (2) (which relates to
section 27 : management agreements).

24. Omit section 46 of the Housing Act 1985 (definition of " service
charge " for the purposes of certain provisions of Part II).

25. In section 57 of the Housing Act 1985 (the index to Part II),
in the entries relating to the expressions " payee and payer ",
" relevant costs " and " service charge " for " section 46 " substitute
" section 621A ".

26. In section 80 of the Housing Act 1985 (the landlord condition
for secure tenancies), for subsection (4) (housing co-operatives to
which the section applies) substitute—

" (4) This section applies to a housing co-operative within
the meaning of section 27B (agreements under certain superseded provisions) where the dwelling-house is comprised in a
housing co-operative agreement within the meaning of that
section.".

27. In section 117 of the Housing Act 1985 (the index to Part IV)
at the appropriate places insert—

" consent (in Schedule 3A)   paragraph 2(3) of that
                                    Schedule "

" landlord (in Part V of   paragraph 5 of that Part "
   Schedule 2)

" management agreement   sections 27(2) and 27B(4) ".
   and manager

28. In section 127(1) of the Housing Act 1985, omit the word
" and " at the end of paragraph (a).

Sch. 5
1985 c. 68.

29. In section 130 of the Housing Act 1985 (reduction of discount where previous discount given), in subsection (2) (meaning of " previous discount ") in paragraph (*a*) after " 7 " insert " or 7A " and after that paragraph insert—

" (*aa*) on conveyance of the freehold, or a grant or assignment of a long lease of a dwelling-house by a person against whom the right to buy was exercisable by virtue of section 171A (preservation of right to buy on disposal to private sector landlord) to a person who was a qualifying person for the purposes of the preserved right to buy and in relation to whom that dwelling-house was the qualifying dwelling-house, or ".

30.—(1) Section 187 of the Housing Act 1985 (minor definitions for purposes of Part V (the right to buy)) is amended as follows.

(2) In the definition of " improvement "—

(*a*) after " means " insert ", in relation to a dwelling-house,",

(*b*) for " a dwelling-house ", in both places, substitute " the dwelling-house ", and

(*c*) at the end (full-out after paragraph (*c*)) insert " and shall be similarly construed in relation to any other building or land ; ".

(3) At the appropriate place insert—

" ' improvement contribution ' means an amount payable by a tenant of a flat in respect of improvements to the flat, the building in which it is situated or any other building or land, other than works carried out in discharge of any such obligations as are referred to in paragraph 16A(1) of Schedule 6 (obligations to repair, reinstate, etc.) ; ".

31. In section 188 of the Housing Act 1985 (the index to Part V) at the appropriate places insert—

" disposal and instrument effecting disposal (in Schedule 9A)	paragraph 10 of that Schedule "
" former landlord and former secure tenant (in relation to a qualifying disposal)	section 171A(2)(*c*) "
" improvement contribution	section 187 "
" preserved right to buy	section 171A(2)(*a*) "
" qualifying disposal (in relation to the preserved right to buy)	section 171A(2)(*b*) "
" qualifying dwelling-house and qualifying person (in relation to the preserved right to buy)	section 171B(1) "
" reference period (for purposes of s.125A or 125B)	section 125C "
" service charge	section 621A "

32. In Part XIII of the Housing Act 1985 (general financial provisions), after section 427 insert—

"Entitlement   427A. The fact that a local housing authority or other
to subsidy in   body has entered into a management agreement, and any
case of land
subject to   letting of land in connection with such an agreement—
management   (*a*) shall be disregarded in determining that authority
agreement.   or body's reckonable income or expenditure for
                        the purposes of housing subsidy, and
                    (*b*) shall not be regarded as a ground for recovering,
                        withholding or reducing any sum under sec-
                        tion 427 (recoupment of housing subsidy).".

33. In section 434 of the Housing Act 1985 (the index to Part
XIII) at the appropriate place insert—

" management agreement   sections 27(2) and 27B(4) ".

34. In section 444(4) of the Housing Act 1985 (advances relevant
to certain powers of local authority to give assistance), for the
words from " by " to the end substitute " a housing authority ".

35. In section 452 of the Housing Act 1985 (vesting of house in
authority entitled to exercise power of sale), in subsection (2) omit
the definition of " housing authority ".

36. In section 453 of the Housing Act 1985 (power of authority
which has granted shared ownership lease to make further advances),
omit subsection (2) (which defines " housing authority ").

37. In section 458 of the Housing Act 1985 (minor definitions), at
the appropriate place insert—

" ' housing authority ' includes any local authority, an urban
    development corporation, the Housing Corporation and a
    registered housing association ; ".

38. In section 459 of the Housing Act 1985 (the index to Part
XIV), at the appropriate places insert—

" housing authority   sections 4(*a*) and 458 "
" service charge   section 621 A ".

39. After section 621 of the Housing Act 1985 insert—

" Meaning   621A.—(1) In this Act ' service charge ' means an
of ' service   amount payable by a purchaser or lessee of premises—
charge ' and
related   (*a*) which is payable, directly or indirectly, for ser-
expressions.   vices, repairs, maintenance or insurance or the
                       vendor's or lessor's costs of management, and
                   (*b*) the whole or part of which varies or may vary
                       according to the relevant costs.

(2) The relevant costs are the costs or estimated costs
incurred or to be incurred by or on behalf of the payee,
or (in the case of a lease) a superior landlord, in connection with the matters for which the service charge is
payable.

(3) For this purpose—

(a) ' costs ' includes overheads, and

(b) costs are relevant costs in relation to a service charge whether they are incurred, or to be incurred, in the period for which the service charge is payable or in an earlier or later period.

(4) In relation to a service charge—

(a) the ' payee ' means the person entitled to enforce payment of the charge, and

(b) the ' payer ' means the person liable to pay it.".

40.—(1) Schedule 4 to the Housing Act 1985 (the qualifying period for the right to buy) is amended as follows.

(2) After paragraph 5 insert—

" *Periods during which right to buy is preserved*

5A. A period qualifies under this paragraph if it is a period during which, before the relevant time—

(a) the secure tenant, or

(b) his spouse (if they are living together at the relevant time), or

(c) a deceased spouse of his (if they were living together at the time of the death),

was a qualifying person for the purposes of the preserved right to buy or was the spouse of such a person and occupied the qualifying dwelling-house as his only or principal home.".

(3) In paragraph 7 (the landlord condition for qualifying period)—

(a) in sub-paragraph (1), in the opening words, after " subject to " insert " paragraph 7A and to ", and omit the words from " a housing co-operative " to " management functions) ";

(b) in sub-paragraph (2), omit the words from " a housing co-operative " to " 1975 ".

(4) After paragraph 7 insert—

" 7A.—(1) The landlord condition shall be treated as having been satisfied in the case of a dwelling-house comprised in a housing co-operative agreement made—

(a) in England and Wales, by a local housing authority, new town corporation or the Development Board for Rural Wales, or

(b) in Scotland, by an islands or district council,

if the interest of the landlord belonged to the housing co-operative.

(2) In sub-paragraph (1) " housing co-operative agreement " and " housing co-operative "—

(a) as regards England and Wales have the same meaning as in section 27B (agreements with housing co-operatives under superseded provisions), and

(*b*) as regards Scotland mean an agreement made under Sᴄʜ. 5
section 5 of the Housing Rents and Subsidies (Scotland)
Act 1975 and a housing co-operative within the meaning of that section.".

41.—(1) Paragraph 14 of Schedule 6 to the Housing Act 1985 1985 c. 68.
(terms of lease granted in pursuance of right to buy: implied
covenants by landlord) is amended as follows.

(2) In sub-paragraph (2), omit the words following paragraph (*c*).

(3) In sub-paragraph (3), for the words from the beginning to
"requirement" insert "There is an implied covenant".

(4) After sub-paragraph (3) insert—

"(3A) Sub-paragraphs (2) and (3) have effect subject to paragraph 15(3) (certain obligations not to be imposed, where landlord's title is leasehold, by reason of provisions of superior
lease).".

Housing Associations Act 1985

42. In Part II of the Housing Associations Act 1985 (financial 1985 c. 69.
provisions), after section 69 insert—

"Land   69A. A housing association is not entitled to a housing
subject to   association grant, revenue deficit grant or hostel deficit
housing
management grant in respect of land comprised in—
agreement.   (*a*) a management agreement within the meaning of
                    the Housing Act 1985 (see sections 27(2) and
                    27B(4) of that Act: delegation of housing
                    management functions by certain authorities), or

        (*b*) an agreement to which section 5 of the Hous-
                    ing Rents and Subsidies (Scotland) Act 1975
                    applies (agreements for exercise by housing co-
                    operatives of certain local authority housing
                    functions).".

SCHEDULE 6

Sections 25(2)
(3), 26(2), (3).

Sɪᴍᴘʟɪꜰɪᴇᴅ Pʟᴀɴɴɪɴɢ Zᴏɴᴇs: Fᴜʀᴛʜᴇʀ Pʀᴏᴠɪsɪᴏɴs

Pᴀʀᴛ I

Sᴄʜᴇᴅᴜʟᴇ ᴛᴏ ʙᴇ Iɴsᴇʀᴛᴇᴅ ɪɴ ᴛʜᴇ Tᴏᴡɴ ᴀɴᴅ Cᴏᴜɴᴛʀʏ Pʟᴀɴɴɪɴɢ Aᴄᴛ 1971

Sᴄʜᴇᴅᴜʟᴇ 8A

Sɪᴍᴘʟɪꜰɪᴇᴅ Pʟᴀɴɴɪɴɢ Zᴏɴᴇs

General

1. A simplified planning zone scheme shall consist of a map
and a written statement, and such diagrams, illustrations and descriptive matter as the local planning authority think appropriate for

SCH. 6   explaining or illustrating the provisions of the scheme, and shall specify—

> (a) the development or classes of development permitted by the scheme,
> (b) the land in relation to which permission is granted, and
> (c) any conditions, limitations or exceptions subject to which it is granted ;

and shall contain such other matters as may be prescribed.

Proposals to make or alter scheme

2.—(1) A local planning authority may at any time decide to make a simplified planning zone scheme or to alter a scheme adopted by them or, with the consent of the Secretary of State, to alter a scheme approved by him.

(2) An authority who decide to make or alter a simplified planning zone scheme shall—

> (a) notify the Secretary of State of their decision as soon as practicable, and
> (b) determine the date on which they will begin to prepare the scheme or the alterations.

Power of Secretary of State to direct making or alteration of scheme

3.—(1) If a person requests a local planning authority to make or alter a simplified planning zone scheme but the authority—

> (a) refuse to do so, or
> (b) do not within the period of three months from the date of the request decide to do so,

he may, subject to sub-paragraph (2), require them to refer the matter to the Secretary of State.

(2) A person may not require the reference of the matter to the Secretary of State if—

> (a) in the case of a request to make a scheme, a simplified planning zone scheme relating to the whole or part of the land specified in the request has been adopted or approved within the twelve months preceding his request ;
> (b) in the case of a request to alter a scheme, the scheme to which the request relates was adopted or approved, or any alteration to it has been adopted or approved, within that period.

(3) The Secretary of State shall, as soon as practicable after a matter is referred to him—

> (a) send the authority a copy of any representations made to him by the applicant which have not been made to the authority, and
> (b) notify the authority that if they wish to make any representations in the matter they should do so, in writing, within 28 days.

(4) The Secretary of State may, after—

(a) considering the matter and any written representations made by the applicant or the authority, and

(b) carrying out such consultations with such persons as he thinks fit,

give the authority a simplified planning zone direction.

(5) The Secretary of State shall notify the applicant and the authority of his decision and of his reasons for it.

4.—(1) A simplified planning zone direction is—

(a) if the request was for the making of a scheme, a direction to make a scheme which the Secretary of State considers appropriate ; and

(b) if the request was for the alteration of a scheme, a direction to alter it in such manner as he considers appropriate.

(2) In either case the direction may extend to—

(a) the land specified in the request to the authority,

(b) any part of the land so specified, or

(c) land which includes the whole or part of the land so specified ;

and, accordingly, may direct that land shall be added to or excluded from an existing simplified planning zone.

Publicity and consultation: general

5.—(1) A local planning authority who propose to make or alter a simplified planning zone scheme shall proceed in accordance with this paragraph, unless paragraph 6 applies (short procedure for certain alterations).

(2) They shall take such steps as will in their opinion secure—

(a) that adequate publicity for their proposals is given in the area to which the scheme relates,

(b) that persons who may be expected to wish to make representations about the proposals are made aware that they are entitled to do so, and

(c) that such persons are given an adequate opportunity of making such representations ;

and they shall consider any representations made to them within the prescribed period.

(3) They shall then, having prepared the relevant documents, that is, the proposed scheme or alterations—

(a) make copies of the documents available for inspection at their office, and

(b) send a copy of them to the Secretary of State.

(4) Each copy of the documents made available for inspection shall be accompanied by a statement of the time within which objections may be made.

(5) The local planning authority shall before preparing the proposed scheme or alterations consult the Secretary of State having

responsibility for highways as to the effect of their proposals on existing or future highways ; and when they have prepared the proposed scheme or alterations they shall send him a copy.

(6) A district planning authority in a non-metropolitan county shall also, before preparing the proposed scheme or alterations, consult the county council as planning authority and as to the effect of their proposals on existing or future highways ; and when they have prepared the scheme or alterations they shall send the county council a copy.

Publicity and consultation : short procedure for certain alterations

6.—(1) Where a local planning authority propose to alter a simplified planning zone scheme and it appears to them that the issues involved are not of sufficient importance to warrant the full procedure set out in paragraph 5, they may proceed instead in accordance with this section.

(2) They shall prepare the proposed alterations and shall—

(a) make copies of them available for inspection at their office, and

(b) send a copy of them to the Secretary of State.

(3) Each copy of the documents made available for inspection shall be accompanied by a statement of the time within which representations or objections may be made.

(4) They shall then take such steps as may be prescribed for the purpose of—

(a) advertising the fact that the proposed alterations are available for inspection and the places and times at which, and the period during which, they may be inspected, and

(b) inviting the making of representations or objections in accordance with regulations ;

and they shall consider any representations made to them within the prescribed period.

(5) The local planning authority shall send a copy of the proposed alterations to the Secretary of State having responsibility for highways.

(6) A district planning authority in a non-metropolitan county shall also send a copy of the proposed alterations to the county council.

Powers of Secretary of State to secure adequate publicity and consultation

7.—(1) The documents sent by the local planning authority to the Secretary of State under paragraph 5(3) shall be accompanied by a statement—

(a) of the steps which the authority have taken to comply with paragraph 5(2), and

(b) of the authority's consultations with other persons and their consideration of the views of those persons.

(2) The documents sent by the local planning authority to the Secretary of State under paragraph 6(2) shall be accompanied by a statement of the steps which the authority are taking to comply with paragraph 6(4).

(3) If, on considering the statement and the proposals and any other information provided by the local planning authority, the Secretary of State is not satisfied with the steps taken by the authority, he may, within 21 days of the receipt of the statement, direct the authority not to take further steps for the adoption of the proposals without—

(a) if they have proceeded in accordance with paragraph 6, proceeding instead in accordance with paragraph 5, or

(b) in any case, taking such further steps as he may specify,

and satisfying him that they have done so.

(4) A local planning authority who are given directions by the Secretary of State shall—

(a) forthwith withdraw the copies of the documents made available for inspection as required by paragraph 5(3)(a) or 6(2)(a), and

(b) notify any person by whom objections to the proposals have been made to the authority that the Secretary of State has given such directions.

Objections : local inquiry or other hearing

8.—(1) The local planning authority may cause a local inquiry or other hearing to be held for the purpose of considering objections to their proposals for the making or alteration of a simplified planning zone scheme.

(2) They shall hold such a local inquiry or other hearing in the case of objections made in accordance with regulations unless all the persons who have made such objections have indicated in writing that they do not wish to appear.

(3) A local inquiry or other hearing shall be held by a person appointed by the Secretary of State or, in such cases as may be prescribed, by the authority themselves.

(4) Regulations may—

(a) make provision with respect to the appointment, and qualifications for appointment, of persons to hold a local inquiry or other hearing ;

(b) include provision enabling the Secretary of State to direct a local planning authority to appoint a particular person, or one of a specified list or class of persons ;

(c) make provision with respect to the remuneration and allowances of the person appointed.

(5) Subsections (2) and (3) of section 250 of the Local Government Act 1972 (power to summon and examine witnesses) apply to an inquiry held under this paragraph.

(6) The Tribunals and Inquiries Act 1971 applies to a local inquiry or other hearing held under this paragraph as it applies to a statutory inquiry held by the Secretary of State, with the substitution in section 12(1) (statement of reasons for decision) for the references to a decision taken by the Secretary of State of references to a decision taken by a local authority.

Adoption of proposals by local planning authority

9.—(1) After the expiry of the period afforded for making objections to proposals for the making or alteration of a simplified planning zone scheme or, if such objections were duly made within that period, after considering the objections so made, the local planning authority may, subject to the following provisions of this paragraph and to paragraph 10 (calling in of proposals by Secretary of State), by resolution adopt the proposals.

(2) They may adopt the proposals as originally prepared or as modified so as to take account of—

(a) any such objections as are mentioned in sub-paragraph (1) or any other objections to the proposals, or

(b) any other considerations which appear to the authority to be material.

(3) After copies of the proposals have been sent to the Secretary of State and before they have been adopted by the local planning authority, the Secretary of State may, if it appears to him that the proposals are unsatisfactory, direct the authority to consider modifying the proposals in such respects as are indicated in the direction.

(4) An authority to whom a direction is given shall not adopt the proposals unless they satisfy the Secretary of State that they have made the modifications necessary to conform with the direction or the direction is withdrawn.

Calling in of proposals for approval by Secretary of State

10.—(1) After copies of proposals have been sent to the Secretary of State and before they have been adopted by the local planning authority, the Secretary of State may direct that the proposals shall be submitted to him for his approval.

(2) In that event—

(a) the authority shall not take any further steps for the adoption of the proposals, and in particular shall not hold or proceed with a local inquiry or other hearing in respect of the proposals under paragraph 8 ; and

(b) the proposals shall not have effect unless approved by the Secretary of State and shall not require adoption by the authority.

Approval of proposals by Secretary of State

11.—(1) The Secretary of State may after considering proposals submitted to him under paragraph 10 either approve them, in whole or in part and with or without modifications, or reject them.

(2) In considering the proposals he may take into account any matters he thinks are relevant, whether or not they were taken into account in the proposals as submitted to him.

(3) Where on taking the proposals into consideration the Secretary of State does not determine then to reject them, he shall, before determining whether or not to approve them—

> (a) consider any objections to them made in accordance with regulations,
>
> (b) afford to any person who made such an objection which has not been withdrawn an opportunity of appearing before and being heard by a person appointed by him for the purpose, and
>
> (c) if a local inquiry or other hearing is held, also afford such an opportunity to the authority and such other persons as he thinks fit,

except so far as objections have already been considered, or a local inquiry or other hearing into the objections has already been held, by the authority.

(4) In considering the proposals the Secretary of State may consult with, or consider the views of, any local planning authority or any other person ; but he is under no obligation to do so, or to afford an opportunity for the making of representations or objections, or to cause a local inquiry or other hearing to be held, except as provided by sub-paragraph (3).

Default powers

12.—(1) Where by virtue of any of the preceding provisions of this Schedule—

> (a) a simplified planning zone scheme or proposals for the alteration of such a scheme are required to be prepared, or
>
> (b) steps are required to be taken for the adoption of any such scheme or proposals,

then, if the Secretary of State is satisfied, after holding a local inquiry or other hearing, that the local planning authority are not taking the steps necessary to enable them to prepare or adopt such a scheme or proposals within a reasonable period, he may make the scheme or the alterations, as he thinks fit.

(2) Where under this paragraph anything which ought to have been done by a local planning authority is done by the Secretary of State, the preceding provisions of this Schedule apply, so far as practicable, with any necessary modifications, in relation to the doing of that thing by the Secretary of State and the thing so done.

(3) Where the Secretary of State incurs expenses under this paragraph in connection with the doing of anything which should have been done by a local planning authority, so much of those expenses as may be certified by the Secretary of State to have been incurred in the performance of functions of that authority shall on demand be repaid by the authority to the Secretary of State.

Regulations and directions

13.—(1) Without prejudice to the preceding provisions of this Schedule, the Secretary of State may make regulations with respect to the form and content of simplified planning zone schemes and with respect to the procedure to be followed in connection with their preparation, withdrawal, adoption, submission, approval, making or alteration.

(2) Any such regulations may in particular—

(a) provide for the notice to be given of, or the publicity to be given to, matters included or proposed to be included in a simplified planning zone scheme and the adoption or approval of such a scheme, or of any alteration of it, or any other prescribed procedural step, and for publicity to be given to the procedure to be followed in these respects ;

(b) make provision with respect to the making and consideration of representations as to matters to be included in, or objections to, any such scheme or proposals for its alteration ;

(c) without prejudice to paragraph (b), provide for notice to be given to particular persons of the adoption or approval of a simplified planning zone scheme, or an alteration to such a scheme, if they have objected to the proposals and have notified the local planning authority of their wish to receive notice, subject (if the regulations so provide) to the payment of a reasonable charge ;

(d) require or authorise a local planning authority to consult with, or consider the views of, other persons before taking any prescribed procedural step ;

(e) require a local planning authority, in such cases as may be prescribed or in such particular cases as the Secretary of State may direct, to provide persons making a request in that behalf with copies of any document which has been made public for the purpose mentioned in paragraph 5(2) or 6(3) or has been made available for inspection under paragraph 5(3) or 6(2), subject (if the regulations so provide) to the payment of a reasonable charge ;

(f) provide for the publication and inspection of a simplified planning zone scheme which has been adopted or approved, or any document adopted or approved altering such a scheme, and for copies of any such scheme or document to be made available on sale.

(3) Regulations under this paragraph may extend throughout England and Wales or to specified areas only and may make different provision for different cases.

(4) Subject to the preceding provisions of this Schedule and to any regulations under this paragraph, the Secretary of State may give directions to any local planning authority or to local planning authorities generally—

(a) for formulating the procedure for the carrying out of their functions under this Schedule ;

(*b*) for requiring them to give him such information as he may   SCH. 6
require for carrying out any of his functions under this
Schedule.

PART II

CONSEQUENTIAL AMENDMENTS—ENGLAND AND WALES

1. In section 34(1) of the Town and Country Planning Act 1971 1971 c. 78.
(registers to be kept by local planning authorities) at the end add
" and also containing such information as may be so prescribed with
respect to simplified planning zone schemes relating to zones in the
authority's area ".

2. In section 41 of the Town and Country Planning Act 1971
(limit of duration of planning permission), in subsection (3) (exceptions) after paragraph (*aa*) insert—

" (*ab*) to any planning permission granted by a simplified planning zone scheme ; ".

3. In section 53(1) of the Town and Country Planning Act 1971
(application to determine whether planning permission required)
after " scheme " insert " or simplified planning zone scheme ".

4. In section 242(1) of the Town and Country Planning Act 1971
(validity of certain instruments to be questioned under that Act and
not otherwise), after paragraph (*a*) insert—

" (*aa*) a simplified planning zone scheme or an alteration of
such a scheme whether before or after the adoption or
approval of the scheme or alteration ; ".

5. In section 244 of the Town and Country Planning Act 1971
(procedure for questioning certain instruments), after subsection (6)
insert—

" (7) Subsections (1) and (2) of this section apply to a simplified planning zone scheme or an alteration of such a scheme as
they apply to a structure plan and an alteration of such a plan,
with the following modifications—

(*a*) for the references to Part II of this Act substitute references to Part III of this Act, and

(*b*) for the reference to regulations under section 18(1) of
this Act substitute a reference to regulations under
paragraph 13 of Schedule 8A to this Act,

and with any other necessary modifications.".

6. In section 287 of the Town and Country Planning Act 1971
(general provisions as to regulations and orders)—

(*a*) in subsection (4) (orders to be made by statutory instrument)
after " 24," insert " 24E,", and

(*b*) in subsection (5)(*b*) (orders subject to negative resolution
procedure), after " section " insert " 24E, ".

7. In section 290(1) of the Town and Country Planning Act 1971 (interpretation), at the appropriate place insert—

" simplified planning zone " and " simplified planning zone scheme " shall be construed in accordance with section 24A of this Act ; ".

Part III

Schedule to be Inserted in the Town and Country Planning (Scotland) Act 1972

Schedule 6A

Simplified Planning Zone Schemes

General

1. A simplified planning zone scheme shall consist of a map and a written statement, and such diagrams, illustrations and descriptive matter as the planning authority think appropriate for explaining or illustrating the provisions of the scheme, and shall specify—

(a) the development or classes of development permitted by the scheme,

(b) the land in relation to which permission is granted ; and

(c) any conditions, limitations or exceptions subject to which it is granted ;

and shall contain such other matters as may be prescribed.

Proposals to make or alter scheme

2.—(1) A planning authority may at any time decide to make a simplified planning zone scheme or to alter a scheme adopted by them or, with the consent of the Secretary of State, to alter a scheme approved by him.

(2) An authority who decide to make or alter a simplified planning zone scheme shall—

(a) notify the Secretary of State of their decision as soon as practicable, and

(b) determine the date on which they will begin to prepare the scheme or the alterations.

Power of Secretary of State to direct making or alteration of scheme

3.—(1) If a person requests a planning authority to make or alter a simplified planning zone scheme but the authority—

(a) refuse to do so, or

(b) do not within the period of three months from the date of the request decide to do so,

he may, subject to sub-paragraph (2), require them to refer the matter to the Secretary of State.

(2) A person may not require the reference of the matter to the SCH. 6
Secretary of State if—

(a) in the case of a request to make a scheme, a simplified planning zone scheme relating to the whole or part of the land specified in the request has been adopted or approved within the twelve months preceding his request ;

(b) in the case of a request to alter a scheme, the scheme to which the request relates was adopted or approved, or any alteration to it has been adopted or approved, within that period.

(3) The Secretary of State shall, as soon as practicable after a matter is referred to him—

(a) send the authority a copy of any representations made to him by the applicant which have not been made to the authority, and

(b) notify the authority that if they wish to make any representations in the matter they should do so, in writing, within 28 days.

(4) The Secretary of State may, after—

(a) considering the matter and any written representations made by the applicant or the authority, and

(b) carrying out such consultations with such persons as he thinks fit,

give the authority a simplified planning zone direction.

(5) The Secretary of State shall notify the applicant and the authority of his decision and of his reasons for it.

4.—(1) A simplified planning zone direction is—

(a) if the request was for the making of a scheme, a direction to make a scheme which the Secretary of State considers appropriate ; and

(b) if the request was for the alteration of a scheme, a direction to alter it in such manner as he considers appropriate.

(2) In either case the direction may extend to—

(a) the land specified in the request to the authority,

(b) any part of the land so specified, or

(c) land which includes the whole or part of the land so specified ;

and, accordingly, may direct that land shall be added to or excluded from an existing simplified planning zone.

Publicity and consultation : general

5.—(1) A planning authority who propose to make or alter a simplified planning zone scheme shall proceed in accordance with this paragraph.

(2) Subject to paragraph 6(2) below, they shall take such steps as will in their opinion secure—

(a) that adequate publicity for their proposals is given in the area to which the scheme relates, (*b*) that persons who may be expected to wish to make representations about the proposals are made aware that they are entitled to do so, and

    (*c*) that such persons are given an adequate opportunity of making such representations ;

and they shall consider any representations made to them within the prescribed period.

    (3) They shall then, having prepared the relevant documents, that is, the proposed scheme or alterations—

    (*a*) make copies of the documents available for inspection at their office, and

    (*b*) send a copy of them to the Secretary of State.

    (4) Each copy of the documents made available for inspection shall be accompanied by a statement of the time within which objections may be made.

    (5) The planning authority shall before preparing the proposed scheme or alterations consult the Secretary of State and any local roads authority in whose district the proposed zone or any part of it lies as to the effect of their proposals on existing or future roads ; and when they have prepared the proposed scheme or alterations they shall send a copy to the Secretary of State and any such local roads authority.

Publicity and consultation : expedited procedure

    6.—(1) The documents sent by the planning authority to the Secretary of State under paragraph 5(3) shall be accompanied by a statement—

    (*a*) of the steps which the authority have taken to comply with paragraph 5(2), and

    (*b*) of the authority's consultations with other persons and their consideration of the views of those persons.

    (2) Where a planning authority do not consider it appropriate to take the steps required by paragraph 5(2) of this Schedule in relation to proposals made by them under sub-paragraph (1) of that paragraph for the alteration of a simplified planning zone scheme, they may instead include, with the copies of those proposals made available for inspection and with the copy sent to the Secretary of State under paragraph (3) of that paragraph, a statement of their reasons for not taking such steps.

Objections : local inquiry or other hearing

    7.—(1) The planning authority may cause a local inquiry or other hearing to be held for the purpose of considering objections to their proposals for the making or alteration of a simplified planning zone scheme.

    (2) They shall hold such a local inquiry or other hearing in the case of objections made in accordance with regulations unless all the persons who have made such objections have indicated in writing that they do not wish to appear.

SCH. 6

(3) A local inquiry or other hearing shall be held by a person appointed by the Secretary of State or, in such cases as may be prescribed, by the authority themselves.

(4) Regulations may—

> (a) make provision with respect to the appointment, and quali- fications for appointment, of persons to hold a local inquiry or other hearing ;
>
> (b) include provision enabling the Secretary of State to direct a planning authority to appoint a particular person, or one of a specified list or class of persons ;
>
> (c) make provision with respect to the remuneration and allow- ances of the person appointed.

(5) The Tribunals and Inquiries Act 1971 applies to a local inquiry 1971 c. 62. or other hearing held under this paragraph as it applies to a statutory inquiry held by the Secretary of State, with the substitution in sec- tion 12(1) (statement of reasons for decision) for the references to a decision taken by the Secretary of State of references to a decision taken by a planning authority.

Adoption of proposals by planning authority

8.—(1) After the expiry of the period afforded for making objec- tions to proposals for the making or alteration of a simplified plan- ning zone scheme or, if such objections were duly made within that period, after considering the objections so made, the planning authority may, subject to the following provisions of this paragraph and to paragraph 9 (calling in of proposals by Secretary of State), by resolution adopt the proposals.

(2) They may adopt the proposals as originally prepared or as modified so as to take account of—

> (a) any such objections as are mentioned in sub-paragraph (1) any other objections to the proposals, or
>
> (b) any other considerations which appear to the authority to be material.

(3) After copies of the proposals have been sent to the Secretary of State and before they have been adopted by the planning aut- hority, the Secretary of State may, if it appears to him that the proposals are unsatisfactory, direct the authority to consider modify- ing the proposals in such respects as are indicated in the direction.

(4) An authority to whom a direction is given shall not adopt the proposals unless they satisfy the Secretary of State that they have made the modification necessary to conform with the direction or the direction is withdrawn.

Calling in of proposals for approval by Secretary of State

9.—(1) After copies of proposals have been sent to the Secretary of State and before they have been adopted by the planning authority, the Secretary of State may direct that the proposals shall be submitted to him for his approval.

(2) In that event—

(*a*) the authority shall not take any further steps for the adoption of the proposals, and in particular shall not hold or proceed with a local inquiry or other hearing in respect of the proposals under paragraph 7 ; and

(*b*) the proposals shall not have effect unless approved by the Secretary of State and shall not require adoption by the authority.

Approval of proposals by Secretary of State

10.—(1) The Secretary of State may after considering proposals submitted to him under paragraph 9 either approve them, in whole or in part and with or without modifications, or reject them.

(2) In considering the proposals he may take into account any matters he thinks are relevant, whether or not they were taken into account in the proposals as submitted to him.

(3) Where on taking the proposals into consideration the Secretary of State does not determine then to reject them, he shall, before determining whether or not to approve them—

(*a*) consider any objections to them in accordance with regulations,

(*b*) afford to any person who made such an objection which has not been withdrawn an opportunity of appearing before and being heard by a person appointed by him for the purpose, and

(*c*) if a local inquiry or other hearing is held, also afford such an opportunity to the authority and such other persons as he thinks fit,

except so far as objections have already been considered, or a local inquiry or other hearing into the objections has already been held, by the authority.

(4) In considering the proposals the Secretary of State may consult with, or consider the views of, any planning authority or any other person ; but he is under no obligation to do so, or to afford an opportunity for the making of representations or objections, or to cause a local inquiry or other hearing to be held, except as provided by sub-paragraph (3).

Default powers

11.—(1) Where by virtue of any of the preceding provisions of this Schedule—

(*a*) a simplified planning zone scheme or proposals for the alteration of such a scheme are required to be prepared, or

(*b*) steps are required to be taken for the adoption of any such scheme or proposals,

then, if the Secretary of State is satisfied, after holding a local inquiry or other hearing, that the planning authority are not taking the steps necessary to enable them to prepare or adopt such a scheme or proposals within a reasonable period, he may make the scheme, or the alterations, as he thinks fit.

(2) Where under this paragraph anything which ought to have been done by a planning authority is done by the Secretary of State, the preceding provisions of this Schedule apply, so far as practicable, with any necessary modifications in relation to the doing of that thing by the Secretary of State and the thing so done.

(3) Where the Secretary of State incurs expenses under this paragraph in connection with the doing of anything which should have been done by a planning authority, so much of those expenses as may be certified by the Secretary of State to have been incurred in the performance of functions of that authority shall on demand be repaid by the authority to the Secretary of State.

Regulations and directions

12.—(1) Without prejudice to the preceding provisions of this Schedule, the Secretary of State may make regulations with respect to the form and content of simplified planning zone schemes and with respect to the procedure to be followed in connection with their preparation, withdrawal, adoption, submission, approval, making or alteration.

(2) Any such regulations may in particular—

(a) provide for the notice to be given of, or the publicity to be given to, matters included or proposed to be included in a simplified planning zone scheme and the adoption or approval of such a scheme, or of any alteration of it, or any other prescribed procedural step, and for publicity to be given to the procedure to be followed in these respects ;

(b) make provision with respect to the making and consideration of representations as to matters to be included in, or objections to, any such scheme or proposals for its alteration ;

(c) without prejudice to paragraph (b), provide for notice to be given to particular persons of the adoption or approval of a simplified planning zone scheme, or an alteration to such a scheme, if they have objected to the proposals and have notified the planning authority of their wish to receive notice, subject (if the regulations so provide) to the payment of a reasonable charge ;

(d) require or authorise a planning authority to consult with, or consider the views of, other persons before taking any prescribed procedural step ;

(e) require a planning authority, in such cases as may be prescribed or in such particular cases as the Secretary of State may direct, to provide persons making a request in that behalf with copies of any document which has been made public for the purpose mentioned in paragraph 5(2) or has been made available for inspection under paragraph 5(3), subject (if the regulations so provide) to the payment of a reasonable charge ;

(f) provide for the publication and inspection of a simplified planning zone scheme which has been adopted or approved, or any document adopted or approved altering such a scheme, and for copies of any such scheme or document to be made available on sale.

(3) Regulations under this paragraph may extend throughout Scotland or to specified areas only and may make different provision for different cases.

(4) Subject to the preceding provisions of this Schedule and to any regulations under this paragraph, the Secretary of State may give directions to any planning authority or to planning authorities generally—

    (*a*) for formulating the procedure for the carrying out of their functions under this Schedule ;

    (*b*) for requiring them to give him such information as he may require for carrying out any of his functions under this Schedule.

Part IV
Consequential Amendments—Scotland

1. At the end of subsection (2) of section 31 of the Town and Country Planning (Scotland) Act 1972 (registers) insert " and also containing such information as may be so prescribed with respect to simplified planning zone schemes relating to zones in the authority's area ".

2. In section 38 of the Town and Country Planning (Scotland) Act 1972 (limit of duration of planning permission), in subsection (3) (exceptions) after paragraph (*aa*) insert—

    " (*ab*) to any planning permission granted by a simplified planning zone scheme ; ".

3. In section 51(1) of the Town and Country Planning (Scotland) Act 1972 (applications to determine whether planning permission required) after the word " scheme " insert " or simplified planning zone scheme ".

4. After subsection (1)(*a*) of section 231 of the Town and Country Planning (Scotland) Act 1972 (validity of plans, &c.) insert—

    " (*aa*) a simplified planning zone scheme or any alteration of any such scheme whether before or after the adoption or approval of the scheme or alteration ; or ".

5. In section 232 of the Town and Country Planning (Scotland) Act 1972 (proceedings for questioning plans, &c.), after subsection (3) insert—

    " (4) Subsections (1) and (2) of this section apply to a simplified planning zone scheme or an alteration of such a scheme as they apply to a structure plan and an alteration of such a plan, with the following modifications—

        (*a*) for the references to Part II of this Act substitute references to Part III of this Act, and

(*b*) for the reference to regulations under section 16(1) of   Sch. 6
     this Act substitute a reference to regulations under
     paragraph 12 of Schedule 6A to this Act,

and with any other necessary modifications.".

6. In section 273 of the Town and Country Planning (Scotland) Act 1972 c. 52.
1972 (orders)—

   (*a*) in subsection (4), after " 21," insert "21E,", and

   (*b*) in subsection (5), after " 1(3)," insert "21E,".

7. In section 275(1) of the Town and Country Planning (Scotland)
Act 1972 after the definition of " road " insert—

   " ' simplified planning zone ' and ' simplified planning zone
      scheme ' shall be construed in accordance with section
      21A of this Act ; ".

SCHEDULE 7

Sections 33 and
37.

Hazardous Substances: Consequential Amendments

Part I

England and Wales

Radioactive Substances Act 1960 (c.34)

1. The following paragraph shall be inserted after paragraph
8A of Schedule 1 to the Radioactive Substances Act 1960 (duty of
public and local authorities not to take account of any radioactivity
in performing their functions)—

   " 8AA. Sections 58B to 58M and 101B of the Town and 1971 c. 78.
   Country Planning Act 1971.".

Town and Country Planning Act 1971 (c.78)

2. In subsection (3) (action on the part of the Secretary of State
that may be questioned in legal proceedings) of section 242 of the
Town and Country Planning Act 1971, the following paragraph shall
be inserted after paragraph (*d*)—

   " (*dd*) any decision by the Secretary of State relating to an
      application for hazardous substances consent ; ".

3. In subsection (2)(*a*) of section 266 of that Act (orders which,
in relation to Crown land, may only be made with consent of appropriate authority)—

   (*a*) after " 51B " there shall be inserted " 58H " ; and

   (*b*) for " or 96 " there shall be substituted " 96 or 101B "

4. Section 269 of that Act (application to Isles of Scilly) shall have
effect as if sections 58B to 58N and 101B were included among the
provisions specified in Part III of Schedule 21 (provisions that may
be applied to Isles as if they were a district).

5. The following section shall be inserted after section 271 of that Act—

"Application to certain hazardous substances authorities of provisions as to hazardous substances control.

271A.—(1) The provisions of this Act relating to hazardous substances shall have effect subject to such exceptions and modifications as may be prescribed in relation to granting hazardous substances consent for authorities who are hazardous substances authorities by virtue of section 1A of this Act.

(2) Subject to the provisions of section 58F of this Act, any such regulations may in particular provide for securing—

(*a*) that any application by such an authority for hazardous substances consent in respect of the presence of a hazardous substance on, over, or under land shall be made to the Secretary of State and not to the hazardous substances authority ;

(*b*) that any order or notice authorised to be made, issued or served under those provisions shall be made, issued or served by the Secretary of State and not by the hazardous substances authority."

6. In section 280 of that Act (rights of entry)—

(*a*) the following subsection shall be inserted after subsection (1)—

"(1A) Any person duly authorised in writing by the Secretary of State or by a hazardous substances authority may at any reasonable time enter any land for the purpose of surveying it in connection with—

(*a*) any application for hazardous substances consent ;

(*b*) any proposal to issue a hazardous substances contravention notice." ;

(*b*) at the end of subsection (4) there shall be added the words " and any person duly authorised in writing by the Secretary of State or by a hazardous substances authority may at any reasonable time enter any land for the purpose of ascertaining whether an offence appears to have been committed under section 58K of this Act." ;

(*c*) the following subsection shall be inserted after subsection (6)—

"(6A) Subsection (6) above shall have effect for the purposes of a claim for compensation made by virtue of section 58H(8) or 58J(12) of this Act as if a reference to a local planning authority were a reference to a hazardous substances authority." ; and

(*d*) in subsection (8), after the word " section " there shall be inserted the words " or a hazardous substances contravention notice has been issued ".

7. In section 290(1) of that Act (Interpretation)—

(*a*) the following shall be inserted after the definition of " conservation area "—

" " contravention of hazardous substances control " has the meaning assigned to it by section 58K(2) of this Act ; " ;

(*b*) the following shall be inserted after the definition of " the Greater London development plan "—

" " hazardous substances authority " is to be construed in accordance with sections 1A and 1B of this Act ;

" hazardous substances consent " means consent required by section 58B of this Act ;

" hazardous substances contravention notice " has the meaning assigned to it by section 101B(3) of this Act ; " ; and

(*c*) the following shall be inserted after the definition of " tree preservation order "—

" " urban development area " and " urban development corporation " have the same meaning as in Part XVI of the Local Government, Planning and Land Act 1980 ; ". 1980 c. 65.

Town and Country Planning Act 1984 (c.10)

8. In section 1 of the Town and Country Planning Act 1984 (applications in anticipation of disposal of Crown interest)—

(*a*) in subsection (1)(*a*), after the words " listed building consent " there shall be inserted the words " , hazardous substances consent " ; and

(*b*) the following subsection shall be inserted after subsection (3)—

" (3A) Any hazardous substances consent granted by virtue of this section shall apply only—

(*a*) to the presence of the substance to which the consent relates after the land in question has ceased to be Crown land ; and

(*b*) so long as that land continues to be Crown land, to the presence of the substance by virtue of a private interest in the land.".

Gas Act 1986 (c.44.)

9. In sub-paragraph (1)(xxiv) of paragraph 2 of Schedule 7 to the Gas Act 1986 (enactments for the purposes of which a public gas supplier is deemed to be a statutory undertaker and his undertaking a statutory undertaking)—

(*a*) after " sections " there shall be inserted " 1B, " ; and

(*b*) after " 49," there shall be inserted " 58F,".

Part II

Scotland

Radioactive Substances Act 1960 (c.34)

1968 c. 47.

1. The following paragraph shall be inserted after the entry relating to the Sewerage (Scotland) Act 1968 in Part II of the first Schedule to the Radioactive Substances Act 1960 (duty of public and local authorities not to take account of any radioactivity in performing their functions)—

1972 c. 52.

" 17A. Sections 56A to 56N and 97B of the Town and Country Planning (Scotland) Act 1972.".

Town and Country Planning (Scotland) Act 1972 (c.52)

2. In subsection (3) (action on the part of the Secretary of State that may be questioned in legal proceedings) of section 231 of the Town and Country Planning (Scotland) Act 1972, the following paragraph shall be inserted after paragraph (*d*)—

" (*dd*) any decision by the Secretary of State relating to an application for hazardous substances consent ; ".

3. In subsection (2)(*a*) of section 253 of that Act (orders which, in relation to Crown land, may only be made with consent of appropriate authority)—

(*a*) after " 49B " there shall be inserted " 56J " ; and

(*b*) for " or 92 " there shall be substituted " 92 or 97B ".

4. The following section shall be inserted after section 257 of that Act—

"Application to planning authorities of provisions as to hazardous substances control.

257A.—(1) The provisions of this Act relating to hazardous substances shall have effect subject to such exceptions and modifications as may be prescribed in relation to hazardous substances consent for planning authorities.

(2) Subject to the provisions of section 56G of this Act, any such regulations may in particular provide for securing—

(*a*) that any application by such an authority for hazardous substances consent in respect of the presence of a hazardous substance on, over or under such land shall be made to the Secretary of State and not to the planning authority ;

(*b*) that any order or notice authorised to be made, issued or served under those provisions shall be made, issued or served by the Secretary of State and not by the planning authority.".

5. In section 265 of that Act (rights of entry)—

(*a*) the following subsection shall be inserted after subsection (1)—

" (1A) Any person duly authorised in writing by the Secretary of State or by a planning authority may at any reasonable time enter any land for the purpose of surveying it in connection with—

> (*a*) any application for hazardous substances consent ;
>
> (*b*) any proposal to issue a hazardous substances contravention notice." ;

(*b*) the following subsection shall be inserted after subsection (4)—

> " (4A) Any person duly authorised in writing by the Secretary of State or by a planning authority may at any reasonable time enter any land for the purpose of ascertaining whether an offence appears to have been committed under section 56L of this Act." ; and

(*c*) the following subsection shall be inserted after subsection (7)—

> " (7A) Any person duly authorised in writing by the Secretary of State or a planning authority may at any reasonable time enter any land in respect of which a hazardous substances contravention notice has been served for the purpose of ascertaining whether the notice has been complied with.".

6. In section 275(1) of that Act (interpretation)—

(*a*) the following shall be inserted after the definition of " conservation area "—

> " " contravention of hazardous substances control " has the meaning assigned to it by section 56L(2) of this Act ; " ;

(*b*) the following shall be inserted after the definition of " government department "—

> " " hazardous substances consent " means consent required by section 56C of this Act ;
>
> " hazardous substances contravention notice " has the meaning assigned to it by section 97B(3) of this Act ; " ; and

(*c*) the following shall be inserted after the definition of " tree preservation order "—

> " " urban development area " and " urban development corporation " have the same meaning as in Part XVI of the Local Government, Planning and Land Act 1980 ; ".   1980 c. 65.

Town and Country Planning Act 1984 (c.10)

7. In section 1 of the Town and Country Planning Act 1984 (applications in anticipation of disposal of Crown interests)—

(*a*) in subsection (1)(*a*), after the words " listed building consent " there shall be inserted the words ", hazardous substances consent " ; and

SCH. 7

(*b*) the following subsection shall be inserted after subsection (3)—

" (3A) Any hazardous substances consent granted by virtue of this section shall apply only—

(*a*) to the presence of the substance to which the consent relates after the land in question has ceased to be Crown land ; and

(*b*) so long as that land continues to be Crown land to the presence of the substance by virtue of a private interest in the land.".

Gas Act 1986 (c.44)

8. In sub-paragraph (1)(xxv) of paragraph 2 of Schedule 7 to the Gas Act 1986 after " 46 ", there shall be inserted " 56B, 56G,".

Section 39(3).

SCHEDULE 8

OPENCAST COAL — MISCELLANEOUS AMENDMENTS

PART I

THE 1958 ACT

1. The following section shall be substituted for section 3—

" Preservation of amenity.

3.—(1) Where the Board are formulating any proposals as to the working of coal by opencast operations or the carrying out of operations incidental to such working, the Board, having regard to the desirability of preserving natural beauty, of conserving flora, fauna, and geological or physiographical features of special interests, and of protecting buildings and other objects of architectural or historic interest, shall take into account any effect which the proposals would have on the natural beauty of the countryside or on any such flora, fauna, features, buildings, or objects.

(2) The provisions of the preceding subsection shall also apply, with the necessary modifications, where the Board are formulating any proposals as to the restoration of land affected by the working of coal by opencast operations or by operations incidental to such working.".

2.—(1) In section 4(1), for the words " the land comprised in an authorisation under section 1 of this Act " there shall be substituted the words " any land on which they desire to work coal by such operations or to carry out operations incidental to such working ".

(2) The following subsections shall be substituted for section 4(6)—

" (6) A compulsory rights order may only be made if opencast planning permission has been applied for or granted in respect of the land comprised in the order or is deemed to have been granted in respect of it.

(6A) Where a compulsory rights order is made before opencast planning permission has been granted in respect of the land comprised in the order, the Secretary of State shall not confirm it unless such permission in respect of that land has first been granted.

(6B) Where a compulsory rights order is made in a case where opencast planning permission has been granted or is deemed to have been granted, the order, as from the time when it is made, shall include a reference to the permission.

(6C) If opencast planning permission is granted in respect of land comprised in a compulsory rights order and the Secretary of State subsequently confirms the order, the order as confirmed shall include a reference to the permission.

(6D) No compulsory rights order, as confirmed, shall extend to any land which is not comprised in the permission or deemed permission referred to in the order.".

3. In section 5(5)—

(*a*) for the word " authorisation " there shall be substituted the words " opencast planning permission " ; and

(*b*) for the words " fulfilment of the authorised purposes " there shall be substituted the words " permitted activities ".

4. In section 13, the words " in respect of which opencast planning permission has been granted " shall be substituted—

(*a*) in subsection (1)—

(i) for the words from " which ", in the second place where it occurs, to " Act ", in the second place where it occurs ; and

(ii) for the words from " comprised ", in the second place where it occurs, to " Act ", in the third place where it occurs ;

(*b*) in subsection (2), for the words from " which " to " Act " ;

(*c*) in subsection (4)—

(i) for the words from " which " to " Act " ; and

(ii) for the words "comprised in such an authorisation " ; and

(*d*) in subsectioin (5), for the words from " which ", in the second place where it occurs, to the end of the subsection.

5. The following sections shall be substituted for section 14—

"Provisions
as to
agricultural
tenancies in
England and
Wales.

14.—(1) Without prejudice to the provisions of Part III of this Act as to matters arising between landlords and tenants in consequence of compulsory rights orders, the provisions of this section shall have effect where—

T 3

    (*a*) opencast planning permission has been granted subject to a restoration condition and to an aftercare condition in which the use specified is use for agriculture or use for forestry, and

    (*b*) immediately before that permission is granted, any of the land comprised therein consists of an agricultural holding or part of an agricultural holding,

whether any of that land is comprised in a compulsory rights order or not.

(2) For the purposes of the Agricultural Holdings Act 1986 (in this Act referred to as " the Act of 1986 ")—

    (*a*) the holding shall not be taken to have ceased to be an agricultural holding ; and

    (*b*) where only part of the holding is comprised in opencast planning permission, that part shall not be taken to have ceased to form part of an agricultural holding,

by reason only that, while occupied or used for the permitted activities, the land is not being used for agriculture within the meaning of that Act.

(3) For the purposes of the Act of 1986, the tenant of the holding shall not be taken to have failed to fulfill his responsibilities to farm in accordance with the rules of good husbandry—

    (*a*) by reason of his having permitted any of the land comprised in the opencast planning permission to be occupied for the purpose of carrying on any of the permitted activities, or by reason of any other thing done or omitted by him for facilitating the use of any of that land for that purpose ;

    (*b*) where any of that land is comprised in a compulsory rights order, by reason of the occupation or use of any of that land in the exercise of rights conferred by the order, in so far as that occupation or use was not permitted or facilitated by the tenant as mentioned in the preceding paragraph.

(4) For the purposes of the Act of 1986 nothing done or omitted by the tenant or by the landlord of the holding by way of permitting any of the land in respect of which opencast planning permission has been granted to be occupied for the purpose of carrying on any of the permitted activities, or by way of facilitating the use of any of that land for that purpose, shall be taken to be a breach of any term or condition of the tenancy, either on the part of the tenant or on the part of the landlord.

SCH 8

(5) For the purposes of subsections (1) to (3) of section 27 of the Act of 1986 (Agricultural Land Tribunal's consent to operation of notice to quit) the condition specified in paragraph (*f*) of subsection (3) of that section shall not be treated as satisfied if the use for the purpose for which the landlord proposes to terminate the tenancy is the use of the land for carrying on any of the permitted activities.

(6) On a reference to arbitration under section 12 of the Act of 1986 with respect to the rent which should be properly payable for the holding, in respect of any period for which the Board are in occupation of the holding, or of any part thereof, for the purpose of carrying on any of the permitted activities, the arbitrator shall not take into account any increase or diminution in the rental value of the holding in so far as that increase or diminution is attributable to the occupation of the holding, or of that part of the holding, by the Board for the purpose of carrying on any of the permitted activities.

(7) For the purpose of the operation of section 13 of the Act of 1986 (increases of rent for landlord's improvements) in relation to improvements carried out on the holding, in a case where the improvements have been affected by anything done for the purpose of carrying on any of the permitted activities, the increase (if any) of the rental value of the holding attributable to the carrying out of the improvements shall be assessed as if it had not been done.

(8) This section does not extend to Scotland.

Provisions as to agricultural tenancies in Scotland.

14A.—(1) Without prejudice to the provisions of Part III of this Act as to matters arising between landlords and tenants in consequence of compulsory rights orders, the provisions of this section shall have effect in Scotland where—

(*a*) opencast planning permission has been granted subject to a restoration condition and to an aftercare condition in which the use specified is use for agriculture, and

(*b*) immediately before that permission is granted, any of the land comprised therein consists of an agricultural holding or part of an agricultural holding,

whether any of that land is comprised in a compulsory rights order or not.

(2) In this section—

"aftercare condition" means a condition requiring that such steps shall be taken as may be necessary to bring land to the standard required for use for agriculture ; and

T4

SCH. 8
1972 c. 52.

1949 c. 75.

" restoration condition " has the meaning given to it in section 27A(2) of the Town and Country Planning (Scotland) Act 1972.

(3) For the purposes of the Agricultural Holdings (Scotland) Act 1949 (in this Act referred to as " the Scottish Act of 1949 ")—

(a) the holding shall not be taken to have ceased to be an agricultural holding ; and

(b) where only part of the holding is comprised in the opencast planning permission, that part shall not be taken to have ceased to form part of an agricultural holding,

by reason only that, while occupied or used for the permitted activities, the land is not being used for agriculture within the meaning of that Act.

(4) For the purposes of the Scottish Act of 1949, the tenant of the holding shall not be taken to have failed to fulfil his responsibilities to farm in accordance with the rules of good husbandry—

(a) by reason of his having permitted any of the land comprised in the opencast planning permission to be occupied for the purpose of carrying on any of the permitted activities, or by reason of any other thing done or omitted by him for facilitating the use of any of that land for that purpose ;

(b) where any of that land is comprised in a compulsory rights order, by reason of the occupation or use of any of that land in the exercise of rights conferred by the order, in so far as that occupation or use was not permitted or facilitated by the tenant as mentioned in the preceding paragraph.

(5) For the purposes of the Scottish Act of 1949 nothing done or omitted by the tenant or by the landlord of the holding by way of permitting any of the land in respect of which opencast planning permission has been granted to be occupied for the purpose of carrying on any of the permitted activities, or by way of facilitating the use of any of that land for that purpose, shall be taken to be a breach of any term or condition of the tenancy, either on the part of the tenant or on the part of the landlord.

(6) For the purposes of section 25(2) of the Scottish Act of 1949, no account is to be taken of permission granted as mentioned in paragraph (c) of that subsection if the permission—

(a) is granted on an application by the National Coal Board ; and

(b) relates to the working of coal by opencast operations ; and (*c*) is granted subject to a restoration condition and an aftercare condition.

(7) For the purposes of section 26 of the Scottish Act of 1949 (in which subsection (1) specifies conditions for the giving of consent under section 25 of that Act to the operation of a notice to quit) the condition specified in paragraph (*e*) of subsection (1) shall not be treated as satisfied if the use for the purpose of which the landlord proposes to terminate the tenancy is the use of the land for carrying on any of the permitted activities.

(8) On a reference to arbitration under section 7 of the Scottish Act of 1949 with respect to the rent which should be properly payable for the holding, in respect of any period for which the Board are in occupation of the holding, or of any part thereof, for the purpose of carrying on any of the permitted activities, the arbiter shall not take into account any increase or diminution in the rental value of the holding in so far as that increase or diminution is attributable to the occupation of the holding, or of that part of the holding, by the Board for the purpose of carrying on any of the permitted activities.

(9) For the purpose of the operation of section 8 of the Scottish Act of 1949 (which relates to increases of rent for improvements carried out by the landlord) in relation to an improvement carried out on the holding, in a case where the improvement has been affected by anything done for the purpose of carrying on any of the permitted activities, the increase (if any) of the rental value of the holding attributable to the carrying out of the improvement shall be assessed as if the improvement had not been so affected.

(10) The use of land for the working of coal by opencast operations shall not be a use for the purposes of which a landlord shall be entitled to resume the land.".

6. The following sections shall be substituted for section 15—

" Suspension
of certain
public rights
of ways.

15.—(1) Where—

(*a*) the Board apply for opencast planning permission ; and

(*b*) over any part of the land to which the application relates there subsists a public right of way, not being a right enjoyed by vehicular traffic,

the Board may also apply to the Secretary of State for an order suspending the public right of way.

(2) The Secretary of State shall not make such an order unless—

(*a*) opencast planning permission is granted ; and

(*b*) he is satisfied—

(i) that a suitable alternative way will be

SCH. 8

made available by the Board (whether on land comprised in the opencast planning permission or on other land) for use by the public during the period for which the order remains in force ; or

(ii) that the provision of such an alternative way is not required.

(3) An order under this section shall specify the date, which shall not be earlier than the making of the order, with effect from which the right of way is suspended.

(4) Where an order has been made under this section the Secretary of State shall revoke it—

(*a*) if—

(i) no permitted activities have been carried on pursuant to the opencast planning permission on the land over which the right of way subsisted ; and

(ii) he is satisfied that there is no early prospect of such activities being so carried on ; or

(*b*) as soon after such permitted activities have been so carried on as he is satisfied that it is no longer necessary for the purpose of carrying on such permitted activities that the right of way should be suspended.

(5) An order under this section shall include such provisions as may appear to the Secretary of State to be appropriate for securing the reconstruction of the way on the restoration of the land over which the right of way subsisted immediately before the order was made.

(6) Where an order is made under this section then, in connection with the provision of such a suitable alternative way as is referred to in subsection (2) above,—

(*a*) the order under this section may provide that, in so far as the carrying out of any operations, or any change in the use of land, involved in making the alternative way available or in permitting it to be used by the public, constitutes development within the meaning of the Act of 1971, permission for that development shall be deemed to be granted under Part III of that Act subject to such conditions (if any) as may be specified in the order ;

(*b*) where the order under this section includes provisions in accordance with paragraph (*a*) above, the Act of 1971 shall have effect as if they were conditions subject to which the opencast planning permission was granted ;

(c) if a compulsory rights order referring to the open-   Sc 8
cast planning permission is made, then, in the
application to that order of section 5(5) above,
the permitted activities shall be taken to include
making an alternative way available for use by
the public, and the right exercisable in accordance with that subsection, as against all persons directly concerned, shall include the right
to permit the public to use any way so made
available ; and

(d) if the land on which the alternative way is to be
made available is specified in the order under
this section and is land which does not form part
of, but it contiguous with, the land to which the
opencast planning permission relates, a compulsory rights order referring to the opencast planning permission may include that land as if it
were part of the land comprised in the permission.

(7) In the application of this section to Scotland, it
shall be read as if for " the Act of 1971 " there were
substituted " the Town and Country Planning (Scotland) 1972 c. 52.
Act 1972 ".

Suspension
of public
rights of
way—
supple-
mentary.

15A.—(1) Before submitting to the Secretary of State
an application for an order under section 15 of this Act,
the Board shall publish a notice in the prescribed form
identifying the right of way and stating—

(a) that the Board are proposing to apply for an
order suspending it in connection with the
working of coal by opencast operations ;

(b) that opencast planning permission has been applied for, or, as the case may be, has been
granted ; and

(c) that objections to the application for the order
may be made in writing to the Secretary of
State within such time, not being less than 28
days from the publication of the notice, as may
be specified.

(2) The duty to publish a notice imposed by subsection
(1) above is a duty to publish it—

(a) in two successive weeks in one or more local
newspapers circulating in the locality in which the
land over which the right of way subsists is situated ; and

(b) in the same or any other two successive weeks, in
the appropriate Gazette.

(3) The period within which objections may be made
expires when the period specified in the last publication

of the notice expires ; and any period specified in earlier publications is to be treated as extended accordingly.

(4) A notice under subsection (1) above shall name a place in the locality where a copy of the application and of a map showing the right of way can be inspected.

(5) The Board shall also, before submitting such an application to the Secretary of State,—

    (*a*) inform—

        (i) in England and Wales, the district council and, except in the case of a metropolitan district, the county council, and any parish or community council or parish meeting ; and

        (ii) in Scotland, every local authority in whose area any part of the land over which the right of way subsists is situated of the right to object conferred by subsection (1) above ;

    (*b*) send them a map showing the right of way and a copy of their notice under subsection (1) above ; and

    (*c*) affix to some conspicuous object at either end of the right of way a notice giving in the prescribed form the prescribed particulars of their proposed application concerning it and of the right to object.

(6) If no objection is made by any such authority, other than a parish or community council or parish meeting, as is mentioned in subsection (5)(*a*) above, or if all objections which are made by any such authority are withdrawn, the Secretary of State, upon being satisfied that the Board have complied with subsections (1) to (5) above, may if he thinks fit make the order.

(7) The Secretary of State may, if he thinks fit, cause a public local inquiry to be held before determining whether to make an order, and shall cause such an inquiry to be held if an objection is made by any such authority and is not withdrawn.

(8) If the Secretary of State causes such an inquiry to be held, he shall consider all objections to the application which are duly made by any person and not withdrawn and the report of the person who held the inquiry before determining whether to make the order.

(9) An order under section 15 of this Act may be made either in accordance with the Board's application or subject to such modifications as the Secretary of State may determine.

(10) If the Secretary of State makes an order, the Board, as soon as may be after the order is made, shall publish a notice in the prescribed form that the order

has been made, describing the right of way which is
suspended, stating the date on which the order comes
into operation and naming a place in the locality where
a copy of the order and of any map to which it refers
can be inspected at all reasonable hours, and shall serve
a like notice and a copy of the order on any body required under this section to be informed of the application
for the order.

(11) The duty to publish a notice imposed by subsection
(10) above is a duty to publish it—
  (*a*) in one or more local newspapers such as are
       mentioned in subsection (1) above ; and
  (*b*) in the appropriate Gazette.

(12) In this section " the appropriate Gazette " means—
  (*a*) the London Gazette in a case where the land over
       which the right of way subsists is situated in
       England or Wales ; and
  (*b*) the Edinburgh Gazette in a case where it is
       situated in Scotland.".

7. In section 16—
  (*a*) in subsections (1) and (2), for the words from " which " to
       " Act " there shall be substituted the words " in respect of
       which opencast planning permission has been granted " ;
  (*b*) in subsection (3), for the words from " comprised " to " Act "
       there shall be substituted the words " in respect of which
       the permission was granted ".

8. In sections 18(3)(*a*) and 19(4)(*a*)—
  (*a*) for the word " authorisation ", in the first place where it
       occurs, there shall be substituted the words " opencast plan-
       ning permission " ; and
  (*b*) for the words " an authorisation " there shall be substituted
       the word " permission ".

9. In section 38—
  (*a*) in paragraph (*a*)—
       (i) for the words from " which " to " Act " there shall
       be substituted the words " in respect of which opencast
       planning permission has been granted " ; and
       (ii) for the words " authorised purposes " there shall
       be substituted the words " purpose of carrying on the
       permitted activities " ;
  (*b*) in paragraph (*b*), for the words " comprised in the authorisa-
       tion " there shall be substituted the words " in respect of
       which the permission was granted and " ; and
  (*c*) for the words from " fulfilment " to the end of the sub-
       section there shall be substituted the words " permitted
       activities "

10. In section 39(3)—

   (*a*) in paragraph (*a*), for the words " an authorisation under section one of this Act " there shall be substituted the words " opencast planning permission " ;

   (*b*) in paragraph (*b*)—

      (i) for the words from " an " to " Act ", in the first place where it occurs, there shall be substituted the words " opencast planning permission " ; and

      (ii) for the words " out of any authorised operations " there shall be substituted the words " on of any of the permitted activities " ; and

   (*c*) in paragraph (*d*), for the words " any of the provisions of the First " there shall be substituted the words " section 15A(4)(*c*) or any of the provisions of the ".

11. In the proviso to section 39(5), for the words " any of the provisions of the First " there shall be substituted the words " section 15A(4)(*c*) or any of the provisions of the ".

12. In section 45(2)—

   (*a*) for the words from " an " to " Act " there shall be substituted the words " opencast planning permission has been granted " ; and

   (*b*) for the words " authorised operations ", there shall be substituted the words " permitted activities ".

13. In section 51(1)—

   (*a*) the following definition shall be inserted after the definition of " National Trust "—

      " " opencast planning permission " means planning permission which permits the Board to work coal by opencast operations or to carry out operations incidental to such working ; " ;

   (*b*) the following definition shall be inserted after the definition of " period of occupation "—

      " " permitted activities " means—

         (*a*) the working of coal by opencast operations pursuant to opencast planning permission and the carrying out of operations incidental to such working ; and

         (*b*) the carrying out of any conditions subject to which opencast planning permission has been granted ; " ; and

   (*c*) the following definition shall be inserted after the definition of " persons directly concerned "—

      " " planning permission " means planning permission under Part III of the Act of 1971 ; ".

14. In section 52(2), the following definition shall be inserted after the definition of " owner "—

" " planning permission " means planning permission under Part III of the Act of 1972 ; ".

15. In paragraph 5(1) of Part I of Schedule 2 (compulsory rights orders)—

(*a*) for the words " an authorisation under section one of this Act " there shall be substituted the words " opencast planning permission " ; and

(*b*) for the words from " an authorisation ", in the second place where those words occur, to " operations " there shall be substituted the words " opencast planning permission should be granted or should have been granted.".

16. In Schedule 6, in paragraph 18(2)(*c*I, for the words from " purposes ", in the first place where it occurs, to the end there shall be substituted the words " activities which, in relation to the opencast planning permission referred to in the order, constitute the permitted activities ".

17. In Schedule 7, in paragraph 24(3)(*a*)—

(*a*) for the word " authorisation ", in the first place where it occurs, there shall be substituted the words " opencast planning permission " ; and

(*b*) for the words " had been made for such an authorisation " there shall be substituted the words " for opencast planning permission had been made ".

PART II

ACQUISITION OF LAND ACT 1981 (*c.*67)

18. In section 29—

(*a*) in subsection (6)—

(i) for the words " an authorisation under section 1 of the Opencast Coal Act 1958 " there shall be substituted the words " opencast planning permission " ; and

(ii) for the words from " an authorisation ", in the second place where they occur, to " operations " there shall be substituted the words " opencast planning permission should be granted or should have been granted " ; and

(*b*) the following subsection shall be substituted for subsection (11)—

" (11) In this section " opencast planning permission " and " persons directly concerned " have the same meanings as in the Opencast Coal Act 1958.".

SCHEDULE 9

LISTED BUILDINGS AND CONSERVATION AREAS

PART I

ENGLAND AND WALES

*Free-standing objects and structures within curtilage of
listed building*

1.—(1) In section 54(9) of the Town and Country Planning Act
1971 (definition of " listed building "), for the words from " and for
the purposes " to the end substitute—

" and, for the purposes of the provisions of this Act relating to
listed buildings and building preservation notices, the following
shall be treated as part of the building—

   (a) any object or structure fixed to the building ;

   (b) any object or structure within the curtilage of the building which, although not fixed to the building, forms
   part of the land and has done so since before 1st July
   1948.".

(2) Where by virtue of this paragraph an object or structure
ceases to be treated as part of a listed building—

   (a) liabilities incurred before the commencement of this paragraph by reason of the object or structure being so treated
   cease to have effect, and

   (b) a condition attached to a listed building consent ceases to
   have effect if, or to the extent that, it could not have been
   attached if this paragraph had been in force ;

except for the purposes of criminal proceedings begun before the
commencement of this paragraph.

Scope of exception for urgent works

2.—(1) In section 55 of the Town and Country Planning Act 1971
(control of works for demolition, alteration or extension of listed
buildings), for subsection (6) (exception for certain urgent works)
substitute—

" (6) In proceedings for an offence under this section it shall
be a defence to prove the following matters—

   (a) that works to the building were urgently necessary in
   the interests of safety or health or for the preservation
   of the building,

   (b) that it was not practicable to secure safety or health or,
   as the case may be, the preservation of the building by
   works of repair or works for affording temporary support or shelter,

   (c) that the works carried out were limited to the minimum
   measures immediately necessary, and

(*d*) that notice in writing justifying in detail the carrying out of the works was given to the local planning authority as soon as reasonably practicable.".

(2) In section 97 of the Town and Country Planning Act 1971 (appeal against listed building enforcement notice) in subsection (1) (grounds of appeal), for paragraph (*d*) substitute—

(*d*) that works to the building were urgently necessary in the interests of safety or health or for the preservation of the building, that it was not practicable to secure safety or health or, as the case may be, the preservation of the building by works of repair or works for affording temporary support or shelter, and that the works carried out were limited to the minimum measures immediately necessary ; ".

Grant of listed building consent subject to subsequent approval of detail

3.—(1) In section 56 of the Town and Country Planning Act 1971 (supplementary provisions with respect to listed building consent), after subsection (4A) insert—

" (4B) Listed building consent may be granted subject to a condtion reserving specified details of the works (whether or not set out in the application) for subsequent approval by the local planning authority or, in the case of consent granted by the Secretary of State, specifying whether the reserved details are to be approved by the local planning authority or by him. ".

(2) In paragraph 8(1) of Schedule 11 to the Town and Country Planning Act 1971 (listed building consent: appeal against decision), for the words from the beginning to " and the consent is refused " substitute—

"Where an application is made to the local planning authority—

 (*a*) for listed building consent, or

 (*b*) for approval of the authority required by a condition imposed on the granting of listed building consent with respect to details of the works,

and the consent or approval is refused ".

(3) Renumber paragraph 9 of Schedule 11 to the Town and Country Planning Act 1971 (appeal in default of decision) as sub-paragraph (1) of that paragraph and after it insert—

" (2) Sub-paragraph (1) of this paragraph applies to an application to the local planning authority for approval by the authority required by a condition imposed on the granting of listed building consent with respect to details of the works as it applies to an application for listed building consent, with the following modifications—

(a) for references to the prescribed period substitute references to the period of eight weeks from the date of the receipt of the application, and

(b) omit paragraph (b) and the word ' or ' preceding it.".

Application to modify or discharge conditions attached to listed building consent

4. After section 56A of the Town and Country Planning Act 1971 insert—

" Application for variation or discharge of conditions. 56B.—(1) Any person interested in a listed building with respect to which listed building consent has been granted subject to conditions may apply to the local planning authority for the variation or discharge of the conditions.

(2) The application shall indicate what variation or discharge of conditions is applied for and the provisions of Part I of Schedule 11 to this Act apply to such an application as they apply to an application for listed building consent.

(3) On such an application the local planning authority or, as the case may be, the Secretary of State may vary or discharge the conditions attached to the consent, and may add new conditions consequential upon the variation or discharge, as they or he thinks fit.".

Extent of exemption according to ecclesiastical buildings

5.—(1) After section 58A of the Town and Country Planning Act 1971 insert—

" Power to restrict exemption of certain ecclesiastical buildings. 58AA.—(1) The Secretary of State may by order provide for restricting or excluding in such cases as may be specified in the order the operation in relation to ecclesiastical buildings of section 56(1) and 58(2) of this Act (buildings excepted from provisions relating to listed buildings and building preservation notices).

(2) An order under this section may—

(a) make provision for buildings generally, for descriptions of building or for particular buildings ;

(b) make different provision for buildings in different areas, for buildings of different religious faiths or denominations or according to the use made of the building ;

(c) make such provision in relation to a part of a building (including, in particular, an object or structure falling to be treated as part of the building by virtue of section 54(9) of this Act) as may be made in relation to a building and make different provision for different parts of the same building ;

    (*d*) make different provision with respect to works   Sch. 9
of different descriptions or according to the
extent of the works ;

    (*e*) make such consequential adaptations or modifi-
cations of the operation of any other provision
of this Act, or of any instrument made under
this Act, as appear to the Secretary of State to
be appropriate.".

(2) In section 287 of the Town and Country Planning Act 1971 1971 c. 78.
(regulations and orders)—

    (*a*) in subsection (4) (orders to be made by statutory instru-
ment), after " 55(3) " insert " 58AA " ;

    (*b*) in subsection (5) (orders subject to negative resolution),
after "section " insert " 58AA " ;

    (*c*) in subsection (9) (power to include supplementary and in-
cidental provisions), after " section " insert " 58AA ".

Dangerous structure orders in respect of listed buildings

6.—(1) In the Town and Country Planning Act 1971, after the
section inserted by paragraph 4 above insert—

" Danger-   56C.—(1) Before taking any steps with a view to the
ous struc- making of a dangerous structure order in respect of a
ture orders listed building, a local planning authority shall consider
in respect whether they should instead exercise their powers under—
of listed
buildings.

    (*a*) section 101 of this Act (power to carry out urgent
works for preservation of building), or

    (*b*) sections 114 and 115 of this Act (power to acquire
building in need of repair).

    (2) In this section " dangerous structure order " means
an order or notice under section 77(1)(*a*) or 79(1) of the
Building Act 1984 or section 62(2), 65 or 69(1) of the
London Building Acts (Amendment) Act 1939.".

(2) In sections 77 and 79 of the Building Act 1984 and in sections 1984 c. 55.
62, 65 and 69 of the London Building Acts (Amendment) Act 1939 1939 c. xcv ii.
insert as the final subsection—

    " ( ) This section has effect subject to the provisions of the
Town and Country Planning Act 1971 relating to listed buildings, buildings subject to building preservation orders and buildings in conservation areas.".

Works for preservation of buildings

7. For section 101 of the Town and Country Planning Act 1971
(urgent works for preservation of unoccupied buildings) substitute—

" Urgent   101.—(1) Where it appears to the local authority or
works to the Secretary of State that works are urgently necessary
preserve for the preservation of—
building.

    (*a*) a listed building, or

(*b*) a building in respect of which a direction has been given by the Secretary of State that this section shall apply,

they or he may, subject to the following provisions of this section, execute the works, which may consist of or include works for affording temporary support or shelter for the building.

(2) The ground on which the Secretary of State may give a direction that this section shall apply to a building is that the building is in a conservation area and it appears to him that its preservation is important for maintaining the character or appearance of the conservation area.

(3) If the building is occupied works may be carried out only to those parts which are not in use; and no action may be taken in respect of an excepted building within the meaning of section 58(2) of this Act.

(4) The owner of the building shall be given not less than seven days' notice in writing of the intention to carry out the works and the notice shall describe the works proposed to be carried out.

(5) The Historic Buildings and Monuments Commission for England have the following functions under this section—

(*a*) as respects buildings in Greater London the Commission have concurrently with the relevant London borough council the functions of a local authority;

(*b*) the Secretary of State shall consult the Commission before giving a direction under subsection (1)(*b*) in respect of a building in England; and

(*c*) if it appears to the Secretary of State in accordance with subsection (1) that works are required for the preservation of a building in England, he shall not himself carry out the works but shall instead authorise the Commission to do so, specifying the works in the authorisation, and it shall be for the Commission to give notice to the owner under subsection (4).

Recovery of expenses of works under s. 101.

101A.—(1) This section has effect for enabling the expenses of works executed under section 101 of this Act to be recovered by the authority who carried out the works, that is, the local authority, the Historic Buildings and Monuments Commission for England or the Secretary of State or, in the case of works carried out by the Historic Buildings and Monuments Commission for England on behalf of the Secretary of State, by the Secretary of State.

(2) The authority or, as the case may be, the Secretary of State may give notice to the owner of the building requiring him to pay the expenses of the works.

(3) Where the works consist of or include works for affording temporary support or shelter for the building—

(*a*) the expenses which may be recovered include any continuing expenses involved in making available the apparatus or materials used, and

(*b*) notices under subsection (2) in respect of any such continuing expenses may be given from time to time.

(4) The owner may within 28 days of the service of the notice represent to the Secretary of State—

(*a*) that some or all of the works were unnecessary for the preservation of the building,

(*b*) in the case of works for affording temporary support or shelter, that the temporary arrangements have continued for an unreasonable length of time, or

(*c*) that the amount specified in the notice is unreasonable or that the recovery of it would cause him hardship,

and the Secretary of State shall determine to what extent the representations are justified.

(5) The Secretary of State shall give notice of his determination, the reasons for it and the amount recoverable—

(*a*) to the owner of the building, and

(*b*) to the local authority or the Historic Buildings and Monuments Commission for England, if they carried out the works.".

Control of demolition in conservation areas

8.—(1) Section 277A of the Town and Country Planning Act 1971 (control of demolition in conservation areas) is amended as follows.

1971 c. 78.

(2) For subsection (8) (application of provisions relating to listed buildings) substitute—

" (8) The following provisions of this Act have effect in relation to buildings to which this section applies as they have effect in relation to listed buildings, subject to such exceptions and modifications as may be prescribed by regulations—

sections 55 to 56C and 58AA and Parts I and II of Schedule 11 (requirement of consent to works: application for and revocation of consent),

sections 96 to 100 (enforcement),

section 172 (compensation where consent revoked or modified),

section 190 and Schedule 19 (purchase notice on refusal of consent),

sections 242, 243, 245 and 246 (validity of orders, proceedings for review and appeals),

section 255 (contributions by local authorities and statutory undertakers) ;

section 266(1)(*b*), (4) and (5) (application to Crown land), and

section 271 and Part VI of Schedule 21 (application of provisions to works by local planning authority).".

(3) In subsection (11) (authorities exercising functions of local planning authority), in paragraph (*c*) (non-metropolitan counties, excluding areas in National Parks) omit "the county planning authority and ".

Form of application for listed building consent

9. For paragraph 1(1) of Schedule 11 to the Town and Country Planning Act 1971 (regulations as to form and manner of application for listed building consent) substitute—

"(1) An application for listed building consent shall be made in such form as the local planning authority may require and shall contain—

(*a*) sufficient particulars to identify the building to which it relates, including a plan, and

(*b*) such other plans and drawings as are necessary to describe the works which are the subject of the application,

and such other particulars as may be required by the local planning authority.

(1A) Provision may be made by regulations under this Act with respect to the manner in which applications for listed building consent are to be made, the manner in which such applications are to be advertised and the time within which they are to be dealt with by local planning authorities or, as the case may be, by the Secretary of State.".

Listed building consent : consideration whether to call in application

10.—(1) In paragraph 5(2) of Schedule 11 to the Town and Country Planning Act 1971 (notice to local planning authority that Secretary of State requires further time to consider whether to call in an application for listed building consent), for the words from " and sub-paragraph (1) " to the end substitute " ; and if he gives such a notice the authority shall not grant the listed building consent until he has notified them that he does not intend to require the reference of the application.".

(2) In paragraph 6(4) of Schedule 11 to the Town and Country Planning Act 1971 (notice to Historic Buildings and Monuments Commission that Secretary of State requires further time to consider whether to call in an application for listed building consent), for the words from " and sub-paragraph (3) " to the end substitute " ; and if he gives such a notice the Commission shall not authorise the local planning authority as mentioned in sub-paragraph (2)(a) of this paragraph, nor under sub-paragraph (2)(b) of this paragraph direct them to grant listed building consent, until he has notified them that he does not intend to require the reference of the application.".

(3) In paragraph 6(6) of Schedule 11 to the Town and Country Planning Act 1971 (notice to local planning authority that Secretary of State requires further time to consider whether to call in application for listed building consent which the Historic Buildings and Monuments Commission have directed the authority to refuse), for the words from " and sub-paragraph (5)(a) " to the end substitute " ; and if he gives such a notice the authority shall not give effect to the Commission's direction until he has notified them that he does not intend to require the reference of the application.".

Listed building consent: directions as to which applications need not be notified to the Secretary of State

11.—(1) Paragraph 7 of Schedule 11 to the Town and Country Planning Act 1971 (directions as to which applications need not be notified to Secretary of State) is amended as follows.

(2) In paragraph 7(1) (power to direct that certain descriptions of application need not be notified) omit, " other than such consent for the demolition of a building " and after that sub-paragraph insert—

" (1A) Before giving a direction under sub-paragraph (1) of this paragraph in respect of any description of application for consent to the demolition of a building in England, the Secretary of State shall consult the Historic Buildings and Monuments Commission for England.".

(3) For paragraph 7(1A) and (1B) (power to except applications from direction under sub-paragraph (1)) substitute—

" (1B) Where a direction is in force under sub-paragraph (1) of this paragraph, the Secretary of State may give to a local planning authority a direction that paragraph 5 or (as the case may be) paragraph 6 of this Schedule shall nevertheless apply—

(a) to a particular application for listed building consent, or

(b) to such descriptions of application for listed building consent as are specified in the direction ;

and such a direction has effect in relation to any such application which has not been disposed of by the authority by their granting or refusing consent.".

(4) At the end of the paragraph add—

" (3) Directions under sub-paragraph (1) or (2) of this paragraph may be given to authorities generally or to particular authorities or descriptions of authority.".

*Application to local planning authorities of provisions
relating to listed buildings*

12. In Part VI of Schedule 21 to the Town and Country Planning Act 1971 (provisions of Act applying to applications by local planning authorities with respect to listed buildings), at the appropriate place insert " Sections 242, 243, 245 and 246.".

PART II

SCOTLAND

Free-standing objects and structures within curtilage of listed building

13.—(1) In section 52(7) of the Town and Country Planning (Scotland) Act 1972 (definition of " listed building "), for the words from " and for the purposes " to the end substitute—

" and, for the purposes of the provisions of this Act relating to listed buildings and building preservation notices, the following shall be treated as part of the building—

(a) any object or structure fixed to the building ;

(b) any object or structure within the curtilage of the building which, although not fixed to the building, forms part of the land and has done so much before 1st July 1948.".

(2) Where by virtue of this paragraph an object or structure ceases to be treated as part of a listed building—

(a) liabilities incurred before the commencement of this paragraph by reason of the object or structure being so treated cease to have effect, and

(b) a condition attached to listed building consent ceases to have effect if, or to the extent that, it could not have been attached if this paragraph had been in force ;

except for the purposes of criminal proceedings begun before the commencement of this paragraph.

Late application for listed building consent

14.—(1) In subsection (1) of section 53 (control of works for demolition, alteration or extension of listed buildings) of the Town and Country Planning (Scotland) Act 1972, for the words " this Part of this Act " where they appear for the second time, substitute " subsection (2) of this section ".

(2) After subsection (2) of the said section 53 insert—

" (2A) If written consent is granted by the planning authority or the Secretary of State for the retention of works for the demolition, alteration or extension of a listed building which have been executed without consent under subsection (2) of this section, the works are authorised under this Part of this Act from the grant of the consent under this subsection."

(3) After subsection (3) of the said section insert—

" (3A) Consent under subsection (2) or (2A) of this section is referred to in this Part of this Act as " listed building consent ".".

(4) At the end of section 54A (limit on duration of listed building consent) of the Town and Country Planning (Scotland) Act 1972 there 1972 c. 52. shall be added—

" (5) Nothing in this section applies to any consent to the retention of works granted under section 53(2A) of this Act.".

Defence to proceedings under section 53

15.—(1) In section 53 of the Town and Country Planning (Scotland) Act 1972 (control of works for demolition, alteration or extension of listed buildings), for subsection (6) (exception for certain urgent works) substitute—

" (6) In proceedings for an offence under this section it shall be a defence to prove the following matters—

(*a*) that works to the building were urgently necessary in the interests of safety or health or for the preservation of the building ;

(*b*) that it was not practicable to secure safety or health or, as the case may be, the preservation of the building by works of repair or works for affording temporary support or shelter ;

(*c*) that the works carried out were limited to the minimum measures immediately necessary, and

(*d*) that notice in writing justifying in detail the carrying out of the works was given to the planning authority as soon as reasonably practicable.".

(2) In section 93 of the Town and Country Planning (Scotland) Act 1972 (appeal against listed building enforcement notice), in subsection (1) (grounds of appeal), for paragraph (*c*) substitute—

(*c*) that works to the building were urgently necessary in the interests of safety or health or for the preservation of the building, that it was not practicable to secure safety or health or, as the case may be, the preservation of the building by works of repair or works for affording temporary support or shelter, and that the works carried out were limited to the minimum measures immediately necessary ; ".

Grant of listed building consent subject to subsequent approval of detail

16.—(1) In section 54 of the Town and Country Planning (Scotland Act 1972 (supplementary provisions with respect to listed building consent), after subsection (4) insert—

" (4A) Listed building consent may be granted subject to a condition reserving specified details of the works (whether or not set out in the application) for subsequent approval by the planning authority or, in the case of consent granted by the Secretary of State, specifying whether the reserved details are to be approved by the planning authority or by him.".

(2) In paragraph 7(1) of the said Schedule 10 to the 1972 Act (listed building consent: appeal against decision), for the words from the beginning to " and the consent is refused " substitute—

" Where an application is made to the planning authority—

(a) for listed building consent, or

(b) for approval of the authority required by a condition imposed on the granting of listed building consent with respect to details of the works,

and the consent or approval is refused ".

(3) Renumber paragraph 8 of that Schedule (appeal in default of decision) as sub-paragraph (1) of that paragraph and after it insert—

" (2) Sub-paragraph (1) of this paragraph applies to an application to the planning authority for approval by the authority required by a condition imposed on the granting of listed building consent with respect to details of the works as it applies to an application for listed building consent, with the following modifications—

(a) for references to the prescribed period substitute references to the period of two months from the date of the receipt of the application, and

(b) omit paragraph (b) and the word ' or ' preceding it.".

Application to modify or discharge conditions attached to listed building consent

17. After section 54C of the Town and Country Planning (Scotland) Act 1972 insert—

"Application, for variation or discharge of conditions. 54D.—(1) Any person interested in a listed building with respect to which listed building consent has been granted subject to conditions may apply to the planning authority for the variation or discharge of the conditions.

(2) The application shall indicate what variation or discharge of conditions is applied for and the provisions of Part I of Schedule 10 to this Act apply to such an application as they apply to an application for listed building consent.

(3) On such an application the planning authority or, as the case may be, the Secretary of State may vary or discharge the conditions attached to the consent, and may add new conditions consequential upon the variation or discharge, as they or he think fit.".

Extent of exemption accorded to ecclesiastical buildings   Sch. 9

18.—(1) After section 56 of the Town and Country Planning (Scot- 1972 c. 52. land Act 1972 insert—

" Power to restrict exemption of certain ecclesiastical buildings.   56AA.—(1) The Secretary of State may by order provide for restricting or excluding in such cases as may be specified in the order the operation in relation to ecclesiastical buildings of sections 54(1) and 56(2) of this Act (buildings excepted from provisions relating to listed buildings and building preservation notices).

(2) An order under this section may—

(a) make provision for buildings generally, for descriptions of building or for particular buildings ;

(b) make different provision for buildings in different areas, for buildings of different religious faiths or denominations or according to the use made of the building ;

(c) make such provision in relation to a part of a building (including, in particular, an object or structure falling to be treated as part of the building by virtue of section 52(7) of this Act) as may be made in relation to a building and make different provision for different parts of the same building ;

(d) make different provision with respect to works of different descriptions or according to the extent of the works ;

(e) make such consequential adaptations or modifications of the operation of any other provision of this Act, or of any instrument made under this Act, as appear to the Secretary of State to be appropriate.

(3) This section is without prejudice to the Church of 1921 c. 29. Scotland Act 1921.".

(2) In section 273 (regulations and orders) of the Town and Country Planning (Scotland) Act 1972—

(a) in subsection (4) (orders to be made by statutory instrument), after " 53(3) " insert " 56AA " ;

(b) in subsection (5) (orders subject to negative resolution), after " 1(3) " insert " 56AA " ;

(c) in subsection (9) (power to include supplementary and incidental provision), after " section " insert " 56AA ".

Effect of listed building enforcement notice

19. After section 95 of the Town and Country Planning (Scotland) Act 1972 insert—

" Effect of listed building consent on listed building enforcement notice.   95A.—(1) If, after the issue of a listed building enforcement notice, consent is granted under section 53(2A) of this Act for the retention of any work to which the listed building enforcement notice relates, the notice shall cease to have effect in so far as it requires steps to be taken which would involve the works not being retained in accordance with the consent.

(2) If the consent is granted so as to permit the retention of works without complying with some condition subject to which a previous listed building consent was granted, the listed building enforcement notice shall cease to have effect in so far as it requires steps to be taken for complying with that condition.

(3) The preceding provisions of this section shall be without prejudice to the liability of any person for an offence in respect of a failure to comply with the listed building enforcement notice before the relevant provisions of that notice ceased to have effect.".

Works for preservation of buildings

1972 c. 52.   20. For section 97 of the Town and Country Planning (Scotland) Act 1972 (urgent works for preservation of unoccupied buildings) substitute—

"Urgent works to preserve building.   97.—(1) Where it appears to the planning authority or the Secretary of State that works are urgently necessary for the preservation of—

    (*a*) a listed building, or

    (*b*) a building in respect of which a direction has been given by the Secretary of State that this section shall apply,

they or he may, subject to the following provisions of this section, execute the works, which may consist of or include works for affording temporary support or shelter for the building.

(2) The ground on which the Secretary of State may give a direction that this section shall apply to a building is that the building is in a conservation area and it appears to him that its preservation is important for maintaining the character or appearance of the conservation area.

(3) If the building is occupied works may be carried out only to those parts which are not in use ; and no action may be taken in respect of an excepted building within the meaning of section 56(2) of this Act.

(4) The owner of the building shall be given not less than 7 days' notice in writing of the intention to carry out the works and the notice shall describe the works proposed to be carried out.

Recovery of expenses of works under s. 97.   97A.—(1) This section has effect for enabling the expenses of works executed under section 97 of this Act to be recovered.

(2) The planning authority or, as the case may be, the Secretary of State may give notice to the owner of the building requiring him to pay the expenses of the works.

(3) Where the works consist of or include works for affording temporary support or shelter for the building—

    (*a*) the expenses which may be recovered include any continuing expenses involved in making available the apparatus or materials used, and

    (*b*) notices under subsection (2) in respect of any such continuing expenses may be given from time to time.

(4) The owner may within 28 days of the service of the notice represent to the Secretary of State—

    (*a*) that some or all of the works were unnecessary for the preservation of the building,

    (*b*) in the case of works for affording temporary support or shelter, that the temporary arrangements have continued for an unreasonable length of time, or

    (*c*) that the amount specified in the notice is unreasonable or that the recovery of it would cause him hardship,

and the Secretary of State shall determine to what extent the representations are justified.

(5) The Secretary of State shall give notice of his determination, the reasons for it and the amount recoverable—

    (*a*) to the owner of the building, and

    (*b*) to the planning authority, if they carried out the works.".

SCH. 9

Control of demolition in conservation areas

21. Section 262A(8) of the Town and Country Planning (Scotland) Act 1972 (application to buildings in conservation areas of provisions relating to listed buildings) is amended as follows— 1972 c. 52.

    (*a*) for the words from " section 53 " to " section 54C " substitute " sections 53 to 54D and 56AA " ;

    (*b*) for " sections 92 to 95 " substitute " sections 92 to 96 " ;

    (*c*) after " section 179 " insert " sections 231 and 233, section 242 " ;

    (*d*) after " section 253(1)(*b*) " insert " , (4) and (5), section 257 ";

    (*e*) after " Schedule 17 " insert " Part IV of Schedule 19 ".

Form of application for listed building consent

22. For paragraph 1(1) of Schedule 10 of the Town and Country Planning (Scotland) Act 1972 (regulations as to form and manner of application for listed building consent) substitute—

    " (1) An application for listed building consent shall be made

SCH. 9

in such form as the planning authority may require and shall contain—

> (a) sufficient particulars to identify the building to which it relates, including a plan, and
>
> (b) such other plans and drawings as are necessary to describe the works which are the subject of the application.

and such other particulars as may be required by the planning authority.

(1A) Provision may be made by regulations under this Act with respect to the manner in which applications for listed building consent are to be made, the manner in which such applications are to be advertised and the time within which they are to be dealt with by planning authorities or, as the case may be, by the Secretary of State.".

Calling in of application for listed building consent

1972 c. 52.

23. In paragraph 5(2) of Schedule 10 to the Town and Country Planning (Scotland) Act 1972 (notice to planning authority that Secretary of State requires further time to consider whether to call in application for listed building consent), for the words from " and sub-paragraph (1) " to the end substitute " ; and if he gives such a notice the authority shall not grant the listed building consent until he has notified them that he does not intend to require the reference of the application.".

Application to planning authorities of provisions relating to listed buildings

24. In Part IV of Schedule 19 to the Town and Country Planning (Scotland) Act 1972 (provisions of Act applying to applications by planning authorities with respect to listed buildings), at the appropriate place insert " Sections 231 and 233 ".

Section 41(1) and (3).

SCHEDULE 10

LOCAL PLANS AND UNITARY DEVELOPMENT PLANS

PART I

SECTIONS 11 TO 15B OF TOWN AND COUNTRY PLANNING ACT 1971 (c.78), AS SUBSTITUTED

ARRANGEMENT OF SECTIONS

Local Plans

11.   Local plans.

11A.   Local plan schemes.

11B.   Power of Secretary of State to direct making of local plan,   Sch. 10
          &c.

12.   Publicity and consultation: general.

12A.   Publicity and consultation: short procedure for certain alterations, &c.

12B.   Powers of Secretary of State to secure adequate publicity and consultation.

13.   Objections: local inquiry or other hearing.

14.   Adoption of proposals.

14A.   Calling in of proposals for approval by Secretary of State.

14B.   Approval of proposals by Secretary of State.

15.   Conformity between plans: certificate of conformity.

15A.   Conformity between plans: alteration of structure plan.

15B.   Conformity between plans: local plan prevails.

*   *   *   *   *

Local plans

11.—(1) A local plan shall consist of—   Local plans.

(a) a written statement formulating in such detail as the local planning authority think appropriate their proposals for the development or other use of land in their area, or for any description of development or other use of such land, including such measures as the authority think fit for the improvement of the physical environment and the management of traffic ;

(b) a map showing those proposals ; and

(c) such diagrams, illustrations or other descriptive matter as the authority think appropriate to explain or illustrate the proposals in the plan, or as may be prescribed.

(2) Different local plans may be prepared for different purposes for the same area.

(3) In formulating their proposals in a local plan the local planning authority shall have regard to any information and any other considerations which appear to them to be relevant or which may be prescribed or which the Secretary of State may in any particular case direct them to take into account.

(4) The proposals in a local plan shall be in general conformity with the structure plan.

(5) A local planning authority may prepare a local plan for a part of their area (an " action area ") which they have selected for the commencement during a prescribed period of comprehensive treatment, by development, redevelopment or improvement of the whole or part of the area selected, or partly by one method and partly by another ; and a local plan prepared for such an action area shall indicate the nature of the treatment selected for the area.

SCH. 10

(6) For the purpose of discharging their functions with respect to local plans a district planning authority may, in so far as it appears to them necessary to do so having regard to the survey made by the county planning authority under section 6 of this Act, examine the matters mentioned in subsections (1) and (3) of that section so far as relevant to their area.

(7) In preparing a local plan a local planning authority shall take into account the provisions of any scheme under paragraph 3 of Schedule 32 to the Local Government, Planning and Land Act 1980 relating to land in their area which has been designated under that Schedule as an enterprise zone.

Local plan schemes.

11A.—(1) A local plan scheme for each county shall be maintained in accordance with this section setting out a programme for the making, alteration, repeal or replacement of local plans for areas in the county, except any part of the county included in a National Park.

(2) The scheme shall, as regards each local plan for which it provides—

    (*a*) specify the title and nature of the plan and the area to which it is to apply and give an indication of its scope,

    (*b*) indicate where appropriate its relationship with the other local plans provided for by the scheme, and

    (*c*) designate the local planning authority, whether county or district, responsible for the plan ;

and may contain any appropriate incidental, consequential, transitional and supplementary provisions.

(3) The district planning authorities shall keep under review the need for, and adequacy of, local plans for their area and may make recommendations to the county planning authority for incorporation into the local plan scheme.

(4) The county planning authority shall, in the light of the recommendations of the district planning authorities and in consultation with those authorities, make and thereafter keep under review and from time to time amend the local plan scheme.

(5) As soon as practicable after making or amending a local plan scheme the county planning authority shall send a copy of the scheme, or the scheme as amended, to the Secretary of State.

(6) If a district planning authority make representations to the Secretary of State that they are dissatisfied with a local plan scheme, the Secretary of State may amend the scheme.

(7) A local planning authority may prepare proposals for the making, alteration, repeal or replacement of a local plan—

    (*a*) in any case, except in the case of proposals relating only to land in a National Park, only where authorised to do so by the local plan scheme, and

    (*b*) in the case of proposals for the alteration, repeal or replacement of a local plan approved by the Secretary of

State, only with the consent of the Secretary of State ; but subject to any direction of the Secretary of State under section 11B.

11B.—(1) The Secretary of State may, after consulting a local planning authority, direct them to make, alter, repeal or replace a local plan with respect to their area or part of it.

Power of Secretary of State to direct making of local plan, &c.

(2) A direction for the making, alteration or replacement of a local plan shall specify the nature of the plan or, as the case may be, the nature of the alteration required.

(3) The authority shall comply with the direction as soon as possible.

(4) The county planning authority shall make such amendments of the relevant local plan scheme as appear to them appropriate in consequence of the direction.

12.—(1) A local planning authority who propose to make, alter, repeal or replace a local plan shall proceed in accordance with this section, unless section 12A applies (short procedure for certain alterations, &c.).

Publicity and consultation: general.

(2) They shall take such steps as will in their opinion secure—

(a) that adequate publicity is given to the proposals in the area to which the plan relates,

(b) that persons who may be expected to wish to make representations about the proposals are made aware that they are entitled to do so, and

(c) that such persons are given an adequate opportunity of making such representations ;

and they shall consider any representations made to them within the prescribed period.

(3) They shall consult the county planning authority or, as the case may be, the district planning authority with respect to their proposals, shall afford that authority a reasonable opportunity to express their views and shall take those views into consideration.

(4) They shall then, having prepared the relevant documents, that is, the proposed plan, alterations, instrument of repeal or replacement plan, as the case may be, and having obtained any certificate required by section 15 (certificate of conformity with structure plan)—

(a) make copies of the documents available for inspection at their office,

(b) send a copy of them to the Secretary of State, and

(c) send a copy of them to the district or county planning authority, as the case may require.

(5) Each copy of the documents made available for inspection shall be accompanied by a statement of the time within which objections may be made.

SCH. 10

Publicity and
consultation:
short procedure
for certain
alterations, &c.

12A.—(1) Where a local planning authority propose to alter, repeal or replace a local plan and it appears to them that the issues involved are not of sufficient importance to warrant the full procedure set out in section 12, they may proceed instead in accordance with this section.

(2) They shall prepare the relevant documents, that is, the proposed alterations, instrument of repeal or replacement plan, as the case may be, and, having obtained any certificate required by section 15 (certificate of conformity with structure plan) shall—

(*a*) make copies of the documents available for inspection at their office,

(*b*) send a copy of them to the Secretary of State, and

(*c*) send a copy of them to the county or district planning authority, as the case may require.

(3) Each copy of the documents made available for inspection shall be accompanied by a statement of the time within which representation or objections may be made.

(4) They shall then take such steps as may be prescribed for the purpose of—

(*a*) advertising the fact that the documents are available for inspection and the places and times at which, and period during which, they may be inspected, and

(*b*) inviting the making of representations or objections in accordance with regulations ;

and they shall consider any representations made to them within the prescribed period.

Powers of
Secretary of
State to secure
adequate
publicity and
consultation.

12B.—(1) The documents sent by the local planning authority to the Secretary of State under section 12 shall be accompanied by a statement—

(*a*) of the steps which the authority have taken to comply with subsection (2) of that section, and

(*b*) of the authority's consultations with other persons and their consideration of the views of those persons.

(2) The documents sent by the local planning authority to the Secretary of State under section 12A shall be accompanied by a statement of the steps which the authority are taking to comply with subsection (4) of that section.

(3) If, on considering the statement and the proposals and any other information provided by the local planning authority, the Secretary of State is not satisfied with the steps taken by the authority, he may, within 21 days of the receipt of the statement, direct the authority not to take further steps for the adoption of the proposals without—

(*a*) if they have proceeded in accordance with section 12A, proceeding instead in accordance with section 12, or

(*b*) in any case, taking such further steps as he may specify,

and satisfying him that they have done so.

(4) A local planning authority who are given directions by the Secretary of State shall—

Sch. 10

> (*a*) forthwith withdraw the copies of the documents made available for inspection as required by section 12(4) or 12A(2). and
>
> (*b*) notify any person by whom objections to the proposals have been made to the authority that the Secretary of State has given such directions.

13.—(1) The local planning authority may cause a local inquiry or other hearing to be held for the purpose of considering objections to their proposals for the making, alteration, repeal or replacement of a local plan.

Objections
local inquiry or
other hearing.

(2) They shall hold such a local inquiry or other hearing in the case of objections made in accordance with regulations unless all the persons who have made such objections have indicated in writing that they do not wish to appear.

(3) A local inquiry or other hearing shall be held by a person appointed by the Secretary of State or, in such cases as may be prescribed, by the authority themselves.

(4) Regulations may—

> (*a*) make provision with respect to the appointment, and qualifications for appointment, of persons to hold a local inquiry or other hearing ;
>
> (*b*) include provision enabling the Secretary of State to direct a local planning authority to appoint a particular person, or one of a specified list or class of persons ;
>
> (*c*) make provision with respect to the remuneration and allowances of the person appointed.

(5) Subsections (2) and (3) of section 250 of the Local Government Act 1972 (power to summon and examine witnesses) apply to an inquiry held under this section.

1972 c. 70.

(6) The Tribunals and Inquiries Act 1971 applies to a local inquiry or other hearing under this section as it applies to a statutory inquiry held by the Secretary of State, with the substitution in section 12(1) (statement of reasons for decision) for the references to a decision taken by the Secretary of State of references to a decision taken by a local authority.

1971 c. 62.

14.—(1) After the expiry of the period afforded for making objections to proposals for the making, alteration, repeal or replacement of a local plan or, if such objections were duly made within that period, after considering the objections so made, the local planning authority may, subject to the following provisions of this section and to section 14A (calling in of proposals by Secretary of State), by resolution adopt the proposals.

Adoption of
proposals.

(2) They may adopt the proposals as originally prepared or as modified so as to take account of—

> (*a*) any such objections as are mentioned in subsection (1) or any other objections to the proposals, or

U 2

(*b*) any other considerations which appear to the authority to be material.

(3) The authority shall not adopt any proposals which do not conform generally to the structure plan.

(4) After copies of the proposals have been sent to the Secretary of State and before they have been adopted by the local planning authority, the Secretary of State may, if it appears to him that the proposals are unsatisfactory, direct the authority to consider modifying the proposals in such respects as are indicated in the direction.

(5) An authority to whom a direction is given shall not adopt the proposals unless they satisfy the Secretary of State that they have made the modifications necessary to conform with the direction or the direction is withdrawn.

(6) Where an objection to the proposals has been made by the Minister of Agriculture, Fisheries and Food and the local planning authority do not propose to modify their proposals to take account of the objection—

(*a*) the authority shall send particulars of the objection to the Secretary of State, together with a statement of their reasons for not modifying their proposals to take account of it, and

(*b*) they shall not adopt the proposals unless the Secretary of State authorises them to do so.

Calling in of proposals for approval by Secretary of State.

14A.—(1) After copies of proposals have been sent to the Secretary of State and before they have been adopted by the local planning authority, the Secretary of State may direct that the proposals shall be submitted to him for his approval.

(2) In that event—

(*a*) the authority shall not take any further steps for the adoption of the proposals, and in particular shall not hold or proceed with a local inquiry or other hearing in respect of the proposals under section 13 ; and

(*b*) the proposals shall not have effect unless approved by the Secretary of State and shall not require adoption by the authority.

(3) Where particulars of an objection made by the Minister of Agriculture, Fisheries and Food have been sent to the Secretary of State under section 14(6), then, unless the Secretary of State is satisfied that that Minister no longer objects to the proposals, he shall give a direction in respect of the proposals under this section.

Approval of proposals by Secretary of State.

14B.—(1) The Secretary of State may after considering proposals submitted to him under section 14A either approve them, in whole or in part and with or without modifications or reservations, or reject them.

(2) In considering the proposals he may take into account any matters he thinks are relevant, whether or not they were taken into account in the proposals as submitted to him.

(3) Where on taking the proposals into consideration the Secretary of State does not determine then to reject them, he shall, before determining whether or not to approve them—

    (*a*) consider any objections to them made in accordance with regulations,

    (*b*) afford to any person who made such an objection which has not been withdrawn an opportunity of appearing before and being heard by a person appointed by him for the purpose, and

    (*c*) if a local inquiry or other hearing is held, also afford such an opportunity to the authority and such other persons as he thinks fit,

except so far as the objections have already been considered, or a local inquiry or other hearing into the objections has already been held, by the authority.

(4) In considering the proposals the Secretary of State may consult with, or consider the views of, any local planning authority or any other person ; but he is under no obligation to do so, or to afford an opportunity for the making of representations or objections, or to cause a local inquiry or other hearing to be held, except as provided by subsection (3).

15.—(1) A district planning authority who have prepared proposals for the making, alteration, repeal or replacement of a local plan shall not take the steps mentioned in section 12(4) or 12A(2) (deposit of documents for inspection, &c.) unless a certificate that the proposals conform generally to the structure plan has been issued in accordance with this section.

(2) The district planning authority shall request the county planning authority to certify that their proposals so conform and that authority shall, within a month of receiving the request, or such longer period as may be agreed between the authorities, consider the matter and, if satisfied that the proposals do so conform, issue a certificate to that effect.

(3) If it appears to the county planning authority that the proposals do not so conform in any respect, they shall, during or as soon as possible after the end of that period, refer the question whether they so conform in that respect to the Secretary of State to be determined by him.

(4) The Secretary of State may in any case by direction to a county planning authority reserve for his own determination the question whether proposals for the making, alteration, repeal or replacement of a local plan conform generally to the structure plan.

(5) On determining a question so referred to or reserved for him, the Secretary of State—

    (*a*) if he is of opinion that the proposals do so conform, may issue, or direct the county planning authority to issue, a certificate to that effect, and

    (*b*) if he is of the contrary opinion, may direct the district planning authority to revise their proposals in such respects as he thinks appropriate so that they will so conform.

15A.—(1) Where proposals for the alteration or replacement of a structure plan have been prepared and submitted to the Secretary of State, he may, on the application of a local planning authority proposing to make, alter, repeal or replace a local plan, direct that it shall be assumed for that purpose that the structure plan proposals have been approved by him, subject to such modifications as may from time to time be proposed by him and notified to the county planning authority.

(2) A direction ceases to have effect if the Secretary of State rejects the proposals for the alteration or replacement of the structure plan.

(3) Before giving a direction the Secretary of State shall consult—

    (*a*) in the case of an application by a county planning authority, any district planning authority whose area is affected by the relevant local plan proposals ;

    (*b*) in the case of an application by a district planning authority, the county planning authority.

(4) A county planning authority shall, on the approval of proposals for the alteration or replacement of a structure plan, consider whether the local plans for areas affected conform generally to the structure plan as altered or to the new plan, as the case may be.

(5) Within the period of one month from the date on which they receive notice of the Secretary of State's approval of the proposals, the county planning authority shall send—

    (*a*) to the Secretary of State, and

    (*b*) to every district planning authority responsible for such a local plan,

lists of the local plans so affected which, in their opinion, do and do not so conform.

15B.—(1) Where there is a conflict between any of the provisions of a local plan in force for an area and the provisions of the relevant structure plan, the provisions of the local plan shall be taken to prevail for all purposes.

(2) Where the structure plan is altered or replaced and the local plan is specified in a list under section 15A(5) as a plan which does not conform to the structure plan as altered or replaced, subsection (1) above does not apply until a proposal for the alteration of the local plan, or for its repeal and replacement, has been adopted or approved by the Secretary of State and the alteration, or replacement plan, has come into force.

PART II

UNITARY DEVELOPMENT PLANS

1. Part I of Schedule 1 to the Local Government Act 1985 (unitary development plans) is amended as follows.

2. After paragraph 6 insert—

    " *Direction to reconsider proposals*

      6A.—(1) After a copy of a unitary development plan has been sent to the Secretary of State and before it is adopted

by the local planning authority, the Secretary of State
may, if it appears to him that the plan is unsatisfactory,
direct the authority to consider modifying the proposals
in such respects as are indicated in the direction.

(2) An authority to whom a direction is given shall not
adopt the plan unless they satisfy the Secretary of State
that they have made the modifications necessary to conform with the direction or the direction is withdrawn.".

3. In paragraph 10(2) (provisions applicable to making of unitary
development plan also apply to alteration or replacement of plan), at
the beginning insert " Subject to paragraph 10A below,".

4. After paragraph 10 insert—

" *Short procedure for certain alterations*

10A.—(1) Where a local planning authority propose to
alter or replace a unitary development plan and it appears
to them that the issues involved are not of sufficient importance to warrant the full procedure set out in paragraph 3(1) and (2), they may instead proceed as follows.

(2) They shall prepare the relevant documents, that is,
the proposed alterations or replacement plan, and shall
make a copy of them available for inspection at their
office and at such other places as may be prescribed and
send a copy to the Secretary of State.

(3) Each copy of the documents made available for
inspection shall be accompanied by a statement of the
time within which representations or objections may be
made.

(4) They shall then take such steps as may be prescribed for the purpose of—

    (*a*) advertising the fact that the documents are avail-
    able for inspection, and the places and times
    at which and period during which they may be
    inspected, and

    (*b*) inviting the making of representations or objec-
    tions in accordance with regulations ;

and they shall consider any representations made to them
within the prescribed period.

(5) The documents sent by the local planning authority
to the Secretary of State under sub-paragraph (2) above
shall be accompanied by a statement of the steps which
the authority are taking to comply with sub-paragraph
(4) above.

(6) If, on considering the statement submitted with
and the matters contained in the documents sent to him
under sub-paragraph (2) above and any other information
provided by the local planning authority, the Secretary
of State is not satisfied with the steps taken by the

U 4

SCH. 10 authority he may, within twenty-one days of the receipt of the statement, direct the authority not to take further steps for the adoption of their proposals without—

(a) proceeding in accordance with paragraph 3(1) and (2) above, or

(b) taking such further action as he may specify,

and satisfying him that they have done so.

(7) A local planning authority who are given directions by the Secretary of State under sub-paragraph (6) above shall—

(a) forthwith withdraw the copies of documents made available for inspection as required by sub-paragraph (2) above ; and

(b) notify any person by whom objections to the proposals have been made to the authority that the Secretary of State has given such directions as aforesaid.

(8) Where a local planning authority proceed in accordance with this paragraph, the references in paragraphs 4(2)(a) and (4) and 7(1) to copies made available or sent to the Secretary of State under paragraph 3(2) shall be construed as references to copies made available or sent to the Secretary of State under sub-paragraph (2) of this paragraph.".

Sections 49 and 53.

SCHEDULE 11

PLANNING: MINOR AND CONSEQUENTIAL AMENDMENDS

PART I

ENGLAND AND WALES

Operation of Use Classes Order on subdivision of planning unit

1971 c. 78. 1. In section 22(2) of the Town and Country Planning Act 1971 (operations and changes of use not amounting to development), in paragraph (f) (use of same prescribed class as existing use) for " the use thereof " substitute " the use of the buildings or other land or, subject to the provisions of the order, of any part thereof ".

Development orders

2.—(1) In section 24 of the Town and Country Planning Act 1971 (development orders), for subsection (3) (general and special orders) substitute—

" (3) A development order may be made either—

(a) as a general order applicable, except so far as the order otherwise provides, to all land, but which may make different provision with respect to different descriptions of land, or

(b) as a special order applicable only to such land or descriptions of land as may be specified in the order.".

(2) In paragraph 17 of Schedule 16 to the Local Government   Sch. 11
Act 1972 (inclusion of provision in development orders empowering 1972 c. 70.
local highway authority to impose restrictions on grant of planning
permission in certain cases) for " shall include in a development
order under section 24 provision " substitute " may include in a
development order under section 24 such provision as he thinks fit ".

Disabled persons : *construction of references to certain documents*

3.—(1) In section 29A of the Town and Country Planning Act 1971 c. 78.
1971 (duty to draw attention to certain provisions for the benefit of
the disabled: public buildings and places of work), in subsection (1)
for paragraph (ii) substitute—

" (ii) the Code of Practice for Access of the Disabled to Buildings (British Standards Institution code of practice BS 5810:
1979) or any prescribed document replacing that code.".

(2) In section 29B of the Town and Country Planning Act 1971
(duty to draw attention to certain provisions for the benefit of the
disabled: educational buildings), in subsection (1) for paragraph (ii)
substitute—

" (ii) to Design Note 18 ' Access for Disabled People to Educational Buildings ' published in 1984 on behalf of the Secretary
of State, or any prescribed document replacing that Note.".

Applications to vary or revoke conditions attached to planning
permission

4. After section 31 of the Town and Country Planning Act 1971
insert—

" Permission   31A.—(1) This section applies to applications for plan-
to develop   ning permission for the development of land without
land without complying with conditions subject to which a previous
compliance   planning permission was granted.
with
conditions
previously   (2) Special provision may be made with respect to such
attached.   applications—

> (*a*) by regulations under section 25 of this Act as
> regards the form and content of the application,
> and
>
> (*b*) by a development order as regards the procedure
> to be followed in connection with the application.

(3) On such an application the local planning authority
shall consider only the question of the conditions subject
to which planning permission should be granted, and—

> (*a*) if they decide that planning permission should
> be granted subject to conditions differing from
> those subject to which the previous permission
> was granted, or that it should be granted uncon-
> ditionally, they shall grant planning permission
> accordingly, and

(*b*) if they decide that planning permission should be granted subject to the same conditions as those subject to which the previous permission was granted, they shall refuse the application.

(4) This section does not apply where the application is made after the previous planning permission has become time-expired, that is to say, the previous permission having been granted subject to a condition as to the time within which the development to which it related was to be begun, that time has expired without the development having been begun.".

Purchase notices : transmission of documents to Secretary of State

1971 c. 78.   5.—(1) In section 181 of the Town and Country Planning Act 1971 (action by council on whom purchase notice is served)—

(*a*) in subsection (1)(c) (notice of unwillingness to comply with purchase notice: contents of notice) for the words from "and that they have transmitted" to the end substitute " and that they have transmitted to the Secretary of State a copy of the purchase notice and of the notice under this subsection " ;

(*b*) in subsection (3) (duty of council to transmit documents to Secretary of State) for the words from " they shall transmit " to the end substitute " then, before they take steps to serve that notice, they shall transmit to the Secretary of State a copy of the purchase notice together with a copy of the notice which they propose to serve ".

(2) In paragraph 1 of Schedule 19 to the Town and Country Planning Act 1971 (action by council on whom listed building purchase notice is served)—

(*a*) in sub-paragraph (1)(c) (notice of unwillingness to comply with purchase notice: contents of notice) for the words from " and that they have transmitted " to the end substitute " and that they have transmitted to the Secretary of State a copy of the purchase notice and of the notice under this sub-paragraph " ;

(*b*) in sub-paragraph (3) (duty of council to transmit documents to Secretary of State) for the words from " they shall transmit " to " reasons " substitute " then, before they take steps to serve that notice, they shall transmit to the Secretary of State a copy of the purchase notice together with a copy of the notice which they propose to serve under sub-paragraph (1)(c) ".

Purchase notice relating to land where use restricted by virtue of previous planning permission

6. In section 184 of the Town and Country Planning Act 1971 (power to refuse to confirm purchase notice where land has re-stricted use by virtue of previous planning permission)—

(*a*) in subsection (1) (cases to which the section applies) for

" land which has a restricted use " substitute " land which consists in whole or in part of land which has a restricted use " ; and

(b) in subsection (3) (power of Secretary of State to refuse to confirm purchase notice), for the words " the land ought, in accordance with the previous planning permission ", substitute " the land having a restricted use by virtue of a previous planning permission ought, in accordance with that permission,",

Consideration of purchase notice concurrently with related planning appeal

7.—(1) In section 186(3) of the Town and Country Planning Act 1971 (relevant period at end of which purchase notice is deemed to have been confirmed) after " relevant period is " insert " , subject to subsection (3A) of this section,", and after that subsection insert—

" (3A) The relevant period does not run if the Secretary of State has before him at the same time both a copy of the purchase notice transmitted to him under section 181(3) of this Act and an appeal notice under any of the following provisions of this Act relating to any of the land to which the purchase notice relates—

    section 36 (appeal against refusal of planning permission, &c.),

    section 88 (appeal against enforcement notice),

    section 95 (appeal against refusal of established use certificate),

    section 97 (appeal against listed building enforcement notice), or

    paragraph 8 or 9 of Schedule 11 (appeal against refusal of listed building consent, &c.).".

(2) In paragraph 3(3)(b) of Schedule 19 to the Town and Country Planning Act 1971 (relevant period at end of which listed building purchase notice is deemed to have been confirmed) after " ' the relevant period ' is " insert " , subject to sub-paragraph (3A) of this paragraph,", and after that sub-paragraph insert—

" (3A) The relevant period does not run if the Secretary of State has before him at the same time both a copy of the listed building purchase notice transmitted to him under paragraph 1(3) of this Schedule and an appeal notice under any of the following provisions of this Act relating to any of the land to which the purchase notice relates—

    section 97 (appeal against listed building enforcement notice), or

    paragraph 8 or 9 of Schedule 11 (appeal against refusal of listed building consent, &c.).".

Local inquiries : application of general provisions of Local Government Act

8.—(1) In section 282 of the Town and Country Planning Act 1971

Sch. 11   (local inquiries held by Secretary of State), for subsection (2) substitute—

> " (2) The provisions of subsections (2) to (5) of section 250 of the Local Government Act 1972 (local inquiries: evidence and costs) apply to an inquiry held by virtue of this section.".

1971 c. 78.   (2) In Schedule 9 to the Town and Country Planning Act 1971 (determination of certain appeals by person appointed by the Secretary of State), in paragraph 5 (local inquiries and hearings held by appointed person) for sub-paragraph (3) substitute—

> " (3) The provisions of subsections (2) to (5) of section 250 of the Local Government Act 1972 (local inquiries: evidence and costs) apply to an inquiry held by virtue of this paragraph, with the following adaptations—
>
> > (*a*) for the references in subsection (4) (recovery of costs of holding the inquiry) to the Minister causing the inquiry to be held, substitute the Secretary of State ; and
> >
> > (*b*) for the reference in subsection (5) (orders as to the costs of the parties) to the Minister causing the inquiry to be held, substitute a reference to the person appointed to determine the appeal or the Secretary of State.".

Orders as to costs of parties where no local inquiry held

9.—(1) After section 282 of the Town and Country Planning Act 1971 (local inquiries: application of general provisions of Local Government Act) insert—

" Orders as to costs of parties where no local inquiry held.   282A.—(1) The Secretary of State has the same power to make orders under section 250(5) of the Local Government Act 1972 (orders with respect to the costs of the parties) in relation to proceedings to which this section applies which do not give rise to a local inquiry as he has in relation to a local inquiry.

> (2) This section applies to proceedings under this Act where the Secretary of State is required, before reaching a decision, to afford any person an opportunity of appearing before and being heard by a person appointed by him.".

(2) In Schedule 9 to the Town and Country Planning Act 1971 (determination of certain appeals by persons appointed by the Secretary of State), in paragraph 5 (local inquiries and hearings held by appointed person) at the end add—

> " (4) The person appointed to determine the appeal or the Secretary of State has the same power to make orders under section 250(5) of the Local Government Act 1972 (orders with respect to the costs of the parties) in relation to proceedings under this Schedule which do not give rise to an inquiry under this paragraph as he has in relation to such an inquiry.".

Procedure on applications and appeals disposed of without inquiry or hearing SCH. 11

10. After section 282A of the Town and Country Planning Act 1971 c. 78.
1971 insert—

" Procedure on certain appeals and applications.

282B.—(1) The Secretary of State may by regulations prescribe the procedure to be followed in connection with proceedings under this Act where he is required, before reaching a decision, to afford any person an opportunity of appearing before and being heard by a person appointed by him and which are to be disposed of without an inquiry or hearing to which rules under section 11 of the Tribunals and Inquiries Act 1971 apply.

(2) The regulations may in particular make provision as to the procedure to be followed—

(a) where steps have been taken with a view to the holding of such an inquiry or hearing which does not take place, or

(b) where steps have been taken with a view to the determination of any matter by a person appointed by the Secretary of State and the proceedings are the subject of a direction that the matter shall instead be determined by the Secretary of State, or

(c) where steps have been taken in pursuance of such a direction and a further direction is made revoking that direction,

and may provide that such steps shall be treated as compliance, in whole or in part, with the requirements of the regulations.

(3) The regulations may also—

(a) provide for a time limit within which any party to the proceedings must submit representations in writing and any supporting documents ;

(b) prescribe the time limit (which may be different for different classes of proceedings) or enable the Secretary of State to give directions setting the time limit in a particular case or class of case ;

(c) empower the Secretary of State to proceed to a decision taking into account only such written representations and supporting documents as were submitted within the time limit ; and

(d) empower the Secretary of State after giving the parties written notice of his intention to do so, to proceed to a decision notwithstanding that no written representations were made within the time limit, if it appears to him that he has sufficient material before him to enable him to reach a decision on the merits of the case.".

Power to return appeal for determination by inspector

11. In Schedule 9 to the Town and Country Planning Act 1971 (determination of certain appeals by persons appointed by the Secretary of State), after paragraph 3 (power of Secretary of State to direct that appeal should be determined by him) insert—

" 3A.—(1) The Secretary of State may by a further direction revoke a direction under paragraph 3 of this Schedule at any time before the determination of the appeal.

(2) A direction under this paragraph shall state the reasons for which it is given and shall be served on the person, if any, previously appointed to determine the appeal, the applicant or appellant, the local planning authority and any person who has made representations relating to the subject matter of the appeal which the authority are required to take into account under section 29(3)(*a*) of this Act.

(3) Where a direction under this paragraph has been given, the provisions of this Schedule relevant to the appeal shall apply, subject to sub-paragraph (4), as if no direction under paragraph 3 had been given.

(4) Anything done by or on behalf of the Secretary of State in connection with the appeal which might have been done by the person appointed to determine the appeal (including any arrangements made for the holding of a hearing or local inquiry) shall, unless that person directs otherwise, be treated as having been done by him.".

Appointment of assessors

12. In Schedule 9 to the Town and Country Planning Act 1971 (determination of certain appeals by persons appointed by the Secretary of State), in paragraph 5 (local inquiries and hearings) after sub-paragraph (1) insert—

" (1A) Where a person appointed under this Schedule to determine an appeal—

(*a*) holds a hearing by virtue of paragraph 2(2)(*b*) of this Schedule, or

(*b*) holds an inquiry by virtue of this paragraph,

an assessor may be appointed by the Secretary of State to sit with the appointed person at the hearing or inquiry to advise him on any matters arising notwithstanding that the appointed person is to determine the appeal.".

Increase of daily penalties for offences

13.—(1) In the provisions of the Town and Country Planning Act 1971 listed in column 1 of the following Table, which impose daily penalties for certain offences whose general nature is indicated in column 2, for the amount shown in column 3 substitute the amount shown in column 4.

TABLE

Provision of 1971 Act	*Nature of offence*	*Present maximum daily fine*	*New maximum daily fine*
Section 57(3)	Damage to listed building.	£20	£40
Section 89(4)	Non-compliance with enforcement notice.	£100	£200
Section 89(5)	Use of land in contravention of enforcement notice.	£100	£200
Section 90(7)	Non-compliance with stop notice.	£100	£200
Section 98(4)	Failure to secure compliance with listed building enforcement notice.	£100	£200
Section 104(7)	Failure to secure compliance with notice as to condition of land.	£20	£40
Section 109(2)	Contravention of advertisement control regulations.	£20	£40

(2) The increased amounts applicable by virtue of sub-paragraph (1) apply to every day after the commencement of this paragraph, notwithstanding that the offence began before.

Consequential amendments of the Town and Country Planning Act 1971

14. In section 1 of the Town and Country Planning Act 1971 1971 c. 78. for subsection (2A) substitute—

" (2A) References in this Act to a local planning authority in relation to a non-metropolitan county shall be construed, subject to any express provision to the contrary as references to both the county planning authority and the district planning authorities.".

15. In section 18(1)(*f*) of that Act, except as respects Greater London—

(*a*) for "section 12(1)(*a*) " substitute " section 12(2)(*a*) ", and

(*b*) for " section 12(2) " substitute " section 12(4) or 12A(2) ".

16. In section 29(1)(*a*) of that Act for " sections 41, 42, 70 and 77 to 80 " substitute " sections 41 and 42 ".

17. In sections 35(4) and 36(5) of that Act for " and 30A " substitute " , 30A and 31A ".

18. In sections 36(7) of that Act for " sections 29(1), 30(1), 67 and 74 " substitute " sections 29(1) and 30(1) ".

19. In section 55(4) of that Act omit " under section 56 of this Act ".

20. In section 105 of that Act—

(*a*) in paragraph (*a*) for " seriously injure " substitute " adversely affect ",

(*b*) omit paragraph (*c*), and

(*c*) in paragraph (*d*) for " seriously injuring " substitute " adversely affecting ".

21. In Schedule 21, in Parts I and V for "Sections 63 to 68" substitute "Sections 63 to 65".

Consequential amendments of other enactments

22. In section 182(5) of the Local Government Act 1972 (functions exercisable in National Park concurrently by county planning authority and district planning authority), for the words "(waste
land)", which describe the subject-matter of section 65 of the Town and Country Planning Act 1971, substitute "(power to require proper maintenance of land)".

23.—(1) Part I of Schedule 16 to the Local Government Act 1972 (functions under and modification of Town and Country Planning Act 1971) is amended as follows.

(2) For paragraphs 10 to 12 (joint local plans) substitute, except as respects Greater London—

"10.—(1) This paragraph applies where two or more local planning authorities jointly prepare proposals for the making, alteration, repeal or replacement of a local plan.

(2) The local planning authorities are jointly responsible for taking the steps required by section 12 or 12A, except that they each have the duty imposed by section 12(4)(*a*) or 12A(2)(*a*) of making copies of the relevant documents available for inspection and objections to the proposals may be made to any of those authorities and the statement required by section 12(5) or 12A(3) to accompany the relevant documents shall state that objections may be so made.

(3) It shall be for each of the local planning authorities to adopt the proposals under section 14(1) and they may do so as respects any part of their area to which the proposals relate, but any modifications subject to which the proposals are adopted must have the agreement of all those authorities.

11. Where in a non-metropolitan county—

(*a*) a structure plan has been jointly prepared by two or more county planning authorities, or

(*b*) a local plan has been jointly prepared by two or more district planning authorities,

a request for a certificate under section 15 that the local plan conforms generally to the structure plan shall be made by each district planning authority to the county planning authority for the area comprising the district planning authority's area and it shall be for that county planning authority to deal with the request.

12. Where a local plan has been made jointly, the power of making proposals for its alteration, repeal or replacement may be exercised as respects their respective areas by any of the authorities by whom it was made,

in accordance with the provisions of the relevant local   Sch. 11
plan scheme, and the Secretary of State may under section 11B direct any of them to make proposals as respects their respective areas.".

(3) In paragraph 19(2) (planning applications subject to duty to
consult county planning authority)—
  (*a*) in sub-paragraph (vi), for the words from " section 12 " to
    the end substitute " section 12 or 12A (publicity and consulta-
    tion regarding local plans) ", and
  (*b*) in sub-paragraph (vii), for the words from " the said section
    12 " to the end substitute " section 12 or 12A (publicity and
    consultation regarding local plans) ".

24. In section 8(3) of the Refuse Disposal (Amenity) Act 1978   1978 c. 3.
(application of general provisions of Town and Country Planning Act
1971 relating to local inquiries and service of notices) for " to 284 "
substitute " 283 and 284 ".

25.—(1) The Industrial Development Act 1982 is amended as fol-   1982 c. 52.
lows.

(2) In section 14 (power of Secretary of State to provide premises
and sites), in subsection (2) (restriction on acquisition of buildings)
for " section 66 of the Town and Country Planning Act 1971 "
substitute " section 14A of this Act ".

(3) After that section insert—

" Meaning   14A.—(1) In section 14(2) of this Act " industrial
of ' industrial building " means a building which is used or designed
buildings'.   for use for carrying on, in the course of a trade or
business, a process for or incidental to any of the following purposes—
  (*a*) the making of any article or part of any article,
  (*b*) the altering, repairing, ornamenting, finishing,
    cleaning, washing, freezing, packing or can-
    ning, or adapting for sale, or breaking up or
    demolition, of any article, or
  (*c*) the getting, dressing or preparation for sale of
    minerals or the extraction or preparation for
    sale of oil or brine,
or which is used or designed for use for carrying on, in
the course of a trade or business, scientific research.

(2) For the purposes of subsection (1) premises which—
  (*a*) are used or designed for use for providing services
    or facilities ancillary to the use of other premises
    for the carrying on of any such process or re-
    search as is mentioned in that subsection, and
  (*b*) are or are to be comprised in the same building
    or the same curtilage as those other premises,
shall themselves be treated as used or designed for use for
the carrying on of such a process or, as the case may be,
of such research.

(3) In this section—

'article' means an article of any description, including a ship or vessel;

'building' includes part of a building;

'minerals' includes all minerals and substances in or under land of a kind ordinarily worked for removal by underground or surface working, except that it does not include peat cut for purposes other than sale;

'scientific research' means any activity in the fields of natural or applied science for the extension of knowledge.".

26. In Part I of Schedule 1 to the Local Government Act 1985 (unitary development plans), in paragraph 12 (joint plans), for sub-paragraph (7) substitute—

" (7) In relation to any proposals made jointly under paragraph 10 above, the references—

(a) in sub-paragraph (2) of that paragraph to paragraphs 2 to 9 above, and

(b) in paragraph 10A(1) above to paragraph 3(1) above, shall include a reference to sub-paragraph (2) above.

(7A) In relation to such joint proposals the references in paragraph 10A above to the local planning authority shall be construed as references to the authorities acting jointly, except that—

(a) each of the authorities shall have the duty under sub-paragraph (2) of making copies of the relevant documents available for inspection, and

(b) representations or objections may be made to any of the authorities, and the statement required by sub-paragraph (3) of that paragraph shall state that objections may be so made.

27.—(1) In Part II of Schedule 1 to the Local Government Act 1985 (transitional provisions), paragraph 20 (local plans between abolition date and commencement of unitary planning provisions is amended as follows.

(2) In sub-paragraph (2) (application of provisions of Part II of Town and Country Planning Act 1971) omit the words from " and in respect of those matters " to the end.

(3) After that sub-paragraph insert—

" (2A) In respect of the matters referred to in sub-paragraph (2) the following provisions (which relate to county planning authorities) do not apply to metropolitan district councils, namely, sections 11A, 11B(4), 12(3) and (4)(c), 12A(2)(c), 15, 15A and 15B(2).".

(4) For sub-paragraph (3) substitute—

" (3) In section 15(1) and (2) (alteration of local plans), as applying in Greater London, the reference to a local plan adopted by a local planning authority includes, in the case of a London borough council, a local plan adopted by the Greater London Council and in force in respect of the area of that authority on the abolition date.

(3A) A metropolitan district council may at any time—

(a) make proposals for the preparation, alteration, repeal or replacement of a local plan adopted by them or adopted by the metropolitan county council and in force in the area of that authority on the abolition date ;

(b) with the consent of the Secretary of State, make proposals for the alteration, repeal or replacement of a local plan approved by him.".

PART II
SCOTLAND

Directions as to modifications of local plans

28.—(1) After subsection (2) of section 12 of the Town and Country Planning (Scotland) Act 1972 (adoption and approval of local plans) insert— 1972 c. 52.

" (2A) After copies of a local plan have been sent to the Secretary of State and before it has been adopted by the planning authority, the Secretary of State may, if it appears to him that any part of it is unsatisfactory, and without prejudice to his power to make a direction under subsection (3) below, direct the authority to consider modifying the plan in such respects as are indicated in the direction.

(2B) An authority to whom a direction is given shall not adopt the plan unless they satisfy the Secretary of State that they have made the modifications necessary to confirm with the direction or the direction is withdrawn.".

(2) In subsection (1) of that section for the words " (2) and (3) " substitute " (2), (2A), (2B) and (3) ".

Operation of Use Classes Order on subdivision of planning unit

29. In section 19(2) of the Town and Country Planning (Scotland) Act 1972 (operations and changes of use not amounting to development), in paragraph (f) (use of same prescribed class as existing use) for " the use thereof " substitute " the use of the buildings or other land or, subject to the provisions of the order, of any part thereof ".

Development orders

30. In section 21 of the Town and Country Planning (Scotland) Act 1972 (development orders), for subsection (3) (general and special orders) substitute—

" (3) A development order may be made either—

    (*a*) as a general order applicable, except so far as the order otherwise provides, to all land, but which may make different provision with respect to different descriptions of land, or

    (*b*) as a special order applicable only to such land or descriptions of land as may be specified in the order.".

Applications to vary or revoke conditions attached to planning permission

1972 c. 52.
31. After section 28 of the Town and Country Planning (Scotland) Act 1972 insert—

" Permission to develop land without compliance with conditions previously attached.
28A.—(1) This section applies to applications for planning permission for the development of land without complying with conditions subject to which a previous planning permission was granted.

(2) Special provision may be made with respect to such applications—

    (*a*) by regulations under section 22 of this Act as regards the form and content of the application, and

    (*b*) by a development order as regards the procedure to be followed in connection with the application.

(3) On such an application the planning authority shall consider only the question of the conditions subject to which planning permission should be granted, and—

    (*a*) if they decide that planning permission should be granted subject to conditions differing from those subject to which the previous permission was granted, or that it should be granted unconditionally, they shall grant planning permission accordingly, and

    (*b*) if they decide that planning permission should be granted subject to the same conditions as those subject to which the previous permission was granted, they shall refuse the application.

(4) This section does not apply where the application is made after the previous planning permission has become time-expired, that is to say, the previous permission having been granted subject to a condition as to the time within which the development to which it related was to have begun, that time has expired without the development having been begun.".

Land adversely affecting amenity of neighbourhood

32.—(1) For subsection (1) of section 63 of the Town and Country Planning (Scotland) Act 1972 (proper maintenance of waste land) substitute—

    " (1) If it appears to a planning authority that the amenity of any part of their district, or an adjoining district, is adversely affected by the condition of any land in their district, they may serve on the owner, lessee and occupier of the land a notice under this section requiring such steps for abating the adverse effect as may be specified in the notice to be taken within such period as may be so specified.".

(2) In subsections (1B) and (1C) of the said section, for the words " waste land notice " substitute " notice under this section ".

33.—(1) In subsections (1) and (5) of section 63A (appeals against waste land notices) of the Town and Country Planning (Scotland) Act 1972, for the words " waste land notice " substitute " notice under section 63 of this Act ".

(2) For paragraph (*a*) of the said subsection (1) substitute—

" (*a*) that neither the amenity of any part of the planning authority's district nor that of any adjoining district has been adversely affected ; ".

(3) In paragraph (*b*) of the said subsection (1), for the word " injury " substitute " adverse effect ".

Appeals against notices under section 63A

34.—(1) After subsection (6) of section 63A insert—

" (7) Subject to section 279 of this Act, Schedule 7 to this Act applies to appeals under this section.".

(2) After sub-paragraph (1)(*a*) of paragraph 2 of Schedule 7 (determination of appeals by person appointed by Secretary of State) to the Town and Country Planning (Scotland) Act 1972, insert—

" (*aa*) in relation to appeals under section 63A, subsections (4) and (6) ; ".

Purchase notices : transmission of documents to the Secretary of State

35—(1) In section 170 of the Town and Country Planning (Scotland) Act 1972 (action by planning authority on whom purchase notice is served)—

(*a*) in subsection (1)(*c*) (notice of unwillingness to comply with purchase notice: contents of notice) for the words from " and that they have transmitted " to the end substitute " and that they have transmitted to the Secretary of State a copy of the purchase notice and of the notice under this subsection " ;

(*b*) in subsection (3) (duty of planning authority to transmit documents to Secretary of State) for the words from " they shall transmit " to the end substitute " then, before they take steps to serve that notice, they shall transmit to the Secretary of State a copy of the purchase notice together with a copy of the notice which they propose to serve ".

(2) In paragraph 1 of Schedule 17 to the Town and Country Planning (Scotland) Act 1972 (action by planning authority on whom listed building purchase notice is served)—

Sch. 11

    (*a*) in sub-paragraph (1)(*c*) (notice of unwillingness to comply with purchase notice: contents of notice) for the words from " and that they have transmitted " to the end substitute " and that they have transmitted to the Secretary of State a copy of the purchase notice and of the notice under this sub-paragraph." ;

    (*b*) in sub-paragraph (3) (duty of planning authority to transmit documents to Secretary of State) for the words from " they shall transmit " to " reasons " substitute " then, before they take steps to serve that notice, they shall transmit to the Secretary of State a copy of the purchase notice together with a copy of the notice which they propose to serve under sub-paragraph (1)(*c*) ".

Purchase notice relating to land where use restricted by virtue of previous planning permission

1972 c. 52.

    36. In section 173 of the Town and Country Planning (Scotland) Act 1972 (power to refuse to confirm purchase notice where land has restricted use by virtue of previous planning permission)—

    (*a*) in subsection (1) (cases to which the section applies) for " land which has a restricted use " substitute " land which consists in whole or in part of land which has a restricted use " ; and

    (*b*) in subsection (3) (power of Secretary of State to refuse to confirm purchase notice), for the words " the land ought, in accordance with the previous planning permission," substitute " the land having a restricted use by virtue of a previous planning permission ought, in accordance with that permission,".

Consideration of purchase notice concurrently with related planning appeal

    37.—(1) In section 175(3) of the Town and Country Planning (Scotland) Act 1972 (relevant period at end of which purchase notice is deemed to have been confirmed) after " relevant period is " insert ", subject to subsection (3A) of this section,", and after that subsection insert—

    " (3A) The relevant period does not run if the Secretary of State has before him at the same time both a copy of the purchase notice transmitted to him under section 170(3) of this Act and an appeal notice under any of the following provisions of this Act relating to any of the land to which the purchase notice relates—

        section 33 (appeal against refusal of planning permission, &c.),

        section 85 (appeal against enforcement notice),

        section 91 (appeal against refusal of established use certificate),

        section 93 (appeal against listed building enforcement notice), or

paragraph 7 or 8 of Schedule 10 (appeal against refusal
of listed building consent, &c.).".

(2) In paragraph 3(3)(*b*) of Schedule 17 to the Town and Country
Planning (Scotland) Act 1972 (relevant period at end of which
listed building purchase notice is deemed to have been confirmed)
after " " the relevant period " is " insert ", subject to sub-paragraph
(3A) of this paragraph,", and after that sub-paragraph insert—

" (3A) The relevant period does not run if the Secretary of
State has before him at the same time both a copy of the listed
building purchase notice transmitted to him under paragraph
1(3) of this Schedule and an appeal notice under any of the
following provisions of this Act relating to any of the land to
which the purchase notice relates—

section 93 (appeal against listed building enforcement
notice), or

paragraph 7 or 8 of Schedule 10 (appeal against refusal of
listed building consent, &c.).".

National Scenic Areas

38. After section 262B of the Town and Country Planning (Scotland) Act 1972 insert—

" National   262C.—(1) Where it appears to the Secretary of State,
Scenic Areas. after such consultation with the Countryside Commission for Scotland and such other persons or bodies as
he thinks fit, that an area is of outstanding scenic value
and beauty in a national context, and that special protection measures are appropriate for it, he may designate the
area by a direction under this section as a National Scenic
Area ; and any such designation may be varied or cancelled by a subsequent direction.

(2) Notice of any such designation, variation, or cancellation as is mentioned in subsection (1) above shall be
published in the Edinburgh Gazette and in at least one
newspaper circulating in the vicinity of the Area by the
Secretary of State.

(3) Every planning authority shall compile and make
available for inspection free of charge at reasonable
hours and at a convenient place a list containing such
particulars as the Secretary of State may determine of any
area in their district which has been designated as a National Scenic Area.

(4) Where any area is for the time being designated as
a National Scenic Area, special attention shall be paid to
the desirability of preserving or enhancing its character
or appearance in the exercise, with respect to any land
in that area, of any powers under this Act.".

Recovery of expenses of local inquiry

39.—(1) For subsection (7) of section 267 (local inquiries) of the

SCH. 11
1972 c. 52.
1973 c. 65.

Town and Country Planning (Scotland) Act 1972 and subsections (7) and (8) of section 210 (power to direct inquiries) of the Local Government (Scotland) Act 1973 substitute—

" (7) The Minister may make orders as to the expenses incurred—

(*a*) by the Minister in relation to—
(i) the inquiry ;
(ii) arrangements made for an inquiry which does not take place ; and

(*b*) by the parties to the inquiry,

and as to the parties by whom any of the expenses mentioned in paragraphs (*a*) and (*b*) above shall be paid.

(7A) What may be recovered by the Minister is the entire administrative expense of the inquiry, so that, in particular—

(*a*) there shall be treated as expenses incurred in relation to the inquiry such reasonable sum as the Minister may determine in respect of the general staff expenses and overheads of his department, and

(*b*) there shall be treated as expenses incurred by the Minister holding the inquiry any expenses incurred in relation to the inquiry by any other Minister or Government department and, where appropriate, such reasonable sum as that Minister or department may determine in respect of general staff expenses and overheads.

(7B) The Minister may by regulations prescribe for any description of inquiry a standard daily amount and where an inquiry of that description does take place what may be recovered is—

(*a*) the prescribed standard amount in respect of each day (or an appropriate proportion of that amount in respect of a part of a day) on which the inquiry sits or the person appointed to hold the inquiry is otherwise engaged on work connected with the inquiry,

(*b*) expenses actually incurred in connection with the inquiry on travelling or subsistence allowances or the provision of accommodation or other facilities for the inquiry, and

(*c*) any expenses attributable to the appointment of an assessor to assist the person appointed to hold the inquiry, and

(*d*) any legal expenses or disbursements incurred or made by or on behalf of the Minister in connection with the inquiry.".

1973 c. 65.

(2) After subsection (7B) of the said section 210 of the Local Government (Scotland) Act 1973 insert—

" (8) Where the Minister has made an order under subsection (7) of this section requiring any party to pay expenses to him he shall certify the amount of the expenses, and any amount so certified shall be a debt due by that party to the Crown and shall be recoverable accordingly.".

(3) In subsection (1) of section 233 of the Local Government 1973 c. 65. (Scotland) Act 1973 (orders, rules and regulations), after " 104(1) " insert " 210(7) ".

(4) After section 210 of the Local Government (Scotland) Act 1973 insert—

" Recovery of expenses of local inquiry.

210A.—(1) The following provisions of this section apply where a Minister is authorised under or by virtue of any of the following statutory provisions to recover expenses incurred by him in relation to an inquiry—

section 129(1)(*d*) of the Road Traffic Regulation Act 1984 c. 27. 1984 (expenses of inquiry under that Act),

any other statutory provision to which this section is applied by order of the Minister.

(2) What may be recovered by the Minister is the entire administrative expense of the inquiry, so that, in particular—

(*a*) there shall be treated as expenses incurred in relation to the inquiry such reasonable sum as the Minister may determine in respect of the general staff expenses and overheads of his department, and

(*b*) there shall be treated as expenses incurred by the Minister holding the inquiry any expenses incurred in relation to the inquiry by any other Minister or Government department and, where appropriate, such reasonable sum as that Minister or department may determine in respect of general staff expenses and overheads.

(3) The expense of an inquiry which does not take place may be recovered by the Minister from any person who would have been a party to the inquiry to the same extent, and in the same way, as the expense of an inquiry which does take place.

(4) The Minister may by regulations prescribe for any description of inquiry a standard daily amount and where an inquiry of that description does take place what may be recovered is—

(*a*) the prescribed standard amount in respect of each day (or an appropriate proportion of that amount in respect of a part of a day) on which the inquiry sits or the person appointed to hold the inquiry is otherwise engaged on work connected with the inquiry,

Sch. 11

(*b*) expenses actually incurred in connection with the inquiry on travelling or subsistence allowances or the provision of accommodation or other facilities for the inquiry,

(*c*) any expenses attributable to the appointment of an assessor to assist the person appointed to hold the inquiry, and

(*d*) any legal expenses or disbursements incurred or made by or on behalf of the Minister in connection with the inquiry.

(5) An order or regulation under this section shall be made by statutory instrument which shall be subject to annulment in pursuance of a resolution of either House of Parliament.

(6) An order applying this section to a statutory provision may provide for the consequential repeal of so much of that provision, or any other provision, as restricts the sum recoverable by the Minister in respect of the services of any officer engaged in the inquiry or is otherwise inconsistent with the application of the provisions of this section.".

Orders as to expenses of parties where no local inquiry held

1972 c. 52.

40.—(1) After the said section 267 of the Town and Country Planning (Scotland) Act 1972 insert—

"Orders as to expenses of parties where no local inquiry held.

267A.—(1) The Secretary of State has the same power to make orders under section 267(7) above in relation to proceedings to which this section applies which do not give rise to a local inquiry as he has in relation to a local inquiry.

(2) This section applies to proceedings under this Act where the Secretary of State is required, before reaching a decision, to afford any person an opportunity of appearing before and being heard by a person appointed by him.".

(2) In Schedule 7 to the Town and Country Planning (Scotland) Act 1972 (determination of certain appeals by person appointed by the Secretary of State), in paragraph 5 (local inquiries and hearings)—

(*a*) in sub-paragraph (3) after the word " shall " insert " subject to sub-paragraph (4) below ".

(*b*) after sub-paragraph (3) insert—

" (4) The person appointed to determine the appeal has the same power to make orders under section 267(7) of this Act in relation to proceedings under this Schedule which do not give rise to an inquiry as he has in relation to such an inquiry.

(5) For the purposes of this paragraph, references to   Sch. 11
the Minister in subsections (7) and (8) of section 267
shall be read as references to the person appointed by
the Secretary of State to determine the appeal.".

*Procedure on applications and appeals disposed of without inquiry
or hearing*

41. After section 267A of the Town and Country Planning (Scot- 1972 c. 52.
land) Act 1972 insert—

" Procedure   267B.—(1) The Secretary of State may by regulations
on certain   prescribe the procedure to be followed in connection
appeals and   with proceedings under this Act where he is required,
applications. before reaching a decision, to afford any person an
opportunity of appearing before and being heard by a
person appointed by him and which are to be disposed
of without an inquiry or hearing to which rules under
section 11 of the Tribunals and Inquiries Act 1971 apply. 1971 c. 62.

(2) The regulations may in particular make provision
as to the procedure to be followed—

> (a) where steps have been taken with a view to the
> holding of such an inquiry or hearing which
> does not take place, or

> (b) where steps have been taken with a view to the
> determination of any matter by a person ap-
> pointed by the Secretary of State and the pro-
> ceedings are the subject of a direction that the
> matter shall instead be determined by the Sec-
> retary of State, or

> (c) where steps have been taken in pursuance of
> such a direction and a further direction is made
> revoking that direction,

and may provide that such steps shall be treated as
compliance, in whole or in part, with the requirements
of the regulations.

(3) The regulations may also—

> (a) provide for a time limit within which any party
> to the proceedings must lodge written submis-
> sions and any supporting documents ;

> (b) prescribe the time limit (which may be different
> for different classes of proceedings) or enable
> the Secretary of State to give directions setting
> the time limit in a particular case or class of
> case ;

> (c) empower the Secretary of State to proceed to a
> decision taking into account only such written
> submissions and supporting documents as were
> lodged within the time limit ; and

SCH. 11

(*d*) empower the Secretary of State, after giving the parties written notice of his intention to do so, to proceed to a decision notwithstanding that no written submissions were lodged within the time limit, if it appears to him that he has sufficient material before him to enable him to reach a decision on the merits of the case.".

Power to return appeal for determination by appointed person

1972 c. 52.

42. In Schedule 7 to the Town and Country Planning (Scotland) Act 1972 (determination of certain appeals by persons appointed by the Secretary of State), after paragraph 3 (power of Secretary of State to direct that appeal should be determined by him) insert—

"3A.—(1) The Secretary of State may by a further direction revoke a direction under paragraph 3 of this Schedule at any time before the determination of the appeal.

(2) A direction under this paragraph shall state the reasons for which it is given and shall be served on the person, if any, previously appointed to determine the appeal, the applicant or appellant, the planning authority and any person who has made representations relating to the subject matter of the appeal which the authority are required to take into account under section 26(3)(*a*) of this Act.

(3) Where a direction under this paragraph has been given, the provisions of this Schedule relevant to the appeal shall apply, subject to sub-paragraph (4), as if no direction under paragraph 3 had been given.

(4) Anything done by or on behalf of the Secretary of State in connection with the appeal which might have been done by the person appointed to determine the appeal (including any arrangements made for the holding of a hearing or local inquiry) shall, unless that person directs otherwise, be treated as having been done by him.".

Appointment of assessors

43. In Schedule 7 to the Town and Country Planning (Scotland) Act 1972 (determination of certain appeals by persons appointed by the Secretary of State), in paragraph 5 (local inquiries and hearings), after sub-paragraph (1) insert—

"(1A) Where a person appointed under this Schedule to determine an appeal—

(*a*) holds a hearing by virtue of paragraph 2(2)(*b*) of this Schedule, or

(*b*) holds an inquiry by virtue of this paragraph,

an assessor may be appointed by the Secretary of State to sit with the appointed person at the hearing or inquiry to advise him on any matters arising notwithstanding that the appointed person is to determine the appeal.".

Increase of daily penalties for offences

44.—(1) In the provisions of the Town and Country Planning 1972 c. 52. (Scotland) Act 1972 listed in column 1 of the following Table, which imposes daily penalties for certain offences whose general nature is indicated in column 2, for the amount shown in column 3 substitute the amount shown in column 4.

TABLE

Provision of 1972 Act	Nature of offence	Present maximum daily fine	New maximum daily fine
Section 55(3)	Damage to listed building.	£20	£40
Section 86.	Non-compliance with enforcement notice.	£100	£200
Section 87(8)(*b*).	Non-compliance with stop notice.	£100	£200
Section 94(2)(*a*).	Failure to secure compliance with listed building enforcement notice.	£100	£200
Section 98(3).	Failure to secure compliance with tree preservation order.	£50	£100
Section 100(1)(*a*).	Non-compliance with discontinuance order.	£100	£200
Section 101(2).	Contravention of advertisement control regulations.	£20	£40

(2) The increased amounts applicable by virtue of sub-paragraph (1) apply to every day after the commencement of this paragraph, notwithstanding that the offence began before.

Other minor amendments of the Town and Country Planning (Scotland) Act 1972

45. In section 84(7) of the Town and Country Planning (Scotland) Act 1972 (power to serve enforcement notice) after " place " insert " or, (according to the particular circumstances of the breach) to secure compliance with the conditions or limitations subject to which planning permission was granted ".

46. In section 99 (enforcement of duties as to replacement of trees) of the Town and Country Planning (Scotland) Act 1972, in subsection (3), after " 85(2) " insert " to (2D) ".

47. In section 158(6)(*b*) of the Town and Country Planning (Scotland) Act 1972 (compensation for planning decisions restricting development other than new development) for the word " 7 " there shall be substituted the word " 8 ".

48. In section 205(3)(*a*) and 205A(3)(*a*) of the Town and Country Planning (Scotland) Act 1972 (procedure in anticipation of planning permission, &c.) after " authority " insert " or ".

49. In section 205(5) of the Town and Country Planning (Scotland) Act 1972 for " 204(5) " substitute " 204(4) ".

50. In section 231 of the Town and Country Planning (Scotland) Act 1972 (validity of development plans and certain orders, decision and directions)—

(*a*) at the end of subsection (2)(*a*) insert " or as applied under

section 181 of the Local Government (Scotland) Act 1973 ",
and

(b) at the end of subsection (2)(b) insert " or under the provisions of that section as applied by or under any other provision of this Act or as applied under section 181 of the Local Government (Scotland) Act 1973.".

51. In section 260 of the Town and Country Planning (Scotland) Act 1972 (default powers of the Secretary of State), at the end of subsection (1) insert " or, in the case of a tree preservation order under section 58 of this Act, as if it had been made and confirmed by the planning authority ".

52. In section 270 of the Town and Country Planning (Scotland) Act 1972 (power to require information as to interest in land) insert—

" (d) the time when that use began ;.

(e) the name and address of any person known to the person on whom the notice is served as having used the premises for those purposes ;

(f) the time when any activities being carried out on the premises began.".

53. In sub-paragraph 2(2) of Schedule 7 (determination of certain appeals by person appointed by Secretary of State) of the Town and Country (Scotland) Act 1972, for " 85(2) " substitute " 85(2D) ".

Consequential amendments of the Town and Country Planning (Scotland) Act 1972

54. In section 26(1)(a) of the Town and Country Planning (Scotland) Act 1972, for the words " sections 38, 39, 68 and 75 to 78 " there shall be substituted the words " sections 38 and 39 ".

55. In sections 32(4) and 33(5) of the Town and Country Planning (Scotland) Act 1972 for the words " and 27A " substitute " 27A and 28A ".

56. In section 33(7) of the Town and Country Planning (Scotland) Act 1972 for the words ", 27(1) and 65 " there shall be substituted the words " and 27(1) ".

57. In section 53(4) of the Town and Country Planning (Scotland) Act 1972 omit " under section 54 of this Act ".

58. In section 267 (local inquiries) of the Town and Country Planning (Scotland) Act 1972, in subsection (9), after " section " insert ", except where the context otherwise requires,".

59. In section 275(1) of the Town and Country Planning (Scotland) Act 1972 (interpretation) the following shall be inserted after the definition of " Minister "—

" ' National Scenic Area ' has the meaning assigned to it by section 262C of this Act.".

60. In Parts I and III of Schedule 19 to the Town and Country Planning (Scotland) Act 1972 for " Sections 61 to 66 " substitute " Sections 61 to 63A ".

Consequential amendments of other enactments

61. In subsection (5) of section 179 (reference of applications to regional planning authority) of the Local Government (Scotland) Act 1973, after " 27A " insert " 28A,". 1973 c. 65.

62. In subsection 8(4) of the Refuse Disposal (Amenity) Act 1978 (application of general provisions of the Town and Country Planning (Scotland) Act 1972 relating to local inquiries and services of notices) for " to 270 " substitute " and 268 to 270 ". 1978 c. 3. 1972 c. 52.

SCHEDULE 12

REPEALS

PART I

HOUSING

Repeals coming into force on passing of Act

Chapter	Short title	Extent of Repeal
1985 c. 71.	Housing (Consequential Provisions) Act 1985.	In Schedule 2, in paragraph 24(8)— (*a*) in sub-paragraph (*d*), the words from " for ' section 60 " to " 1985 ' and "; (*b*) in sub-paragraph (*e*), the words from " for the " to " Schedule ' and "; (*c*) sub-paragraph (*f*).

Repeals coming into force on appointed day

Chapter	Short title	Extent of repeal
1975 c. 28.	Housing Rents and Subsidies (Scotland) Act 1975.	Section 5(6).
1977 c. 42.	Rent Act 1977.	In section 69(1), the words " (to be known as a certificate of fair rent) ". In section 70(1), the word " and " before paragraph (*b*). In Schedule 12, in paragraph 3, the words " unless the dwelling-house is subject to a regulated tenancy ".
1980 c. 51.	Housing Act 1980.	Section 56(3). Section 140.
1980 c. 65.	Local Government, Planning and Land Act 1980.	Section 156(3).
1981 c. 64.	New Towns Act 1981.	Section 43(3) and (4). Section 49(*b*) and (*c*).
1985 c. 51.	Local Government Act 1985.	In Schedule 13, in paragrapʼn 14, sub-paragraph (*d*) and the word " and " preceding it. In Schedule 14, paragraph 58(*e*).
1985 c. 68.	Housing Act 1985.	Section 30(2). Section 46. In section 127, the word " and " at the end of paragraph (*a*). In section 452(2), the definition of " housing authority ". Section 453(2). In Schedule 4, in paragraph 7(1), the words from " a housing co-operative " to " management functions)".

Chapter	Short title	Extent of Repeal
1985 c. 71.	Housing (Consequential Provisions) Act 1985.	In Schedule 6, in paragraph 14(2), the words following paragraph (*c*). In Schedule 2, paragraphs 27, 35(3), 44(3), and 45(2).

PART II

OPENCAST COAL

Chapter	Short title	Extent of repeal
6 & 7 Eliz. 2 c. 69.	Opencast Coal Act 1958.	Sections 1 and 2. Section 9(2). In section 18(2), the words "(apart from this Act)". In section 39(10), the words " First or ". Section 46(2). Section 48. In section 51, in subsection (1), the definitions of " the authorised purposes " and " authorised operations ". Section 53(2). Schedule 1. In Schedule 9, in paragraph 3(2), the words " under the First Schedule to this Act, or ". Schedule 10.
1971 c. 78.	Town and Country Planning Act 1971.	Section 60(10)(*a*). In section 216(3), in paragraph (*a*), the words "or the National Coal Board" and in paragraph (*b*), the words from " or " to " 1958 ".
1972 c. 52.	Town and Country Planning (Scotland) Act 1972.	Section 58(10)(*a*). In section 205(3) and 205A(3), in paragraph (*a*) the words " or the National Coal Board " and in paragraph (*b*) the words from " or " to " 1958 ".
1975 c. 56.	Coal Industry Act 1975.	Section 5. In Schedule 3, paragraphs 3 and 11. Schedule 4.
1981 c. 67.	Acquisition of Land Act 1981.	In Schedule 4, paragraph 11(5).
1986 c. 5.	Agricultural Holdings Act 1986.	In Schedule 14, paragraph 25.

Part III

Miscellaneous (England and Wales)

Chapter	Short title	Extent of repeal
62 & 63 Vict. c. 19.	Electric Lighting (Clauses) Act 1899.	In the Schedule, in section 10(*b*), the words " and the express consent of the local authority also ".
16 & 17 Geo. 5 c. 51.	Electricity (Supply) Act 1926.	In Schedule 6, the entry relating to section 21 of the Electricity (Supply) Act 1919.
8 & 9 Geo. 6 c. 43.	Requisitioned Land and War Works Act 1945.	Section 52.
10 & 11 Geo. 6 c. 51.	Town and Country Planning Act 1947.	In Schedule 8, the entry relating to section 21 of the Electricity (Supply) Act 1919.
10 & 11 Geo. 6 c. 54.	Electricity Act 1947.	In Part I of Schedule 4, the entry relating to section 21 of the Electricity (Supply) Act 1919.
11 & 12 Geo. 6 c. 17.	Requisitioned Land and War Works Act 1948.	In the Schedule, paragraph 10.
5 & 6 Eliz. 2 c. 48.	Electricity Act 1957.	In section 33(3), the words " and the next following ".
1968 c. 14.	Public Expenditure and Receipts Act 1968.	In Schedule 3, in paragraph 6, the entry relating to section 290(4) of the Local Government Act 1933.
1971 c. 78.	Town and Country Planning Act 1971.	In section 29A— (*a*) in subsection (2), the definition of " the Code of Practice for Access of the Disabled to Buildings "; (*b*) subsection (3). Section 29B(2) and (3). In section 32(2), in the proviso, the words " of sections 66 to 86 ". In section 55(4), the words " under section 56 of this Act ". Sections 66 to 86. Section 88B(4). Section 105(1)(*c*). Section 110(1). In section 147(3), the words from " or in respect of " to the end. Section 151. Section 165(4). In section 169— (*a*) subsection (5); (*b*) in subsection (7), the words from " and no compensation" to the end. In section 180(4), the words from " and no account " to the end.

Chapter	Short title	Extent of Repeal
1971 c. 78 —*cont.*	Town and Country Planning Act 1971.—*cont.*	Section 185. Section 191(2). In section 237(5), the words from " and no compensation " to the end. Sections 250 to 252. In section 260(1)(*d*), the words " grants in accordance with regulations made under section 250 of this Act or ". In section 287— (*a*) in subsection (4), the words " 69, 73(6), 74(4), 75(8)"; (*b*) in subsection (5)(*b*), the words " 69, 73(6), 75(8) or " and the words from " or an order under section 74(4)" to the end; (*c*) subsection (7); (*d*) subsection (9). In section 290(1)— (*a*) in the definition of "building ", the words in parenthesis; (*b*) the definition of " industrial development certificate ". Schedules 12 and 13. In Schedule 21— (*a*) in Part I, the references to sections 250, 251(1) and 252; (*b*) in Part II, the references to sections 79 to 81; (*c*) in Part III, the references to sections 72 and 251(2) to (5); (*d*) in Part V, the references to sections 72 and 73 to 86. In Schedule 24, paragraphs 20A, 26 to 30 and 70.
1972 c. 42.	Town and Country Planning (Amendment) Act 1972.	Sections 5 and 6.
1972 c. 70.	Local Government Act 1972.	In section 182(1), the words from " (2A) " to the end. Section 183(2). In section 250(4), the words from " (including " to " in the inquiry) ". In Schedule 16, paragraphs 1 to 3.
1974 c. 7.	Local Government Act 1974.	In Schedule 6, paragraph 25(4).
1974 c. 32.	Town and Country Amenities Act 1974.	Section 3(1). Section 5.

Chapter	Short title	Extent of repeal
1976 c. 70.	Land Drainage Act 1976.	In section 96(5), the words from "including" to "in the inquiry)".
1977 c. 40.	Control of Office Development Act 1977.	The whole Act.
1980 c. 65.	Local Government, Planning and Land Act 1980.	Section 88. In section 134— (*a*) in subsection (1), the words "Subject to subsection (2) below,"; (*b*) subsection (2). In Schedule 14, paragraphs 6 to 8. In Schedule 15, paragraphs 1 and 16. In Part I of Schedule 29, in the entry relating to section 65, the word "waste".
1981 c. 67.	Acquisition of Land Act 1981.	In Schedule 4, in paragraph 1, in the entry relating to the Local Government Act 1972, the words "section 125(4) and (7)".
1982 c. 30.	Local Government (Miscellaneous Provisions) Act 1982.	In Schedule 6, in the Table in paragraph 7(*b*) the entries relating to ss. 15 and 15A of the Town and Country Planning Act 1971.
1982 c. 52.	Industrial Development Act 1982.	Section 15(1)(*b*). In Part II of Schedule 2, paragraph 7(1).
1983 c. 47.	National Heritage Act 1983.	In Schedule 4, paragraph 18. Schedule 5, paragraph 6.
1984 c. 27.	Road Traffic Regulation Act 1984.	In section 129(1)(*d*), the words from "(including" to "in the inquiry)".
1985 c. 51.	Local Government Act 1985.	Section 3(2). In Schedule 2, paragraph 1(8).

PART IV

MISCELLANEOUS (SCOTLAND)

Chapter	Short title	Extent of repeal
1968 c. 14.	Public Expenditure and Receipts Act 1968.	In Schedule 3, in paragraph 6, the entry relating to section 355(8) of the Local Government (Scotland) Act 1947.

Chapter	Short title	Extent of Repeal
1972 c. 52.	Town and Country Planning (Scotland) Act 1972.	In section 29(2), in the proviso, the words " of sections 64 to 83 ". In section 53(2), the word " only " and the words " (in this Act referred to as listed building consent) ". In section 53(4) the words " under section 54 of this Act,". In section 63(1A), the words from " ; and references " to " construed ". Sections 64 to 83. Section 85(8). In section 136(3) the words from " or in respect of " to the end. Section 140. Section 154(4). In section 158— (a) Subsection (5). (b) In subsection (7) the words from " and no compensation " to the end. In section 169(4) the words from " and no account " to the end. Section 174. Section 180(2). In section 226(5) the words from " and no compensation" to the end. Section 231(2)(e). In section 233(3), the words "(other than an order under section 203(1)(a) of this Act)". Sections 237 to 239. In section 247(1)(d), the words from " in accordance " to " grants ". In section 273— (a) In subsection (4), the words " 67, 71(6), 72(4), 73(8)". (b) In subsection (5) the words " 67, 71(6), 73(8)". (c) Subsections (7) to (9). In section 275(1)— (a) In the definition of "building", the words ", except in sections 71 to 83 of this Act, ". (b) the definition of " industrial development certificate ".

Sch. 12

Chapter	Short title	Extent of repeal
1972 c. 52. —*cont.*	Town and Country Planning (Scotland) Act 1972.—*cont.*	In Schedule 19— (a) in Part I, the reference to sections 237, 238(1) and 239; (b) in Part II, the references to sections 77 to 79 and 83; (c) in Part III, the reference to section 70. In Schedule 22, paragraphs 22 to 25 and 60.
1974 c. 32.	Town and Country Amenities Act 1974.	Section 5.
1980 c. 65.	Local Government, Planning and Land Act 1980.	In section 134(1) the words " Subject to subsection (2) below, ". In Part I of Schedule 30, in the entry relating to section 63, the word " waste ".
1982 c. 52.	Industrial Development Act 1982.	Section 15(1)(b). Paragraph 10 of Part II of Schedule 2.
1984 c. 27.	Road Traffic Regulation Act 1984.	In section 129(1)(d) the words from " (including " to " in the inquiry) ".

Public Order Act 1986

1986 CHAPTER 64

An Act to abolish the common law offences of riot, rout, unlawful assembly and affray and certain statutory offences relating to public order; to create new offences relating to public order; to control public processions and assemblies; to control the stirring up of racial hatred; to provide for the exclusion of certain offenders from sporting events; to create a new offence relating to the contamination of or interference with goods; to confer power to direct certain trespassers to leave land; to amend section 7 of the Conspiracy and Protection of Property Act 1875, section 1 of the Prevention of Crime Act 1953, Part V of the Criminal Justice (Scotland) Act 1980 and the Sporting Events (Control of Alcohol etc.) Act 1985; to repeal certain obsolete or unnecessary enactments; and for connected purposes.

[7th November 1986]

BE IT ENACTED by the Queen's most Excellent Majesty, by and with the advice and consent of the Lords Spiritual and Temporal, and Commons, in this present Parliament assembled, and by the authority of the same, as follows:—

PART I

NEW OFFENCES

1.—(1) Where 12 or more persons who are present together Riot. use or threaten unlawful violence for a common purpose and the conduct of them (taken together) is such as would cause a person of reasonable firmness present at the scene to fear for

X 4

his personal safety, each of the persons using unlawful violence for the common purpose is guilty of riot.

(2) It is immaterial whether or not the 12 or more use or threaten unlawful violence simultaneously.

(3) The common purpose may be inferred from conduct.

(4) No person of reasonable firmness need actually be, or be likely to be, present at the scene.

(5) Riot may be committed in private as well as in public places.

(6) A person guilty of riot is liable on conviction on indictment to imprisonment for a term not exceeding ten years or a fine or both.

Violent
disorder.

2.—(1) Where 3 or more persons who are present together use or threaten unlawful violence and the conduct of them (taken together) is such as would cause a person of reasonable firmness present at the scene to fear for his personal safety, each of the persons using or threatening unlawful violence is guilty of violent disorder.

(2) It is immaterial whether or not the 3 or more use or threaten unlawful violence simultaneously.

(3) No person of reasonable firmness need actually be, or be likely to be, present at the scene.

(4) Violent disorder may be committed in private as well as in public places.

(5) A person guilty of violent disorder is liable on conviction on indictment to imprisonment for a term not exceeding 5 years or a fine or both, or on summary conviction to imprisonment for a term not exceeding 6 months or a fine not exceeding the statutory maximum or both.

Affray.

3.—(1) A person is guilty of affray if he uses or threatens unlawful violence towards another and his conduct is such as would cause a person of reasonable firmness present at the scene to fear for his personal safety.

(2) Where 2 or more persons use or threaten the unlawful violence, it is the conduct of them taken together that must be considered for the purposes of subsection (1).

(3) For the purposes of this section a threat cannot be made by the use of words alone.

(4) No person of reasonable firmness need actually be, or be likely to be, present at the scene.

(5) Affray may be committed in private as well as in public places.

(6) A constable may arrest without warrant anyone he reasonably suspects is committing affray.

(7) A person guilty of affray is liable on conviction on indictment to imprisonment for a term not exceeding 3 years or a fine or both, or on summary conviction to imprisonment for a term not exceeding 6 months or a fine not exceeding the statutory maximum or both.

4.—(1) A person is guilty of an offence if he—

    (*a*) uses towards another person threatening, abusive or insulting words or behaviour, or

    (*b*) distributes or displays to another person any writing, sign or other visible representation which is threatening, abusive or insulting,

Fear or provocation of violence.

with intent to cause that person to believe that immediate unlawful violence will be used against him or another by any person, or to provoke the immediate use of unlawful violence by that person or another, or whereby that person is likely to believe that such violence will be used or it is likely that such violence will be provoked.

(2) An offence under this section may be committed in a public or a private place, except that no offence is committed where the words or behaviour are used, or the writing, sign or other visible representation is distributed or displayed, by a person inside a dwelling and the other person is also inside that or another dwelling.

(3) A constable may arrest without warrant anyone he reasonably suspects is committing an offence under this section.

(4) A person guilty of an offence under this section is liable on summary conviction to imprisonment for a term not exceeding 6 months or a fine not exceeding level 5 on the standard scale or both.

5.—(1) A person is guilty of an offence if he—

    (*a*) uses threatening, abusive or insulting words or behaviour, or disorderly behaviour, or

    (*b*) displays any writing, sign or other visible representation which is threatening, abusive or insulting,

Harassment, alarm or distress.

within the hearing or sight of a person likely to be caused harassment, alarm or distress thereby.

(2) An offence under this section may be committed in a public or a private place, except that no offence is committed

PART I

where the words or behaviour are used, or the writing, sign or other visible representation is displayed, by a person inside a dwelling and the other person is also inside that or another dwelling.

(3) It is a defence for the accused to prove—

(a) that he had no reason to believe that there was any person within hearing or sight who was likely to be caused harassment, alarm or distress, or

(b) that he was inside a dwelling and had no reason to believe that the words or behaviour used, or the writing, sign or other visible representation displayed, would be heard or seen by a person outside that or any other dwelling, or

(c) that his conduct was reasonable.

(4) A constable may arrest a person without warrant if—

(a) he engages in offensive conduct which the constable warns him to stop, and

(b) he engages in further offensive conduct immediately or shortly after the warning.

(5) In subsection (4) " offensive conduct " means conduct the constable reasonably suspects to constitute an offence under this section, and the conduct mentioned in paragraph (a) and the further conduct need not be of the same nature.

(6) A person guilty of an offence under this section is liable on summary conviction to a fine not exceeding level 3 on the standard scale.

Mental element: miscellaneous.

6.—(1) A person is guilty of riot only if he intends to use violence or is aware that his conduct may be violent.

(2) A person is guilty of violent disorder or affray only if he intends to use or threaten violence or is aware that his conduct may be violent or threaten violence.

(3) A person is guilty of an offence under section 4 only if he intends his words or behaviour, or the writing, sign or other visible representation, to be threatening, abusive or insulting, or is aware that it may be threatening, abusive or insulting.

(4) A person is guilty of an offence under section 5 only if he intends his words or behaviour, or the writing, sign or other visible representation, to be threatening, abusive or insulting, or is aware that it may be threatening, abusive or insulting or (as the case may be) he intends his behaviour to be or is aware that it may be disorderly.

(5) For the purposes of this section a person whose awareness is impaired by intoxication shall be taken to be aware of that of which he would be aware if not intoxicated, unless he shows

either that his intoxication was not self-induced or that it was
caused solely by the taking or administration of a substance in
the course of medical treatment.

(6) In subsection (5) " intoxication " means any intoxication,
whether caused by drink, drugs or other means, or by a combination of means.

(7) Subsections (1) and (2) do not affect the determination for
the purposes of riot or violent disorder of the number of
persons who use or threaten violence.

7.—(1) No prosecution for an offence of riot or incitement Procedure:
to riot may be instituted except by or with the consent of the miscellaneous.
Director of Public Prosecutions.

(2) For the purposes of the rules against charging more
than one offence in the same count or information, each of
sections 1 to 5 creates one offence.

(3) If on the trial on indictment of a person charged with
violent disorder or affray the jury find him not guilty of the
offence charged, they may (without prejudice to section 6(3) of
the Criminal Law Act 1967) find him guilty of an offence under 1967 c. 58.
section 4.

(4) The Crown Court has the same powers and duties in
relation to a person who is by virtue of subsection (3) convicted before it of an offence under section 4 as a magistrates'
court would have on convicting him of the offence.

8. In this Part—   Interpretation.
    " dwelling " means any structure or part of a structure occu-
          pied as a person's home or as other living accommoda-
          tion (whether the occupation is separate or shared with
          others) but does not include any part not so occupied,
          and for this purpose " structure " includes a tent, cara-
          van, vehicle, vessel or other temporary or movable
          structure ;
    " violence " means any violent conduct, so that—
          (*a*) except in the context of affray, it includes
          violent conduct towards property as well as violent
          conduct towards persons, and
          (*b*) it is not restricted to conduct causing or in-
          tended to cause injury or damage but includes any
          other violent conduct (for example, throwing at or
          towards a person a missile of a kind capable of caus-
          ing injury which does not hit or falls short).

9.—(1) The common law offences of riot, rout, unlawful assembly and affray are abolished.

(2) The offences under the following enactments are abolished—

    (*a*) section 1 of the Tumultuous Petitioning Act 1661 (presentation of petition to monarch or Parliament accompanied by excessive number of persons),

    (*b*) section 1 of the Shipping Offences Act 1793 (interference with operation of vessel by persons riotously assembled),

    (*c*) section 23 of the Seditious Meetings Act 1817 (prohibition of certain meetings within one mile of Westminster Hall when Parliament sitting), and

    (*d*) section 5 of the Public Order Act 1936 (conduct conducive to breach of the peace).

Construction
of other
instruments.
1886 c. 38.
1894 c. 60.
1906 c. 41.

10.—(1) In the Riot (Damages) Act 1886 and in section 515 of the Merchant Shipping Act 1894 (compensation for riot damage) " riotous " and " riotously " shall be construed in accordance with section 1 above.

(2) In Schedule 1 to the Marine Insurance Act 1906 (form and rules for the construction of certain insurance policies) " rioters " in rule 8 and " riot " in rule 10 shall, in the application of the rules to any policy taking effect on or after the coming into force of this section, be construed in accordance with section 1 above unless a different intention appears.

(3) " Riot " and cognate expressions in any enactment in force before the coming into force of this section (other than the enactments mentioned in subsections (1) and (2) above) shall be construed in accordance with section 1 above if they would have been construed in accordance with the common law offence of riot apart from this Part.

(4) Subject to subsections (1) to (3) above and unless a different intention appears, nothing in this Part affects the meaning of " riot " or any cognate expression in any enactment in force, or other instrument taking effect, before the coming into force of this section.

PART II

PROCESSIONS AND ASSEMBLIES

11.—(1) Written notice shall be given in accordance with this section of any proposal to hold a public procession intended—

    (*a*) to demonstrate support for or opposition to the views or actions of any person or body of persons, (*b*) to publicise a cause or campaign, or

(*c*) to mark or commemorate an event,

unless it is not reasonably practicable to give any advance notice of the procession.

(2) Subsection (1) does not apply where the procession is one commonly or customarily held in the police area (or areas) in which it is proposed to be held or is a funeral procession organised by a funeral director acting in the normal course of his business.

(3) The notice must specify the date when it is intended to hold the procession, the time when it is intended to start it, its proposed route, and the name and address of the person (or of one of the persons) proposing to organise it.

(4) Notice must be delivered to a police station—

(*a*) in the police area in which it is proposed the procession will start, or

(*b*) where it is proposed the procession will start in Scotland and cross into England, in the first police area in England on the proposed route.

(5) If delivered not less than 6 clear days before the date when the procession is intended to be held, the notice may be delivered by post by the recorded delivery service ; but section 7 of the Interpretation Act 1978 (under which a document sent by post is 1978 c. 30. deemed to have been served when posted and to have been delivered in the ordinary course of post) does not apply.

(6) If not delivered in accordance with subsection (5), the notice must be delivered by hand not less than 6 clear days before the date when the procession is intended to be held or, if that is not reasonably practicable, as soon as delivery is reasonably practicable.

(7) Where a public procession is held, each of the persons organising it is guilty of an offence if—

(*a*) the requirements of this section as to notice have not been satisfied, or

(*b*) the date when it is held, the time when it starts, or its route, differs from the date, time or route specified in the notice.

(8) It is a defence for the accused to prove that he did not know of, and neither suspected nor had reason to suspect, the failure to satisfy the requirements or (as the case may be) the difference of date, time or route.

(9) To the extent that an alleged offence turns on a difference of date, time or route, it is a defence for the accused to prove that the difference arose from circumstances beyond his control

or from something done with the agreement of a police officer or by his direction.

(10) A person guilty of an offence under subsection (7) is liable on summary conviction to a fine not exceeding level 3 on the standard scale.

12.—(1) If the senior police officer, having regard to the time or place at which and the circumstances in which any public procession is being held or is intended to be held and to its route or proposed route, reasonably believes that—

(a) it may result in serious public disorder, serious damage to property or serious disruption to the life of the community, or

(b) the purpose of the persons organising it is the intimidation of others with a view to compelling them not to do an act they have a right to do, or to do an act they have a right not to do,

he may give directions imposing on the persons organising or taking part in the procession such conditions as appear to him necessary to prevent such disorder, damage, disruption or intimidation, including conditions as to the route of the procession or prohibiting it from entering any public place specified in the directions.

(2) In subsection (1) " the senior police officer " means—

(a) in relation to a procession being held, or to a procession intended to be held in a case where persons are assembling with a view to taking part in it, the most senior in rank of the police officers present at the scene, and

(b) in relation to a procession intended to be held in a case where paragraph (a) does not apply, the chief officer of police.

(3) A direction given by a chief officer of police by virtue of subsection (2)(b) shall be given in writing.

(4) A person who organises a public procession and knowingly fails to comply with a condition imposed under this section is guilty of an offence, but it is a defence for him to prove that the failure arose from circumstances beyond his control.

(5) A person who takes part in a public procession and knowingly fails to comply with a condition imposed under this section is guilty of an offence, but it is a defence for him to prove that the failure arose from circumstances beyond his control.

(6) A person who incites another to commit an offence under subsection (5) is guilty of an offence.

(7) A constable in uniform may arrest without warrant anyone he reasonably suspects is committing an offence under subsection (4), (5) or (6).

(8) A person guilty of an offence under subsection (4) is liable on summary conviction to imprisonment for a term not exceeding 3 months or a fine not exceeding level 4 on the standard scale or both.

(9) A person guilty of an offence under subsection (5) is liable on summary conviction to a fine not exceeding level 3 on the standard scale.

(10) A person guilty of an offence under subsection (6) is liable on summary conviction to imprisonment for a term not exceeding 3 months or a fine not exceeding level 4 on the standard scale or both, notwithstanding section 45(3) of the Magistrates' Courts Act 1980 (inciter liable to same penalty as incited).

1980 c. 43.

(11) In Scotland this section applies only in relation to a procession being held, and to a procession intended to be held in a case where persons are assembling with a view to taking part in it.

13.—(1) If at any time the chief officer of police reasonably believes that, because of particular circumstances existing in any district or part of a district, the powers under section 12 will not be sufficient to prevent the holding of public processions in that district or part from resulting in serious public disorder, he shall apply to the council of the district for an order prohibiting for such period not exceeding 3 months as may be specified in the application the holding of all public processions (or of any class of public procession so specified) in the district or part concerned.

Prohibiting public processions.

(2) On receiving such an application, a council may with the consent of the Secretary of State make an order either in the terms of the application or with such modifications as may be approved by the Secretary of State.

(3) Subsection (1) does not apply in the City of London or the metropolitan police district.

(4) If at any time the Commissioner of Police for the City of London or the Commissioner of Police of the Metropolis reasonably believes that, because of particular circumstances existing in his police area or part of it, the powers under section 12 will not be sufficient to prevent the holding of public processions in that area or part from resulting in serious public disorder, he may with the consent of the Secretary of State make an order prohibiting for such period not exceeding 3 months as may be specified in the order the holding of all public processions (or

PART II   of any class of public procession so specified) in the area or part concerned.

(5) An order made under this section may be revoked or varied by a subsequent order made in the same way, that is, in accordance with subsections (1) and (2) or subsection (4), as the case may be.

(6) Any order under this section shall, if not made in writing, be recorded in writing as soon as practicable after being made.

(7) A person who organises a public procession the holding of which he knows is prohibited by virtue of an order under this section is guilty of an offence.

(8) A person who takes part in a public procession the holding of which he knows is prohibited by virtue of an order under this section is guilty of an offence.

(9) A person who incites another to commit an offence under subsection (8) is guilty of an offence.

(10) A constable in uniform may arrest without warrant anyone he reasonably suspects is committing an offence under subsection (7), (8) or (9).

(11) A person guilty of an offence under subsection (7) is liable on summary conviction to imprisonment for a term not exceeding 3 months or a fine not exceeding level 4 on the standard scale or both.

(12) A person guilty of an offence under subsection (8) is liable on summary conviction to a fine not exceeding level 3 on the standard scale.

(13) A person guilty of an offence under subsection (9) is liable on summary conviction to imprisonment for a term not exceeding 3 months or a fine not exceeding level 4 on the standard scale or both, notwithstanding section 45(3) of the Magistrates' Courts Act 1980.

1980 c. 43.

Imposing conditions on public assemblies.

14.—(1) If the senior police officer, having regard to the time or place at which and the circumstances in which any public assembly is being held or is intended to be held, reasonably believes that—

    (a) it may result in serious public disorder, serious damage to property or serious disruption to the life of the community, or

    (b) the purpose of the persons organising it is the intimidation of others with a view to compelling them not to do an act they have a right to do, or to do an act they have a right not to do,

he may give directions imposing on the persons organising or taking part in the assembly such conditions as to the place at

which the assembly may be (or continue to be) held, its maximum duration, or the maximum number of persons who may
constitute it, as appear to him necessary to prevent such disorder,
damage, disruption or intimidation.

(2) In subsection (1) " the senior police officer " means—

　　(a) in relation to an assembly being held, the most senior
　　　　in rank of the police officers present at the scene, and

　　(b) in relation to an assembly intended to be held, the chief
　　　　officer of police.

(3) A direction given by a chief officer of police by virtue of
subsection (2)(b) shall be given in writing.

(4) A person who organises a public assembly and knowingly
fails to comply with a condition imposed under this section is
guilty of an offence, but it is a defence for him to prove that
the failure arose from circumstances beyond his control.

(5) A person who takes part in a public assembly and knowingly fails to comply with a condition imposed under this section is guilty of an offence, but it is a defence for him to prove
that the failure arose from circumstances beyond his control.

(6) A person who incites another to commit an offence under
subsection (5) is guilty of an offence.

(7) A constable in uniform may arrest without warrant anyone he reasonably suspects is committing an offence under subsection (4), (5) or (6).

(8) A person guilty of an offence under subsection (4) is liable
on summary conviction to imprisonment for a term not exceeding 3 months or a fine not exceeding level 4 on the standard
scale or both.

(9) A person guilty of an offence under subsection (5) is liable
on summary conviction to a fine not exceeding level 3 on the
standard scale.

(10) A person guilty of an offence under subsection (6) is
liable on summary conviction to imprisonment for a term not
exceeding 3 months or a fine not exceeding level 4 on the standard scale or both, notwithstanding section 45(3) of the Magi-   1980 c. 43.
strates' Courts Act 1980.

15.—(1) The chief officer of police may delegate, to such   Delegation.
extent and subject to such conditions as he may specify, any of
his functions under sections 12 to 14 to a deputy or assistant
chief constable ; and references in those sections to the person
delegating shall be construed accordingly.

(2) Subsection (1) shall have effect in the City of London and
the metropolitan police district as if " a deputy or assistant chief
constable " read " an assistant commissioner of police ".

PART II
Interpretation.

1963 c. 33.

1984 c. 54.

16. In this Part—

"the City of London" means the City as defined for the purposes of the Acts relating to the City of London police ;

"the metropolitan police district" means that district as defined in section 76 of the London Government Act 1963 ;

"public assembly" means an assembly of 20 or more persons in a public place which is wholly or partly open to the air ;

"public place" means—

(a) any highway, or in Scotland any road within the meaning of the Roads (Scotland) Act 1984, and

(b) any place to which at the material time the public or any section of the public has access, on payment or otherwise, as of right or by virtue of express or implied permission ;

"public procession" means a procession in a public place.

PART III

RACIAL HATRED

Meaning of " racial hatred "

Meaning of
" racial
hatred ".

17. In this Part " racial hatred " means hatred against a group of persons in Great Britain defined by reference to colour, race, nationality (including citizenship) or ethnic or national origins.

Acts intended or likely to stir up racial hatred

Use of words
or behaviour
or display of
written
material

18.—(1) A person who uses threatening, abusive or insulting words or behaviour, or displays any written material which is threatening, abusive or insulting, is guilty of an offence if—

(a) he intends thereby to stir up racial hatred, or

(b) having regard to all the circumstances racial hatred is likely to be stirred up thereby.

(2) An offence under this section may be committed in a public or a private place, except that no offence is committed where the words or behaviour are used, or the written material is displayed, by a person inside a dwelling and are not heard or seen except by other persons in that or another dwelling.

(3) A constable may arrest without warrant anyone he reasonably suspects is committing an offence under this section.

(4) In proceedings for an offence under this section it is a defence for the accused to prove that he was inside a dwelling and had no reason to believe that the words or behaviour used,

or the written material displayed, would be heard or seen by a person outside that or any other dwelling.

(5) A person who is not shown to have intended to stir up racial hatred is not guilty of an offence under this section if he did not intend his words or behaviour, or the written material, to be, and was not aware that it might be, threatening, abusive or insulting.

(6) This section does not apply to words or behaviour used, or written material displayed, solely for the purpose of being included in a programme broadcast or included in a cable programme service.

19.—(1) A person who publishes or distributes written material Publishing or which is threatening, abusive or insulting is guilty of an offence distributing if— material.

    (*a*) he intends thereby to stir up racial hatred, or

    (*b*) having regard to all the circumstances racial hatred is likely to be stirred up thereby.

(2) In proceedings for an offence under this section it is a defence for an accused who is not shown to have intended to stir up racial hatred to prove that he was not aware of the content of the material and did not suspect, and had no reason to suspect, that it was threatening, abusive or insulting.

(3) References in this Part to the publication or distribution of written material are to its publication or distribution to the public or a section of the public.

20.—(1) If a public performance of a play is given which Public involves the use of threatening, abusive or insulting words or performance behaviour, any person who presents or directs the performance of play. is guilty of an offence if—

    (*a*) he intends thereby to stir up racial hatred, or

    (*b*) having regard to all the circumstances (and, in particular, taking the performance as a whole) racial hatred is likely to be stirred up thereby.

(2) If a person presenting or directing the performance is not shown to have intended to stir up racial hatred, it is a defence for him to prove—

    (*a*) that he did not know and had no reason to suspect that the performance would involve the use of the offending words or behaviour, or

    (*b*) that he did not know and had no reason to suspect that the offending words or behaviour were threatening, abusive or insulting, or (*c*) that he did not know and had no reason to suspect that the circumstances in which the performance would be given would be such that racial hatred would be likely to be stirred up.

(3) This section does not apply to a performance given solely or primarily for one or more of the following purposes—

(*a*) rehearsal,

(*b*) making a recording of the performance, or

(*c*) enabling the performance to be broadcast or included in a cable programme service ;

but if it is proved that the performance was attended by persons other than those directly connected with the giving of the performance or the doing in relation to it of the things mentioned in paragraph (*b*) or (*c*), the performance shall, unless the contrary is shown, be taken not to have been given solely or primarily for the purposes mentioned above.

(4) For the purposes of this section—

(*a*) a person shall not be treated as presenting a performance of a play by reason only of his taking part in it as a performer,

(*b*) a person taking part as a performer in a performance directed by another shall be treated as a person who directed the performance if without reasonable excuse he performs otherwise than in accordance with that person's direction, and

(*c*) a person shall be taken to have directed a performance of a play given under his direction notwithstanding that he was not present during the performance ;

and a person shall not be treated as aiding or abetting the commission of an offence under this section by reason only of his taking part in a performance as a performer.

(5) In this section " play " and " public performance " have the same meaning as in the Theatres Act 1968.

1968 c. 54.

(6) The following provisions of the Theatres Act 1968 apply in relation to an offence under this section as they apply to an offence under section 2 of that Act—

section 9 (script as evidence of what was performed),

section 10 (power to make copies of script),

section 15 (powers of entry and inspection).

Distributing, showing or playing a recording.

21.—(1) A person who distributes, or shows or plays, a recording of visual images or sounds which are threatening, abusive or insulting is guilty of an offence if—

(*a*) he intends thereby to stir up racial hatred, or

(*b*) having regard to all the circumstances racial hatred is likely to be stirred up thereby.

(2) In this Part "recording" means any record from which PART III
visual images or sounds may, by any means, be reproduced;
and references to the distribution, showing or playing of a
recording are to its distribution, showing or playing to the public
or a section of the public.

(3) In proceedings for an offence under this section it is a
defence for an accused who is not shown to have intended to
stir up racial hatred to prove that he was not aware of the
content of the recording and did not suspect, and had no reason
to suspect, that it was threatening, abusive or insulting.

(4) This section does not apply to the showing or playing of a
recording solely for the purpose of enabling the recording to be
broadcast or included in a cable programme service.

22.—(1) If a programme involving threatening, abusive or Broadcasting
insulting visual images or sounds is broadcast, or included in or including
a cable programme service, each of the persons mentioned in programme
subsection (2) is guilty of an offence if— in cable
programme
  (a) he intends thereby to stir up racial hatred, or service.

  (b) having regard to all the circumstances racial hatred is
      likely to be stirred up thereby.

(2) The persons are—

  (a) the person providing the broadcasting or cable pro-
      gramme service,

  (b) any person by whom the programme is produced or
      directed, and

  (c) any person by whom offending words or behaviour are
      used.

(3) If the person providing the service, or a person by whom
the programme was produced or directed, is not shown to have
intended to stir up racial hatred, it is a defence for him to prove
that—

  (a) he did not know and had no reason to suspect that the
      programme would involve the offending material, and

  (b) having regard to the circumstances in which the pro-
      gramme was broadcast, or included in a cable pro-
      gramme service, it was not reasonably practicable for
      him to secure the removal of the material.

(4) It is a defence for a person by whom the programme was
produced or directed who is not shown to have intended to stir
up racial hatred to prove that he did not know and had no
reason to suspect—

  (a) that the programme would be broadcast or included in
      a cable programme service, or

(*b*) that the circumstances in which the programme would be broadcast or so included would be such that racial hatred would be likely to be stirred up.

(5) It is a defence for a person by whom offending words or behaviour were used and who is not shown to have intended to stir up racial hatred to prove that he did not know and had no reason to suspect—

(*a*) that a programme involving the use of the offending material would be broadcast or included in a cable programme service, or

(*b*) that the circumstances in which a programme involving the use of the offending material would be broadcast, or so included, or in which a programme broadcast or so included would involve the use of the offending material, would be such that racial hatred would be likely to be stirred up.

(6) A person who is not shown to have intended to stir up racial hatred is not guilty of an offence under this section if he did not know, and had no reason to suspect, that the offending material was threatening, abusive or insulting.

(7) This section does not apply—

(*a*) to the broadcasting of a programme by the British Broadcasting Corporation or the Independent Broadcasting Authority, or

(*b*) to the inclusion of a programme in a cable programme service by the reception and immediate re-transmission of a broadcast by either of those authorities.

1984 c. 46.

(8) The following provisions of the Cable and Broadcasting Act 1984 apply to an offence under this section as they apply to a " relevant offence " as defined in section 33(2) of that Act—

section 33 (scripts as evidence),

section 34 (power to make copies of scripts and records),

section 35 (availability of visual and sound records) ;

and sections 33 and 34 of that Act apply to an offence under this section in connection with the broadcasting of a programme as they apply to an offence in connection with the inclusion of a programme in a cable programme service.

Racially inflammatory material

Possession of racially inflammatory material.

23.—(1) A person who has in his possession written material which is threatening, abusive or insulting, or a recording of visual images or sounds which are threatening, abusive or insulting, with a view to—

(*a*) in the case of written material, its being displayed, published, distributed, broadcast or included in a cable programme service, whether by himself or another, or (*b*) in the case of a recording, its being distributed, shown, played, broadcast or included in a cable programme service, whether by himself or another,

is guilty of an offence if he intends racial hatred to be stirred up thereby or, having regard to all the circumstances, racial hatred is likely to be stirred up thereby.

(2) For this purpose regard shall be had to such display, publication, distribution, showing, playing, broadcasting or inclusion in a cable programme service as he has, or it may reasonably be inferred that he has, in view.

(3) In proceedings for an offence under this section it is a defence for an accused who is not shown to have intended to stir up racial hatred to prove that he was not aware of the content of the written material or recording and did not suspect, and had no reason to suspect, that it was threatening, abusive or insulting.

(4) This section does not apply to the possession of written material or a recording by or on behalf of the British Broadcasting Corporation or the Independent Broadcasting Authority or with a view to its being broadcast by either of those authorities.

24.—(1) If in England and Wales a justice of the peace is satisfied by information on oath laid by a constable that there are reasonable grounds for suspecting that a person has possession of written material or a recording in contravention of section 23, the justice may issue a warrant under his hand authorising any constable to enter and search the premises where it is suspected the material or recording is situated.

Powers of entry and search.

(2) If in Scotland a sheriff or justice of the peace is satisfied by evidence on oath that there are reasonable grounds for suspecting that a person has possession of written material or a recording in contravention of section 23, the sheriff or justice may issue a warrant authorising any constable to enter and search the premises where it is suspected the material or recording is situated.

(3) A constable entering or searching premises in pursuance of a warrant issued under this section may use reasonable force if necessary.

(4) In this section " premises " means any place and, in particular, includes—

(*a*) any vehicle, vessel, aircraft or hovercraft,

(*b*) any offshore installation as defined in section 1(3) (*b*) of the Mineral Workings (Offshore Installations) Act 1971, and

1971 c. 61.

(*c*) any tent or movable structure.

PART III
Power to order
forfeiture.

25.—(1) A court by or before which a person is convicted of—

　(*a*) an offence under section 18 relating to the display of written material, or

　(*b*) an offence under section 19, 21 or 23,

shall order to be forfeited any written material or recording produced to the court and shown to its satisfaction to be written material or a recording to which the offence relates.

(2) An order made under this section shall not take effect—

　(*a*) in the case of an order made in proceedings in England and Wales, until the expiry of the ordinary time within which an appeal may be instituted or, where an appeal is duly instituted, until it is finally decided or abandoned ;

　(*b*) in the case of an order made in proceedings in Scotland, until the expiration of the time within which, by virtue of any statute, an appeal may be instituted or, where such an appeal is duly instituted, until the appeal is finally decided or abandoned.

(3) For the purposes of subsection (2)(*a*)—

　(*a*) an application for a case stated or for leave to appeal shall be treated as the institution of an appeal, and

　(*b*) where a decision on appeal is subject to a further appeal, the appeal is not finally determined until the expiry of the ordinary time within which a further appeal may be instituted or, where a further appeal is duly instituted, until the further appeal is finally decided or abandoned.

(4) For the purposes of subsection (2)(*b*) the lodging of an application for a stated case or note of appeal against sentence shall be treated as the institution of an appeal.

Supplementary provisions

Savings for
reports of
parliamentary
or judicial
proceedings.

26.—(1) Nothing in this Part applies to a fair and accurate report of proceedings in Parliament.

(2) Nothing in this Part applies to a fair and accurate report of proceedings publicly heard before a court or tribunal exercising judicial authority where the report is published contemporaneously with the proceedings or, if it is not reasonably practicable or would be unlawful to publish a report of them contemporaneously, as soon as publication is reasonably practicable and lawful.

Procedure and
punishment.

27.—(1) No proceedings for an offence under this Part may be instituted in England and Wales except by or with the consent of the Attorney General.

(2) For the purposes of the rules in England and Wales against charging more than one offence in the same count or information, each of sections 18 to 23 creates one offence.

(3) A person guilty of an offence under this Part is liable—

(a) on conviction on indictment to imprisonment for a term not exceeding two years or a fine or both ;

(b) on summary conviction to imprisonment for a term not exceeding six months or a fine not exceeding the statutory maximum or both.

28.—(1) Where a body corporate is guilty of an offence under this Part and it is shown that the offence was committed with the consent or connivance of a director, manager, secretary or other similar officer of the body, or a person purporting to act in any such capacity, he as well as the body corporate is guilty of the offence and liable to be proceeded against and punished accordingly.

(2) Where the affairs of a body corporate are managed by its members, subsection (1) applies in relation to the acts and defaults of a member in connection with his functions of management as it applies to a director.

29. In this Part—

" broadcast " means broadcast by wireless telegraphy (within the meaning of the Wireless Telegraphy Act 1949) for general reception, whether by way of sound broadcasting or television ;

" cable programme service " has the same meaning as in the Cable and Broadcasting Act 1984 ;

" distribute ", and related expressions, shall be construed in accordance with section 19(3) (written material) and section 21(2) (recordings) ;

" dwelling " means any structure or part of a structure occupied as a person's home or other living accommodation (whether the occupation is separate or shared with others) but does not include any part not so occupied, and for this purpose " structure " includes a tent, caravan, vehicle, vessel or other temporary or movable structure ;

" programme " means any item which is broadcast or included in a cable programme service ;

" publish ", and related expressions, in relation to written material, shall be construed in accordance with section 19 (3);

" racial hatred " has the meaning given by section 17 ;

PART III

" recording " has the meaning given by section 21(2), and " play " and " show ", and related expressions, in relation to a recording, shall be construed in accordance with that provision ;

" written material " includes any sign or other visible representation.

PART IV

EXCLUSION ORDERS

Exclusion orders.

30.—(1) A court by or before which a person is convicted of an offence to which section 31 applies may make an order (an exclusion order) prohibiting him from entering any premises for the purpose of attending any prescribed football match there.

(2) No exclusion order may be made unless the court is satisfied that making such an order in relation to the accused would help to prevent violence or disorder at or in connection with prescribed football matches.

(3) An exclusion order may only be made—

(a) in addition to a sentence imposed in respect of the offence of which the accused is convicted, or

(b) in addition to a probation order or an order discharging him absolutely or conditionally.

1973 c. 62.

(4) An exclusion order may be made as mentioned in subsection (3)(b) notwithstanding anything in sections 2, 7 and 13 of the Powers of Criminal Courts Act 1973 (which relate to orders there mentioned and their effect).

Offences connected with football.

31.—(1) This section applies to any offence which fulfils one or more of the following three conditions.

(2) The first condition is that the offence was committed during any period relevant to a prescribed football match (as determined under subsections (6) to (8)), while the accused was at, or was entering or leaving or trying to enter or leave, the football ground concerned.

(3) The second condition is that the offence—

(a) involved the use or threat of violence by the accused towards another person and was committed while one or each of them was on a journey to or from an association football match,

(b) involved the use or threat of violence towards property and was committed while the accused was on such a journey, or

(c) was committed under section 5 or Part III while the accused was on such a journey.

(4) The third condition is that the offence was committed under section 1(3) or (4) or 1A(3) or (4) of the Sporting Events (Control of Alcohol etc.) Act 1985 (alcohol on journeys to or from certain sporting events) and the designated sporting event concerned was an association football match.

(5) For the purposes of subsection (3) a person's journey includes breaks (including overnight breaks).

(6) The period beginning 2 hours before the start of the match or (if earlier) 2 hours before the time at which it is advertised to start, and ending 1 hour after the end of it, is a period relevant to it.

(7) Where the match is advertised to start at a particular time on a particular day and is postponed to a later day, the period in the advertised day beginning 2 hours before and ending 1 hour after that time is also a period relevant to it.

(8) Where the match is advertised to start at a particular time on a particular day and does not take place, the period in that day beginning 2 hours before and ending 1 hour after that time is a period relevant to it.

32.—(1) An exclusion order shall have effect for such period Effect of as is specified in the order. order.

(2) The period shall be not less than three months or, in the case of a person already subject to an exclusion order, not less than three months plus the unexpired period of the earlier order or, if there is more than one earlier order, of the most recent order.

(3) A person who enters premises in breach of an exclusion order is guilty of an offence and liable on summary conviction to imprisonment for a term not exceeding 1 month or a fine not exceeding level 3 on the standard scale or both.

(4) A constable who reasonably suspects that a person has entered premises in breach of an exclusion order may arrest him without warrant.

33.—(1) A person in relation to whom an exclusion order has Application had effect for at least one year may apply to the court by which to terminate it was made to terminate it. order.

(2) On such an application the court may, having regard to the person's character, his conduct since the order was made, the nature of the offence which led to it and any other circumstances of the case, either by order terminate the order (as from a date specified in the terminating order) or refuse the application.

PART IV

(3) Where an application under this section is refused, a further application in respect of the exclusion order shall not be entertained if made within the period of six months beginning with the day of the refusal.

(4) The court may order the applicant to pay all or any part of the costs of an application under this section.

(5) In the case of an exclusion order made by a magistrates' court, the reference in subsection (1) to the court by which it was made includes a reference to any magistrates' court acting for the same petty sessions area as that court.

1980 c. 43.

(6) Section 63(2) of the Magistrates' Courts Act 1980 (power to suspend or rescind orders) does not apply to an exclusion order.

Information.

34.—(1) Where a court makes an exclusion order, the clerk of the court (in the case of a magistrates' court) or the appropriate officer (in the case of the Crown Court)—

(a) shall give a copy of it to the person to whom it relates,

(b) shall (as soon as reasonably practicable) send a copy of it to the chief officer of police for the police area in which the offence leading to the order was committed, and

(c) shall (as soon as reasonably practicable) send a copy of it to any prescribed person.

(2) Where a court terminates an exclusion order under section 33, the clerk of the court (in the case of a magistrates' court) or the appropriate officer (in the case of the Crown Court)—

(a) shall give a copy of the terminating order to the person to whom the exclusion order relates,

(b) shall (as soon as reasonably practicable) send a copy of the terminating order to the chief officer of police for the police area in which the offence leading to the exclusion order was committed, and

(c) shall (as soon as reasonably practicable) send a copy of the terminating order to any prescribed person.

1980 c. 43.

(3) References in this section to the clerk of a magistrates' court shall be construed in accordance with section 141 of the Magistrates' Courts Act 1980, reading references to that Act as references to this section.

(4) In this section "prescribed" means prescribed by order made by the Secretary of State.

(5) The power to make an order under this section shall be exercisable by statutory instrument subject to annulment in pursuance of a resolution of either House of Parliament.

35.—(1) The court by which an exclusion order is made may make an order which—

    (*a*) requires a constable to take a photograph of the person to whom the exclusion order relates or to cause such a photograph to be taken, and

    (*b*) requires that person to go to a specified police station not later than 7 clear days after the day on which the order under this section is made, and at a specified time of day or between specified times of day, in order to have his photograph taken.

(2) In subsection (1) " specified " means specified in the order made under this section.

(3) No order may be made under this section unless an application to make it is made to the court by or on behalf of the person who is the prosecutor in respect of the offence leading to the exclusion order.

(4) If the person to whom the exclusion order relates fails to comply with an order under this section a constable may arrest him without warrant in order that his photograph may be taken.

36.—(1) In this Part " prescribed football match " means an association football match of any description prescribed by order made by the Secretary of State.

(2) The power to make an order under this section shall be exercisable by statutory instrument subject to annulment in pursuance of a resolution of either House of Parliament.

37.—(1) The Secretary of State may by order provide for sections 30 to 35 to apply as if—

    (*a*) any reference to an association football match included a reference to a sporting event of a kind specified in the order, and

    (*b*) any reference to a prescribed football match included a reference to such a sporting event of a description specified in the order.

(2) An order under subsection (1) may make such modifications of those sections, as they apply by virtue of the order, as the Secretary of State thinks fit.

(3) The power to make an order under this section shall be exercisable by statutory instrument, and no such order shall be made unless a draft of the order has been laid before and approved by resolution of each House of Parliament.

PART V

MISCELLANEOUS AND GENERAL

Contamination
of or
interference
with goods
with intention
of causing
public alarm or
anxiety, etc.

38.—(1) It is an offence for a person, with the intention—

(a) of causing public alarm or anxiety, or

(b) of causing injury to members of the public consuming or using the goods, or

(c) of causing economic loss to any person by reason of the goods being shunned by members of the public, or

(d) of causing economic loss to any person by reason of steps taken to avoid any such alarm or anxiety, injury or loss,

to contaminate or interfere with goods, or make it appear that goods have been contaminated or interfered with, or to place goods which have been contaminated or interfered with, or which appear to have been contaminated or interfered with, in a place where goods of that description are consumed, used, sold or otherwise supplied.

(2) It is also an offence for a person, with any such intention as is mentioned in paragraph (a), (c) or (d) of subsection (1), to threaten that he or another will do, or to claim that he or another has done, any of the acts mentioned in that subsection.

(3) It is an offence for a person to be in possession of any of the following articles with a view to the commission of an offence under subsection (1)—

(a) materials to be used for contaminating or interfering with goods or making it appear that goods have been contaminated or interfered with, or

(b) goods which have been contaminated or interfered with, or which appear to have been contaminated or interfered with.

(4) A person guilty of an offence under this section is liable—

(a) on conviction on indictment to imprisonment for a term not exceeding 10 years or a fine or both, or

(b) on summary conviction to imprisonment for a term not exceeding six months or a fine not exceeding the statutory maximum or both.

(5) In this section " goods " includes substances whether natural or manufactured and whether or not incorporated in or mixed with other goods.

(6) The reference in subsection (2) to a person claiming that certain acts have been committed does not include a person who in good faith reports or warns that such acts have been, or appear to have been committed.

39.—(1) If the senior police officer reasonably believes that   PART V
two or more persons have entered land as trespassers and are   Power to direct
present there with the common purpose of residing there for   trespassers to
any period, that reasonable steps have been taken by or on   leave land.
behalf of the occupier to ask them to leave and—

  (*a*) that any of those persons has caused damage to pro-
      perty on the land or used threatening, abusive or
      insulting words or behaviour towards the occupier, a
      member of his family or an employee or agent of his,
      or

  (*b*) that those persons have between them brought twelve
      or more vehicles on to the land,

he may direct those persons, or any of them, to leave the land.

(2) If a person knowing that such a direction has been given
which applies to him—

  (*a*) fails to leave the land as soon as reasonably practicable,
      or

  (*b*) having left again enters the land as a trespasser within
      the period of three months beginning with the day on
      which the direction was given,

he commits an offence and is liable on summary conviction to
imprisonment for a term not exceeding three months or a fine
not exceeding level 4 on the standard scale, or both.

(3) A constable in uniform who reasonably suspects that a
person is committing an offence under this section may arrest
him without warrant.

(4) In proceedings for an offence under this section it is a
defence for the accused to show—

  (*a*) that his original entry on the land was not as a tres-
      passer, or

  (*b*) that he had a reasonable excuse for failing to leave the
      land as soon as reasonably practicable or, as the case
      may be, for again entering the land as a trespasser.

(5) In this section—

  " land " does not include—

      (*a*) buildings other than—

          (i) agricultural buildings within the meaning of
              section 26(4) of the General Rate Act 1967,   1967 c. 9.
              or

          (ii) scheduled monuments within the meaning of
              the Ancient Monuments and Archaeological   1979 c. 46.
              Areas Act 1979 ;

      (*b*) land forming part of a highway ;

" occupier " means the person entitled to possession of the land by virtue of an estate or interest held by him ;

" property " means property within the meaning of section 1971 c. 48. 10(1) of the Criminal Damage Act 1971 ;

" senior police officer " means the most senior in rank of the police officers present at the scene ;

" trespasser ", in relation to land, means a person who is a trespasser as against the occupier of the land ;

" vehicle " includes a caravan as defined in section 29(1) 1960 c. 62. of the Caravan Sites and Control of Development Act 1960 ;

and a person may be regarded for the purposes of this section as having the purpose of residing in a place notwithstanding that he has a home elsewhere.

Amendments, repeals and savings.
1985 c. 57.
1980 c. 62. **40.**—(1) Schedule 1, which amends the Sporting Events (Control of Alcohol etc.) Act 1985 and Part V of the Criminal Justice (Scotland) Act 1980, shall have effect.

(2) Schedule 2, which contains miscellaneous and consequential amendments, shall have effect.

(3) The enactments mentioned in Schedule 3 (which include enactments related to the subject matter of this Act but already obsolete or unnecessary) are repealed to the extent specified in column 3.

(4) Nothing in this Act affects the common law powers in England and Wales to deal with or prevent a breach of the peace.

(5) As respects Scotland, nothing in this Act affects any power of a constable under any rule of law.

Commence-
ment. **41.**—(1) This Act shall come into force on such day as the Secretary of State may appoint by order made by statutory instrument, and different days may be appointed for different provisions or different purposes.

(2) Nothing in a provision of this Act applies in relation to an offence committed or act done before the provision comes into force.

(3) Where a provision of this Act comes into force for certain purposes only, the references in subsection (2) to the provision are references to it so far as it relates to those purposes.

Extent. **42.**—(1) The provisions of this Act extend to England and Wales except so far as they—

(a) amend or repeal an enactment which does not so extend, or (*b*) relate to the extent of provisions to Scotland or Northern Ireland.

(2) The following provisions of this Act extend to Scotland—

in Part I, section 9(2) except paragraph (*a*) ;

in Part II, sections 12 and 14 to 16 ;

Part III ;

Part V, except sections 38, 39, 40(4), subsections (1) and (3) of this section and any provision amending or repealing an enactment which does not extend to Scotland.

(3) The following provisions of this Act extend to Northern Ireland—

sections 38, 41, this subsection, section 43 and paragraph 6 of Schedule 2.

43. This Act may be cited as the Public Order Act 1986. Short title.

SCHEDULES

Section 40 (1).

SCHEDULE 1

SPORTING EVENTS

PART I

ENGLAND AND WALES

Introduction

1985 c. 57.   1. The Sporting Events (Control of Alcohol etc.) Act 1985 shall be amended as mentioned in this Part.

Vehicles

2. The following shall be inserted after section 1 (offences in connection with alcohol on coaches and trains)—

"Alcohol on certain other vehicles.   1A.—(1) This section applies to a motor vehicle which—

    (*a*) is not a public service vehicle but is adapted to carry more than 8 passengers, and

    (*b*) is being used for the principal purpose of carrying two or more passengers for the whole or part of a journey to or from a designated sporting event.

(2) A person who knowingly causes or permits intoxicating liquor to be carried on a motor vehicle to which this section applies is guilty of an offence—

    (*a*) if he is its driver, or

    (*b*) if he is not its driver but is its keeper, the servant or agent of its keeper, a person to whom it is made available (by hire, loan or otherwise) by its keeper or the keeper's servant or agent, or the servant or agent of a person to whom it is so made available.

(3) A person who has intoxicating liquor in his possession while on a motor vehicle to which this section applies is guilty of an offence.

(4) A person who is drunk on a motor vehicle to which this section applies is guilty of an offence.

(5) In this section—

    " keeper ", in relation to a vehicle, means the person having the duty to take out a licence for it under section 1(1) of the Vehicles (Excise) Act 1971,

1971 c. 10.

    " motor vehicle " means a mechanically propelled vehicle intended or adapted for use on roads, and

" public service vehicle " has the same meaning as in
the Public Passenger Vehicles Act 1981.".

Fireworks etc.

3. The following shall be inserted after section 2 (offences in connection with alcohol, containers etc. at sports grounds)—

" Fireworks
etc.
     2A.—(1) A person is guilty of an offence if he has an
article or substance to which this section applies in his
possession—

     (*a*) at any time during the period of a designated
          sporting event when he is in any area of a
          designated sports ground from which the event
          may be directly viewed, or

     (*b*) while entering or trying to enter a designated
          sports ground at any time during the period of a
          designated sporting event at the ground.

     (2) It is a defence for the accused to prove that he
had possession with lawful authority.

     (3) This section applies to any article or substance
whose main purpose is the emission of a flare for purposes
of illuminating or signalling (as opposed to igniting or
heating) or the emission of smoke or a visible gas ; and
in particular it applies to distress flares, fog signals, and
pellets and capsules intended to be used as fumigators
or for testing pipes, but not to matches, cigarette lighters
or heaters.

     (4) This section also applies to any article which is a
firework.".

Licensing etc.

4. The following shall be inserted after section 5—

" Private
facilities for
viewing
events.
     5A.—(1) In relation to a room in a designated sports
ground—

     (*a*) from which designated sporting events may be
          directly viewed, and

     (*b*) to which the general public are not admitted,

sections 2(1) (*a*) and 3(1) (*a*) of this Act have effect with
the substitution for the reference to the period of a designated sporting event of a reference to the restricted period
defined below.

     (2) Subject to any order under subsection (3) below,
the restricted period of a designated sporting event for the
purposes of this section is the period beginning 15 minutes
before the start of the event or (if earlier) 15 minutes before
the time at which it is advertised to start and ending 15
minutes after the end of the event, but—

     (*a*) where an event advertised to start at a particular
          time on a particular day is postponed to a later

day, the restricted period includes the period in the day on which it is advertised to take place beginning 15 minutes before and ending 15 minutes after that time, and

(b) where an event advertised to start at a particular time on a particular day does not take place, the period is the period referred to in paragraph (a) above.

(3) The Secretary of State may by order provide, in relation to all designated sporting events or in relation to such descriptions of event as are specified in the order—

(a) that the restricted period shall be such period, shorter than that mentioned in subsection (2) above, as may be specified in the order, or

(b) that there shall be no restricted period.

(4) An order under this section shall be made by statutory instrument which shall be subject to annulment in pursuance of a resolution of either House of Parliament.

Occasional licences.

5B.—(1) An occasional licence which is in force for any place situated in the area of a designated sports ground, and which would (apart from this section) authorise the sale of intoxicating liquor at the place during the whole or part of the period of a designated sporting event at the ground, shall not authorise such sale.

(2) Where the sale of intoxicating liquor would (apart from this section) be authorised by an occasional licence, its holder is guilty of an offence if he sells or authorises the sale of such liquor and by virtue of this section the licence does not authorise the sale.

(3) A person is guilty of an offence if he consumes intoxicating liquor at a place, or takes such liquor from a place, at a time when an occasional licence which would (apart from this section) authorise the sale of the liquor at the place does not do so by virtue of this section.

Clubs.

1964 c. 26.

5C.—(1) Subsections (3) and (5) of section 39 of the Licensing Act 1964 (clubs), and subsection (4) of that section as it applies to subsection (3), shall not apply as regards the supply of intoxicating liquor in the area of a designated sports ground during the period of a designated sporting event at the ground or as regards the keeping of intoxicating liquor for such supply ; but subsections (2) to (5) below shall apply.

(2) During the period of such an event at the ground, intoxicating liquor shall not be supplied by or on behalf of a registered club to a member or guest in the area of the ground except at premises in respect of which the club is registered.

(3) A person supplying or authorising the supply of intoxicating liquor in contravention of subsection (2) above is guilty of an offence.

(4) A person who, during the period of such an event, obtains or consumes intoxicating liquor supplied in contravention of subsection (2) above is guilty of an offence.

(5) If intoxicating liquor is kept in any premises or place by or on behalf of a club for supply to members or their guests in contravention of subsection (2) above, every officer of the club is guilty of an offence unless he shows that it was so kept without his knowledge or consent.

Non-retail sales.

5D.—(1) During the period of a designated sporting event at a designated sports ground, intoxicating liquor shall not be sold in the area of the ground except by sale by retail.

(2) A person selling or authorising the sale of intoxicating liquor in contravention of subsection (1) above is guilty of an offence.

(3) A person who, during the period of such an event, obtains or consumes intoxicating liquor sold in contravention of subsection (1) above is guilty of an offence.".

Supplementary

5. In sections 2 and 3, after subsection (1) insert—

"(1A) Subsection (1)(a) above has effect subject to section 5A(1) of this Act."

6. In section 7(3) (power to stop and search vehicles), after " public service vehicle (within the meaning of section 1 of this Act) " insert " or a motor vehicle to which section 1A of this Act applies ".

7.—(1) Section 8 (penalties) shall be amended as follows.

(2) In paragraph (a) after " 1(2) " there shall be inserted " or 1A(2) ".

(3) In paragraph (b) after " 1(3) " there shall be inserted " , 1A(3) ", after " 2(1) " there shall be inserted " , 2A(1) " and after " 3(10) " there shall be inserted ", 5B(2), 5C(3), 5D(2) ".

(4) In paragraph (c) after " 1(4) " there shall be inserted " , 1A(4) ".

(5) At the end there shall be inserted—

" (d) in the case of an offence under section 5B(3), 5C(4) or 5D(3), to a fine not exceeding level 3 on the standard scale, and

(e) in the case of an offence under section 5C(5), to a fine not exceeding level 1 on the standard scale.".

SCH. 1

Minor amendment

8. Section 3(9) (notice varying order about sale or supply of intoxicating liquor) shall have effect, and be taken always to have had effect, as if in paragraph (*b*) " order " read " notice ".

PART II

SCOTLAND

Introduction

1980 c. 62.

9. Part V of the Criminal Justice (Scotland) Act 1980 (sporting events: control of alcohol etc.) shall be amended as mentioned in this Part.

Vehicles

10. After section 70 there shall be inserted the following—

"Alcohol on certain other vehicles.   70A.—(1) This section applies to a motor vehicle which is not a public service vehicle but is adapted to carry more than 8 passengers and is being operated for the principal purpose of conveying two or more passengers for the whole or part of a journey to or from a designated sporting event.

(2) Any person in possession of alcohol on a vehicle to which this section applies shall be guilty of an offence and liable on summary conviction to imprisonment for a period not exceeding 60 days or a fine not exceeding level 3 on the standard scale or both.

(3) Any person who is drunk on a vehicle to which this section applies shall be guilty of an offence and liable on summary conviction to a fine not exceeding level 2 on the standard scale.

(4) Any person who permits alcohol to be carried on a vehicle to which this section applies and—

    (*a*) is the driver of the vehicle, or

    (*b*) where he is not its driver, is the keeper of the vehicle, the employee or agent of the keeper, a person to whom it is made available (by hire, loan or otherwise) by the keeper or the keeper's employee or agent, or the employee or agent of a person to whom it is so made available,

shall, subject to section 71 of this Act, be guilty of an offence and liable on summary conviction to a fine not exceeding level 3 on the standard scale.".

11. In section 71 (defences in connection with carriage of alcohol) for " or 70 " there shall be substituted " , 70 or 70A(4) ".

12. In section 75 (police powers of enforcement) for " or 70 " there shall be substituted " , 70 or 70A ".

13. In section 77 (interpretation of Part V)— Sch. 1

    (*a*) the following definitions shall be inserted in the appropriate places alphabetically—

        " " keeper ", in relation to a vehicle, means the person having the duty to take out a licence for it under section 1(1) of the Vehicles (Excise) Act 1971 ; 1971 c. 10.

        " motor vehicle " means a mechanically propelled vehicle intended or adapted for use on roads ; " ; and

    (*b*) in the definition of " public service vehicle " for the words " Part I of the Transport Act 1980 " there shall be substituted the words " the Public Passenger Vehicles Act 1981 " ; ". 1981 c. 14.

Fireworks etc.

14.—(1) After section 72 there shall be inserted the following—

" Possession of fireworks etc. at sporting events.

    72A.—(1) Any person who has entered the relevant area of a designated sports ground and is in possession of a controlled article or substance at any time during the period of a designated sporting event shall be guilty of an offence.

    (2) Any person who, while in possession of a controlled article or substance, attempts to enter the relevant area of a designated sports ground at any time during the period of a designated sporting event at the ground shall be guilty of an offence.

    (3) A person guilty of an offence under subsection (1) or (2) above shall be liable on summary conviction to imprisonment for a period not exceeding 60 days or to a fine not exceeding level 3 on the standard scale or both.

    (4) It shall be a defence for a person charged with an offence under subsection (1) or (2) above to show that he had lawful authority to be in possession of the controlled article or substance.

    (5) In subsections (1) and (2) above " controlled article or substance " means—

        (*a*) any article or substance whose main purpose is the emission of a flare for purposes of illuminating or signalling (as opposed to igniting or heating) or the emission of smoke or a visible gas ; and in particular it includes distress flares, fog signals, and pellets and capsules intended to be used as fumigators or for testing pipes, but not matches, cigarette lighters or heaters ; and

        (*b*) any article which is a firework.".

  (2) In section 75 (police powers of enforcement) at the end of sub-paragraph (ii) of paragraph (*e*) there shall be inserted—

    " ; or

        (iii) a controlled article or substance as defined in section 72A(5) of this Act.".

Y 4

SCHEDULE 2

OTHER AMENDMENTS

Conspiracy and Protection of Property Act 1875 (c.86)

1.—(1) In section 7 of the Conspiracy and Protection of Property Act 1875 (offence to intimidate etc. with a view to compelling another to abstain from doing or to do an act) for the words from " shall " to the end there shall be substituted " shall be liable on summary conviction to imprisonment for a term not exceeding 6 months or a fine not exceeding level 5 on the standard scale or both.".

(2) And the following shall be added at the end of that section—

" A constable may arrest without warrant anyone he reasonably suspects is committing an offence under this section.".

Prevention of Crime Act 1953 (c.14)

2. In section 1 of the Prevention of Crime Act 1953 (offence to have offensive weapon) at the end of subsection (4) (offensive weapon includes article intended by person having it for use by him) there shall be added " or by some other person ".

Civic Government (Scotland) Act 1982 (c.45)

3.—(1) Part V of the Civic Government (Scotland) Act 1982 (public processions) shall be amended in accordance with this paragraph.

(2) In section 62 (notification of processions)—

(*a*) in subsection (1)—

    (i) after " below " there shall be inserted " (*a*) " ; and

    (ii) at the end there shall be inserted—

" ; and

    (*b*) to the chief constable." ;

(*b*) in subsection (2)—

    (i) in paragraph (*a*), after " council " there shall be inserted " and to the office of the chief constable " ;

    (ii) in paragraph (*b*), for " that office " there shall be substituted " those offices " ;

(*c*) in subsection (4)—

    (i) after " area " there shall be inserted " (*a*) " ; and

    (ii) after " them " there shall be inserted—

" ; and

    (*b*) intimated to the chief constable." ; and

(*d*) in subsection (12), in the definition of " public place ", for " the Public Order Act 1936 " there shall be substituted " Part II of the Public Order Act 1986 ".

(3) In section 63 (functions of regional and islands councils in relation to processions)—

(*a*) after subsection (1) there shall be inserted—

"(1A) Where notice of a proposal to hold a procession has been given or falls to be treated as having been given in accordance with section 62(1) of this Act—

(*a*) if a regional or islands council have made an order under subsection (1) above they may at any time thereafter, after consulting the chief constable, vary or revoke the order and, where they revoke it, make any order which they were empowered to make under that subsection ;

(*b*) if they have decided not to make an order they may at any time thereafter, after consulting the chief constable, make any order which they were empowered to make under that subsection." ;

(*b*) in subsection (2) after " (1) " there shall be inserted " or (1A) " ;

(*c*) in subsection (3)—

(i) in paragraph (*a*)(i), after "(1)" there shall be inserted or (1A) above " ;

(ii) in paragraph (*a*)(ii), for " such an order " there shall be substituted " an order under subsection (1) above or to revoke an order already made under subsection (1) or (1A) above " ;

(iii) at the end of paragraph (*a*)(ii), for " and " there shall be substituted—

" (iii) where they have, under subsection (1A) above, varied such an order, a copy of the order as varied and a written statement of the reasons for the variation ; and " ;

(iv) in paragraph (*b*), after " (1) " there shall be inserted " or (1A) ", and after " made " where third occurring there shall be inserted " and, if the order has been varied under subsection (1A) above, that it has been so varied " ; and

(v) at the end of paragraph (*b*) there shall be inserted— " ; and

(*c*) where they have revoked an order made under subsection (1) or (1A) above in relation to a proposal to hold a procession, make such arrangements as will ensure that persons who might take or are taking part in that procession are made aware of the fact that the order has been revoked.".

SCH. 2   (4) In section 64 (appeals against orders under section 63)—

(*a*) in subsection (1) for the words from " against " to the end there shall be substituted—

" against—

(*a*) an order made under section 63(1) or (1A) of this Act ; or

(*b*) a variation under section 63(1A) of this Act of an order made under section 63(1) or (1A), in relation to the procession." ;

(*b*) in subsection (4) after " make " there shall be inserted " or, as the case may be, to vary " ; and

(*c*) in subsection (7) after " order " there shall be inserted " or, as the case may be, the variation of whose order ".

(5) In section 65 (offences and enforcement)—

(*a*) in paragraphs (*b*) and (*c*) of subsection (1), after " (1) " there shall be inserted " or (1A) " ; and

(*b*) in paragraphs (*b*) and (*c*) of subsection (2), after " (1) " there shall be inserted " or (1A) ".

(6) In section 66 (relationship with Public Order Act 1936)—

(*a*) for " the Public Order Act 1936 " there shall be substituted " Part II of the Public Order Act 1986 " ;

(*b*) in paragraph (*a*), for " or order made under section 3 " there shall be substituted " under section 12 ", and " or that order " shall be omitted ; and

(*c*) in paragraph (*b*), " or order under the said section 3 " shall be omitted.

Criminal Justice Act 1982 (c.48)

4. The following shall be inserted at the end of Part II of Schedule 1 to the Criminal Justice Act 1982 (statutory offences excluded from provisions for early release of prisoners)—

PUBLIC ORDER ACT 1986

27. Section 1 (riot).
28. Section 2 (violent disorder).
29. Section 3 (affray).".

Cable and Broadcasting Act 1984 (c.46)

5.—(1) The Cable and Broadcasting Act 1984 as it extends to England and Wales and Scotland is amended as follows.

(2) Omit section 27 (inclusion of programme in cable programme service likely to stir up racial hatred).

(3) In section 28 (amendment of the law of defamation), at the end add—

" (6) In this section " words " includes pictures, visual images, gestures and other methods of signifying meaning.".

(4) In section 33(2), in the definition of " relevant offence " omit
" an offence under section 27 above or ".

6.—(1) Section 27 of the Cable and Broadcasting Act 1984 as it extends to Northern Ireland is amended as follows.

(2) For subsections (1) to (5) substitute—

" (1) If a programme involving threatening, abusive or insulting visual images or sounds is included in a cable programme service, each of the persons mentioned in subsection (2) below is guilty of an offence if—

(a) he intends thereby to stir up racial hatred, or

(b) having regard to all the circumstances racial hatred is likely to be stirred up thereby.

(2) The persons are—

(a) the person providing the cable programme service,

(b) any person by whom the programme is produced or directed, and

(c) any person by whom offending words or behaviour are used.

(3) If the person providing the service, or a person by whom the programme was produced or directed, is not shown to have intended to stir up racial hatred, it is a defence for him to prove that—

(a) he did not know and had no reason to suspect that the programme would involve the offending material, and

(b) having regard to the circumstances in which the programme was included in a cable programme service, it was not reasonably practicable for him to secure the removal of the material.

(4) It is a defence for a person by whom the programme was produced or directed who is not shown to have intended to stir up racial hatred to prove that he did not know and had no reason to suspect—

(a) that the programme would be included in a cable programme service, or

(b) that the circumstances in which the programme would be so included would be such that racial hatred would be likely to be stirred up.

(5) It is a defence for a person by whom offending words or behaviour were used and who is not shown to have intended to stir up racial hatred to prove that he did not know and had no reason to suspect—

(a) that a programme involving the use of the offending material would be included in a cable programme service, or

(b) that the circumstances in which a programme involving the use of the offending material would be so included,

SCH. 2

or in which a programme so included would involve the use of the offending material, would be such that racial hatred would be likely to be stirred up.

(5A) A person who is not shown to have intended to stir up racial hatred is not guilty of an offence under this section if he did not know, and had no reason to suspect, that the offending material was threatening, abusive or insulting.

(5B) A person guilty of an offence under this section is liable—

(*a*) on conviction on indictment to imprisonment for a term not exceeding two years or a fine or both ;

(*b*) on summary conviction to imprisonment for a term not exceeding six months or a fine not exceeding the statutory maximum or both.".

(3) In subsection (8) (consents to prosecutions), for the words from " shall not be instituted " to the end substitute " shall not be instituted except by or with the consent of the Attorney General for Northern Ireland.".

(4) In subsection (9) (interpretation) for " ' racial group ' means a group of persons " substitute " ' racial hatred ' means hatred against a group of persons in Northern Ireland ".

(5) After subsection (10) insert—
" (11) This section extends to Northern Ireland only.".

Police and Criminal Evidence Act 1984 (c.60)

7. In section 17(1)(*c*) of the Police and Criminal Evidence Act 1984 (entry for purpose of arrest for certain offences) in sub-paragraph (i) the words from " 4 " to " peace) " shall be omitted and after sub-paragraph (ii) there shall be inserted—
" (iii) section 4 of the Public Order Act 1986 (fear or provocation of violence) ; ".

Section 40 (3).

SCHEDULE 3
REPEALS

Chapter	Short title	Extent of repeal
13 Chas. 2. Stat. 1. c. 5.	Tumultuous Petitioning Act 1661.	The whole Act.
33 Geo. 3. c. 67.	Shipping Offences Act 1793.	The whole Act.
57 Geo. 3. c. 19.	Seditious Meetings Act 1817.	The whole Act.
5 Geo. 4. c. 83.	Vagrancy Act 1824.	In section 4, the words from " every person being armed " to " arrestable offence " and from " and every such gun " to the end.
2 & 3 Vict. c. 47.	Metropolitan Police Act 1839.	In section 54, paragraph 13.
2 & 3 Vict. c. xciv.	City of London Police Act 1839.	In section 35, paragraph 13.

Chapter	Short title	Extent of repeal
3 Edw. 7.c .ccl.	Erith Tramways and Improvement Act 1903.	Section 171.
1 Edw. 8 & 1 Geo. 6. c. 6.	Public Order Act 1936.	Section 3. Section 4. Section 5. Section 5A. In section 7, in subsection (2) the words " or section 5 or 5A " and in subsection (3) the words " , four or five ". Section 8 (6). In section 9, in subsection (1) the definition of " public procession " and in subsection (3) the words " by the council of any borough or district or ".
7 & 8 Geo. 6. c.xxi.	Middlesex County Council Act 1944.	Section 309.
1967 c. 58.	Criminal Law Act 1967.	Section 11(3). In Schedule 2, paragraph 2(1) (*b*).
1968 c. 54.	Theatres Act 1968.	Section 5. In sections 7(2), 8, 9(1), 10 (1) (*a*) and (*b*), 15(1)(*a*) and 18(2), the references to section 5.
1976 c. 74.	Race Relations Act 1976.	Section 70. Section 79(6).
1976 c. xxxv.	County of South Glamorgan Act 1976.	Section 25. In Part I of Schedule 3, the entry relating to section 25.
1980 c. 62.	Criminal Justice (Scotland) Act 1980.	In section 75(*e*)(i), the word " or " at the end.
1980 c. x.	County of Merseyside Act 1980.	In section 30(2), paragraph (*b*), the word " and " preceding that paragraph and the words from " and may make " to the end. In section 30(5), the words " in the said section 31 or ". Section 31. In section 137(2), the reference to section 31.
1980 c. xi.	West Midlands County Council Act 1980.	Section 38, except subsection (4). In section 116(2), the reference to section 38.
1980 c. xiii.	Cheshire County Council Act 1980.	Section 28, except subsection (4). In section 108(2), the reference to section 28.
1980 c. xv.	Isle of Wight Act 1980.	Section 26, except subsection (4). In section 63(2), the reference to section 26.
1981 c. ix.	Greater Manchester Act 1981.	Section 56, except subsection (4). In section 179(2), the reference to section 56.

Sch. 3

Chapter	Short title	Extent of repeal
1981 c. xxv.	East Sussex Act 1981.	Section 29. In section 102(2), the reference to section 29.
1982 c. 45.	Civic Government (Scotland) Act 1982.	Section 62(10). In section 63(3)(*a*)(i), the word " or " at the end. In section 66, in paragraph (*a*), the words " or that order ", and in paragraph (*b*) the words " or order under the said section 3 ".
1982 c. 48.	Criminal Justice Act 1982.	In Part I of Schedule 1, the entries relating to riot and affray.
1984 c. 46.	Cable and Broadcasting Act 1984.	Section 27. In section 33 (2), the words "an offence under section 27 above or".
1984 c. 60.	Police and Criminal Evidence Act 1984.	In section 17(1)(*c*)(i) the words from " 4 " to " peace) ".
1985 c. 57.	Sporting Events (Control of Alcohol etc.) Act 1985.	In section 8, the word " and " at the end of paragraph (*b*).

Housing (Scotland) Act 1986

1986 CHAPTER 65

An Act to amend the Tenants' Rights, Etc. (Scotland) Act 1980, the Housing Associations Act 1985 in its application to Scotland and the Building (Scotland) Act 1959; to make further provision as regards housing in Scotland; and for connected purposes. [7th November 1986.]

BE IT ENACTED by the Queen's most Excellent Majesty, by and with the advice and consent of the Lords Spiritual and Temporal, and Commons, in this present Parliament assembled, and by the authority of the same, as follows:—

Amendment of Tenants' Rights, Etc. (Scotland) Act 1980

1.—(1) In section 1(3) of the 1980 Act (dwelling-houses to which right to purchase applies), for the words " of paragraphs (*a*), (*b*), (*c*) or (*f*) " there shall be substituted the words " paragraph, other than (*g*),".

(2) In section 10(2) of the 1980 Act (landlords in secure tenancies)—

    (*a*) after paragraph (*a*) there shall be inserted the following paragraph—

        " (*aa*) a regional council, or a joint board or joint committee of two or more regional councils, or any trust under the control of a regional council ; " ; and

Extension of right to purchase and of " secure tenancy ".

1980 c. 52.

(*b*) after paragraph (*g*) there shall be inserted the following paragraphs—

1967 c. 77.

" (*h*) a police authority within the meaning of section 2(1), as read with subsection (9)(*b*) of section 19, of the Police (Scotland) Act 1967 or a joint police committee constituted by virtue of subsection (2)(*b*) of the said section 19 ; and

1947 c. 41.

(*i*) a fire authority in Scotland for the purposes of the Fire Services Acts 1947 to 1959 (or a joint committee constituted by virtue of section 36(4)(*b*) of the Fire Services Act 1947).".

Increased
discount
where
dwelling-
house
purchased is
a flat.

2.—(1) Subject to subsection (3) below, in section 1(5)(*b*) of the 1980 Act (discount for purposes of calculation of purchase price of dwelling-house)—

(*a*) in sub-paragraph (i), after the words " 32 per cent." there shall be inserted the words " , or where the dwelling-house is a flat 44 per cent.," ;

(*b*) in sub-paragraph (ii), after the words " one per cent." there shall be inserted the words " , or where the dwelling-house is a flat two per cent.," ;

(*c*) after the words " 60 per cent." there shall be inserted the words " , or where the dwelling-house is a flat 70 per cent.," ; and

(*d*) at the end there shall be added the words " For the purposes of the foregoing provisions of this paragraph a " flat " is a separate and self-contained set of premises, whether or not on the same floor, forming part of a building from some other part of which it is divided horizontally.".

(2) Subject to subsection (3) below, in section 9A of the 1980 Act (application of Part I of that Act when dwelling-house is repurchased as defective), after the words " ' 30 per cent.' ;" there shall be inserted the words " (AA) for the words ' 44 per cent.' there shall be substituted the words ' 40 per cent.' ; ".

(3) Subsections (1) and (2) above shall have no effect as regards the exercise of a right to purchase by application under section 2(1) of the 1980 Act if the offer to sell has been duly served (whether by the landlord or, under section 7(3)(*a*) of that Act, by the Lands Tribunal for Scotland) before the date of coming into force of this section.

3.—(1) Subject to subsection (6) below, in subsection (7) of section 1 of the 1980 Act (fixing of price at which tenant entitled to purchase dwelling-house)—

> (*a*) for the words " 15 May 1975 " there shall be substituted the words " 31 December 1978 " ; and
>
> (*b*) in paragraph (*a*), for the words " in providing the dwelling-house " there shall be substituted the words—
>
>> " after that date (either or both)—
>>
>>> (i) in providing ;
>>>
>>> (ii) in making improvements (other than by way of repair or maintenance) to,
>>
>> the dwelling-house ".

Amendment of date after which certain restrictions may apply as regards price fixed for purchase of dwelling-house; and extension of those restrictions.

(2) Subject to subsection (6) below, after the said subsection (7) there shall be inserted the following subsection—

> " (7A) Where the dwelling-house was first let under a tenancy which, if Part II of this Act had then been in force, would have been a secure tenancy, on or before the date mentioned in subsection (7) above but an outstanding debt has been incurred after that date in making improvements (other than by way of repair or maintenance) to the dwelling-house, the price fixed under subsection (5) above shall not be less than—
>
>> (*a*) that outstanding debt ; or
>>
>> (*b*) the market value of the dwelling-house determined under subsection (5)(*a*) above,
>
> whichever is the lesser except in such cases as the Secretary of State may, by order made as is mentioned in subsection (7) above, prescribe.".

(3) Subject to subsection (6) below, in subsection (8) of the said section 1 (interpretation of " outstanding debt ")—

> (*a*) after the word " means " there shall be inserted the words ", in relation to paragraph (*a*)(i) of that subsection," ; and
>
> (*b*) at the end there shall be added the words " ; and
>
>> (*e*) where the landlord is a body mentioned in paragraph (*d*) or (*e*) of section 10(2) of this Act, any proportion of capital grants which it must repay on the dwelling-house being sold ;
>>
>> but in relation to paragraph (*a*)(ii) of that subsection and in subsection (7A) above its meaning is confined to any undischarged debt arising from the cost of the works of improvement together with—
>>
>>> (i) administrative costs attributable to those works : and

(ii) where the landlord is such body as is mentioned in paragraph (*e*) above, any such proportion as is there mentioned.".

(4) With the consent of the Treasury the Secretary of State may by order made by statutory instrument—

(*a*) amend subsection (7) of the said section 1 so as to substitute a later date for—

(i) the words substituted by subsection (1) above ; or

(ii) words substituted by virtue of this subsection ; or

(*b*) provide that subsections (7)(*a*)(ii), (7A) and (8) of the said section 1 shall apply with such modifications as he may specify in the order ;

and such order may make different provision in relation to different areas, cases or classes of case and may exclude certain areas, cases or classes of case.

(5) A statutory instrument under subsection (4) above shall be subject to annulment in pursuance of a resolution of either House of Parliament.

(6) The foregoing provisions of this section shall have no effect as regards the exercise of a right to purchase by application under section 2(1) of the 1980 Act if the offer to sell has been duly served (whether by the landlord or, under section 7(3)(*a*) of that Act, by the Lands Tribunal for Scotland) before the date of coming into force of this section.

Secretary of State's power to give directions as to conditions in offers to sell.

4. After section 4 of the 1980 Act there shall be inserted the following section—

" Further limitations on conditions of sale.

4A.—(1) Where it appears to the Secretary of State that the inclusion of conditions of a particular kind in offers to sell would be unreasonable he may by direction require landlords generally, landlords of a particular description, or particular landlords not to include conditions of that kind (or not to include conditions of that kind unless modified in such manner as may be specified in the direction) in offers to sell served on or after a date so specified.

(2) Where a condition's inclusion in an offer to sell—

(*a*) is in contravention of a direction under subsection (1) above ; or

(*b*) in a case where the tenant has not by the date specified in such a direction served

a relative notice of acceptance on the landlord, would have been in such contravention had the offer to sell been served on or
after that date,

the condition shall have no effect as regards the
offer to sell.

(3) A direction under subsection (1) above may—

   (*a*) make different provision in relation to dif-
      ferent areas, cases or classes of case and
      may exclude certain areas, cases or classes
      of case ; and

   (*b*) be varied or withdrawn by a subsequent
      direction so given.

(4) Section 211 of the Local Government (Scot- 1973 c. 65.
land) Act 1973 (provision for default of local authority) shall apply as regards a failure to comply with
a requirement in a direction under subsection (1)
above as that section applies as regards such failure
as is mentioned in subsection (1) thereof.".

5. After section 9A of the 1980 Act there shall be inserted the Financial and
following section— other
assistance for
   " Financial   9B.—(1) Where, in relation to any proceedings, or tenants
and other involved in
assistance prospective proceedings, to which this section ap- proceedings
for tenants plies, a tenant or purchaser is an actual or prospec- under Part I
involved in tive party, the Secretary of State may on written of 1980 Act
proceedings etc.
under Part I application to him by the tenant or purchaser give
etc. financial or other assistance to the applicant, if the
Secretary of State thinks fit to do so :

   Provided that assistance under this section shall
be given only where the Secretary of State con
siders—

   (*a*) that the case raises a question of principle
      and that it is in the public interest to give
      the applicant such assistance ; or

   (*b*) that there is some other special considera-
      tion.

   (2) This section applies to—

   (*a*) any proceedings under this Part of this Act ;
      and

   (*b*) any proceedings to determine any question
      arising under or in connection with this
      Part of this Act other than a question as
      to market value for the purposes of section
      1(5) of this Act.

(3) Assistance by the Secretary of State under this section may include—

(a) giving advice ;

(b) procuring or attempting to procure the settlement of the matter in dispute ;

(c) arranging for the giving of advice or assistance by a solicitor or counsel ;

(d) arranging for representation by a solicitor or counsel ;

(e) any other form of assistance which the Secretary of State may consider appropriate.

(4) In so far as expenses are incurred by the Secretary of State in providing the applicant with assistance under this section, any sums recovered by virtue of an award of expenses, or of an agreement as to expenses, in the applicant's favour with respect to the matter in connection with which the assistance is given shall, subject to any charge or obligation for payment in priority to other debts under the Legal Aid and Advice (Scotland) Acts 1967 and 1972 and to any provision of those Acts for payment of any sum into the legal aid fund, be paid to the Secretary of State in priority to any other debts.

(5) Any expenses incurred by the Secretary of State in providing assistance under this section shall be paid out of money provided by Parliament ; and any sums received by the Secretary of State under subsection (4) above shall be paid into the Consolidated Fund.".

Information from landlords in relation to Secretary of State's powers under Part I of 1980 Act.

1973 c. 65.

6. After the section inserted into the 1980 Act by section 5 of this Act there shall be inserted the following section—

" Information from landlords in relation to Secretary of State's powers under this Part.

9C.—(1) Without prejudice to section 199 of the Local Government (Scotland) Act 1973 (reports and returns by local authorities etc.), where it appears to the Secretary of State necessary or expedient, in relation to the exercise of his powers under this Part of this Act, he may by notice in writing to a landlord require it—

(a) at such time and at such place as may be specified in the notice, to produce any document ; or

(b) within such period as may be so specified or such longer period as the Secretary of State may allow, to furnish a copy of any document or supply any information.

(2) Any officer of the landlord designated in the notice for that purpose or having custody or control of the document or in a position to give that information shall, without instructions from the landlord, take all reasonable steps to ensure that the notice is complied with.".

7. After section 25 of the 1980 Act there shall be inserted the following cross-heading and section—

Contributions towards the cost of transfers and exchanges.

" *Transfers and Exchanges*

Contributions towards the cost of transfers and exchanges.

25A.—(1) The Secretary of State may with the consent of the Treasury make out of money provided by Parliament grants or loans towards the cost of arrangements for facilitating moves to and from homes by which—

> (*a*) a secure tenant of one landlord (the " first landlord ") becomes, at his own request, the secure tenant of a different landlord (whether or not by means of an exchange whereby a secure tenant of the different landlord becomes the secure tenant of the first landlord) ; or

> (*b*) each of two or more tenants of dwelling-houses, one at least of which is let under a secure tenancy, becomes the tenant of the other dwelling house (or, as the case may be, of one of the other dwelling houses).

(2) The grants or loans may be made subject to such conditions as the Secretary of State may determine, and may be made so as to be repayable (or, as the case may be, repayable earlier) if there is a breach of such a condition.

(3) In subsection (1) above, the reference to a " secure tenant " is to a tenant under a secure tenancy within the meaning of this Act or of the Housing Act 1985 or of Chapter II of Part II of the Housing (Northern Ireland) Order 1983.".

1985 c. 68.
S.I.: 1983 No. 1118 (N.I. 15).

8. For subsection (1A) of section 27 of the 1980 Act (publication of rules as to housing lists etc.) there shall be substituted the following subsections—

Duty of housing association to make rules governing housing list etc.

> " (1A) It shall be the duty of every registered housing association (within the meaning of the Housing Associations Act 1985)—

1985 c. 69.

> > (*a*) within the period of six months commencing with the date of coming into force of section 8 of the

Housing (Scotland) Act 1986 to make rules governing the matters mentioned in paragraphs (*a*) to (*d*)
of subsection (1) above (unless it has, in accordance with subsections (2) and (2A) below, published such rules before that date and those rules
remain current) ;

(*b*) within six months of the making of rules under
paragraph (*a*) above, and within six months of
any alteration of such rules (whether or not made
under that paragraph)—

(i) to send a copy of them to each of the
bodies mentioned in subsection (1B) below ;
and

(ii) to publish them in accordance with subsections (2) and (2A) below.

(1B) The bodies referred to in subsection (1A)(*b*)(i) above
are—

(i) the Housing Corporation ; and

(ii) every islands or district council within whose area
there is a dwelling house let, or to be let, by the
association under a secure tenancy.".

Extension of
power of
islands and
district
councils to
indemnify
certain
heritable
creditors.

9. In section 31 of the 1980 Act (local authority indemnities
for building societies)—

(*a*) in subsection (1)—

(i) after the words " (Northern Ireland) 1967) "
and, at the second and third places where they occur,
" building society " there shall in each case be inserted the words " or recognised body " ;

(ii) for the words " the standard security " there
shall be substituted the words " a heritable
security " ;

(*b*) in subsection (2) for the words " under the standard
security " there shall be substituted the words ", or
recognised body, under the heritable security " ;

(*c*) in subsection (5) after the words " building societies "
there shall be inserted the words " or recognised
bodies " ; and

(*d*) after subsection (5) there shall be inserted the following
subsections—

" (5A) In this section " recognised body " means a
body designated, or of a class or description designated, in an order made under this subsection by
statutory instrument by the Secretary of State with the
consent of the Treasury.

(5B) Before making an order under subsection (5A) above varying or revoking an order previously so made, the Secretary of State shall give an opportunity for representations to be made on behalf of a recognised body which, if the order were made, would cease to be such a body.".

10. In Schedule 1 to the 1980 Act, paragraph 1 (tenancy not to be secure tenancy if for period exceeding 20 years) shall cease to have effect.

Removal of restriction on security of tenure.

11. In Schedule 2 to the 1980 Act (grounds for recovery of possession of dwelling-houses let under secure tenancies), after paragraph 5 there shall be inserted the following paragraph—

Restoration of ground for recovery of possession of dwelling-house.

" 6. The landlord wishes to transfer the secure tenancy of the dwelling-house to—

> (*a*) the tenant's spouse (or former spouse) ; or
>
> (*b*) a person with whom the tenant has been living as husband and wife,

who has applied to the landlord for such transfer ; and either the tenant or the (as the case may be) spouse, former spouse or person, no longer wishes to live together with the other in the dwelling-house.".

12. The 1980 Act shall have effect subject to the amendments specified in Schedule 1 to this Act.

Further amendment of 1980 Act.

Amendment of Housing Associations Act 1985

13.—(1) In section 4 of the 1985 Act (eligibility of housing associations for registration), at the end of subsection (3) there shall be added the following paragraph—

Shared ownership agreements.
1985 c. 69.

" (*h*) in Scotland, acquiring, or repairing and improving, or building, or creating by the conversion of dwellings or other property, dwellings to be disposed of under shared ownership agreements.".

(2) In section 106(2) of the 1985 Act (interpretation for purposes of application to Scotland), for the definition of " shared ownership lease " there shall be substituted the following definition—

'" shared ownership agreement " means an agreement whereby a registered housing association—

> (*a*) sells a *pro indiviso* right in a dwelling to a person and leases the remaining *pro indiviso* rights therein to him subject to his being entitled, from time to time, to purchase those remaining rights until he has purchased the entire dwelling ; or

(b) conveys *pro indiviso* rights in dwellings to trustees to hold on behalf of persons each of whom, by purchasing a share in those dwellings, becomes entitled to exclusive occupancy of one of the dwellings but with any such person who wishes to sell or otherwise dispose of his share being required to do so through the agency of the trustees,

or such other agreement as may be approved whereby a person acquires from a registered housing association a *pro indiviso* right in a dwelling or dwellings and thereby becomes entitled to exclusive occupancy of the dwelling or, as the case may be, of one of the dwellings ; '.

Payments etc. in community-based housing associations.

14. After section 15 of the 1985 Act there shall be inserted the following section—

" Payments etc. in community-based housing associations in Scotland.

15A.—(1) In relation to a community-based housing association in Scotland the following are also permitted, notwithstanding section 15(1) of this Act—

(a) payments made by the association in respect of the purchase of a dwelling, or part of a dwelling, owned and occupied by a person described in subsection (2) below who is not an employee of the association ; but only if—

(i) such payments constitute expenditure in connection with housing projects undertaken for the purpose of improving or repairing dwellings, being expenditure in respect of which housing association grants may be made under section 41(1) of this Act ; and

(ii) the purchase price does not exceed such value as may be placed on the dwelling, or as the case may be part, by the district valuer ;

(b) the granting of the tenancy of a dwelling, or part of a dwelling, to such a person ; but only if the person—

(i) lives in the dwelling or in another dwelling owned by the association ; or

(ii) has at any time within the period of twelve months immediately preceding the granting of the tenancy lived in the dwelling (or such other dwelling) whether or not it belonged to the housing association when he lived there.

(2) The persons mentioned in subsection (1) above are—

(a) a committee member or voluntary officer of the association ; or

(b) a person who at any time in the twelve months preceding the payment (or as the case may be the granting of the tenancy) has been such a member or officer ; or

(c) a close relative of a person described in paragraph (a), or (b), above.

(3) For the purposes of subsection (1) above, a housing association is " community-based " if it is designated as such by the Housing Corporation.

(4) The Housing Corporation—

(a) shall make a designation under subsection (3) above only if it considers that the activities of the housing association relate wholly or mainly to the improvement of dwellings, or the management of improved dwellings, within a particular community (whether or not identified by reference to a geographical area entirely within any one administrative area) ; and

(b) may revoke such a designation if it considers, after giving the association an opportunity to make representations to it as regards such revocation, that the association's activities have ceased so to relate.".

15. Sections 44 (projects qualifying for housing association grant: repair or improvement after exercise of right to buy etc.) and 45 (projects qualifying for such grant: disposal to tenant of charitable housing association etc.) of the 1985 Act shall apply to Scotland ; and accordingly— Extension of sections 44 and 45 of 1985 Act to Scotland.

(a) in the said section 44—

(i) in subsection (1), after the word " exercise " there shall be inserted the word " — (a) " ; and after the words " 1985 " there shall be inserted the following paragraph—

" ; or

(b) in Scotland, his right to purchase under section 1 of the Tenants' Rights, Etc. (Scotland) Act 1980," ; 1980 c. 52.

(ii) in subsection (2), after the word " exercised " there shall be inserted the word " — (a) " ; and after the word " lease " there shall be inserted the following paragraph—

" ; or

(b) in Scotland, the right to purchase," ; and

(iii) for subsection (3) there shall be substituted the following subsection—

" (3) " Dwelling-house ", in the application of this section to—

(a) England and Wales, has the same meaning as in Part V of the Housing Act 1985 ; and

1985 c. 68.

(b) Scotland, means a house." ; and

(b) in the said section 45—

(i) in subsection (2), after the word " for " there shall be inserted the word " — (a) " and at the end there shall be added the following words—

" ; or

1980 c. 52.

(b) subsection (11)(e) or (f) of section 1 of the Tenants' Rights, Etc. (Scotland) Act 1980 (analogous Scottish provision) would have a right to purchase under that section." ;

(ii) in subsection (3), at the end there shall be added the words " ; and a dwelling is also publicly funded for this purpose if it is in Scotland and housing association grant has been paid in respect of a project which included its improvement or repair or, where it and another dwelling are both provided for letting under the project, the improvement or repair of that other dwelling." ;

(iii) in subsection (4), at the beginning there shall be inserted the words " In England and Wales," ; and

(iv) after subsection (4) there shall be added the following subsection—

" (5) In Scotland, where a registered housing association concludes missives for the acquisition of a house and, without taking title, disposes of its interest to a tenant to whom this section applies, subsection (1) and the following provisions have effect as if the association first acquired the house and then disposed of it to the tenant—

section 8 (disposal of land by registered housing associations),

section 9 (consent of Housing Corporation to disposals),

> section 79(2) (power of Housing Corpora-
> tion to lend to person acquiring
> interest from registered housing asso-
> ciation), and
>
> section 6 of the Tenants' Rights, Etc. (Scot- 1980 c. 52.
> land) Act 1980 (recovery of discount
> on early re-sale).".

16.—(1) In section 52 of the 1985 Act (reduction, suspension Repayment
or reclamation of housing association grant), at the end of of housing
subsection (1) there shall be added the following words— association
grant.

" or

> (*f*) there is paid to the association, in respect of land
> to which the grant relates, an amount payable in
> pursuance of section 6 of the Tenants' Rights
> Etc. (Scotland) Act 1980 (recovery of discount on
> early re-sale), or
>
> (*g*) in Scotland, there is paid to the association, in
> respect of land to which the grant relates, an
> amount payable as regards the purchase, under
> a shared ownership agreement, of a *pro indiviso*
> share in a dwelling by a person who already has
> such a share in the dwelling under that agree-
> ment.".

(2) In subsection (3)(*b*) of the said section 52, for the words
" or (*e*) " there shall be substituted the words " (*e*), (*f*) or (*g*) ".

Housing Expenditure and Grants

17. In paragraph 22(2) of Schedule 3 to the Local Govern- Precondition
ment (Scotland) Act 1975 (restrictions on use of capital and as regards use
renewal and repair funds), after the word " restaurant " there of renewal
shall be inserted the words " ; and if the renewal and repair fund and repairs
is used so to meet expenditure incurred by the authority in rela- certain
tion to any house, or other property, to which their housing housing
revenue account relates, the amount in question shall, subject to expenditure.
paragraph 1(7) of Schedule 4 to the Housing (Financial Pro- 1975 c. 30.
visions (Scotland) Act 1972, first to be carried to the credit of 1972 c. 46.
that account ".

18.—(1) In section 4 of the Housing (Financial Provisions) Grants to
(Scotland) Act 1978 (grants to Scottish Special Housing Associa- Scottish
tion and development corporations)— Special
Housing
> (*a*) for subsection (1) there shall be substituted the following Association
> subsection— and
>
> > " (1) The Secretary of State may each year make development
> > grants, of such amount and subject to such con- corporations.
> > ditions as he may determine, to the Scottish Special 1978 c. 14.

Housing Association (in this Act referred to as " the Association ") and to development corporations in accordance with the provisions of this section." ; and

(*b*) in subsection (2), for the words from " calculated " to " State " there shall be substituted the words " approved by the Secretary of State and calculated in accordance with rules made by him ".

(2) After the said section 4 there shall be inserted the following section—

" Grants for affording tax relief to Scottish Special Housing Association.

4A.—(1) The Secretary of State may, on the application of the Association, make grants to the Association for affording relief from—

(*a*) income tax (other than income tax which the Association is entitled to deduct on making any payment) ; and

(*b*) corporation tax.

(2) A grant under this section shall be of such amount, shall be made at such times and shall be subject to such conditions as the Secretary of State thinks fit.

(3) The conditions mentioned in subsection (2) above may include conditions for securing the repayment in whole or in part of a grant made to the Association in the event of tax in respect of which the grant was made subsequently being found not to be chargeable or in such other events as the Secretary of State may determine.

(4) An application under this section shall be made in such manner and shall be supported by such evidence as the Secretary of State may direct.

(5) The Commissioners of Inland Revenue and their officers may disclose to the Secretary of State such particulars as he may reasonably require for determining whether a grant should be made under this section or whether a grant so made should be repaid or the amount of such grant or repayment.".

Amendment of Building (Scotland) Act 1959

Amendment of Building (Scotland) Act 1959.
1959 c. 24.

19.—(1) The Building (Scotland) Act 1959 shall be amended in accordance with the following provisions of this section.

(2) In section 3(4)(*b*) (circumstances in which building standards regulations are not to apply), after the words " exempted classes " there shall be inserted the words " , to such extent as may be specified in the regulations ".

(3) For section 4B (power of Secretary of State to approve types of building, etc.), there shall be substituted the following section—

" Class warrants.

4B.—(1) The following provisions of this section shall have effect with a view to enabling the Secretary of State, on an application being made to him under this section, to issue a certificate (to be known as a " class warrant ") that a particular design (including specification of materials) of building conforms, either generally or in any class of case, to particular provisions of the building standards regulations.

(2) A person intending to apply for a class warrant under this section shall send a copy of the prospective application in the prescribed manner to a body designated by the Secretary of State which, if it is satisfied that the design in respect of which the warrant is sought conforms to the building standards regulations, shall recommend that the class warrant be issued.

(3) An application to the Secretary of State for a class warrant under this section shall be made in the prescribed manner and shall be accompanied by a relevant recommendation made under subsection (2) above.

(4) The Secretary of State may, where a recommendation under subsection (2) above is made in respect of a design of building, issue a class warrant in respect of that design ; and a class warant so issued shall be accepted by a local authority as conclusive of the matters stated therein.

(5) A body designated under subsection (2) above may charge such fee for considering a design in respect of which a copy application has been sent to it under that subsection as may be agreed between the applicant and the body.

(6) A class warrant shall, if it so provides, cease to have effect at the end of such period as may be specified in it.

(7) The Secretary of State may at any time vary or revoke a class warrant ; but before doing so he shall give the person on whose application it was issued reasonable notice that he proposes so to do.

(8) Where the Secretary of State varies or revokes a class warrant he shall publish notice of that fact in such manner as he thinks fit.

(9) There may be prescribed—

(a) the type, part or parts of building to which the provisions of this section shall apply ;

(b) the terms and conditions on which a class warrant may be issued ;

(c) procedures incidental to any provisions of this section ;

(d) the fee, if any, to be charged for issuing a class warrant ;

(e) any variations in the design of building which will be permitted.

(10) Where a fee is chargeable by virtue of subsection (9)(d) above, the regulations under which it is chargeable may make different provision (which, without prejudice to the generality of this subsection, may include provision for remission of the fee in whole or in part) for—

(a) different cases or classes of case ; or

(b) different circumstances or classes of circumstances,

(difference being determined by reference to any factor or factors whatsoever).".

(4) After section 6 there shall be inserted the following section—

" Self-
certification
of design.

6AA.—(1) On making an application for a warrant under section 6 of this Act, an applicant may submit a certificate issued under this section certifying that the design (including the specification of material to be used) of the building complies with building standards regulations prescribed under paragraph (a) of subsection (2) below ; and in determining whether to issue the warrant, the local authority shall accept the certificate as conclusive of the facts to which it relates.

(2) There may be prescribed—

(a) the part or parts of the building standards regulations in relation to which a certificate under this section may be submitted and different provision may be made in respect of different parts of the regulations and in respect of different types of building ;

(b) whether or not by reference to specific criteria, such person or persons as shall be entitled to issue such certificate ;

(c) the form of such certificate ;

(d) the drawings, plans, specifications or other material which shall be submitted with the certificate.".

(5) In section 9 (certificate of completion), after subsection (2) there shall be inserted the following subsection—

" (2A) Where the Secretary of State has issued a relevant class warrant, a local authority shall grant a certificate of completion in respect of any building unless—

(i) the approved design (or an approved variation) has not been complied with whether by reason of faulty workmanship or otherwise ; or

(ii) the building standards regulations in relation to any part of the building to which section 4B of this Act does not apply have not been complied with.".

(6) For section 20 (fees chargeable by local authorities) there shall be substituted the following section—

" Fees chargeable by local authorities.

20.—(1) A local authority may in respect of the performance of their functions under this Act charge such fees as may be prescribed ; but there may also be prescribed cases or classes of case for which, or circumstances or classes of circumstances where, no fee shall be chargeable.

(2) Where a fee is chargeable by virtue of subsection (1) above, the regulations under which it is so chargeable may make different provision (which, without prejudice to the generality of this subsection, may include provision for remission of the fee in whole or in part) for—

(a) different cases or classes of case ;

(b) different circumstances or classes of circumstances ;

(c) different items or classes of business,

(difference being determined by reference to any factor or factors whatsoever).".

Amendment of Land Compensation (Scotland) Act 1973

20.—(1) The Land Compensation (Scotland) Act 1973 shall be amended in accordance with the following provisions of this section.

(2) In section 27(1) (right to home loss payment where person displaced from dwelling)—

(a) after paragraph (e) there shall be inserted the following paragraph—

" (f) an order for recovery of possession of the dwelling under section 15(2) of the Tenants' Rights, Etc. (Scotland) Act 1980, on the ground set out in paragraph 10 of Part I of Schedule 2 to that Act," ; and

[margin notes] Compensation for person displaced from dwelling-house let under secure tenancy.
1973 c. 56.
1980 c. 52.

(b) after sub-paragraph (v) there shall be inserted the following sub-paragraph—

"(vi) where paragraph (f) above applies, the landlord.".

(3) In section 29 (supplementary provisions about home loss payments), after subsection (7) there shall be inserted the following subsection—

"(7AA) If a landlord recovers possession of a dwelling by agreement—

1980 c. 52.

(a) after serving notice under section 14 of the Tenants' Rights, Etc. (Scotland) Act 1980 on the tenant specifying the ground set out in paragraph 10 of Part I of Schedule 2 to that Act ; or

(b) where, but for that agreement, it would have served such notice on him specifying that ground,

it may, in connection with the recovery, make to him a payment corresponding to any home loss payment which it would be required to make to him if the recovery were by order under section 15(2) of that Act.".

Amendment of Housing (Homeless Persons) Act 1977

Functions of local authorities with respect to persons who are homeless or threatened with homelessness.

1977 c. 48.
1966 c. 49.

21.—(1) The Housing (Homeless Persons) Act 1977 shall be amended in accordance with the following provisions of this section.

(2) In section 1(2) (homeless persons and persons threatened with homelessness) after paragraph (c) there shall be inserted the following paragraph—

"(d) it is overcrowded as defined in section 89 of the Housing (Scotland) Act 1966 and may endanger the health of the occupants."

(3) In section 4 (duties of housing authorities to homeless persons and persons threatened with homelessness) after subsection (6) there shall be inserted the following subsection—

"(7) Where a local authority has a duty under subsections (4) and (5) above "accommodation" shall be defined as accommodation that shall not be overcrowded as defined in section 89 of the Housing (Scotland) Act 1966 and which does not pose a threat to the health of the occupants.".

Supplemental

Interpretation.

22. In this Act—

"the 1980 Act " means the Tenants' Rights, Etc. (Scotland) Act 1980 ; and

1985 c. 69.

"the 1985 Act " means the Housing Associations Act 1985.

23.—(1) The Secretary of State may by order made by statutory instrument make such incidental, consequential, transitional or supplementary provision as appears to him to be necessary or proper for giving full effect to, or in consequence of any of the provisions of, this Act.

Consequential, transitional and supplementary provision.

(2) A statutory instrument made under subsection (1) above shall be subject to annulment in pursuance of a resolution of either House of Parliament.

(3) Paragraph 7(*a*)(ii) and (*b*)(ii) of Schedule 1 to this Act shall have no effect as regards any case in which repayment has become exigible under subsection (1) of section 6 of the 1980 Act before the coming into force of that paragraph ; but in any other case the terms of any standard security, offer to sell or concluded missives shall, in so far as they are inconsistent with the period of years specified in that subsection, or with the proportions specified in subsection (3) of that section, have effect as if so modified as to obviate that inconsistency.

24. There shall be paid out of the money provided by Parliament any—

Expenses.

- (*a*) sums required by the Secretary of State for making grants, loans or other payments by virtue of this Act ;
- (*b*) administrative expenses incurred by him by virtue of this Act ;
- (*c*) increase attributable to the provisions of this Act in the sums which under any other enactment are paid out of money so provided.

25.—(1) The enactments specified in Schedule 2 to this Act shall have effect subject to the amendments there specified, (being minor amendments or amendments consequential on the provisions of this Act).

Minor amendments and repeals.

(2) The enactments specified in Schedule 3 to this Act are repealed to the extent specified in the third column of that Schedule.

26.—(1) This Act may be cited as the Housing (Scotland) Act 1986.

Citation, commencement and extent.

(2) This Act, except this section, shall come into force on such day as the Secretary of State may appoint by order made by statutory instrument ; and different days may be so appointed for different provisions and for different purposes.

(3) This Act applies to Scotland only.

SCHEDULES

SCHEDULE 1

AMENDMENT OF 1980 ACT

1. In section 1 (secure tenant's right to purchase)—

(a) in subsection (1A)—

(i) after the word " Act " there shall be inserted the word " —(a) " ;

(ii) in the proviso, for the word " subsection " there shall be substituted the word " paragraph " ; and

(iii) after the proviso there shall be added the following paragraph—

" (b) a landlord mentioned in paragraph (a) or (aa) of section 10(2) of this Act is required neither to enter into, nor to induce (or seek to induce) any person to enter into, such agreement as is mentioned in paragraph (a) above or into any agreement which purports to restrict that person's rights under this Act." ;

(b) in subsection (4)(a), for the words " over the age of 18 years and at the relevant date the dwelling-house has been their only or principal home for a continuous period of 6 months, and " there shall be substituted the words " at least 18 years of age, that they have, during the period of 6 months ending with the relevant date, had their only or principal home with the tenant and that " ;

(c) in subsection (5)—

(i) for the words " subsection (7) " there shall be substituted the words " subsections (7) and (7A) " ; and

(ii) in paragraph (b)(ii), for the words "tenant or by any one of the joint tenants or by his spouse " there shall be substituted the words " appropriate person " ;

(d) after subsection (5) there shall be inserted the following subsection—

" (5A) for the purposes of subsection (5)(b)(ii) above, the " appropriate person " is the tenant or, if it would result in a higher discount and if she is cohabiting with him as at the relevant date, his spouse ; and where joint tenants are joint purchasers the " appropriate person " shall be whichever tenant (or as the case may be spouse) has the longer or longest such occupation." ;

(e) in subsection (10)—

(i) after paragraph (d) there shall be inserted the following paragraphs—

1985 c. 69.
" (dd) a registered housing association within the meaning of the Housing Associations Act 1985 ;

(ddd) the Housing Corporation ; " ;

(ii) in paragraph (*h*), for the words " or section 19(9)(*b*) of the Police (Scotland) Act 1967 " there shall be substi- 1967 c. 77. tuted the words " , as read with subsection (9)(*b*) of section 19, of the Police (Scotland) Act 1967 or a joint police committee constituted by virtue of subsection (2)(*b*) of the said section 19 " ;

(iii) in paragraph (*i*), after the words " 1959 " there shall be inserted the words " (or a joint committee constituted by virtue of section 36(4)(*b*) of the Fire Services 1947 c. 41. Act 1947) " ; and

(iv) in paragraph (*l*), for the words " by the tenant or occupier " there shall be substituted the words " , whether by the tenant or his spouse," ;

(*f*) in subsection (11)—

(i) in paragraph (*a*), for the words " of paragraphs (*a*), (*b*) or (*c*) " there shall be substituted the words " paragraph, other than (*g*)," ; and

(ii) at the end of paragraph (*c*) there shall be added the following paragraphs—

" ;

(*d*) where a landlord mentioned in paragraph (*e*) of section 10(2) of this Act has at no time received a grant under—

(i) any enactment mentioned in paragraph 2 of Schedule 1 to the Housing Associations Act 1985 (grants under enactments superse- 1974 c. 44. ded by the Housing Act 1974) ;

(ii) section 31 of the Housing Act 1974 (management grants) ;

(iii) section 41 of the Housing Associations 1985 c. 69. Act 1985 (housing association grants) ;

(iv) section 54 of that Act (revenue deficit grants) ;

(v) section 55 of that Act (hostel deficit grants) ; or

(vi) section 59(2) of that Act (grants by local authorities) ; or

(*e*) where a landlord so mentioned has at no time let (or had available for letting) more than 100 dwellings ; or

(*f*) where a landlord so mentioned is a charity—

(i) entered in the register of charities maintained under the Charities Act 1960 by the 1960 c. 58. Charity Commissioners for England and Wales ; or

(ii) which but for section 4(4) of, and paragraph (*g*) of the Second Schedule to, that Act (exempt charities) would require to be so entered ; or (*g*) where by virtue of section 49(2) of the said Act of 1960 (extent) a landlord so mentioned is not one to which Part II of that Act (registration of charities etc.) applies, but—

(i) the landlord has, in respect of all periods from 14th November 1985, or from the date of first being registered by the Housing Corporation (whichever is the later), claimed and been granted (whether or not retrospectively) under section 360(1) of the Income and Corporation Taxes Act 1970 (special exemptions for charities) exemption from tax ; and

(ii) where such exemption has not been claimed and granted in respect of all periods from the said date of registration, the rules of the landlord, registered under the Industrial and Provident Societies Act 1965 and in force at that date were such as would have admitted of such exemption had it been claimed as at that date ; or

(*h*) where, within a neighbourhood, the dwelling-house is one of a number (not exceeding 14) of dwelling-houses with a common landlord, being a landlord so mentioned, and it is the practice of that landlord to let at least one half of those dwelling-houses for occupation by any or all of the following—

(i) persons who have suffered from, or are suffering from, mental disorder (as defined in the Mental Health (Scotland) Act 1984), physical handicap or addiction to alcohol or other drugs ;

(ii) persons who have been released from prison or other institutions ;

(iii) young persons who have left the care of a local authority,

and a social service is, or special facilities are, provided wholly or partly for the purpose of assisting those persons." ;

(*g*) after subsection (11) there shall be inserted the following subsections—

"(11A) The Secretary of State may by order amend, or add to, the list of classes set out in sub-paragraphs (i) to (iii) of paragraph (*h*) of subsection (11) above.

(11B) The Commissioners of Inland Revenue shall, as regards any registered housing association, at the request of the Secretary of State, provide him and the Housing Corporation with such information as will enable them to determine whether that association is a landlord in

respect of which this section will not, by virtue of sub-   Sᴄʜ. 1
section (11) (g) above, apply ; and where a registered
housing association is refused exemption on a claim
under section 360(1) of the Income and Corporation 1970 c. 10.
Taxes Act 1970 the Commissioners shall forthwith inform
the Secretary of State and the Housing Corporation of
that fact.

(11C) Where information has been received by the
Housing Corporation under subsection (11B) above and
having regard to that information the Corporation is
satisfied that the housing association to which it relates
is not a landlord in respect of which this section applies,
they shall make an entry to that effect in the register
of housing associations maintained by them under section
3(1) of the Housing Associations Act 1985 ; and they 1985 c. 69.
shall cancel that entry where subsequent information so
received in relation to that housing association is inconsistent with their being so satisfied." ; and

(*h*) in subsection (12), in the definition of " occupation "—

(i) for paragraph (iii) there shall be substituted the
following paragraphs—

" (iii) as a child, or as the spouse of a child, of a
person mentioned in paragraph (i) above who
has succeeded, directly or indirectly, to the rights
of that person in a dwelling-house occupation of
which would be reckonable for the purposes
of this section ; but only in relation to any
period when the child, or as the case may be
spouse of the child, is at least 16 years of age ;
or

(iv) in the discretion of the landlord, as a member
of the family of a person mentioned in paragraph (i) above who, not being that person's
spouse or child (or child's spouse), has succeeded, directly or indirectly, to such rights as
are mentioned in paragraph (iii) above ; but
only in relation to any period when the member
of the family is at least 16 years of age ; and " ;

(ii) for the word " disregarded " there shall be substituted the words " regarded as not affecting continuity " ;

(iii) for the word " subsection " there shall be substituted the words " subsections (3) and " ; and

(iv) for the words " in connection with service by the
tenant or occupier as a member of the regular armed
forces of the Crown " there shall be substituted the words
" as is mentioned in subsection (10)(*l*) above ".

2. In section 1A(2) (restriction on order vesting in landlord heri-
table proprietor's interest), for the words " of paragraphs (*a*), (*b*), (*c*)
and (*f*) " there shall be substituted the words " paragraph, other than
(*g***),".**

3. After section 1A there shall be inserted the following section—

" Provision of information to secure tenants.

1B.—(1) Whenever a new secure tenancy is to be created, if—

    (*a*) by virtue of subsection (11) of section 1 of this Act, the dwelling-house is not one to which that section applies ; or

    (*b*) subsection (7) or (7A) of that section may (assuming no change in the date for the time being specified in the former subsection and disregarding any order made, or which might be made, by the Secretary of State under section 3(4)(*b*) of the Housing (Scotland) Act 1986) affect any price fixed, as regards the dwelling-house, under subsection (5) of that section,

the landlord shall so inform the prospective tenant by written notice.

(2) Where in the course of a secure tenancy the dwelling-house, by virtue of subsection (11) of the said section 1, ceases to be one to which that section applies, the landlord shall forthwith so inform the tenant by written notice.".

4. In section 2(6) (time for serving notice of acceptance), after sub-paragraph (iii*a*) there shall be inserted the following sub-paragraph—

" (iii*b*) a finding or determination by the Lands Tribunal for Scotland in a matter referred to it under subsection (2)(*d*) of the said section 7 where no order is made under the said subsection (3)(*b*) ;".

5. In section 4—

    (*a*) in subsection (7)(*a*) (order affecting right of pre-emption where unreasonable proportion of dwelling-houses in rural area sold other than as principal homes), for the words " the number of dwelling-houses of which the council concerned is the landlord at the date of commencement of this Part of this Act " there shall be substituted the words " all relevant dwelling houses " ; and

    (*b*) after subsection (7) there shall be inserted the following subsection—

" (7A) For the purposes of subsection (7)(*a*) above, a " relevant dwelling house " is one of which, at the date of—

    (*a*) commencement of this Part of this Act, the council concerned ; or

    (*b*) coming into force of paragraph 5 of Schedule 1 to the Housing (Scotland) Act 1986, a registered housing association,

is landlord.".

6. In section 5(1) (loan to purchase dwelling-house), after the word " body ; " there shall be inserted the following paragraph—

" *(aa)* in the case where the landlord is the Housing Corporation or a registered housing association, to the Housing Corporation ;".

7. In section 6 (recovery of discount on early re-sale)—

  (a) in subsection (1), for the words—

    (i) from " (otherwise than " to " compulsory purchase) " there shall be substituted the words—

      " (except as provided for in section 6A of this Act) " ;

    (ii) " 5 years " there shall be substituted the words " 3 years " ; and

    (iii) " a proportion of the discount under section 1(5)(*b*) of this Act in accordance with subsection (3) below " there shall be substituted the words " , in accordance with subsection (3) below, a proportion of the difference between the market value determined, in respect of the dwelling-house, under section 1(5)(*a*) of this Act and the price at which the dwelling-house was so purchased " ;

  (b) in subsection (3)—

    (i) for the word " discount " there shall be substituted the word " difference " ;

    (ii) for the words from " 80 " to the end there shall be substituted the words " 66 per cent where it occurs in the second such year and 33 per cent where it occurs in the third such year." ;

  (c) in subsection (5), at the end there shall be added the words " For the avoidance of doubt, paragraph (*a*) above applies to a standard security granted in security both for the purpose mentioned in sub-paragraph (i) and for that mentioned in sub-paragraph (ii) thereof as it applies to a standard security so granted for but one of those purposes." ; and

  (d) in each of subsections (5) and (6), for the words " repay a proportion of discount under this section " there shall be substituted the words " make a repayment under subsection (1) above ".

8. After section 6 there shall be inserted the following section—

" Cases where discount etc. is not recoverable. 6A.—(1) There shall be no liability to make a repayment under section 6(1) of this Act where the disposal is made—

    (a) by the executor of the deceased owner acting in that capacity ; or

    (b) as a result of a compulsory purchase order ; or

    (c) in the circumstances specified in subsection (2) below.

(2) The circumstances mentioned in subsection (1)(c) above are that the disposal—

    (a) is to a member of the owner's family who has lived with him for a period of 12 months before the disposal ; and

    (b) is for no consideration:

Provided that, if the disponee disposes of the house before the expiry of the 3 year period mentioned in subsection (1) of section 6 of this Act, the provisions of that section will apply to him as if this was the first disposal and he was the original purchaser.".

9. In section 8(1) (powers of local authorities to sell houses), for the words "Notwithstanding anything contained in any" there shall be substituted the words "Subject to section 74(2) of the Local Government (Scotland) Act 1973 (restriction on disposal of land) but notwithstanding anything contained in any other".

10. In section 10(4)(b) (application of certain provisions to tenancies which are not secure tenancies), after the word "2" there shall be inserted the words "or 9".

11. In section 13(2) (succession to secure tenancy)—

    (a) for paragraph (a) there shall be substituted the following paragraph—

        " (a) a person whose only or principal home at the time of the tenant's death was the dwelling house and who was at that time either—

            (i) the tenant's spouse ; or

            (ii) living with the tenant as husband and wife ; " ; and

    (b) in paragraph (c), for the word " over " there shall be substituted the words " who has attained ".

12. In section 15 (power of court to adjourn proceedings for possession of dwelling-house)—

    (a) in subsection (1), for the words from "1 to" to "Part I" there shall be substituted the words " 1 to 7 and 16 of Part I";

    (b) for subsection (2) there shall be substituted the following subsection—

        "(2) Subject to subsection (1) above, in proceedings under the said section 14 the court shall make an order for recovery of possession if it appears to the court that the landlord has a ground for recovery of possession, being—

            (a) a ground set out in any of paragraphs 1 to 5, 7 and 16 of the said Part I and specified in the notice required by the said section 14 and that it is reasonable to make the order ; or

            (b) a ground set out in any of paragraphs 8 to 15 of the said Part I and so specified and that other suitable accommodation will be available for the tenant when the order takes effect ; or

    (*c*) the ground set out in paragraph 6 of the said Part I and so specified and both that it is reasonable to make the order and that other suitable accommodation will be available as aforesaid," ; and

  (*c*) in subsection (3), after the words " (2)(*b*) " there shall be inserted the words " or (*c*) ".

13. For section 26 (restriction on residential requirements) there shall be substituted the following sections—

"Admission to housing list.

26.—(1) In considering whether an applicant for local authority housing is entitled to be admitted to a housing list, an islands or district council shall take no account of—

    (*a*) the age of the applicant provided that he has attained the age of 16 years ; or

    (*b*) the income of the applicant and his family ; or

    (*c*) whether, or to what value, the applicant or any of his family owns or has owned (or any of them own or have owned) heritable or moveable property ; or

    (*d*) any outstanding liability (for payment of rent or otherwise) attributable to the tenancy of any dwelling-house of which the applicant is not, and was not when the liability accrued, a tenant ; or

    (*e*) whether the applicant is living with, or in the same dwelling-house as—

        (i) his spouse ; or

        (ii) a person with whom he has been living as husband and wife.

    (2) Where an applicant—

    (*a*) is employed in the area of the islands or district council ; or

    (*b*) has been offered employment in the area of the council ; or

    (*c*) wishes to move into the area of the council and the council is satisfied that his purpose in doing so is to seek employment ; or

    (*d*) has attained the age of 60 years and wishes to move into the area of the council to be near a younger relative ; or

    (*e*) has special social or medical reasons for requiring to be housed within the area of the council,

admission to a housing list shall not depend on the applicant being resident in the area.

    (3) Where an islands or district council has rules which give priority to applicants on its housing list it shall apply

2 A 3

those rules to an applicant to whom subsection (2) above applies no less favourably than it applies them to a tenant of the council whose housing needs are similar to those of the applicant and who is seeking a transfer to another dwelling-house belonging to the council.

(4) In this section and in section 27 of this Act " housing list " means a list of applicants for local authority housing which is kept by an islands or district council in connection with allocation of housing.

Allocation of local authority housing.

26A. In the allocation of local authority housing an islands or district council—

(*a*) shall take no account of—

(i) the length of time for which an applicant has resided in its area ; or

(ii) any of the matters mentioned in paragraphs (*a*) to (*d*) of section 26(1) of this Act ; and

(*b*) shall not impose a requirement—

(i) that an application must have remained in force for a minimum period ; or

(ii) that a divorce or judicial separation be obtained ; or

(iii) that the applicant no longer be living with, or in the same dwelling-house as, some other person,

before the applicant is eligible for the allocation of housing.".

14. In section 27(2A) (certain registered housing association rules to be available for perusal), for the words " (1A)(*a*)(ii) " there shall be substituted the words " (1A)(*b*)(i) ".

15. In section 30—

(*a*) in subsection (4) (home loan interest rate chargeable) at the beginning there shall be inserted the words " Subject to subsection (8) below," ; and

(*b*) for subsection (8) (variation of home loan interest rate), there shall be substituted the following subsections—

" (8) Where the declaration of a new standard rate or, as the case may be, the determination of a new locally determined rate, affects the rate of interest chargeable under subsection (4) above by an islands or district council the council shall, as soon as practicable after such declaration or determination, serve in respect of each of its variable interest home loans a notice on the borrower which shall, as from the appropriate day—

(*a*) vary the rate of interest payable by him ; and

(*b*) where, as the result of the variation, the amount outstanding under the advance or security would increase if the periodic repayments were not increased, increase the amount of the periodic

repayments to such an amount as will ensure that
the said outstanding amount will not increase.

(8A) In subsection (8) above, " the appropriate day "
means such day as shall be specified in the notice, being—

> (*a*) in the case of a new standard rate, a day not less
> than 2 weeks, nor more than 6 weeks, after ser-
> vice of the notice ; and

> (*b*) in the case of a new locally determined rate, the
> first day of the relevant period of 6 months.".

16. In section 82 (interpretation), for the definition of "family"
there shall be substituted the following definition—

' "family", and any reference to membership thereof, shall be
construed in accordance with section 82A of this Act ; '.

17. After section 82 there shall be inserted the following section—

" Members 82A.—(1) A person is a member of another's family
of a person's for the purposes of this Act if—
family.

> (*a*) he is the spouse of that person or he and that
> person live together as husband and wife ; or

> (*b*) he is that person's parent, grandparent, child,
> grandchild, brother, sister, uncle, aunt, nephew
> or niece.

(2) For the purposes of subsection (1)(*b*) above—

> (*a*) a relationship by marriage shall be treated as a
> relationship by blood ;

> (*b*) a relationship of the half-blood shall be treated
> as a relationship of the whole blood ;

> (*c*) the stepchild of a person shall be treated as his
> child ; and

> (*d*) an illegitimate child shall be treated as the legiti-
> mate child of his mother and reputed father.".

18. At the end of Schedule 1 (tenancies which are not secure tenancies) there shall be added the following cross-headings and paragraphs—

" Police and fire authorities

8. A tenancy shall not be a secure tenancy if the landlord is an authority or committee mentioned in—

> (*a*) section 10(2)(*h*) of this Act and the tenant—

>> (i) is a constable of a police force, within
>> the meaning of the Police (Scotland) Act 1967, 1967 c. 77.
>> who in pursuance of regulations under section
>> 26 of that Act occupies the dwelling-house
>> without obligation to pay rent or rates ; or

>> (ii) in a case where head (i) above does not
>> apply, is let the dwelling-house expressly on
>> a temporary basis pending its being required
>> for the purposes of such a police force ; or

SCH. 1

1947 c. 41.

(b) section 10(2)(i) of this Act and the tenant—

(i) is a member of a fire brigade, maintained in pursuance of the Fire Services Act 1947, who occupies the dwelling-house in consequence of a condition in his contract of employment that he live in close proximity to a particular fire station ; or

(ii) in a case where head (i) above does not apply, is let the dwelling-house expressly on a temporary basis pending its being required for the purposes of such a fire brigade.

Dwelling-houses part of, or within curtilage of, certain other buildings

9. A tenancy shall not be a secure tenancy if the dwelling-house forms part of, or is within the curtilage of, a building which mainly—

(a) is held by the landlord for purposes other than the provision of housing accommodation ; and

(b) consists of accommodation other than housing accommodation.".

19. In Part I of Schedule 2 (grounds on which courts may order recovery of possession of dwelling-house)—

(a) in paragraph 10—

(i) for the words " The landlord intends " there shall be substituted the words " It is intended " ;

(ii) for the word " it " there shall be substituted the words " such demolition or work " ; and

(iii) for the words " do so without " there shall be substituted the words " take place without the landlord " ; and

(b) at the end there shall be added the following paragraph—

" 16. The tenant is the person, or one of the persons, to whom the tenancy was granted and the landlord was induced to grant the tenancy by a false statement made knowingly or recklessly by the tenant.".

Section 25(1).

SCHEDULE 2

MINOR AND CONSEQUENTIAL AMENDMENTS

The Building (Scotland) Act 1959 (c. 24)

1. In section 17(2) of the Building (Scotland) Act 1959 (restriction on effect of requirement to demolish, or carry out operations in relation to, a building), after paragraph (b) there shall be inserted the following paragraph—

" (bb) a building to which section 262A of the said Act of 1972 (control of demolition in conservation areas) applies ; ".

The Housing (Financial Provisions) (Scotland) Act 1972 (c. 46)

2. In the proviso to paragraph 2 of Schedule 4 to the Housing (Financial Provisions) (Scotland) Act 1972 (debits to housing revenue

account in respect of loan charges payable as regards certain sold, Sch. 2 or demolished, houses), for the words " to which the account relates and which is demolished after the coming into force of this Act or in respect of any house to which the account relates and which is " there shall be substituted the words " which, being a house to which the account related—

    (*a*) was demolished after the coming into force of this Act ; or

    (*b*) was ".

The Land Tenure Reform (Scotland) Act 1974 (c. 38)

3. In section 8(7) of the Land Tenure Reform (Scotland) Act 1974 (saving)—

    (*a*) for the words " 1971 " there shall be substituted the words " 1984 or a secure tenancy within the meaning of the Tenants' Rights, Etc. (Scotland) Act 1980 " ; and 1980 c. 52.

    (*b*) for the words " that Act " there shall be substituted the words " either of those Acts ".

The Housing Associations Act 1985 (c. 69)

4.—(1) The Housing Associations Act 1985 shall be amended in accordance with this paragraph.

(2) In section 8(1) (power of registered housing associations to dispose of land), after the word " buy) " there shall be inserted the words " and Part I of the Tenants' Rights, Etc. (Scotland) Act 1980 (analogous Scottish provisions) ".

(3) In section 15(1) (prohibition on payments etc. by certain registered housing associations), at the end there shall be added the words " or by section 15A of this Act ".

(4) In section 40 (index of defined expressions), after the entry relating to a shared ownership lease there shall be inserted the following entry—

    " shared ownership agreement (in relation   section 106 ".
       to Scotland)

(5) In section 42 (projects qualifying for housing association grant: accommodation for letting, hostels), in subsection (2)(*a*)—

    (*a*) after the word " includes " there shall be inserted the words " —(i) In England and Wales," ; and

    (*b*) after the word " lease," there shall be inserted the following sub-paragraph—

        " (ii) in Scotland, disposal under a shared ownership agreement,".

(6) In section 86 (Housing Corporation indemnities for building societies)—

    (*a*) in subsection (1)—

        (i) after the words " building society " in each of the three places where they occur there shall be inserted the words " or recognised body " ; and

    (ii) in paragraph (*b*), for the word " the " where it last occurs there shall be substituted the word " a ";

    (*b*) in subsection (2), after the words " building society " there shall be inserted the words " or recognised body " ;

    (*c*) in subsection (5), after the words " building societies " there shall be inserted the words " or recognised bodies " ; and

    (*d*) at the end there shall be added the following subsections—

    " (6) In this section, " recognised body " means a body designated, or of a class or description designated, in an order made under this subsection by statutory instrument by the Secretary of State with the consent of the Treasury.

    (7) Before making an order under subsection (6) above varying or revoking an order previously so made, the Secretary of State shall give an opportunity for representations to be made on behalf of a recognised body which, if the order were made, would cease to be such a body.".

    (7) In section 106 (interpretation), at the end there shall be added the following subsection—

    " (3) In the definition of " shared ownership agreement " in subsection (2) above, " approved " means approved by the Secretary of State after consultation with the Housing Corporation.".

    (8) In section 107—

    (*a*) in subsection (3) (list of provisions of Act applying to England and Wales only), for the words " 4(3)(*g*) " there shall be substituted the words " 4(3)(*d*) " ; and

    (*b*) in subsection (4) (list of provisions of Act applying to Scotland only), after the word " only— " there shall be inserted the words—

    " section 4(3)(*h*),

    section 15A,".

SCHEDULE 3

REPEALS

Chapter	Short title	Extent of repeal
10 & 11 Eliz. 2. c. 37.	The Building Societies Act 1962.	In Schedule 3.3(2)(*b*), the word " and " where it first occurs.
1968 c. 31.	The Housing (Financial Provisions) (Scotland) Act 1968.	Section 25(1)(*d*).
1980 c. 52.	The Tenants' Rights, Etc. (Scotland) Act 1980.	In section 1(8), the word " and " at the end of paragraph (*c*). In section 1(11), the word " nor " at the end of paragraph (*b*). In section 10(2), the word " and " at the end of paragraph (*f*). In section 30(5), the words " and the standard rate shall be effective from the date when it is declared by the Secretary of State ". In Schedule 1, paragraph 1.
1985 c. 69.	The Housing Associations Act 1985.	Section 100. In section 106(2), the definition of " heritable security ". In section 107(3), the words " 17(4)," ; the words " sections 44 and 45," ; the word " (3) " where it occurs in the entry relating to section 52; and the words " section 105,".

National Health Service (Amendment) Act 1986

1986 CHAPTER 66

An Act to apply certain enactments, orders and regulations relating to food and health and safety to certain health service bodies and premises; to make further provision as to pharmaceutical services under the National Health Service Act 1977 and the National Health Service (Scotland) Act 1978 and the remuneration of persons providing those services, general medical services, general dental services or general ophthalmic services under those Acts; to provide further, as respects Scotland, as to co-operation among certain bodies in securing and advancing the health of disabled persons, the elderly and others; and for connected purposes.   [7th November 1986]

BE IT ENACTED by the Queen's most Excellent Majesty, by and with the advice and consent of the Lords Spiritual and Temporal, and Commons, in this present Parliament assembled, and by the authority of the same, as follows:—

1.—(1) For the purposes of food legislation—

(*a*) a health authority shall not be regarded as the servant or agent of the Crown, or as enjoying any status, immunity or privilege of the Crown ; and

(*b*) premises used by a health authority shall not be regarded as property of or property held on behalf of the Crown.

Application of food legislation to health authorities and health service premises.

(2) The appropriate authority may by regulations—

(*a*) provide who is to be treated as the occupier or owner of any such premises for any of those purposes ; and

(b) make such modifications of the food legislation, in its application to health authorities, as appear to the authority to be necessary for its effective operation in relation to them.

(3) The powers to make regulations conferred by subsection (2) above shall be exercisable by statutory instrument.

(4) A statutory instrument containing regulations made in the exercise of the power conferred by paragraph (a) of that subsection shall be subject to annulment in pursuance of a resolution of either House of Parliament.

(5) A statutory instrument containing regulations made in the exercise of the power conferred by paragraph (b) shall not be made unless a draft of the instrument has been laid before Parliament and approved by a resolution of each House.

(6) Section 125 of the 1977 Act and section 101 of the 1978 Act shall have no effect in relation to any action, liability, claim or demand arising out of the food legislation.

(7) In this section—

    (a) as respects England Wales—

1984 c. 30.

        (i) " the appropriate authority " means the Ministers, as defined in section 132(1) of the Food Act 1984 ;

        (ii) " the food legislation " means the Food Act 1984 and any regulations or order made under it ;

        (iii) " health authority " has the meaning assigned to it by section 128 of the 1977 Act ;

    (b) as respects Scotland—

        (i) " the appropriate authority " means the Secretary of State ;

1956 c. 30.
1977 c. 28.

        (ii) " the food legislation " means the Milk and Dairies (Scotland) Acts 1914 to 1949, the Food and Drugs (Scotland) Act 1956 and the Control of Food Premises (Scotland) Act 1977 and any regulations or order made under those Acts ;

1984 c. 36.

        (iii) " health authority " means a Health Board constituted under section 2 of the 1978 Act, the Common Services Agency constituted under section 10 of that Act or a State Hospital Management Committee constituted under section 91 of the Mental Health (Scotland) Act 1984.

(8) This section shall have no effect in relation to anything done or omitted before its commencement.

2.—(1) For the purposes of health and safety legislation— Health and safety legislation.

    (*a*) a health authority shall not be regarded as the servant or agent of the Crown, or as enjoying any status, immunity or privilege of the Crown ; and

    (*b*) premises used by a health atuhority shall not be regarded as property of or property held on behalf of the Crown.

(2) In this section—

" health authority "—

    (*a*) as respects England and Wales, has the meaning assigned to it by section 128 of the 1977 Act ; and

    (*b*) as respects Scotland, means a Health Board constituted under section 2 of the 1978 Act, the Common Services Agency constituted under section 10 of that Act or a State Hospital Management Committee constituted under section 91 of the Mental Health (Scotland) Act 1984 ; and 1984 c. 36.

" the health and safety legislation " means—

    (*a*) the Health and Safety at Work etc. Act 1974 and the regulations, orders and other instruments in force under it ; and 1974 c. 37.

    (*b*) the enactments specified in the third column of Schedule 1 to that Act and the regulations, orders and other instruments in force under those enactments.

(3) Section 125 of the 1977 Act and section 101 of the 1978 Act shall have no effect in relation to any action, liability, claim or demand arising out of the health and safety legislation.

(4) This section shall have no effect in relation to anything done or omitted before its commencement.

3.—(1) The following section shall be substituted for section 42 of the 1977 Act— Pharmaceutical services.

" Regulations as to pharmaceutical services.   **42.**—(1) Regulations shall provide for securing that arrangements made by a Family Practitioner Committee under section 41 above will enable persons in the Comittee's locality for whom drugs, medicines or appliances mentioned in that section are ordered as there mentioned to receive them from persons with whom such arrangements have been made.

    (2) The regulations shall include provision—

        (*a*) for the preparation and publication by a Committee of one or more lists of persons, other than medical practitioners and dental practitioners, who undertake to provide pharmaceutical services from premises in the Committee's locality ;

(b) that an application to a Committee for inclusion in such a list shall be made in the prescribed manner and shall state—

   (i) the services which the applicant will undertake to provide and, if they consist of or include the supply of appliances, which appliances he will undertake to supply ; and

   (ii) the premises from which he will undertaken to provide those services ;

(c) that, except in prescribed cases—

   (i) an application for inclusion in such a list by a person not already included ; and

   (ii) an application by a person already included in such a list for inclusion also in respect of services or premises other than those already listed in relation to him.

shall be granted only if the Committee is satisfied, in accordance with the regulations, that it is necessary or desirable to grant it in order to secure in the neighbourhood in which the premises are located the adequate provision by persons included in the list of the services, or some of the services, specified in the application ; and

(d) for the removal of an entry in respect of premises from a list if it has been determined in the prescribed manner that the person to whom the entry relates—

   (i) has never provided from those premises ; or

   (ii) has ceased to provide from them, the services, or any of the services, which he is listed as undertaking to provide from them.

(3) The regulations may include provision—

(a) that an application to a Committee may be granted in respect of some only of the services specified in it ;

(b) that an application to a Committee relating to services of a prescribed description shall be granted only if it appears to the

Committee that the applicant has satisfied such conditions with regard to the provision of those services as may be prescribed ;

(c) that the inclusion of a person in a list in pursuance of such an application may be for a fixed period ;

(d) that, where the premises from which an application states that the applicant will undertake to provide services are in an area of a prescribed description, the applicant shall not be included in the list unless his inclusion is approved by a prescribed body and by reference to a prescribed criterion ; and

(e) that the prescribed body may give its approval subject to conditions.

(4) The regulations shall include provision conferring on such persons as may be prescribed rights of appeal from decisions made by virtue of this section.

(5) The regulations shall be so framed as to preclude—

(a) a person included in a list published under subsection (2)(a) above ; and

(b) an employee of such a person ;

from taking part in the decision whether an application such as is mentioned in subsection (2)(c) above should be granted or an appeal against such a decision brought by virtue of subsection (4) above should be allowed.".

(2) Regulations purporting to be made under section 42(b) of the 1977 Act and made before the passing of this Act shall be treated as being and always having been valid.

(3) The following subsections shall be substituted for subsection (2) of section 27 of the 1978 Act—

" (2) Regulations shall provide for securing that arrangements made by a Health Board under subsection (1) will enable persons in the Board's area for whom drugs, medicines or apliances mentioned in that subsection are ordered as there mentioned to receive them from persons with whom such arrangements have been made.

(3) The regulations shall include provision—

(a) for the preparation and publication by a Health Board of one or more lists of persons, other than medical practitioners and dental practitioners, who undertake to provide pharmaceutical services from premises in the Board's area ;

(*b*) that an application to a Health Board for inclusion in such a list shall be made in the prescribed manner and shall state—

(i) the services which the applicant will undertake to provide and, if they consist of or include the supply of appliances, which appliances he will undertake to supply ; and

(ii) the premises from which he will undertake to provide those services ;

(*c*) that, except in prescribed cases—

(i) an application for inclusion in such a list by a person not already included ; and

(ii) an application by a person already included in such a list for inclusion also in respect of services or premises other than those already listed in relation to him,

shall be granted only if the Health Board is satisfied, in accordance with the regulations, that it is necessary or desirable to grant it in order to secure in the neighbourhood in which the premises are located the adequate provision by persons included in the list of the services, or some of the services, specified in the application ; and

(*d*) for the removal of an entry in respect of premises from a list if it has been determined in the prescribed manner that the person to whom the entry relates—

(i) has never provided from those premises ; or

(ii) has ceased to provide from them,

the services, or any of the services, which he is listed as undertaking to provide from them.

(4) The regulations may include provision—

(*a*) that an application to a Health Board may be granted in respect of some only of the services specified in it ;

(*b*) that an application to a Health Board relating to services of a prescribed description shall be granted only if it appears to the Board that the applicant has satisfied such conditions with regard to the provision of those services as may be prescribed ;

(*c*) that the inclusion of a person in a list in pursuance of such an application may be for a fixed period ;

(*d*) that, where the premises from which an application states that the applicant will undertake to provide services are in an area of a prescribed description, the applicant shall not be included in the list unless his inclusion is approved by a prescribed body and by reference to a prescribed criterion ; and

(e) that the prescribed body may give its approval subject to conditions.

(5) The regulations shall include provision conferring on such persons as may be prescribed rights of appeal from decisions made by virtue of subsection (3) or (4).

(6) The regulations shall be so framed as to preclude—

(a) a person included in a list published under subsection (3)(a) above ; and

(b) an employee of such a person ;

from taking part in the decision whether an application such as is mentioned in subsection (3)(c) above should be granted or an appeal against such a decision brought by virtue of subsection (5) above should be allowed.".

(4) In section 28 of the 1978 Act, after the word " by " where it first occurs in each of subsections (1) and (2) there shall be inserted the words " or under ".

4.—(1) On a determination of remuneration for any of the descriptions of services mentioned in section 43A(1) of the 1977 Act or section 28A(1) of the 1978 Act or any category of services falling within such a description the determining authority may adjust the amount of the remuneration in either or both of the following ways— Remuneration of persons providing general medical services etc.

(a) by deducting an amount to take account of any overpayment ;

(b) by adding an amount to take account of any underpayment,

if it appears to the authority that an earlier determination was unsatisfactory.

(2) An earlier determination is to be taken to have been unsatisfactory only if, had it fallen to the authority to make it at the time of the later determination, the authority would have made it on the basis of different information.

(3) If an amount falls to be deducted by virtue of subsection (1)(a) above, the determining authority, in fixing amounts of remuneration for persons to whom the determination relates, may have regard to the period within which they first provided services of the description to which it relates.

(4) In this section—

" earlier determination " means an earlier determination of remuneration of the same or other persons for services of the same description or any category of services falling within that description and includes such a determination made before the passing of this Act ;

" overpayment " means the aggregate of any amounts which were properly paid under the earlier determination but which in the authority's opinion were paid because that determination was unsatisfactory, exclusive of any portion of that aggregate in respect of which a deduction under subsection (1) above has already been made ; and

" underpayment " means the aggregate of any amounts which in the authority's opinion would have been paid under the earlier determination if that determination had not been unsatisfactory, exclusive of any portion of that aggregate in respect of which an addition under subsection (1) above has already been made.

(5) If the later determination is of remuneration for a category of services falling within one of the descriptions of services mentioned in section 43A(1) of the 1977 Act or section 28A(1) of the 1978 Act, it is immaterial whether the earlier determination was of remuneration for the same category of services or for any other category of services falling within the same description.

(6) In subsection (7) of section 43B of the 1977 Act and of section 28B of the 1978 Act—

(a) in paragraph (a), for the words " a kind to which the determination will relate " there shall be substituted the words " the description to which the determination will relate or of any category falling within that description " ; and

(b) the following paragraph shall be substituted for paragraph (d)—

" (d) the extent to which it is desirable to encourage the provision, either generally or in particular places, of the description or category of services to which the determination will relate ; ".

(7) The following subsection shall be inserted after each of those subsection—

" (8) If the determination is of remuneration for a category of services falling within one of the descriptions of services mentioned in subsection (1) of the preceding section, the reference in subsection (7)(a) above to a category of services is a reference to the same category of services or to any other category of services falling within the same description.".

5.—(1) After section 13 of the 1978 Act there shall be inserted the following sections—

Co-operation and advice in relation to disabled persons, the elderly and others.

" Co-operation in planning of services for disabled persons, the elderly and others.

    13A.—(1) The duty under section 13, in relation to persons to whom this section applies, includes—

      (a) joint planning of—

         (i) services for those persons ; and

          (ii) the development of those services, being services which are of common concern to Health Boards and either or both of the authorities mentioned in that section ;

      (b) such consultation with voluntary organisations providing services similar to those mentioned in paragraph (a) as might be expected to contribute substantially to the joint planning of the services mentioned in that paragraph ;

      (c) the publication, at such times and in such manner as the bodies who have made joint plans under paragraph (a) consider appropriate, of those joint plans.

    (2) This section applies to—

      (a) disabled persons within the meaning of the Disabled Persons (Services, Consultation and Representation) Act 1986 ;

1986 c. 33.

      (b) persons aged 65 or more ; and

      (c) such other categories of persons as the Secretary of State may by order specify.

Joint Liaison Committees.

    13B.—(1) The Secretary of State may, after consultation with such Health Boards, local authorities, education authorities, associations of such authorities and other organisations and persons as appear to him to be appropriate, by order provide for the formation and as to the functions of committees, to be known as joint liaison committees, to advise Health Boards and local and education authorities on the performance of such of their duties under section 13 as consist of co-operation in the planning and operation of services of common concern to Health Boards and such authorities.

    (2) An order under subsection (1) may contain provisions relating to the role of voluntary organisations in joint liaison committees.".

  (2) Section 15 of the Disabled Persons (Services, Consultation and Representation) Act 1986 is hereby repealed.

Expenses.

6. There shall be paid out of money provided by Parliament any increase attributable to this Act in sums so provided under any other Act.

Orders in Council making corresponding provision for Northern Ireland.

1974 c. 28.

7. An Order in Council under paragraph 1(1)(*b*) of Schedule 1 to the Northern Ireland Act 1974 (legislation for Northern Ireland in the interim period) which states that it is made for purposes corresponding to those of this Act—

(*a*) shall not be subject to paragraph 1(4) and (5) of that Schedule (affirmative resolution of both Houses of Parliament) ; but

(*b*) shall be subject to annulment in pursuance of a resolution of either House.

Short title, etc.

8.—(1) This Act may be cited as the National Health Service (Amendment) Act 1986.

(2) In this Act—

1977 c. 49.

" the 1977 Act " means the National Health Service Act 1977 ; and

1978 c. 29.

" the 1978 Act " means the National Health Service (Scotland) Act 1978.

1980 c. 53.

(3) Section 21(1) of the Health Services Act 1980 and paragraph 54 of Schedule 1 to that Act shall cease to have effect.

(4) Sections 1 and 2 above shall come into force at the end of the period of three months beginning with the day on which this Act is passed.

(5) Each of the following provisions of this Act—

(*a*) section 3 above ; and

(*b*) to the extent that it inserts section 13B of the 1978 Act into that Act, secion 5 above,

shall come into force on such day as the Secretary of State may by order made by statutory instrument appoint in relation to it.

(6) Section 7 above extends to Northern Ireland only, but apart from that section, subsection (1) above and this subsection, this Act does not extend to Northern Ireland.

Consolidated Fund (No. 2) Act 1986

1986 CHAPTER 67

Apply certain sums out of the Consolidated Fund to the service of the years ending on 31st March 1987 and 1988.

[18th December 1986.]

Most Gracious Sovereign,

WE, Your Majesty's most dutiful and loyal subjects, the Commons of the United Kingdom in Parliament assembled, towards making good the supply which we have cheerfully granted to Your Majesty in this Session of Parliament, have resolved to grant unto Your Majesty the sums hereinafter mentioned; and do therefore most humbly beseech Your Majesty that it may be enacted, and be it enacted by the Queen's most Excellent Majesty, by and with the advice and consent of the Lords Spiritual and Temporal, and Commons, in this present Parliament assembled, and by the authority of the same, as follows:—

1. The Treasury may issue out of the Consolidated Fund of the United Kingdom and apply towards making good the supply granted to Her Majesty for the service of the year ending on 31st March 1987 the sum of £2,206,135,000.

Issue out of the Consolidated Fund for the year ending 31st March 1987.

2. The Treasury may issue out of the Consolidated Fund of the United Kingdom and apply towards making good the supply granted to Her Majesty for the service of the year ending on 31st March 1988 the sum of £44,907,033,000.

Issue out of the Consolidated Fund for the year ending 31st March 1988.

3. This Act may be cited as the Consolidated Fund (No. 2) Act 1986.

Short title.

Advance Petroleum Revenue Tax Act 1986

1986 CHAPTER 68

An Act to provide for the repayment of certain amounts of advance petroleum revenue tax.   [18th December 1986]

BE IT ENACTED by the Queen's most Excellent Majesty, by and with the advice and consent of the Lords Spiritual and Temporal, and Commons, in this present Parliament assembled, and by the authority of the same, as follows:—

1.—(1) In accordance with the provisions of this Act, advance petroleum revenue tax shall be repaid to a participator in an oil field—

    (a) in respect of whom none of the chargeable periods ending before 1st July 1986 is his net profit period for the purposes of this Act; and

    (b) who was a participator in that field on 6th November 1986 and who, on that date, was entitled to a share of the oil won from that field during the chargeable period ending on 31st December 1986;

and the Schedule to this Act shall have effect for determining whether any chargeable period is for the purposes of this Act a participator's net profit period in relation to a particular oil field.

Repayment of APRT where net profit period not yet reached.

(2) In this section " relevant participator " means any such participator as is referred to in subsection (1) above; and other expressions used in this Act have the same meaning as in Chapter II of Part VI of the Finance Act 1982 (advance petroleum revenue tax).

1982 c. 39.

(3) There shall be determined in the case of every relevant participator the amount by which his APRT credit for the chargeable period ending on 31st December 1986 exceeds his provisional liability for petroleum revenue tax for that period in respect of the field in question and, subject to subsection (5) below, on a claim made in that behalf, there shall be repaid to the participator so much of that excess as does not exceed £15 million.

(4) The reference in subsection (3) above to a participator's provisional liability for petroleum revenue tax for a chargeable period is a reference to the amount of tax shown to be payable by him for that period in the statement delivered under section 1(1)(a) of the Petroleum Revenue Tax Act 1980.

(5) A claim under subsection (3) above shall be made in such form as the Board may prescribe (whether before or after the passing of this Act) and shall be made not later than 28th February 1987 and, for the purposes of this Act, the Board may have regard to claims made before as well as after the passing of this Act.

(6) Paragraph 10(4) of Schedule 19 to the Finance Act 1982 (interest on certain repayments of APRT) shall not apply to any amount of APRT which is repayable only by virtue of this Act.

(7) A repayment of APRT made to a relevant participator pursuant to this Act,—

(a) shall be presumed to be a repayment of APRT which was paid later in priority to APRT which was paid earlier ; and

(b) shall be disregarded in computing his income for the purposes of income tax or corporation tax.

2.—(1) This Act may be cited as the Advance Petroleum Revenue Tax Act 1986.

(2) This Act shall be construed as one with Part I of the Oil Taxation Act 1975.

SCHEDULE

NET PROFIT PERIOD

1. In this Schedule—

    (a) " the principal Act " means the Oil Taxation Act 1975 ;

    (b) " statement ", in relation to an oil field and a chargeable period, means the statement delivered by a participator in that oil field in respect of that period under section 1(1)(a) of the Petroleum Revenue Tax Act 1980 ;

    (c) " the material date ", in relation to a participator in an oil field, means the date on which he delivers his statement in respect of that field for the chargeable period ending on 31st December 1986 ; and

    (d) " section 111 " means section 111 of the Finance Act 1981 (restriction of expenditure supplement).

2. Subject to the following provisions of this Schedule, if a chargeable period is a participator's net profit period for the purposes of section 111, that period is also his net profit period for the purposes of this Act.

3.—(1) If, before the material date, no notice of assessment or determination under paragraph 10 of Schedule 2 to the principal Act has been given to a participator with respect to any of the chargeable periods ending before 1st July 1986, the question whether one of those periods is his net profit period for the purposes of this Act shall be determined, subject to sub-paragraphs (2) and (3) below, on the assumption that, before making any modifications under subsections (3) to (5) of section 111, the amount of the assessable profit or allowable loss which accrued to the participator in each of the chargeable periods ending before 1st July 1986 was as set out in the statement delivered in respect of that period.

(2) If the expenditure treated as allowed in determining the assessable profit or allowable loss set out in the statement delivered in respect of any of the chargeable periods referred to in sub-paragraph (1) above is less than could have been treated as so allowed by virtue of paragraph 2(4) of the Schedule to the Petroleum Revenue Tax Act 1980, the assessable profit or allowable loss set out in that statement shall be taken for the purposes of sub-paragraph (1) above to be what it would have been if account had been taken of all the expenditure which could have been treated as so allowed.

(3) In any case where—

    (a) by virtue of sub-paragraph (2) above, any amount of expenditure is treated as allowed in determining the assessable profit or allowable loss which is taken to be set out in the statement for any chargeable period, and

    (b) the whole or any part of that amount is in fact treated as allowed in determining the assessable profit or allowable loss set out in the statement delivered in respect of any subsequent period,

the assessable profit or allowable loss of that subsequent period as set out in the statement delivered in respect of that period shall be taken for the purposes of sub-paragraph (1) above to be adjusted so as to prevent any amount of expenditure being taken into account more than once.

4.—(1) If, in a case where paragraph 3(1) above does not apply in relation to a participator,—

    (a) one of the chargeable periods ending before 1st July 1986 is the participator's net profit period for the purposes of section 111, and

    (b) a claim has been made under Schedule 5 or Schedule 6 to the principal Act in respect of expenditure incurred before 1st July 1986, and

(c) as to the whole or any part of that expenditure, at the material date either the Board have not notified their decision on the claim or an appeal against their decision on the claim has not been finally determined or abandoned (or treated as abandoned),

the question whether one of the periods referred to in paragraph (a) above is the participator's net profit period for the purposes of this Act shall be determined on the assumptions in sub-paragraph (2) below.

(2) The assumptions referred to in sub-paragraph (1) above are—

(a) that so much of any expenditure as falls within paragraph (c) of that sub-paragraph has been allowed and, in the case of expenditure claimed as qualifying for supplement under paragraph (b)(ii) or paragraph (c)(ii) of section 2(9) of the principal Act, has been allowed as so qualifying ; and

(b) that the participator's share of any of that expenditure which is the subject of a claim under Schedule 5 to the principal Act is the share proposed in the claim under paragraph 2(4)(b) of that Schedule.

5. Any reference in paragraph 3 or paragraph 4 above to a question whether a chargeable period is a participator's net profit period being determined on particular assumptions is a reference to that question being determined (on the basis of those assumptions) in accordance with sections 111 and 112 of the Finance Act 1981.

1981 c. 35.

Bishops (Retirement) Measure 1986

1986 No. 1

A Measure passed by the General Synod of the Church of England to make fresh provision with respect to the resignation or retirement of archbishops and bishops and for purposes connected therewith.   [18th March 1986]

PART I

Bishops

1.—(1) Where a person holding the office of diocesan bishop or suffragan bishop wishes to resign his office he shall, after consultation with the archbishop, tender his resignation to the archbishop in a written instrument in the prescribed form.

Resignation of bishop.

(2) If the archbishop decides to accept the resignation, he shall, within 28 days of receiving the instrument, by endorsement upon the instrument in the prescribed form declare the bishopric vacant as from a date specified in the endorsement (which shall subject to the provisions of sections 1(3) and 3 of the Ecclesiastical Offices (Age Limit) Measure 1975, be the date proposed by the bishop in the instrument or such later date as may be agreed by the archbishop and bishop concerned) ; and the instrument shall be filed in the provincial registry.

1975 No. 2.

2.—(1) Not less than six months before the date on which a person holding the office of diocesan bishop or suffragan bishop is required to vacate his office in accordance with section 1 of the Ecclesiastical Offices (Age Limit) Measure 1975, the archbishop shall by written instrument in the prescribed form declare

Retirement of bishop on reaching age-limit.

PART I

the bishopric vacant as from that date or, if his continance in office beyond that date is authorised under section 3(1) of that Measure, from the later date so authorised.

(2) Where after the making of an instrument under subsection (1) above—

1975 No. 2.

(a) in the case of an instrument relating to a diocesan bishop, the archbishop authorises his continuance in office under section 3(1) of the Ecclesiastical Offices (Age Limit) Measure 1975, or

(b) in the case of an instrument relating to a suffragan bishop, the diocesan bishop authorises his continuance in office under that section,

the archbishop may by written instrument in the prescribed form substitute for the date specified in the instrument made under subsection (1) above the date of the expiration of the period for which continuance in office is so authorised.

(3) Any instrument made under this section shall be filed in the provincial registry.

Retirement of bishop in case of disability.

3.—(1) Where it appears to the archbishop that a person holding the office of diocesan bishop or suffragan bishop is incapacitated by physical or mental disability from the due performance of his episcopal duties, the archbishop may, with the concurrence of the two senior diocesan bishops of the province, and subject to subsection (2) below, request the bishop to tender his resignation to the archbishop in a written instrument in the prescribed form.

(2) Before making any such request the archbishop shall send to the bishop notice of his intention to do so, and if within 15 days after receiving such notice or within such extended period as the archbishop may allow the bishop sends to the archbishop a demand for a medical examination, the archbishop shall not request the bishop to tender his resignation until the report of the medical examination has been considered by the archbishop and the said senior bishops.

(3) The expenses of the medical examination shall be defrayed by the Church Commissioners.

(4) On receiving an instrument of resignation under subsection (1) above, the archbishop shall by endorsement on the instrument in the prescribed form declare the bishopric vacant as from a date specified in the endorsement.

(5) If the bishop to whom a request has been made by the archbishop under this section refuses or fails within 2 months of the receipt of the request to tender his resignation or is

prevented by his infirmity from so doing, the archbishop may by written instrument in the prescribed form declare the bishopric vacant as from a date specified in the instrument.

(6) The date from which a bishopric may be declared vacant under this section shall not be earlier than the date of the endorsement under subsection (4) above or the date of the instrument under subsection (5) above, as the case may be ; and any instrument made under this section shall be filed in the provincial registry.

PART II

Archbishops

4. Where an archbishop wishes to resign his archbishopric Resignation of he shall tender his resignation to Her Majesty in a written instru- archbishop. ment in the prescribed form and Her Majesty may by Order in Council declare the archbishopric vacant as from a date specified in the Order (which date shall not be earlier than the date of the Order).

5. Not less than six months before the date on which an Retirement of archbishop is required to vacate his office in accordance with archbishop on section 1 of the Ecclesiastical Offices (Age Limit) Measure 1975, reaching the archbishop shall tender his resignation to Her Majesty in age-limit. a written instrument in the prescribed form and Her Majesty 1975 No. 2. may by Order in Council declare the archbishopric vacant as from that date or, if Her Majesty decides to exercise Her discretion under section 2 thereof, as from such later date as Her Majesty may determine under that section.

6.—(1) Where it appears to the two senior bishops of the Retirement of province that the archbishop of that province is incapacitated archbishop in by physical or mental disability from the due performance of case of his duties, the two senior bishops may, with the concurrence disability. of the archbishop of the other province and subject to subsection (2) below, request the archbishop to tender his resignation to Her Majesty in a written instrument in the prescribed form, and Her Majesty, on receiving the resignation, may by Order in Council declare the archbishopric vacant as from a date specified in the Order.

(2) Before making any such request the two senior bishops shall send to the archbishop notice of their intention to do so, and if within 15 days after receiving such notice or within such extended period as the two senior bishops may allow the archbishop sends to the two senior bishops a demand for a medical examination, the two senior bishops shall not request the archbishop to tender his resignation until the report of the medical examination has been considered by the two senior bishops and the archbishop of the other province.

PART II

(3) The expenses of the medical examination shall be defrayed by the Church Commissioners.

(4) If the archbishop to whom a request has been made by the two senior bishops under this section refuses or fails within two months of the receipt of the request to tender his resignation or is prevented by his infirmity from so doing, the two senior bishops may with the concurrence of the archbishop of the other province petition Her Majesty to declare the archbishopric vacant.

(5) Upon receiving any such petition Her Majesty may by Order in Council declare the archbishopric vacant as from a date specified in the Order.

(6) The date from which an archbishopric may be declared vacant by an Order in Council under subsection (1) or (5) above shall not be earlier than the date of the Order.

PART III

General provisions

Provisions as to pensions.

1961 No. 3.

7. Where a bishopric is declared vacant under section 3 or an archbishopric is declared vacant under section 6 of this Measure, the bishop or archbishop shall be treated for the purposes of sections 1 of the Clergy Pensions Measure 1961 as having retired on the ground of infirmity on the date from which the bishopric or archbishopric is declared vacant.

Effect of declaration of vacancy.

8.—Where a bishopric or archbishopric has been declared vacant under this Measure, any other preferment held by the bishop or archbishop shall also be vacated unless in the case of a bishopric the archbishop, or in the case of an archbishopric Her Majesty, declares that it shall not be vacated.

(2) Any such declaration shall be made in the written instrument, endorsement or Order in Council declaring the bishopric or archbishopric vacant.

Fee for legal officers.

1962 No. 1.

9. No fee shall be prescribed under the Ecclesiastical Fees Measure 1962 in respect of any specific duty imposed on any legal officer by virtue of the provisions of this Measure ; in this section " legal officer " has the same meaning as in the Ecclesiastical Fees Measure 1962.

Interpretation.

10.—(1) In this Measure the following expressions have the meanings hereby respectively assigned to them unless the context otherwise requires, that is to say :—

"archbishop" in relation to any diocesan bishop means the archbishop of the province in which his diocese is situated and in relation to any suffragan bishop means the archbishop of the province in which the diocese of the bishop to whom he is suffragan is situated ;

" medical examination " means an examination into the physical or mental abilities of the person demanding the examination by a medical practitioner agreed on between that person and the person or persons requesting his resignation or, failing such agreement, appointed by the President of the Royal College of Physicians;

" preferment " includes an archbishopric, a bishopric, archdeaconry, deanery or office in a cathedral or collegiate church, and a benefice, and every curacy, lectureship, readership, chaplaincy, office or place which requires the discharge of any spiritual duty ;

" prescribed " means prescribed by the Vicars-General of the provinces of Canterbury and York acting jointly.

(2) In this Measure the expression " diocesan bishop " shall not include an archbishop.

(3) The powers exercisable by an archbishop under this Measure shall, during the absence abroad or incapacity through illness of the archbishop or a vacancy in the see, be exercisable by the archbishop of the other province.

(4) For the purposes of this Measure, the seniority of a diocesan bishop after the Bishops of London and Winchester in the province of Canterbury and after the Bishop of Durham in the province of York shall be determined by length of service as a diocesan bishop within the provinces except that any diocesan bishop who by reason of illness or absence is unable to act or whose retirement is in question shall be disregarded.

11.—(1) In section 3(1) of the Ecclesiastical Offices (Age Limit) Measure 1975 there shall be added at the end the words " except that a diocesan bishop may exercise his powers under this subsection in relation to a suffragan bishop only after consultation with the archbishop of the province."

Minor and consequential amendments.
1975 No. 2.

(2) In subsections (1), (9) and (13) of section 8 of the Church of England (Miscellaneous Provisions) Measure 1983 for any reference to a deed there shall be substituted a reference to an instrument.

1983 No. 2.

12.—(1) Any rule of law or custom with respect to the resignation or retirement of an archbishop or a bishop is hereby abrogated.

Repeals.

Part IV

2 B

PART III

(2) The enactments specified in the Schedule to this Measure are hereby repealed to the extent specified in column 3 of that Schedule.

Short title, extent and commencement.

13.—(1) This Measure may be cited as the Bishops (Retirement) Measure 1986.

(2) This Measure shall extend to the whole of the provinces of Canterbury and York.

(3) This Measure shall come into force on such day as the Archbishops of Canterbury and York may jointly appoint.

SCHEDULE

S. 12(2).

REPEALS

Provision	Short title	Extent of repeal
1951 No. 2.	The Bishops (Retirement) Measure 1951.	The whole Measure.
1961 No. 3.	The Clergy Pensions Measure 1961.	In Schedule 2, the amendments to the Bishops (Retirement) Measure 1951.
1975 No. 2.	The Ecclesiastical Offices (Age Limit) Measure 1975.	Section 4.
1983 No. 2.	The Church of England (Miscellaneous Provisions) Measure 1983.	Section 7.

Ecclesiastical Fees Measure 1986

1986 No. 2

A Measure passed by the General Synod of the Church of England to make further provision with respect to ecclesiastical fees and for purposes connected therewith.
[18th March 1986]

PART I

Parochial Fees

1.—(1) The Church Commissioners may prepare a draft of an order (to be known as a " Parochial Fees Order ") which prescribes the amount of the parochial fees to be paid to the persons specified in that order in relation to the matters so specified.

Preparation of draft Parochial Fees Orders.

(2) A draft order prepared under subsection (1) above may contain such incidental provisions as the Church Commissioners consider necessary or desirable.

2.—(1) Every draft Parochial Fees Order shall be laid before the General Synod and if it is approved by the General Synod, whether with or without amendment, the draft order as so approved shall be referred to the Church Commissioners.

Procedure for making Parochial Fees Orders.

(2) Where a draft order is referred to the Church Commissioners under subsection (1) above then—

(a) if it has been approved by the General Synod without amendment, the Church Commissioners shall, by applying their seal, make the order ;

(*b*) if it has been approved by the General Synod with amendment, the Church Commissioners may either—

(i) by applying their seal make the order as so amended, or

(ii) withdraw the draft order for further consideration in view of any amendment made by the General Synod ;

and a Parochial Fees Order shall not come into force until it has been sealed by the Church Commissioners.

(3) Where the Standing Committee of the General Synod determines that a draft Parochial Fees Order does not need to be debated by the General Synod, then, unless—

(*a*) notice is given by a member of the General Synod in accordance with its Standing Orders that he wishes the draft order to be debated, or

(*b*) notice is so given by any such member that he wishes to move an amendment to the draft order and at least twenty-five other members of the Synod indicate when the amendment is called that they wish the amendment to be moved,

the draft order shall for the purposes of subsections (1) and (2) above be deemed to have been approved by the General Synod without amendment.

1946 c 36.

(4) The Statutory Instruments Act 1946 shall apply to a Parochial Fees Order sealed by the Church Commissioners under subsection (2) above as if it were a statutory instrument and were made when sealed by the Commissioners and as if this Measure were an Act providing that any such order shall be subject to annulment in pursuance of a resolution of either House of Parliament.

Provisions as to persons to whom parochial fees are to be paid.

3.—(1) During a vacancy in a benefice parochial fees which, but for the vacancy, would be paid to the incumbent of the benefice shall be paid to the diocesan board of finance or to such other person as the said board, after consultation with the bishop, may direct.

(2) Where a licence of a chapel includes a provision fixing a fee for the solemnization of a marriage or any other matter for which a parochial fee is prescribed by a Parochial Fees Order then, notwithstanding anything in the licence, the fee to be paid in respect of that matter shall be the fee prescribed by the order, but any provision of the licence as to the person to whom the fee in respect of that matter is to be paid shall continue to apply and where the licence provides for the fee to be paid to two or more persons the fee prescribed by the order shall be payable to those persons in the same proportions as under the provisions of the licence.

PART II

Ecclesiastical Judges' and Legal Officers' Fees

4.—(1) After every ordinary election to the General Synod the Constitution Archbishops of Canterbury and York shall jointly request— of Fees Advisory

 (*a*) the Lord Chancellor to appoint a person who is or has Commission. been a judge of the Court of Appeal or of the High Court of Justice, a circuit judge or a recorder ;

 (*b*) the chairman of the Bar Council to appoint a barrister ; and

 (*c*) the president of the Law Society to appoint a solicitor ;

and the three persons so appointed together with—

 (*d*) the person who holds the appointments of First Church Estates Commissioner and Chairman of the Central Board of Finance, and

 (*e*) a member of the Standing Committee of the General Synod appointed for the purposes of this Measure by that Committee,

shall constitute the Fees Advisory Commission.

(2) If at any time the appointments of First Church Estates Commissioner and Chairman of the Central Board of Finance are not both held by the same person, subsection (1) above shall have effect as if for paragraphs (*d*) and (*e*) there were substituted the following paragraphs—

 " (*d*) the First Church Estates Commissioner and

 (*e*) the Chairman of the Central Board of Finance."

(3) The members of the Fees Advisory Commission appointed under paragraphs (*a*) to (*c*) of subsection (1) above and (unless the appointments of First Church Estates Commissioner and Chairman of the Central Board of Finance are not held by the same person) the member appointed under paragraph (*e*) of that subsection (the " appointed members ") shall hold office until, after the next following ordinary election to the General Synod, further appointments are made under this section.

(4) If an appointed member of the Fees Advisory Commission dies or resigns, then—

 (*a*) if he was appointed under paragraph (*a*), (*b*) or (*c*) of subsection (1) above, the Archbishops of Canterbury and York shall jointly request the person who appointed him to appoint as a member of the Commission another person who is qualified for appointment under the paragraph in question ;

 (*b*) if he was appointed under paragraph (*e*) of that subsection, the Standing Committee of the General Synod

PART II

shall appoint as a member of the Commission another member of that Committee,

and a person appointed under this subsection shall hold office for the period for which the person who has died or resigned would have held office.

(5) The Fees Advisory Commission shall be entitled to act notwithstanding any temporary vacancy caused by the death or resignation of any of its members.

(6) An appointed member of the Fees Advisory Commission whose term of office comes to an end shall be eligible for re-appointment.

Legal Officers (Annual Fees) Orders.

5.—(1) The Fees Advisory Commission may make recommendations as to the annual fees to be paid to legal officers in respect of such of the duties of their office as are specified by the Commission, and the Commission may make an order (to be known as a " Legal Officers (Annual Fees) Order ") to give effect to their recommendations.

(2) Any order made under subsection (1) above may contain such incidental provisions as the Fees Advisory Commission considers necessary or desirable.

(3) Any order made under subsection (1) above shall be laid before the General Synod and shall not come into force until it has been approved by the General Synod.

(4) Where the Standing Committee of the General Synod determines that a Legal Officers (Annual Fees) Order does not need to be debated by the General Synod, then, unless notice is given by a member of the General Synod in accordance with its Standing Orders that he wishes the order to be debated, the order shall for the purposes of subsection (3) above be deemed to have been approved by the General Synod.

1946 c. 36.

(5) The Statutory Instruments Act 1946 shall apply to a Legal Officers (Annual Fees) Order approved by the General Synod as if it were a statutory instrument and were made when so approved and as if this Measure were an Act providing that any such order shall be subject to annulment in pursuance of a resolution of either House of Parliament.

Ecclesiastical Judges and Legal Officers (Fees) Orders.

6.—(1) The Fees Advisory Commission may make recommendations as to the fees to be paid in respect of such duties performed by ecclesiastical judges and legal officers as are specified by the Commission (not, in the case of legal officers, being duties covered by the annual fees payable under a Legal Officers (Annual Fees) Order), and the Commission may make an order (to be known as an " Ecclesiastical Judges and Legal Officers (Fees) Order ") to give effect to their recommendations.

(2) Any order made under subsection (1) above may contain such incidental provisions as the Fees Advisory Commission considers necessary or desirable.

(3) Any order made under subsection (1) above shall be laid before the General Synod and shall not come into force until it has been approved by the General Synod, whether with or without amendment.

(4) Where the Standing Committee of the General Synod determines that an Ecclesiastical Judges and Legal Officers (Fees) Order does not need to be debated by the General Synod, then, unless—

> (a) notice is given by a member of the General Synod in accordance with its Standing Orders that he wishes the order to be debated, or

> (b) notice is so given by any such member that he wishes to move an amendment to the order and at least twenty-five other members of the Synod indicate when the amendment is called that they wish the amendment to be moved,

the order shall for the purposes of subsection (3) above be deemed to have been approved by the General Synod without amendment.

(5) The Statutory Instruments Act 1946 shall apply to an Ecclesiastical Judges and Legal Officers (Fees) Order approved by the General Synod as if it were a statutory instrument and were made when so approved and as if this Measure were an Act providing that any such order shall be subject to annulment in pursuance of a resolution of either House of Parliament.

1946 c. 36

PART III

Miscellaneous and General

7. Any fee payable by virtue of an order made under this Measure shall be recoverable as a debt.

Recovery of fees.

8. Where an archbishop or bishop has paid any sum by virtue of any order made or deemed to be made under this Measure and the liability to pay that sum was imposed on him as archbishop or bishop, the Church Commissioners shall reimburse that sum to the archbishop or bishop.

Reimbursement of archbishops or bishops.

Private, local
and personal
Acts which are
inconsistent
with Parochial
Fees Orders.

9. Schedule 1 to this Measure which relates to private, local and personal Acts which are inconsistent with a Parochial Fees Order shall have effect.

Interpretation.

10. In this Measure the following expressions have the meanings hereby respectively assigned to them—

" ecclesiastical judges " means the Dean of the Court of Arches and the Auditor of the Chancery Court of York, the Vicars General of the provinces of Canterbury and York, the Commissary General and Diocesan Chancellors ;

" legal officers " means the provincial registrars, diocesan registrars, bishops' legal secretaries and chapter clerks ;

" parish " means any ecclesiastical parish or other place the incumbent or minister whereof either is entitled to retain for his own benefit or is under a duty to pay over to any other person the parochial fees chargeable ;

" parochial fees " mean any fees payable to a parochial church council, to a clerk in Holy Orders, or to any other person performing duties in connection with a parish for, or in respect of, the solemnization or performance of church offices or the erection of monuments in churchyards or such other services or matters as may by law or custom be included in a Parochial Fees Order and such other services or matters for which, in the opinion of the Church Commissioners, the payment of fees is appropriate, except fees or other charges payable under section 214 of, and Schedule 26 to, the Local Government Act 1972 (burial fees) or fees payable under section 62 of the Cremation Act 1902 (cremation service fees).

1972 c. 70.

1902 c. 8.

Repeals,
consequential
amendments
and
transitional
provisions.

11.—(1) The Ecclesiastical Fees Measure 1962 is hereby repealed.

(2) In section 63 of the Ecclesiastical Jurisdiction Measure 1963 for the words from " Ecclesiastical Fees " to the end of the section there shall be substituted the words " Ecclesiastical Fees Measure 1986 " and in section 6(3) of the Faculty Jurisdiction Measure 1964 for the words " Ecclesiastical Fees Measure 1962 " there shall be substituted the words " Ecclesiastical Fees Measure 1986."

1962 No. 1.

1963 No. 1.

1964 No. 5.

(3) The transitional provisions in Schedule 2 to this Measure shall have effect.

12.—(1) This Measure may be cited as the Ecclesiastical Fees
Measure 1986.

(2) This Measure shall extend to the whole of the provinces
of Canterbury and York except the Channel Islands and the
Isle of Man, but may be applied to the Channel Islands, as
defined by the Channel Islands (Church Legislation) Measures
1931 and 1957, or either of them, in accordance with the provisions of those Measures and may be extended to the Isle of Man
by or under Act of Tynwald.

(3) This Measure shall come into force on such day as the
Archbishops of Canterbury and York may jointly appoint and
different days may be so appointed for different provisions.

PART III

Short title,
extent and
commence-
ment.

1931 No. 4.
1957 No. 1.

SCHEDULES

SCHEDULE 1

PRIVATE, LOCAL AND PERSONAL ACTS WHICH ARE INCONSISTENT WITH PAROCHIAL FEES ORDERS

1. Where a Parochial Fees Order is inconsistent with a private, local or personal Act which affects a parish, the parochial church council or, if there is no parochial church council, the incumbent or minister may apply to the Church Commissioners requesting them to prepare an order providing for the amendment or repeal of that Act in order to permit the Parochial Fees Order to apply to the parish ; and, on receiving such an application, the Church Commissioners may prepare a draft order accordingly.

2. Where the Church Commissioners prepare a draft order under paragraph 1 above, they shall—

(*a*) send a copy of that order to the bishop of the diocese in which the parish is situated, the parochial church council (if any) and the incumbent or minister of the parish, and any person whose power of fixing fees or whose right to receive fees is affected by the order, together with a notice that consideration will be given to any representations sent in writing to them before such date (which shall not be less than one month from the date of the sending of the notice) as may be specified in the notice ; and

(*b*) cause a copy of the order to be posted for a period of not less than one month on or near the principal door of the church of the parish, or at least one of such churches if there be more than one, together with a notice that consideration will be given to any representations sent in writing to them before such date (which shall not be less than one month from the date when the copy of the order was first posted), as may be specified in the notice ; and

(*c*) publish an advertisement in at least one local newspaper circulating in the parish stating the purport of the draft order and at what place in the parish it may be inspected (which may be on or near the church door mentioned in sub-paragraph (*b*) above or such other place as the Church Commissioners may decide) and that consideration will be given to any representations sent in writing to them before such date (which shall not be less than one month from the date when the advertisement was published) as may be specified in the advertisement.

3. The Church Commissioners shall consider all representations made to them under paragraph 2 above and may make such amendments in the order as they think fit.

4. When the periods during which representations may be made under paragraph 2 above have all expired and the Church Commis-

sioners have considered all representations made to them, they may, by applying their seal, make the order or, as the case may be, the order as amended under paragraph 3 above.   Sch. 1

5. The Statutory Instruments Act 1946 shall apply to an order 1946 c. 36. sealed by the Church Commissioners under paragraph 4 above as if it were a statutory instrument and were made when sealed by the Commissioners and as if this Measure were an Act providing that the order shall be subject to annulment in pursuance of a resolution of either House of Parliament.

6. The Church Commissioners shall send copies of any order made under this Schedule to every person or body specified in sub-paragraph 2(*a*) above and shall publish in the London Gazette a notice stating they have made the order and specifying a place where copies of the order may be obtained.

SCHEDULE 2
Transitional Provisions

1. No order made under Part I of this Measure shall be binding on a clerk in Holy Orders or other person performing duties in connection with a parish to whom the provisions of section 2(4) of the Ecclesiastical Fees Measure 1962 applied immediately before the 1962 No. 1. coming into force of this provision without his consent in writing; but such consent when given shall be irrevocable.

2. Until the Fees Advisory Commission is constituted under this Measure, the members of the Fees Committee appointed under section 1(3) of the Ecclesiastical Fees Measure 1962 shall, notwithstanding the repeal of that Measure by this Measure, continue to hold office and may perform any of the functions of the Fees Advisory Commission under this Measure.

3. Notwithstanding the repeal by this Measure of the Ecclesiastical Fees Measure 1962, any order made under that Measure relating to legal officers' fees or parochial fees shall be deemed to have been made under this Measure; and any fee payable at the coming into force of this Measure under an existing order relating to legal officers' fees or parochial fees shall be deemed to be payable under this Measure.

4. Any sum payable to any person under the provisions of section 5 of the Ecclesiastical Fees Measure 1962 shall, if reimbursible by the Church Commissioners at the coming into force of this provision, be deemed to be reimbursible under this Measure.

5. Nothing in this Schedule shall be taken as prejudicing the application of sections 16 and 17 of the Interpretation Act 1978.   1978 c. 30.

Patronage (Benefices) Measure 1986

1986 No. 3

A MEASURE passed by the General Synod of the Church of England to amend the law relating to patronage of benefices.   [18th July 1986]

PART I

REGISTRATION AND TRANSFER OF RIGHTS OF PATRONAGE

1.—(1) Subject to the provisions of this Measure, the registrar of each diocese shall compile and maintain a register indicating in relation to every benefice in the diocese the person who is the patron of the benefice and containing such other information as may be prescribed. *Registration of patrons.*

(2) Except as provided by this Measure, no person shall be entitled, after the expiration of the period of fifteen months beginning with the date on which this section comes into force, to exercise any of the functions of a patron of a benefice unless he is registered as patron of that benefice, and the said period is in this Measure referred to as the " registration period ".

(3) The provisions of Schedule 1 to this Measure shall have effect with respect to the registration of patrons of benefices and other matters relating thereto.

(4) The registration under this Measure of any person as a patron of a benefice shall be conclusive evidence of the matters registered.

(5) Any register maintained under this Measure shall be open to inspection by the public at all reasonable times.

PART I
Registration
of patronage
belonging
to an office.

2. In the case of a right of patronage of a benefice which belongs to an office, the duty of the registrar of the diocese under section 1(1) of this Measure to register in relation to that benefice the person who is the patron thereof shall be construed as a duty to register that office as a patron of that benefice ; and section 1(4) shall apply in relation to an office which is registered as a patron as it applies in relation to a person who is so registered.

Transfer of
rights of
patronage.

3.—(1) No right of patronage of a benefice shall be capable of sale and any transfer thereof for valuable consideration shall be void.

(2) Subject to the provisions of this section, a right of patronage vested in an ecclesiastical corporation shall not be transferred to any body or person unless—

    (a) the consent of the bishop or, if the bishop is the proposed transferor, the consent of the archbishop has been obtained ; or

    (b) the transfer is made by a pastoral scheme or order.

(3) Where a right of patronage of a benefice is proposed to be transferred otherwise than by a pastoral scheme or order, the proposed transferor shall send to the bishop (or, if the bishop is the proposed transferor, to the archbishop) and to the registrar of the diocese a notice stating—

    (a) his intention to transfer that right ;

    (b) the name and address of the proposed transferee ; and

    (c) particulars of the terms of the proposed transfer.

(4) On receiving a notice under subsection (3) above, the registrar shall send to the secretary of the parochial church council of the parish concerned a notice informing him of the proposed transfer and stating that before the expiration of the period of one month beginning with the date on which the notice is sent to him representations with respect to the proposed transfer may be made to the registrar by the parochial church council ; and the registrar shall notify the bishop and the proposed transferor, or, if the bishop is the proposed transferor, the bishop and the archbishop, of any representations made to him within that period.

(5) After the expiration of the period of one month mentioned in subsection (4) above, the bishop or, if the bishop is the proposed transferor, the archbishop shall consider any representations made under that subsection and, whether or not any such representations have been made, the bishop or archbishop may request the proposed transferor (either personally or through some person appointed by the proposed transferor) to confer with him (or with some person appointed by the bishop or, as

the case may be, the archbishop) as to the proposed transfer ; and the bishop or, as the case may be, the archbishop shall not give any consent required under this section until after any such representations have been considered and any such request has been complied with.

(6) Any transfer of a right of patronage otherwise than by a pastoral scheme or order shall be in the prescribed form.

(7) Where a right of patronage of a benefice is transferred otherwise than by a pastoral scheme or order, the registrar shall not register the transferee as a patron of that benefice unless—

> (*a*) he is satisfied that the requirements of this section have been complied with ; and
>
> (*b*) an application for registration is made in accordance with Schedule 1 to this Measure before the expiration of the period of twelve months from the date of the execution of the transfer ;

and if no such application for registration is made before the expiration of that period of twelve months the transfer shall be of no effect.

(8) No transfer of a right of patronage of a benefice shall take effect during the period of a vacancy in that benefice.

(9) In this section " transfer " means a transfer *inter vivos* including a transfer by way of exchange ; but it does not include a transfer by operation of law, a transfer upon the appointment of a new trustee or a transfer by the personal representatives of a deceased person.

4.—(1) The registrar of a diocese may rectify an entry in the register of patrons in any case— Rectification of register.

> (*a*) where all the persons interested agree to the rectification of the entry ; or
>
> (*b*) where the registrar decides that the entry should be rectified—
>
>> (i) because a person is, or is not, entitled to be registered as patron of a benefice, or
>>
>> (ii) because information registered as to the exercise of a right of presentation to a benefice is incorrect,
>
> and, in either case, no appeal against the registrar's decision has been brought within the period specified in paragraph 8 of Schedule 1 to this Measure or the appeal has been dismissed ; or
>
> (*c*) where any rectification of the entry is required by reason of a decision of the chancellor of the diocese under that Schedule.

PART I

(2) Where in the case of an entry in the register relating to any benefice—

(a) the entry has been adverse to the claim of any person for a period of more than thirty years, or

(b) if the period of thirty years from the end of the registration period has not expired, the benefice has been held adversely to the claim of any person for a period of more than thirty years,

then, notwithstanding anything in subsection (1) above or in paragraph 5 of Schedule 1 to this Measure, no rectification of that entry may be made in favour of that person unless all the persons interested agree to that rectification.

1980 c. 58.

(3) Section 25 of the Limitation Act 1980 (time limits for actions to enforce advowsons) shall cease to have effect at the end of the registration period.

Rights of patronage exercisable otherwise than by registered patron.

5.—(1) Where an office is registered as a patron of a benefice, the person who is for the time being the holder of that office shall, subject to the provisions of Part II of this Measure, be entitled to discharge all the functions of a patron of that benefice.

(2) Where a registered patron of a benefice dies then, until the person to whom the right of patronage is to be transferred is registered as a patron of that benefice, the personal representatives of the deceased patron shall, subject to the provisions of Part II of this Measure, be entitled to discharge all the functions of a patron of that benefice.

(3) A registered patron of a benefice may by an instrument creating a power of attorney confer on the donee of the power authority to discharge on his behalf all the functions of a patron of that benefice, and where such a power is created the donee shall, subject to the provisions of Part II of this Measure, be entitled to discharge those functions until the power is revoked.

(4) Any person entitled to discharge any functions in relation to a benefice by virtue of this section shall be entitled to discharge those functions notwithstanding that he is not registered in the register of patrons in relation to that benefice.

Abolition of registration of advowsons at Land Registry.

6.—(1) After the date on which section 1 of this Measure comes into force, no advowson shall be registered in the register of title to freehold and leasehold land kept at Her Majesty's Land Registry, and after the expiration of the registration period under this Measure all titles to advowsons registered in that register shall be deemed, by operation of this Measure and without any entry being made in the register, to have been closed and removed from that register.

(2) In section 3 of the Land Registration Act 1925 in para- PART I
graph (viii) (definition of " land ") the words " an advowson " 1925 c. 21.
shall cease to have effect at the end of the registration period.

PART II

EXERCISE OF RIGHTS OF PRESENTATION

General provisions as to filling of vacancies

7.—(1) Subject to section 70 of the Pastoral Measure 1983, Notification
where a benefice becomes vacant by reason of the death of the of vacancies.
incumbent, the bishop shall, as soon as practicable after he be- 1983 No. 1.
comes aware of the vacancy, give notice of that fact to the designated officer of the diocese.

(2) Subject to section 70 of the Pastoral Measure 1983, where
the bishop is aware that a benefice is shortly to become vacant by
reason of resignation or cession, the bishop shall give such notice
of that fact as he considers reasonable in all the circumstances to
the designated officer of the diocese.

(3) Any notice required to be given to the designated officer
under subsection (1) or (2) above shall also be given to the registrar of the diocese, unless he is the designated officer.

(4) As soon as practicable after receiving a notice under subsection (1) or (2) above the designated officer shall send notice of
the vacancy to the registered patron of the benefice and to the
secretary of the parochial church council of the parish belonging
to the benefice ; and any such notice shall include such information as may be prescribed.

(5) In this Measure " the designated officer ", in relation to
a diocese, means such person as the bishop, after consulting the
bishop's council, may designate or, if no person is designated, the
secretary of the pastoral committee of the diocese.

8.—(1) Where the registered patron of a benefice is an Provisions as
individual and is not a clerk in Holy Orders, he shall on receiv- to declarations
ing notice of a vacancy in the benefice under section 7(4) of of
this Measure— membership.

(a) if able to do so, make a written declaration (in this
Measure referred to as " the declaration of membership ") declaring that he is an actual communicant
member of the Church of England or of a Church
in communion with that Church ; or

(b) if unable to make the declaration himself, appoint some
other person, being an individual who is able and willing to make it or is a clerk in Holy Orders or one of
the bodies mentioned in subsection (7) below, to act
as his representative to discharge in his place the functions of a registered patron.

(2) Where the registered patron of a benefice is a body of persons corporate or unincorporate then, on receiving notice of a vacancy in the benefice under section 7(4) of this Measure, that body shall appoint an individual who is able and willing to make the declaration of membership or is a clerk in Holy Orders to act as its representative to discharge in its place the functions of a registered patron.

(3) Notwithstanding anything in subsection (1) above, where the registered patron of a benefice who is an individual and is not the bishop of a diocese is of the opinion, on receiving notice of a vacancy in the benefice under section 7(4) of this Measure, that he will be unable for any reason to discharge his functions as a patron of that benefice he may, notwithstanding that he is able to make the declaration of membership, appoint such a representative as is mentioned in subsection (1)(b) above to discharge those functions in his place.

(4) Where a benefice the right of presentation to which belongs to an office (other than an ecclesiastical office) becomes vacant, the person who holds that office on the date on which the benefice becomes vacant shall be entitled to present on that vacancy and shall as soon as practicable after that date—

    (a) if able to do so, make the declaration of membership, or

    (b) if unable to make the declaration himself, appoint some other person, being a person who may be appointed as a representative under subsection (1)(b) above, to act as his representative to discharge in his place the functions of a registered patron.

(5) Where the right of presentation to a benefice is exercisable by the donee of a power of attorney, the donee shall as soon as practicable after receiving notice of the vacancy in the benefice (or, if the power is created during the vacancy, as soon as practicable after it is created)—

    (a) if able to do so, make the declaration of membership, or

    (b) if unable to make the declaration himself, appoint some other person, being a person who may be appointed as a representative under subsection (1)(b) above, to act as his representative to discharge in his place the functions of a registered patron.

(6) Where under the preceding provisions of this section a body mentioned in subsection (7) below is appointed to discharge the functions of a registered patron, that body shall as soon as practicable after being so appointed appoint as its representative an individual who is able and willing to make the declaration of membership or is a clerk in Holy Orders.

(7) The bodies referred to in subsection (1)(*b*) above are—

- (*a*) the dean and chapter or the cathedral chapter of the cathedral church of the diocese ;
- (*b*) the dean and chapter of the collegiate church of St. Peter in Westminster ;
- (*c*) the dean and canons of the collegiate church of St. George, Windsor ;
- (*d*) any diocesan board of patronage ;
- (*e*) any patronage board constituted by a pastoral scheme ;
- (*f*) any university in England or any college or hall in such a university ; and
- (*g*) the colleges of Eton and Winchester.

9.—(1) Before the expiration of the period of two months Information beginning with the date on which a benefice becomes vacant, a to be sent to registered patron who is an individual shall send to the designated designated officer of the diocese— officer.

- (*a*) the declaration of membership made by him, or
- (*b*) the name and address of his representative and the declaration of membership made by that representative.

(2) Before the expiration of the said period of two months, a registered patron which is a body of persons corporate or unincorporate shall send to the designated officer of the diocese the name and address of the individual who is to act as its representative and the declaration of membership made by that representative.

(3) Where the functions of a registered patron are to be discharged by the holder of an office, subsection (1) above shall apply to the person who holds that office on the date on which the benefice becomes vacant as it applies to the registered patron.

(4) Where the functions of a registered patron are to be discharged by the donee of a power of attorney, subsection (1) above shall apply to the donee as it applies to the registered patron except that, if the power is created during the vacancy concerned, there shall be substituted for the period of two months mentioned in that subsection the period of two months beginning with the date on which the power is created, and the information required to be sent under that subsection shall include information as to that date.

(5) Where the registered patron or his representative is a clerk in Holy Orders, the registered patron shall, before the expiration of the period during which the declaration of membership is required to be sent to the designated officer under the preceding

PART II

provisions of this section, notify the designated officer of that fact, and a declaration of membership made by that clerk shall not be required to be sent to the designated officer under this section.

(6) As soon as practicable after receiving information under this section as to the appointment of a representative, the designated officer shall send to the secretary of the parochial church council the name and address of that representative.

Disqualification for presentation.

10. Where the registered patron of a benefice or the representative of that patron, is a clerk in Holy Orders or is the wife of such a clerk, that clerk shall be disqualified for presentation to that benefice.

Requirements as to meetings of parochial church council.

11.—(1) Before the expiration of the period of four weeks beginning with the date on which the notice under section 7(4) of this Measure is sent to the secretary of the parochial church council, one or more meetings of that council shall be held for the purposes of—

(a) preparing a statement describing the conditions, needs and traditions of the parish ;

(b) appointing two lay members of the council to act as representatives of the council in connection with the selection of an incumbent ;

(c) deciding whether to request the registered patron to consider advertising the vacancy ;

(d) deciding whether to request a meeting under section 12 of this Measure ; and

(e) deciding whether to request a statement in writing from the bishop describing in relation to the benefice the needs of the diocese and the wider interests of the Church.

(2) A meeting of the parochial church council for which subsection (1) above provides shall be convened by the secretary thereof, and no member of that council who is—

(a) the outgoing incumbent or the wife of the outgoing incumbent, or

(b) the registered patron, or

(c) the representative of the registered patron,

shall attend that meeting.

(3) None of the following members of the parochial church council, that is to say—

(a) any person mentioned in subsection (2) above, and

(b) any deaconess or lay worker licensed to the parish,

shall be qualified for appointment under subsection (1)(b) above.

(4) If before the vacancy in the benefice is filled any person appointed under subsection (1)(*b*) above dies or becomes unable for any reason to act as the representative of, or ceases to be a member of, the council by which he was appointed, then, except where he ceases to be such a member and the council decides that he shall continue to act as its representative, his appointment shall be deemed to have been revoked and the council shall appoint another lay member of the council (not being a member disqualified under subsection (3) above) to act in his place for the remainder of the proceedings under this Part of this Measure.

(5) If a parochial church council holds a meeting under subsection (1) above but does not appoint any representatives at that meeting, then, subject to subsection (6) below, two churchwardens who are members of that council (or, if there are more than two churchwardens who are members of the council, two churchwardens chosen by all the churchwardens who are members) shall act as representatives of the council in connection with the selection of an incumbent.

(6) A churchwarden who is the registered patron of a benefice shall not be qualified under subsection (5) above to act as a representative of the parochial church council or to choose any other churchwarden so to act, and in any case where there is only one churchwarden qualified to act as such a representative that churchwarden may act as the sole representative of that council in connection with the selection of the incumbent.

(7) Any representative of the parochial church council appointed under subsection (1) or (4) above and any churchwarden acting as such a representative by virtue of subsection (5) or (6) above is in this Part of this Measure referred to as a " parish representative ", and where a churchwarden is entitled to act as the sole parish representative any reference in this Part to the parish representatives shall be construed as a reference to that churchwarden.

(8) A copy of the statement prepared under subsection (1)(*a*) above together with the names and addresses of the parish representatives shall, as soon as practicable after the holding of the meeting under that subsection, be sent by the secretary of the parochial church council to the registered patron and, unless the bishop is the registered patron, to the bishop.

12.—(1) Where a request for a meeting under this section is made—

    (*a*) by a notice sent by the registered patron or the bishop to the secretary of the parochial church council, or

    (*b*) by a resolution of the parochial church council, passed at a meeting held under section 11 of this Measure,

Joint meeting of parochial church council with bishop and patron.

PART II a joint meeting of the parochial church council with the registered patron and (if the bishop is not the registered patron) the bishop shall be held for the purpose of enabling those present at the meeting to exchange views on the statement prepared under section 11(1)(*a*) of this Measure (needs of the parish) and the statement presented under subsection (2) below (needs of the diocese).

(2) At any meeting held under this section the bishop shall present either orally or, if a request for a statement in writing has been made by the registered patron or the parochial church council, in writing a statement describing in relation to the benefice the needs of the diocese and the wider interests of the Church.

(3) Any notice given under subsection (1)(*d*) above shall be of no effect unless it is sent to the secretary of the parochial church council not later than ten days after a copy of the statement prepared under subsection (1)(*a*) of section 11 of this Measure is received by the persons mentioned in subsection (8) of that section.

(4) The outgoing incumbent and the wife of the outgoing incumbent shall not be entitled to attend a meeting held under this section.

(5) A meeting requested under this section shall be held before the expiration of the period of six weeks beginning with the date on which the request for the meeting was first made (whether by the sending of a notice as mentioned in subsection (1)(*a*) above or by the passing of a resolution as mentioned in subsection (1)(*b*) above), and at least fourteen days' notice (unless a shorter period is agreed by all the persons concerned) of the time and place at which the meeting is to be held shall be given by the secretary of the parochial church council to the registered patron, the bishop (if he is not the registered patron) and the members of the parochial church council.

(6) If either the registered patron or the bishop is unable to attend a meeting held under this section, he shall appoint some other person to attend on his behalf.

(7) The chairman of any meeting held under this section shall be such person as the persons who are entitled to attend and are present at the meeting may determine.

(8) No meeting requested under this section shall be treated for the purposes of this Measure as having been held unless there were present at the meeting—

    (*a*) the bishop or the person appointed by the bishop to attend on his behalf, and

(b) the registered patron or the person appointed by the
    patron to attend on his behalf, and

(c) at least one third of the members of the parochial church
    council who were entitled to attend.

(9) The secretary of the parochial church council shall invite
both the rural dean of the deanery in which the parish is (unless
he is the outgoing incumbent) and the lay chairman of the
deanery synod of that deanery to attend a meeting held under
this section.

13.—(1) The registered patron of a vacant benefice shall not
make to any priest an offer to present him to a benefice until—

   (a) if a request for a meeting under section 12 of this Measure has been made, either—

      (i) that meeting has been held, or

      (ii) all the parties concerned have agreed that no
such meeting should be held, or

      (iii) the period of six weeks mentioned in section
12(5) has expired ; and

   (b) (whether or not such a request has been made) the
making of the offer to the priest in question has been
approved—

      (i) by the parish representatives, and

      (ii) if the registered patron is a person other than
the bishop of the diocese in which the benefice is,
by that bishop.

*Provisions
with respect
to the selection
of incumbent.*

(2) If, before the expiration of the period of four weeks
beginning with the date on which the registered patron sent
to the bishop a request for him to approve under paragraph (b)
of subsection (1) above the making of the offer to the priest
named in the request, no notice is received from the bishop of
his refusal to approve the making of the offer, the bishop shall
be deemed to have given his approval under that paragraph.

(3) If, before the expiration of the period of two weeks
beginning with the date on which the registered patron sent to
the parish representatives a request for them to approve under
paragraph (b) of subsection (1) above the making of the offer to
the priest named in the request, no notice is received from any
representative of his refusal to approve the making of the offer,
the representatives shall be deemed to have given their approval
under that paragraph.

(4) If—

   (a) the bishop refuses to approve under paragraph (b) of
subsection (1) above the making of the offer to the
priest named in the request, or

    (*b*) any parish representative refuses to approve under that
        paragraph the making of that offer,

the bishop or the representative, as the case may be, shall notify
the registered patron in writing of the grounds on which the refusal is made.

(5) Where approval of an offer is refused under subsection
(4) above, the registered patron may request the archbishop to
review the matter and if, after review, the archbishop authorises
the registered patron to make the offer in question, the patron
may make that offer accordingly.

(6) Where a priest accepts an offer made in accordance with
the provisions of this section to present him to a benefice and
the registered patron is a person other than the bishop, the patron
shall send the bishop a notice presenting the priest to him for
admission to the benefice.

Failure of
registered
patron to
comply with
s. 9.

14.—(1) Where any declaration of membership or other
information required to be sent to the designated officer under
section 9 of this Measure is not sent to that officer before the
expiration of the period during which it is required to be so sent
and the registered patron is a person other than the bishop then,
after the expiration of that period—

    (*a*) no meeting shall be held under section 12 of this
        Measure by reason of any request made by the reg-
        istered patron and subsections (2), (5), (6) and (8) of that
        section shall not apply in relation to that patron ; and

    (*b*) no offer shall be made to any priest under section 13
        of this Measure ;

but the bishop may, subject to subsection (2) below, make to
such priest as he thinks fit an offer to collate him to the benefice.

(2) The bishop shall not make an offer under subsection (1)
above unless the making of the offer has been approved by the
parish representatives, and subsections (3), (4)(*b*) and (5) of
section 13 of this Measure shall apply in relation to a request
sent by the bishop to those representatives by virtue of this
subsection as if for any reference to the registered patron there
were substituted a reference to the bishop.

(3) Where under subsection (1) above the bishop makes to a
priest an offer to collate him to a benefice in respect of which
there is more than one person registered under this Measure,
the registered patron whose turn it was to present to the benefice
shall be treated for the purposes of this Measure as having
exercised that turn.

15. If a copy of the statement prepared under section 11(1)(*a*) of this Measure is not sent under subsection (8) of that section to the persons mentioned in that subsection or if notice is not given under section 12(5) of this Measure of any joint meeting requested under subsection (1)(*a*) of the said section 12 then— PART II Failure of council to comply with s. 11 or 12.

    (*a*) if the bishop is the registered patron, he may, without making any request for the approval of the parish representatives, make to such priest as he thinks fit an offer to collate him to the benefice ; and

    (*b*) if the bishop is not the registered patron, that patron shall be entitled to proceed under section 13 of this Measure as if paragraphs (*a*) and (*b*)(i) of subsection (1), subsection (3) and paragraph (*b*) of subsection (4) thereof had not been enacted.

Provisions which apply where benefice remains vacant for nine months

16.—(1) If at the expiration of the period of nine months beginning with the date on which a benefice becomes vacant— Presentation to benefices remaining vacant for nine months.

    (*a*) no notice of presentation under section 13(6) of this Measure has been received by the bishop, or

    (*b*) where the bishop is the registered patron, he has not received an acceptance of any offer made by him to collate a priest to the benefice,

the right of presentation to that benefice shall be exercisable by the archbishop in accordance with the provision of this section ; and a notice to that effect shall be sent by the bishop to the archbishop.

(2) In calculating the period of nine months mentioned in subsection (1) above, no account shall be taken of any of the following periods, that is to say—

    (*a*) a period during which the decision of the bishop to refuse to approve the making to a priest of an offer to present him to a benefice is under review by an archbishop,

    (*b*) a suspension period within the meaning of the Pastoral Measure 1983, and 1983 No. 1.

    (*c*) a period during which the exercise of rights of presentation is restricted under section 24 or 69 of that Measure.

(3) As soon as practicable after a right of presentation becomes exercisable by an archbishop under this section, the archbishop shall send to the secretary of the parochial church council of the parish concerned a notice requiring him within three weeks after receiving the notice to send to the archbishop copies of the statement describing the conditions, needs and traditions

PART II

of the parish prepared in accordance with section 11 of this Measure together with copies of any additional observations which the council wishes the archbishop to consider.

(4) The bishop may, and if the archbishop so requests shall, send to the archbishop a statement describing in relation to the benefice the needs of the diocese and the wider interests of the Church.

(5) Before the archbishop decides on the priest to whom an offer to present him to the benefice is to be made he shall consult the bishop, the parish representatives and such other persons as he thinks fit, including other persons who in his opinion can also represent the views of the parishioners and, if during the period of nine months mentioned in subsection (1) above the approval of the bishop or the parish representatives to the making of an offer to a priest by the registered patron of the vacant benefice has been refused under section 13 of this Measure, the archbishop shall not make any offer to that priest under this section unless the consent of the bishop or, as the case may be, the parish representatives has been obtained.

(6) Where a priest accepts an offer to present him to a benefice made in accordance with the provisions of this section, the archbishop shall send to the bishop a notice presenting the priest to him for admission to the benefice.

Institution and collation

Provisions to have effect where bishop refuses to institute presentee.

1898 c. 48.

1972 No. 3.

17.—(1) Nothing in the preceding provisions of this Measure shall be taken as affecting the power of a bishop under section 2(1)(b) of the Benefices Act 1898 or section 1 of the Benefices Measure 1972 or any rule of law to refuse to institute or admit a presentee to the benefice.

(2) Where in exercise of any such power a bishop refuses to institute or admit a presentee to a benefice, and either no legal proceedings in respect of the refusal are brought or the refusal of the bishop is upheld in such proceedings, the presentation to the benefice affected shall be made by the registered patron whose turn it was to present when the vacancy first occurred; and for the purposes of sections 7, 9, 11 and 12 of this Measure a new vacancy shall not be treated as having occurred by virtue of this section.

Amendment of Benefices Act 1898.

18.—(1) Section 3 of the Benefices Act 1898 (appeal against refusal to institute) shall have effect subject to the following amendments—

    (a) in subsection (1) for the words from " require that the matter " to the end of the subsection there shall be substituted the words "appeal to the archbishop and the Dean of the Arches and Auditor who shall decide whether to uphold the bishop's refusal or direct him to institute or admit the presentee ".

(*b*) for subsections (2) and (3) there shall be substituted the following subsection—

"(2) Any proceedings on an appeal under this section shall be held in public and any party to such proceedings shall be entitled to appear by counsel or a solicitor."

(*c*) in subsection (4) for the words "judgment of the court" there shall be substituted the words "decision of the archbishop and Dean ";

(*d*) for subsection (6) there shall be substituted the following subsections—

"(6) The Dean of the Arches and Auditor may nominate a chancellor to hear, in his place, an appeal under this section with the archbishop, and where any such nomination is made any reference in subsection (1) or (4) above to the Dean shall be construed accordingly.

(7) In this section 'the archbishop' means the archbishop of the province in which the benefice is or, where the benefice is in the diocese of the archbishop of that province or the archbishopric of that province is vacant or the archbishop is patron of that benefice, the archbishop of the other province."

(2) For section 11 of that Act (rules) there shall be substituted the following section—

"Rules.   11. The Patronage (Appeals) Committee constituted under Schedule 1 to the Patronage (Benefices) Measure 1986 shall have power to make rules—

(*a*) prescribing anything to be prescribed under this Act,

(*b*) regulating the procedure and practice on or in connection with proceedings on an appeal under section 3 of this Act including, without prejudice to the generality of the preceding provision, rules regulating matters relating to costs, fees and expenses in respect of any such proceedings."

19.—(1) Subject to subsection (3) below, a bishop shall not on a vacancy in a benefice institute or collate any person to the benefice unless after the occurrence of the vacancy a notice in the prescribed form, signed by or on behalf of the bishop, is **Notice of intention of bishop to institute or collate person to benefice.**

PART II

served on the secretary of the parochial church council of the parish concerned informing him of the bishop's intention to institute or collate that person to the benefice specified in the notice and a period of three weeks has expired since the date of the service of the notice.

(2) As soon as practicable after receiving a notice under subsection (1) above the secretary shall cause the notice or a copy thereof to be fixed on or near the principal door of every church in the parish and every building licensed for public worship in the parish and to remain affixed thereon for two weeks.

(3) Subsection (1) above shall not apply in relation to a person designated by or selected under a pastoral scheme or order as the incumbent of any benefice.

Provisions relating to benefice of which an incumbent is patron

Bishop to act in place of incumbent patron in certain cases.

20. Where a benefice (" the ancillary benefice ") becomes vacant and it is the turn of the incumbent of another benefice (" the principal benefice "), being the registered patron of the ancillary benefice, to present to that benefice, then if, when the ancillary benefice becomes vacant or at any time during the vacancy thereof and before a notice of presentation under section 13(6) of this Measure is sent to the bishop by the incumbent of the principal benefice—

(a) the principal benefice is or becomes vacant, or

(b) the principal benefice is under sequestration, or

(c) the incumbent of the principal benefice is suspended or inhibited from discharging all or any of the duties attached to his preferment,

the bishop shall discharge in his place the functions of a registered patron.

Exercise of patronage by personal representatives

Exercise of patronage by personal representatives.

21. Where a benefice becomes vacant and either—

(a) the registered patron who would have been entitled to present upon the vacancy is dead and the person to whom the right of patronage is to be transferred has not before the vacancy occurs been registered as a patron of that benefice, or

(b) the registered patron dies during the vacancy,

then, notwithstanding anything in section 3(8) of this Measure the right of presentation to that benefice upon that vacancy shall be exercisable by that patron's personal representatives; but, before they exercise that right, they shall comply with the requirements of sections 8 and 9 of this Measure as if they were the registered patron.

Exchange of benefices

22.—(1) Two incumbents may by instrument in writing agree to exchange their benefices if the agreement of the following persons has been obtained—

(a) the bishop of the diocese in which each benefice is,

(b) any registered patron whose turn it is to present to either of the benefices, and

(c) the parochial church council of the parish of each benefice, the agreement having in each case been given by resolution of the council.

(2) Where a registered patron whose turn it is to present to a benefice has given his agreement under subsection (1) above to an exchange by the incumbent of that benefice, he shall be treated for the purposes of this Measure as having exercised that turn.

Special provisions as to certain benefices

23. The provisions of this Part of this Measure shall in their application to—

(a) a benefice which comprises two or more parishes,

(b) a benefice of which the parochial church council of the parish belonging to the benefice is the registered patron, and

(c) benefices held in plurality,

have effect subject to the provisions of Schedule 2 to this Measure.

Interpretation of Part II

24.—(1) Subject to subsections (2) and (3) below, in this Part of this Measure, except in sections 7(4) and 10, any reference to a registered patron, in relation to any vacancy in a benefice in respect of which there is more than one patron registered under this Measure, shall be construed as a reference to the registered patron whose turn it is, according to the information in the register of patrons on the date on which the vacancy occurs, to present on that vacancy.

(2) In a case where the functions of the registered patron of a benefice in relation to a vacancy in the benefice are to be discharged by the holder of an office or the donee of a power of attorney, any reference in this Part of this Measure (except in sections 8, 9(1) to (4) and 21) to the registered patron shall (subject to subsection (3) below) be construed as a reference to that office-holder or donee as the case may be.

PART II

(3) In sections 11 and 12 of this Measure any reference to the registered patron of a benefice (except the reference in section 11(2)(*b*)) shall in a case where the functions of the patron in relation to a vacancy in the benefice are to be discharged by a representative be construed as a reference to that representative, and in section 13 of this Measure any reference to the registered patron of a benefice shall, in a case where the registered patron, being an individual, has appointed a body mentioned in section 8(7) of this Measure or another individual to discharge those functions, be construed as a reference to that body or that other individual, as the case may be.

(4) In this Part of this Measure, except in section 8, "representative", in relation to a registered patron, means—

(*a*) in the case of a registered patron who is an individual, the individual appointed under section 8(1)(*b*), (3) or (6);

(*b*) in the case of a registered patron which is a body of persons, the individual appointed under section 8(2);

(*c*) in the case of a registered patron which is an office, the individual appointed under section 8(4) or (6);

(*d*) in a case where the functions of a registered patron are to be discharged by the donee of a power of attorney, the individual appointed under section 8(5) or (6).

(5) In this Part of this Measure " parish representative " has the meaning assigned to it by section 11(7) of this Measure.

PART III

MISCELLANEOUS PROVISIONS AS TO PATRONAGE

Appointment of patron of benefice which has no registered patron

Appointment of patron of benefice which has no registered patron.

25. Where at the expiration of the registration period or at any subsequent time no person is registered as the patron of a benefice, then unless in relation to that benefice—

(*a*) a notice under paragraph 7 of Schedule 1 to this Measure has been served on any person by the registrar of the diocese in which the benefice is and either the period mentioned in paragraph 8 of that Schedule has not expired or an appeal under paragraph 9 thereof has not been determined ; or

(*b*) the right of presentation to the benefice is exercisable by the personal representatives of a deceased patron,

the Diocesan Board of Patronage for the diocese shall become   Part III
the patron of that benefice, and the registrar of the diocese shall
register that Board as patron accordingly.

Diocesan Boards of Patronage

26.—(1) There shall continue to be a body corporate in every Diocesan
diocese called the Diocesan Board of Patronage.   Board of
    Patronage.
(2) The constitution and rules of procedure of Diocesan
Boards of Patronage shall be those set out in Schedule 3 to this
Measure.

27.—(1) Subject to subsection (2) below, a Diocesan Board Powers of
of Patronage shall have power to acquire, hold and transfer any Diocesan
right of patronage and to exercise any right of presentation or Boards of
other right incident to a right of patronage held by the Board. Patronage.

(2) Subject to subsection (3) below, a Diocesan Board of
Patronage shall not transfer any right of patronage held by it to
any other person without the consent of the parochial church
council of the parish or each of the parishes belonging to the
benefice concerned unless the transfer is authorised by or under
any enactment.

(3) If a parish is transferred from a benefice in one diocese
to a benefice in another diocese, the Diocesan Board of Patronage for the first-mentioned diocese may transfer its right of
patronage to the Diocesan Board of Patronage of that other
diocese without the consent of the parochial church council of
that parish.

(4) Where the transfer of a right of patronage requires the consent of a parochial church council under this section, any transfer of the right effected without that consent shall be void.

28. Where a benefice becomes void under section 4 of the Presentation
Simony Act 1588 (simoniacal presentation etc. to a benefice by Diocesan
declared void and the presentation to be made by the Crown Board of
for that turn) the presentation to that benefice upon that vacancy Patronage in
shall be made by the Diocesan Board of Patronage. case of void
    benefice.
    1588 c. 6.

Benefices affected by pastoral re-organisation

29.—(1) In section 32 of the Pastoral Measure 1983 (pro- Provisions as
visions as to patronage) in subsection (1) for the word " patron " to patronage
there shall be substituted the words " registered patron " and for affected by
subsection (3) there shall be substituted the following subsec- pastoral
tions— schemes.
    1983 No. 1.
    " (3) Without prejudice to the generality of subsections
(1) and (2) above, a pastoral scheme (whether it relates

PART III

only to an existing benefice or provides for the creation of a new benefice) may with the consent of the registered patron or patrons of any benefice affected by the scheme provide for the transfer of existing rights of patronage to, or for the vesting of new rights of patronage in, a special patronage board constituted by the scheme.

(3A) A special patronage board constituted by a pastoral scheme by virtue of subsection (3) shall consist of such members as the scheme may provide, and the scheme may designate the member who is to be chairman of the board; and the following provisions of paragraph 1 of Schedule 3 shall apply to such a patronage board as they apply to a patronage board constituted by a pastoral scheme establishing a team ministry, that is to say—

(a) sub-paragraph (6) so far as it relates to any member of a board;

(b) sub-paragraph (7) so far as it relates to the entitlement to votes of any member of a board;

(c) sub-paragraph (8), and

(d) sub-paragraph (10) so far as it relates to the transfer of the rights to be members of a board."

(2) Where any right of patronage of a benefice is transferred to or becomes vested in any person by virtue of a pastoral scheme the registrar of the diocese in which that benefice is shall, on receiving a copy of the Order in Council confirming the scheme, register him as the patron of that benefice.

(3) Subject to any provision for the designation or selection of the first incumbent of a new benefice created by a pastoral scheme, sections 7 to 16 of this Measure shall apply to the making of the first presentation to the benefice as if the coming into operation of the scheme were the occurrence of a vacancy in the benefice.

Other amendments of the law relating to rights of patronage etc.

Removal of certain disabilities.

3 Jas. 1. c. 5.
1 Will. &
Mary c. 26.
13 Anne c. 13.

30.—(1) The following enactments (which impose disabilities on patrons practising the Roman Catholic religion etc.) that is to say—

(a) section 13 of the Presentation of Benefices Act 1605;

(b) section 2 of the Presentation of Benefices Act 1688; and

(c) section 1 of the Presentation of Benefices Act 1713,

shall cease to have effect.

(2) Section 15 of the Roman Catholic Relief Act 1829 Part III
(Roman Catholic member of lay body corporate not to vote in 1829 c. 7.
election, presentation or appointment of persons to ecclesiastical
benefice, etc., in the gift, patronage or disposal of that body)
shall cease to have effect in so far as it relates to benefices.

(3) Section 17 of the Roman Catholic Relief Act 1829 (right
of presentation to benefice to devolve upon the Archbishop of
Canterbury for the time being where right belongs to office which
is held by person professing the Roman Catholic religion) and,
in section 4 of the Jews Relief Act 1858, the words from the be- 1858 c. 49.
ginning to " being ; and " (similar provision relating to right of
presentation belonging to office held by person professing the
Jewish religion) shall cease to have effect.

31.—(1) Without prejudice to the provisions of section 16 of this Abrogation
Measure, any rule of law whereby the right of patronage of a of rules as
benefice lapses to a bishop or archbishop or to Her Majesty in to lapse.
right of Her Crown shall cease to have effect.

(2) Nothing in this section shall affect any right of presentation which on a vacancy in a benefice is exercisable by Her
Majesty—

   (*a*) by reason of the appointment to a diocesan bishopric
      of the incumbent of the benefice concerned , or

   (*b*) by reason of a vacancy in the see of a diocesan bishop
      who is a registered patron of the benefice concerned.

32.—(1) Every advowson which immediately before the date Advowsons
on which this section comes into force is appendant to any land appendant
or any manor shall by virtue of this section be severed from that to become
land or manor and become an advowson in gross which— advowsons in
gross.

   (*a*) in the case of land belonging at that date to a charity,
      shall belong to that charity ;

   (*b*) in any other case, shall belong in his personal capacity
      to the person who at that date is the owner in fee simple
      of that land or the lord of that manor, as the case
      may be.

(2) Every advowson which immediately before the said date
is appendant to any rectory, not being a rectory with cure of
souls, shall by virtue of this section be severed from that rectory
and become an advowson in gross belonging in his personal capacity to the person who at that date is the rector of that rectory.

(3) Nothing in this section shall affect the trusts, if any, on
which any advowson is held.

PART III
Transfer of
advowson
held on trust
for sale or
comprised in
settled land.

33.—(1) Where any advowson is held by any trustee on trust for sale, or on a trust which would be a trust for sale if the advowson were capable of sale, it shall be lawful for the trustees to transfer the advowson gratuitously to any person who has agreed to accept it and—

(*a*) being an individual—

(i) is an ecclesiastical corporation sole, or

(ii) is an actual communicant member of the Church of England, or

(*b*) being a body of persons, corporate or unincorporate,—

(i) is one of the bodies mentioned in section 8(7) of this Measure, or

(ii) has the furtherance of the work of the Church of England as one of its objects.

(2) Where the consent of any person is by any instrument containing such a trust, or by any statutory provision, made requisite to the execution of the trust, then, subject to section 26(1) and

1925 c. 20.

(2) of the Law of Property Act 1925 (consents to the execution of a trust for sale), the trustees shall obtain the consent of that person to the execution of a transfer made lawful by subsection (1) above.

(3) The tenant for life of settled land may make a grant in fee simple of any advowson comprised in the settled land gratuitously to any such person as is referred to in subsection (1) above.

1925 c. 18.

(4) Subsection (3) above shall be construed as one with the Settled Land Act 1925, and that Act shall apply as if the power conferred by subsection (3) had been conferred by that Act.

(5) Nothing in any local Act or trust deed shall prevent the transfer inter vivos by trustees of an advowson which is the subject of a trust.

Abolition of
certain rights
etc. of
patronage.
1938 No. 3.

34.—(1) The right of pre-emption of the patron of a benefice under section 4 of the Parsonages Measure 1938 over any property belonging to the benefice in respect of which it is proposed to exercise a power of sale conferred by that Measure is hereby abolished.

(2) The requirement to obtain the consent of the patron of a benefice to the exercise of the power conferred by—

(*a*) section 2A of the Parsonages Measure 1938 (power of bishop during vacancy in benefice to divide, enlarge or improve parsonage house) ; or

1960 No. 1.

(*b*) section 9(1) of the Church Property (Miscellaneous Provisions) Measure 1960 (power of incumbent or bishop

to take or grant easements over land belonging to bene- PART III
fice), or

(*c*) section 11(1) of that Measure (power of incumbent to
dedicate certain land belonging to benefice for purpose
of a highway),

is hereby abolished.

(3) The requirement to obtain the consent of the patron of a
church to the exercise of the power conferred by section 20(1)
of the Marriage Act 1949 (power of bishop to license chapel 1949 c. 83.
for publication of banns and solemnisation of marriages) is hereby abolished.

(4) The obligation imposed by section 4 of the Army Chap- 1868 c. 83.
lains Act 1868 to transmit to the patron or patrons of a church
or chapel affected a copy of the draft of a scheme for constituting
a precinct or district an extra parochial district for the purpose
of that Act in order that he or they may have an opportunity
of making observations or objections is hereby abolished.

(5) The Parsonages Board within the meaning of the Repair 1972 No. 2.
of Benefice Buildings Measure 1972 shall consult the registered
patron, if any, of the benefice affected before—

(*a*) determining on the alterations (if any) with which damage
to the parsonage house is to be made good under
section 12(3) of that Measure, or

(*b*) determining that the whole or part of the damage be not
made good,

but shall not, in either case, be prohibited from making its
determination without the consent of that patron.

(6) No incumbent shall be prohibited under section 21(1) of
the Repair of Benefice Buildings Measure 1972 from making
additions or alterations to the buildings of the parsonage house
without the consent of the patron, but before making any such
addition or alteration he shall consult the registered patron, if
any, of the benefice.

PART IV

GENERAL AND SUPPLEMENTARY PROVISIONS

*Benefices in the patronage of the Crown, Duke of Cornwall or
Lord Chancellor*

35.—(1) Without prejudice to the application of sections 28 Provisions
and 31 of this Measure to the Crown and except as provided by with respect to
this section, nothing in this Measure shall apply in relation to any benefices in
benefice the patronage or any share in the patronage of which the patronage
is vested in or exercisable by Her Majesty, whether in right of or Duke of

2 C 3 Cornwall.

PART IV Her Crown or Her Duchy of Lancaster or otherwise, or is vested in or exercisable by the possessor for the time being of the Duchy of Cornwall, whether Her Majesty or a Duke of Cornwall (in this Measure referred to as a " Crown benefice ").

(2) Where it appears to the registrar of a diocese that a benefice is a Crown benefice, the registrar shall, as soon as practicable after the date on which section 1 of this Measure comes into force, notify Her Majesty or the possessor for the time being of the Duchy of Cornwall that he proposes to register Her Majesty or the possessor for the time being of the Duchy of Cornwall, as the case may be, as patron of the benefice specified in the notice.

(3) Where in the case of a Crown benefice a share only in the patronage is vested in Her Majesty or the possessor for the time being of the Duchy of Cornwall (in this section referred to as a " shared benefice ") sections 1 and 2 of this Measure shall apply for the purpose of enabling any patron other than Her Majesty or the possessor for the time being of the Duchy of Cornwall to be registered as a patron of that benefice and sections 5 and 21 of this Measure shall apply in relation to a registered patron of a shared benefice other than Her Majesty or the possessor for the time being of the Duchy of Cornwall.

(4) Where a right of patronage in a Crown benefice is transferred to any person other than Her Majesty or the Duke of Cornwall the registrar shall not register the transferee as patron of the benefice unless the application for transfer is made in accordance with Schedule 1 to this Measure before the expiration of the period of twelve months beginning with the date of execution of the transfer.

(5) Where a right of patronage of a benefice is proposed to be transferred to Her Majesty or to the possessor for the time being of the Duchy of Cornwall, section 3(2) to (7) of this Measure shall not apply but the transferor shall send a notice to the registrar to inform him of the transfer and the registrar shall notify Her Majesty or the possessor for the time being of the Duchy of Cornwall that he proposes to register Her Majesty or, as the case may be, the possessor of the Duchy of Cornwall as patron of that benefice.

(6) Section 3(1) of this Measure shall apply to the transfer of a right of patronage of a Crown benefice.

(7) Section 7 of this Measure shall apply in relation to a Crown benefice, and where the designated officer of a diocese receives a notice under that section in respect of a Crown benefice then—

(a) if the patronage is vested wholly in Her Majesty or the possessor for the time being of the Duchy of Cornwall or, in the case of a shared benefice, if the right of presentation upon the vacancy in question is exercisable by Her Majesty or the Duke of Cornwall, any parochial church council to which notice is given under section 7(4) of this Measure may send to Her Majesty or the Duke of Cornwall, as the case may be, a statement describing the conditions, needs and traditions of the parish, and a copy of any such statement shall be sent to the bishop;

(b) if the benefice is a shared benefice and the right of presentation upon the vacancy in question is exercisable by a person other than Her Majesty or the Duke of Cornwall, sections 8 to 21 of this Measure shall apply in relation to the benefice.

(8) Section 22 of this Measure shall apply in relation to a Crown benefice and where the consent of Her Majesty or the possessor for the time being of the Duchy of Corwall is required by that section that consent may be given in accordance with the provisions of paragraphs (a) to (d) of section 81(2) of the Pastoral Measure 1983 and those provisions shall have effect accordingly with the necessary modifications.

1983 No. 1.

(9) Section 34 of this Measure shall apply in relation to a Crown benefice.

36. Without prejudice to the provisions of the Lord Chancellor (Tenure of Office and Discharge of Ecclesiastical Functions) Act 1974, the provisions of section 35 of this Measure shall apply in relation to a benefice the patronage or a share of the patronage of which is vested in the Lord Chancellor as it applies in relation to a Crown benefice, and accordingly any reference in that section to Her Majesty shall in relation to any benefice the patronage or a share of the patronage of which is so vested be construed as including a reference to the Lord Chancellor.

Provisions with respect to benefices in patronage of Lord Chancellor.

1974 c. 25.

Supplementary provisions

37.—(1) All notices, agreements, approvals, consents and requests required or authorised by this Measure to be served, sent, given or made shall be in writing, and all such notices, other than notices under paragraphs 7 and 8 of Schedule 1 to this Measure shall be in the prescribed form.

Provisions as to notices and other documents.

(2) Any notice or other document required or authorised by this Measure to be served on or sent or given to any person may be served, sent or given by delivering it to him, or by leaving it at his proper address, or by post.

PART IV

(3) Any notice or other document required or authorised to be served, sent or given to a corporation or to an unincorporated body having a secretary or clerk or to a firm, shall be duly served, sent or given if it is served on or sent or given to, as the case may be, the secretary or clerk of the corporation or body or a partner of the firm.

1978 c. 30.

(4) Subject to subsection (5) below, for the purposes of this section and of section 7 of the Interpretation Act 1978 in its application to this section, the proper address of the person on or to whom any such notice or other document is required or authorised to be served, sent or given shall be his last known address, except that in the case of the secretary or clerk of a corporation, it shall be that of the registered or principal office of the corporation, and in the case of the secretary or clerk of an unincorporated body or a partner of a firm, it shall be that of the principal office of the body or firm.

(5) If the person on or to whom any such notice or other document is to be served, sent or given has specified an address within the United Kingdom for the serving, sending or giving of the notice or other document, his proper address for the said purposes shall be that address.

Patronage
(Procedure)
Committee.

38.—(1) There shall be a committee, to be known as the Patronage (Procedure) Committee, which shall consist of a chairman and four other members appointed by the Standing Committee.

(2) The Patronage (Procedure) Committee shall have power to make rules with regard to any matter of procedure arising under this Measure and in particular with regard to any matter to be prescribed thereunder, except that no rules may be made under this subsection with regard to any matter in respect of which rules may be made by the Patronage (Appeals) Committee under paragraph 11 of Schedule 1 to this Measure.

(3) Any three members of the Patronage (Procedure) Committee may exercise all the powers of the Committee.

(4) Any rules made by the Patronage (Procedure) Committee shall be laid before the General Synod and shall not come into force until approved by the General Synod, whether with or without amendment.

(5) Where the Standing Committee determines that the rules do not need to be debated by the General Synod, then, unless—

(a) notice is given by a member of the General Synod in accordance with its Standing Orders that he wishes the rules to be debated, or

(b) notice is so given by any such member that he wishes
to move an amendment to the rules and at least
twenty-five other members of the Synod indicate when
the amendment is called that they wish the amendment to be moved,

the rules shall for the purposes of subsection (4) above be
deemed to have been approved by the General Synod without
amendment.

(6) The Statutory Instruments Act 1946 shall apply to rules 1946 c. 36
approved by the General Synod under this section as if they were
statutory instruments and were made when so approved, and
as if this Measure were an Act providing that any such rules
shall be subject to annulment in pursuance of a resolution of
either House of Parliament.

39.—(1) In this Measure, unless the context otherwise re- Interpre-
quires— tation.

" actual communicant member of the Church of England "
means a member of the Church of England who is confirmed or ready and desirous of being confirmed and
has received Communion according to the use of the
Church of England or of a Church in communion with
the Church of England at least three times during the
twelve months preceding the date on which he makes
the declaration of membership ;

" actual communicant member of a Church in communion
with the Church of England " means a communicant
member of a Church in communion with the Church
of England who has received Communion according
to the use of the Church of England or of a Church in
communion with the Church of England at least three
times during the twelve months preceding the date on
which he makes the declaration of membership ;

" archbishop " means the archbishop of the province in
which the benefice is or, where the benefice is in the
diocese of the archbishop of that province or the archbishopric of that province is vacant or the archbishop
is the patron of that benefice, the archbishop of the
other province ;

" benefice " means the office of rector or vicar of a parish
or parishes, with cure of souls, but not including the
office of vicar in a team ministry or any office in a
cathedral church ;

" the bishop " means the bishop of the diocese concerned ;

" clerk in Holy Orders " means a priest or deacon of the
Church of England and " priest " includes a bishop ;

PART IV

" the declaration of membership " has the meaning assigned to it by section 8(1) ;

" the designated officer " has the meaning assigned to it by section 7(5) ;

" parish " means a parish constituted for ecclesiastical purposes and does not include a conventional district ;

" pastoral committee ", " pastoral order " and " pastoral scheme " have the same meanings respectively as in the Pastoral Measure 1983 ;

1983 No. 1.

" patron ", in relation to any benefice, means the person or persons entitled, otherwise than by virtue of section 16, to present to that benefice upon a vacancy, including—

(a) in any case where the right to present is vested in different persons jointly, every person whose concurrence would be required for the exercise of the joint right, and

(b) in any case where the patronage is vested in different persons by way of alternate or successive right of presentation, every person who would be entitled to present on the next or any subsequent turn ;

" register of patrons " means a register compiled and maintained under section 1 ;

" registered " means registered under this Measure in a register of patrons ;

" registered patron ", in relation to a benefice, means any person who or office which is for the time being registered as a patron of that benefice ;

" registration period " has the meaning assigned to it by section 1(2) ;

" the Standing Committee " means the Standing Committee of the General Synod.

(2) Where a pastoral scheme or pastoral order provides for the holding of benefices in plurality any reference in this Measure to a benefice shall be construed as including a reference to benefices held in plurality.

(3) If any question arises whether a Church is a Church in communion with the Church of England, it shall be conclusively determined for the purposes of this Measure by the Archbishops of Canterbury and York.

Temporary provision with respect to filling of certain vacancies.

40. Where a benefice is vacant at the date on which section 1 of this Measure comes into force, or becomes vacant after that date and before the end of the registration period, the vacancy shall be filled in accordance with the law in force immediately before that date, except that if a suspension period has been declared in respect of the benefice under section 67 PART IV of the Pastoral Measure 1983 or any restriction has been im- 1983 No. 1. posed by section 69 of that Measure in respect of the benefice and the suspension period does not come to an end, or the restriction does not cease to be in force, until after the end of the registration period, the vacancy shall be filled in accordance with the provisions of this Measure.

41.—(1) The enactments specified in Schedule 4 to this Amendments Measure shall have effect subject to the amendments specified in and repeals. that Schedule, being minor amendments or amendments consequential on the provisions of this Measure.

(2) Subject to section 40 of this Measure, the enactments specified in Schedule 5 to this Measure (which include enactments which were obsolete, spent or unnecessary before the passing of this Measure) and the instrument there specified are hereby repealed to the extent specified in column 3 of that Schedule.

42.—(1) This Measure may be cited as the Patronage (Bene- Short title, fices) Measure 1986. extent and
commence-

(2) This Measure shall extend to the whole of the provinces ment. of Canterbury and York, except the Channel Islands and the Isle of Man, but may be applied to the Channel Islands, as defined in the Channel Islands (Church Legislation) Measures 1931 and 1957, or either of them, in accordance with those Measures, and may be extended to the Isle of Man by or under Act of Tynwald.

(3) This Measure shall come into operation on such date as the Archbishops of Canterbury and York may jointly appoint; and different dates may be appointed for different provisions.

SCHEDULES

SCHEDULE 1

REGISTRATION OF PATRONS

Preparation of list of patrons

1. The registrar of each diocese shall before the expiration of the period of one month beginning with the date on which section 1 of this Measure comes into force prepare a list of all the benefices in the diocese which shall specify in relation to each benefice the person who in the opinion of the registrar is entitled to be registered under this Measure as the patron thereof and shall contain, in a case where he considers that more than one person is entitled to be so registered, such information as may be prescribed as to the exercise of the right to present to that benefice upon a vacancy.

2.—(1) Before the expiration of the period of six weeks beginning with the date on which section 1 of this Measure comes into force the registrar shall—

    (*a*) send to each person who is named in the list prepared under paragraph 1 above a notice specifying the benefice or benefices in respect of which the registrar considers he is entitled to be registered and containing such information as may be prescribed (including, in the case of patronage vested in more than one person, prescribed information as to the exercise of the right of presentation),

    (*b*) advertise in the prescribed manner such information concerning the list prepared by the registrar and the provisions of this Measure as may be prescribed.

(2) Any notice under sub-paragraph (1)(*a*) above shall inform the person to whom the notice is sent that the registrar proposes at the end of the registration period to register that person as a patron of the benefice specified in the notice and also to register the information contained in the notice unless before that date some other person applies to be registered in respect of the same right of patronage or expresses disagreement with that information ; and the person to whom the notice is sent shall be required to acknowledge in the prescribed form the receipt of the notice.

(3) The registrar shall send to the incumbent of the benefice concerned and to the secretary of the parochial church council concerned a copy of any notice sent by him under sub-paragraph (1)(*a*) above.

Application for registration

3. Any person who claims to be a patron of a benefice at the date on which section 1 of this Measure comes into force may before the end of the registration period apply to the registrar of the diocese in which the benefice is situated to be registered as a patron of that benefice, notwithstanding that he is not named on the list prepared by that registrar under paragraph 1 above.

4. Any person to whom a right of patronage of a benefice is transferred after the date on which section 1 of this Measure comes into force shall before the expiration of the period of twelve months beginning with the date on which the transfer takes effect apply to the registrar of the diocese to be registered as a patron of that benefice.

5. Any person who claims in relation to any benefice—

    (*a*) that he is entitled to be registered as a patron of that benefice in place of, or in addition to, any person who is so registered, or

    (*b*) that any information registered as to the exercise of a right of presentation to that benefice is incorrect,

may at any time apply to the registrar of the diocese for the register to be rectified under section 4 of this Measure.

6. Any application made under paragraph 3, 4 or 5 above shall be accompanied by such documents and other information as may be prescribed.

Determination of disputes

7. Where the registrar—

    (*a*) decides that any person—

        (i) who is named in a list prepared under paragraph 1 above, or

        (ii) who has made an application under paragraph 3, 4 or 5 above,

    is not entitled to be registered as a patron of the benefice concerned ; or

    (*b*) decides that information which any patron of a benefice wishes to be registered as to the exercise of his right to present to that benefice ought not to be registered ; or

    (*c*) decides that any person who is registered as a patron of a benefice was not entitled to be so registered ; or

    (*d*) decides that any information which is registered as to the exercise of a right to present to a benefice is incorrect,

he shall serve a notice on that person informing him of his decision and of the effect of paragraphs 8 and 9 below.

8. A person on whom a notice is served under paragraph 7 above may, before the expiration of the period of twenty-eight days beginning with the date of the notice, appeal against the registrar's decision by sending him a notice of appeal.

9.—(1) On receiving a notice of appeal under paragraph 8 above the registrar shall refer the appeal to the chancellor of the diocese and the chancellor shall decide whether to uphold the appeal or dismiss it and shall inform the registrar and the appellant of his decision.

(2) Any proceedings on an appeal to the chancellor of a diocese under this paragraph shall be held in public and any party to such proceedings shall be entitled to appear by counsel or a solicitor.

Rules

10.—(1) There shall be a committee to be known as the Patronage (Appeals) Committee which shall consist of—

> the Dean of the Arches and Auditor or, if the Dean nominates the Vicar-General of the Province of Canterbury or the Vicar-General of the Province of York to act in his place, the Vicar-General so nominated ;

> one chancellor and one diocesan registrar nominated jointly by the Archbishops of Canterbury and York ; and

> two persons nominated by the Standing Committee.

(2) Any three members of the Patronage (Appeals) Committee, one of whom shall be the Dean of the Arches and Auditor or the Vicar-General nominated by the Dean under sub-paragraph (1) above, may exercise all the powers of the Committee.

11. The Patronage (Appeals) Committee shall have power to make rules regulating the procedure and practice on or in connection with proceedings on an appeal under this Schedule including, without prejudice to the generality of the preceding provision, rules regulating matters relating to costs, fees and expenses in respect of any such proceedings.

12.—(1) Any rules made by the Patronage (Appeals) Committee shall be laid before the General Synod and shall not come into force until approved by the General Synod, whether with or without amendment.

(2) Where the Standing Committee determines that the rules do not need to be debated by the General Synod, then, unless—

(a) notice is given by a member of the General Synod in accordance with its Standing Orders that he wishes the rules to be debated, or

(b) notice is so given by any such member that he wishes to move and amendment to the rules and at least twenty-five other members of the Synod indicate when the amendment is called that they wish the amendment to be moved,

the rules shall for the purposes of sub-paragraph (1) above be deemed to have been approved by the General Synod without amendment.

1946 c. 36.   (3) The Statutory Instruments Act 1946 shall apply to rules approved by the General Synod under this paragraph as if they were statutory instruments and were made when so approved, and as if this Measure were an Act providing that any such rules shall be subject to annulment in pursuance of a resolution of either House of Parliament.

Registration

13.—(1) In the case of any disagreement as to the person entitled to be registered as patron of a benefice or as to the exercise of the right of presentation, the registrar as soon as practicable after he—

(a) has determined that a person is entitled to be registered as a patron of a benefice (and has determined the information, if any, to be registered as to the exercise of the right of presentation) and either the period mentioned in paragraph 8 above has expired or the appeal has been dismissed ; or

(b) has been informed of the decision of the chancellor on an appeal brought under paragraph 9 above, being a decision as to the person entitled to be registered as a patron of that benefice or as to any information to be registered in respect of the exercise of right of presentation,

shall register that person as a patron of that benefice in the register of patrons accordingly (together with any information to be registered as to the exercise of the right of presentation) and shall inform him that he has done so.

(2) Unless the person entitled to the right of patronage in question has already been registered under sub-paragraph (1) above, the registrar shall at the end of the registration period register in the register of patrons as a patron of the benefice specified in a notice under paragraph 2 above the person to whom the notice was sent (and the information in that notice) and shall inform him that he has done so.

Notices to parishes

14. After the registrar has registered any person as a patron of a benefice he shall within one month from the end of the registration period or, in the case of a right of patronage registered after the end of that period, as soon as practicable after the registration, send to the secretary of the parochial church council of the parish, or of each of the parishes, belonging to the benefice a notice stating that that person has been registered and giving the name and address of that person and particulars of the benefice and of the information which has been registered in relation thereto.

Benefices held in plurality

15. The preceding provisions of this Schedule shall have effect for the purpose of enabling any person who is a patron of two or more benefices which are for the time being held in plurality, to be registered as a patron of those benefices while so held subject to the modification that for references to a benefice there shall be substituted references to benefices so held.

Rights of patronage belonging to an office

16. Where a right of patronage of a benefice belongs to, or is claimed to belong to, an office, the provisions of this Schedule shall have effect subject to the following modifications—

  (*a*) the notice required to be sent under paragraph 2(1)(*a*) shall be sent to the person who then holds that office and shall state the intention of the registrar to register that office as a patron of that benefice ;

  (*b*) any person who at the time of the application holds that office, and claims that on the date on which section 1 of this Measure comes into force a right of patronage of that benefice belonged to that office, may apply under paragraph 3 for that office to be registered as a patron of that benefice ;

  (*c*) any person who at the time of the application holds that office (being an office to which a right of patronage has been transferred after the said date) may apply under paragraph 4 for that office to be registered as a patron of that benefice ;

  (*d*) any notice required to be served under paragraph 7 or information required to be given under paragraph 9 or 13 shall be served on or given to the person who then holds that office.

Section 23.
SCHEDULE 2

Modification of Part II in its Application to Certain Benefices

Benefice comprising two or more parishes

1. Where a benefice comprises two or more parishes then, except in a case in which paragraph 19 or 20 below applies, the provisions of Part II of this Measure shall have effect subject to the modifications for which paragraphs 2 to 18 below provide.

2. In section 7(4), for the words " the parish " there shall be substituted the words " each of the parishes ".

3. In section 9(6) for the words " secretary of the parochial church council " there shall be substituted the words " secretaries of the parochial church councils ".

4. For section 11(1) there shall be substituted :—

  " (1) Before the expiration of the period of four weeks beginning with the date on which the notice under section 7(4) of this Measure is sent to the secretaries of the parochial church councils concerned one or more joint meetings of those councils shall be held for the purposes of—

    (*a*) discharging the duties imposed on them by subsection (1A) below ;

    (*b*) appointing such number of persons, but not less than four, as will enable each of those councils to have at least one representative, to act as representatives of those councils in connection with the selection of an incumbent :

    (c) deciding whether to request the registered patron to consider advertising the vacancy ;

    (d) deciding whether to request a meeting under section 12 of this Measure ;

    (e) deciding whether to request a statement in writing from the bishop describing in relation to the benefice the needs of the diocese and the wider interests of the church ;

and each person appointed under paragraph (b) shall be a member of one of the parochial church councils concerned.

(1A) At the meeting, or the first meeting, convened under this section, the parochial church councils shall decide whether they will join in preparing a statement describing the conditions, needs and traditions of the parishes belonging to the benefice or whether the parochial church council of each parish will prepare such a statement in relation to that parish, and that decision having been made, the parochial church councils of those parishes or the parochial church council of each parish, as the circumstances require, shall prepare such a statement."

5. In section 11(2), for the words from the beginning to " council ", in the second place where it occurs ; there shall be substituted the words " A joint meeting of the parochial church councils for which subsection (1) above provides shall be convened by the secretaries of those councils, and no member of any of those councils ".

6. In section 11(3), for the words " the parochial church council " there shall be substituted the words " any of the parochial church councils " and for the words " the parish " there shall be substituted the words " any of the parishes ".

7. In section 11(4), for the words from " the council by which he was appointed " to the end there shall be substituted the words " any of the councils by which he was appointed then, except where he ceases to be such a member and those councils decide that he shall continue to act as their representative, his appointment shall be deemed to have been revoked and those councils shall appoint another lay member of any of those councils in his place ".

8. For section 11(5) there shall be substituted—

" (5) If the parochial church councils concerned hold a joint meeting under subsection (1) above but do not appoint representatives under paragraph (b) of that subsection, all the church-wardens who are members of any of the councils concerned shall appoint not more than five of those churchwardens to act as representatives of those councils in connection with the selection of an incumbent."

9. In section 11(8) for " 1(a) " there shall be substituted " (1A) " and for the words " secretary of the parochial church council " there

SCH. 2   shall be substituted the words " secretaries of the parochial church councils ".

10. For section 12(1) there shall be substituted—

" (1) Where a request for a meeting under this section is made—

(a) by a notice sent by the registered patron or the bishop to the secretaries of the parochial church councils concerned or

(b) by a resolution of those councils passed at a joint meeting held under section 11 of this Measure,

a joint meeting of those councils with the registered patron and (if the bishop is not the registered patron) the bishop shall be held for the purpose of enabling those present at the meeting to exchange views on the statement or statements prepared under section 11(1A) of this Measure (needs of the parish) and the statement presented under subsection (2) below (needs of the diocese)."

11. In section 12(2) for the word " council " there shall be substituted the word " councils ".

12. In section 12(3) for the words " the parochial church council " there shall be substituted the words " each of the parochial church councils concerned " and for " (1)(a) " there shall be substituted " (1A)."

13. In section 12(5) for the words " secretary of the parochial church council " there shall be substituted the words " secretaries of the parochial church councils " and for the words " parochial church council " in the second place where those words occur there shall be substituted the words " parochial church councils concerned ".

14. In section 12(8)(c) for the word " council " there shall be substituted the words " councils concerned ".

15. In section 12(9) for the words " The secretary of the parochial church council shall invite both the rural dean of the deanery in which the parish is " there shall be substituted the words " The secretaries of the parochial church councils concerned shall invite both the rural dean of the deanery which comprises the parishes concerned."

16. In section 16(3) for the words " of the parish ", in the first place where those words occur, there shall be substituted the words " of each of the parishes belonging to the benefice ".

17. In section 19(1) for the words " of the parish " there shall be substituted the words " of each of the parishes ".

18. In section 22(1) for the words " the parish of each benefice " there shall be substituted the words " every parish belonging to each benefice ".

Benefices having team council or joint parochial church council

19. Where, by a pastoral scheme or by a scheme made under the Church Representation Rules, a team council is established in respect of a benefice which comprises more than one parish, the functions under Part II of this Measure of the parochial church councils of those parishes shall be exercisable by the team council.

20. Where, by a pastoral scheme or by a scheme made under the Church Representation Rules, a joint parochial church council is established for all the parishes of a benefice, the functions under Part II of this Measure of the parochial church councils of those parishes shall be exercisable by the joint parochial church council.

*Benefice of which parochial church council
is the registered patron*

21. Where the parochial church council of the parish belonging to a benefice is the registered patron of the benefice, Part II of this Measure shall have effect in relation to that benefice as if the provisions thereof requiring the appointment of parish representatives and the approval of such representatives to the making of an offer to present a priest to the benefice, and any other provisions thereof referring to such representatives, were omitted.

Benefices held in plurality

22. Where two or more benefices are held in plurality, the provision of Part II of this Measure shall have effect in relation to them as if they were a single benefice comprising two or more parishes.

SCHEDULE 3

CONSTITUTION AND PROCEDURE OF A DIOCESAN BOARD OF PATRONAGE

1.—(1) A Diocesan Board of Patronage (hereinafter referred to as "the Board") shall consist of—

(a) the bishop of the diocese ;

(b) three clerks in Holy Orders beneficed in or licensed to any parish in the diocese elected by the house of clergy of the diocesan synod by the method of the single transferable vote ;

(c) five lay persons elected by the house of laity of that synod by the method of the single transferable vote ; and

(d) for the purpose of transacting any business relating to a particular benefice, the archdeacon in whose archdeaconry, and both chairmen of the deanery synod of the deanery in which, that benefice is.

(2) An archdeacon shall not be qualified to be elected under subparagraph (1)(b).

2. The bishop of the diocese may nominate any suffragan bishop or assistant bishop holding office in the diocese to act in his place as a member of the Board on such occasions as he may determine.

3. The Board shall elect one of its members other than the bishop to be the chairman of the Board.

4.—(1) The election of members of the Board shall take place every six years in the same year as, but after, the election of members of the diocesan synod, and the elected members of the Board shall hold office for a term of six years beginning with 1st January next following their election.

(2) Where a casual vacancy occurs among the elected members of the Board, then—

(*a*) if the vacancy is among the members elected under paragraph 1(1)(*b*) above, the vacancy shall be filled by the election by the elected clerical members of the Bishop's Council of a person qualified to be elected under that paragraph,

(*b*) if the vacancy is among the members elected under paragraph 1(1)(*c*) above, the vacancy shall be filled by the election by the elected lay members of the Bishop's Council of a lay person.

(3) Any person elected to fill a casual vacancy shall hold office only for the unexpired portion of the term of office of the person in whose place he is elected.

(4) An elected member of the Board, if qualified for election, shall be eligible for re-election on the termination of any period of office.

5.—(1) The quorum of the Board shall be six.

(2) Subject to sub-paragraph (1), the Board may act notwithstanding any vacancy in its membership.

6. A clerical member of the Board shall not take part in any proceedings of the Board connected with the exercise of a right of presentation in favour of himself.

7. Subject to the preceding provisions and to any directions as to procedure given by the diocesan synod, the Board shall have power to regulate its own procedure.

8. No election shall be held under this Schedule until after the election of members of the diocesan synod to be held in the year 1988 and any member of a diocesan board of patronage who holds office on the date on which this Schedule comes into force shall, subject to paragraph 4(2) and (3) above, continue in office until the 31st December 1988.

SCHEDULE 4

Section 41.

MINOR AND CONSEQUENTIAL AMENDMENTS

Pluralities Act 1838

1838 c. 106.

1. In section 58 of the Pluralities Act 1838 for the words from " upon any such " to the end there shall be substituted the words " no offer of any benefice which becomes void under this section shall be made under any provision of the Patronage (Benefices) Measure 1986 or otherwise to the person by reason of whose non-residence the benefice so became void ".

Parsonages Measure 1938

1938 No. 3.

2. In section 2A of the Parsonages Measure 1938 for the words " the Diocesan Dilapidations Board and the patron of the benefice " there shall be substituted the words " and the Diocesan Dilapidations Board ".

3. In section 3(1) of that Measure for the words " the patron ", where first occurring, there shall be substituted the words " the registered patron ", and the words from " Provided " to the end shall be omitted.

4. In section 7 of that Measure immediately before the word " patron " wherever occurring, there shall be inserted the word " registered ".

5. In section 13 of that Measure immediately before the word " patron ", wherever occurring, there shall be inserted the word " registered ".

6. In section 15(1) of that Measure paragraph (i) shall be omitted and in paragraphs (ii) and (iii) immediately before the word " patron " there shall be inserted the word " registered ".

7. In section 16 of that Measure immediately before the word " patron ", where first occurring, there shall be inserted the word " registered ", and at the end of that section there shall be inserted the words " and for the purposes of this Measure Her Majesty shall be deemed to be the registered patron of a benefice the patronage of which is vested in the Crown or is part of the possessions of the Duchy of Lancaster, and the possessor for the time being of the Duchy of Cornwall shall be deemed to be the registered patron of a benefice the patronage of which is part of the possessions of that Duchy ".

8. At the end of section 20 of that Measure there shall be inserted the words " and ' registered patron ' has the same meaning as in the Patronage (Benefices) Measure 1986 ".

New Parishes Measure 1943

9. In section 28 of the New Parishes Measure 1943 for the words " parochial church council or patron " there shall be substituted the words " or parochial church council ".

Parsonages (Amendment) Measure 1947

10. In section 1 of the Parsonages (Amendment) Measure 1947 immediately before the word " patron " there shall be inserted the word " registered ", and at the end of that section there shall be added the following paragraph—

" In this section ' registered patron ' has the same meaning as in the Patronage (Benefices) Measure 1986."

City of London (Guild Churches) Act 1952

11. In section 9(6) of the City of London (Guild Churches) Act 1952 for the words from the beginning to " 1931 " there shall be substituted the words " The Patronage (Benefices) Measure 1986 ".

12. In section 10(1) of that Act for the word " is " there shall be substituted the words " was at the passing of this Act ".

Synodical Government Measure 1969

13. In Schedule 3 of the Synodical Government Measure 1969 (Church Representation Rules)—

    (*a*) in rule 16(3) there shall be inserted at the end the words " or the functions of a parochial church council under Part II of the Patronage (Benefices) Measure 1986 ";

    (*b*) in rule 17—

        (i) in paragraph (1)(*c*) there shall be inserted at the beginning the words " subject to paragraph 20 of Schedule 2 to the Patronage (Benefices) Measure 1986 ";

        (ii) in paragraph (2) after the words " said Measure " there shall be inserted the words " and to paragraph 20 of Schedule 2 to the Patronage (Benefices) Measure 1986 ";

    (*c*) in rule 17A—

        (i) in paragraph (1)(*c*) there shall be inserted at the beginning the words " subject to paragraph 19 of Schedule 2 to the Patronage (Benefices) Measure 1986 ";

        (ii) in paragraph (2) after the words " the said Measure " there shall be inserted the words " and to paragraph 19 of Schedule 2 to the Patronage (Benefices) Measure 1986 ";

    (*d*) in rule 17B—

        (i) in paragraph (1)(*c*) after " 1983 " there shall be inserted the words " and its functions under Part II of the Patronage (Benefices) Measure 1986 ";

(ii) at the end of paragraph 3 there shall be added the words "except that the functions of a parochial church council under Part II of the Patronage (Benefices) Measure 1986 may not be delegated to a group council ".

Repair of Benefice Buildings Measure 1972

14. In the proviso to section 12(3) of the Repair of Benefice Buildings Measure 1972 for the words "the patron" there shall be substituted the words "after consulting the registered patron", and after the word "consent", where last occurring, there shall be inserted the words "and after such consultation ".

15. In section 21(1) of that Measure for the words from "without" to "patron" there shall be substituted the words "until after he has consulted the registered patron, and obtained the consent of the Board ".

16. In section 31(1) of that Measure for the definition of "patron" there shall be substituted the words "'registered patron' has the same meaning as in the Patronage (Benefices) Measure 1986 ".

Pastoral Measure 1983

17. In section 18(2) of the Pastoral Measure 1983—

(a) in the proviso for the words "section 1 of the Benefices (Exercise of Rights of Presentation) Measure 1931 " there shall be substituted the words "section 7 of the Patronage (Benefices) Measure 1986 " ;

(b) in paragraph (b) of the proviso for the words "section 1 " there shall be substituted the words "section 7 ".

18. In section 67 of that Measure—

(a) in subsection (1) for the word "patron", in each place where it occurs, there shall be substituted the words "registered patron " ;

(b) in subsection (6) for paragraph (b) there shall be substituted—

"(b) the registered patron of the benefice, unless the only registered patron is the bishop ; ".

19. In section 68(2) of that Measure for the word "patron" there shall be substituted the words "registered patron ".

20. In section 69 of that Measure—

(a) in subsection (1) for the word patron, in both places where that word occurs, there shall be substituted the words "registered patron " ;

(b) in subsection (2) for paragraph (a) there shall be substituted—

"(a) the registered patron, unless the only registered patron is the bishop ; " ;

for the word "patron" in the second place where it occurs there shall be substituted the words "registered patron" and for the words from "and the requirement" to the end of the subsection there shall be substituted the words "and the provisions of section 7 of the Patronage (Benefices) Measure 1986 shall, subject to the modifications made by section 70 of this Measure, apply ".

21. In section 70 of that Measure—

(a) in paragraph (a) for the words "section 1 of the Benefices (Exercise of Rights of Presentation) Measure 1931 " there shall be substituted the words " section 7 of the Patronage (Benefices) Measure 1986 " ;

(b) in paragraph (d) for the words " section 1 " there shall be substituted the words " section 7(4) ".

22. For section 80(1) of that Measure there shall be substituted the following subsection—

"(1) Where it is necessary for the purposes of this Measure or any scheme or order made thereunder to find the registered patron of a benefice and it appears to the Commissioners that it is not possible or is not reasonably practicable to find that patron, the Commissioners may direct that the diocesan board of patronage shall be treated for those purposes as the registered patron of that benefice, and any such direction shall be conclusive for the said purposes."

23. In section 82 of that Measure for the word " patron " there shall be substituted the words " registered patron ".

24. In section 87(1) of that Measure the following definition shall be inserted after the definition of " redundancy scheme "—

" registered patron ", in relation to a benefice or to benefices held in plurality, means every person who is for the time being registered under the Patronage (Benefices) Measure 1986 in a register of patrons as a patron of that benefice or those benefices "

25. In Schedule 3 to that Measure—

(a) in paragraph 1—

(i) in sub-paragraph (3) for the words from the beginning to " any other enactment " there shall be substituted the words " Any enactment " ;

(ii) in sub-paragraph (6) there shall be inserted at the end of the words " being a person who has made the declaration of membership within the meaning of the Patronage (Benefices) Measure 1986 " ;

(iii) in sub-paragraph (9) for the words " presentation of the rector by " there shall be substituted the words " patron to be " ;

(b) for paragraph 3 there shall be substituted the following paragraph—

" 3. Where a group ministry is established by a pastoral scheme for a group of benefices, the registered patron of a benefice in the group shall consult the other incumbents and any priests in charge in the group before he makes a request under section 13 of the Patronage (Benefices) Measure 1986 for the approval of the parish representatives (as defined in section 11(7) of that Measure), and (unless the registered patron is the bishop) of the bishop, to the making to a priest of an offer to present him to the benefice " ;

(c) in paragraph 4(3)(c) there shall be inserted at the beginning the words " subject to paragraph 19 of Schedule 2 to the Patronage (Benefices) Measure 1986," ;

(d) in paragraph 13(1)(c) there shall be inserted at the beginning the words " subject to paragraph 20 of Schedule 2 to the Patronage (Benefices) Measure 1986,".

SCHEDULE 5
REPEALS
Acts

Chapter	Short title	Extent of repeal
31 Eliz. 1. c. 6.	The Simony Act 1588.	In section 4, the words from "And that it shall " to " turne onlye ". In section 5, the words from " and that the patron " to the end. Section 6. In section 9, the words from " and that the patron " to " notwithstandinge ".
3 Jas. 1. c. 5.	The Presentation of Benefices Act 1605.	Section 13.
1 Will. & Mar. c. 26.	The Presentation of Benefices Act 1688.	The whole Act.
13 Anne c. 13.	The Presentation of Benefices Act 1713.	The whole Act except sections 9 and 11.
1 Geo. 1. stat. 2. c. 10.	The Queen Anne's Bounty Act 1714.	In section 6, the words from the beginning to " benefices, and " in the second place where those words occur. Sections 7 and 8.
11 Geo. 2. c. 17.	The Church Patronage Act 1737.	The whole Act.
44 Geo. 3. c. 43.	The Clergy Ordination Act 1804.	In section 1, the words from " Provided " to the end.
10 Geo. 4. c. 7.	The Roman Catholic Relief Act 1829.	Section 15 insofar as it relates to ecclesiastical benefices. In section 16, the words from " Provided ", where last occurring, to the end. Section 17.
1 & 2 Vict. c. 106.	The Pluralities Act 1838.	In section 31, the word " benefice ", where it occurs for the second and sixth time, and the words " or benefice ". In section 58, the words from " and it shall be lawful " to " second publication thereof as aforesaid ".
3 & 4 Vict. c. 20.	The Queen Anne's Bounty Act 1840.	Sections 2 to 4.
3 & 4 Vict. c. 113.	The Ecclesiastical Commissioners Act 1840.	Sections 42, 48 and 73.
4 & 5 Vict. c. 39.	The Ecclesiastical Commissioners Act 1841.	Section 22.
9 & 10 Vict. c. 88.	The Church Patronage Act 1846.	The whole Act.
16 & 17 Vict. c. 50.	The Ecclesiastical Commissioners (Exchange & Patronage) Act 1853.	The whole Act.

Chapter	Short title	Extent of repeal
19 & 20 Vict. c. 50.	The Sale of Advowsons Act 1856.	The whole Act.
21 & 22 Vict. c. 49.	The Jews Relief Act 1858.	In section 4, the words from the beginning to " being; and ".
23 & 24 Vict. c. 124.	The Ecclesiastical Commissioners Act 1860.	Section 42.
31 & 32 Vict. c. 83.	The Army Chaplains Act 1868.	In section 4, the words " and to the patron or patrons ", the words " patron or patrons " in the second place where they occur and the words " and patron or patrons ".
31 & 32 Vict. c. 114.	The Ecclesiastical Commission Act 1868.	Section 12.
33 & 34 Vict. c. 39.	The Church Patronage Act 1870.	The whole Act.
34 & 35 Vict. c. 45.	The Sequestration Act 1871.	Section 6.
61 & 62 Vict. c. 48.	The Benefices Act 1898.	Section 1. In section 2, paragraph (*a*) of subsection (1) and subsection (2). Sections 5 and 6.
12 & 13 Geo. 6. c. 76.	The Marriage Act 1949.	In section 20, in subsections (1) to (3) and (6), the words " patron and " and the words " patron or ", wherever they occur, and in subsection (7) the words " ' patron ' and " and the words " patron or " and the words, " as the case may be ".

Measures

Chapter	Short title	Extent of repeal
14 & 15 Geo. 5. No. 1.	The Benefices Act 1898 (Amendment) Measure 1923.	The whole Measure.
20 & 21 Geo. 5. No. 8.	The Benefices (Transfer of Rights of Patronage) Measure 1930.	The whole Measure except as applied by section 6(3) of the City of London (Guild Churches) Act 1960.
21 & 22 Geo. 5. No. 3.	The Benefices (Exercise of Rights of Presentation) Measure 1931.	The whole Measure.
22 & 23 Geo. 5. No. 1.	The Benefices (Diocesan Boards of Patronage) Measure 1932.	The whole Measure.

SCH. 5

Chapter	Short title	Extent of repeal
23 Geo. 5. No. 1.	The Benefices (Purchase of Rights of Patronage) Measure 1933.	The whole Measure.
1 & 2 Geo. 6. No. 3.	The Parsonages Measure 1938.	In section 3(1), the proviso. Section 4. In section 15(1), paragraph (i). Section 19.
6 & 7 Geo. 6. No. 1.	The New Parishes Measure 1943.	Section 29(2).
7 & 8 Eliz. 2. No. 2.	The Vacancies in Sees Measure 1959.	Section 1 and the Schedule.
8 & 9 Eliz. 2. No. 1.	The Church Property (Miscellaneous Provisions) Measure 1960.	In section 3(2), the words from " and at " to the end. In section 9(1), the words " the patron ". In section 11(1), the words " the patron ".
1972 No. 2.	The Repair of Benefice Buildings Measure 1972.	Section 27(2).
1978 No. 1.	The Dioceses Measure 1978.	In the Schedule, in paragraph 10, the words from " and for " to the end.
1983 No. 1.	The Pastoral Measure 1983.	Section 32(10). Sections 71 and 72. In section 81(1) the words from the beginning to " Crown ", where it first occurs. In Schedule 3, paragraphs 5(4) and 6.

Instrument

Number	Title	Extent of repeal
1938 No. 636.	Rules made by Queen Anne's Bounty pursuant to section 15 of the Parsonages Measure 1938.	Rule 1. In rule 2, the words " as defined by these Rules ". In rule 3, the words " (as defined by these Rules) ". Rule 7. In the Schedule, Form No. 4.

Deacons (Ordination of Women) Measure 1986

1986 No. 4

A MEASURE passed by the General Synod of the Church of England to make provision for the ordination of women as deacons, and for connected purposes.

[7th November 1986]

1.—(1) It shall be lawful for the General Synod to make provision by Canon for enabling a woman to be ordained to the office of deacon if she otherwise satisfies the requirements of Canon Law as to the persons who may be ordained as deacons. *Provision for ordination of women as deacons.*

(2) In the case of a deaconess who is licensed or holds a bishop's permission to officiate, a Canon made in pursuance of subsection (1) above may make provision for enabling the deaconess to be ordained to the office of deacon notwithstanding—

(a) that she has not after applying to be so ordained been further examined concerning her knowledge of holy scripture or of the doctrine, discipline and worship of the Church of England, or

(b) that she has not exhibited to the bishop of the diocese any certificate or other document which is required to be so exhibited by every person who is to be made a deacon.

(3) In section 1(1) of the Clergy (Ordination and Miscellaneous Provisions) Measure 1964 there shall be inserted at the beginning the words "Subject to the provisions of section 1(2) of the Deacons (Ordination of Women) Measure 1986". *1964 No. 6.*

(4) Nothing in this Measure shall make it lawful for a woman to be ordained to the office of priest.

Provisions as to the order of deaconesses.

2.—(1) It shall be lawful for the General Synod to provide by Canon that no woman shall be admitted to the order of deaconesses unless before the date on which this Measure comes into force she has been accepted for training for admission to that order.

(2) Nothing in this Measure shall affect the rights of a deaconess who does not become a deacon.

Provisions as to pensions etc.

1961 No. 3.

3.—(1) Subject to subsection (2) below, the provisions of Parts I, III and IV of the Clergy Pensions Measure 1961 (in this section referred to as " the 1961 Measure ") shall, so far as material, apply in relation to a woman who becomes a clerk in Holy Orders within the meaning of that Measure by virtue of being ordained to the office of deacon, and in relation to the husband or widower of any such woman, as they apply in relation to a male clerk in Holy Orders and the wife or widow of any such clerk.

(2) For the purposes of section 46 of the 1961 Measure the retiring age of a woman shall be the age of sixty years or such other age as the General Synod may by resolution from time to time determine.

(3) In consequence of the foregoing provisions of this section the 1961 Measure shall have effect subject to the amendments specified in the Schedule to this Measure.

Interpretation.

4. In any Canon, order, rule or regulation relating to deacons, words importing the masculine gender include the feminine, unless the contrary intention appears.

Short title, commencement and extent.

5.—(1) This Measure may be cited as the Deacons (Ordination of Women) Measure 1986.

(2) This Measure shall come into force on such day as the Archbishops of Canterbury and York may jointly appoint.

(3) This Measure shall extend to the provinces of Canterbury and York except that it shall only extend to the Isle of Man and the Channel Islands in accordance with the following provisions of this section.

(4) Sections 1, 2, 4 and 5 shall extend to the Isle of Man and section 3 may by or under Act of Tynwald be extended to the Isle of Man with such exceptions, adaptations and modifications as may be specified in such Act or instrument thereunder.

(5) This Measure may be applied to the Channel Islands as defined in the Channel Islands (Church Legislation) Measures 1931 and 1957, or either of them, in accordance with those Measures.

SCHEDULE

AMENDMENTS OF CLERGY PENSIONS MEASURE 1961

1. In section 2(3) for the words " his wife ", in both places where those words occur, there shall be substituted the words " his spouse ".

2. In section 19 for paragraph (*b*) there shall be substituted the following paragraph—

   " (*b*) for the provision of homes of residence for retired clerks and their spouses, and for the widows, widowers and dependants of deceased clerks, in accordance with the provisions of section twenty-six of this Measure ; ".

3. In section 26—

   (*a*) in subsection (1)(*a*) for the words "wives and for the widows " there shall be substituted the words " spouses and for the widows, widowers " ;

   (*b*) in subsection (3A)—

   (i) for paragraph (*a*) there shall be substituted the following paragraph—

   " (*a*) a retired clerk or retired church worker or the spouse of a retired clerk or retired church worker ; " ;

   (ii) in paragraph (*b*) for the words "wife of such clerk or the spouse of such church worker " there shall be substituted the words " spouse of such clerk or such church worker " ;

   (iii) for paragraph (*c*) there shall be substituted the following paragraph—

   (*c*) the widow or widower of a deceased clerk or deceased church worker ; " ;

   (iv) in the definition of " the retiring age " for the words " a clerk " there shall be substituted the words " a male clerk " and for the words " female church worker " there shall be substituted the words " female clerk or female church worker " ;

4. In section 46 for the definition of " retiring age " there shall be substituted the following definition—

   " ' retiring age ' means in the case of a man the age of 65 years or such earlier age as the General Synod may by resolution from time to time determine and in the case of a woman the age of 60 years or such other age as the General Synod may so determine ; ".

INDEX

TO THE

PUBLIC GENERAL ACTS

AND

GENERAL SYNOD MEASURES 1986

A

PART I

INTRODUCTORY

PART II

PROVISIONS AFFECTING TENANCY DURING ITS CONTINUANCE

Written tenancy agreements

Fixed equipment

ANIMALS (SCIENTIFIC PROCEDURES) ACT 1986 c.14 ... ... I, p. 227

Miscellaneous and supplementary

APPEALS. Under—

APPROPRIATION ACT 1986 c. 42 ... ... II, p. 839

ARMED FORCES ACT 1986: c. 21 ... ... I, p. 273

PART I

CONTINUANCE OF SERVICES ACTS

PART II

AMENDMENTS OF SERVICES ACTS ETC.

Offences

Sentence, reconsideration and limitation

Civilians

D

E

FINANCE ACT 1986 c. 41   ...   .   I. p. 573

PART I

CUSTOMS AND EXCISE AND VALUE ADDED TAX

CHAPTER I

CUSTOMS AND EXCISE

The rates of duty

PART I

REGULATION OF INVESTMENTS BUSINESS

CHAPTER I

PRELIMINARY

CHAPTER II

RESTRICTION ON CARRYING ON BUSINESS

CHAPTER III

AUTHORISED PERSONS

Members of recognised self-regulating organisations

Persons authorised by recognised professional bodies

Insurance companies

Friendly societies

PART I

GAS SUPPLY

Introductory

HOUSING (SCOTLAND) ACT 1986 c. 65   ...   .   IV, p. 2731

Amendment of Tenants' Rights, Etc. (Scotland) Act 1980

I

INCEST AND RELATED OFFENCES (SCOTLAND) ACT 1986 c. 36   I, p. 531.

INDUSTRIAL TRAINING ACT 1986 c. 15 ...   .   I, p. 251.

INSOLVENCY ACT 1986 c. 45   ...   .   II, p. 1027

THE FIRST GROUP OF PARTS

COMPANY INSOLVENCY; COMPANIES WINDING UP

PART I

COMPANY VOLUNTARY ARRANGEMENTS

The proposal

CHAPTER V

EFFECT OF BANKRUPTCY ON CERTAIN RIGHTS, TRANSACTIONS, ETC.

Rights of occupation

CHAPTER VI

BANKRUPTCY OFFENCES

Preliminary

LOCAL GOVERNMENT ACT 1986 c. 10   ...   .   I, p. 179

PART I

RATING

PART II

LOCAL AUTHORITY PUBLICITY

PART III

TRANSFER OF LOCAL AUTHORITY MORTGAGES

PART IV

MISCELLANEOUS AND GENERAL

Miscellaneous

General

M

MAGISTRATES COURT. Appeal to, Under—
Agricultural Holdings Act (c. 5, s. 19 (2)) ... ... I, p. 34.
Animals (Scientific Procedures) Act (c. 14, s. 26 (3)) ... I, p. 244.

MARRIAGE (PROHIBITED DEGREES OF RELATIONSHIP) ACT 1986 c. 16   I, p. 253.

§ 1(4) and schedule 1.   Marriage between certain persons related by affinity not to be void, I, p. 253.
2 and schedule 2.   Marriage between certain persons related by affinity—Scotland, I, p. 254.
3.   Marriage according to rites of Church of England or the Church in Wales, I, p. 255.
4.   Amendment of s.3 of Perjury Act 1911, I, p. 255.
5.   Amendment of Schedule 1 to Supreme Court Act 1981, I, p. 255.
6.   Short title, citation, commencement and extent, I, p. 255.
Schedule 1.—Amendment of Marriage Act 1949, I, p. 256.
Schedule 2.—Amendment of Marriage (Scotland) Act 1977, I, p. 260.

MARRIAGE (WALES) ACT 1986 c. 7   ...   .   I, p. 154

§ 1.   Benefices held in plurality, I, p. 154.
2.   Short title and citation, I, p. 154.

MUSEUM OF LONDON ACT 1986 c. 8   ...   .   I, p. 155

§ 1.   Composition of Board of Governers, I, p. 155.
2.   Functions of Board of Governers, I, p.156.
3.   Funding of general expenses in respect of Museum, I, p. 157.
4.   Funding of Greater London archaeological service, I, p. 158.
5.   Reports, I, p. 158.
6.   Expenses, I, p. 158.
7(3) and schedule .   Short title, commencement and repeals, I, p. 158.
Schedule Repeals, I, p. 159.

NATIONAL HEALTH SERVICE (AMENDMENT) ACT 1986 c. 66   ...   IV, p. 2765

§ 1.   Application of food legislation to health authorities and health service premises, IV, p. 2765
2.   Health and safety legislation, IV, p. 2767
3.   Pharmaceutical services, IV, p. 2767
4.   Remuneration of persons providing general medical services etc., IV, p. 2771
5.   Co-operation and advice in relation to disabled persons, the elderly and others, IV, p. 2773
6.   Expenses, IV, p. 2774
7.   Orders in Council making corresponding provision for Northern Ireland, IV, p. 2774
8.   Short title, etc., IV, p. 2774

NORTHERN IRELAND. Application to, or power to extend to, under—
Agriculture Act (c. 49, s. 24(7)) ... ... II, p. 1461
Airports Act (c. 31, s. 85(8)) ... ... I, p. 433
Animals (Scientific Procedures) Act (c. 14, s. 29) ... ... I, p. 244
Atomic Energy Authority Act (c. 3, s. 10(3)) ... ... I, p .16
British Shipbuilders (Borrowing Powers) Act (c. 19, s. 2(2)) I, p. 268
Building Societies Act (c. 53, s. 122(1)) ... ... III, p. 1839
Commonwealth Development Corporation Act (c. 25, s. 2(3)) I, p. 315
Consumer Safety (Amendment) Act (c. 29, s. 17(4)) ... I, p. 341
Drug Trafficking Offences Act (c. 32, s. 40(5)) ... ... I, p. 494
Education (No. 2) Act (c. 61, s. 67(7)(*b*)) ... ... IV, p. 2400
Family Law Act (c. 55, s. 69(7)) ... ... III, p. 1997
Finance Act (c. 41, s. 6) ... ... I, p. 576
Financial Services Act (c. 60, s. 209) ... ... IV, p. 2231
Gas Act (c. 44, s. 68(6)) ... ... II, p. 973
Housing and Planning Act (c. 63, s. 58(3)) ... ... IV, p. 2572

OUTER SPACE ACT 1986 c. 38 ... ... I, p. 543

Application of Act

§ 1. Activities to which this Act applies., I, p. 543
2. Persons to whom this Act applies., I, p. 543

Licensing of activities

3. Prohibition of unlicensed activities., I, p. 544
4. Grant of licence., I, p. 544
5. Terms of licence., I, p. 545
6. Transfer, variation, suspension or termination of licence., I, p. 546

Other controls

7. Register of space objects., I, p. 546
8. Power to give directions., I, p. 547
9. Warrant authorising direct action., I, p. 547
10. Obligation to indemnify government against claims., I, p. 548

General

11. Regulations., I, p. 548
12. Offences., I, p. 548
13. Minor definitions., I, p. 549
14. Index of defined expressions., I, p. 550
15. Short title, commencement and extent., I, p. 550

PARLIAMENT—

Approval of each House of Parliament required for draft orders, regulations under:—
Agricultural Holdings Act (c. 5, ss. 22(4), 94(3), sch. 11 para. 1(2))
I, pp. 36, 90, 121
Agriculture Act (c. 49, ss. 6(1)(4)(5)) ... ... II, pp. 1446, 1447
Airports Act (c. 31, ss. 32, 79(3)), ... I, pp. 379, 429
Armed Forces Act (c. 31, s. 1(2)(4)) ... ... I, p. 273
Building Societies Act (c. 53, s. 14(1)(7)(a), 19(1)(7), 20(4)(7), 26(12)(13), 27(6)(7), 34(2)(9)(a), 41(15)(16), 82(9)(10), 104, sch. 7 para. 1)
III, pp. 1686, 1688, 1697, 1698, 1699, 1707, 1708, 1716, 1717, 1730, 1796, 1822, 1879
Drug Trafficking Offences Act (c. 32, ss. 25, 26) ... I, pp. 477, 478
Financial Services Act (c.60, s. 46(1)(b)(2), 48(8)(9), 58(3)(d)(5), 109(2)(4), 115, 135(1) (adding s. 21A(2)(4) to the Insurance Companies Act 1982 c. 50), 157, 160(6)(d)(9), sch. 11 paras. 28, 36(3)(4)
IV, pp. 2077, 2080, 2081, 2092, 2135, 2136, 2141, 2159, 2176, 2180, 2181, 2285, 2290
Housing and Planning Act (c. 63, ss. 2(1) (adding s. 129(2A)(2B) to the Housing Act 1985 c. 68), 3(2) (adding s. 1(5B)(5C) to the Tenants' Rights, Etc (S.)

PART VII

MISCELLANEOUS, GENERAL AND SUPPLEMENTARY

Miscellaneous

General

Northern Ireland

Supplementary

T

W